# NEW TRADITIONS FROM NIGERIA

# NEW TRADITIONS FROM NIGERIA

## SEVEN ARTISTS OF THE NSUKKA GROUP

## SIMON OTTENBERG

SMITHSONIAN INSTITUTION PRESS

IN ASSOCIATION WITH

THE NATIONAL MUSEUM OF AFRICAN ART

WASHINGTON AND LONDON

Copy editor: Frances Kianka
Production editors: Jenelle Walthour, Jack Kirshbaum
Designer: Linda McKnight

Library of Congress Cataloging-in-Publication Data
Ottenberg, Simon.
     New traditions from Nigeria : seven artists of the Nsukka group /
  Simon Ottenberg.
         p.     cm.
     Includes bibliographical references and index.
     ISBN 1-56098-800-2 (alk. paper)
     1. Art, Nigerian—Nigeria—Nsukka. 2. Art, Modern—20th century—
  Nigeria—Nsukka. 3. Art, Igbo—Influence. 4. Artists—Nigeria—
  Nsukka—Attitudes. I. Title.
  N7399.N52N786   1997
  709′.699′409045—dc21                                          97-7666

British Library Cataloguing-in-Publication Data is available.

Manufactured in the United States of America
04  03  02  01  00  99  98  97    5  4  3  2  1

⊗ The paper used in this publication meets the minimum requirements of the
American National Standard for Information Sciences—Permanence of Paper
for Printed Library Materials ANSI Z39.48-1984.

For permission to reproduce illustrations appearing in this book, please corre-
spond directly with the photographers. Unless otherwise noted, photographs are
by Simon Ottenberg. The Smithsonian Institution Press does not retain reproduction rights for these illustrations individually, or maintain a file of addresses for
photo sources.

IN MEMORY

SYLVIA H. WILLIAMS

DIRECTOR

NATIONAL MUSEUM OF AFRICAN ART

SMITHSONIAN INSTITUTION

1983    1996

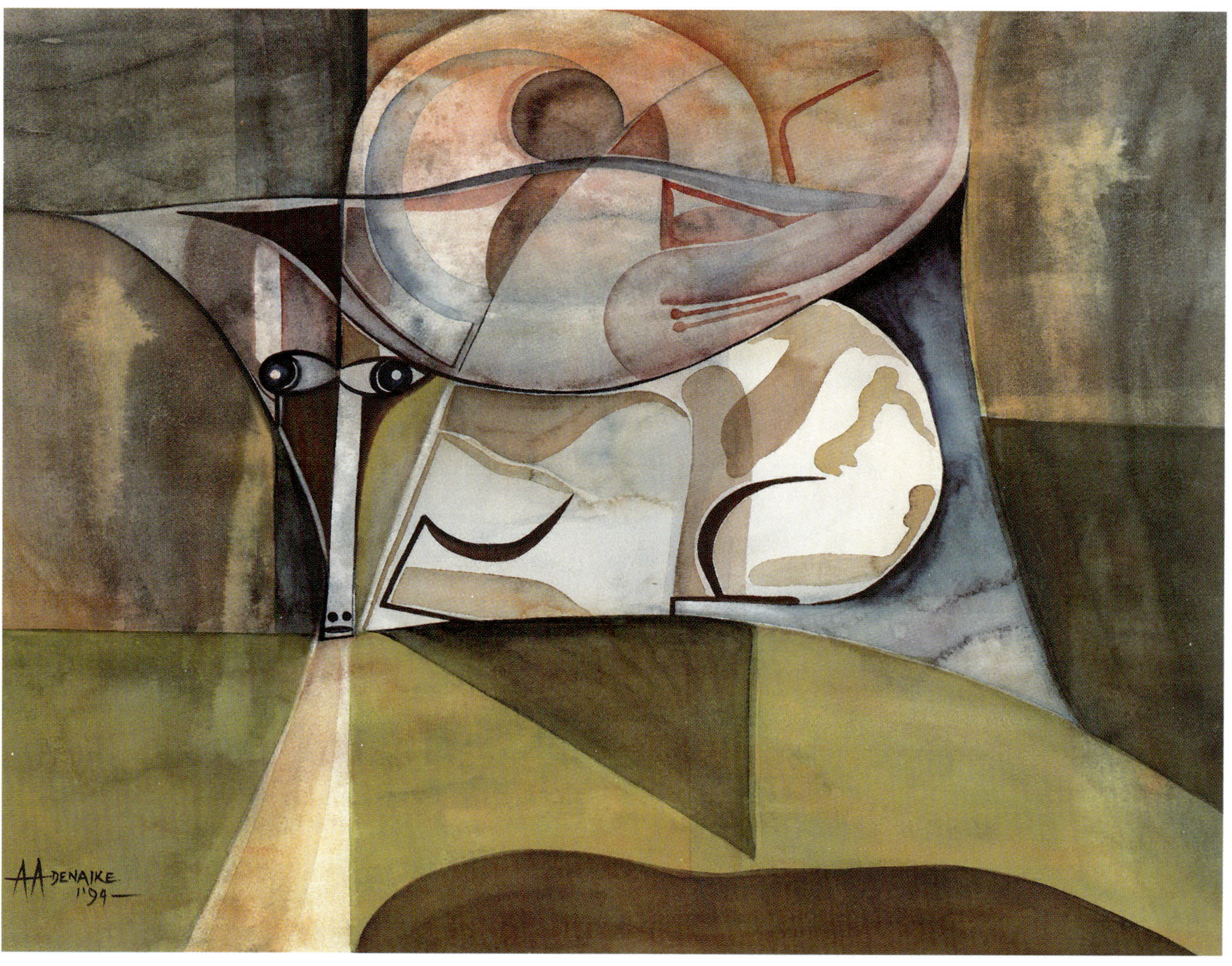

Fig. 147

# CONTENTS

# FOREWORD

In his discussion of the eclectic art of Ọlu Ọguibe in this remarkable volume, Simon Ottenberg refers to the artist's 1994 work on canvas, *Two Lovers by the Rio Santa Catarina,* which "shows an indistinctly portrayed pair standing side by side in semidarkness, a blue crescent moon overhead and a blue river running down the center from top to bottom." This work is part of the artist's record of a Mexican experience but, despite its invocation of a recent encounter, manages to reveal a nostalgia for a past that simply refuses to go away. Ottenberg is right in celebrating "the very human feeling of love [Ọguibe] projects" in this work, but one could go further by seeing this painting in relation to a spirit that hovers over the work of nearly all the artists presented in this volume. I am referring to the late Nigerian poet Christopher Okigbo, whose early poem "Love Apart" contains images that are strikingly close to those in Ọguibe's piece:

> The moon has ascended between us
> Between two pines
> That bow to each other
>
> Love with the moon has ascended
> Has fed on our solitary pines
>
> And we are now shadows
> That cling to each other
> But kiss the air only.

Indeed, Okigbo's career provides a fitting context within which both the achievement and predicament of these Nsukka artists may be read. He was born, grew up, and received his elementary and secondary schooling in Igbo country east of the Niger, but then studied at the University College, Ibadan (now the University of Ibadan), in the Yoruba west. He taught secondary school in the same Yoruba west before moving back east to work, in the early 1960s, at the library of the new University of Nigeria, Nsukka. At Nsukka he formed a close friendship with an American poet, Peter Thomas, both of them constituting the nucleus of what was to become a vibrant artistic culture that continued to thrive even after Okigbo left Nsukka to return to Ibadan as representative of Cambridge University Press.

This was a momentous move in many ways. First, the literary culture of Nigeria was now centered in the western part of the country. Most of the book publishing houses were—and still are—based in Ibadan. Chinua Achebe, who had published his first two novels, was director of Radio Nigeria in Lagos, an hour away by road. Cyprian Ekwensi, also an established writer at this time, was director at the Federal Ministry of Information, also in Lagos. Wọle Ṣoyinka had published his early drama, was working at the University of Ibadan, and had formed a theater company based at Ibadan. The poet J. P. Clark had worked as a journalist at Ibadan and, after an interrupted stint at Princeton, had returned to the University of Ibadan as a research scholar, working on what was to become the epoch-making epic *The Ozidi Saga* and also writing poems and plays. There were other writers, visual artists, dramatists (especially of the new and thriving culture of Yoruba folk opera or traveling theater), and musicians who made Ibadan very much the cultural capital of the country. And then there was the German ethnologist and promoter of culture, Ulli Beier, who undertook to bring this lively company of artists into a club (the Mbari Club) where they periodically met to present their work in an atmosphere of combined seriousness and conviviality—a veritable symposium.

Okigbo, very much a key figure in this group, had married a woman from the Muslim north (he had been raised a Catholic), and they had a daughter together. By the mid-1960s the political situation in the country had begun to deteriorate speedily, and not even the relationships formed between these kindred spirits in the arts were spared the trauma bred by the interethnic distrust that was in a fundamental way responsible for the crisis that erupted into the civil war in 1967. Okigbo left Ibadan for Lagos and soon after joined his fellow Igbo in the newly formed Republic of Biafra where he died fighting in a front close to Nsukka.

In both his personal life and his career, then, Okigbo had united the three main regions of Nigeria well before ethnic or cultural identity became such a touchy issue in the political life of the country. But the content of his poetry is just as revealing. In his first major collection of poems, *Labyrinths,* he addressed himself to questions about the relationship of traditional African culture to ideas and outlooks that colonialism had introduced into his society and by which he would seem to have been drawn away. Much of this early poetry was therefore set within the structure of a ritual experience in which these influences were brought into a mantic confrontation with one another. At the end of this long, searing rite, in the final movement of the sequence, "Distances," the poet reemerges to declare that, although he cannot pretend to have solved the conundrums raised by the clash of images in his personality, he remains beholden to the protective spirits of his community from which he would seem to have strayed.

Okigbo never renounced his curiosity about other cultures, but the poetry he wrote shortly before he died had the tone of a traditional minstrel whose vision had been honed by the harsh realities of the times. Combining rhetorical stridency with the oblique thrusts of proverbial wit, he decried the dangers posed for the nation by leaders threatening our lives with foreign instruments of destruction, and could glean from the country's political horizon a bleak and uncertain future in which

An old star departs, leaves us here on the shore
Gazing heavenward for a new star approaching;
The new star appears, foreshadows its going
Before a going and coming that goes on forever . . .
("Elegy for Alto," in *Path of Thunder*)

We can therefore see why the spirit of Christopher Okigbo hovers over the careers of the Nsukka artists—all but one of whom is a poet as well as visual artist—discussed by Ottenberg in this book. For a start, during his brief stint at that university, Okigbo had lit a creative spark that was waiting for the right moment to burst into flame. The moment came during the civil crisis, when many Igbo intellectuals were forced to return to their native region to complement those already there, providing Nsukka with perhaps the highest concentration of stellar scholars and artists—Michael Echeruo, Emmanuel Obiechina, Adiele Afigbo, Uche Okeke, Mẹki Nzewi, Ikenna Nzimiro, and many others—to converge on any Nigerian campus at that time.

The synergy must have been amazing. To their counterparts in "federal territory," the Nsukka scholars may have appeared to be experiencing a certain cultural inbreeding in their enclave. But if some of the work that came out of that period is anything to go by, it was also an opportunity for some needed stocktaking. So much at least is clear enough from the volume *Igbo Traditional Life, Culture and Literature* (1971), jointly edited by Echeruo and Obiechina, with contributions by Afigbo, Nzewi, Nzimiro, and others and published by Sunday Anọzie (then at the State University of New York College at New Paltz), who one year later published a magisterial study, *Christopher Okigbo: Creative Rhetoric.* Although resources at Nsukka dwindled steadily as the federal government and army tightened the noose on secessionist Biafra, there was a superabundance of both a sense of right and the will to survive.

That will was tested to the full in the thirty months of the civil war. Enough has been written about that war, I think, by both historians and political analysts, that it is fairly clear now what really happened and why Biafra fell. The usefulness of books like Ottenberg's is in helping us see the impress of the war on the cultural history of this region.

Here again the presence and absence of Okigbo were emblematic. For many Nigerians in federal territory who knew Okigbo and his work, the war took on a different meaning the moment his death was announced by the media. Many people began to ask "Why?" Whatever the question meant, there was at least the general sense of a sad and pointless waste about the whole enterprise. From the evidence of the visual arts and poetry discussed by Ottenberg in this book, there must have been a general sense among the Biafrans of a certain wealth—call it a heroic spirit, a cultural heritage, whatever you will—that desperately needed to be defended against the ravages of the war. In rededicating himself to the protective spirits of his people, Okigbo helped, perhaps more in death than in life, to cement the determination of a people that their "way" was worth everything to them. This is equally clear from two collections of creative writing co-edited by another Igbo literary giant, Chinua Achebe, and dedicated to the spirit of Christopher Okigbo: *Aka Weta* and *Don't Let Him Die,* the former containing, among other works, poems by authors who strain consciously for the styles and touches of traditional Igbo minstrelsy.

I think it would be correct to say that the most defining element in the works of the Nsukka artists presented here by Ottenberg is their attachment to traditional artistic principles. They do not all show this loyalty to the same degree, of course. It is reasonably clear that the younger ones in this group—Ada Udechukwu and Ọlu Oguibe—feel the bonds with tradition a little less than their elders, perhaps because they are that much further removed from the sources of its inspiration (Okigbo, Achebe, and others) and so are more susceptible to the pressures of contemporary reality. But so deeply has the imprint of *uli* been etched into the psychology of this school, that again and again its "image insists"—to borrow a phrase from Okigbo—even in the works of its least representative devotees. Indeed, Ọlu Ọguibe's current achievements seem to indicate that, the further the artist moves away from his traditional sources and into cultural circles where those sources are painfully marginalized, the more he feels the need to return to his roots with a hurt sense of pride.

Still, the record of the Nsukka school has demonstrated that the survival of the tradition is guaranteed not by a narcissistic withdrawal into itself but by a calculated openness to external influences. A notable achievement of this book is the author's choice of representative figures whose backgrounds and styles define a spectrum that reveals various levels of stress between Igbo and non-Igbo worlds. At one end of the spectrum is Uche Okeke, who spent most of his formative youth in the Muslim Hausa north of Nigeria and so came to Igbo tradition from the outside. Chike Aniakọr studied art at the Nigerian College of Arts, Science and Technology, Zaria (northern Nigeria)—a contemporary of Okeke's there—in a program run along British lines by British teachers but, unlike Okeke, settled immediately back into life in Igboland upon graduation. Obiọra Udechukwu's art studies in Zaria were interrupted by the civil crisis, which forced him to pursue and (after the war) complete his degree at Nsukka, becoming one of the first truly homebred students of Igbo artistic tradition in a program developed by Okeke and Aniakọr.

Obiọra Udechukwu represents the point of stabilization of this tradition in Ottenberg's spectrum, for after him we come to Nsukka artists who in one way or another reinscribe the external relations of the tradition. El Anatsui is from Ghana and has made imaginative connections between the styles favored by the Nsukka school and the resources, especially the *kente* and *adinkra* designs, provided by his native land. Tayọ Adenaike is from the Yoruba west of the country, and though he has identified himself intimately with Igbo culture and the *uli* imprint of the school, he has also found some room for his native Yoruba sensibilities within the aesthetic armature of the host tradition. Born of an Igbo father and an American mother, Ada Udechukwu spent part of her childhood in the United States and has a rather limited contact with traditional Igbo culture. Though she makes a nodding concession to *uli* aesthetics, her work seems subtly marked by an underlying feminist revolt against the patriarchalism of the tradition, and certainly by some distance from that tradition due no doubt to a lingering attachment to her American background.

The most mercurial of the group, however, is Ọlu Ọguibe. He grew up with sufficiently firm roots in Igbo society, and, though he lived through the civil war and was somewhat scarred by it, he survived well enough to commit himself to a Nigeria that seemed to take the task of reconstruction rather seriously. But things only got worse, filling him with utter despair and forcing him, like many of his compatriots, to leave the country permanently. It has frequently been said that exile easily breeds a sense of rootlessness and a certain postmodernist distrust of the concept of the nation-state. Ọguibe once taught at Goldsmiths' College of London University with the notable anti-Afrocentrist sociologist Paul Gilroy—they both wore dreadlocks—and has settled for now in the United States. He does not evince the deep anti-essentialism of Gilroy, but in both his art and art criticism he appears more inclined than before to see reality in a multicultural light in which *uli* no longer enjoys a special spot.

As we come to the end of the spectrum defined by Ottenberg's sampling, it might well be said that the Nsukka school—if Ọguibe may be taken to represent its developmental potential—has merely brought the history of Nigerian art full circle. After all, the stellar artists of the earlier days, such as Aina Ọnabolu and Ben Enwọnwu, were best known for employing European artistic styles in articulating their African subjects. Enwọnwu may have come closer to the indigenous sensibility by embracing the ideology of Négritude in his subjects, but these were in the final analysis circumscribed by an approach bred by a too long apprenticeship in the art schools of Europe.

Whatever the multicultural affinities between the earlier generations of Nigerian artists and the younger stars of the Nsukka or any other school in Nigerian art history, there is a qualitative difference. The art of the former was more readily given to the service of celebration than the work of the latter, no doubt because the country desperately needed to advertise the milestones of its political and cultural growth. Enwọnwu's giant bronze portrait of Queen Elizabeth II still sits magisterially in front of the old National Parliament in Lagos—in the eyes of many, a mockery of the political independence into which Nigeria was emerging when the sculpture was commissioned. In the art of Felix Idubọr and Ẹrhabọr Ẹmọkpae, there was a particular emphasis on celebration no less of the varied cultural achievement of the young nation than of the classic traditions of ancient Benin.

Among these Nsukka artists, however, the mood is different. Some of them have on occasion been called upon to represent their nation at international cultural events and even to grace certain landmarks within the country with their skills. But, given the political climate within which those skills have been honed, it would be reasonable to expect the same pattern of relationships noted above in the career of Okigbo: on the one hand, an intense introspection into a destabilized personal or cultural identity, as in the art of Ada Udechukwu and Ọlu Ọguibe; on the other, a confrontation with the collapse of reason in Nigeria's social and political life. This latter element is perhaps best represented in the art of Obiọra Udechukwu and Ọlu Ọguibe, both of whom have been nearly as energetic in the use of verbal as of visual art in drumming their lament of Nigeria's sociopolitical decline. Ọguibe's major poetry collection, *A Gathering Fear,* won the All-Africa Okigbo Prize for Literature in 1992 and has been favorably compared by Chinua Achebe with Okigbo's work. Obiọra Udechukwu had much earlier edited a *Homage to Christopher Okigbo* (1975) under the imprint of Ọdunke, an association of literary and visual artists in Nsukka, the Ọdunke Artists, dedicated to keeping alive the creative fire and legacy of the late poet. In discussing Udechukwu's art, Ottenberg is sensitive in identifying the lines from the artist's own poetry collection (*What the Madman Said,* 1990) that capture—with that flavor of folk minstrelsy characteristic of the later, elegiac Okigbo—the tragic reversal of fortune in the Nigerian state:

> *We were once poor but wealthy*
> *We are now rich but poor.*

It has made sense, then, to see the careers of these Nsukka artists in light of Okigbo's life and legacy. For not only does he epitomize the social, political, and cultural challenges facing the artist in his country, but, as we read Ottenberg's excellent portraits of the Nsukka group and view their creations, the bonds between poetry and visual art become abundantly clear: *ut pictura poesis.* Both activities are, of course, marked by an expressive economy that dictates a judicious deployment of signs within a compact space. But, in the works of these Nsukka artists, there is so much *brio*—look how effortlessly Obiọra Udechukwu matches flourish with frugality, or how confidently El Anatsui limns his pieces so that, however you choose to arrange them, their impact is hardly impaired— that we soon lose a sense of the constraints on sign and space.

Ottenberg has also shown himself abundantly equal to the challenge of capturing this key segment of Nigeria's cultural history. I say *cultural* rather than *art* history, because the anthropologist in him has seen fit to locate the phenomenon of the Nsukka school within the complex intersection of art and life that is especially crucial in understanding the frustrating conditions surrounding every honest endeavor in Nigeria today. Ottenberg's prose is measured and economical, not necessarily because he has chosen to tread cautiously in a discipline where (as he tells us) he is somewhat of a newcomer, but more perhaps because one can hardly undertake to celebrate any achievement in Nigerian history without some sobering sense of the apparent futility of it all. Ottenberg is nonetheless wise in keeping his discussion tame, unsententious, and on the whole remarkably free of the pretentious theoretical jargon that some of the work—especially Oguibe's, and to some extent Anatsui's—might invite.

*New Traditions from Nigeria* also recommends itself to specialist and nonspecialist alike in other ways. On the one hand, in its careful and detailed consultation of numerous creative and critical works in the field, it admirably complements studies that other writers have done on the arts of the Igbo, notably G. I. Jones, Herbert M. Cole (both alone and in collaboration with Chike Aniakọr), and others. In his own anthropological works, especially in relation to the Afikpo Igbo—most notably *The Masked Rituals of Afikpo* (1975)—Ottenberg has probed the broad cultural milieu within which artistic creativity is carried on.

On the other hand, the discussion is richly illuminated by the author's intimate look at the lives of these Nsukka artists. Claims are never glibly made about the works and lives in question. Every formulation is substantiated either by reference to the artist's published position on the issue or by opinions volunteered in an interview or both; indeed, there are so many interviews that the reader gets nearly as vivid a sense of the arts in creation as of history in the making. This is a book for which we should be truly grateful.

ISIDORE OKPEWHO
DEPARTMENT OF AFRICAN STUDIES
STATE UNIVERSITY OF NEW YORK AT BINGHAMTON

# ACKNOWLEDGMENTS

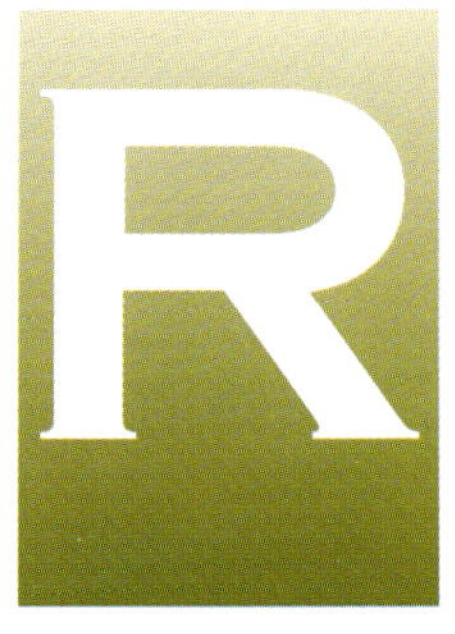

oy Sieber, formerly associate director for collections and research, National Museum of African Art, encouraged me to apply for a Regents Fellowship at the museum, which I held in the academic year 1993–94, during which time he ably helped me conceive my project on contemporary African art. The late Sylvia Williams, director of the museum, worked closely on the project with me until her death in 1996. She taught me many things about museums, exhibitions, and contemporary art and encouraged my field research and my overall project, which fitted into her view of the growing importance of this art. Sieber and Williams were my pioneer guides in America, the essential first scholars of this book.

In the spring of 1992, in Nigeria, I met Obiọra Udechukwu, one of the artists described in this work; from our subsequent meetings came the idea for this book and the accompanying exhibition. He and his wife, Ada, also in this book, housed and fed me with patience and care on most of my six trips to Nigeria. They provided me with a generous base from which to operate. Obiọra guided me through the history and the artists of the Nsukka group, although the final selection was entirely my own. He also made major improvements to a draft of this book, with patience and intelligence, allowing me to draw from his library and his memory of Nigerian art, events, and artists.

In addition to the Udechukwus, I am extremely grateful for the very considerable assistance of the other five artists discussed in this work: Uche Okeke, Chike Aniakọr, El Anatsui, Tayọ Adenaike, and Ọlu Ọguibe. They patiently answered my sometimes groping questions and allowed me to see and photograph their art, to interview them with pen and notebook, and also to videotape them on various occasions. Uche Okeke and his wife, Kaego, kindly put me up a number of times at their impressive home at the Asele Institute in Nimo and opened their grand art collection to me, as well as their collection of books and papers, providing much information and personal reminiscences amidst generous helpings of food and palm wine. Six of the seven artists in the book kindly read the chapters written about them and made very helpful comments. A young Nsukka artist, Chika Okeke, assisted me in numerous ways, providing me with valuable insights on the artists. Ọla Ọlọidi, then head of the Department of Fine and Applied Arts at the University of Nigeria, Nsukka, helped me with advice and assistance in obtaining theses and other relevant materials.

I interviewed a wide range of artists, sometimes once, sometimes twice or more, some of whom were not in the Nsukka group, but all of whom helped me understand its nature. Among them were Sylvester Ogbechie, the late Uzọ Egọnu, C. S. Okeke, C. Krydz Ikwuemesi, Paul Igboanugo, the late Chuka Amaefunah, Marcia Kure, Kaego Uche-Okeke, Obiọra Anidi, Chris Afuba, Gbubemi Amas Amanoritsewor, Ndidi Dike, Ifediọramma Dike, the late Okpu Eze, Blaise Gbaden, Bridget Egbeji, Bona Ezeudu, Nsikak Essien, Okay Ikenegbu, Benjo N. Igwilo, Barthosa Nkurumeh, Rowland Ndefo, Emmanuel A. J. Ulasi, Uzọ Ndubisi, Tony Nwachukwu, Boniface Okafọr, Ray Ọbeta, Ọkpan Oyeọku, Chijioke Ọnuọra, Samson Uchendu, Greg Odo, and Chinwe Uwatse. Mẹki Nzewi kindly led me to and explained the Nsugbe *uli* project, and Ernest Ezeanya patiently and pleasantly drove me over the bad roads of eastern Nigeria in his sturdy vehicle.

In Lagos, Emeka Ọkpara kindly arranged to put me up at the University of Nigeria Guest House numerous times. James Callahan, director of the United States Information Service, and Ray Orley, its cultural affairs officer, were extremely helpful on a recent trip to Nigeria. In London, the artist and scholar Elizabeth Willis, who has carried out the best historical studies of Igbo *uli* designs, was generous with her time and knowledge, and John Picton's perspectives on contemporary African art have been invaluable. In Bayreuth, Norbert Aas, who has followed the Nsukka artists over the years, kindly housed me with his friendly family; he was of great assistance in terms of personal knowledge, archival material, photographs, and in directing me to Uche Okeke's art in Munich. In the United States, Herbert M. Cole, an expert on Igbo art, patiently read sections of earlier versions of this manuscript, making thoughtful comments. Sarah Adams, who studied *uli* motifs on a Fulbright Scholarship in 1994–95, has added considerably to my knowledge of this art.

At the National Museum of African Art in Washington, D.C., in addition to Sieber and Williams, many persons assisted me in this project. I worked very closely with Andrea Nicolls, assistant curator, whose efficiency and practical wisdom I much admire. Janet Stanley, the museum's chief librarian, was impressively helpful; the library's collection on contemporary Nigerian artists is unsurpassed. Philip Ravenhill, chief curator at the museum, who was not initially involved in the project but assisted after the passing of Williams, has had insightful ideas and perspectives. Patricia Fiske, assistant director of the museum, ably guided me through many problems in this project. Amy Staples taught me how to use video for interviews, though I did not really meet her expectations. Chris Geary ably supported my photographic needs, as did Anita Jenkins, and Franko Khoury who took many of the photographs in this book. Others in the museum who aided me include Roslyn Walker, the museum's new director, who supported my work in numerous ways. Holly Laffoon and Toni Evans-Mayo did valuable secretarial work for me; the assistance of Julie Haifley, the museum's registrar, was invaluable. Sylvester Ogbechie kindly made the African diacritical notations and the drawings of the *uli* and *nsibidi* motifs, and Susan Cook prepared the maps. I wish to thank the National Museum of African Art for generous financial support toward the publication of this book. And many thanks to Frances Kianka for her careful and thoughtful editing of the text.

In Seattle, G. and H. Printing provided much valuable help, as did Pro-Lab, a photographic service. Occasional talks with René Bravmann stimulated me to explore in new directions. Most of all, my wife, Carol, provided immense support for my work on this book, at times giving up her own personal interests to see that I was free to pursue mine.

# A NOTE ON ORTHOGRAPHY

For the Igbo language, the ọ sound is pronounced as in "ought," the ẹ sound as in "wet," and the ụ sound as in "dunce." Generally, in the Igbo language when two consonants begin a word, the first is voiced and the second is not, as in Nsukka, *mma,* and *nka.* In the Yoruba language, ọ and ẹ are similar to the Igbo, and ṣ has the sound of "sh."

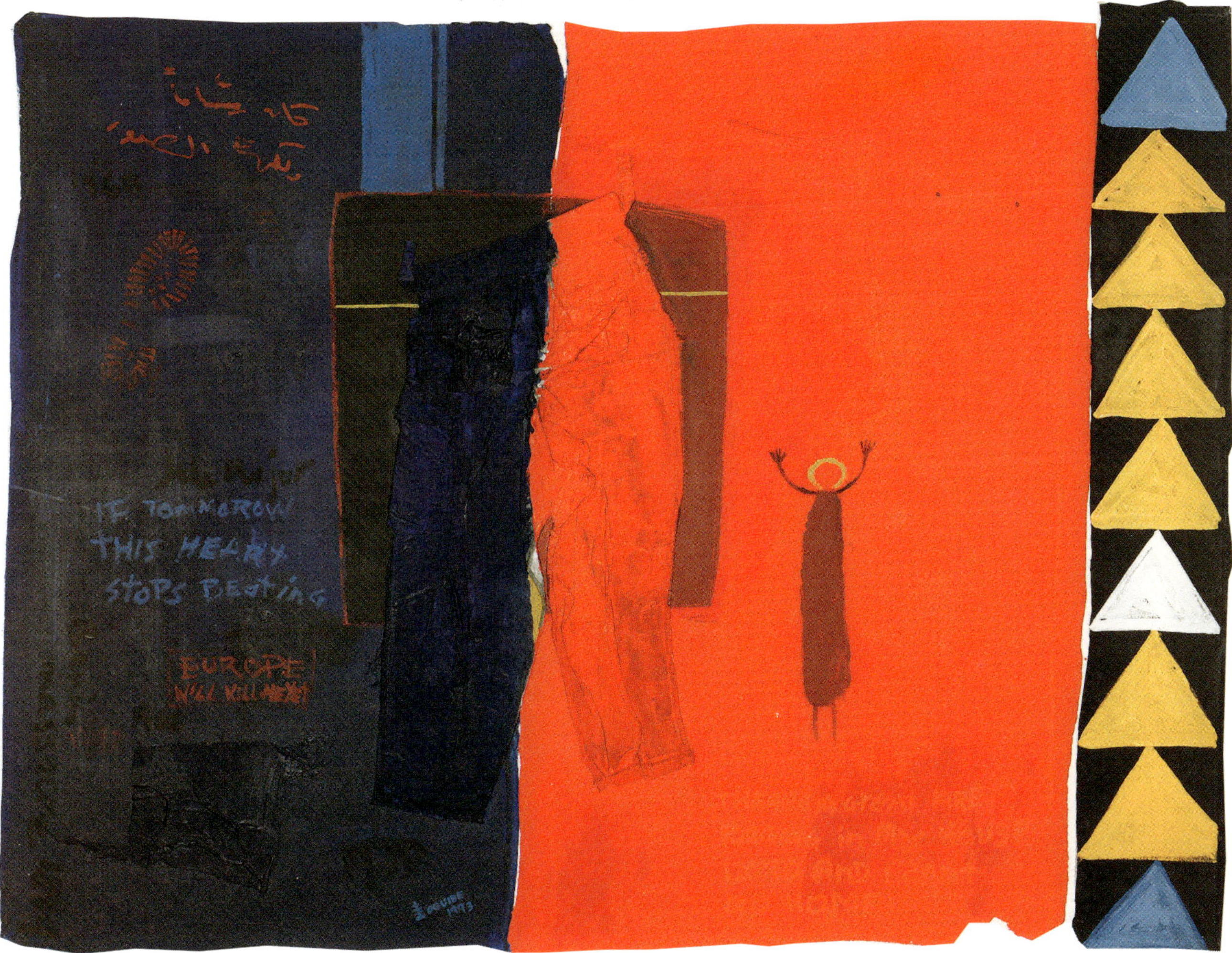

Fig. 191

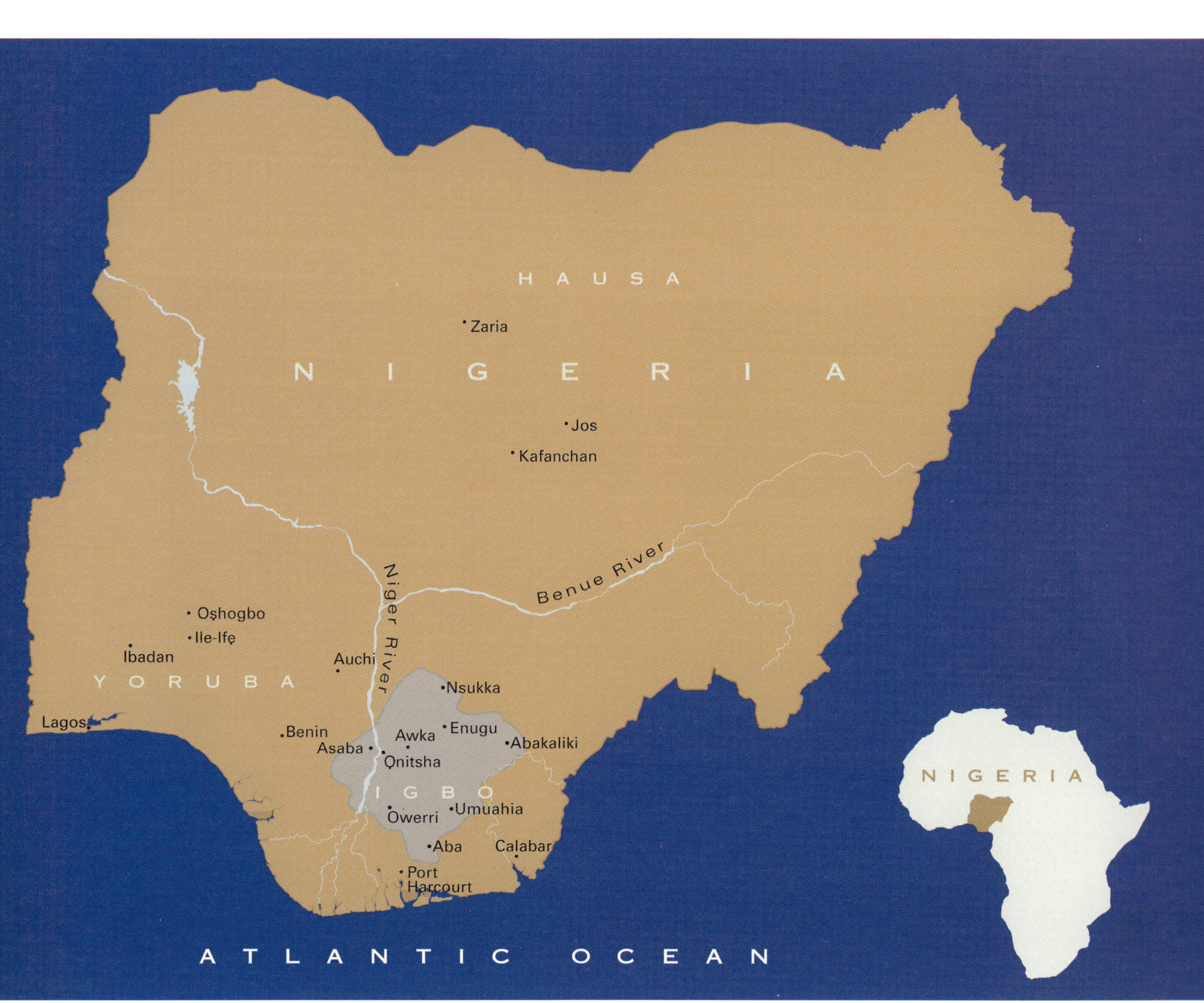

HAUSA
Zaria
NIGERIA
Jos
Kafanchan
Oshogbo
Ile-Ifẹ
Ibadan
Auchi
YORUBA
Niger River
Benue River
Nsukka
Lagos
Benin
Awka
Enugu
Abakaliki
Asaba
Ọnitsha
IGBO
Owerri
Umuahia
Aba
Calabar
Port Harcourt
ATLANTIC OCEAN
NIGERIA

# INTRODUCTION

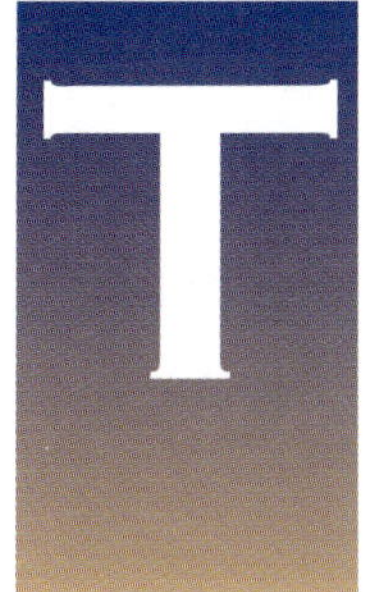

his book describes the creative work of seven contemporary artists within the framework of a larger number of artists whom I call the Nsukka group, who live or have lived in southeastern Nigeria. The group came into being in the 1960s and 1970s and still flourishes today. Its members are well educated and, either as students or teachers, are or have been connected with the University of Nigeria, Nsukka, a major federal government school founded in 1960, the year Nigeria gained independence.[1] The Nsukka artists form a regionally cohesive group mostly living or having once resided in the Nsukka area or in nearby Igbo centers.[2] The Igbo form one of the three largest cultural groups in Nigeria. Generally but not exclusively of Igbo background, the Nsukka artists draw on traditional Igbo body painting and wall murals called *uli* (in southern and eastern Igbo areas, the term is *uri*), associated with rituals and other events, art forms virtually gone today. The Nsukka artists use *uli* designs but employ Euro/American art media to create outside of traditional settings. The contemporary artists are mostly males; changes in gender, time, and setting are important transformations.

In recent years some of the artists have employed designs of another kind, *nsibidi,* from the southeastern Igbo area but originally from non-Igbo peoples further east, particularly the Ejagham. This traditional, largely male-produced and male-controlled design system is associated with male secret organizations, while *uli* was not. Some of the Nsukka artists employ both *uli* and *nsibidi,* others only one of them.

**MAP 1**. Nigeria.

While using older designs and images, these contemporary artists are frequently concerned in their art with present-day social, economic, and political problems in Nigeria and sometimes all of Africa. Senior members of the group—particularly Uche Okeke, Obiọra Udechukwu, Chike Aniakọr, and the late Chuka Amaefunah—were involved on the Biafran side in the bitter Nigerian civil war of 1967–70, mainly contested in the Igbo homeland. The war sensitized Igbo visual artists, as well as literary figures, dramatists, and musicians, to the mass movements of displaced persons, to refugee problems, hunger, illness, death, and disease, as well as to political hegemony, beyond what they might otherwise have experienced. To this day, many Nsukka artists express considerable sensitivity to issues of military control in Nigeria, the endemic corruption in the country, elitism, economic breakdown, and the collapse of basic facilities generally taken for granted in Europe and America: problems with water, electricity, and telephone service, rapid inflation, low pay, unemployment, the frequent unavailability of basic medicines, and police harassment on the roads. The artists are conscious of many disappointments in the postcolonial evolution of Nigeria. They form part of a well-educated, modernizing Nigerian nation that is today in a state of economic, moral, and social decline, despite the high achievement-orientation of its people and the country's rich natural resources. I will write on the impact of these matters on the artists and their responses to it.

I have framed this study of artists in historical terms, beginning with the awakening of contemporary art in the Nigerian colonial period in the first half of this century, through its growth in the 1950s and 1960s during political agitation leading to independence and the political and military unrest that eventually followed. I then discuss the beginnings of the Nsukka artists' group and the military takeover of Nigeria for long periods of time until today, despite which the Nsukka artists have grown and flourished. The work of these artists is to be understood in the context of national affairs, as this is the way they situate their art.

The Nsukka artists prefer well-established European media and techniques, except for the use of Nigerian woods and items such as cowrie shells and small African metal pieces in mixed-media work. For materials they employ pencil, graphite, pen, brush and ink, crayon, watercolors, pastel, gouache, tempera, oil, and acrylic. They create in mixed media, use a range of printing skills, such as serigraph, etching, and lithograph, and employ modern tools and equipment in woodwork and metalwork. They use the entire range of colors, yet at times some of these artists prefer the colors of *uli* wall murals—reddish-brown, yellow, white, and black—and the black or indigo of *uli* body painting. They seldom use the words "fine art" in reference to their work, an old-fashioned term, yet the art program at their university at Nsukka is called the Department of Fine and Applied Arts. This would suggest locating the Nsukka artists in the Euro/American art world and differentiating them from the older, indigenous arts, but in practice their art lies between the two.

## NIGERIA

Nigeria is a large country with a population of more than 80 million people composed of three major cultural groupings and more than a hundred others, some of substantial size. The Yoruba in the southwest, some 15 million strong, are Christians, Muslims, or traditionalists or merge tradition with one of these two religions. They have had a history of centralized states with extensive court art as well as public masquerading and dancing. The Hausa and Fulani, predominant in the north and numbering more than 30 million people, traditionally lived in highly stratified patron-client Muslim states, with much of their art being nonrepresentational and with impressive architecture in palaces and mosques. The main population group in the southeast, the Igbo, are some 12 million

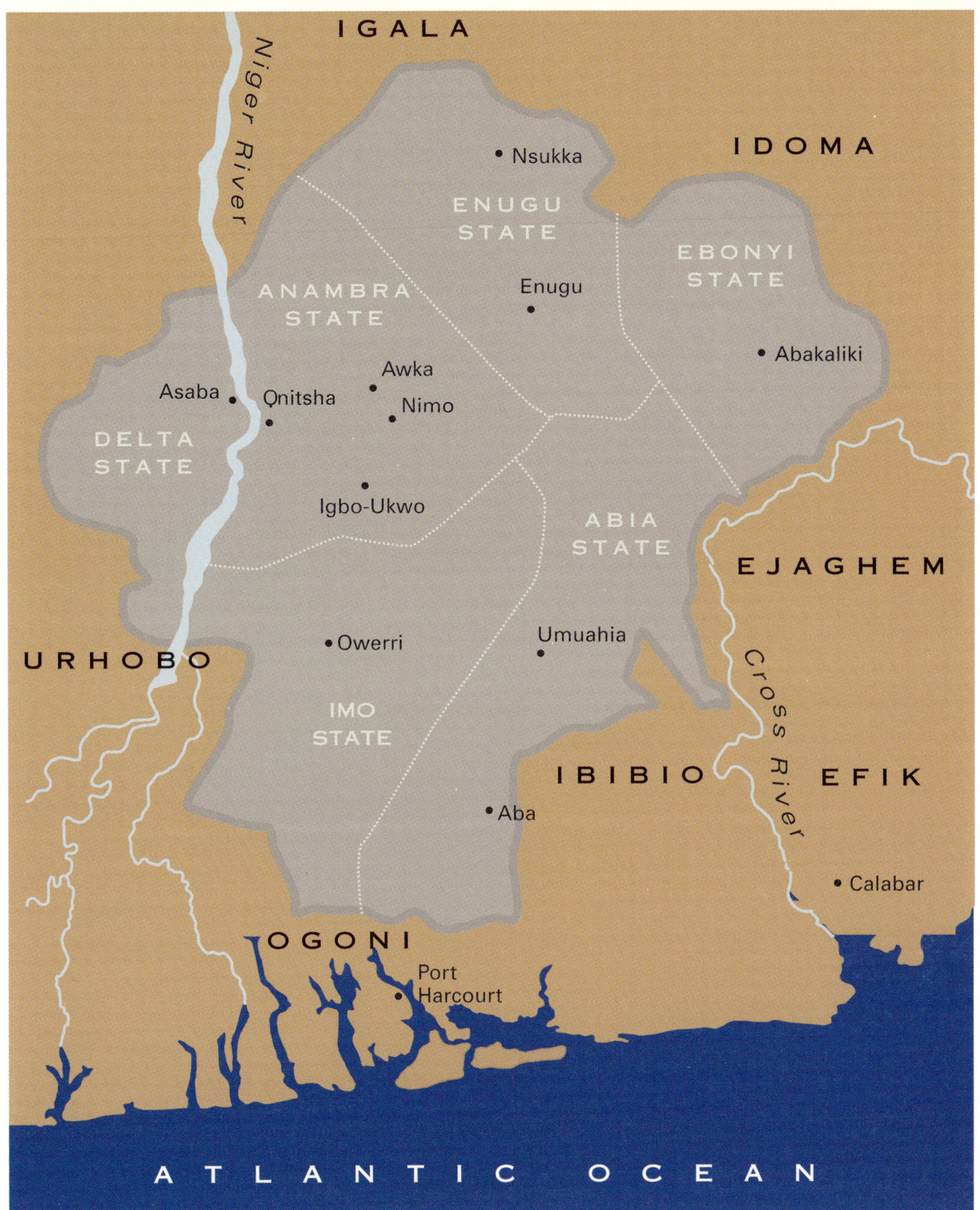


**MAP 2**. The Igbo Region of Nigeria.

strong and primarily Christian. Except for several small traditional states, such as at Ọnitsha, the Igbo formerly consisted of clusters of villages led by elders, titled persons, and priests. Political consensus was often reached by general agreement of community leaders. There have been popular male Igbo masquerade and figure sculpture traditions, as well as female wall and body painting.

In terms of European influence, the southwest region, including Lagos, the country's major port and its capital until a few years ago (it is now at Abuja in north central Nigeria), early felt the impact of the British in conquest, education, Christian influence, and European economic development. Lagos became the center for contemporary Nigerian art early in the century and continues to hold that position. The southeastern area was opened to

European influence at a somewhat later time but responded rapidly to British and Christian influence. The largely Muslim north showed a slower response until after Nigeria's independence in 1960. It is not surprising that most of the earliest contemporary Nigerian artists were Yoruba from the country's southwest.

## IGBO SOCIETY, CULTURE, AND ART

The Department of Fine and Applied Arts, University of Nigeria, Nsukka, is in Enugu State in the northern Igbo area. Most of the artists come from the present Anambra, Enugu, and Imo states, the three most central Igbo ones, rather than Abia State to the east and southeast, Ebonyi State to the northeast, and the western Igbo area in Delta State. It is largely the art of the more central Igbo that informs the contemporary Nsukka artists, although in recent years they have drawn inspiration from a broader area.

The Igbo have been generally patrilineally organized, tropical forest farmers growing root crops such as the African yam, cassava (manioc), and coco-yam (taro), as well as rice, various greens and other vegetables, and harvesting palm trees for their nuts, oil, and palm wine.[3] As an ancient people in the region, the population is dense for African rural farm areas. Because of this density the Igbo have expanded on their borders for hundreds of years, and after British colonialism took root they moved into other Nigerian areas for trade, farming, school-teaching, and business and later as physicians, lawyers, professors, civil servants, politicians, and military personnel, especially in the rapidly growing urban centers. Thus it is no surprise that they have also taken to contemporary art as a profession. Of high entrepreneurial spirit in a country where entrepreneurship is common, they move about to work, trade, and study.[4] Yet most of them keep in touch with their home area, even if they were born and raised away from it, and these home links figure importantly for the artists discussed in this book.

Igbo culture is characterized by strong art traditions and a rich art vocabulary from which its contemporary artists draw. There have been, and still exist, numerous masquerades, particularly the white-faced masked and appliqué-costumed *agbogho mmuo*.[5] There are numerous wood sculpted figures associated with shrines, and decorated doors and stools. Painted earth images occur in elaborately prepared *mbari* houses, a shrine in process, males and females taking part in its construction over time (fig. 1).[6] Female visual arts have included splendidly decorated pottery[7] and the fine *akwete* cloths of the southern Igbo.[8] Only occasionally are there still found *uli* murals, those elegant forms little studied until recently, which play important roles for the Nsukka artists.[9] These contemporary Nsukka artists, and sometimes others, draw on images of *mamiwata*, a female river spirit whose image is found throughout West Africa.

There is a rich and varied tradition of Igbo tales, often involving *mbe*, the tortoise trickster, and minstrels and poets present elaborate oral materials; some Nsukka artists draw on these. There are also significant dramatic traditions within and external to masquerading. Music and dancing skills are developed and frequently found at rites. Igbo architecture involves elaborate men's houses and shrines and interesting village and compound layouts, nowadays increasingly replaced with "palaces" belonging to important persons.[10]

The idea of different art forms joining together, rather than being distinct, is typical of the Igbo, as with other Africans. Body and wall *uli* were painted for title taking and other events at which there was music, dancing, fine dress, and speechmaking—an overall aesthetic. Minstrel songs are also a form of poetry, often accompanied on the *ubo* musical instrument.

Igbo art varies from area to area, as do dialects, kinship practices, religious beliefs, architecture, farming styles, and the degree of European education. Such variations are not surprising in a large population; the works of the Nsukka artists exhibit considerable variation as well.

The contemporary Nsukka artists are not only cognizant of the traditional art but also of the numerous and complex Igbo religious beliefs and practices involving ideas about many spirits from nature, those for divination and fertility and those to cure illnesses. The female earth spirit, Ana (called Ali, Ala, or Ani in various Igbo areas), is everywhere a major force concerned with fertility and general health and welfare. The heavenly god, Chukwu, Ana's counterpart, is frequently called upon in ritual and sacrifice, though he rarely has his own shrine. There is the spirit of the individual's destiny, Chi. Reincarnation beliefs exist, and ancestor spirits play important roles in Igbo life. The Igbo religious world is closely linked to aesthetic forms that symbolize belief and practice in various ways.

Until a few decades ago the Igbo did not have a known classical history on which Nsukka artists might draw, as could the Yoruba, Bini, and some other Nigerian groups, as well as artists in Ethiopia and the Sudan, though they have taken from the ancient non-Igbo Nok culture of Nigeria's north and from elsewhere.[11] However, the publication in 1970 of Thurstan Shaw's Igbo-Ukwu excavations in central Igboland revealed a priestly center at about A.D. 800 with design elements similar to some *uli* and other Igbo art of this century.[12] While Nsukka artists rarely draw specifically from these finds, they have been encouraged by the knowledge that they, too, have a classical artistic background.

The original missions in Igboland were Catholic, Anglican, Scottish Presbyterian, and English Methodist. In later years, American Baptists, Seventh Day Adventists, and other missionaries came in; more recently, numerous

1. *Mbari* house in process, Umuedi Nnorie, 1967. Photo: Herbert M. Cole.

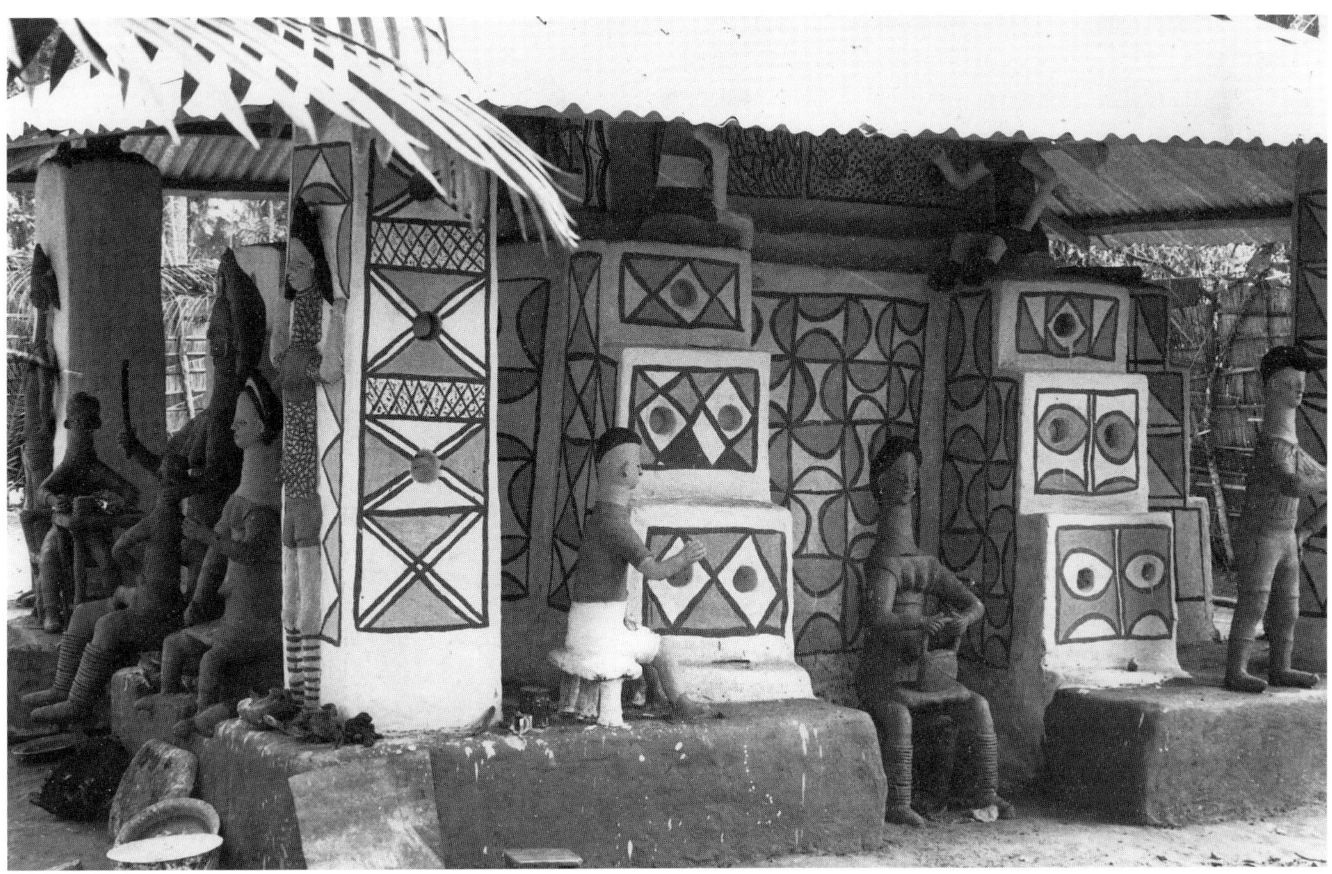

fundamentalist religions and born-again Christian groups have become popular, often with American connections.[13] Syncretist churches blending Christianity and reinterpreted African traditions have existed for some time. Although Nigeria has no official religion, the Igbo area, indeed all of southeastern Nigeria, shows strong Christian influence, despite the continuation of numerous traditional beliefs and practices. The Nsukka artists, as most Igbo, have been exposed to Christian teachings and experience. While not always accepting a particular Christian dogma, such as strictures against polygyny and sacrifice at traditional shrines, the Igbo accommodate some traditional practices with Christianity. Most Nigerian church groups made the transition from external mission control to indigenous leadership by the end of the 1970s. A substantial number of Yoruba of southwestern Nigeria have found Islam congenial. However, the Igbo have not, and there are few Muslims in the Igbo area.

Igbo are often educated in the European style, some of them extremely so. Many speak both Igbo and English, and some know other Nigerian, African, or other tongues. They read and publish a great deal, and some of them have had experience abroad. Yet they retain considerable knowledge of and experience with their own traditions, especially senior Igbo. With the exception of some staunch or fundamentalist Christians, the Igbo generally live without much personal conflict between tradition and the selective Europeanized world that came to them during and after colonialism. Both are ingrained in them. The variety of syntheses of European influence and Igbo culture that occur is impressive. There is a playfulness and an experimental quality to these links, showing the ability to adjust to changing conditions without an overly strong nostalgia for the past or a need to put past tradition totally behind.[14]

The Nsukka artists come from rich and creative artistic, cultural, and religious traditions and are also familiar with forms of Christianity and selective Euro/American life and culture. These provide valuable resources for them to draw upon. The partial decline and the reinterpretation of traditional art forms in Nigeria mean that important creative activity in the visual arts today lies with the contemporary field. The Nsukka artists are an excellent example of this.

## TERMS

In this book, I use the terms *group, Nsukka group,* and *Nsukka artists* for those in this study in preference to other ways of describing them. Some of the artists and some Nigerian art critics use the terms *Ulists* or *Uliists* for the artists and *Ulism* or *Uliism* to refer to their art. I find these terms to be narrow, as they stress only one aspect of the work of these artists who also draw on other areas of cultural tradition, and current Nigerian life and problems, using Euro/American materials and techniques. The term *school,* as in *Nsukka school,* or *Uli* school, is also occasionally used in Nigeria, referring to either the Nsukka university art school or to the idea of a group of artists with related styles. But "school" implies too tight an organization; many of the artists are no longer directly associated with the university and live elsewhere in Nigeria or overseas. Some persons may consider these artists to form an "art movement," though in Euro/America the expression often refers to a radical and ideological break with the past, as with the Surrealists, Impressionists, and Abstract Expressionists. There are elements of a "movement" among the Nsukka artists, as they broke with naturalistic and conventional European art training, and some of the artists are very much interested in social and political change in Nigeria. Yet as the artists draw from Igbo culture, there is continuity, not a break with the past. Thus I hesitate to use the term *art movement* for them.

I employ Euro/American art and art historical terms sparingly, for they have meanings and contexts that are not always useful in Africa. One of the seven Nsukka artists in this book, Olu Oguibe, has been critical of the recent trends toward heavy intellectualization and theorization in postmodern Euro/American art criticism, viewing these as mechanisms for hiding, rather than dealing with, the very basic struggles for survival of African-born artists and others.[15] I tend to agree with this viewpoint; some postmodern ideas seem overly erudite considering the problems of social life in Nigeria and other African countries that I have observed.

If these Nsukka artists are a "group," it must be understood that they are not formally organized as such, except those who are currently faculty and students in the Department of Fine and Applied Arts at the university. Yet there is a good level of interaction among those at the university with those who once taught or studied there but now live elsewhere. Many of them keep in touch, view each other's work, are stimulated by it with reference to their art, and write about each other's creations. There is a spirit of solidarity among many of them, even though some have ceased to produce art.

## THE ARTISTS

Of the thirty-five or more artists in the Nsukka group who are serious, exhibiting professionals, a good many, including some of the younger ones, have traveled abroad to Europe, the United States, or both, to study or for exhibitions, to take part in workshops, to visit, or to pursue careers as artists; some have relatives overseas. In Nigeria these artists' lives are often somewhat enclosed because of conditions in the country and their preoccupation with coping with daily living; yet they are not turned inward, uninterested in or unaware of what goes on in the rest of the world and its arts. This is so even if they rarely depict images from the broader world as a consequence of their travels. They are eager for contact with other world areas and regret that conditions in Nigeria do not allow them more travel time abroad. Only one of the seven artists in this book, Ọlu Ọguibe, who lived in London for six years and is now in the United States, has strongly moved away from the Nsukka artists' traditions in recent years. The artists are not "natural" or naive artists; they are well trained and aware of the wider world about them.

### ARTISTIC QUALITIES

The Nsukka artists strongly base their art on drawing, as might be expected from their integrating traditional Igbo body and mural painting into their work. Their art is often linear, with numerous curvilinear lines, generally

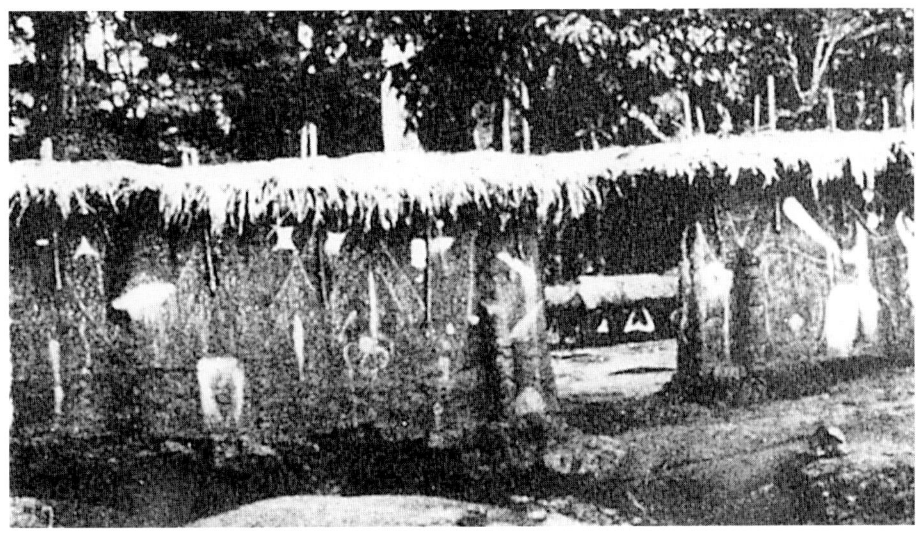

**2.** *Uli* mural on outer wall of an Igbo shrine at Nibo, near Awka, c. 1910. Photo: Northcote Thomas, from Thomas 1913, pl. VIII.

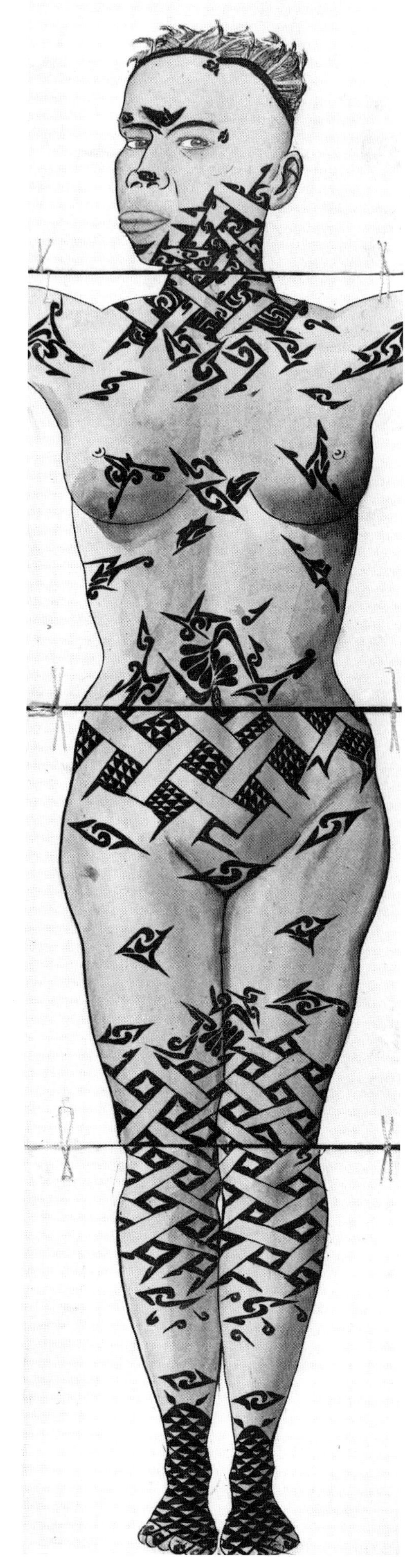

3. *Uli* body designs from Igbo country collected by E. H. Duckworth, possibly from Arochuku, date unknown. Collection and photo: Pitt-Rivers Museum, University of Oxford.

in preference to angular, squarish, and rectangular ones. As one of the artists, Obiọra Udechukwu, has written, *uli* has a lyrical quality that is found in the contemporary art.[16] The art is mostly two-dimensional; even the metalwork has this quality, and much of the wood sculpture is in relief. Perspective is not a predominant feature, as it is not with the traditional *uli* and *nsibidi* art. Delightful ways of playing with positive and negative space draw from *uli* and characterize the contemporary artists' creations.

The Nsukka art often depicts humans rather than animals or objects; African heads, faces, and figures abound. This is a change from traditional *uli* art, which seldom pictured humans but rather depicted many manmade objects such as bowls and farm tools, as well as animals, birds, plants, plant parts, and celestial elements (fig. 2). These *uli* motifs are incorporated into images of human figures in the contemporary art. Yet, as traditional *uli* designs commonly appeared on the faces, arms, legs, and bodies of females, from girls to senior women, and occasionally on males, their association with the human body is evident; and the presence of *uli* murals on houses and compound walls of Igbo living areas suggests human sociability. *Nsibidi* designs tend to express social relationships more directly than *uli*, for example, motifs such as those for lovers or for a married couple with child. Because of this connection with social relationships, they are gaining popularity among the Nsukka artists.

Traditional *uli* was employed in many social situations, such as at title taking, marriages, memorial services for the dead, and harvest rites, even if the designs themselves rarely depicted human situations (figs. 3–5). It is not surprising that the Nsukka artists often depict humans, for the Igbo are a gregarious and talkative people. Lacking some of the rituals and their social relationships of the past, the Nsukka artist puts his or her sociability and concern for other humans into depictions of them, in contrast to the traditional *uli* artists, who employed the design system as an aesthetic adjunct to Igbo rituals and events.

While the art of some Nsukka artists may appear to resemble Euro/American modern art, little of which is found in Nigeria, these

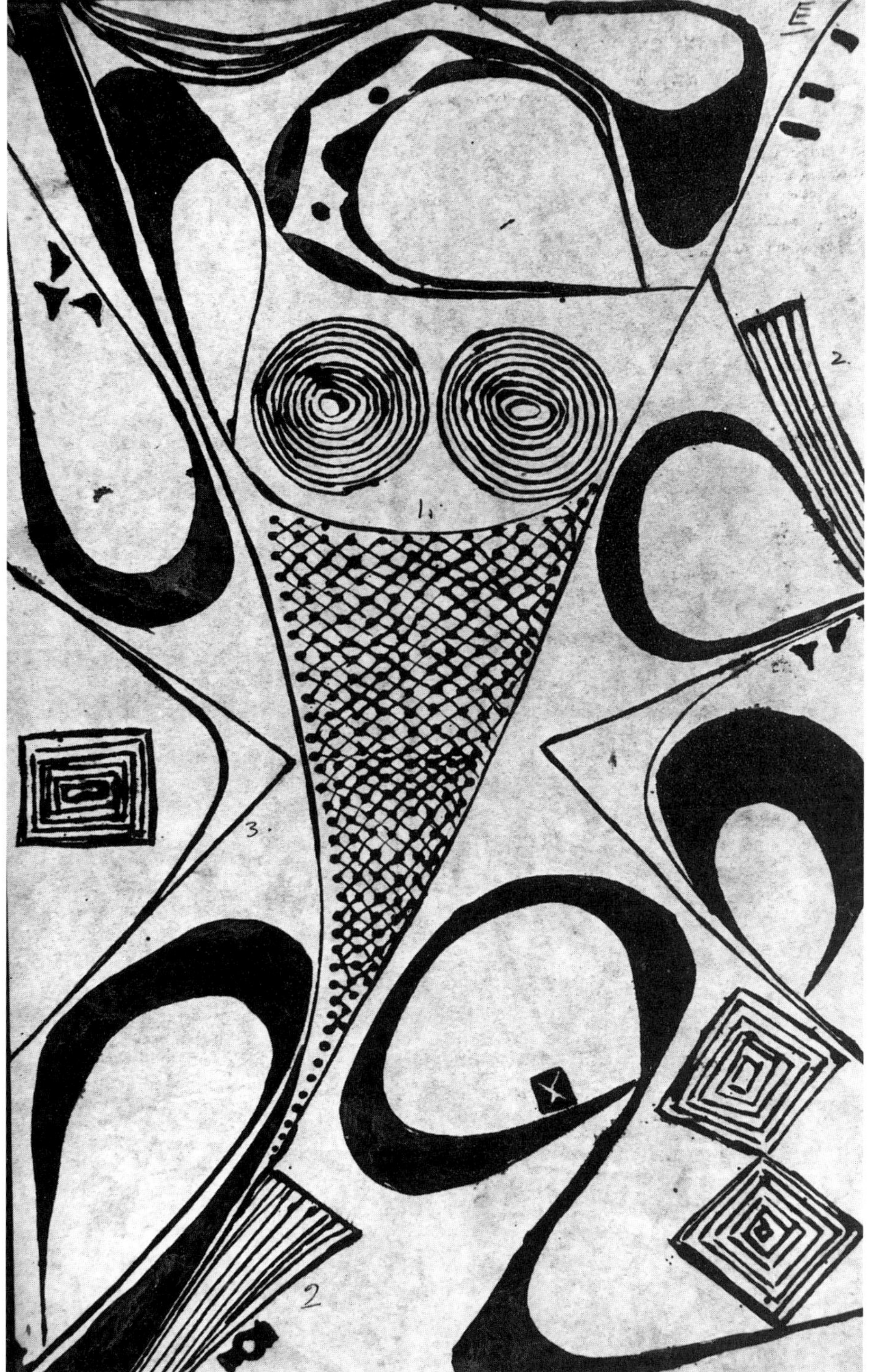

**4.** *Uli* body designs from Awka District collected by W. B. Yeatman, c. 1933. Collection and photo: Pitt-Rivers Museum, University of Oxford.

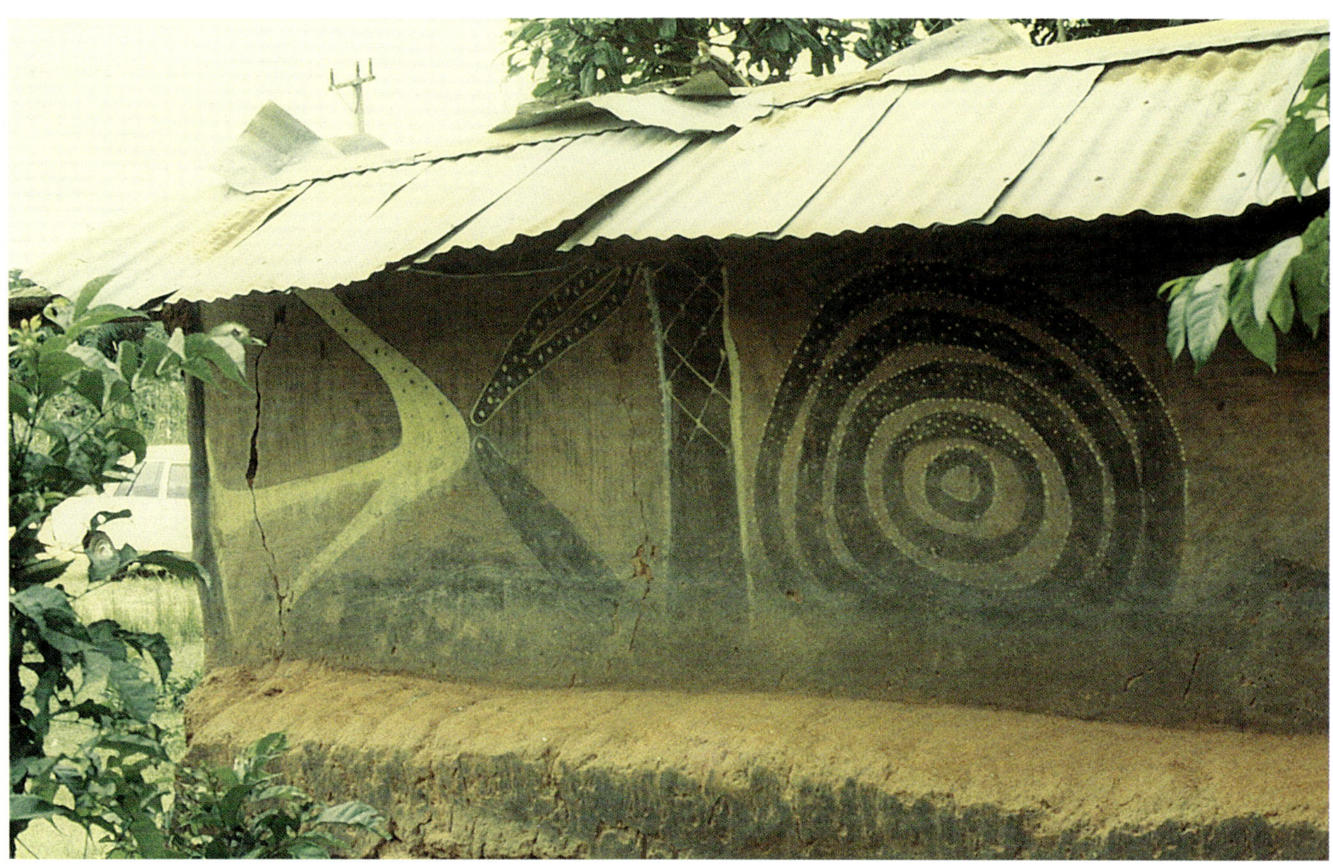

**5**. Section of *uli* shrine wall at Nri, 1994.

artists are familiar with it through books and slides as well as visits abroad.[17] Yet they strive for artistic independence. They blend traditional *uli* motifs and sometimes *nsibidi* designs, draw from Igbo masquerades and dances and other Igbo and African cultural elements, often blending these with current sociopolitical commentaries, scenes from daily life, the seasons, and the lovely hill country of Nsukka and its environs. They do so in characteristic linear styles.

## VARIATIONS

The Nsukka artists do not form a rigidly uniform group, however; some make greater use of *uli* motifs than others, and some emphasize *nsibidi* designs over *uli* motifs. A few are almost apolitical, while others are expressive of social and political life. Some depict Christian scenes—not surprising in a Christian region of Nigeria.[18] A few look mainly to Igbo festivals and dances for their material, while others rarely do. Some employ a variety of media; others prefer one or two forms. El Anatsui, one of the seven artists discussed in this book, is of Ghanaian origin, while another, Tayọ Adenaike, is from the Yoruba in southwest Nigeria. Both artists have lived in Igbo country for years and have absorbed much of its culture, drawing from *uli*, *nsibidi*, and Igbo traditions in their art. There are a number of other non-Igbo artists in the larger Nsukka group. The Nsukka artists are interesting for the varying forms that their art takes, while remaining within a similar general framework of artistic beliefs.

The seven Nsukka artists who are the focus of this book are also the subject of an exhibition sponsored by and held at the National Museum of African Art, Smithsonian Institution, Washington, D.C. (October 21, 1997–April 26, 1998). The selected artists vary in age from their early thirties to early sixties. In my selection I have included the group's founding artist, Uche Okeke, and the other artist who is senior in age, Chike Aniakọr. The next generation includes Obiọra Udechukwu and El Anatsui. Tayọ Adenaike is the next youngest in age, followed by Ọlu Ọguibe and Ada Udechukwu, who is the only female artist among the seven. I describe the work of each artist in sequence according to age, beginning with the most senior. Only a few of the larger Nsukka group of artists are deceased, among them Chuka Amaefunah, who died in 1993, and a younger promising artist, Kevin Echeruo, who died in the late 1960s.[19] This is, therefore, a relatively young artistic tradition, and it has been possible for me to interview most of the artists in person.

My selection of these seven artists, for both this book and the exhibition, probably reflects biases deriving from my own background and American experience, though I have tried to minimize these by steeping myself in the work of many Nsukka artists and by my discussions with them. I have perhaps been overly influenced by certain members of the group whom I have come to know best. I have emphasized painting and printmaking, and in one case wood sculpture, over metal sculpture, ceramics, textiles, and mixed media because this is where I believe the strengths of the Nsukka artists lie at present.



The Nsukka artists also have strong literary interests, writing about their own art and that of other Nigerian artists, generally in English but occasionally in Igbo. Two of the seven artists discussed in this book are also trained art historians. The Nsukka artists are concerned with the low level of art criticism in Nigeria, as are artists elsewhere in the country. One of the seven artists has a bachelor's degree in literature rather than visual art. Many of them write poetry, and three are well known for their verse. The artists' poetry, mostly in English but some in Igbo, is viewed by them and others as another way of expressing their beliefs, experiences, and emotions. Some of them have published poetry illustrated with their own work, and their art is found in literature journals such as *Okike* and *Research in African Literatures* and in books by various authors. Several of the seven artists have been inspired in their poetry and visual art by epic songs of traditional Igbo minstrels. Many have been influenced by the writings of the late, well-known Igbo poet Christopher Okigbo and other authors such as the internationally known Igbo novelist Chinua Achebe, who once taught at the University of Nigeria, Nsukka. A number of the artists have been involved in creating, acting in, and directing drama. Their visual art cannot be satisfactorily explored without an understanding of their roles in related art forms.



By training and life work I am an anthropologist, although for this study I have of course familiarized myself with art historical concepts and theories. In 1952–53, I carried out anthropological research for fifteen months at Afikpo, an Igbo group of villages. In 1959–60, I returned there and to the Igbo town of Abakaliki for a like period of time. Since then I have made a number of briefer trips to Igbo country and have published several studies based on my research there.[20]

Afikpo and Abakaliki are respectively in the eastern and northeastern Igbo areas, distant and culturally somewhat distinct from Nsukka and the more central Igbo regions where most of the artists in this study, and much of the Igbo designs that the artists employ, originate. *Uli* and *nsibidi* were never prominent design elements at Afikpo and Abakaliki when I was there, and I generally overlooked their existence. As other scholars of African art until recent years, I preferred to concentrate on the aspects of African art that Euro/Americans considered more interesting: masks and figures. I published several articles and a book on traditional Afikpo masquerades and became familiar with Igbo culture and art.[21] My anthropological orientation allows me to place art in its cultural and social context, and my Igbo research resulted in publications on family and kinship, traditional forms of leadership and authority, religion, and boys growing to manhood. These studies have not been strongly historical, though much of my Igbo writings deal with what is now Afikpo's and Abakaliki's past, considering that many changes have occurred there. Nevertheless, a study of contemporary art requires understanding the historical background, and I have tried to be sensitive to historical factors.

For an anthropologist, learning the language of art history can be a lengthy process, particularly as much of art history is oriented toward Euro/American art and employs terms and concepts that appear to have little relevance to the kind of societies anthropologists study, particularly noncentralized ones such as the Igbo. Yet a cross-fertilization of ideas on art, art history, and anthropology can be very fruitful.

How well can someone such as myself, from the hegemonic Euro/American world, understand African art and culture and express that understanding in writing? Current critical theory casts doubt on this. Olu Oguibe, one of the younger artists included in this book, is dubious about the ability of non-African scholars from Euro/America to comprehend African art, whether contemporary or more traditional forms, because of hegemonic, acquisitive, and racialistic attitudes and because of their use of African art for non-African ends.[22] I have become increasingly humble (even with my considerable African research, which, in addition to my Nigerian experience, includes a year in Ghana and nearly two in northern Sierra Leone) as to how well I can interpret African art and culture. If it were not for the friendship and encouragement of artists involved in this study, I might have abandoned it. I have tried to make their viewpoints and ideas clear by quoting from their own publications and words, sometimes from videotapes, which form only a small part of discussions with them over the past five years.



I have tried to be aware of Euro/American attitudes toward African art. For nearly a century now, more strongly since World War II, there has been interest in traditional African art, which has led to the appropriation of its art objects in immense quantities in Europe and America and now in Japan. There are rapidly rising prices, the creation of large collections, and numerous African art galleries in Euro/America. Many museum and gallery exhibitions of this art have taken place; there is hardly a major museum that has not had at least one such exhibition. Contemporary African artists are very much aware of this and are critical of the Euro/American appropriation of traditional African work. To see much of it they must leave home or rely on the few available publications in their countries to familiarize themselves with it. When the Nsukka artists draw from their own traditions, they are well aware of the ways that Euro/America has drawn from African traditions and made use of them and perceive this as a major contrast to their own manner of acting. This matter concerns them deeply. While they desire greater contact with Europe and America, and many contemporary African artists wish to sell some of their art there, a few of them are cautious in doing so, preferring that their art remain in their own country or elsewhere in Africa. Contemporary African artists sometimes wonder whether they and their art will be swallowed up by the external world, as traditional art has been.[23] Recently, however, the interest in traditional African art in Europe and America, especially in sculpture, has peaked, shifting to naive art, photography, textiles, and ceramics and to geographic areas of Africa other than the west and central regions. There is also a slowly growing interest in contemporary African art.

## THE EMERGING FIELD

This interest has had to meet several challenges from Euro/America: that the art is either derivative of Euro/American forms or of traditional African art; that it is not as interesting or as skilled as older African work; that the great civilizations of Africa, with their artistic creativity, are in the past; that, at best, contemporary African artists produce premodern or modern art and not the more desirable postmodern art and are out of step with the Euro/American art world. Again, a common belief is that the most interesting African art is that of the untrained artist, a belief that equates such art with the naive art of Europe and America. I hope that this book helps refute some of these mistaken views.

Despite these misconceptions, interest in contemporary African art continues to grow, as it has for Native American, Inuit, and Australian Aboriginal work. Unfortunately, the rise of multiculturalism in Euro/America has sometimes led to a crude selling of cultural materials, to their cheapening and degradation. Some of the best contemporary third and fourth world art derives from peoples in these cultures who are employing their background, rituals, and religions in new and imaginative ways, though frequently using Euro/American art media. The rise of contemporary art in Nigeria and elsewhere in Africa is part of a worldwide movement, not an isolated case.

The growing interest in contemporary African art in Europe and America today is reflected in major exhibitions—such as *Africa Now, Africa Explores, Magiciens de la Terre, Contemporary African Artists: Changing Traditions,* and *Seven Stories*—as well as in smaller ones.[24] There are several useful general studies, particularly Jean Kennedy's survey, a journal in New York devoted to it, and several journals in African countries.[25] In Nigeria, these include *The Eye, Nigeria Magazine, Glendora Review,* and *USO: Nigerian Journal of Art.* There is now a particularly strong interest in black South African art, publications, and exhibitions.[26] There have been occasional gallery exhibits in England, particularly during the Africa '95 celebrations, and others in France, Germany, and the United States. A gallery in London and several in New York regularly exhibit contemporary African art.[27] A few collectors of traditional African work are now turning their attention to contemporary forms as well. This book, then, is written in the context of a newly emerging field of interest in contemporary African art in Europe and America, but tries to separate itself from older established traditions of Euro/American appropriation of traditional African art and scholarly orientations to it.

What seems desirable now in contemporary African art is a series of detailed studies rather than general surveys and exhibits and the short commentaries on individual artists that have appeared. There is a need for detailed analyses of individual artists and their art and of African artistic schools and groups, which are often regionally and culturally sited. Scholarly work on the history of contemporary African art is urgent while some of its pioneers are still alive.

In this book, then, I try to develop one useful approach to the study of this art. My own taste is to blend anthropology and art history, with sensitivity to indigenous African expressions. It is not simply anthropology, art history, or cultural studies. I hope that this work will serve as one possible model for others interested in the field of contemporary African art. If it proves useful in that regard, it will, in addition to presenting the interesting history and intriguing work of one group of artists, have fulfilled a major goal of mine.

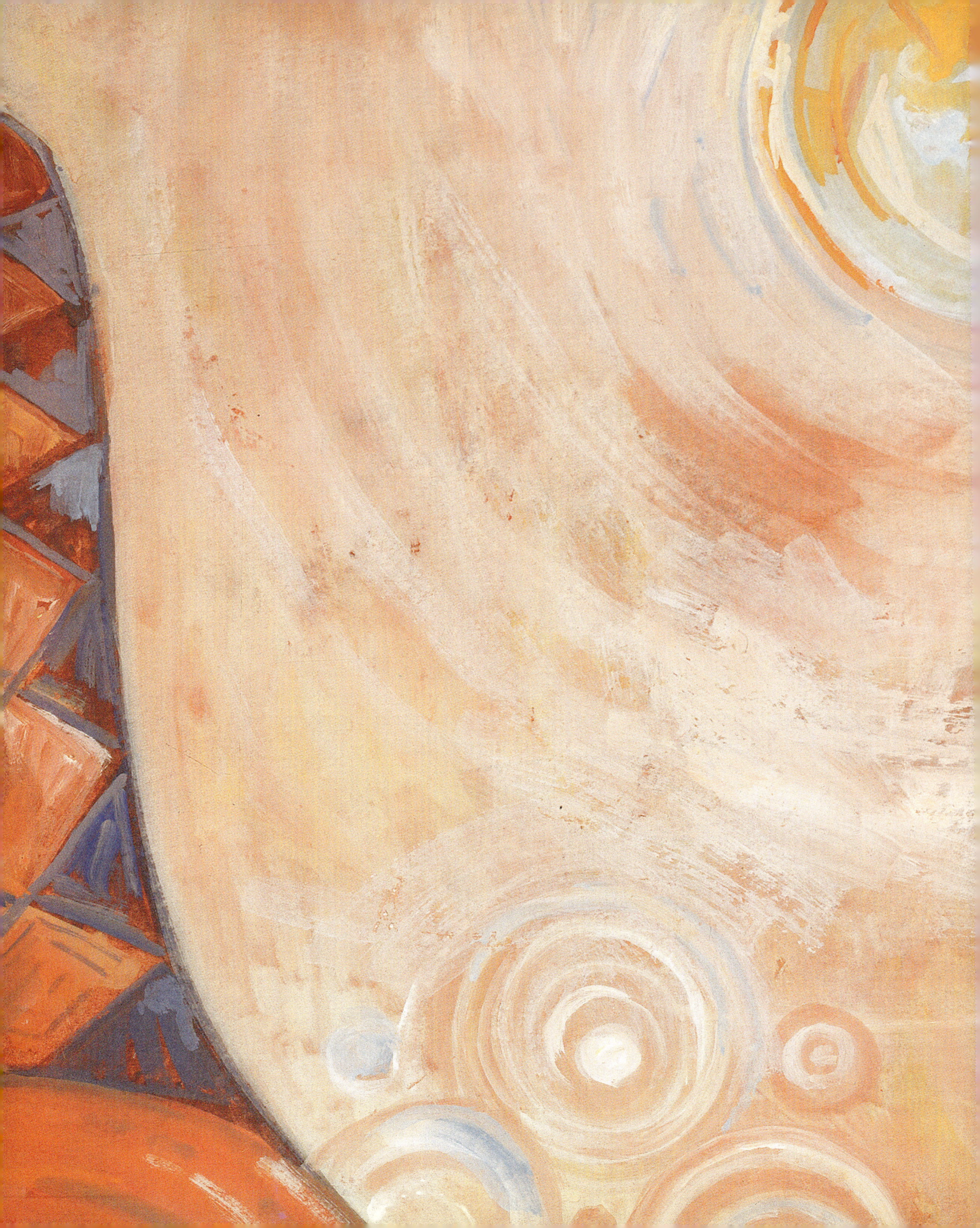

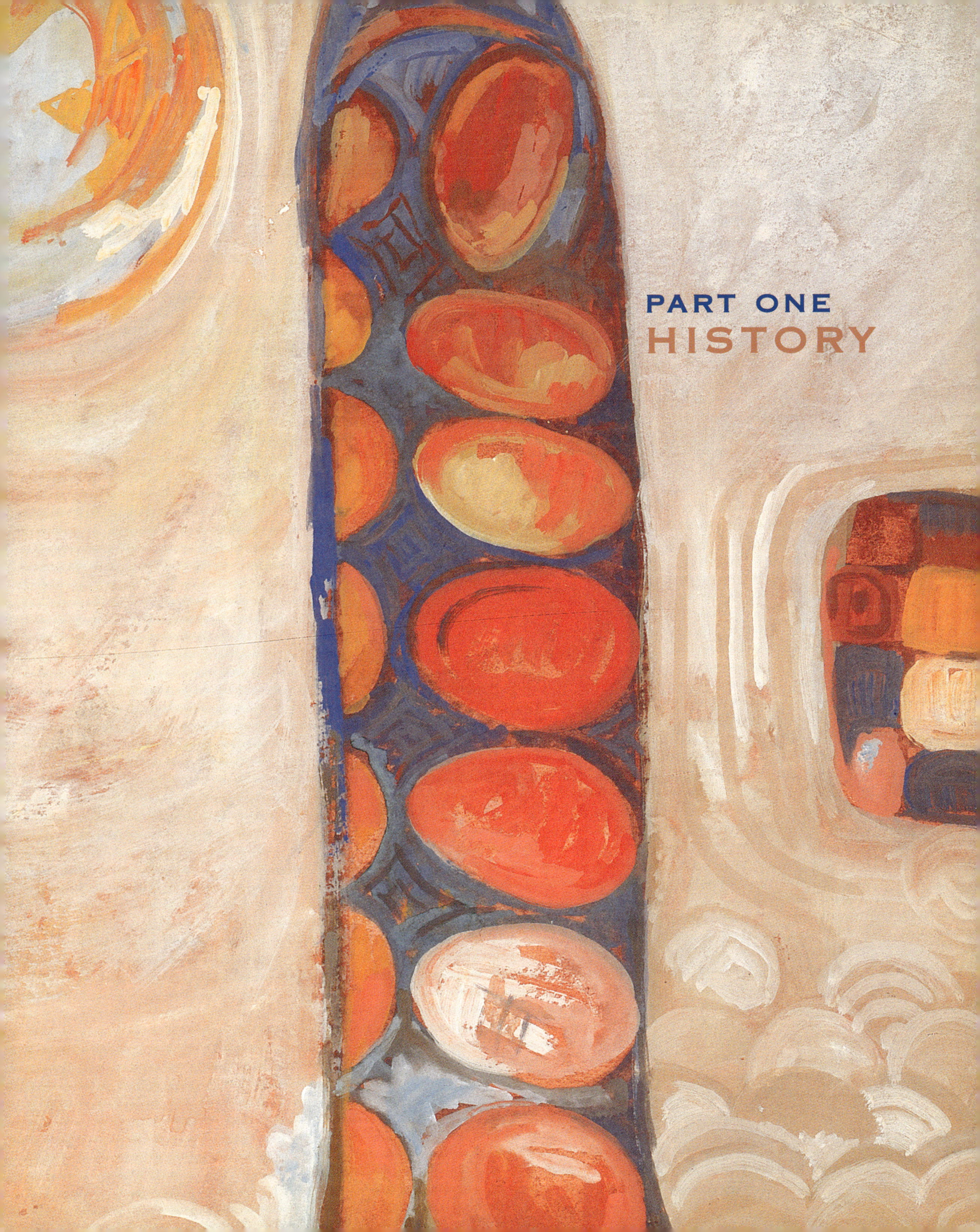
PART ONE
HISTORY

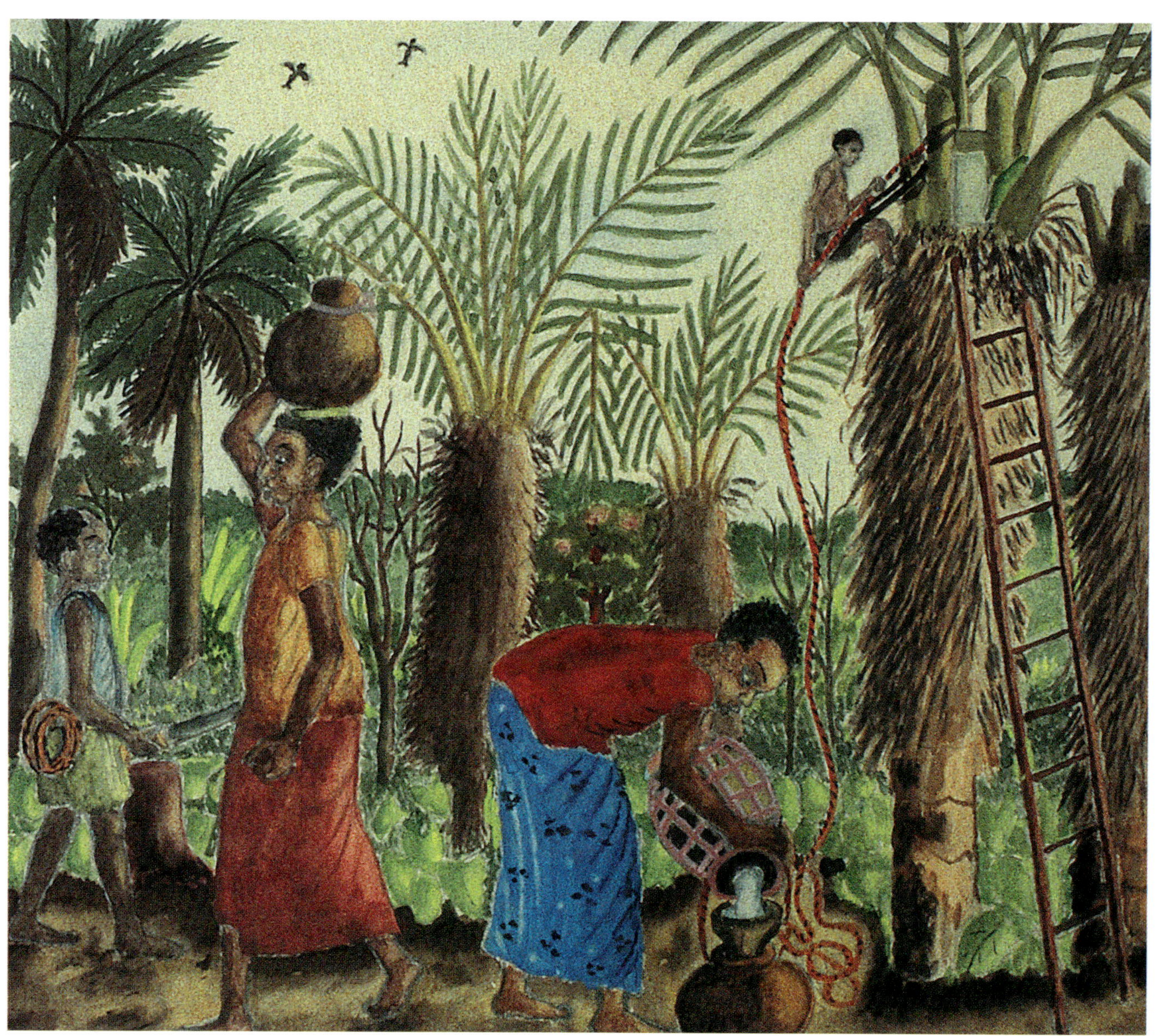

Detail of fig. 6.

# 1. PIONEERS AND PREDECESSORS, 1900–1970

It is no longer possible to look at African art and see nothing but a continuous and rapid process of disintegration. We can now see that African art has responded to the social and political upheavals that have taken place all over the continent. The African artist has refused to be fossilized.

ULLI BEIER[1]

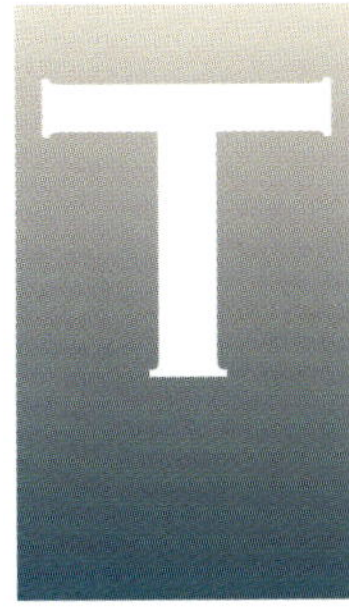

The Nsukka artists did not just spring up; they were preceded by contemporary Nigerian artists going back to the beginning of the twentieth century. From then until about 1950 there were a few pioneers existing even in the heyday of British colonialism with its strong antagonism to traditional art and rituals, but more accepting of conventional British art, of portraits and idyllic scenes of native life. The 1950s and 1960s were marked by an increase in the number of artists and the rise of less conventional and more experimental work during the growth of nationalism and Nigerian independence in 1960. The work of the Nsukka artists was, in part, a reaction to some of the earlier artistic trends.

## THE PIONEERS

Aina Ọnabolu (1882–1963), of Yoruba origin, was the first contemporary artist in Nigeria, possibly in Africa south of the Sahara.[2] He did his first serious painting in Lagos in 1903 and, in 1920, held what was probably the first solo exhibition in Nigeria. He then studied in London and Paris, returning to teach in a number of Lagos secondary schools. Determined to prove to Africans and colonialists that he could be as skilled as European artists, Ọnabolu followed the British Academy style of his time, feeling that portraits, his major art form, "should be seen as history, and himself a history painter."[3] It was not the history of indigenous cultures but of the emerging urban African elite, especially in Lagos, with which he had close ties. Although Ọnabolu is sometimes called the father of modern or contemporary art in Nigeria, Ọla Ọlọidi notes that Ọnabolu was not creating art in the style of Picasso, Braque, or other modernists of the time but in conventional British forms, while these continental artists were

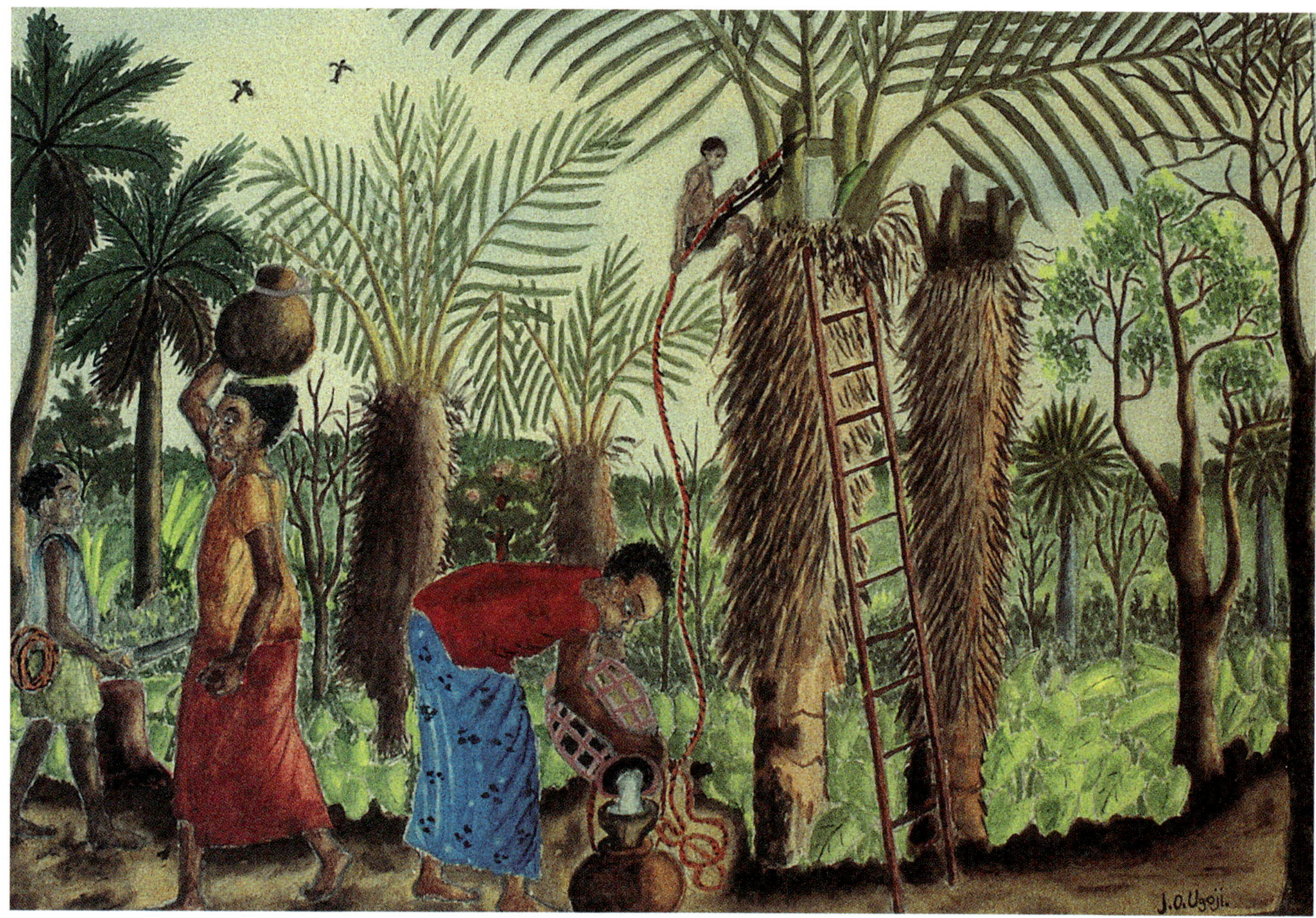

**6**. J. O. Ugọji, *Palm Wine Tapper*, n.d.,
watercolor on paper, dimensions unknown. Collection of the Asele Institute, Nimo.

producing art closer to traditional African styles than Ọnabolu was.[4] Ọnabolu is revered in Nigeria today as the country's first nontraditional African artist, but he is criticized for emulating British art, so different from indigenous Nigerian forms.

Ọnabolu persuaded the Nigerian Department of Education to develop a plan for art education in 1923, which led to the hiring of Kenneth C. Murray from England to teach in Nigerian secondary schools. Moving between several secondary schools in different parts of the country, Murray trained five students together between 1933 and 1936. Some of the students were of differing cultural backgrounds. In this effort to create Nigerian art teachers, Murray's approach opposed Ọnabolu's. Murray had his students draw on traditional cultural themes—market scenes, fishing, palm wine tapping, and so on—often in watercolor, simply painted works without perspective, not in British Academy style and not portraits. As teachers and artists, they later helped develop a tradition of genre art in Nigeria (fig. 6). C. C. Ibeto, Uthman M. Ibrahim, D. L. K. Nnachy, and A. P. Umana remained in this tradition, but the fifth student, Ben Enwọnwu, was to depart from it (see below).[5]

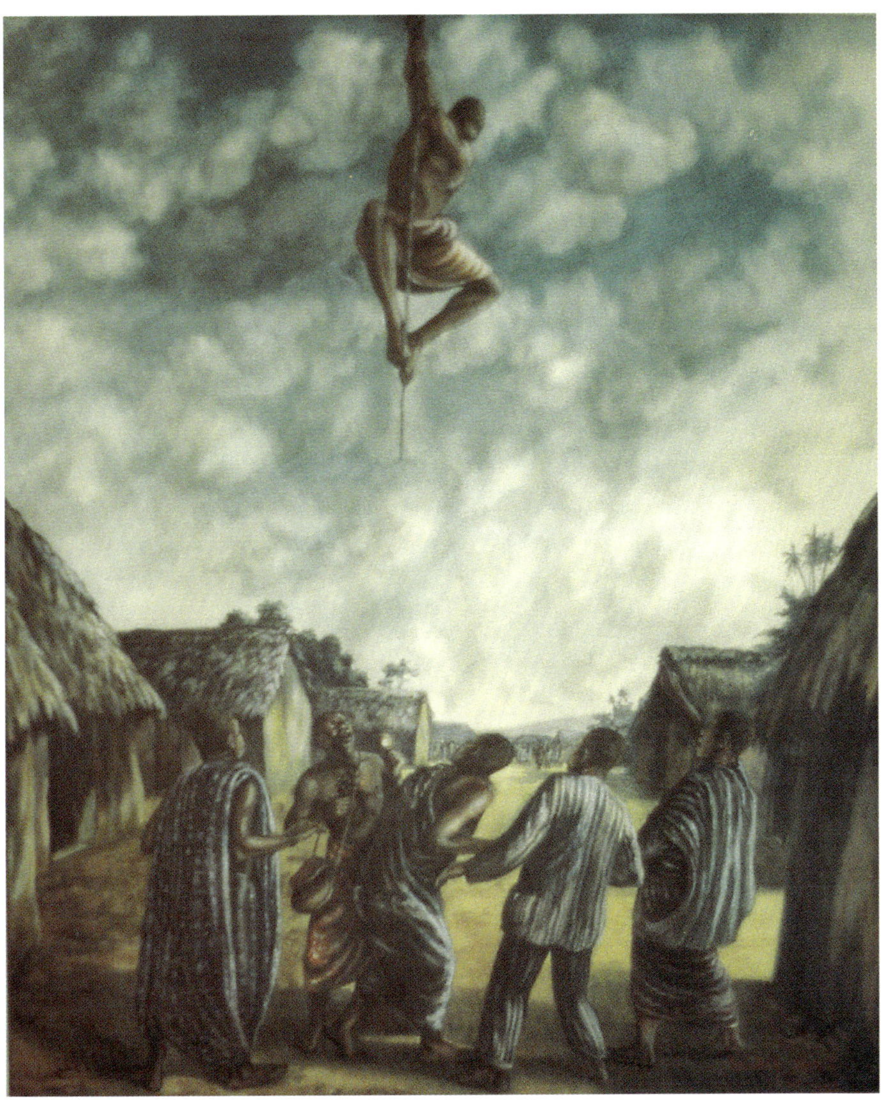



Akinọla Laṣekan (1916–72),[6] also of Yoruba parentage and largely self-taught, unlike Ọnabolu, painted images based on Yoruba myths, such as his *Ajaka of Ọwa* (fig. 7),[7] and scenes and portraits of elites and of ordinary people, as well as doing commercial art in Lagos. He became a political cartoonist, particularly for the *West African Pilot,* an anticolonial nationalist newspaper controlled by the rising politician Nnamdi Azikiwe.[8] The first well-known Nigerian cartoonist, Laṣekan's cartoons criticized not only British colonials but also African elites, whom he often viewed as being conservative. He was a member of a new, upwardly mobile political generation, in contrast to Ọnabolu's associations with conservative Nigerian elites. Yet Laṣekan's portraits were conventionally naturalistic, as were Ọnabolu's.

A close associate of Laṣekan and another Yoruba artist,[9] the sculptor Justus D. Akeredolu (1915–84) pioneered in creating naturalistic thorn sculpture from the silk-cotton tree, especially of traditional African scenes—a woman pounding food, a cattle herder—and Christian views such as crèches.[10] His naturalistic pieces differed stylistically from traditional Yoruba art. He had a host of imitators over the years; thorn carving has become a popular tourist art, but the work does not exhibit Akeredolu's skill.

S. A. O. Chukueggu, born 1915 in Mbaisẹ, Igbo country, represents another early tradition, in which two of his sons joined.[11] He sculpted unusual, often fantastic, wooden human and animal forms and Igbo spiritual figures based on tales and myths, objects differing stylistically from traditional Igbo sculpture and not employed as shrine objects. The Nsukka artist Obiọra Udechukwu has suggested to me that Chukueggu's style resembles contemporary Makonde art of East Africa, although it evolved independently and never reached the same popularity.

These pioneer artists created in diverse styles and media, a trait characteristic of contemporary Nigerian art today. They were variously locating themselves as artists within the framework of colonialism, indigenous cultures, and the emerging consequences of relationships between the two. They often relied on expatriate customers as well as African elites. Ọnabolu's emulation of British art was not so different from the tendency of some other Nigerians of the time to copy British culture. Laṣekan's willingness to paint naturalistic portraits of elites, while also creating political cartoons critical of the British and Nigerian establishment, suggests another typical reaction to colonial influence: working within colonialism yet reaching for one's goals. The genre artists tended to idealize traditional cultures and avoided dealing with changing Nigerian social life. Akeredolu and Chukueggu displayed innovation away from traditional sculptural forms as Nigerians in other fields of endeavor were innovative in other ways in reaction to colonialism.

## THE 1950S AND 1960S

Ben Enwọnwu (1921–94), of Igbo background, mentioned earlier as a genre artist, also belongs in this later period.[12] Not too long after his training with Murray, he studied art in England and Paris. Returning to Nigeria, he created sophisticated naturalistic portrait paintings and sculpture busts of elite Africans in wood and metal; in 1957 he completed a portrait sculpture of Queen Elizabeth at Buckingham Palace. He became the best-known contemporary Nigerian artist in Europe, establishing a residence in London in addition to his home in Nigeria and gradually taking Ọnabolu's place.

Enwọnwu also developed a second style in paint and sculpture, which he occasionally blended with his first, known as his "African Style." This grew out of his attachment to a political and cultural movement of French colonized peoples called Négritude, with centers in Paris and Dakar, of which the Senegalese politician and poet Léopold Senghor was a leader.[13] Négritude extolled the African mother, the family and the larger kin group, the creative aspects of African life, the beauty of black skin, and the supposed antimaterialism of Africans—features that were believed to contrast strongly with Euro/American culture and life. Enwọnwu was not a radical political person as were some other members of this movement, but was gentle about his beliefs. Négritude was never popular in English-speaking Africa, and Enwọnwu had no artistic followers who became prominent.

His "African Style" art took the form of dancing females and masked figures, particularly male masqueraders dressed as young, elegant females, figures largely drawn from his home city of Ọnitsha in Igboland.[14] In both his sculpture and painting, the human figures are elongated, lean, flexible, and beautiful, suggesting elegant movement and dignity. Occasionally these forms were quite simplified and abstract. His art glorified the African female. Enwọnwu's "African Style," in fact, is a form of sophisticated genre art, idealizing aspects of African life. Some of his paintings exhibited *uli* designs, as on masqueraders' costumes.[15]

Enwọnwu won many honors in Nigeria and Britain, becoming probably the best-known Nigerian artist in

Europe after World War II. His place in Nigerian art today is debated, his links to other Nigerian artists yet to be clarified.

Enwọnwu's "African Style" was part of the rapidly changing art scene in the 1950s and 1960s which saw the growth of other art forms that complemented the visual arts. For example, in literature there were the novels of Chinua Achebe, the dramas and poetry of Wọle Ṣoyinka, and the poetry of Christopher Okigbo. New composers, songwriters, and dramatists appeared; indigenous dance was put on stage and in festival settings; and the growth of "Highlife," "Juju," and other popular musical forms occurred. Nigerians were developing rich new cultural traditions, without these being negated by colonials and missionaries. The latter two peoples, in the years before independence, slowly came to realize the importance of the arts in the creation of Nigerian identity and a sense of nationhood.

Changes in the arts occurred during the growth of Nigerian political parties and nationalism in the 1950s, the development of elections at all governmental levels, and the creation of a federal government run by Nigerians by 1960, although the export/import economy was still in foreign hands. But the independence euphoria was soon shaken by internal political and ethnic rivalries, two military coups in 1966, pogroms against southerners in the north in 1966 and 1967, and the bitter Biafran war of 1967–70. These events had a powerful impact on the future Nsukka artists.

Other changes in these two decades included increased foreign and Nigerian business activities, the beginning of universal primary school education and growing secondary school training. There were federal universities, the first being University College, Ibadan in 1948; others were founded in the 1960s at Zaria, Nsukka, Ifẹ, and Lagos. Some types of expatriates differing from the usual colonial officials came to Nigeria. A few of these were eager to assist the growth of the arts, which had been helped before then by only a few pioneering colonials, such as K. C. Murray, G. I. Jones, and E. H. Duckworth. Expatriate archaeologists, museum personnel, teachers, artists, and others, often liberal in politics and representing new interests in the country, were happy to assist Nigerian artistic growth.

The major government museum for indigenous treasures, the National Museum, was opened in Lagos in 1957, and other government museums opened in Esie in 1945, Jos in 1952, Ifẹ in 1954, Ọrọn in 1958, Kano in 1960, and Ọwọ in 1968.[16] There were changing attitudes among some of the educated Nigerian elite, who went from rejecting their past cultures to seeing their importance, with a growing awareness of how much of Nigeria's cultural treasures had left the country. The increasing sensitivity to indigenous cultures was reflected in much of the Nigerian contemporary art of these two decades. The era of Ọnabolu was over. The British conception of Nigeria as a country of pagans who had to be civilized was at an end.

Art training began at Yaba Technical Institute, Lagos (now Yaba College of Technology) in 1952. In 1953 the Nigerian College of Arts, Science and Technology (NCAST) began art courses at Ibadan, the art program being transferred to NCAST Zaria in the north in 1955; this college later became Ahmadu Bello University. A third postsecondary art center arose at the University of Nigeria, Nsukka, in Igbo country in 1961, a year after the university opened. The University of Ifẹ, founded in 1962 at Ile-Ifẹ in Yoruba country (now Ọbafemi Awolowo University), began offering art courses in 1969.[17] Secondary school art teaching was on the increase, although still frequently taught by untrained teachers.

There was substantial growth in the number of skilled artists in this period. Among them were several so-called neotraditionalists, standing intermediate between traditional and contemporary styles. There was Felix Idubọr from Benin, known for his wood-sculpted human heads, the two Yoruba artists Lamidi Fakẹyẹ, famous

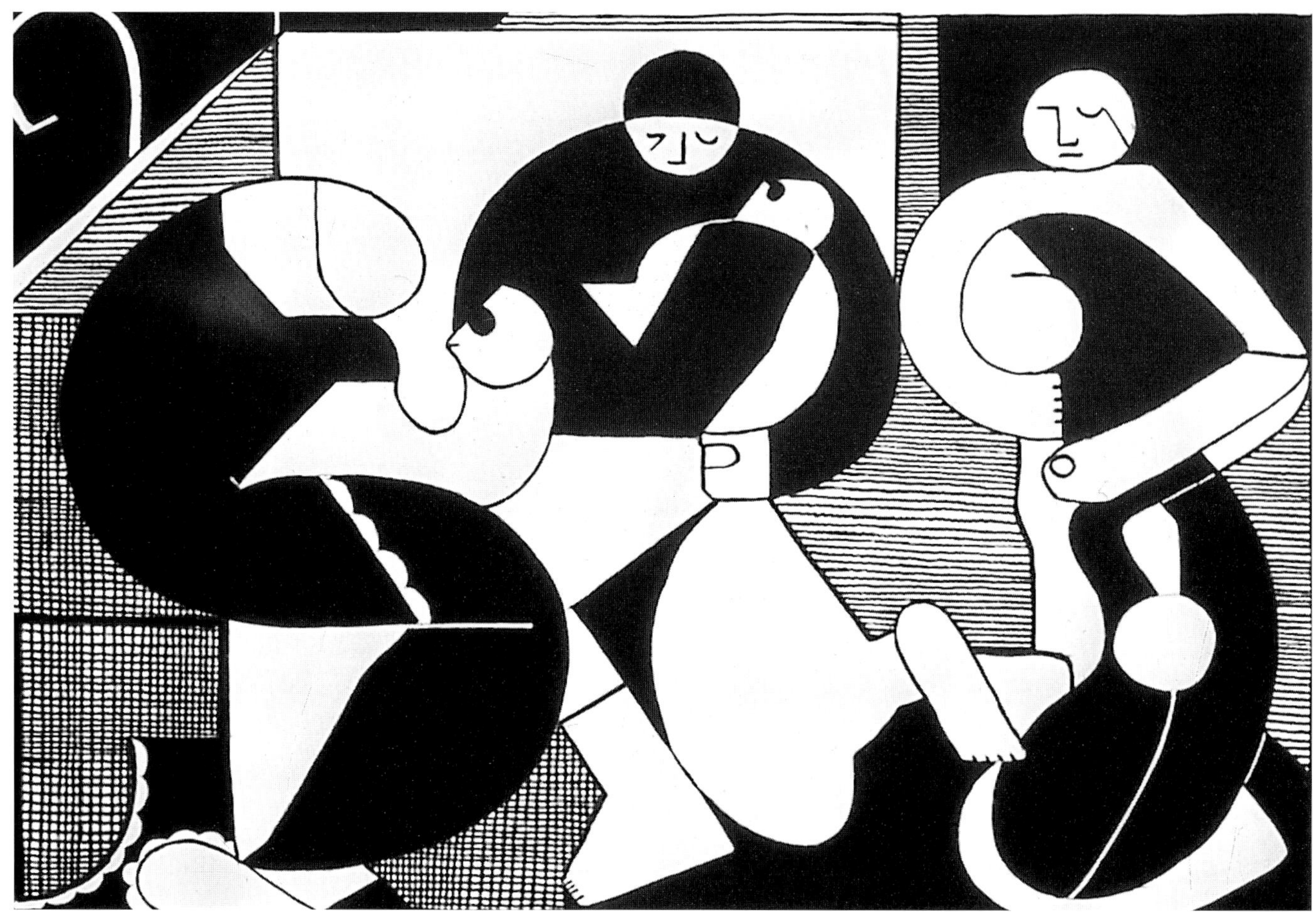

**8**. Uzọ Egọnu, *Gathering of the Villagers,* 1981, black gouache on paper. 58 × 79 cm. Collection of the artist's estate. Photo: the artist.

for his wood-carved doors, and Yẹmi Bisiri, who created lively metal figures. Ovia Idah began as a traditional Benin sculptor but developed his own unique style in wood and in cement. Festus Idẹhẹn, also from Benin, became noted for his art in concrete, sometimes in mural form.[18]

Moving beyond neotraditional art, Ben Osawe developed an unusual, abstract, rounded, and highly polished wood sculptural style. Bruce Onobrakpẹya pioneered in innovative print forms, and Erhabọr O. Ẹmọkpae, a muralist, painter, and sculptor, created unusual works leaning toward the abstract. Uzọ Egọnu, of Igbo background, left Nigeria in 1945 at the age of thirteen for England and lived there and in Germany until his death in 1996. One of the finest Nigerian painters and printmakers (fig. 8), he made a mark for himself in England, though his art is little known in Nigeria, which he rarely visited. There were also Agbo Fọlarin, the Yoruba sculptor and muralist, and the late Okpu Eze, the Igbo painter and sculptor, whose work sometimes was abstract.[19]

There were two prominent female artists, Etso Ugbodaga Ngu, whose work largely involved abstract mask-like figures, and Afi Ekọng, who created naturalistic paintings.[20] The latter's social standing in Lagos and her control of an art gallery meant that she had an important influence on contemporary art, while Ngu reached students through university teaching. The two artists were pioneers at a time when contemporary female artists were rare in Nigeria, though not traditional ones in certain fields of art.

All these artists were from the south of Nigeria. Only Jimọ Akolo, of Yoruba background, was from the north.[21] This disparity reflected the greater concentration at that time on social change and education in Nigeria's south than its north.

Cultural centers developed and played important artistic roles. The first was started by Uche Okeke at Kafanchan in Nigeria's north in 1958.[22] He was later to become the founder of the Nsukka artists' group. Primarily for the visual arts, the center in Kafanchan was moved to Enugu in the 1960s by Okeke, who later joined it with groups in drama, poetry, and music. Just before the Biafran war he moved his center to Nimo (see below, Chapters 2–4). In 1960 another center was begun in Ibadan by Ulli Beier, a German expatriate, who came with his Austrian artist wife, Suzanne Wenger. Beier's center was called the Mbari Club or Mbari Ibadan; the word *mbari* refers to the spectacular Igbo shrine structures with many dried earth-painted figures and abstract wall designs.[23] Mbari Ibadan put on art exhibitions, plays, poetry readings, and other cultural events, attracting the new young people in the arts, and it published literature and art catalogues. Beier and his wife, and later his second wife, Georgina Betts, were involved in another cultural center that opened in 1962 at Oṣogbo in Yoruba country, called the Mbari Club Oṣogbo, Mbari Mbayọ, or Mbari Mbayọ Oṣogbo.[24] The Beiers recruited local Yoruba, some from a traveling theater company, with little or no formal European-style education, and gave them painting and other art equipment with only some guidance (how much is debated today).[25] The artists developed a style called Oṣogbo art, differing from traditional Yoruba art, with often fantastic human and animal creatures in unusual color combinations, often with large oval eyes, works generally in watercolor, paint, and block prints.[26] From this center emerged a group of artists who became well known in Nigeria, including Twins Seven Seven, Jacob Afọlabi, Rufus Ogundele, and Muraina Oyelami.[27] The Beiers did much to bring Oṣogbo art to Europe, art that was also popular with expatriates in Nigeria.

Michael Cardew established and ran the government-supported Abuja Pottery Training Centre at Abuja, north central Nigeria, in the 1950s and early 1960s. Traditional potters, generally Gwari in the area, were trained to employ glazing, the pottery wheel, and other nonindigenous ceramic techniques. A female ceramist, Ladi Kwali, became well known in Nigeria and exhibited in Europe and the United States.[28]

In 1947 a Catholic art center was begun by two fathers at Ọyẹ-Ekiti in Yoruba country for traditional Yoruba craftsmen to produce objects for Catholic churches, from which developed several smaller workshops.[29] Christian images were combined with neotraditional Yoruba sculptural styles. Lamidi Fakẹyẹ became a prominent artist from this experiment.[30] There had been an earlier missionary center at Arochuku in southeast Igbo country in the 1930s to train women in embroidery using Igbo *uli* designs and some *nsibidi* motifs, an attempt to develop a local industry for women. This continued for several decades.[31]

A few of these interesting centers, with diverse orientations and concerns, continued after the end of the civil war in 1970, but most gave way to universities as centers for the arts and to the galleries, museums, and artists organizations that arose. The centers were an important stimulus for the arts in their time; there is no money to develop them today.

During the 1950s and 1960s there was a dramatic expansion of art galleries and other venues for exhibitions, particularly in Lagos. By 1967 there were more than half a dozen Lagos galleries, and by 1969 twenty-five exhibitions had been held there in the previous three years.[32] Some galleries were owned by artists, others by entrepreneurs; the government ran one as well. Several private salons run by expatriates developed. Foreign embassies in Lagos developed cultural centers that sometimes exhibited Nigerian contemporary art, among them the British Council, the Goethe Institut, and the United States Information Service.[33] Some hotels in Lagos and elsewhere had gallery shops and sometimes held exhibitions of contemporary art. Interest in public art increased as independence approached. During this period and for a time after independence, the central and regional Nigerian governments put resources into public art at road intersections, in government buildings, and elsewhere and sponsored some art exhibitions. Newspapers and magazines more and more reviewed art exhibitions, generally without skilled critics. The question of whether there was or should be a characteristic Nigerian style of contemporary art arose, but there was no consensus on the issue. Another question was whether abstract art had a place in Nigerian art or not. And what was the role of tradition in the new art?[34] It was a lively, argumentative time, with skilled Nigerian artists and interested expatriates involved. This was the period in Nigerian contemporary art when expatriates played their strongest roles; in the years after 1970 their influence declined.

Expatriates helped start the journals *Black Orpheus* (1957), *Ibadan* (1957), and *Nigeria,* a government publication from early colonial days (from 1960, *Nigeria Magazine*), all of which contained articles on contemporary visual art as well as the other new arts. Ulli Beier published *Art in Nigeria in 1960* (1960) and *Contemporary Art in Africa* (1968), which had a major section on Nigeria. The British magazines *West Africa* and *West African Review* carried Nigerian art reviews and commentaries.

The Society of Nigerian Artists (SNA) was founded in 1964 with twenty-four members and a Lagos exhibition. These artists had studied at colleges or universities and represented a new generation that desired to speak up for their interests, as a group, to government and others and to hold exhibitions.[35] Later the society admitted non-academically trained artists and developed branch chapters. It has had its successes and its failures over the years.

All these activities indicate that there was already a lively art scene in Nigeria by the time of the full development of the Nsukka artists in the 1970s. The group, in fact, had its early beginnings in the 1950s and 1960s. Thus the Nsukka artists came into being in the context of an actively developing art scene and have added their own unique viewpoints and experience to the Nigerian and African art world.

## CIVIL WAR, 1967–1970

A few brief comments on the background of the war are in order here.[36] In 1966 and 1967 a series of pogroms by Muslim northerners against Igbo and other Christian southerners living and working in the north led to the movement of Igbos and other eastern Nigerians back to their homelands, joined by frightened individuals and families from other parts of Nigeria. Up to a million refugees left work, businesses, farms, and possessions, posing immense resettlement problems in the Igbo area. There followed a brutal civil war fought by the newly created Biafra against Nigeria for independence. The Biafran effort failed in January 1970 after gradual attrition of its blockaded territory in southeastern Nigeria and much death, famine, and suffering. During the war, Igbo artists and art students—some of whom later became the core of the Nsukka artists' group, including writers, dramatists, and musicians—formed a heightened concentration of artists such as the region had never known. They designed currency, stamps, and posters and were involved in magazine and newspaper design as well as various other propaganda activities. As the front decreased, the artists moved from place to place, forming cultural centers for plays, exhibitions, and concerts. A well-known Igbo artist, Simon Okeke, and the Igbo poet Christopher Okigbo died in the conflict. The experience of artists on the Biafran side led them, after the war, to a sensitivity to questions of hunger, suffering, and other calamities to a much greater extent than artists in the rest of Nigeria, who were not much affected by a conflict largely fought on Biafran territory.[37] This sensitivity became a characteristic of the Nsukka group. Peace brought a slow return to normal artistic activities in the east.[38] Exhibitions and other activities in the rest of Nigeria were hampered during the war. In the long run the war did not stop, but only slowed, the growth of contemporary art in Nigeria. For many of the Biafran artists, it provided a perspective different from that of artists on the federal side. Yet the end of the war united all Nigerian artists in many ways.

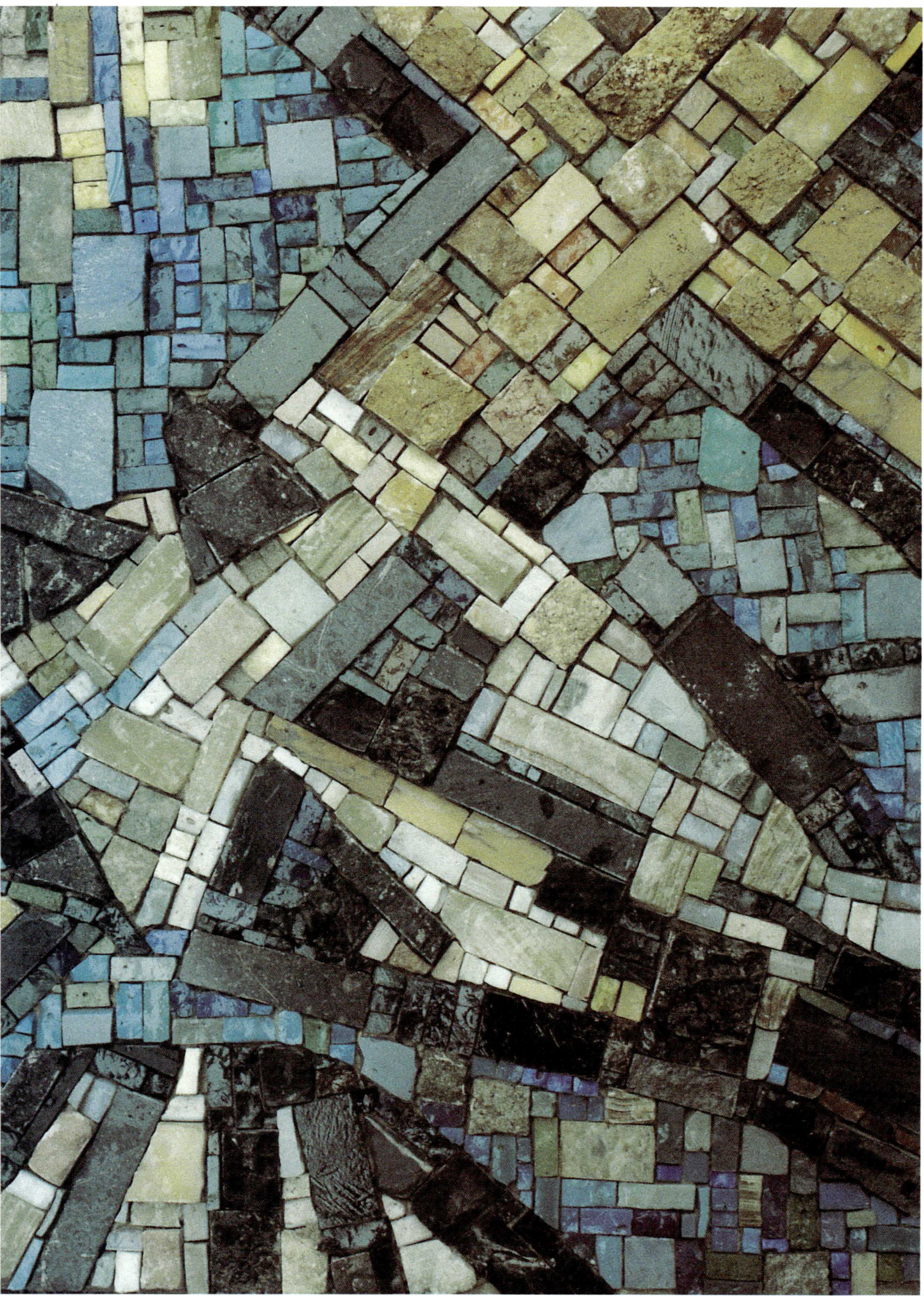

Detail of fig. 26.

# 2. UCHE OKEKE

## I: THE EARLY YEARS

Every artist, any visual artist, who cannot draw
is really for me not a visual artist.

UCHE OKEKE[1]

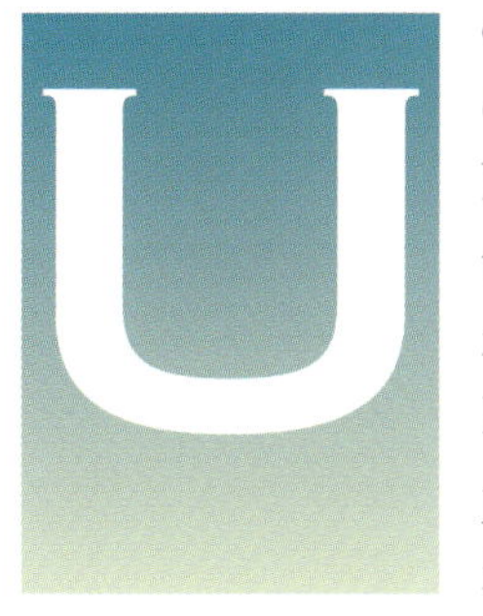

che Okeke, founder of the Nsukka artists, developed creatively in the context of the 1950–60 decades in Nigeria and was a major player in its artistic renaissance.[2] Born in 1933 at Nimo, Njikoka Division, in the present Anambra State, he has had a lifelong association with the town, also his father's birthplace. Near Awka, Ọrlu, Nnewi, and other important Igbo communities, Nimo is in a highly populated area of central Igboland, not far from the large Niger River trading and educational center of Ọnitsha. The region is known for its level of entrepreneurship and education, a conscious interest in its culture and history, and for the strong influence of the Catholic and Anglican churches. Okeke was baptized a Catholic with the name of Christopher, which he rarely employed in his art or adult life, though some of his early work is signed "C. Uche Okeke."

Okeke's mother returned to Nimo to give birth to him—a common Nigerian practice—for she was living with her family in Kafanchan in north central Nigeria, a long way from Igboland. Kafanchan was an important railroad junction at a time when railroads were a useful means of transportation in Nigeria.[3] In savannah and hill country, far from the rainy, tropical forest area of Nimo, Kafanchan was both a Christian and a Muslim community, with a mixture of people from the south—mainly Igbo and Yoruba—and local Birom and Hausa.

Okeke's mother soon returned with him to Kafanchan's Igbo quarters. But he was exposed to a variety of cultures as a child, particularly as two years after his birth the family moved to a culturally mixed area of town, though maintaining close ties with other Igbos at Kafanchan.

Okeke's father, Isaac Okonkwọ Chukwuka Okeke, born about 1901, became a Catholic mission boy in the

1910s. This is not surprising, as Nimo has been strongly Catholic. Briefly a schoolteacher in the early 1920s, and then trained as a carpenter at Adazi Catholic Mission, not far from Nimo, he became a master craftsman, a cabinetmaker and furniture designer, with interests in sculpture and painting. The patrilineal line is known for its traditional medicinal healers, blacksmiths, and woodworkers, including sculptors. After training, the father opened a workshop at Nimo and then in a neighboring town; he later joined the Nigerian Railway as a carpenter, moving to Makurdi and then to Kafanchan in 1929. Okeke and his siblings played in his Kafanchan workshop, though they were too young to learn woodworking.

The father, an important figure in his son's life, was a collector of craft items, art, books and prints, and aphorisms. Okeke has a papier-mâché figure of a colonial officer that his father owned. These objects found about his childhood home are likely connected to Okeke's own later collections of art, crafts, and books. His father loved music and collected gramophone records, including popular Igbo hits of the day. He brought a famous Igbo musician to the house and was a patron of school concerts as well as having an interest in masquerades. He was also a good reader—the Bible, Shakespeare, Greek myths, and legends were part of his fare. His father also encouraged Okeke to serve at Catholic mass.

Okeke's mother, Monica Mgboye Okeke, born in 1910 at Enugu-Ukwu, not far from Nimo, learned *uli* designs when a girl and practiced the art, though not at Kafanchan. Married in 1926, she taught dress designing and knitting in the 1930s and 1940s, had a sewing and knitting workshop, and traded in pottery and textile materials. Two girls were born before Okeke and four siblings after him.

Okeke's father died suddenly in 1943, a profound shock to Okeke and the family. At the funeral he carried the cross to Kafanchan's Catholic cemetery; in 1961 he painted this scene in oil (see fig. 17). The family remained in town, the mother keeping her workshop and opening a maternity center at home. She later became active in politics and was a staunch Catholic who was involved with the church and local Catholic women's organizations.

## FORMATIVE YEARS, 1933–1958

Okeke began drawing in primary school, continuing throughout his school days.[4] At first he imitated illustrations in school texts, in the manner of other Nigerian artists as they began to draw. At times his mother, supportive of his artistic interests, collected his drawings and displayed them at home. Okeke made paper boats and created kites and drums; he still has a small, colored ink drawing on cardboard of Christ on the Cross. He copied illustrations from books about Sir Francis Drake and on pirates. Okeke attended the Catholic St. Claver's Primary School in 1941–47, and by 1944 he was assisting the teacher with visual aids, drawing maps and putting drawings on the blackboard. This was a common experience for budding Nigerian artists. He also had interests in gardening and drumming; at school he was a member of the brass band, and he also played the side-drum for three years. He began acquiring books for himself in 1945 and has never ceased. Okeke also wandered the local countryside, developing a feeling for the excitement of travel, and he loved to see and hear birds.

Tales, particularly Igbo ones, were important in his early mature art; it is not surprising that as a child he lived in a world rich in lore. He learned tales—both spoken and sung—from his mother, who first sparked his interest. His oldest sister, Flora, was a good storyteller, and he was influenced by her as well as by an Igbo friend of his father and by others who told tales at his home. There was *mbe* the Igbo trickster tortoise, *mamiwata*, the mythical female water spirit, *ogbanje*, the powerful spiritual force believed to take a mother's child away to death again and again,[5] wizards, and other beings—a rich fantasy world for Okeke to draw on later in his art.

Okeke clearly came from a family rich in interests in the new world opened up by colonialism as well as in traditional Igbo culture. These two appear to have been rarely in serious conflict at home. Early influences on an artist are not often as clear as Okeke's. His love of collecting, his concern with art and design, his pleasure in Igbo tales, his Christian interest, and his enjoyment of traveling, all seem to derive from childhood. Living away from home also probably increased his curiosity about Igbo culture, which he mainly experienced as a young child in its particular forms at Kafanchan.

### SECONDARY SCHOOL DAYS AND INTERIM PERIOD

Okeke's opportunity to experience Igbo life more fully came when he went to secondary schools in Igboland, all the time continuing to draw and experiment with art. In 1948–49 he was at Metropolitan College, Ọnitsha; both the large city and its huge market fascinated him. He learned photography there, a skill he did not employ in his artwork, and he collected art reproductions. But he was unhappy in the overcrowded and understaffed school, and he planned to transfer elsewhere; thereupon the school authorities dismissed him! In January 1950 he entered Bishop Shanahan College, Ọrlu, run by Marist Brothers, where he remained until graduation in December 1953. He appears to have enjoyed himself there, beginning a diary and writing down tales that he collected at school and in the Ọrlu area. He read widely—biographies, travelogues, and history—including works by H. G. Wells, William Hazlitt, Hilaire Belloc, Dante Alighieri, and George Bernard Shaw. He discovered a book of Igbo tales, but he did not think much of the illustrations, believing he could do better.[6] He was active in sports and in students' societies. By 1951 he was writing poetry, the commencement of a long poetic career.[7] Returning to Kafanchan after graduation, he decided not to follow in his father's footsteps with the railway. Yet it is evident that Okeke shared many of his parents' interests and that he was determined to move ahead.

After leaving secondary school, Okeke was invited by his former primary schoolteacher, Patrick Oteka, a

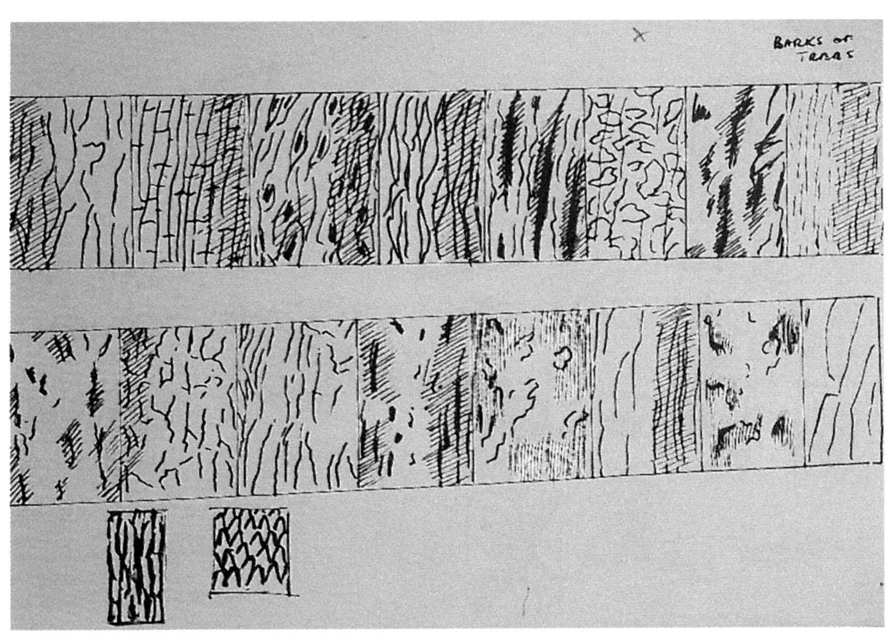


**9**. Uche Okeke, bark designs, 1958, pen and ink on paper, from a sketchbook. 14 × 19 cm. Collection of the artist.

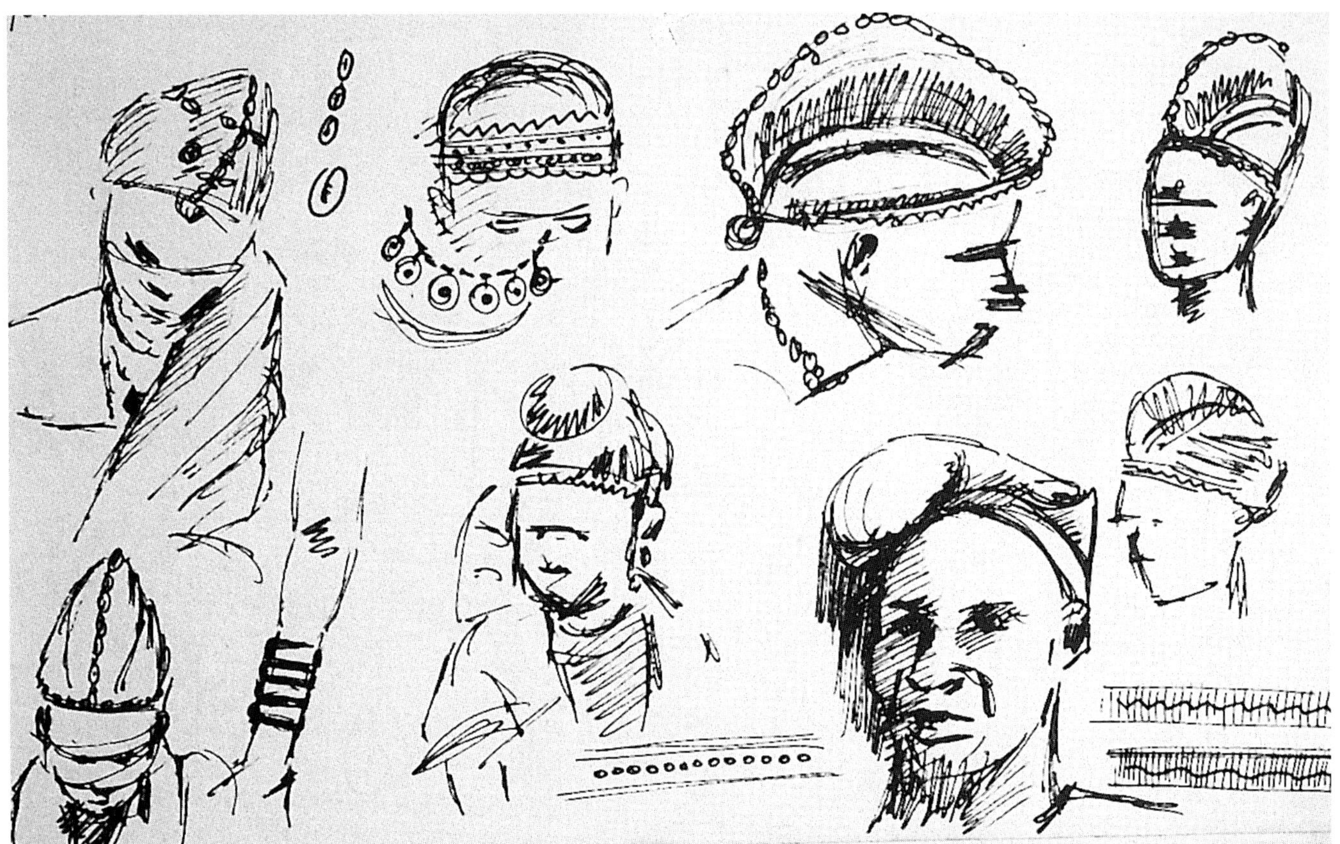

**10**. Uche Okeke, heads and faces,
1958, pen and ink on paper, from a
sketchbook. 14 × 19 cm.
Collection of the artist.

supervisor of schools, to produce visual aids for his old school at Kafanchan, for schools at Kagoro and Kagoma, and for the Teachers Training Preparatory School at Kafanchan.[8] He had taken the Cambridge School Certificate examination, which would allow him to enter a university in Nigeria and take the Civil Service Examination, which would make it possible for him to obtain a civil service position, and he was awaiting the results. Okeke's early interest had been literary, to write poetry and to write up the Igbo tales he was collecting, but after he was invited to prepare instructional aids, his visual art interest became primary, though he has retained interest in writing poetry and in Igbo lore throughout his life.[9]

Ngọzi Ndubisi writes that, at the time Okeke left Bishop Shanahan College, his drawings were "most academic in style; that is naturalistic drawings, frequently in pencil, based on the rules of the academy."[10] They involved life studies and those from nature, including tree bark designs (figs. 9, 10). In 1954, determined to improve his skills, he began a correspondence course with the artist Akinọla Laṣekan (see Chapter 1), another course in art from the International Correspondence School, London, and one in taxidermy from Omaha, Nebraska, reflecting a growing interest in animal forms related to his art concerns. He also subscribed to *Studio* magazine. As he writes of this time: "I was anxious to discover the most effective method of acquiring competence in drawing. I then made sketches and detailed studies of natural forms out-of-doors in the countryside" in the area around Kafanchan.[11] He also had contact with a fitter in the Kafanchan locomotive shop, who was an amateur artist.[12] Okeke's wife, Ego Uche-Okeke, believes that his career as an artist began in earnest in 1954.[13]

In 1955, in order to earn a living, Okeke took a clerk's position in the Department of Labour and Employment Exchange at Jos, a northern city not far from Kafanchan. In his free time he joined the Nigerian Field Society, then composed mostly of expatriates interested in natural history, and he exhibited his taxidermy products at a local meeting of the society. He visited the new government Jos Museum regularly, continuing to practice taxidermy, drawing, and painting.[14] His sketchbooks indicate that he was a keen observer of animals and plants.

In 1956 Okeke helped prepare an exhibition, *Nigerian Drawings and Paintings,* at the federal Jos Museum, with works by Nigerian and expatriate artists. The museum was under the direction of the archaeologist Bernard Fagg, who was assisted in the exhibition by Dennis Duerden, teaching at Keffi Government Secondary School. Okeke exhibited some of his art; a small pastel landscape of his was purchased by Nigerian Governor-General Sir James Robertson. He also showed drawings from nature, northern Nigerian scenes, local Africans, Birom, and others. He writes:

> This exhibition . . . was important because it afforded me the opportunity to study first hand the works of both local and foreign artists living in the country. I saw for the first time the original works of such Nigerian artists as Ben Enwọnwu and Clara Ugbodaga, now Mrs. Ugbodaga-Ngu, and those of students of the Government Secondary School Keffi. I was not so sure how I felt about the entire exhibition. It was rather with mixed feeling and a certain sympathy that I viewed their technical achievement.[15]

Okeke was stimulated by taking part in and viewing the exhibition and by the encouragement of Duerden and Fagg. His statement suggests that he felt he had something to offer that some artists did not.

In May of the same year Okeke held his first solo exhibition at the Jos Town Council Hall, *Life in Northern Nigeria,* which was repeated at Kaduna, another northern Nigerian city. This included landscapes and images of northern peoples. His mother supplied material aid, and the artist Laṣẹkan wrote the foreword for the exhibition brochure, though they had never met.

The following year, 1957, Okeke transferred to the Labour Department in Lagos. There he briefly met Kenneth Murray, but they did not become close, perhaps because of age and status differences. Okeke also met some of the contemporary Nigerian artists. In the same year he returned north, entering the Nigerian College of Arts, Science and Technology at Zaria (a city somewhat north of Kafanchan) as an art student. Here his art style and ideas rapidly developed. Other than his Igbo tale drawings, his work before entering college was conventional, mainly landscapes, human figures, and animal and plant forms, mostly based on his northern experiences.

## THE ASELE PERIOD, 1958–1966

The time that Okeke himself calls his Asele Period was one of intense artistic exploration, with the use of Igbo cultural elements in his art, including those drawn from tales, spiritual figures, and *uli* linear qualities.[16] In the nine years of the Asele Period, which ended shortly before the beginning of the Biafran war in 1967, he established his basic art style, began to be known nationally in Nigeria, held a number of art exhibitions, won recognition as a poet, established his own cultural center, traveled to Germany, and became a leader among Nigerian artists in developing an art philosophy known as natural synthesis. These years largely set the future path of his artistic creations.

Okeke studied for his diploma in fine art at the Nigerian College of Arts, Science and Technology at Zaria between 1957 and 1961.[17] He was a founding member of the Art Society, formed in 1958, composed of ten male art students who became known as the "Zaria Rebels." Their views profoundly altered the direction of contemporary Nigerian art. He was its first elected secretary and its second president, replacing Simon Obiekeziẹ Okeke in the latter position.[18] As a leader, Uche Okeke played a major role in the development of the society's idea of natural synthesis in the arts in Nigeria. This involved the acceptance of much of European media and technique (though not barring experimentation with these) and the development of styles and content close to the students' Nigerian experience, whether it be their own cultural tradition, that of other Nigerian cultures, or current Nigerian life. No single art style or content was implied; the Art Society's students, as other art students at Zaria, developed quite different styles, as can be seen from the art of Simon Okeke, Uche Okeke, Yusuf Grillo, Demas Nwoko, Okechukwu Ọdita, and Bruce Onobrakpẹya.[19] The synthesis was to be natural, unconscious, and unforced, to come from the experience of the individual artist, including from their cultures.[20] With Okeke it was probably rarely or never forced, but it was often consciously done. Natural synthesis can include Christian experience, as it did for Okeke. He writes:[21] "When I illustrate Ibo Folk tales I use new materials and [the] new experience of a new age. The results must be new art expressions and experiences for all. In the same way when I paint *Madonna and Child* or *Christ* it is new because of my experience and conception of the Christian faith."[22]

Nebechianya Eze writes that Okeke told her: "The members of the society were required to do some research on local history, local arts and crafts, and the way these arts or artworks were produced, the techniques and the philosophies underlying this type of manifestation of the Nigerian peoples."[23] Most important were "the philosophies behind these creative disciplines. The philosophy of the traditional should be employed to satisfy contemporary needs." Thus an intellectual approach to art was developing and an early programmatic African approach to art. It was a way for Art Society members to anchor their work in Nigerian culture so as not to lose their bearings. It was a homegrown approach, not derived from the outside, as some of Enwọnwu's art was from Négritude, which arose through Senghor's views, or Ọnabolu's British Academy style.

Such a synthesis in art has not been uncommon among third and fourth world contemporary artists in this century, but the history of its evolution and the forms it has taken vary greatly. The Zaria students seemed unaware that they were part of a broad world art movement and were excited by the growth of their own viewpoints. The idea soon spread to other artists at the college, and elsewhere in Nigeria, through the society members' art as their careers developed and by their own proselytizing after graduating from Zaria in 1960 and 1961.

In fact, some earlier artists, such as Enwọnwu, had employed elements of natural synthesis in their art, drawing from Nigerian cultural traditions, but they did not develop their work into a synthetic art philosophy. The genre art of Kenneth Murray's students was considered too naive by the Zaria students to be natural synthesis, as it was largely limited to an idyllic traditional past and the art techniques were not very sophisticated. But Sylvester Ogbechiẹ, a young art historian, who trained at Nsukka, in an evaluation of the Zaria group, feels that the term *synthesis* was poorly defined, that what occurred at Zaria was less a revolution or rebellion than an evolution, which had its predecessors, particularly Enwọnwu.[24] Yet I believe that it was the Zaria students, largely led by Okeke, who crystallized the concept.

The growth of the Art Society students' views should be seen in the context of their experience at the time. They perceived that they were being taught British Academy art, associated with standards of the Royal Academy of Art in London. The art curriculum followed that of Goldsmiths' School of Art, London, with which their school was affiliated. Both of these institutions stressed a naturalistic style, still life images, figure drawing, painting, composition, and European art history, approaches divorced from African experience and artistic styles. There was no course on African art history at that time at the college. All of the lecturers, including the head of the Department of Fine Arts, were expatriates, except for the Nigerian artist Etso Clara Ugbodaga Ngu, but she was not particularly supportive of the views of the Art Society members; she had been trained in Britain. The society's members were from various cultures in Nigeria's south, as were most other art students at Zaria. They lived in a cultural and geographic setting at Zaria different from that of their various homelands in southern Nigeria. They wished to connect their cultural experiences to their art more than they felt their teachers were interested in doing. Their lecturers, on the whole, had little experience in the south of Nigeria and seemed to lack an understanding of what these cultures, with their rich artistic traditions, were like.[25]

Martin Onwuzurọha suggests that student peer-group behavior may have been a feature in the formation of the Art Society, for the art students were apparently kidded a lot about not being in a "practical" field, particularly by engineering and architecture students.[26] The society's formation was thus also an attempt to raise the art students' standing in the eyes of other students. The activities of the Art Society and the later influence of its members on contemporary Nigerian art have been, for a long time, a topic of discussion among artists, art students, and art historians in the country.

Living in Nigeria's north, the students felt a need to draw from their own traditions as they wished and to explore life in Nigeria. Okeke probably had less experience with his own cultural roots than did other artists in the society, for he had lived much of the time in the north, except for his secondary school years, while others had only come from the south to study at the college. Was this why he played such a leadership role in the society, feeling the neglect of his own culture more deeply than the others?

Okeke has made it clear to me that he never intended, in turning to Igbo culture, to do so for the sake of returning to the past, which he thought impossible; I believe this was also the view of other society members. It was not a return but a recourse to the past, to integrate past and present experience. However, with occasional exceptions by Okeke and other Art Society members, their art was not particularly political at that time, though for some of them it became so later on. It was aesthetic politics that they were engaged in.

In 1958 Okeke wrote the poem "I Will Not Go to Kpaaza," reflecting his protective feelings about Igbo culture:

I'll not go to Kpaaza
I will not go
I will not go to fish in her spring
my fathers did not go
they did not go to her
secluded spring
they did not kill her fish.
But early Enochs said
they must go to Kpaaza
they must kill fish—
fish for troubles
in ancient spring
in sacred spring.
Kpaaza, they said, must go
to nourish and sustain
Christian converts body and soul
with sacred fish of sacred spring
I will not go to Kpaaza
I will not go
to fish in her peaceful water
my fathers did not go.[27]

The poem became a symbol of interest in tradition for the later contemporary Nsukka artists, among whom it is well known, although Okeke recanted its major premise after the civil war. Kpaaza was a sacred spring near his home at Nimo, which Christian converts threatened to destroy through fishing. The poem refers to Chinua Achebe's famous novel, *Things Fall Apart*,[28] where the overzealous Christian convert Enoch tears off the mask of one of nine sacred *egwugwu* masqueraders, and then these figures, with the help of Igbo townsmen, burn the village church, which the straitlaced British missionary and his Igbo interpreter try to defend.[29] Okeke's position at that time, as now, was not anti-Christian but against the excessive activities of its zealots in attacking tradition.

Ulli Beier visited the art students, encouraging them to explore their own cultures and to carry on with their own art outside the classroom. Ironically, he was soon to guide the development of the Oṣogbo artists with artistic views that contrasted with those of the Zaria students. Enwọnwu also visited and addressed the students, but did not appear to convert them to his artistic viewpoint. The students were to go on to solve the problem of their artistic identity in the postcolonial, largely Christian and traditional worlds. As Okeke later argued, they had to search for a theoretical basis for their art in order to attain a true synthesis.[30] There was no point in aping European forms.[31]

The search for identity involved experimentation, for example, Simon Okeke's unusual watercolors based on Igbo culture.[32] The search also ultimately had to do with the hope of substantial art purchases by Nigerians, a chance to depart from art that primarily pleased expatriates to art that related more to Nigerians. For many years, Okeke was reluctant to sell his work to some expatriates in Nigeria.

The Art Society should also be seen in the context of Nigeria's obtaining its independence in 1960. Throughout the students' time at Zaria, there was a sense of political freedom and of future economic independence from Britain. The students wished to decolonize Nigerian art, to make it integral to society. Independence was not only political; it was also to be a cultural and artistic independence. This was easier to posit than it would have been thirty years earlier. It was not difficult in 1960 to be critical of Aina Ọnabolu's slavish copying of British art of an earlier time. Would the Zaria students have acted any differently from Ọnabolu in terms of their art had they been young at the time that he was?[33]

For these young artists, natural synthesis did not come to full fruition until the years after they graduated, when they had the opportunity to research more deeply their own cultures as well as others. Okeke became a strong proponent of the principle that what you do not know of your own culture you should research and learn. Gani Odutokun writes of Demas Nwoko, Bruce Onobrakpẹya, and Uche Okeke that after Zaria "the trio took different methods to arrive at the same objective of realizing in their art a synthesis of the traditional African culture and the evolving 20th century civilization dominated largely by Western influence."[34]

We know little of what the Zaria expatriate teachers thought of the art students' reactions to them, other than that they resisted the students' views. There are accounts from students involved, from Nigerian art historians such as Ọla Ọlọidi and Sylvester Ogbechiẹ, comments from Michael Crowder and Ulli Beier, expatriates sympathetic to the students' viewpoint, but little from the art teachers at Zaria themselves.[35] It appears that some of these instructors were not practicing art in the Academy style, but were following a set curriculum laid down by the school with the Slade School of Art and later with Goldsmiths' School of Art, both of the University of London.[36]

The students, including Okeke, made their views known to their teachers and continued to follow the demands of the curriculum, thus acquiring skill in European media and technique while developing their own styles and content outside the classroom, sharing their art with one another. They were encouraged, however, by their teachers to make use of images from the local countryside but to treat them in the Academy style. Aware of the students' views, the teachers, at Uche Okeke's suggestion, arranged a cultural tour in 1959 for some of the Art Society's members and for college lecturers. They visited famous art centers and important archaeological and historical sites in Nigeria, including Bida, Tada, Esie, Ado Ekiti, Abeokuta, Lagos, and Benin City.[37] Both the students and the lecturers learned firsthand about cultural and artistic features they had been unaware of before, and painting members of the society, at the invitation of the head of the department at Zaria, viewed new painting work done by their lecturers. Whatever the conflict that existed between the society's members and the lecturers, there was also conflict between the members and the official Association of Fine Arts Students at the university, who favored the development of Goldsmiths' College for art certification, while the Art Society students saw it as continuing in the British tradition. Thus there were interesting nuances to the relations between the society's members and their lecturers.

The society disbanded in June 1961, by which time a majority of its members had graduated, including Uche Okeke.[38] The views of its members did not alter the teaching at Zaria during the time they were there or soon afterward; changes occurred only later on. Of the ten members, most majored in painting; only Nwagbara and Ekeada were in graphics and commercial design. Uche Okeke, Simon Okeke, Onobrakpeya, Nwoko, and Grillo became well-known professional Nigerian artists; the others became artists and art teachers or art historians. Uche Okeke's role in the society and as an art student at Zaria was a major one, and he has continued to play artistic leadership roles in Nigeria.


## FANTASTIC FIGURES AND IGBO TALES

What of Okeke's art while at Zaria? After several years of experimentation, in 1958 and 1959 he perfected pen and ink depictions of characters and incidents from his collection of Igbo tales. He had continued to document Igbo tales, for example, collecting Igbo traditions at Aro Ndizogu in the 1959 long vacation. His tale drawings, exhibited at Mbari Ibadan in 1961, received favorable attention; some of them were published there in that year.[39] The tale texts were not published, and Okeke did not feel bound to depict specific scenes relating to them, though he did so in some instances. The tale figures are grotesque, whether animal or human, fitting the artist's idea that the tale's fantasy qualities justified this presentation. His interest in indigenous tales is not unusual for Nigerian contemporary artists, including those from Osogbo; it is also found in contemporary Nigerian literature.[40] Okeke was an early exponent of employing tales in Nigerian contemporary art.

The work is bold and attractive. The images are clearly outlined, their interiors frequently filled with patterns of rows of dots, parallel lines—wavy (figs. 11–13), zigzag, or straight—and rows of small spheres, circles, or triangles. Eyes, mouths, and noses are striking, often enlarged and distended. The art has a strong linear quality, with numerous interlacing lines, but it does not yet draw strongly from *uli* design as Okeke's later art does. Rather, some decorative patterns were derived from masks and wood carvings,[41] and some appear to be from feathers, shells, or scales.[42] As Ulli Beier comments:

> But these weird creatures are certainly haunting. Are they plants? Are they animals? Masks or human beings? In the fantasy world of Okeke everything is possible. There are scaly creatures with flabby wings, maidens whose eyes are cowrie shells, men whose hair is feathers. Many creatures are froglike, fearsome and cold. Others have fluid, slimy plasma forms that seem to change in front of one's eyes. But this is not a contrived world of surrealism.[43]

Beier wrote, with reference to genre art, in the foreword to Okeke's Mbari publication: "The times are gone when

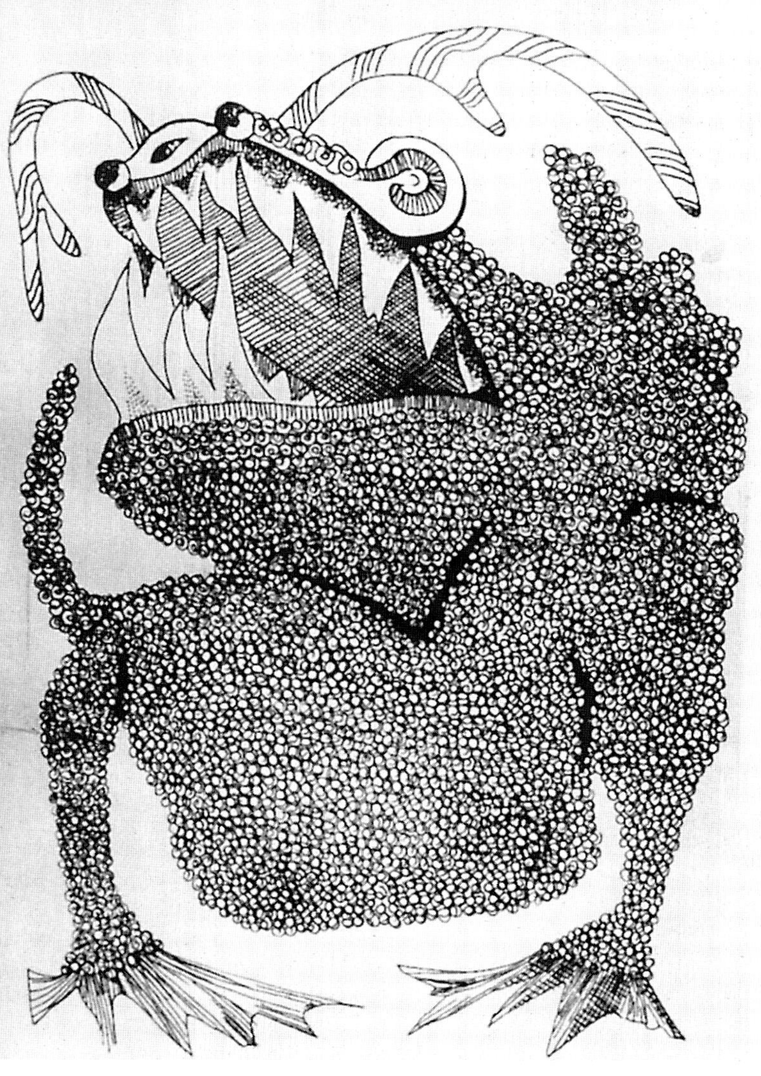

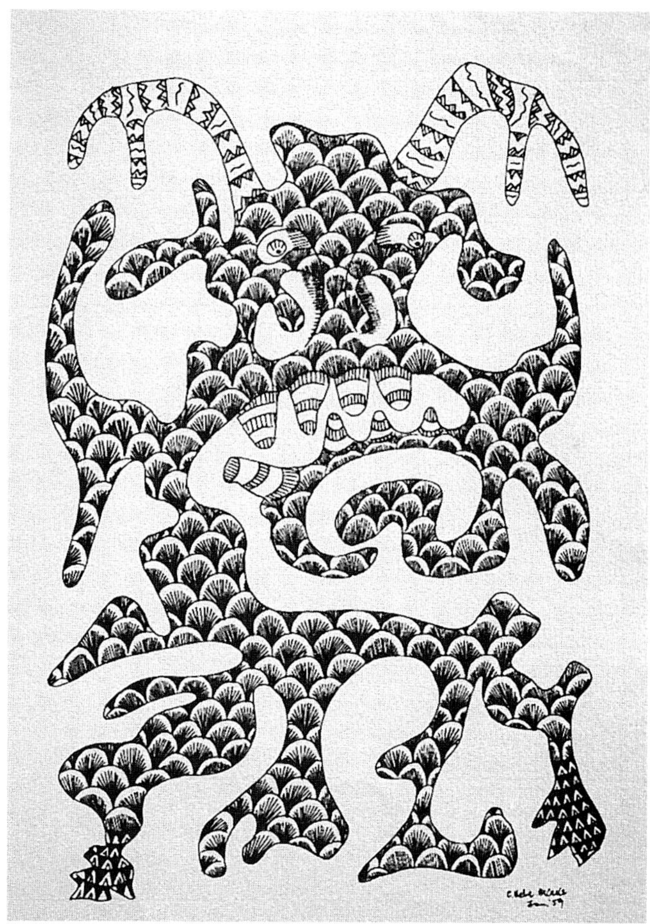

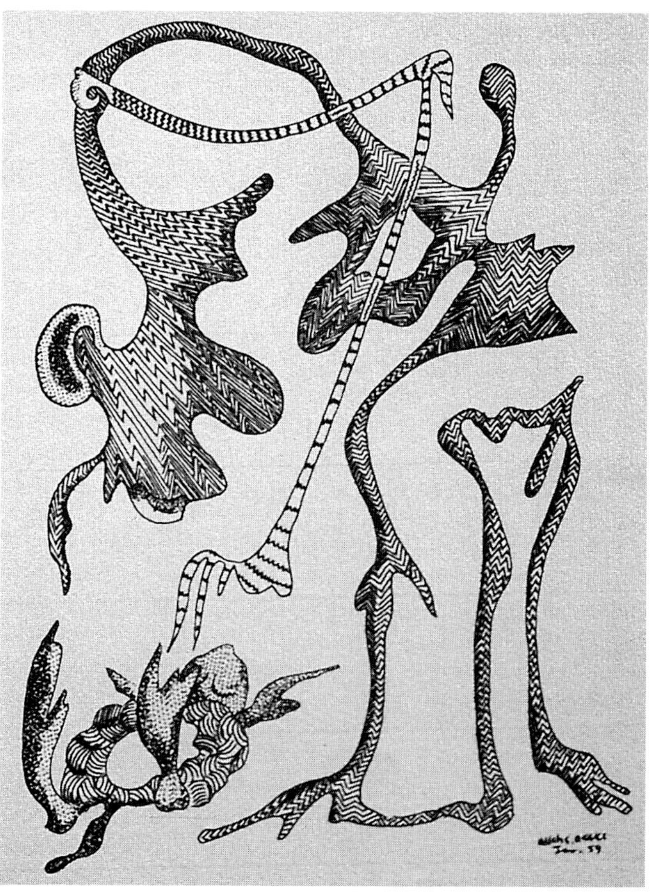

**11 (ABOVE).** Uche Okeke, *Fabled Brute*, 1959, pen and ink on paper, dimensions unknown. Collection of the Asele Institute. Photographer unknown.

**12 (TOP RIGHT).** Uche Okeke, *Wunderlichen Ọmalide (Wondrous Ọmalide),* 1969, pen and ink on paper, dimensions unknown. From U. Okeke 1969b. Collection of the artist.

**13 (BOTTOM RIGHT).** Uche Okeke, *Die Schildkröte,* 1969, pen and ink on paper, dimensions unknown. From U. Okeke 1969b. Collection of the artist.

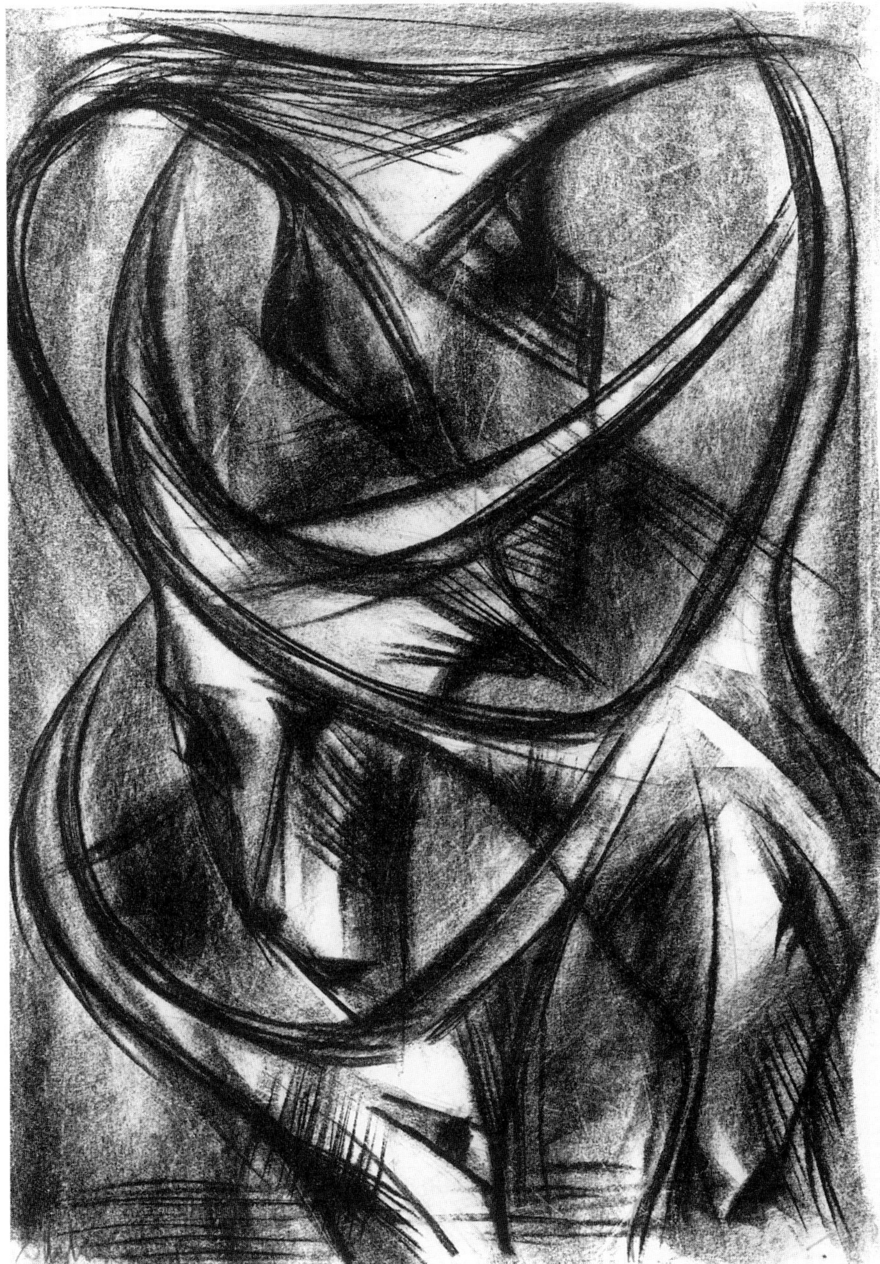



it was considered African to compose market scenes, lagoons with palm trees and women carrying water pots on their heads."[44] Okeke, in a manner strikingly different from that of Enwọnwu, was also drawing upon tradition.

Images and style were not derived from Okeke's teachers at Zaria, though his skill in pen and ink work was undoubtedly enhanced by his training. His observations of plants, animal forms, and tree bark were linked to his knowledge of Igbo tales. That Okeke's earliest substantial work was in drawing is consistent with his lifetime emphasis on the importance of this skill as basic to art, an approach he stressed later in directing art training at the University of Nigeria, Nsukka. In a letter to the Harmon Foundation early in 1962, he wrote: "In recent years I have made hundreds of drawings—I have made many more drawings than any Nigerian artist. I love drawing. I hope that I will be able to let you have some drawings of mine in the future."[45]

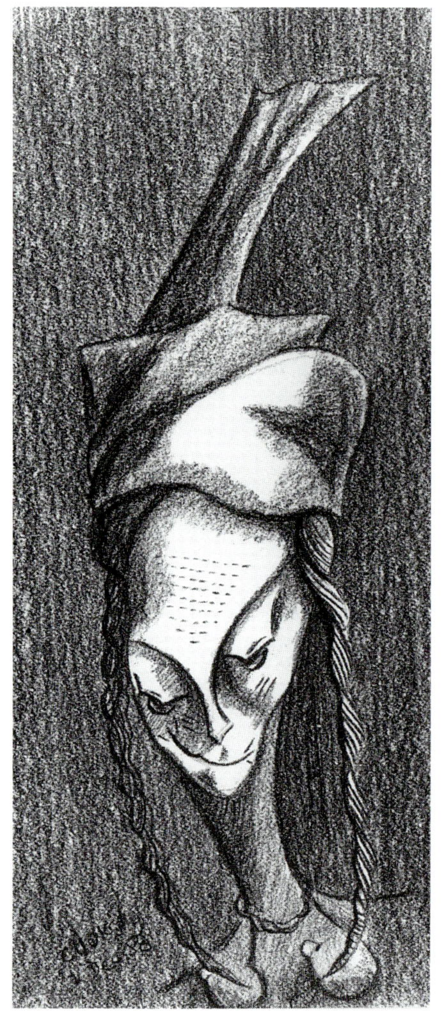

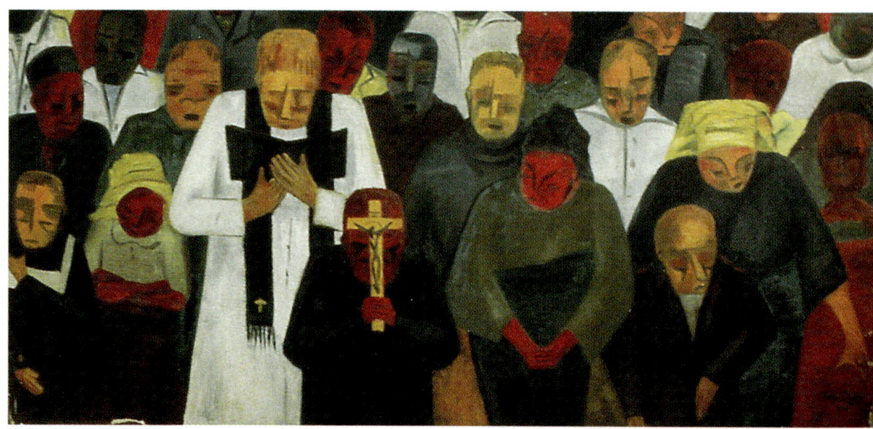

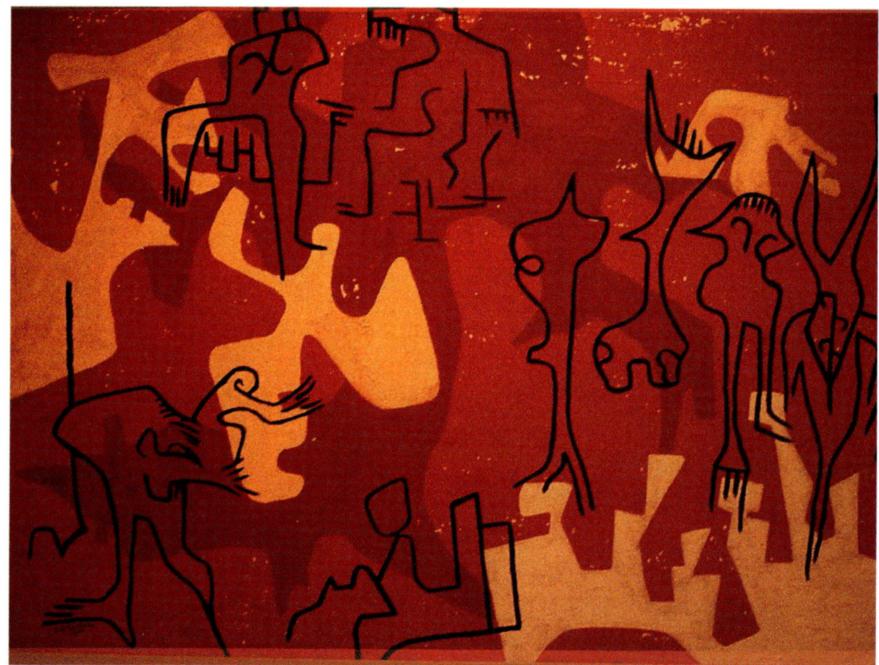

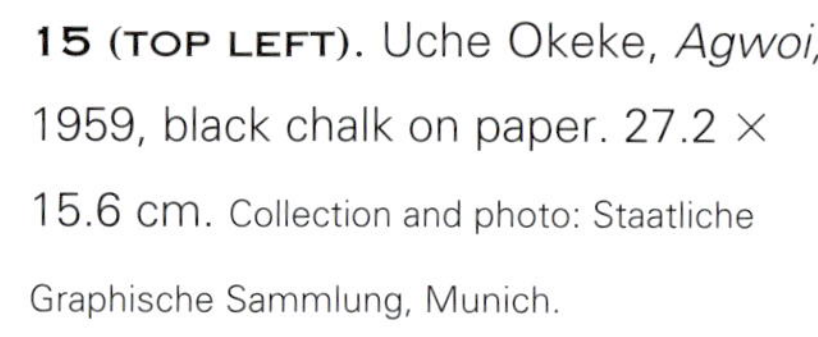

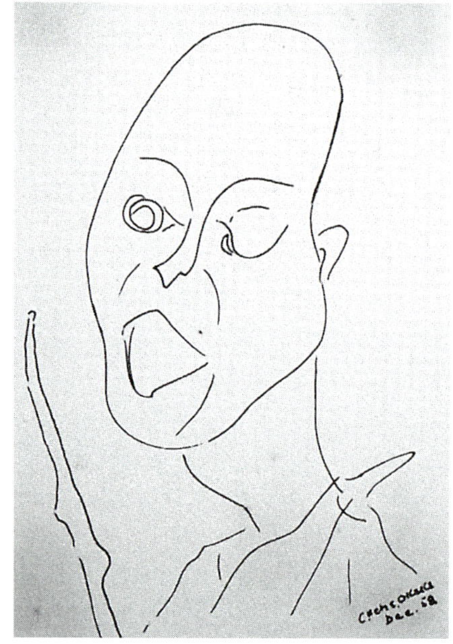

**15 (TOP LEFT)**. Uche Okeke, *Agwoi*, 1959, black chalk on paper. 27.2 × 15.6 cm. Collection and photo: Staatliche Graphische Sammlung, Munich.

**16 (BOTTOM LEFT)**. Uche Okeke, *Head of a Beggar (Nok Suite),* 1958 or 1959, pen and ink on paper. 19 × 14 cm. Collection of the artist.

**17 (TOP RIGHT)**. Uche Okeke, *Burial Procession*, 1961, oil, dimensions unknown. Collection of the artist.

**18 (BOTTOM RIGHT)**. Uche Okeke, *Ana Mmuọ (Land of the Dead)*, 1961, oil. 93.3 × 174.6 cm. Gift of Joanne B. Eicher, and of Cynthia Carolyn Ngọzi and Diana Eicher to the National Museum of African Art.

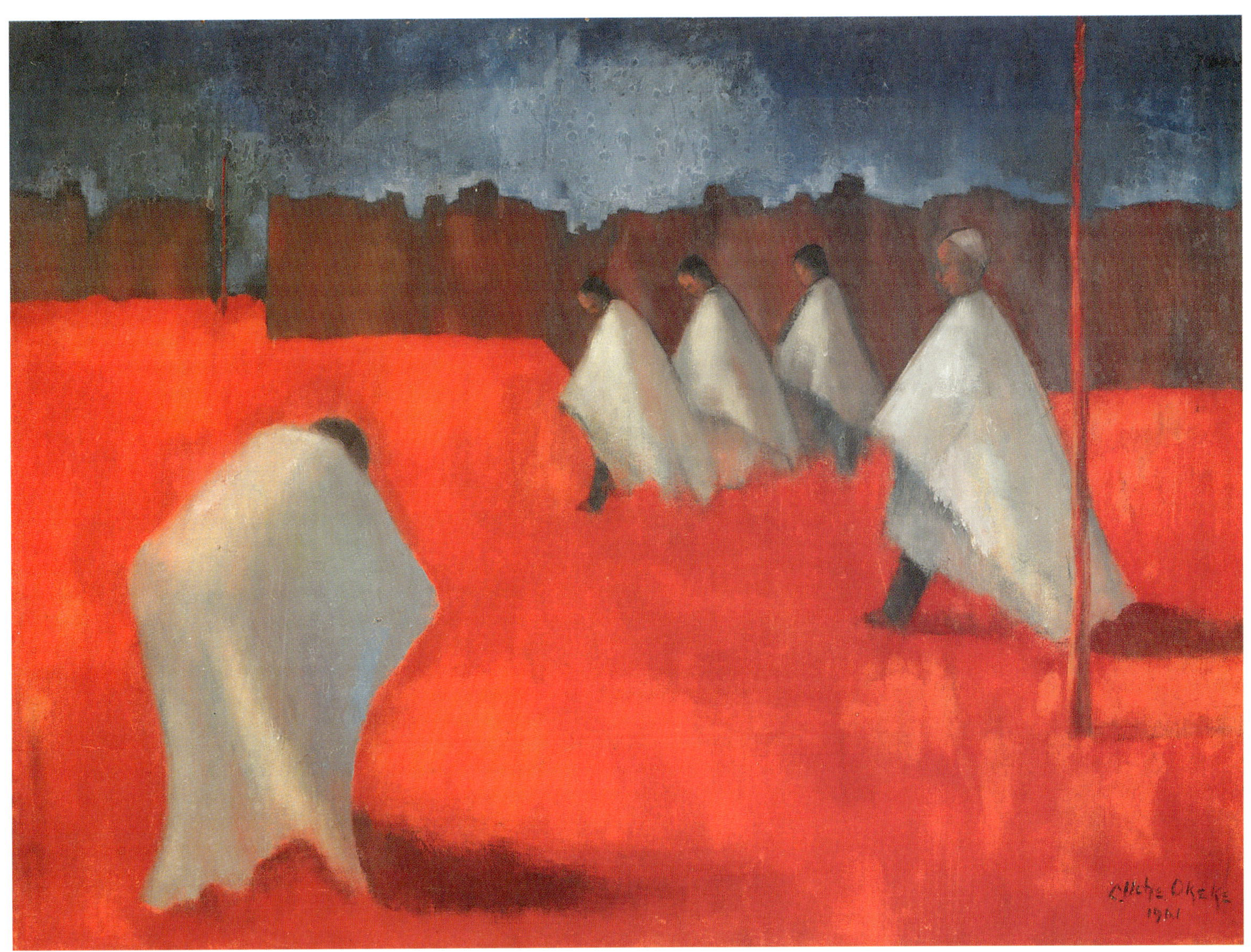

**19**. Uche Okeke, *Jumaa,* 1961, oil on board. 91.4 × 121.9 cm. Collection of the Asele Institute. Photo: Franko Khoury.

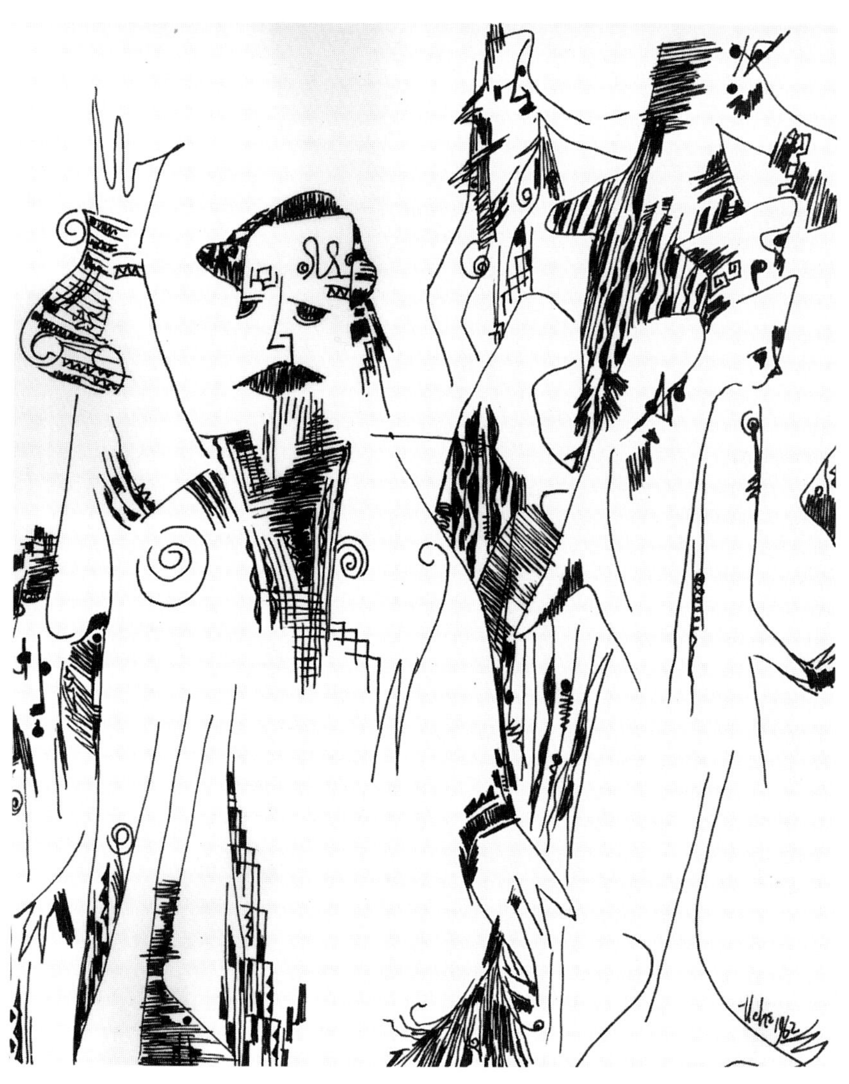

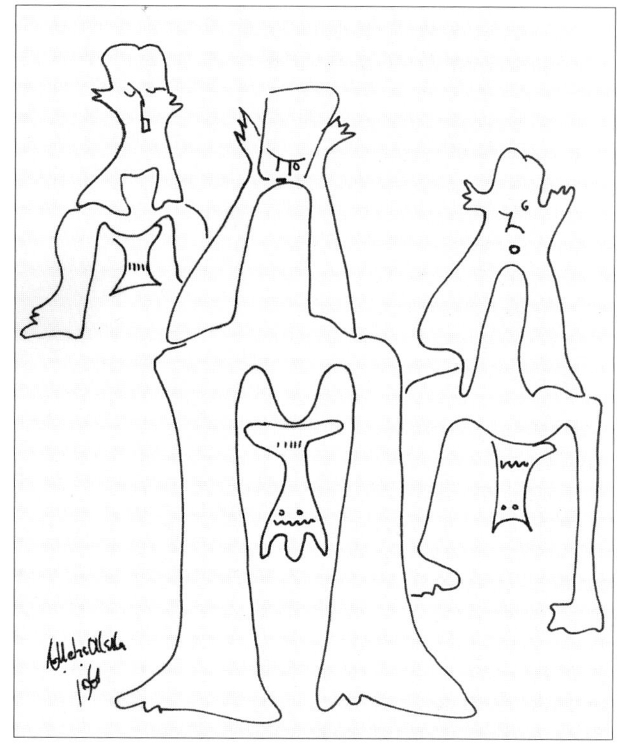

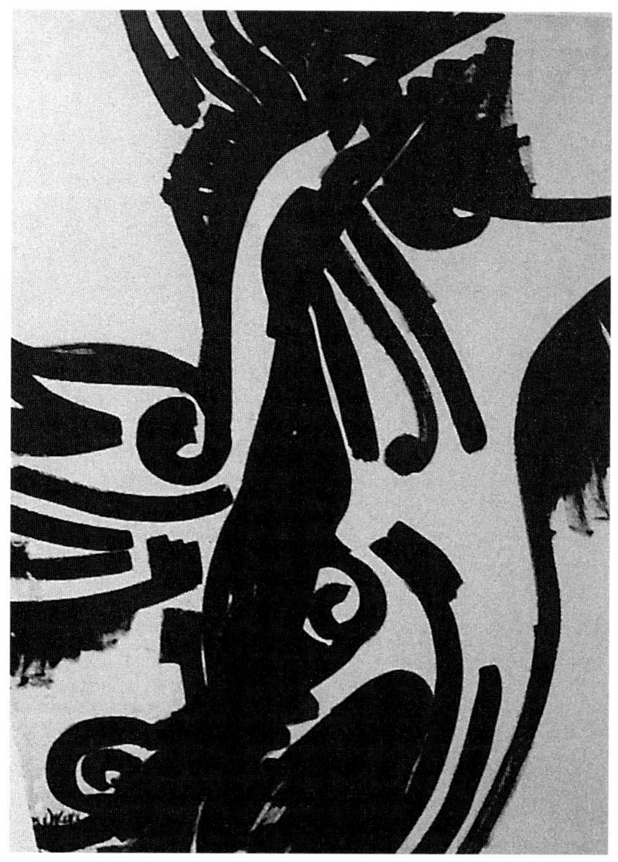

**20 (ABOVE).** Uche Okeke, *Dilemma of the Colonial Politician,* 1962, pen and ink on paper. 25.9 × 20.7 cm.
Collection and photo: Staatliche Graphische Sammlung, Munich.

**21 (TOP RIGHT).** Uche Okeke, *Three Thinkers,* 1961, pen and ink on paper. 18.8 × 14 cm. Collection and photo: Staatliche Graphische Sammlung, Munich.

**22 (BOTTOM RIGHT).** Uche Okeke, *Birds in Flight,* 1962, brush and ink on paper. 51 × 38 cm. Collection of the artist.

Okeke's former student, Obiora Udechukwu, in talking with Okeke, learned that he drew the human figures, as well as the animal ones, in fantastic form because they were all part of nature; there was no point in making the humans realistic because they were not real persons.[46] Udechukwu writes: "A heroic character like Ojaadili is not just represented as a man but is a cross between ape, man and bird, even wood sculpture. The eyes are discs that resemble schematized gramophone records."[47] He also comments that the charges of obscurantism in this art fail if a proper critical attitude exists.[48] He quotes Beier that "even if one is not acquainted with Igbo folklore one is tempted to invent new stories and adventures of *Nza* the Smart, or *Ojaadili*."[49] Okeke's figures sometimes appear to be humorous because of their grotesqueness, a humor otherwise rarely found in his work. He later put some of these strange creatures into other media, such as his *Fabled Brute* in oil and also in gouache.[50]

By choosing tales of his time, Okeke was stating that Igbo culture was not dead but active and could no longer be ignored in contemporary art. To Okeke, tales were not an incidental and amusing form of African culture, as Euro/Americans like to think of them, nor the amusing fantasies of naive people as the term *folktale* suggests, but a very important aspect of culture.

Okeke made other, less well known explorations at the time of his Zaria training. In 1958 and 1959 he produced a series of black chalk drawings, some with intense human faces with sharply delineated features and one with a very abstract snail-like design (figs. 14, 15). These have backgrounds of soft vertical strokes, darkening the drawings.[51] In 1958 and 1959 he created more than eighty pen and ink works of human heads, including a self-portrait, all of which he called the *Nok Suite,* where facial features are almost caricatures.[52] The suite was based on persons in the Kafanchan area, though some works drew from the Nigerian Rivers region (fig. 16). In 1961 he produced a substantial-sized, realistic oil painting of his father's funeral procession, with the family and its friends, in which Okeke, as a boy, carries the cross, with his mother beside him in a black headcloth and a European priest and a male Hausa at the upper left (fig. 17). Another oil, surprisingly abstract and with dark wandering black lines, entitled *Ana Mmuo,* a reference to masked spirit dancers, was also completed at this time (fig. 18).

Images from northern Nigeria appear in his art, for example, a naturalistic oil painting of a beggar (1961) and the oil *Fulani Woman* (1961), with its gatelike background, which emphasizes the qualities of the long, thin, vertical Fulani face in the foreground. An oil, *Jumaa* (1961; fig. 19), originally entitled *Beggardom,* shows Muslims moving toward a walled city.[53] With its strong red foreground, the painting gives the sense of sun and heat on barren ground in contrast to the full white body cloths of the Muslims. Okeke also created a number of drawings and paintings of beggars. He was worried about Nigerian conditions, including the considerable increase of begging in the country. Was Nigeria becoming a begging nation rather than people doing things for themselves?[54] A small linocut Christmas card of 1960, *Bonsue Dancers,* with the design in white against a black background, has impressive angular lines. A brush and ink work, again with the design in white on a black background, *Face of Time* (1959), has largely curvilinear elements in it and is quite abstract in appearance. It became the logo of Okeke's cultural center some years later (see fig. 52). A charcoal *Madonna* (1960) is one of a series of Christian themes that Okeke was to explore in various media in his career.[55]

Okeke drew from both Igbo and northern cultures, the northern generally more realistically than the Igbo. He produced art on Christian and Muslim themes. Overall, his art took fantastic, naturalistic, and abstract forms, and he worked in several media: pen and ink, brush and ink, oil, gouache, and linocut. If his intellectual views on natural synthesis were focused in this period, his production at this time was varied in images and media (figs. 20–22).

The linear qualities of Okeke's art of the time suggest *uli* influence. For several years before entering the college at Zaria, he had become interested in *uli*. He saw it as an important Igbo drawing technique, which sometimes incorporated animal forms, such as the lizard, snake, and tortoise, though in a simplified manner, certainly

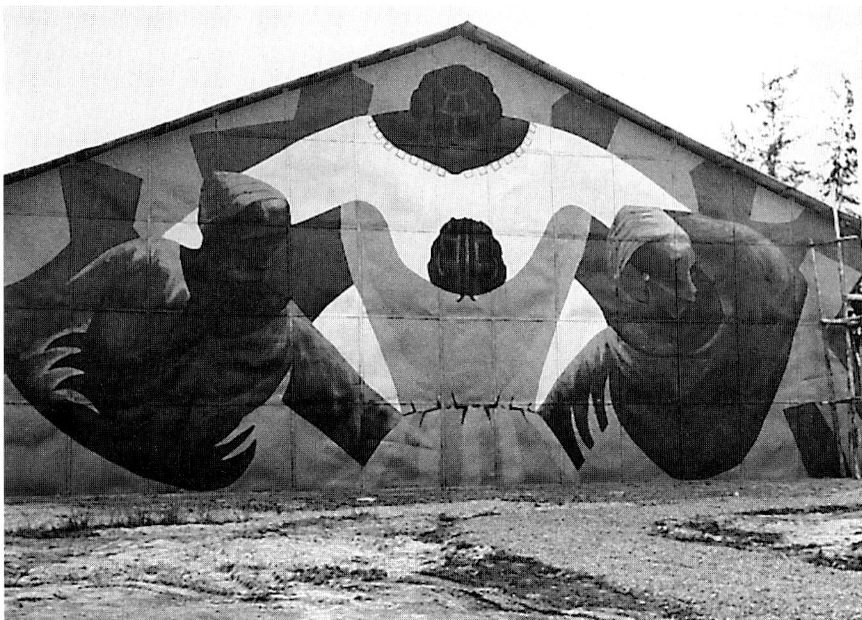



not as Okeke did in his Igbo tale art. As Okeke was interested in drawing, it is not surprising that in 1959 he had his mother draw from memory, in charcoal on paper, a range of *uli* motifs and instruct him as to their meaning. As he says about that period:

> Yes, we had a very rich building architectural tradition in the past, which used everything to decorate and construct a house, a living space. And so I thought that with that kind of background, there was no way I could go on and study other things without knowing and learning about that background that made me Igbo or non-Igbo. So even though I was brought up in the north, I have that consciousness that whatever happened, the folklore we are talking about, everything we did was basically what we learnt from the past, and so I had to go straight to my mother.[56]

Okeke came to realize that there was an association of *uli* with Igbo tales; tales referred to an *uli* forest, and *uli* is also the name of a pod found in the forest from which ink is obtained to draw the body designs. After completing his Igbo tale phase, Okeke more and more employed the linear qualities of *uli,* but without generally using its specific motifs. It perfectly fit his drawing interests, his concern for Igbo culture, and his close association with his mother.

In 1960 Okeke painted a mural (15 × 9 m), entitled *Unity* by Beier and *Mother Nigeria and Her Children* or *Mother Nigeria* by Okeke (fig. 23), at the Arts and Crafts Pavilion in Lagos for the independence celebrations.[57] Painted with commercial paints on raffia mats framed to the wall in sections by thin wood strips, the work was not in his Igbo tale style. It was more realistic, with human figures of both sexes and different ages that lack the considerable design elements within the bodies of the figures found in his Igbo tale art. Two other Art Society members, Demas Nwoko and Bruce Onobrakpẹya, who also painted wall murals at the pavilion, organized the accompanying contemporary art exhibition with Okeke. Okeke and Nwoko also held a joint exhibition sponsored by the British Council at Ibadan in 1960. In 1961 he and Nwoko exhibited at Mbari Ibadan and then at Exhibition Centre, Lagos.[58] Okeke also designed wall murals for Mbari Ibadan the same year. All three artists were startlingly innovative compared to what had come before in Nigeria; this was recognized by Nigerian artists and scholars and by Crowder, Beier, and other expatriates. Okeke also exhibited at the Biennale at São Paulo, Brazil, in 1961. He won first prize in the Esso Independence Calendar painting competition in 1959, and in 1958 he was awarded a federal government scholarship to continue his art training at Zaria. He was involved in the formation of the Nigerian Academy of Fine Arts in Lagos in 1961, being its publicity secretary.[59] Okeke was becoming known in Jos, Zaria, Ibadan, and Lagos as one of the interesting young artists of the coming generation.

Okeke's degree of recognition and exposure, as well as that of other Zaria art students, would have been unusual for a college student in Europe or America, but the Nigerian situation differed.[60] There were few artists, and Okeke's and other Zaria students' art was unusual, attractive to both Africans and expatriates, and received good support. Furthermore, these artists and others from Zaria were ambitious and worked hard at their art and at arranging for exhibitions. Okeke continued to write poetry during this period, winning the first prize for poetry in 1960 from the Nigerian Arts Council in Lagos.

## CULTURAL CENTER

In the midst of his other activities, at the end of 1958 Okeke opened his Cultural Centre in Kafanchan.[61] He had already begun to collect materials for it, and he would continue to do so. The center housed publications on Nigerian and other visual art, poetry, reference books, the works of other Nigerian artists, particularly those at Zaria, photographs, documents, and his own art. He purchased books in Lagos and elsewhere and obtained free donations of publications, including books from the Harmon Foundation in New York. Intent on creating a center to document the development of Nigerian contemporary art, he wrote in July 1961:

> Kafanchan Cultural Centre in Northern Nigeria began in a very humble way in 1959. It was my idea. It is gradually growing. Now there are some 3,000 books and periodicals in its collection (Books on Art, African Literature, Novels, Biographies, Anthropology etc.). There are about 400 art pieces in its growing gallery—drawings, prints, paintings, sculptures, etc., all of contemporary artists.[62]

The cultural center reflects the scholarly side of Okeke, who later published a great deal on contemporary Nigerian art and its history, on *uli* design, and on other topics. The cultural center was also his studio when he was not at Zaria. When away from Kafanchan, his mother and two railway technician friends cared for it. Ulli Beier once visited him there.

Even if there had not been problems at Zaria, Okeke would have started the center, but in the context of the Art Society, the center can be seen as a counter to the college, as artists could use it to create independently of teaching influences and to study the work of other Nigerian artists. Okeke's life indicates that while he later taught for some fifteen years at the University of Nigeria, Nsukka, developing the art department there, and while he believed in academic art training, he also saw cultural centers as a viable alternative for artistic stimulation and learning and for apprentice training. He has maintained the cultural center to the present day, locating it at different sites over the years.

After leaving Zaria, Okeke briefly worked as a graphic artist with the writer Cyprian Ekwensi, who was director of the Federal Information Service, Lagos. In 1962 Okeke returned to his cultural center at Kafanchan, working in his studio. Before he went to Germany toward the end of 1962, he had already exhibited in Europe, in 1960–61 in the *Kunst aus Zentralafrika* exhibition in Berlin, Bremen, Dortmund, and Dormstadt, Germany.[63] In May 1962, Okeke and Demas Nwoko had a successful showing of larger paintings at Galerie Lambert in Paris.[64] Beier wrote the preface of the brochure for the exhibition, extolling the two as representing a new generation of

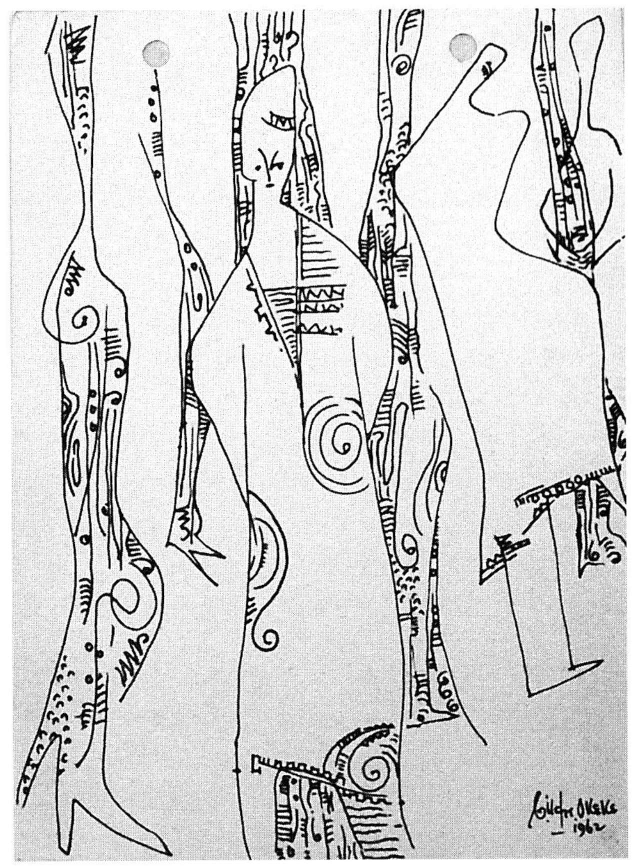

**24 (LEFT).** Uche Okeke, *Punishment (Oja Suite no. 4),* 1962, pen and ink on paper. 19.1 × 13.9 cm. Collection of Simon Ottenberg.

**25 (BELOW).** Uche Okeke, eight works from the *Oja Suite,* 1962, pen and ink on paper. 60 × 88 cm. Collection of the Asele Institute. Photo: Franko Khoury.

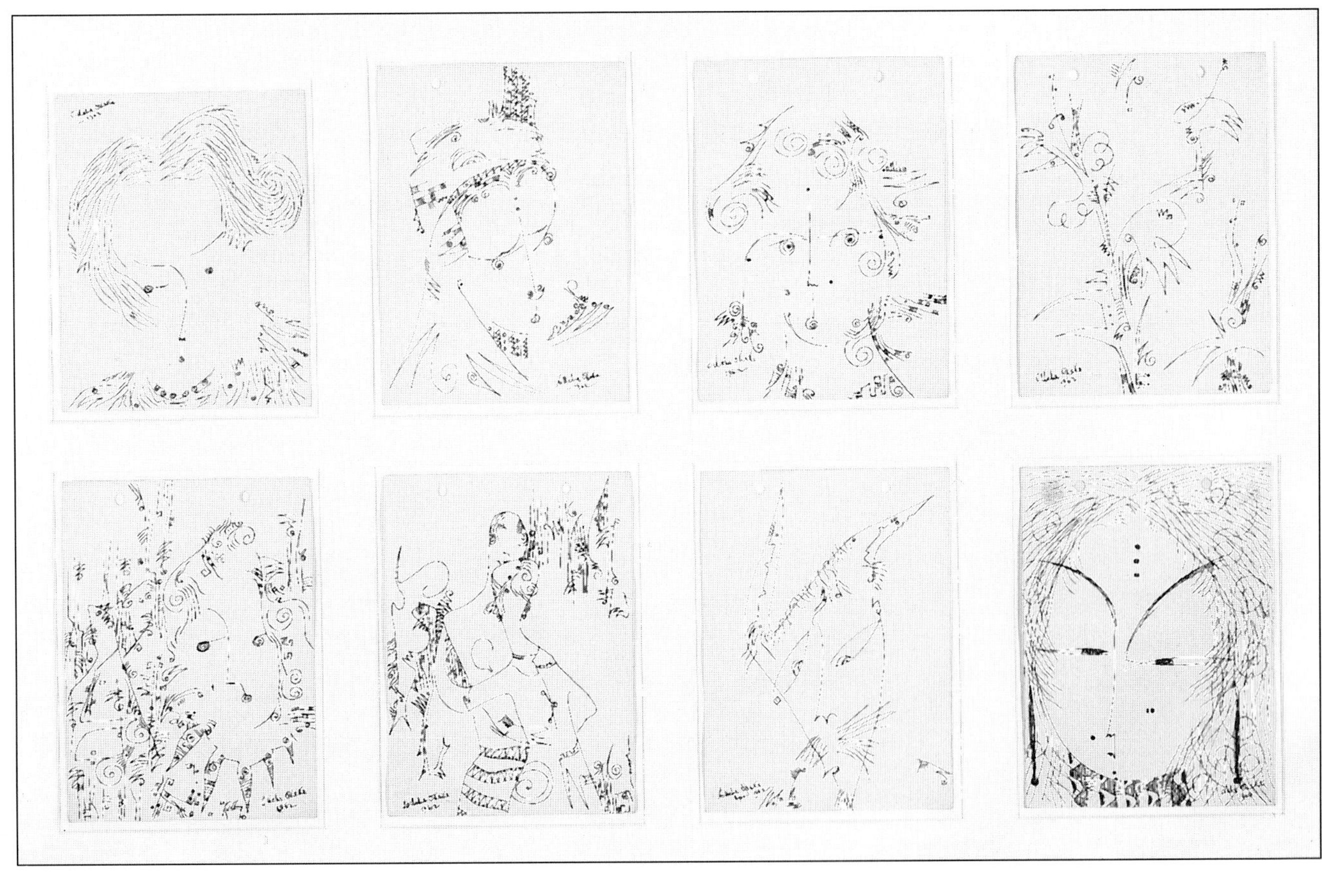

artists. In the same year Okeke exhibited with other artists at the Ugandan Independence Art Exhibition, Kampala, and with the Nigerian National Collection of Antiquities at the National Gallery of Rhodesia, Salisbury.[65]

Okeke wanted foreign experiences. On September 11, 1961, he wrote to the Harmon Foundation that he had "been working very hard to build up our Cultural Centre. I desire to travel out of this country in [the] future in order to meet artists and visit art galleries and museums. Ours is about the first such project [the cultural center] in Nigeria and we are prepared to make it a success."[66] His reactions to his teachers at Zaria had not turned him away from the idea of traveling to Europe and of viewing European art there, nor did it do so for other Art Society members. They felt that there was more to European art and life than they had been exposed to at Zaria. Already in early 1962 he thought of relocating the center to Enugu, a populous place in the heart of Igboland, with educational and government institutions and convenient transportation.[67]

## FIRST GERMAN EXPERIENCE

Toward the end of 1962, Okeke went to West Germany on a German federal scholarship.[68] While in Lagos waiting to travel, he produced his *Oja Suite* (figs. 24, 25), which "display[s] the gestural nuances of *uli.*"[69] In Germany he was attached to Franz Mayer, Hofkunstanstalt, Munich, a factory specializing in stained glass and mosaics, at the time working to restore churches bombed during World War II.[70] Remaining in Germany somewhat less than a year, he studied German for a while at Rott am Inn near Wasserburg, where he had an exhibition of his drawings. At Mayer's workshop he first created a mosaic of flowers in a vase, later destroyed in the Biafran war. After being there a week he decided not just to design and let others assemble his mosaics, but to do the whole process. He cut the colored marble and the smalti, a fine Italian glass mosaic with irregular surfaces, creating interesting shadows and catching light differently at various angles, which the flat marble did not do. He then glued these tesserae to a backing. He had created mosaic tile work as a student at Zaria, and he expressed a wish to work in this form when making arrangements for Germany. Okeke created fourteen small *Stations of the Cross* mosaics, a larger *Madonna and Child,* and a stained glass window, *Christ's Entry into Nimo,* which portrays Christ riding triumphant into the artist's hometown on a fabulous being (figs. 26–28).

"Almost all commissions in our firm are religious. I have already completed a number of designs based on biblical themes," he wrote.[71] An *Exhibition of Mosaics and Stained Glass Windows* of his work was held at the Franz Mayer firm in March 1963. The Staatliche Graphische Sammlung, Munich, acquired eighteen of his drawings and two prints that Okeke had brought along or produced in Germany, including nature studies, works drawn from Igbo culture, and one of his rare political works, *Dilemma of the Colonial Politician* (1962, pen and ink; fig. 20). He produced a brush and ink series in Munich, called the *Munich Suite,* on topics similar to those of his earlier *Oja Suite.* By 1962 he was definitely involved in the use of *uli* in his art. He has continued this interest until today. Other than the work for Franz Mayer, most of his art produced in Germany drew on Nigerian themes.

There he visited art schools, acquiring ideas for his cultural center, went to museums, art galleries, castles, libraries, and to plays and operas. He traveled widely, met many artists, collected work from them for his cultural center, and helped establish a short-lived Mbari center in Munich.

He was struck by two German qualities. Their art scene was much more competitive than the Nigerian one, and he was impressed that in German industry, including Franz Mayer's factory, designers and craftsmen worked hand in hand. Okeke had always had an interest in functional art, which is clear from his talk to the Zaria Art Society of October 1960: "Our new society calls for a synthesis of old and new, of functional art and art for its own sake."[72] In his lifetime, Okeke has done commissions for churches and government buildings, and favors the

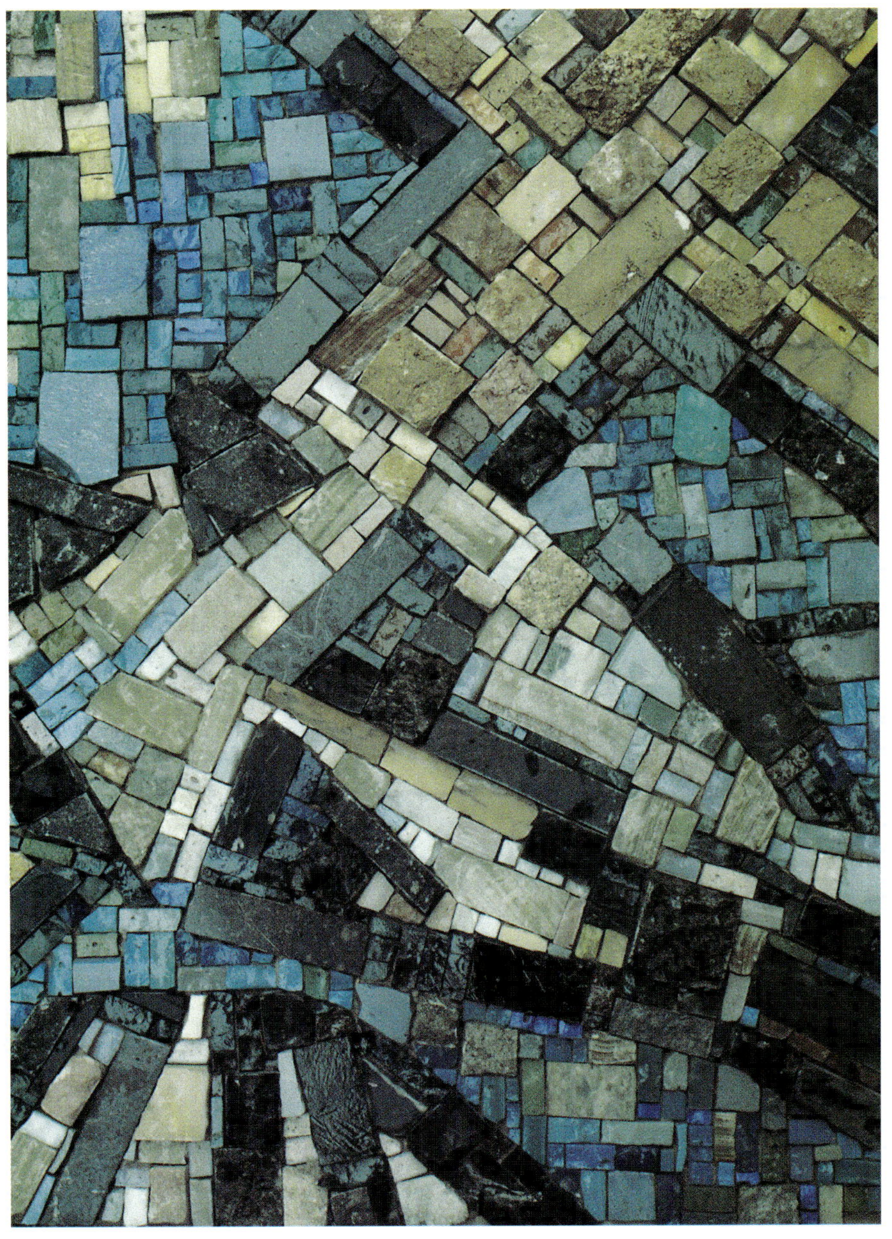

**26**. Uche Okeke, *Stations of the Cross IX,* 1962, mosaic tile. 52.3 × 35 cm. Collection of the artist.

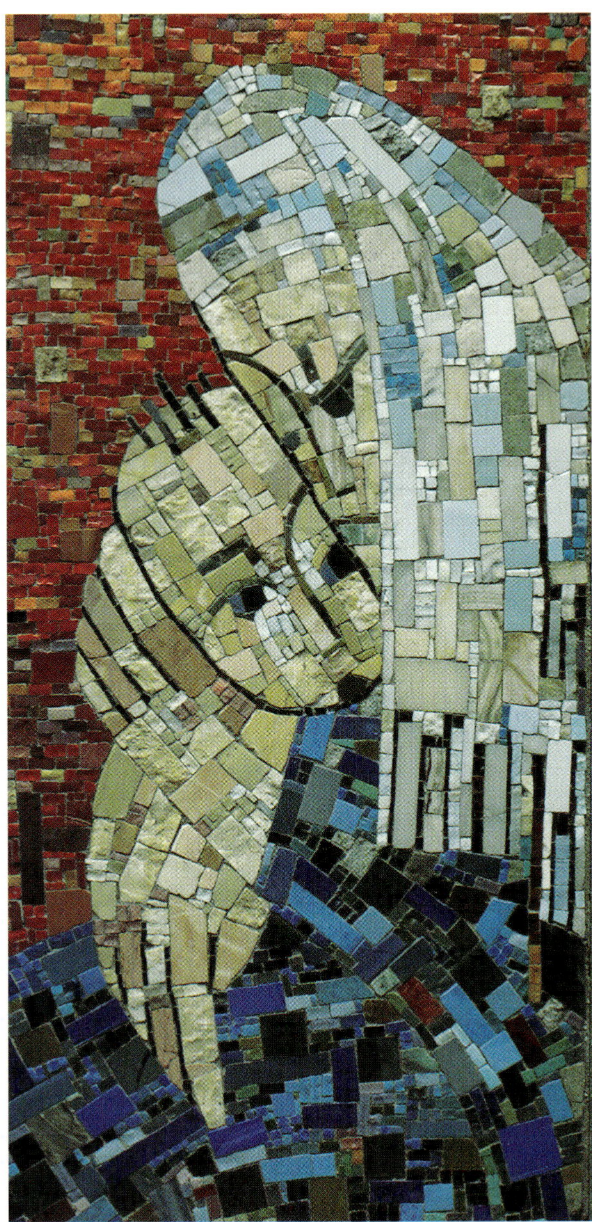

**27**. Uche Okeke, *Madonna and Child,* 1962, mosaic tile. 111.5 × 58 cm. Collection of the artist.

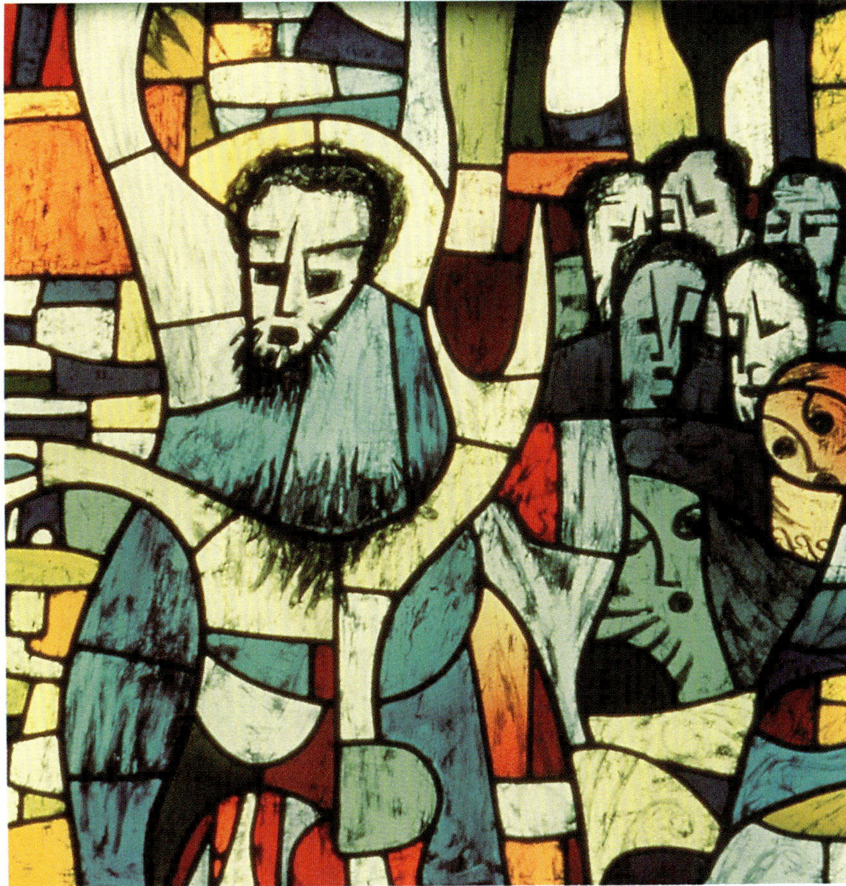



cooperation of architect and artist in their creation; he is aware of the strong functional element in traditional African arts.

Okeke's stained glass window and his flower mosaic came back to Nigeria, as he did in late 1963, although he never worked in either medium again.[73] It is not obvious how his German experience influenced his later art. I once asked him this, and he said I would have to see for myself. I believe it encouraged him to go ahead and experiment in his own creations, to develop his cultural center, and to conceive of what both an apprentice and an academic art training system should involve. Possibly he was influenced by some European artists whose work had qualities relating to *uli* design, such as Paul Klee. In addition to the *uli* experiments, he had the opportunity to explore religious subjects at this time. The German experience was clearly a rich one.

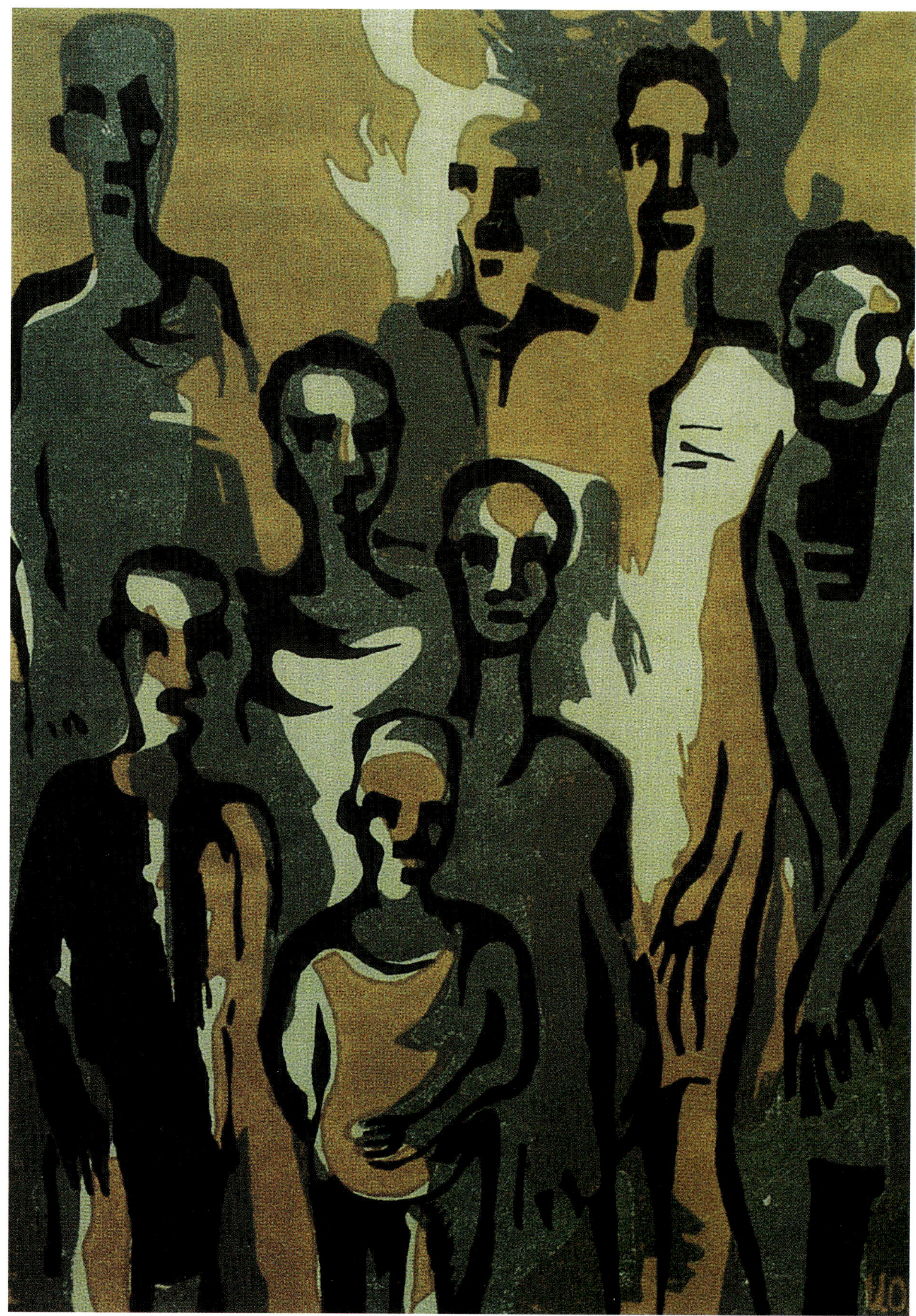

Detail of fig. 45.

# 3. UCHE OKEKE

## II: ENUGU DAYS, *ULI* AND SPIRITUAL FIGURES, BIAFRA

The first thing I did was to take the total concept of the spirit world, the world of man and based on Igbo lore. I had to find a way of reflecting this in my own work.

UCHE OKEKE[1]

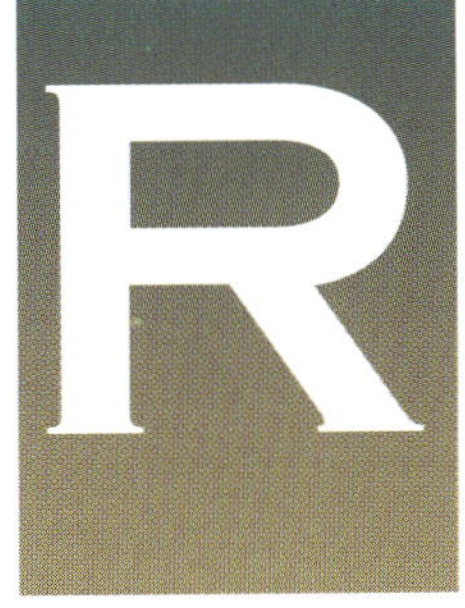

eturning to Kafanchan in 1963, Okeke transferred his cultural center to Agbani Road, in the Uwani section of Enugu, in August of that year. This growing Igbo city was Nigeria's Eastern Region capital at that time, much more a center of artistic activities than Kafanchan. The center's ground floor served as a gallery, the upstairs as Okeke's studio and apartment. Yet he planned someday to move the center to his Nimo home, and in 1964 acquired land there for this purpose.[2] His four-year stay in Enugu was to be productive artistically and in providing interaction with other visual artists, poets, novelists, dramatists, and musicians comparable to the early days of the Mbari Ibadan center.

In 1961, before Okeke arrived, a Regional Art Club was founded by a group of artists in Enugu using facilities of the United States Information Service. In 1962, while Okeke was still in Germany, the Mbari Writers and Artists Club was inaugurated at Ogui Road; the new club was distinct from the Mbari Ibadan one.[3] The Regional Art Club soon associated with Mbari and was joined by two former members of the Zaria Art Society, Oseloka Osadebe and Okechukwu Ọdita, who were teaching in the new art program at the University of Nigeria, Nsukka, not far away (see below).

Okeke's cultural center became the focus for a number of artists and persons interested in the arts (fig. 29). Its gallery displayed art from Okeke's contemporary collection, including Okeke's and that of other former Art Society members—Oseloka Osadebe, Okechukwu Ọdita, and Ogbonnaya Nwagbara—as well as the work of other artists. Evening classes were held there, taught by Okeke and others. In 1965 Okeke established an art supply shop on Zik's Avenue in Enugu, which he named Asele, after the mythic Anambra Igbo female spirit of creativity.

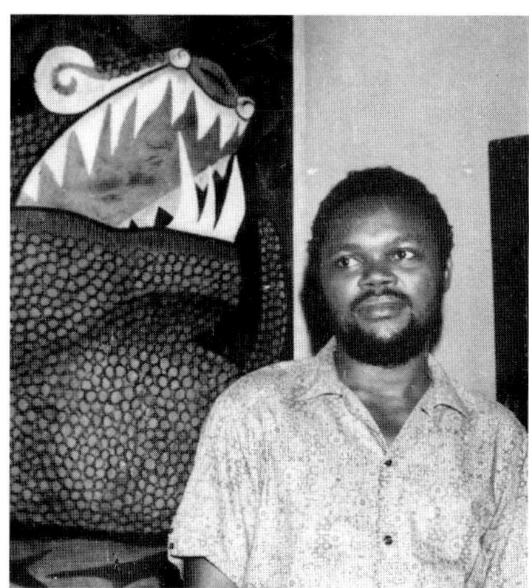

**29**. Uche Okeke at his Cultural Centre, Enugu, c. 1965. Photographer unknown.

Artists in Enugu came to know the work of the important Igbo poet Christopher Okigbo through Mbari.

Okeke's cultural center joined in early 1964 with the Mbari group to form Mbari Enugu, which Okeke directed into 1967. Members of this combined center were active in the annual Eastern Nigeria Festival of the Arts; Okeke was its art organizer in 1965, revising its program.[4] He cooperated with the British Council, which ran an "Art in Education" workshop in 1965, where Okeke was one of four tutors.[5] He also had a promising private art student between 1963 and 1967, Uzọ Ndubisi.[6] Okeke occasionally engaged in this type of teaching and clearly played important roles in art in Enugu.

He was also involved in other arts organizations belonging to Mbari Enugu in his role as artistic director and designer for plays produced by the Eastern Nigerian Theatre Group. These included Andre Obe's *Noah* (1963), Wọle Ṣoyinka's *The Lion and the Jewel* (1964), Sam Iyamu's *The Corps Diplomatique* (1964), and J. P. Clark's *Song of the Goat* and *The Masquerade*. The latter two were staged as well in 1965 at the Commonwealth Arts Festival in London, Glasgow, and Liverpool, providing Okeke the opportunity for a brief trip abroad.[7] The immediate postindependence period had produced a plethora of artistic activities and events in which Okeke was much involved. In addition, Okeke illustrated Chinua Achebe's 1962 edition of his famous novel *Things Fall Apart* and designed the dust jacket and cover for John Munonye's *The Only Son*, published in 1966.[8]

Okeke was very productive during the Enugu period. In 1965 he held a solo exhibition of his drawings at the Goethe Institut, Lagos, and solo exhibitions of his paintings at the Hotel Presidential, Enugu, and at the British Council, Port Harcourt. In 1966 there was an exhibition of his art at the Mbari Art Gallery, Enugu, and an exhibition of his graphics at the British Council in 1967. He took part in some eight group exhibitions in Nigeria in 1963–64, as well as a Harmon Foundation, New York exhibition, and another in Philadelphia, both in 1964. In 1966 he exhibited as part of the Nigerian contingent at the First World Festival of Negro Arts at Dakar. As a founding member of the Society of Nigerian Artists, he showed at their first exhibition in 1964 in Lagos. He also painted murals in the Children's Section of the then Eastern Nigeria Library, Enugu, in 1964.[9]

In Enugu, Okeke was deeply involved in what was to be a lifetime of activities proselytizing to the public and the government for contemporary art. Articles by him appeared in Lagos and Enugu newspapers.[10] He gave an important talk on the history of contemporary Nigerian art, at Queens' School, Enugu, on December 16, 1963, under the auspices of the British Council.[11] His writings considered the need for a strong national artists organization to encourage contemporary art.

In the time between Nigerian independence in 1960 and the beginning of the Biafran conflict in 1967, Enugu's importance in all fields of art rivaled that of Ibadan and Lagos, and Okeke was a major player in it. He writes in 1964 of the speed of change in Nigeria: "I can never return to the mood or feeling of my 1957 to 1958 folktale drawings."[12] The city's artistic growth was to disappear in the Biafran war; it was never to have such a rich, productive period again.

In Enugu in 1966 Okeke married Eunice Nwakaego Ọkadigwe. She later studied art at the University of Nigeria, Nsukka, and became a fabric artist with a lifelong interest in children's art.[13] She has been a strong supporter of and aide to her husband.

There was a visual art center at Nsukka, about an hour's drive north of Enugu, also in Igbo country, in a lovely grassland area with palm groves and other trees. In 1970, after the Biafran war, it became the center of the Nsukka artists group under Okeke. In the 1960s it was known as the Ben Enwọnwu College of Fine Art at the University of Nigeria, Nsukka.[14] The university and its art program were founded in 1960, though art teaching began only in 1961.[15] Modeled after American land grant universities, partially funded through Michigan State University and a U.S. AID program, the school was innovative in a number of ways, having Nigeria's first university law, accounting, music, and business programs.

The art training program had different agendas than that of Zaria. The first head of the art department was an American, Margaret Dunlap, from Michigan State University. There were other expatriate American, British, and Nigerian teachers. Anthony John-Kamen, from the present Anambra State in eastern Nigeria, taught there in 1962–67.[16] The sculptor Francis Osague, from Benin, also taught there for several years.[17] The Yoruba-born artist Akinọla Laṣekan (discussed in Chapter 1), taught at the university between 1961 and 1966, was head of the department at one time, and produced a large painting for the university library depicting the life of Nnamdi Azikiwe, the famous nationalist politician, who had much to do with the university's founding. Although the department was named after Enwọnwu, he did not teach there, though Azikiwe had tried to hire him. As mentioned earlier, Emmanuel Ọdita and Oseloka Osadebe, two former Art Society students from Zaria, were young teachers there for a time. Yet as the art historian Ọlọidi writes: "the pre-war period in the department was saturated mainly with the stylistic and conceptual art philosophy of the Academy through Laṣekan, himself a harbinger of Ọnabolu's naturalism."[18] There was no *uli* training or interest in *uli* design then. However, Ọdita and Osadebe were artists whose work was moving from the naturalistic to new styles; thus it was not surprising that they should have considerable contact with artists at the Enugu art centers. Anyakọra and other art students at Nsukka referred to the work of these two artists as "'bam bam bam,' reflecting the quick application of colours which contrasted with the painstaking realism and photographic representations of Mr. Laṣekan. For the students, it was a matter of choice, which made difficult the emergence of a definite Nsukka style."[19] Thirteen students graduated from the program between 1961 and 1966.

The Nsukka art program and the university before the war were lively. There was a Nsukka Writers Society which student artists also joined. The campus itself was cosmopolitan, with teachers from many parts of the world as well as from different Nigerian cultures. Azikiwe was trying to establish an international university. Art students were exposed to a broad liberal arts program. However, the art program produced few students who became distinguished artists over time. Perhaps the best known is the printmaker Paul Igboanugo, who studied there in 1965–67 and returned to finish his degree in 1972, after the war, under Uche Okeke's regime with a different art program.[20] Babatunde Lawal, who has become a well-known Africanist art historian, studied graphics there.

The Enugu-Nsukka poles represented contrasting styles of art, both within Igbo settings. The Nsukka style was commonly found and popular in Nigeria before the activities of the Zaria Art Society took hold; the Enugu centers largely represented the latter viewpoint. As Uche Okeke wrote: "At Nsukka in 1961, an American style Art Department was opened without due reference to the experience of Zaria."[21] Only with the arrival of Uche Okeke and others at the university after the war was the art department to move toward what had been going on in Enugu before the war.

Yet there was contact between the artists at Enugu and Nsukka. Oseloka Osadebe, teaching at the university, produced a mural for the outside of the Mbari Enugu building, and some Nsukka artists had exhibitions at Enugu cultural centers. And there were some changes at the university in the 1966–67 teaching year, the last before the war closed the university as political tensions increased in Nigeria. Because of the pogroms in the north and the threat of war, art students from the eastern region who were training at Zaria, including Obiọra Udechukwu (one of the artists in this study), Bons Nwabiani, and Gertrude Ezeani,[22] and from elsewhere in Nigeria, transferred from other regions of Nigeria to the university at Nsukka, bringing in some different ideas in art than existed there; there were some tensions between the original students and the new ones. During the time just before the Biafran war, non-eastern Nigerian faculty, including Laṣekan, left as the political situation grew tense. Igbo art faculty from elsewhere joined the university at this time, for example, Chuka Amaefunah, who had done a B.A. at Zaria in 1963 in graphic design; he later became very interested in *uli* motifs.[23] By June 1967 when the university closed, ideas about natural synthesis developed by the Art Society at Zaria had penetrated the Nsukka art program.

## *ULI* MOTIFS, IGBO MYTHOLOGY, UCHE OKEKE, AND THE NSUKKA ARTISTS

By the time of Okeke's Enugu period, his interest in *uli* was well developed, and a characterization of it is in order before discussing his art at this time.

*Uli* designs were formerly painted by females on female bodies, very occasionally on males, in blue black to black color. The women also painted *uli* designs on house, compound, and shrine walls, usually the exterior sides, in red/brown, yellow, black, and white, and occasionally, during the colonial period, in blue from washing blue. In some Igbo areas the wall murals were called *upa,* which literally translates as "laterite"; in other areas they were called *ntite*. But among the contemporary artists, the term *uli* is used for both body and wall painting. The body decorations lasted for a few days or more, the wall paintings about a year, depending on how well they were protected from the rain, for they were water soluble.[24]

Igbo *uli* painting has been little studied by anthropologists and art historians until recent times, who, like myself, concentrated on male-produced wood masks and figures, generally viewed as more exotic and spectacular. Scholars generally neglected the female arts, which were incorrectly seen as only associated with the domestic life of Igbo communities, not the larger ceremonial world. If scholars studied Igbo female arts, it was pottery and cloth; they did not look for an overall design system covering many different kinds of objects that *uli* motifs were more recently found to be associated with. It has largely been contemporary Igbo artists, led by Uche Okeke, who have brought *uli* to full attention and who have viewed it as a whole design system, no matter on what it occurs.[25]

Though the delightful body and wall motifs appear to have been secular, except for wall paintings associated with shrines, *uli* designs did take on a sacred quality, for they were associated with the spiritual world in that both body and wall *uli* appeared at important community rituals with religious aspects: girls' puberty rites, marriages, burials, memorial services, title taking events, the New Yam Festival, and New Year celebrations, among others. Female dance groups arranged to have the same design patterns on their members' bodies.[26] Body *uli* might be seen on females at major market days in a community. A few *uli* motifs had sacred qualities, as *isi ọji* (the head of the kola nut), for kola was an important preliminary ritual to many social meetings and activities, relating to peaceful social relationships and used in shrine sacrifices.[27] The python (*eke*) was another motif with sacred and tabooed qualities. *Uli* designs were sometimes said to have the power to cure measles, to safeguard women in pregnancy, and to ensure fertility, which suggests spiritual power at work.[28] The *uli* moon and sun (*ọnwa* and

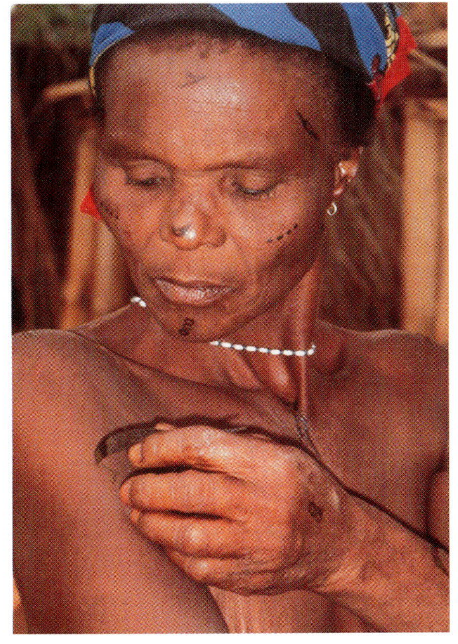

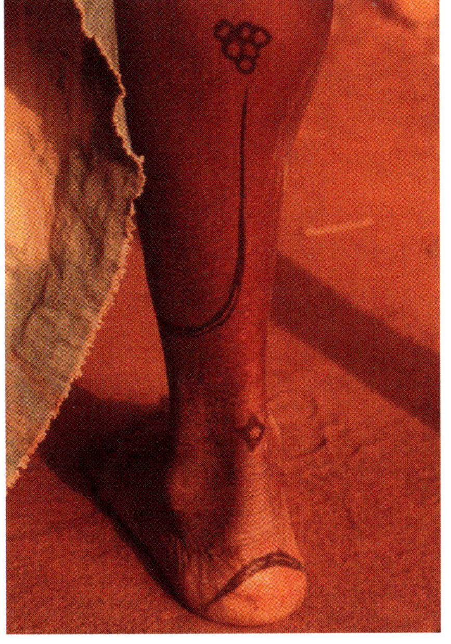

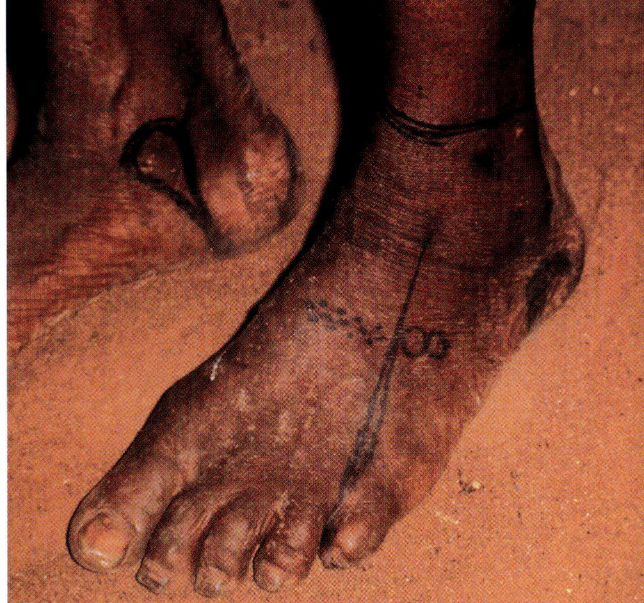

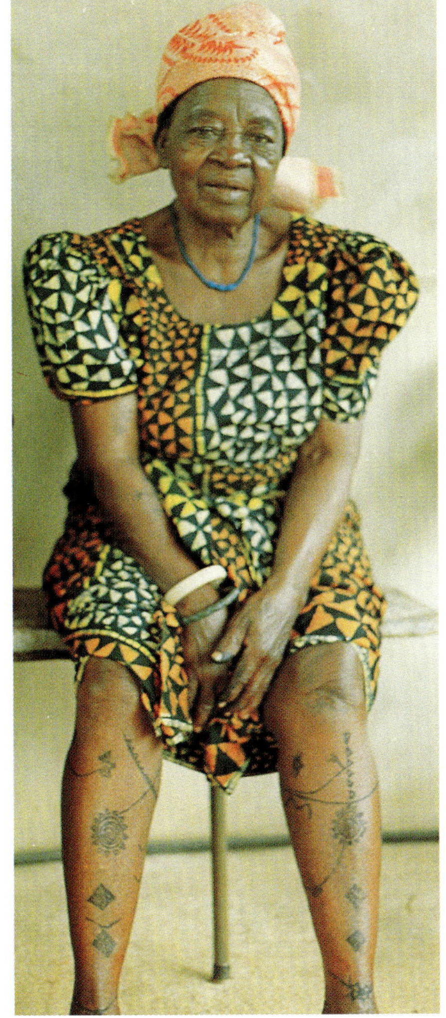

**30 (TOP LEFT).** Ekedinma Ọjiakọr from Agulu painting herself with a dull iron *uli* blade, 1995. Photo: Sarah Adams.

**31 (TOP CENTER).** *Uli* leg designs painted on herself by Ekedinma Ọjiakọr from Agulu, 1995. Photo: Sarah Adams.

**32 (TOP RIGHT).** Foot and ankle *uli* designs painted by Ekedinma Ọjiakọr on herself, 1995. Photo: Sarah Adams.

**33 (BOTTOM LEFT).** A painter of the Earth Shrine, Nimo, October 1994, showing leg *uli* designs. Photo: Elizabeth Willis.

*anyanwu* respectively) were Igbo spiritual figures. Elizabeth Willis suggests, following Okeke, that *uli* may have been inspired by Igbo religion.[29] She sees important associations between women, *uli,* and the major Igbo earth deity Ala or Ana.[30]

But *uli* also had important aesthetic aspects.[31] *Uli* murals visually enhanced the compound and its houses by decorating walls and homes. *Uli* beautified female bodies, who at an earlier time wore less clothing than today; it was possible to place the designs widely on the body as well as the face, and for them to be seen (figs. 30–33; see figs. 3, 4). Girls who had not had their puberty ceremony often wore only waistbands of *jigida* plastic beads, cowrie shells, or some other beads, so the body was available for visible decoration. The individual who was beautiful by nature was made more beautiful, and the less beautiful became more so. The *uli*-decorated female body was viewed by both sexes as aesthetically pleasing. Sexual attractiveness was there, but it was subdued by aesthetic qualities or blended into the aesthetics so as not to be obvious. To beautify the female body and the compound were Igbo ideals. Beauty was related to morality; to be beautiful was to be moral.[32] Other forms of body designs existed, such as *ogaalu* (in which the skin was blistered with concentric circles), *mbubu* incisions, *ichi* facial scarifications, and *nki* skin pricking.[33] These were not of much interest to the contemporary artists.

Myths and proverbs are associated with *uli*. At Ufuma, Lọlọ, the founder's wife, was believed to be a beautiful woman who painted beautiful *uli* on her body; therefore females in the village had the right to do so. And there is a saying, *O tulu agwa ka eke:* "something is as beautiful as a python." [34] And *Nwa agbọghọ dere uri ga de echee na ọdi maa, uri ala a, a mma ala:* "The maiden who goes into marriage with beautiful *uli* patterns thinks she is naturally beautiful; the *uli* patterns fade and her beauty is gone." [35]

*Uli* motifs may have been related to a larger system of designs in Igboland, for designs occurred on wooden masks, figures, doors and panels, incising on pottery, on the *agbọghọ mmụọ* appliqué body costumes of Igbo male masqueraders, in women's ceremonial hairstyles, on cloth, on bronze and ironwork, and on the mud figures and walls of traditional Igbo *mbari* shrine houses.[36]

There is disagreement as to whether all of these designs in Igboland were called *uli* or *uri* or not, and whether they formed a single widespread system of design throughout the Igbo area, as Uche Okeke believes. Some designs may have had other names and meanings and may have belonged to different design systems, though perhaps with some relationship to *uli*, as I believe to be true. Okeke, who has written extensively on *uli* in relation to his own art and that of his students and colleagues, sometimes assumes that the specific *uli* designs found in his home Anambra State were almost universally found elsewhere in Igboland.[37]

However, Elizabeth Willis, an artist and art historian, recently carried out extensive *uli* investigations and made use of *uli* drawings collected early in this century by the colonial officials G. I. Jones, M. D. W. Jeffreys, Kenneth Murray, and others. Willis believes that there are considerable differences in the designs and different meanings for the same design in different Igbo areas.[38] This fits my conception of the considerable variation in Igbo culture that exists in all spheres of Igbo life, from masquerade and art forms to political, religious, and kinship organization, as well as the names for *uli* motifs by dialect region. Even in a single community, the interpretation of the meaning of a specific design might have differed for various females. Yet the Anambra area includes the famous, influential Nri culture, whose influence spread far beyond its borders in religion, art, and blacksmithing.[39] So *uli* designs may have spread from there as well. In any case, Okeke is correct in stressing the importance and widespread nature of design in Igbo culture.

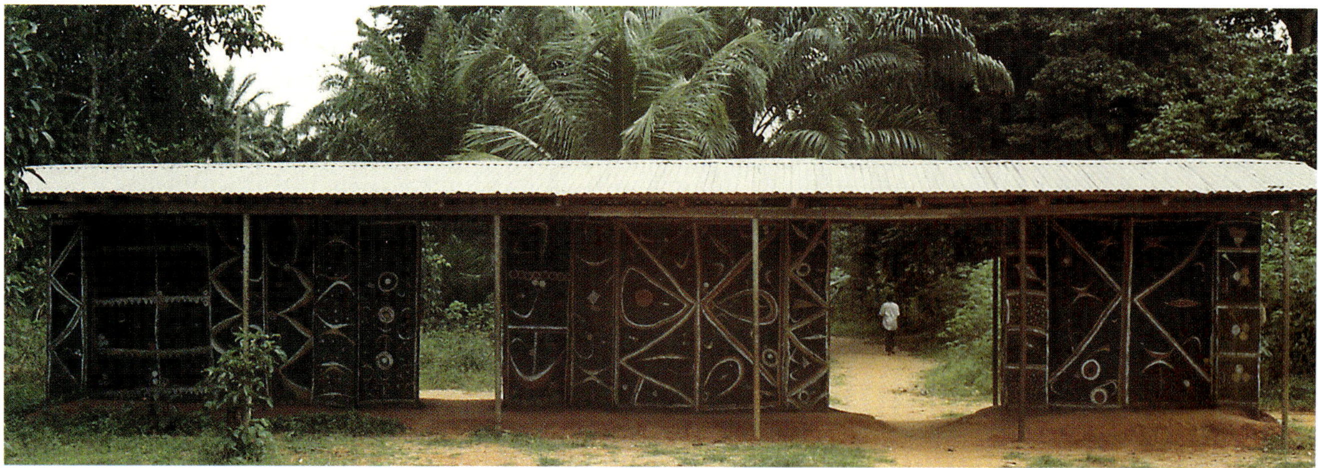

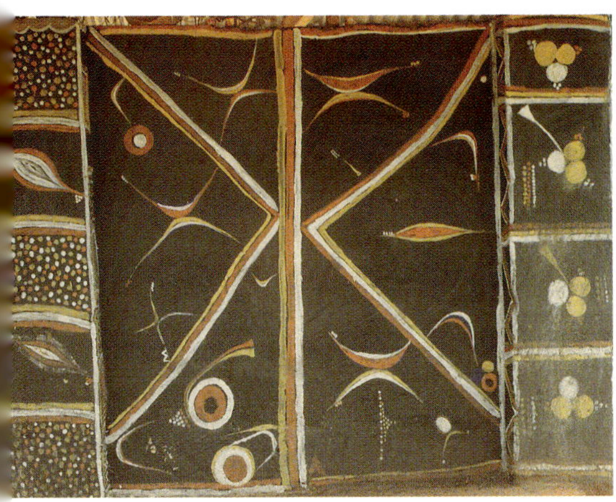

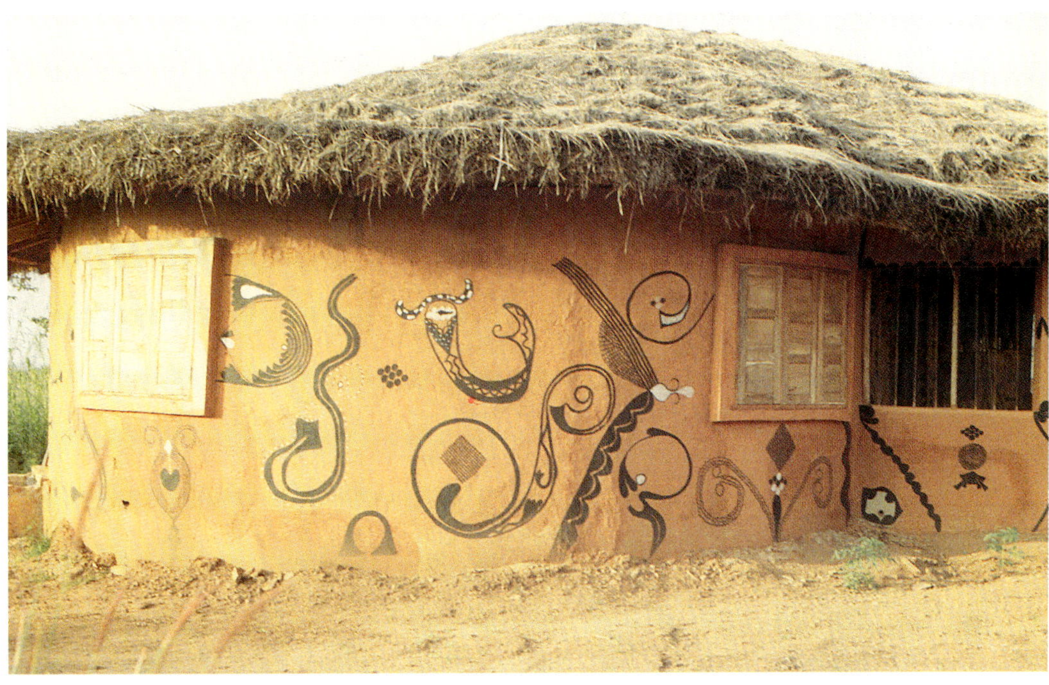

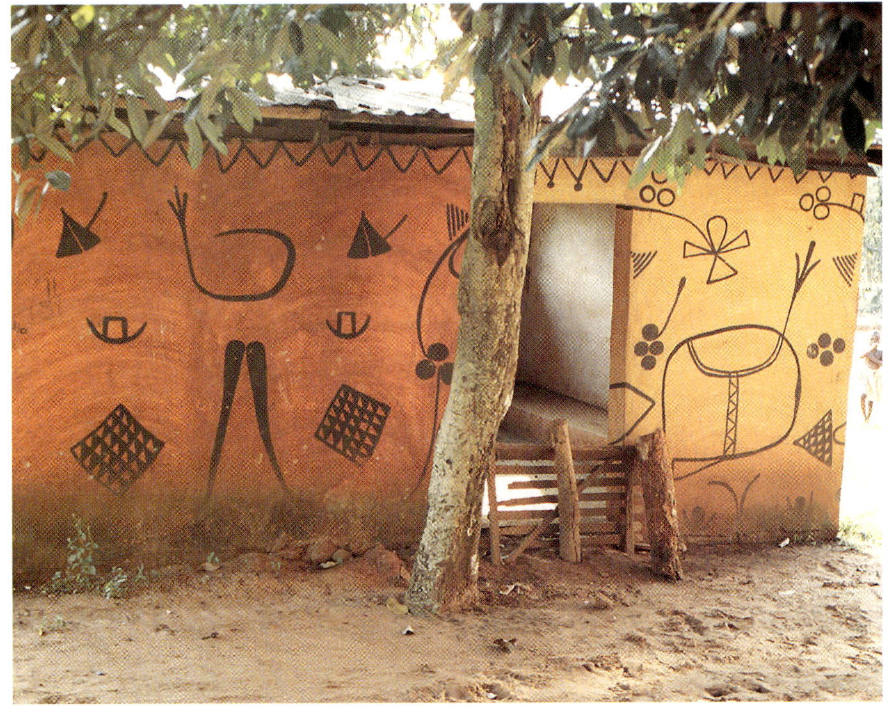

**34 (FACING PAGE)**. *Uli* mural, Earth Shrine, Otenyi Village, Nimo, November 1993, dimensions unknown.

**35 (TOP LEFT)**. *Uli* mural section, Earth Shrine, Otenyi Village, Nimo, November 1993, dimensions unknown.

**36 (TOP RIGHT)**. Murals on central meeting house, Nsugbe, Ama Dialog project, 1993.

**37 (BOTTOM RIGHT)**. Murals on shrine house, Nsugbe, painted through the Ama Dialog project, 1993.

Okeke's focus on the particular forms of *uli* in his Anambra State led to the use of *uli* forms found there and their meanings by himself and many of his art students, who, for various reasons, often came from Anambra, until recent generations. Thus for many of the contemporary artists, *uli* has largely meant Anambra style *uli*, though some artists tend to consider it as general *uli*. This kind of reinterpretation of the past, of course, is not rare in art, ceremony, politics, and other fields.[40]

Today body and wall *uli* have largely died out, as females dress more fully and social, ritual, and building styles have changed. There are still some elderly Igbo women who have knowledge of *uli*; there is also the *uli* on the walls within the Ọdinani Museum at Nri and outside the museum at a shrine (the latter designs are fading; see fig. 5). At Nimo there is still a finely painted triple wall to an earth shrine entrance (figs. 34, 35), and some other *uli* wall sites exist. The German artist Doris Weller and the Nigerian ethnomusicologist Meki Nzewi have had a project, Ama Dialog, for a number of years at Nsugbe, a community north of Ọnitsha, to revive wall *uli*. They have been encouraging Nsugbe women and four women from nearby Omo, one of whom finger paints, to create *uli* designs on large sheets of cloth, equivalent in size to a wall mural section in earlier days of painting, and on smaller sheets of paper. Nzewi and Weller have then exhibited the women's art in Lagos and in Germany. The artists have each developed their own *uli* style. These paintings are made at an Nsugbe *uli* center that has been constructed; its walls are also decorated with *uli* motifs (fig. 36). Four of the local artists have also decorated the outer walls of an important traditional Nsugbe shrine house (fig. 37).[41]

But *uli* survives mainly in contemporary Nsukka art, with artists employing new media, the designs often beautifying and enhancing the art. This new *uli* art form is largely produced by male artists—a significant gender transformation. Whether the contemporary artists' male viewpoints have influenced their selection and use of *uli* is not yet clear.

In body *uli,* the dark dye was produced from a number of plant forms and applied by females on other females, occasionally on themselves.[42] Mothers taught daughters how to body paint, and there were experts who

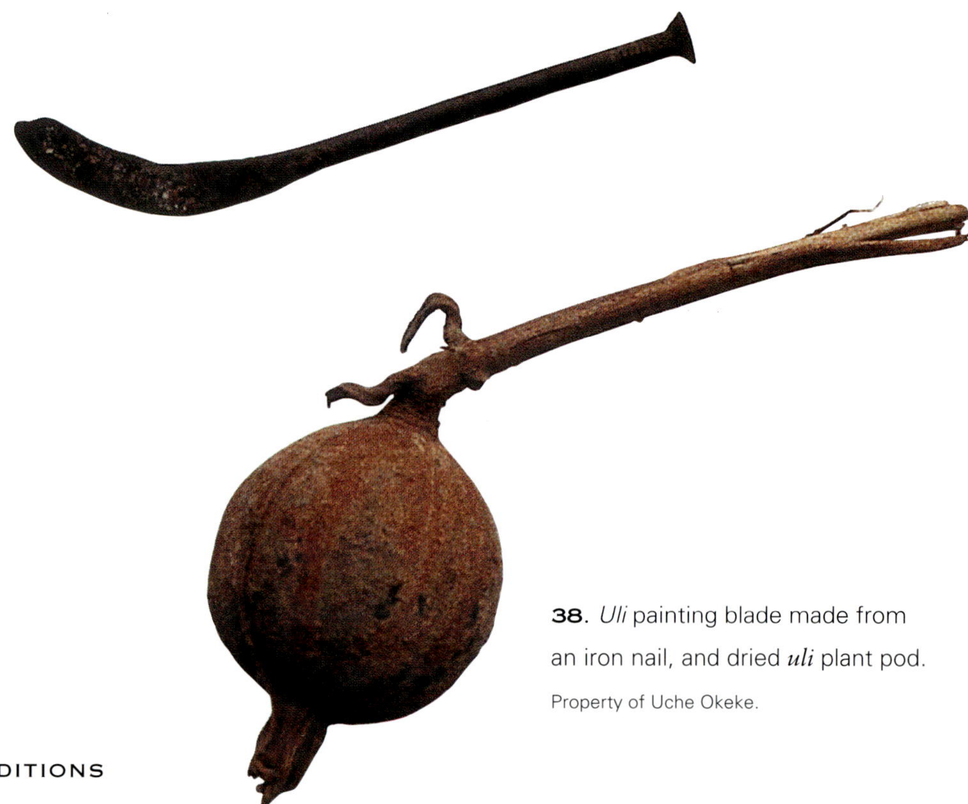

**38.** *Uli* painting blade made from an iron nail, and dried *uli* plant pod.
Property of Uche Okeke.

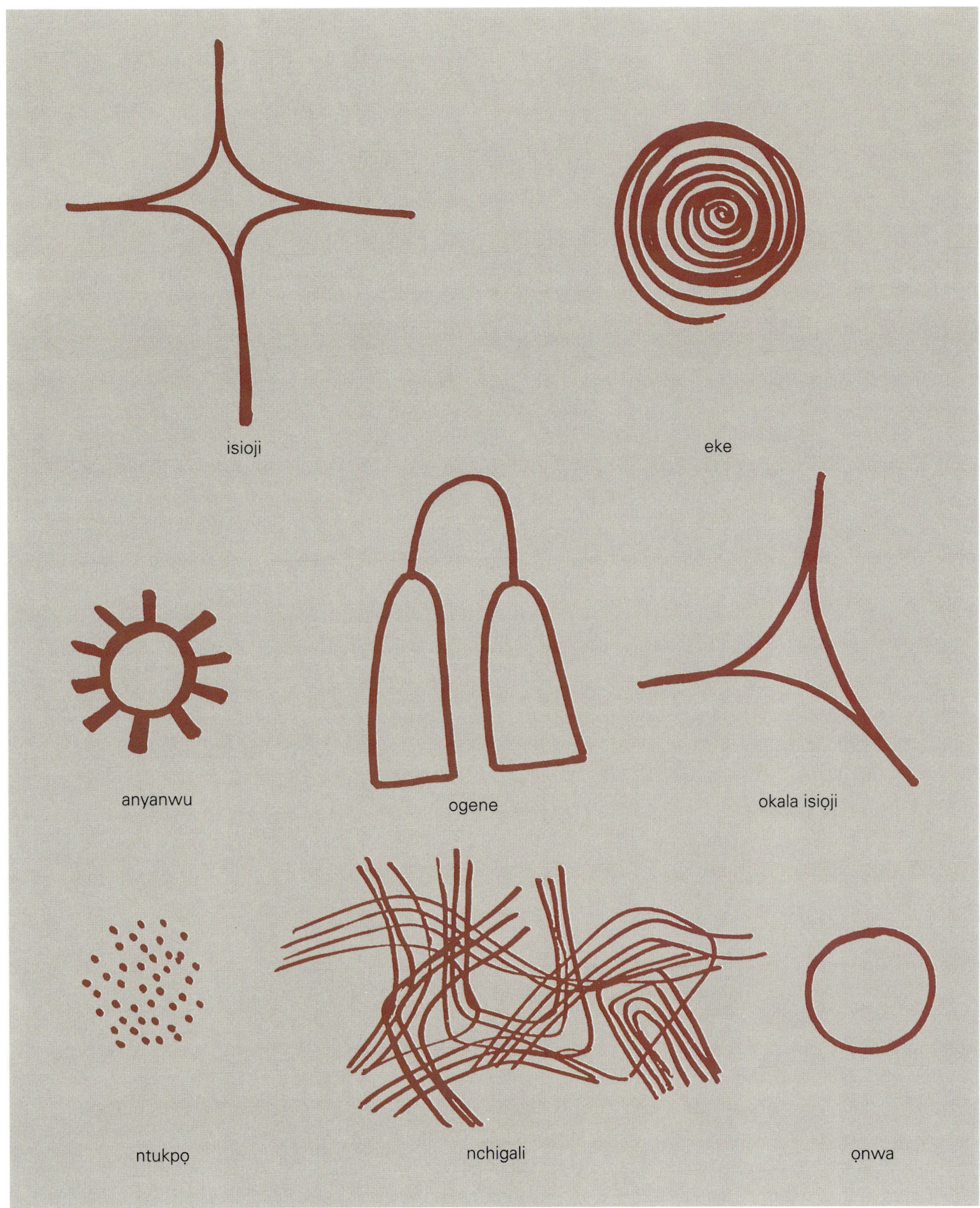


**FIG. A** *Uli* motifs. Drawn by Sylvester Ogbechie.

would decorate other females, sometimes for a fee or a gift. A large number of girls, as well as women of a range of ages, might wear *uli* for a specific community event; it was rare that a single female appeared alone in *uli,* and if many females wore it, it would have been unusual for another female of the group to have refused to do so. The human skin was usually prepared beforehand by shaving its hairs and then rubbing in camwood and palm oil that gave the skin a rich appearance, and often a somewhat lighter tone, to better contrast with *uli.*[43] The motifs were put on with a knife edge, a stick, a strand of raffia palm, or some other implement (fig. 38). In some areas, a stamp made from a mid-rib of the raffia wine palm tree was employed.[44] The receiver sometimes made suggestions of motifs to be employed by the painter, but in other cases let the artist make the decision. Designs might be reserved for particular body areas, such as the lips or the navel, or for special ritual occasions.[45]

Each design had a name, generally that of the object it depicted (fig. A). The motifs were from life's experience. In any community there were hundreds of these; for Igboland as a whole, probably thousands. There were motifs of objects made by humans, such as a hoe (*ogu*) or metal gong (*ogene*). There were animal and bird forms and also plant motifs: the snake, particularly the sacred python (*eke*), the lizard (*ngwele*), the eagle (*ugo*), the kola nut head (*isi ọji*), the cassava leaf (*akwukwọ akpu*). There were motifs from celestial bodies, especially the sun and the moon (respectively *anyanwu* and *ọnwa*). There were some other *uli* forms that were simply abstract designs, as the dot (*ntukpọ*), the line (*akpala*), or parallel lines (*nchiwa*). Cars and airplanes, the draughts gameboard, linoleum designs, bread, and a football are modern motifs.[46] A small number of motifs represented actions or movements, such as *nchigali,* which means turning around and around.[47] *Uli* artists were *bricoleurs,* drawing from the world around them, but occasionally creating a new design.[48] Motifs were not arranged on the body to create a language or to tell a tale, but rather for their aesthetic appeal, to beautify the body. The empty areas between neighboring motifs were frequently generous, creating a sense of positive and negative space that became a playful and important element in the art of the contemporary artists who have made use of *uli* (fig. 39). What Willis writes of wall murals is also true of body *uli:*

> Any representative image seen on a mural is in a way isolated from its own meaning, because the other motifs around
> it will have no connecting theme and no message is being put across. Rather the power and impact of the images lie
> in the way motifs are arranged spatially, the contrasts of scale employed to produce variety and visual dynamism,
> and the quality and accuracy of the draughtsmanship.[49]

The body *uli* motifs were generally small and often quite linear in appearance, as the snake movement design (*ije agwọ*) and the wavy line (*akpala*). The *uli* designs on the body tended to be thin in line rather than thick and bold. *Uli* painters had their own favorite designs and styles, and it is said that certain designs were used to enhance the beauty of fat women, while others were for thin females. There are songs, poems, and proverbs referring to *uli.*[50]

The contemporary Nsukka artist Obiọra Udechukwu, among others, believes that *uli* has a celestial quality, much like the stars, the moon, the planets, and the constellations,[51] and that *uli* exhibits lyrical symbolism, a kind of metaphorical expression of poetry and music.[52] He also sees *uli* as being calligraphic in form, similar to Chinese drawing and painting in some of its features, and he notes that *uli* was done spontaneously, without erasures or other alterations, as some of the Nsukka artists of today attempt to do in their work.[53] To him it is a superb form of the Igbo female aesthetic, with which I agree. He also considers these designs to be semi-abstract or abstract, as they are literally abstractions from the real objects, often portrayed in silhouette or simple outline form, rather than with great detail within the borders. Sometimes they are metonymic, when only a part of an object represents the whole, as the eagle feather (*abuba ugo*), the cassava leaf (*akwukwọ akpu*), and the leopard's claw

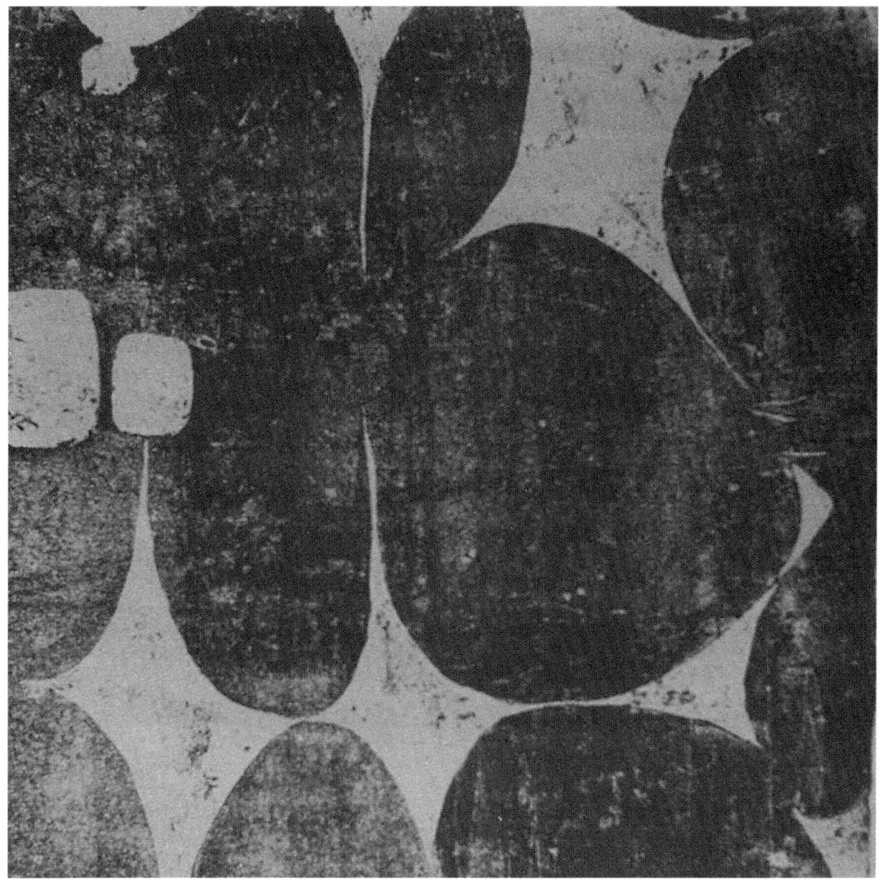



(*mbọ agụ*).[54] These designs could, in fact, be enjoyed aesthetically without knowing their meanings, something that frequently occurs with a modern viewer looking at contemporary art with *uli* designs.[55] *Uli* motifs were portrayed in two-dimensional form on the body and on walls, and this relates to the tendency toward no perspective in much of the drawing and painting of the contemporary Nsukka artists. Despite this, *uli* art is aesthetically rich. As Chike Aniakọr writes:

> At its best, Uli is the rhythmic temper of line like a melodic note plucked from the thumb piano (Ubọ Akwala). In Uli, the line dances, spirals into diverse shapes, elongates, attenuates, thickens, swells and slides, thins and fades out from a slick point, leaving an empty space that sustains it with mute echoes by which silence is part of sound. At once cursive, it creates taut boundaries which it simultaneously relieves with dotted textures; curls up and resolves into a blocked shape hemmed with a contrasting colour boundary.[56]

Uche Okeke considers that *uli* draws from and likely originated from designs in nature, as from the skin designs on the sacred python and other snakes, on certain rodents, such as the spotted squirrel, and on members of the cat family, particularly the leopard.[57] The association of *uli* with nature occurs in another sense, as *uli* is placed on the human body.

With regard to wall *uli,* it is not certain whether it historically preceded or followed body *uli.* Possibly the body form was first, as earlier forms of Igbo wall and house construction may have lacked smooth walls on which to place *uli,* as was true in the eastern Igbo area at Afikpo until recently.[58] On the other hand, some artists feel that *uli* wall painting originated on shrine walls, then moved to more secular walls in the compounds, thus having a religious origin.[59] Though its time of origin is unknown, *uli*-like designs occur on bronze and pottery material from Igbo-Ukwu, which dates to the ninth century.[60] Both body and wall *uli* tended to use the same motifs, though they were generally larger on wall *uli,* which also sometimes placed greater emphasis on animal forms.[61]

The walls were prepared, as the skin of the human body, before *uli* motifs were applied.[62] A wall was smoothed with water and laterite, rubbed with smooth pebbles or a coconut shell, and then rubbed with fiber of some sort or with cloth to create a faintly visible series of swirling designs as background, called *akika,* in reddish or yellowish brown or in some earthlike color. The wall was often divided into vertical sections, frequently marked by dark vertical lines; separate females painted on the designs in each section, sometimes with an expert *uli* designer supervising.[63] Girls learning to paint might help out. Each female made her own designs in her sections as a rule; there was often no overall pattern for the whole decorated wall. Generally all sections of the wall were decorated at the same time. This was also so for body painting for an event; female bodies were painted at about the same time, though by different artists in different parts of the community, at the painters' homes or those of the painted. The timing of both body and wall *uli* suggests a cooperative, communal quality to this art form, despite the individualistic creations of each artist.

The colors of wall *uli* came from natural pigments.[64] Painting was done with sticks, feathers, fibers, or fingers. Colors did not overlap; they were not blended as a rule. The outer borders of a motif were sharp and distinct—there was no blurring—and this was true in body *uli*. The wall mural's motif borders might have rows of dots along them in a color different from that of the motif, perhaps in white, to demarcate it further. Particularly in the wall murals, where individual designs were larger than in body painting, there was some filling in of motifs with elements of the object being depicted, such as the eyes and mouth of an animal, or with the application of simple linear designs. *Uli* was not placed on every house or wall in a compound or village, but according to the event involved, for example, on the outer walls of a man's home who was taking an important title. As in the case of body painting, the effect was strongly aesthetic, to add beauty to the village for important occasions and to show pride in the community when individuals from other areas came for a special occasion.[65] As there were a number of these events in a year, and the murals might last a year or so, a number of decorated walls and houses might be seen at one time, giving the community a lively visual quality against an otherwise neat but generally earth-brown appearance. As in body *uli,* wall murals might have a celestial and lyrical two-dimensional quality.

Okeke divides wall paintings into two types:

(a) Abstract design elements or organic motifs/symbols are generally austerely ordered on shrine walls. The colours here are muted with very occasional flash of light colors or white of *nzu* [chalk]. The *uli* elements are powerful and dynamic and able to dominate the wide and open wall space.
(b) More homely natural design motifs are stylised and rather profuse. The colours are gay and relaxed and express youthful vigour or joy of life. The entire picture or wall space is filled with repeated motifs.[66]

The Nsukka artists draw in various ways from *uli* body and wall motifs. Uche Okeke has made much use of its linear qualities; female hair in his drawings often has the appearance of yam tendrils. But he did not make specific use of many *uli* designs. His linear qualities seem to fit his drawing interests and skills and his happiness with two-dimensional work: "Before I realized the potential of the *uli* idiom, I worked to create an illusion of three dimensions in my paintings."[67] His students and the students of his students tend to employ *uli*'s linear qualities as well, but they often make use of a larger range of specific *uli* designs in their work, either simply as decoration around a major image that they are portraying or in some relationship to that image, as the kola nut head, which represents peace in a painting concerned with issues of peace and conflict. Common *uli* motifs that came to be employed by the Nsukka artists include the kola nut head, half kola nut head, python or snake, crescent moon, full moon, mirror, comb, wavy line, and spiral, so that a small corpus of designs have come to stand for the larger body of them, the latter representing much of the traditional experience and the material and natural world of traditional Igbo life. Different contemporary artists have favorite motifs that they employ again and again. Motifs may also be altered in shape by elongation or some other process. What were rarely symbolized in *uli* motifs were personal interrelationships and human emotions, such as aggression or fear. It is a very object-oriented design sys-

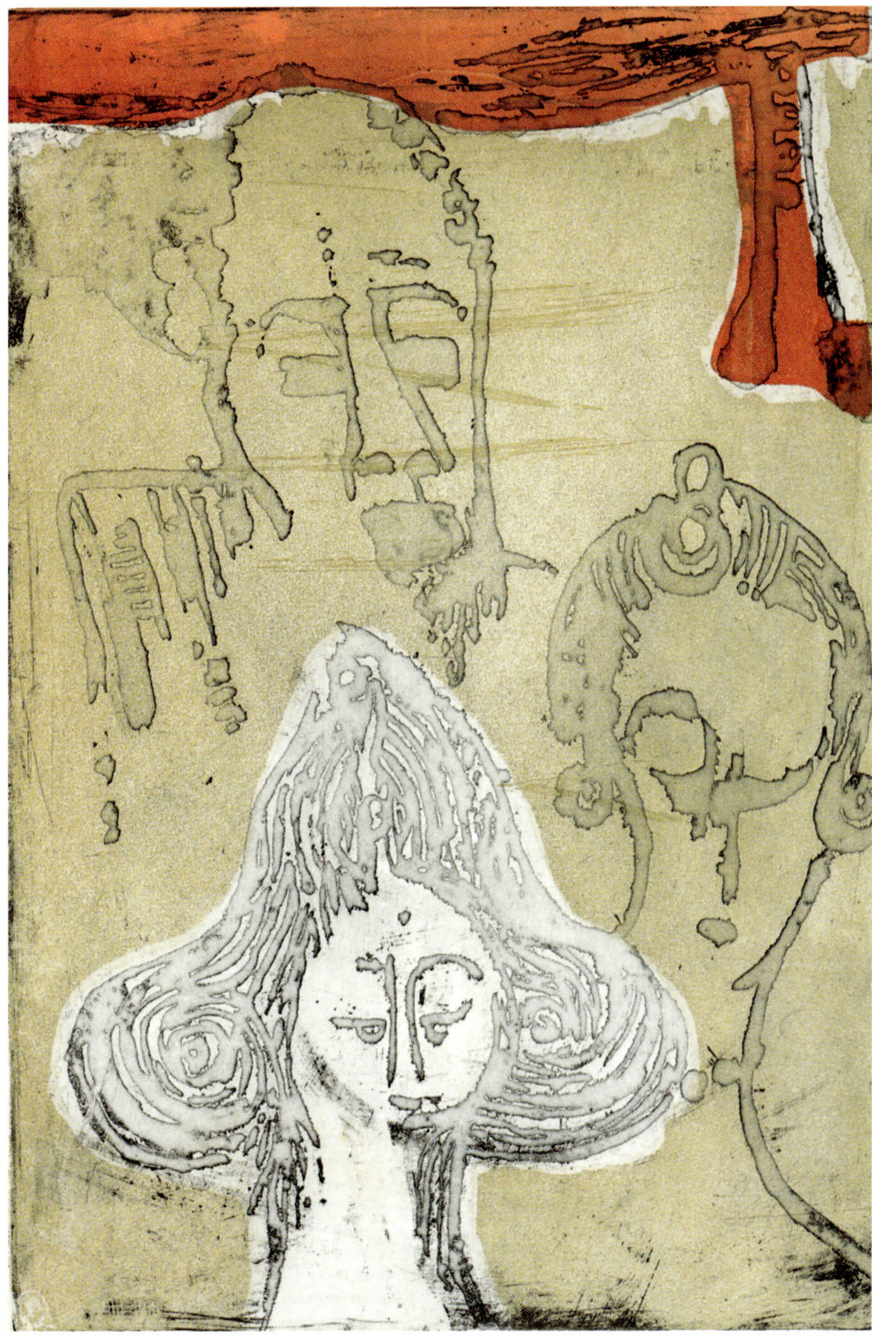

**40**. Uche Okeke, *Ana, Asele and Badunka*, 1982, etching on paper. 45.8 × 30.5 cm. Collection of Dolly J. Fiterman. Photo: Franko Khoury.

tem. Of course, many of the *uli* symbols are also universal designs, such as a circle to represent the sun or moon, crescent moon, wavy line as of a snake, and the spiral. The contemporary Nsukka artists are aware of this; the traditional *uli* painters were not. Finally, not every design in the contemporary art relates to a *uli* motif.

In his art, Uche Okeke has also drawn from Igbo mythology and religious belief, depicting spiritual figures that were and are considered powerful in the Anambra River basin area, including Nimo.[68] As with *uli* motifs, Okeke has tended to extol myths and spiritual figures typical of his home area as if they were general to much of Igboland, though he is aware that this is not so. While Okeke's students and their students occasionally make use of these spiritual figures in their art, this has not been pervasive compared to the attention given to *uli*. Similarly, his colleagues and followers have not focused on Igbo tales as much as Okeke did in his earlier work.[69]

Among the major spiritual figures in Okeke's world is Ana, as she is called at Nimo and surrounding areas, who to Okeke is the source of beauty and the keeper of moral law. (I have already noted this association of beauty and morality in discussing *uli*.) A major Igbo deity, concerned with the fertility and welfare of living things, both the earth and the spirit of the earth, Ana is well represented by earth mounds and other shrines. Eri, on the other hand, is believed to have been the first man in the Anambra River area, coming to earth from the home of Chukwu, the god of the heavens. Eri interacted with nature spirits and with Ana to produce many of the laws of human behavior and to help populate the region.[70]

Asele is another spiritual force Okeke has depicted in his art and for whom he has named his cultural center at Nimo. It also refers to Okeke's own designation of his 1958–66 artistic period. Asele is the finest visual artist, the spirit of design, who excels in *uli* in both the land of the living and the dead. Badunka, her male counterpart, is the master of handicrafts and technology, the genius of manipulative skills. Other spirit figures appear in Okeke's art as well.

Ana, Asele, and Badunka indicate to Okeke that there are spiritual forces that support the visual aesthetics of the Igbo, reinforcing his interest in Igbo tradition (fig. 40). Okeke's interest in spiritual figures complements his concern with *uli,* and he employs *uli* elements to depict them in art, seeing both as interrelated in Igbo art and culture. Okeke's Igbo mythic figures should also be seen in terms of his Christian images, especially of Christ and the Madonna, sometimes depicted with *uli* qualities. Okeke has religious feelings for both Igbo and Christian worlds.[71]

Not only have Igbo tales, mythic figures, and *uli* stimulated Okeke's art, but sometimes music as well: "My reaction . . . depends very much on the mood and the type of work I am executing. *Egwu Torch,* associated with changelings suited fine my mood for my painting *Qyqyo* or *Qgbanje.* Musical notes suggest to me forms, colours, movements and textures."[72]

## UCHE OKEKE'S ART IN HIS ENUGU PERIOD

A striking aspect of Okeke's art in Enugu is a series of oil paintings that he produced in 1965. Larger works than his pen and ink works and prints, they are generally dark in tone, with the exception of *Qgbanje,* which is pinkish. These paintings are frequently in shades of brown and the darker yellows, with dark blues and greens here and there. If Okeke is drawing on wall *uli* in these oils, he is not doing so in the sense of separating colors distinctly, for he blends the colors at the margins of his images. The figures are rarely as distinctly delineated as in his earlier oils, such as *Jumaa* (see fig. 19) and *Burial Procession* (see fig. 17), both produced in 1961. Although there is a linear quality to them, Okeke appears to have employed *uli* more sparingly than in his drawings and prints. The linear quality tends toward the vertical, with broad brush strokes and facial features sometimes distorted from the normal.

Most of these oils draw from traditional Igbo belief or experience, as *Ugolqchanma* (fig. 41), *Bird of Time, Qgbanje* (*Qyqyo*), *Efuru,* and *Primeval Forest.*[73] Tayq Adenaike writes of the last three paintings that they "leave one in solemn or reverential wonder of things of the far beyond."[74] He feels that *Efuru* has two qualities of *uli* wall paintings, the use of space and the economy of design.[75] These aspects are present to some extent in other oils of Okeke's from this time, reminding us that the feel of *uli* can occur in the contemporary work without the use of specific *uli* motifs. In *Bird of Time* we see the upward-sweeping hair of the female head which characterizes some of his female heads in different media, with its linear qualities, in this case involving a blending of the hair into the background forest. In other works the hair is more curvilinear; the female head hair in much of his work is long and sinuous and sometimes quite loose, not the tightly organized hair of Igbo women's ceremonial dress.[76] Okeke's depictions of hair often suggest nature rather than cultural order.

Of these oil paintings drawing on tradition, *Primeval Forest* is a theme Okeke has also done in pen and ink and in prints over the years; the theme echoes the mystery of the deep forest areas of Igboland (now rapidly disappearing), often associated with Igbo spiritual forces. *Qgbanje* refers to a specific belief, popular in southeastern

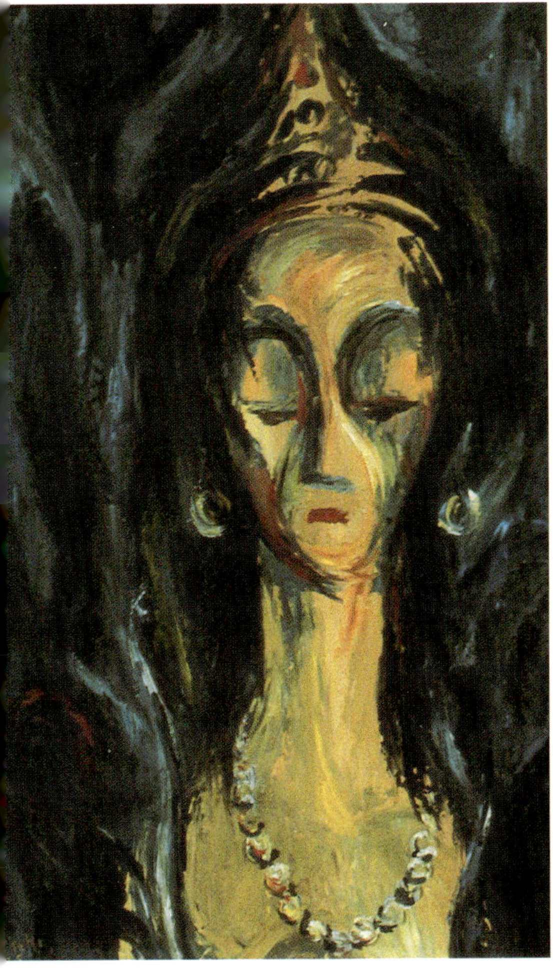

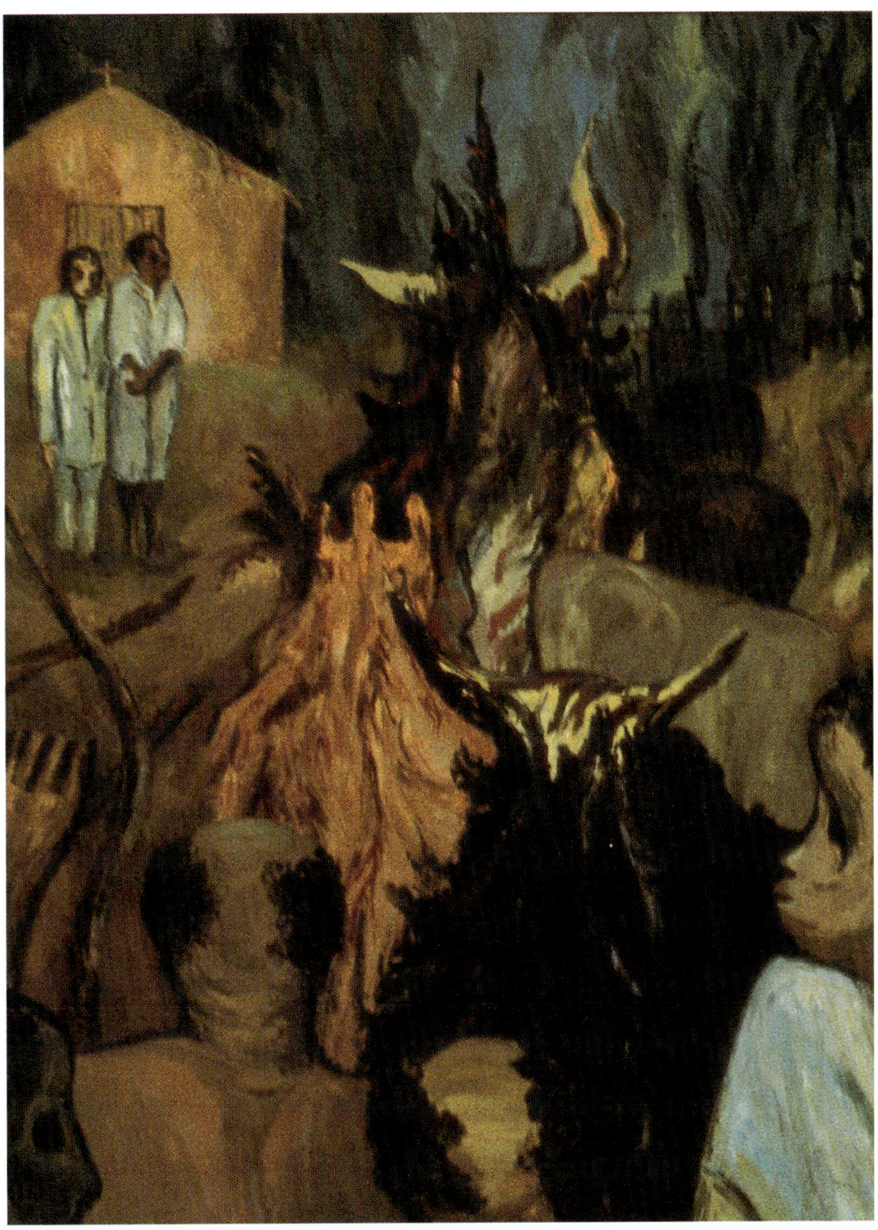

**41 (LEFT)**. Uche Okeke, *Ugolọchanma*, 1965, oil. 76.5 × 50 cm. Collection of the Asele Institute.

**42 (RIGHT)**. Uche Okeke, *The Conflict (After Achebe)*, 1965, oil. 121.9 × 91.4 cm. Collection of the artist.

Nigeria, that the cause of a woman's children continually dying at birth or not long after—unfortunately not rare in the region—is a spiritual force calling the child back to the other world, for which elaborate rites and activities are required.[77] In *Ogbanje*, we see the parents standing at the left looking anxiously at the standing child which is facing the dark forest, as if attracted to return to its spiritual world. There are swirls and brush sweeps, which give the work a sense of unease in its contents; this occurs in other oils of Okeke's from this period.

Two other oils of 1965 have to do with social issues. *The Conflict (After Achebe)* (fig. 42) depicts the scene from Chinua Achebe's novel *Things Fall Apart*, already mentioned in connection with Okeke's poem "Kpaaza."[78] In the painting, *egwugwu* masqueraders and dancers are moving toward the church in the distance, ready to set

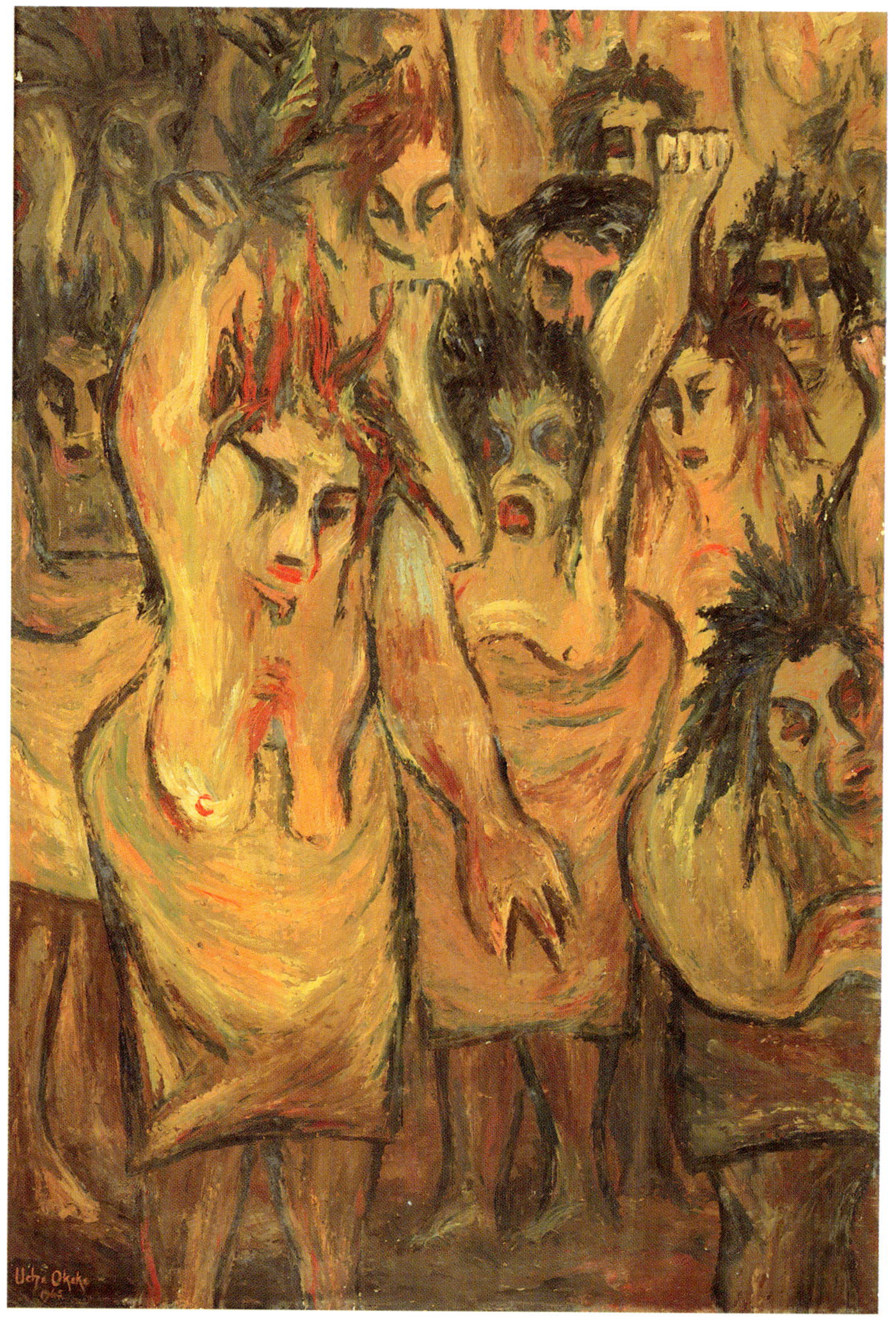

fire to it; the church is being guarded at the front by the lonely figures of the missionary and his Igbo assistant. The painting, as the poem, condemns overzealous aspects of Christianity and asks for respect for native tradition. There is the interesting contrast between the quiet of the two standing Christians at the painting's upper left and the turbulence of the Igbo masquerade dancers at the right.

In *Aba Revolt* (fig. 43), Okeke depicts raging women with large breasts facing the viewer as if to attack. Dark browns predominate, with touches of red. The painting refers to the female revolts against British colonial officials in 1929, starting at Aba and spreading to other Igbo and non-Igbo regions of eastern Nigeria, which caused some destruction and disruptions and which surprised and upset the British, more used to male hostilities in their colonial world.[79] The central female figure with very large breasts refers to the mythic Igbo woman of giant breasts, *nwanyi mgbọlọd'ala,* a powerful Igbo mythic figure.[80] It is said that it was actually she who led the revolt, a female capable of placing her breasts behind her and sitting on them. Breasts here are very much a sign of female power; they also reflect their importance in feeding the infant child with milk in traditional Igboland, nursing sometimes for as long as several years, as well as symbolizing other important female roles in Igbo society. The brown color of the work also suggests the powerful earth spirit Ana, often depicted by Okeke. He is clearly impressed with strong feminine figures. These two paintings are among the few of Okeke's that depict aggression, although conflict does occur in his art based on Igbo tales, as well as in his depictions of refugees and other scenes relating to the Biafran war.

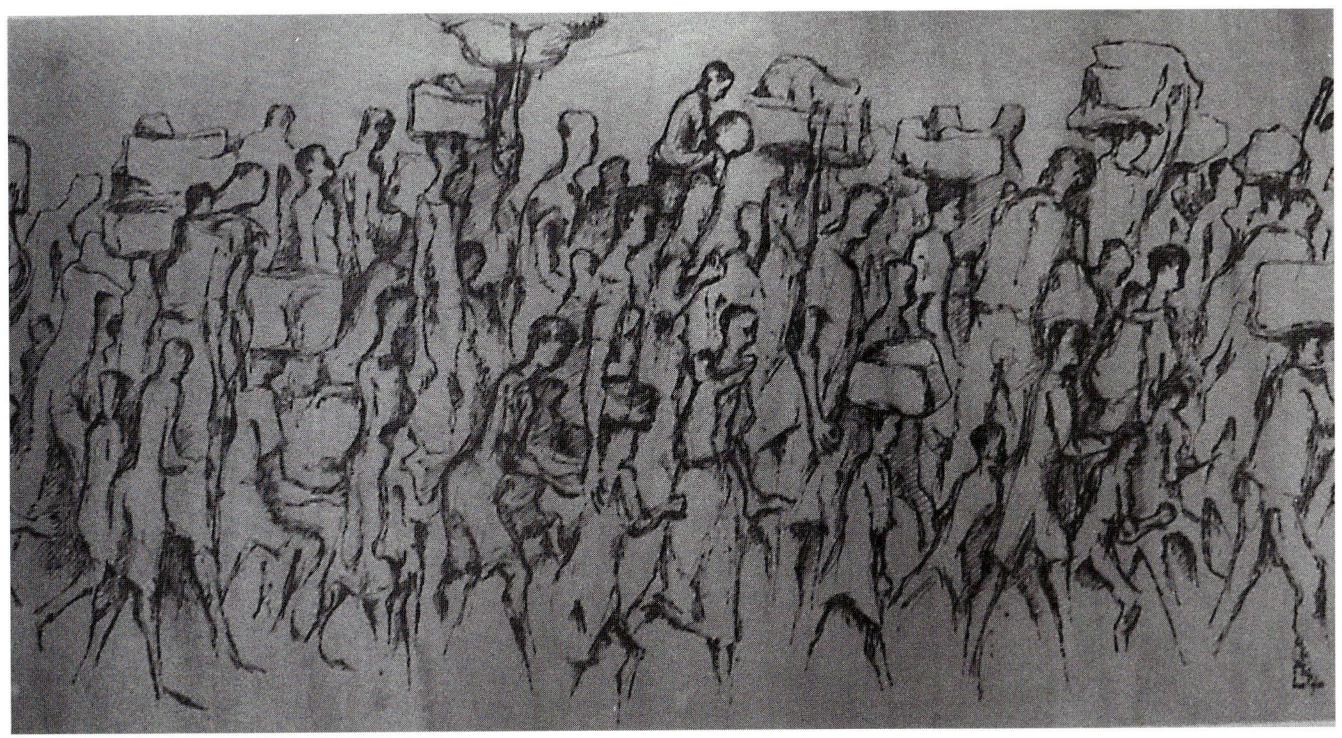

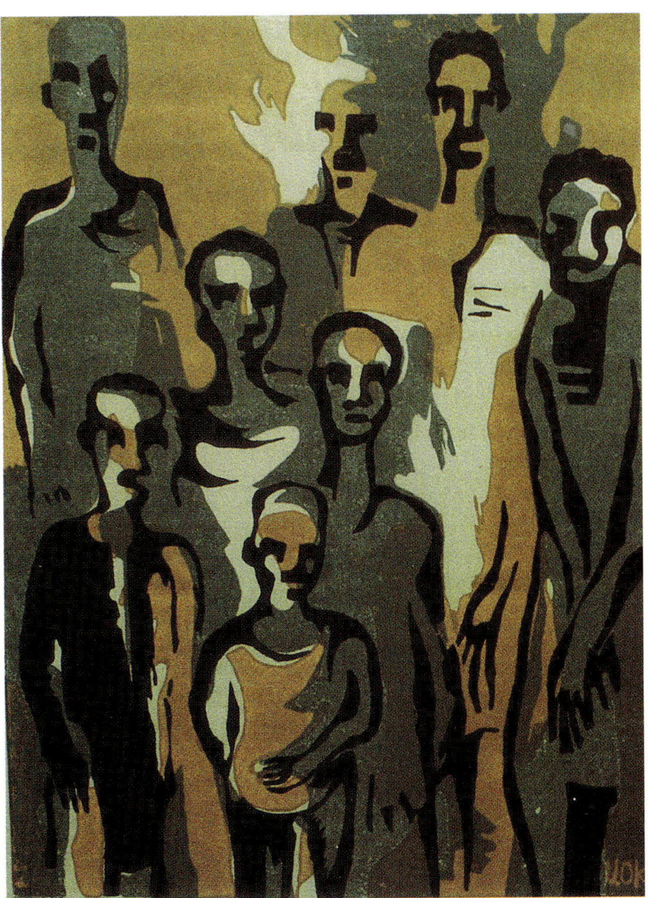

**44 (ABOVE).** Uche Okeke, *Ọsọndu,*
1968, pen, ink, and wash on paper. 38
× 58 cm. Collection of the artist.

**45 (LEFT).** Uche Okeke, *Refugee Family,* 1966, linocut on paper. 41 × 35 cm.
Collection of the artist.

The mid-1960s oils show that by then Okeke had strongly immersed himself in Igbo religion and myth and was preoccupied with it in his art, overcoming his earlier handicap of having been partly brought up away from Igboland. One notes the changes from the earlier genre art, say of Murray's students, where village scenes were simply and nicely depicted, where there were pleasant masqueraders and palm wine tappers and females carrying loads to and from market. Okeke's work is not genre painting; it is much more sophisticated technically and deals more deeply with culture and belief.

In this period Okeke continued to create linear pen and ink work, such as *The Head of Udo's Parrot* (1965) and *Cash Madam* (1966?), the latter dealing with a seated madam holding money at a place of prostitution.[81] This was not a usual image for the artist, though prostitution, by the time he produced this work, was becoming common in eastern Nigeria. His pen and ink work at this time was either in thin or heavy lines, generally curvilinear, and having the sense of some of the more abstract linear elements of *uli*.

As the political situation worsened in Nigeria in 1966 and 1967, Okeke created linocuts depicting refugees returning from the north and elsewhere in Nigeria; pogroms in the north were leading to serious problems of suffering, displacement, and anxiety. Examples are *Ọsọndu* (1968; fig. 44),[82] *Refugee Family* (fig. 45) and *Returnees* (both in 1966), and *The Return* (1967). Possibly these works of simply outlined figures were produced in print formto reach a larger audience than drawings because of Okeke's concern with the deteriorating situation in Nigeria.

## THE BIAFRAN PERIOD

In the first half of 1967, with the threat of war, Uche Okeke's life and art took a radically altered direction. Igbo artists in all fields were affected; the war was to leave a lasting impression on their lives and their work.

In early 1967 Okeke moved his cultural center collection for safety into storage at a bungalow belonging to a chief at Nimo; these became the materials for his later cultural center there, the Asele Institute. Much of the collection remained in storage for thirteen years.[83] Nimo, though threatened, was never attacked by ground forces, though Okeke and others moved elsewhere at one time for safety. The collection suffered deterioration but was not destroyed, as the works of other artists on the Biafran side often were during the conflict. As war threatened, Okeke returned to Nimo, as others went home or entered the military; the various arts organizations in Enugu broke up following the war's beginning in July 1967, and the University of Nigeria closed. At home, during the intermediate period while Biafra's war organization was developing, Okeke directed a drama production of *Danda* at a secondary school, an adaptation of a novel by Nkem Nwankwọ, with former secondary school students and university undergraduates as the players.[84]

At home he also began writing a dance drama, *Ekeama*, about the *ogbanje* phenomenon, and a play, *Unọ Aja (Mud House)*.[85] He was soon involved in the war, for in 1968 he was appointed head of the Visual Art Section, Refugees Affairs Committee, of the Biafran Directorate of Propaganda, located at Aba in southern Igbo country. Before that city fell, the Directorate was moved to Umuahia further north. Okeke's section helped refugees produce local handicrafts—baskets, mats, bags, masks, and cloths—and he organized art exhibitions by non-refugee artists at Umudike and Umuahia. He also produced poster designs, brochures, and magazine covers and wrote war poetry.[86]

At Umuahia he helped organize a small group of writers and artists, who held regular meetings to discuss the role of artists in society and in war and revolution.[87] In November 1968, Okeke wrote from that city: "The dreamer must turn activist in order to rescue our civilisation from destruction and death. He must speak out with all the forces at his command, fight if he must and die in order to safeguard our liberty and survival."[88] Though heartily disliking war, he was fully committed to the Biafran cause. The conflict was a time of introspection for Okeke and other Biafran artists. Though Okeke did not express concern, among some young Biafran writers and artists, disillusionment set in as the war progressed, for the Biafran leaders appeared to become reactionary and there apparently was misappropriation of relief supplies by the influential.[89] In any case, social and political issues played important roles for Okeke and other Biafran artists during the war, rather than artistic questions about the extent to which traditional Igbo culture should be drawn upon and how this should be done. Not that questions of Igbo identity and of the value of Igbo culture were no longer concerns, for the war became largely an Igbo war against the rest of Nigeria, and the question of the survival of Igbo culture and its people was paramount. While the conflict continued, Okeke found time to write two dramas based on Igbo culture and to prepare gouaches to illustrate a book of Igbo tales he had collected, but he did these while living in the quiet of Germany.

In 1969 Okeke, with the assistance of others, gathered together a collection of traditional Igbo arts and crafts and contemporary art from the Biafran side, the latter including some ninety items from his Asele Institute. These were collected for exhibitions in Germany organized by a pro-Biafran group, the Zentrale der Aktions Komitees, Biafra-Sudan, under the sponsorship of its director, Dr. Ruth Bowert. While much Biafran war propaganda was directed toward the hunger, dislocations, and illnesses of Biafrans, and while the contemporary art in this collection sometimes featured images of refugees, war, and suffering, the aim was to show that the Biafrans were skilled people, capable of standing independently on their own with a developed culture.

Okeke was flown in a small plane to São Tomé in Spanish Guinea, and then to Lisbon and Frankfurt by commercial plane, the art moving separately. The exhibition, as it first appeared in Cologne, was large, some 440 objects, of which 297 were contemporary works and 143 traditional arts and crafts. Of the former, 174 were by Okeke. Later shows in Bonn, Essen, Dortmund, Dusseldorf, Trier, and Munich did not necessarily contain all the works. Okeke prepared a catalogue for the exhibition and a publication relating to it.[90] Some twenty-three contemporary Nigerian artists were exhibited, including artists who were at Enugu or Nsukka in the years before the war, all of Igbo background. When fighting began, Biafrans hoped that European nations and the United States might support their side politically, if not militarily, but while people in a number of countries formed pro-Biafran groups for relief purposes, support did not materialize. The German exhibitions were probably futile in this sense, though useful in raising awareness of the plight of blockaded Biafra and encouraging relief contributions.[91]

In Germany, Okeke renewed artistic and other contacts and again had the opportunity to study the art scene. He produced a radio play, *The Long Night,* on commission for the Voice of Germany, Munich, and completed his two plays, *Ekeama, an Ọgbanje Drama* and *Unọ Aja.* The first, on the theme of *ọgbanje,* he had already depicted in his art; the second was concerned with the folly of war.[92] *Ekeama* illustrates the considerable depth of knowledge of Anambra Igbo culture that Okeke had acquired. In Munich in 1969 and 1970 he created monochromic gouaches for his book *Tales of Land of Death: Igbo Folk Tales,* published in 1971 in New York, first making preliminary gouaches in a sketchbook.[93] In that year a book of German translations of some of his poetry with his line illustrations, *Vierzig Gedichte,* was published in Dortmund,[94] and some unbound sheets of some of his first folktale drawing series were also printed in Germany.[95]

The war ended in early January 1970 with the defeat of Biafra. At about this time, in Munich, Okeke wrote a statement, "I Will Now Go to Kpaaza," recanting his previous position stated in his "Kpaaza" poem. The war had changed everything: "In the 1960s, I worked to rediscover my roots, to clear the forest around where I would farm, but there were far too many stumps to be uprooted. I have walked the footpaths of Nimo and listened to

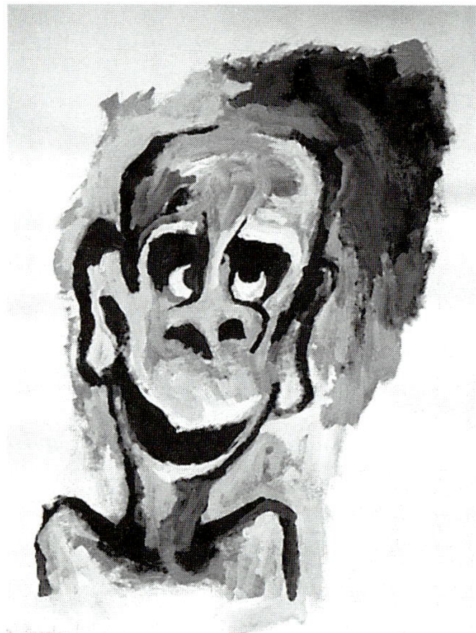

**46 (ABOVE)**. Uche Okeke, *The Witch,* 1969 or 1970, monochromatic gouache on paper, from a sketchbook of the artist, dimensions unknown. Collection of the artist.

**47 (RIGHT)**. Uche Okeke, *The Drug Potion,* 1962, monochromatic gouache on paper, from a sketchbook of the artist, dimensions unknown. Collection of the artist.

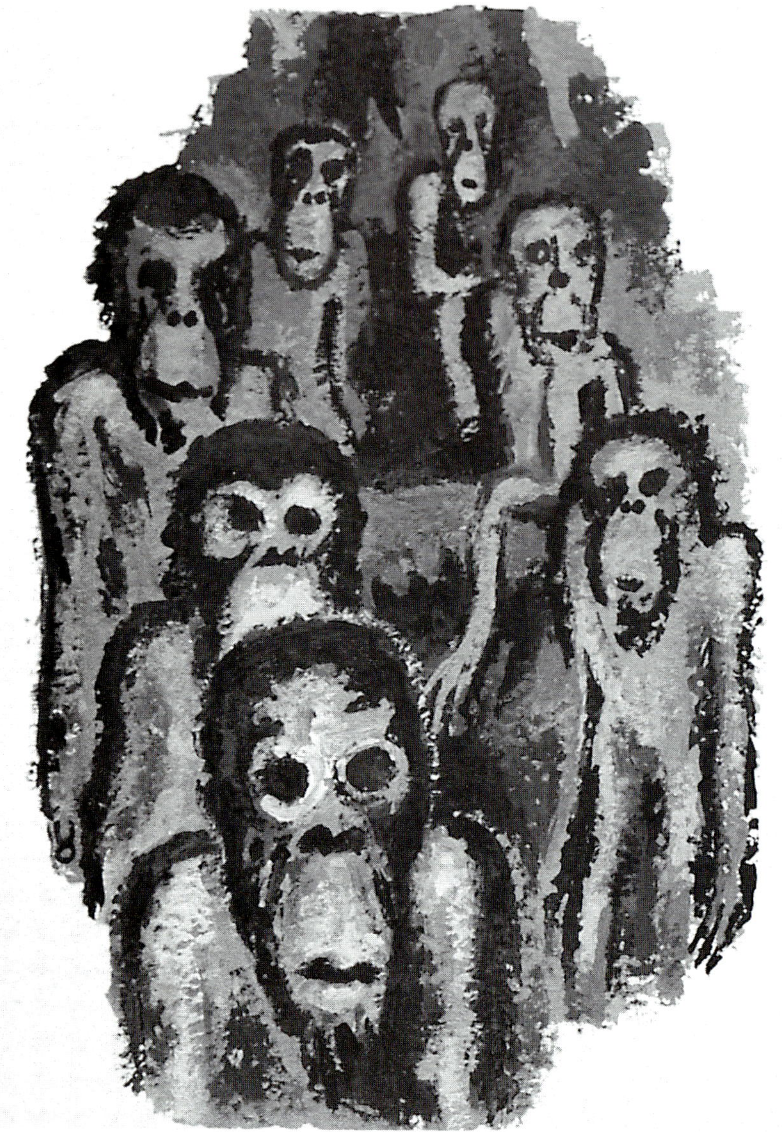

the traditional keepers of wisdom. I find I cannot escape my contemporary time-space, the realities of life now."[96] As he recently explained to me, the young were no longer as interested in tradition, and the war destroyed much of it. Henceforth he was to argue for a gentle merger of tradition and modernity, without undue pressure. But he never gave up his interest in Igbo culture in his art and life.

Okeke returned home at the end of 1970 and was appointed lecturer and acting head of the then Department of Fine Arts at the University of Nigeria, Nsukka, replacing N. W. Udosen as head at a largely destroyed campus that had reopened earlier that year. The art faculty included Udosen and Chuka Amaefunah, the latter having gone to Nsukka to teach the last year before the civil war, and Anthony Ọrah, who had also taught and been a student there before the conflict. They were joined by Chike Aniakọr. This was the start of a new and important phase in Okeke's life, the establishment of a training program to implement his views on art.

Okeke had long wished to publish a book of Igbo tales; his 1961 *Drawings* contained no texts. The new works, in gouache, in his 1971 *Tales of Land of Death: Igbo Folk Tales*, were stylistically a substantial departure from the earlier publication, though many of the same tales were involved.[97] O. Udechukwu points out that these new works differed not only in medium but in their use of halftones, as against the earlier pure lines and considerable patterning within images.[98] In the new work, lines are thicker, often heavy, the images simpler and generally less grotesque in appearance (figs. 46, 47). Where human faces occur, they are often sad, depressed, and sometimes with exaggerated mouths, as if crying out, perhaps reflecting Okeke's feelings about the war and its consequences. Okeke's reply to Udechukwu's queries about this work is revealing:

> The *Tales of Land of Death* (1971) gouaches were different in style from my earlier drawing because I was interested in leaving something for the young. This was the result of the experience of the civil war. I had stripped my work of most of its decorative quality, only essential decorative effects were retained. The uli spirit was very much present, although its linear effect was not immediately obvious. This later style perhaps relates in essence to traditional Igbo painting.[99]

Udechukwu sees Okeke's work in general as deriving "from a mythopoetic kind of vision."[100] In contrasting the two styles of Okeke's Igbo tale art, Udechukwu writes:

> For the present writer, however, the 1961 drawings are more exciting, more remote from everyday reality and therefore closer to the literary or folkloric point of departure. Their forms are far more fantastic and elaborate with eye-arresting patterns, interlacing lines, rhythmic repetitions. The illustrations for *Tales* are bold, highly simplified gouache paintings in white, black and greys. This simplicity which precludes infusion of elaborate details has taken the fantasy and the esoteric air out of the otherwise brilliantly composed pictures.[101]

Not long ago Okeke informed me that he had changed his tale illustration style in gouache from his earlier pen and ink style, because he wished to do something different and in a simpler manner.

Much of Okeke's other art during the Biafran period directly relates to the war and does not generally represent a departure from earlier styles; only the content differs. For example, *Ọsọndu* ("Flight"), pen and ink (1968; fig. 44), created in the heat of the war, after the retreat from Aba, shows a large group of tightly packed walking refugees, some carrying heavy loads, their figures simply drawn in outline. There is a good sense of movement from left to right in the picture. By the time Okeke created this he had had to move several times from his prewar Enugu base; perhaps he was expressing his own experience as well as that of numerous refugees whom he had observed as the front lines changed. In *Faces of War* (charcoal, 1969), Okeke draws four old and weary faces with tired eyes and simply sketched standing figures in the right background. *Lament of the Returnees* (pastel, 1967) consists of faces in agony, with large open mouths, the visages not too differently drawn from those in his gouache tales.[102] This art expressed Okeke's feelings on the effects of the war and were probably effective in arousing sympathy when viewed outside Nigeria. In Germany in 1970 he also created some pen and ink drawings on a variety of topics.[103]

In addition, Okeke produced realistic art for posters and other propaganda use within Biafra during the war, such as the poster *Farm Save Biafra*, with images of various vegetables, a poster to encourage people to grow food.

Despite the war, this was a productive time for Okeke. He had time, while in Germany, to reflect on the conflict, the nature of Igbo culture, and what he wished to do upon his return in the supportive atmosphere of German life, rather than the milieu of the increasing decline and losses for Biafra as time went on.

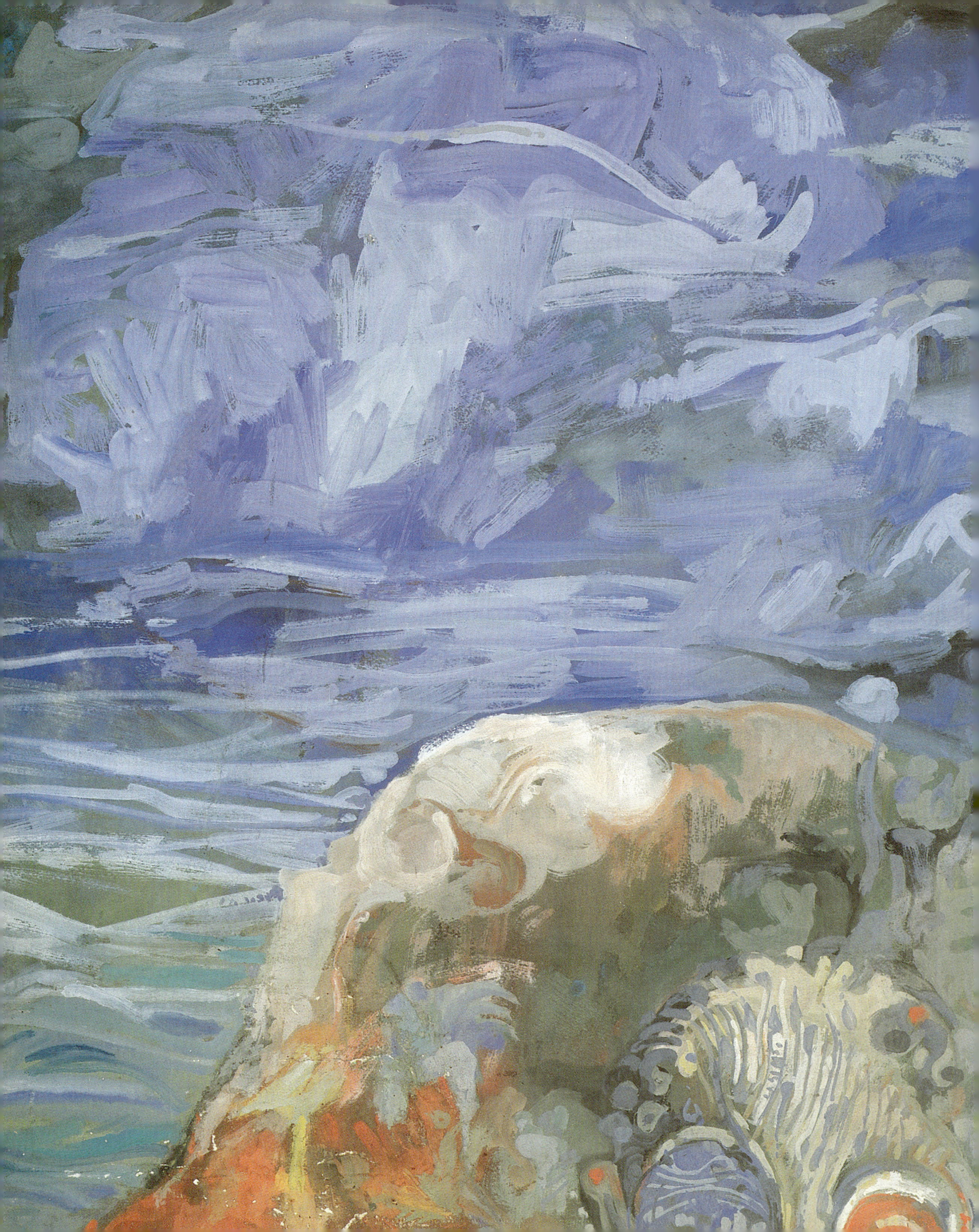

# 4. UCHE OKEKE

## III: THE DEVELOPMENT OF AN ART DEPARTMENT AND RETIREMENT

I see my work as my own contribution to contemporary art. Revival, I don't like the word revival. I don't wake up a dead person and ask him to live. What one would like to see is an organic kind of transformation. You know, change, rather than trying to beat a dead horse to make it live. That is dangerous for any culture or any civilization.

**UCHE OKEKE** [1]

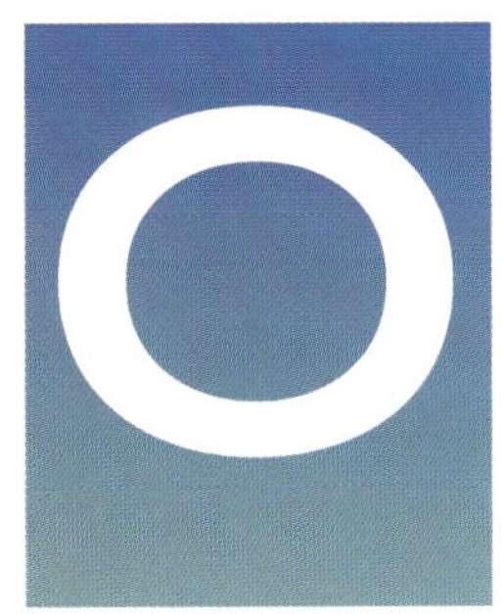

keke's Uli Period, as he calls it, began in December 1970 when he became acting head of the Department of Fine and Applied Arts at the University of Nigeria, Nsukka, and lasted until his retirement from teaching in 1986. During this time he led in creating an art teaching program at the university that drew for inspiration on *uli* design, yet without having a specific course on it. Okeke's ideas on *uli,* and those of some of his teaching colleagues, such as Chike Aniakọr and Chuka Amaefunah, permeated the teaching program and were readily picked up by students. It was a time when Okeke's own art turned from a preoccupation with wartime conditions to draw again from Anambra myth, although other artists continued to create images of the war's horror well into the 1970s. Okeke moved part of his cultural center collection in storage at Nimo to his university home, where he had a workplace, calling it the Asele Art Studio.

The Uli Period was a time when Okeke held three university administrative posts at different times, as well being an artist, art historian, and exhibitor, taking part in group shows and traveling to Europe and America. It was also a period when he vigorously promoted contemporary Nigerian art through speeches, publications, and organizing conferences. At this time he was a man for all seasons.

This was followed by what Okeke calls his Nimo Period, which continues to this day, when he retired to his Asele Institute at Nimo, occasionally creating works, organizing seminars, writing on contemporary Nigerian art, and working with his voluminous collections of books and art.

Detail of fig. 55.

The Uli Period activities occurred at a time of impressive growth in Nigerian contemporary art. There was much more postsecondary teaching in art, many more students graduated, the needs for graphic design professionals for business and industry increased, and new galleries appeared in Lagos and elsewhere in the country. The Mbari style of cultural center largely disappeared, except for Okeke's Asele Institute and one or two others; universities and galleries became the major art centers. The postwar oil boom allowed increasing Nigerian university support for the arts as well as growing art patronage. The number of individual expatriates interested in contemporary art probably declined, but their support was replaced by increasing exhibition support from cultural centers operated by foreign embassies, such as the Goethe Institut, the Italian Cultural Institute, the Alliance Française, all in Lagos, and the British Council in various cities. There was growing influence enjoyed by the Zaria-trained artists from Okeke's time and later and by Nigerian artists trained in other art programs at universities and colleges in the country and abroad. State governments were increasingly supportive of the arts, and there was the massive FESTAC '77 international festival in Lagos, a major art stimulus, as well as the opening of the National Gallery of Modern Art in Lagos in 1981. The contemporary Nigerian art scene became richer, larger, more diverse, and more complex.

Despite Okeke's claim that he would now go to Kpaaza, there was, in the former Biafran area after the war, a rebuilding of traditional cultural institutions as home communities settled down and reconstructed their residences and their communal and business buildings, often with the support of Igbo who in substantial numbers again moved out from their home base for work in other regions of Nigeria.[2] Shrines were rebuilt, masks and statues recreated, masquerades and rituals redeveloped, though these were not necessarily quite the same as before the war. Indigenous *uli* art continued to die out; it probably would have anyway, but the war accelerated the process. The growth of Okeke's training program at Nsukka, supported by his teaching colleagues there, is a part of this cultural revival that placed Igbo tradition strongly into contemporary art through the agency of an increasing number of artists. I believe that given Okeke's ambition, drive, and interest in tradition, this would probably have occurred even if there had not been a war, but the conflict reinforced a wish in some Igbo artists to consider their own culture more deeply.

Okeke's time at the university was another period of intense activity, involving interaction with members of the various art disciplines there, as had occurred at Enugu before the war. This declined by 1986, when Okeke left teaching, as the oil boom had become the oil bust, financial support was tight, and scholars began to leave the university for positions elsewhere. During Okeke's time at the university, however, writers and scholars, such as the novelist Chinua Achebe, the literary critic Donatus Nwọga, and the historian of eastern Nigeria, A. E. Afigbo, all played important university roles that complemented and supported Okeke's.

The Institute of African Studies at the university was active with exhibits, conferences, and the publication of the bulletin *Ikorok* (later *Ikoro,* 1971–) and *Ikenga, a Journal of African Studies* (1972–). Many other journals existed, which in one way or another related to Nigerian visual art. *The Muse: Literary Journal of the English Association at Nsukka,* originally begun in 1963, was revived and frequently contained work by Nsukka artists. *Okike, a Nigerian Journal of New Writing* (1971–) appeared, as well as a few issues of *Nsukkascope* (1971–), both edited by Chinua Achebe. There was *Ụwa Ndi Igbo* (1984–), edited by Chukwuma Azuonye, and *New Culture* (1978–79), edited by Okeke's friend and fellow Zaria art student, Demas Nwoko, for which Okeke wrote a series of articles on contemporary art. *Nigeria Magazine* continued to publish on contemporary work in the visual arts as well as in literature, music, drama, and dance. Again, there was *Anu, a Magazine of Igbo Culture* (1979–, Owerri), *Ugo* (1977–, Enugu), *Nka, a Journal of the Arts* (1983–, Owerri), and *Ọdinani, the Journal of the*

*Ọdinani Museum, Nri* (1972–, Nri), all published sporadically but containing useful articles on the various arts. *The Conch*, started in 1969 in Paris mainly by Igbo scholars in exile, and later published in the United States, had a strong Igbo focus, publishing its first issue in memory of the Igbo poet Christopher Okigbo and a 1971 number entitled "Igbo Traditional Life, Culture and Literature." *African Arts* (1967–, University of California, Los Angeles) contained articles on Nigerian and African contemporary art, partly because its managing editor, John Povey, held a strong interest in these matters. This was an impressive group of publications for Nigerian contemporary artists to explore and to which they might contribute drawings or texts. With Nigeria's current financial difficulties, many of these publications have disappeared.

The university campus lost some of the international flavor that it had before the war. Never again would there be as many expatriates there, but it was a time for very active and famous Nigerian scholars, which made the university an outstanding one in Nigeria; the art program that Okeke founded played an important role in this process. The Nsukka artists gradually emerged as a cohesive collectivity with the consciousness that their art existed with its own qualities, in the context of other visual art centers developing at universities elsewhere in Nigeria and in other areas of Africa.

## OKEKE AT THE HELM

Uche Okeke desired an African-oriented art program at Nsukka, not the Zaria model. The emphasis of his program was on drawing and design; regardless of what field of visual art the student emphasized, he or she had to be competent in drawing. In design, the Western representational model of objects and human figures was taught, but increasingly the emphasis was on drawing based upon *uli* and African culture, not necessarily specific *uli* motifs, but its linear and lyrical qualities, two-dimensionality, and its use of negative and positive space. As Okeke told me: "The tradition of *uli* was transformed and used to teach, and we had to experiment using the media, the different motifs and symbols of the traditional *uli* artists." [3] Students were free to alter, to manipulate the *uli* symbols; there was not a view that they should be rigidly copied. Some of the most intriguing images have come out of the Nsukka artists' work in this regard. Yet some students, when they became professionals, such as Tunde Ṣoyinka and Ike Igwenagu, have not made use of *uli*. Not surprisingly, most of the early students majored in painting or graphics. As the program expanded and new faculty were added, the principles of a background in drawing and design were applied to sculpture, mixed-media, textiles, and ceramics. Okeke taught drawing and painting.

A course in Western art history was retained from the past in modified form, and one on African art history was created and taught by Chike Aniakọr (see Chapter 5), who had obtained a B.A. at Zaria in painting in 1964 and a postgraduate art teacher's certificate in 1965.[4] Aniakọr, just into the teaching program when Okeke arrived, had an interest in *uli* and in Igbo tradition independent of Okeke's. The teaching of traditional African art was considered crucial by faculty members. Later, a new course on contemporary Nigerian art was added. Okeke, expanding the horizons of the program, saw to it that applied arts were added to the department under its new name, the Department of Fine and Applied Arts.[5]

Chuka Amaefunah returned to teach after the war.[6] While his initial concerns were with the naturalistic art, he developed a mixed-media style, drawing explicitly from *uli,* more so than Okeke or Aniakọr, adding strength to the department's *uli* outlook (fig. 48). He taught graphics and printmaking, and later taught photography.

Okeke's new program required art students, whether in studio or art history, to write a B.A. thesis and an M.F.A. thesis, when this degree was introduced in 1975. These writings were generally the result of field research on indigenous art, frequently Igbo, in the context of a community's or area's culture; sometimes research was conducted

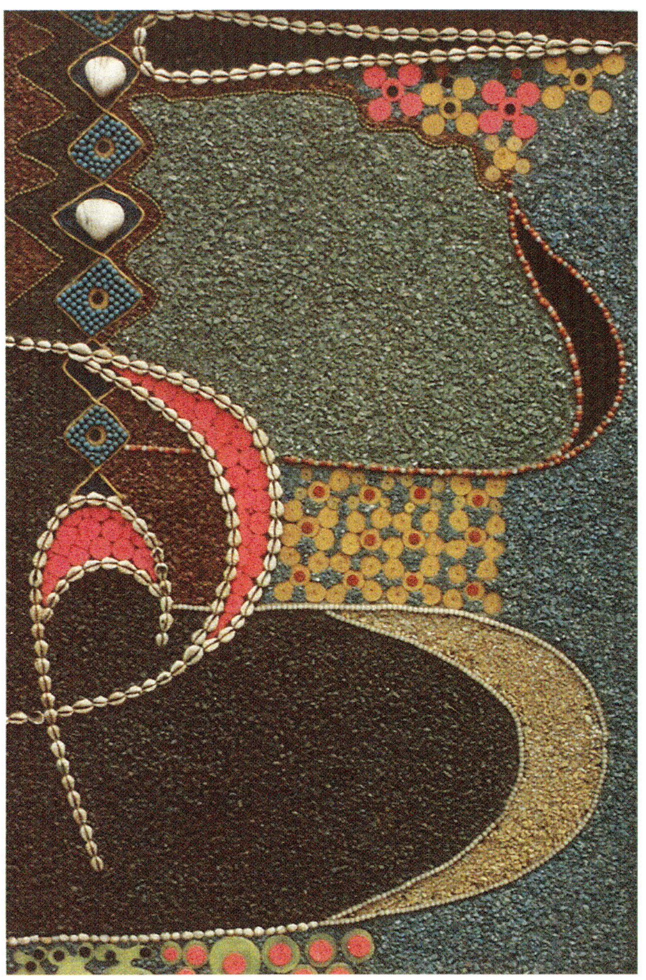

**48**. Chuka Amaefunah, *Early Moon of Maidenhood,* 1973, mixed media, dimensions unknown. Collection of the Amaefunah family.

in the student's own home region. Students returning from research reported on their work at seminars; some collected art and other objects for the university's Institute of African Studies Museum. This research approach, unusual for studio art students, reflected Okeke's, Aniakọr's, and Amaefunah's keen interest in having students learn more of indigenous tradition. Some theses were written on contemporary artists as well. The faculty's insistence that students experience their own or some other culture as part of their training was useful given that many of them had been away from home for schooling or for other reasons. Another function was to establish a corpus of information on *uli* and on other indigenous design forms and art, which were useful for teaching and research.[7] By June 1971 the art department already had a student who wrote his B.A. thesis on Igbo design.[8] From a professional anthropological viewpoint, these theses appear somewhat naive, but they do contain valuable data and interesting interpretations. Today they represent a corpus of more than a hundred useful works.

The first students in the new program had either begun their training at Zaria and transferred to Nsukka as war clouds grew, or their work had been interrupted at Nsukka by the war. While individual students have occasionally reacted negatively to the art program and its *uli* emphasis, this has never been forced on anyone, and nothing like the reaction to the art training at Ahmadu Bello University has ever occurred.

In 1972 Okeke wrote of the first students: "The best of them are at home with Christopher Okigbo's poetry, Chinua Achebe's novels and art literature of contemporary Africa. They have themselves written and in the case of Obiọra Udechukwu, published materials on aspects of Igbo art and culture, old and new."[9] Okeke's interest in poetry and literature, and in research on traditional culture, was being carried on by some of the students, a good number of whom wrote poetry themselves. The program has always been sensitive to Nigerian literary matters.

While Okeke's art was only rarely political with reference to national issues except during the war, some of his colleagues and students, such as Chike Aniakọr and Obiọra Udechukwu, were to comment in their art on social and political conditions in Nigeria. This would later become a hallmark of the Nsukka artists. But Okeke has worried over art degenerating into cartoons by becoming political and over artists who devoted most of their work to social and political issues in Nigeria; balance was necessary. However, he has been very political at the national and regional levels in pushing for art teaching in the schools, colleges, and universities, advocating, as other artists, the establishment of a national museum for contemporary art, the development of a strong Society of Nigerian Artists, and support for the arts at all governmental levels. He has been an artist politician rather than expressing politics in his art. He has written that he is "fully aware of the importance of cultural politics or the politics of culture as a weapon for the collective survival and indeed corporate identity of the Nigerian peoples."[10] Okeke sees art development as an aspect of the broader development of Nigeria.

A feature of Okeke's art prevalent among some former students has been to stress in their art human faces and figures, with landscapes, still life pictures, and animals being less common. It is faces and figures that are dominant, suggesting a strong interest in humans and human interaction, in sociability, not uncharacteristic of Igbo and Nigerian culture.

Another training feature that derives from Okeke and Aniakọr is the considerable focus on pen and ink and on brush and ink work—forms close to traditional *uli* body painting and murals and to Okeke's stress on drawing. Okeke has not worked in acrylic as far as I know; it was during the 1980s that some of his students began to employ it. He has preferred oil and gouache. While Okeke and his students and former students did create some public art, there was no strong stress on it in the art program, though certainly no ideology against it. Often soft-spoken, and teaching by indirection, Okeke could be quite critical of a student's work, calling it like that of a street artist or worse.

The Nsukka art program came to be known as the Nsukka School of Art or the Uli School. Occasionally non-Igbo artists from elsewhere, such as Dele Jẹgẹdẹ and Gani Odutokun, experimented with *uli,* and after Okeke helped develop the art program at the Institute of Management and Technology in Enugu in 1973, Nsukka-trained artists came to teach there, and an interest in *uli* formed a part of their program. But Uliism, as Amaefunah called it, has not spread elsewhere, though ideas of natural synthesis occur widely among Nigerian artists today.

The department gradually grew to full strength.[11] Gerd von Stokar arrived from Germany as department head in 1973, as a professor outranking Okeke, and remained until 1975 when Okeke took over again until 1979 and then again in 1982–83. Whether head or not, Okeke remained a driving force in the program. Ọla Ọlọidi, an art historian and a former department head, was teaching by 1976, finishing his Ph.D. in the department on contemporary Nigerian art in 1984.[12]

Okeke guided the establishment of the art department's Ana Gallery, which opened in 1978. Named after the Igbo earth deity, the gallery has functioned intermittently for student, faculty, and other artists' exhibitions.[13] Okeke helped develop museum space at the Institute of African Studies for a contemporary gallery, also an intermittent affair. Toward the end of Okeke's time at the university, the practice of having printmaking workshops of about three weeks, with an expatriate print expert, was started, the first being held in 1985. These have mostly been led by Germans, under the auspices of the Goethe Institut, Lagos, with one through the British Council, and have involved faculty, students, and outside artists (see Chapter 8). Printmaking fits well into *uli* design principles, but at times there have been problems with print supplies and equipment at the university, so that the workshops have become important supplements to the training program.[14] Okeke also insisted that his faculty arrange for catalogues of their exhibitions to present for consideration for promotion in rank; the use of catalogues probably has characterized the Nsukka artists more than others in Nigeria.

In 1976 Okeke organized an International Symposium on Contemporary Nigerian Art at the university, which drew artists, art historians, and art students from all over Nigeria to present papers, as well as some scholars from abroad.[15] The conference, its accompanying exhibit of contemporary Nigerian art, and the frequent exhibitions of the faculty and graduates on the campus and elsewhere in Nigeria over the years made the art program widely known. At this conference, Okeke restated his positions on art, which I have already explored.[16]

Okeke, promoted to lecturer I in 1973, to reader in 1974, and to professor in 1976, was in 1979 elected dean of the Faculty of Art for two years, following which he spent the 1981–82 academic year at the University of Minnesota in Minneapolis. He returned to Nigeria and became director of the Institute of African Studies at the university in 1983. But as the years went by, he turned his attention more and more to his Asele Institute at Nimo and to the completion of its building, largely designed by himself and his artist and architect friend Demas Nwoko. Thus in his final years at the university (1979–86) he was less closely in touch with the art department. Since leaving in 1986 he has devoted himself full-time to his Asele Institute at Nimo. The art program at the university has pretty much remained within the parameters that Okeke established.[17]

## OKEKE'S ART IN HIS ULI PERIOD

Little change occurred in Okeke's style during his Uli Period. He drew from *uli* and Anambra myth and produced work with Christian themes. He was active artistically from 1971 to 1976, but in the years 1976–80 and 1984–86 he produced little work. He was artistically energetic in the 1981–82 academic year in Minneapolis.[18] While his work remained skillful in the Uli Period, there is a sense of repetition in style and content from earlier times and of intermittent artistic exhaustion, probably related to administrative duties at the university and his growing preoccupation with developing the Asele Institute. His greatest innovations were designing woodwork and crafting a large tapestry, both relatively new media for Okeke.

Between 1974 and 1978 Okeke executed a number of works in Conté crayon, charcoal, and pen and ink.[19] Three pen and ink works from 1978 were *Face of Change: I—Man, II—The Village, III—The City,* suggesting Okeke's increasing concern with problems of change. Some of his most interesting art was in wood. He produced

**49**. Uche Okeke, *XI, Station of the Cross,* 1975, wood relief. 45 × 61.2 cm. Collection of the artist.

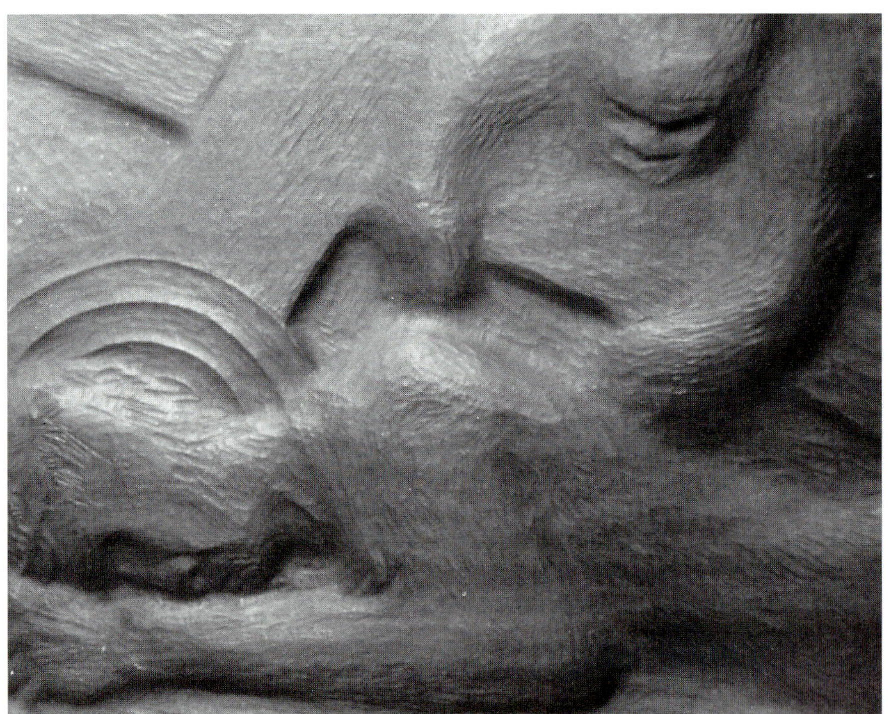

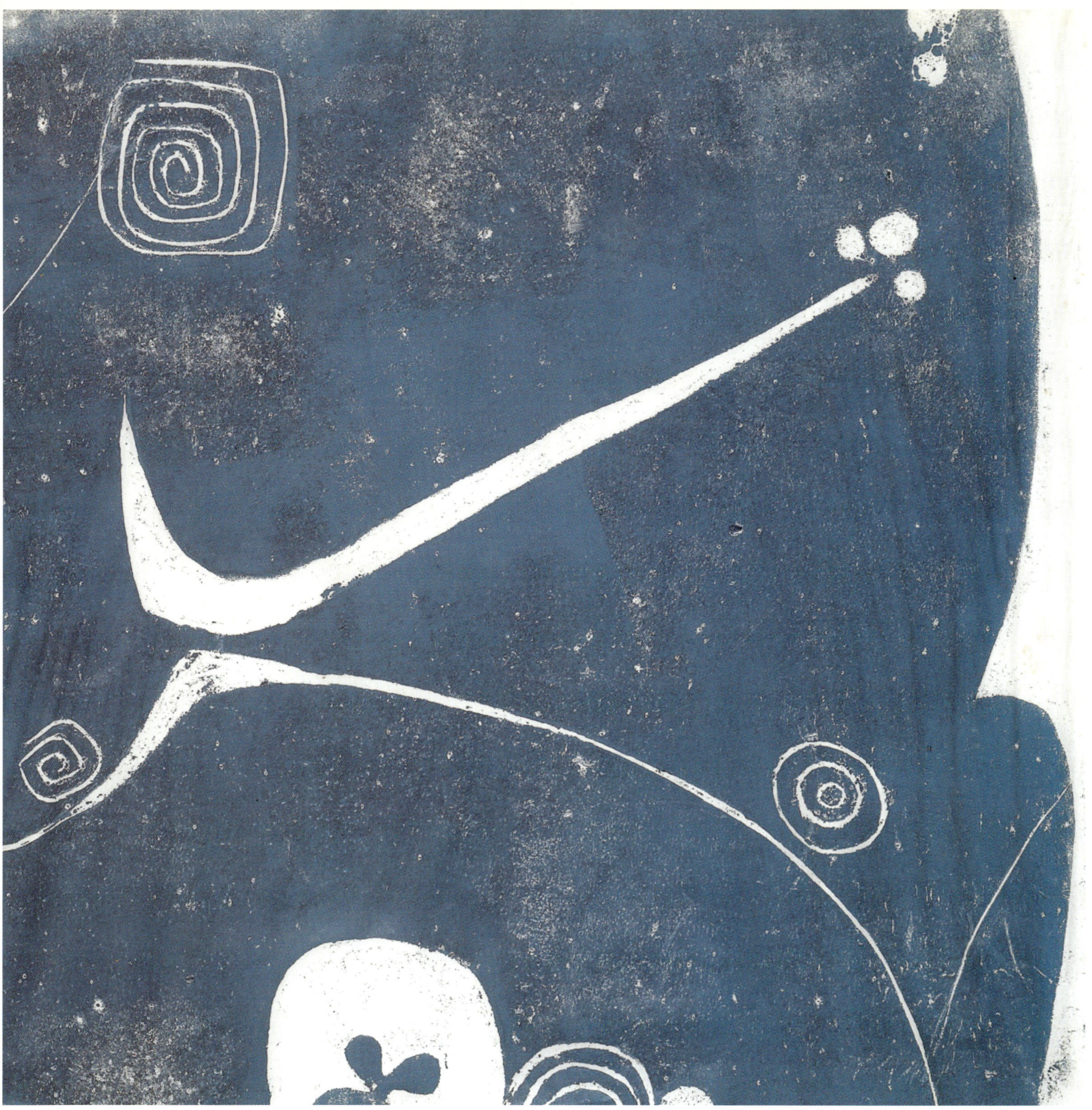

**50.** Uche Okeke, *Mma-Nwa-Uli,* 1972, celotex board cut print on paper. 45.4 × 45.9 cm. Collection of Joanne B. Eicher. Photo: Franko Khoury.

fourteen simply and gracefully executed small wood relief works of the *Stations of the Cross* for St. Peter's Parish Church at the university (fig. 49), but they were never delivered and remain today at the Asele Institute.[20] In 1971 he designed five portals and the archbishop's throne for the Holy Trinity Cathedral, Ọnitsha, the building having been damaged during the war. The portals represent aspects of Christian belief and experience, such as *The Trinity* and *Baptism*. The throne and portals, officially dedicated in 1979, were executed under Okeke's direction by Chris Afuba, who was for a time an apprentice of Okeke's at the university.[21] Afuba had opened an art studio in Nimo in 1971, and then in 1972–73 he lived at Okeke's Asele Art Studio at Nsukka. Afuba also did some carving for Okeke's wood figure, *Ekeama*, finished in 1971, and for another substantial wood carving based on Igbo tradition, *Ukolo Osisi*, produced the same year.[22] Okeke, at the time of this writing, is creating a large cross on commission from Alex Ekwueme, the architect and former vice president of Nigeria, for the new St. John's Church at Oko, Anambra State.

Okeke was commissioned to design a large tapestry of dyed and woven threads for the VIP lounge at the new Murtala Muhammed International Airport in Lagos, along with other works by other contemporary artists in various media at different airport sites for the 1977 Second World Black and African Festival of Arts and Culture (FESTAC '77) held in Lagos.[23] The tapestry, woven at Okeke's Asele Institute, has no human figures in it, but consists of irregularly shaped vertical blocks of white and various colors, one of Okeke's most abstract pieces. During the festival, there was also a large exhibition, *Contemporary Visual Arts* (164 works by professional artists, 141 by students), at which Okeke exhibited his *Ekeama* sculpture and a number of other works, all on traditional Igbo themes.[24]

Okeke's woodcuts shown at the festival were produced in 1972. In the same year he created the woodcut *Isi Nwọji* ("Head of the Kola Nut"); *Mma-Nwa-Uli*, a celotex board print, one of his most explicitly *uli* productions (fig. 50); and a letterpress printing, *The Maiden's Cry*. In 1974 he completed a woodcut *Baptism*, based on one of the portal designs for the Ọnitsha Cathedral (fig. 51). The early 1970s was a period in which Okeke was involved in printing in three media: wood, linoleum, and metal. Ngọzi Ekekwe writes: "He engraves lino or wood and pulls a print from a hand press. This is mostly black and white with occasional colouration. His etchings are done on metal plate and are printed in etching machines."[25]

In 1981 the federal government opened the National Gallery of Modern Art at the National Theatre complex in Lagos, with a collection that it had acquired over the years.[26] Okeke and many other artists and friends of the arts had long advocated such a gallery for modern works, but Okeke's art was not there because of a dispute between him and the government over art policies. Okeke felt that the government had not clearly developed its policies toward contemporary art when the gallery was established. However, works of colleagues and former University of Nigeria students—Adenaike, Amaefunah, Aniakọr, Igboanugo, and O. Udechukwu—were exhibited.

Okeke's University of Minnesota experience was at the invitation of Joanne Eicher, an expert on African cloth, who has researched among the Kalabari over the years in southeastern Nigerian coastal areas. She and her former husband had been friends of Okeke and his family since before the Biafran war. This was a major productive period in Okeke's life. He held four solo exhibitions in Minneapolis (fig. 52), took part in a joint show in Detroit, and produced more than thirty-eight works in gouache, watercolor, charcoal, pen and ink, line and wash, crayon, and etching, as well as drawings for Eicher's summer 1982 course on dress fashion.[27] In addition, two of his major writings on art were published while he was there—a collection of his papers, *Art in Development*, and *Design Inspiration through Uli*—as well as a portfolio of thirty-five reproductions of his art.[28]

Virtually all the art Okeke produced in Minneapolis was on Igbo themes. Some are recreations of works he had previously made in Nigeria, others are not (fig. 53). The art draws strongly on *uli* qualities and is well done.

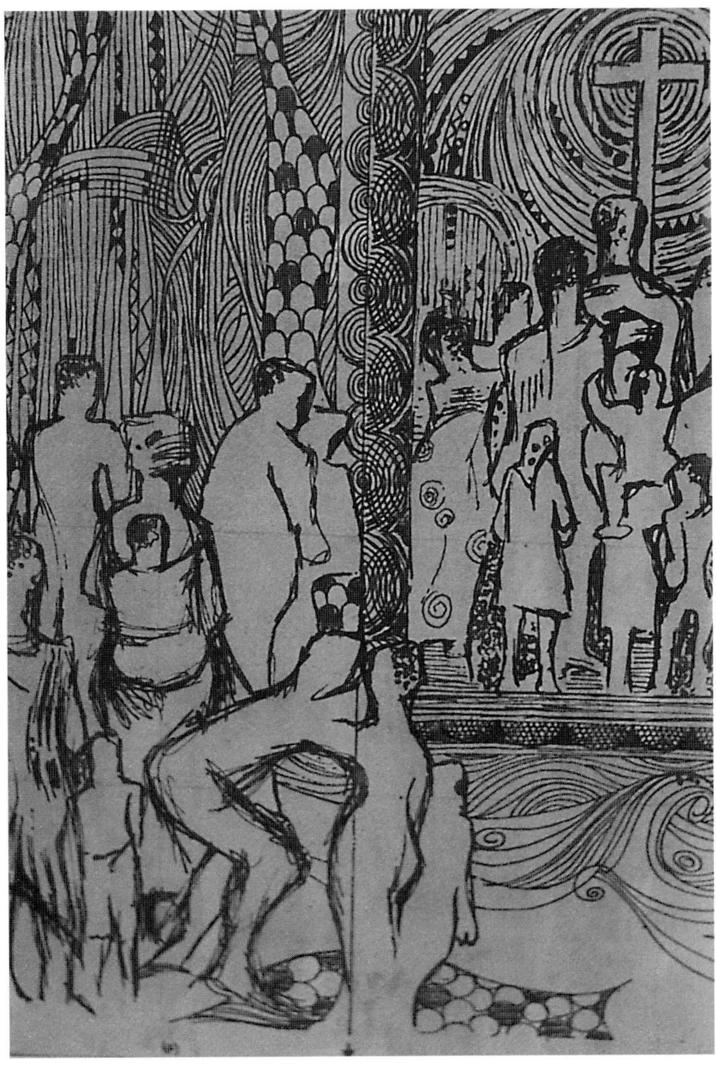

**51 (LEFT)**. Uche Okeke, *Baptism*, 1974, block print on paper, dimensions unknown. Collection of the artist.

**52 (BELOW)**. Uche Okeke, detail from *Homage to Asele: Contemporary Nigerian Prints and Drawings by Uche Okeke,* showing the artist's *Face of Time* logo. Minneapolis, 1982, poster on paper, dimensions unknown. Collection of the artist.

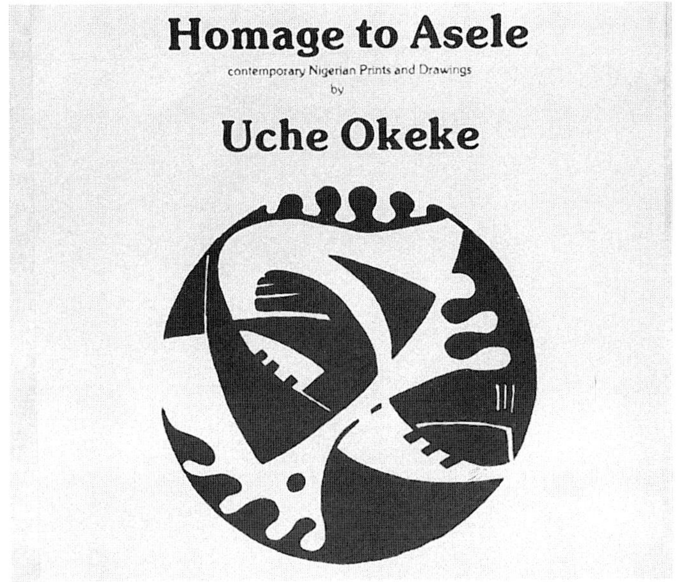



He did few works based on American life but, rather, brought Igbo culture to Minneapolis. Included are images of Ana the earth deity, Onwa the moon, Eri the mythic founder of the Anambra Igbo area, Mamiwata the water spirit, and images of masqueraders. These works demonstrated that he retained his artistic skill.[29]

Back at Nsukka in 1983, Okeke continued to be productive. He created a series of gouaches on Igbo mythic themes (figs. 54, 55). The colors are soft and rich, swirls and circular brushwork abound; the mysterious quality of some of his earlier mythic art is present.[30]

In his Uli Period, Okeke published reproductions of his art in a number of journals, of pen and ink and brush and ink drawings, some from earlier periods of time, art that has proven appropriate for publication, as have similar creations by other Nsukka artists. His reproductions are mainly based on Igbo themes, occasionally using specific *uli* motifs. They do not generally relate to the particular writings of the authors among whose texts they appear.[31]

53 (RIGHT). Uche Okeke, *Procession of Mmuo,* 1981, pen and ink on paper. 15.2 × 23 cm. Collection of Dolly J. Fiterman. Photo: Franko Khoury.

54 (BELOW). Uche Okeke, *Ide, Pillar of Light,* 1983, gouache. 29.8 × 45.1 cm. Collection of Ajie Ukpabi Asika. Photo: Franko Khoury.


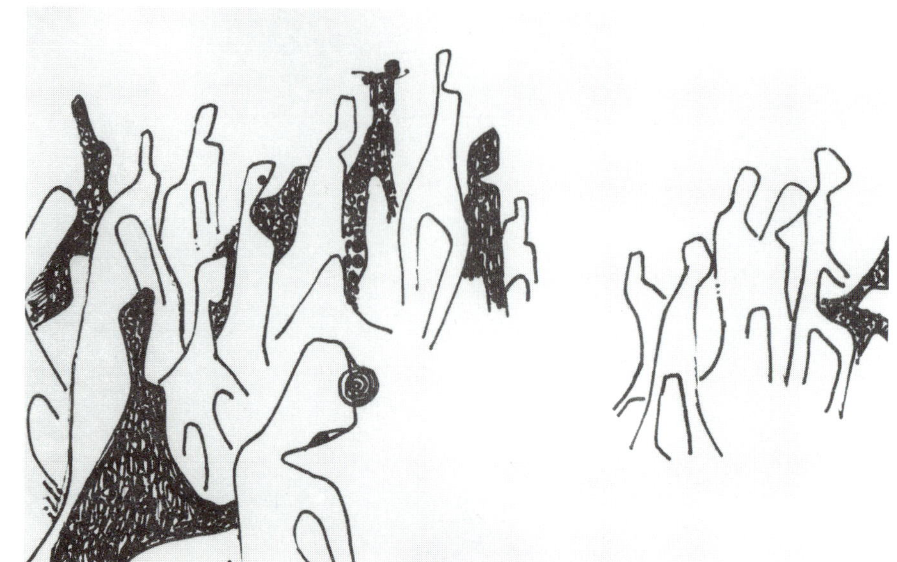

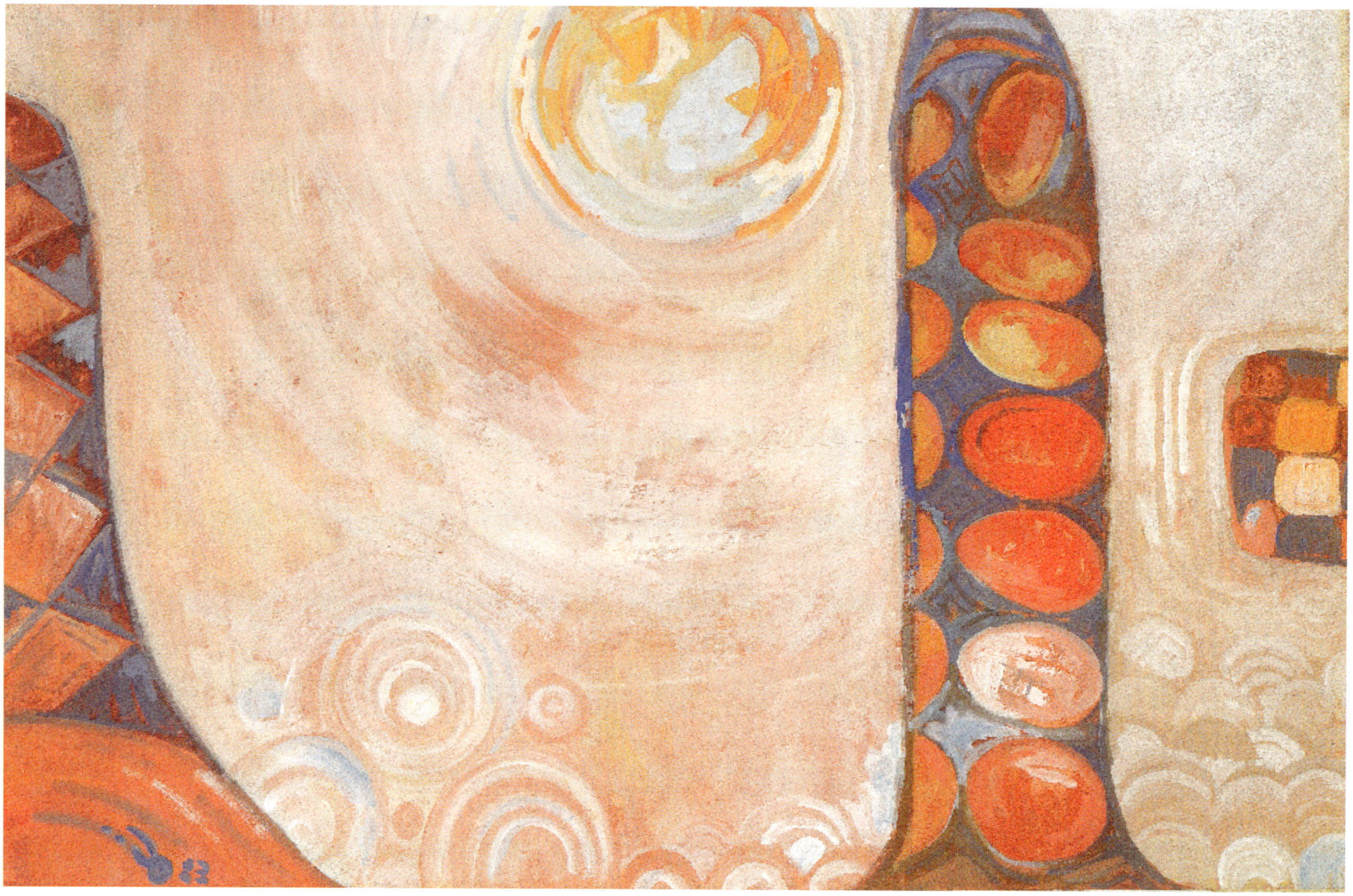

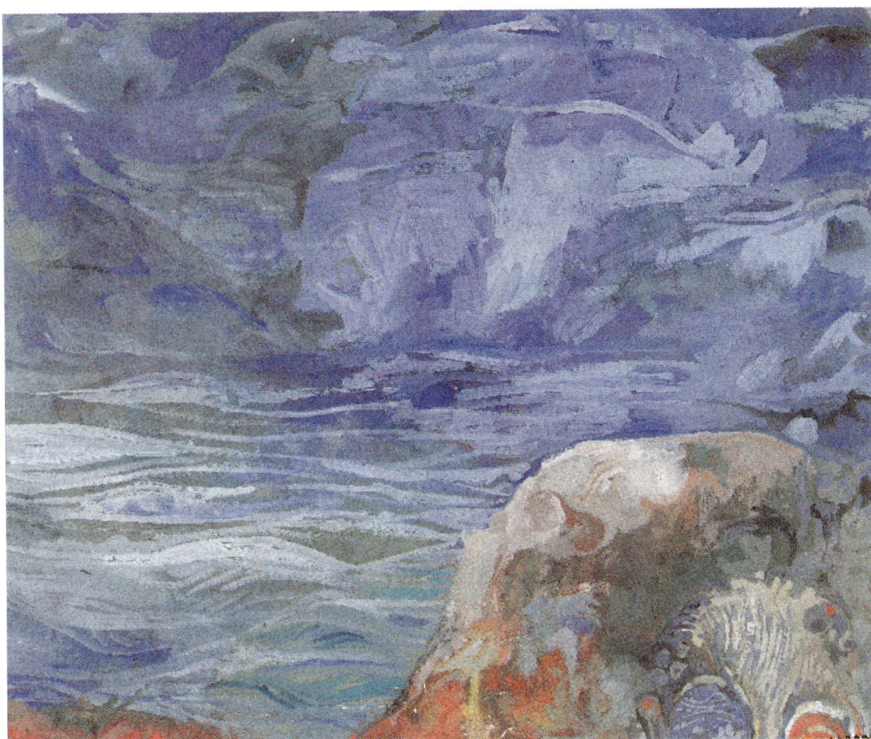



## OKEKE'S OTHER ACTIVITIES IN HIS ULI PERIOD

At this time Okeke exhibited widely.[32] In addition to those in America, he had solo exhibitions at the Institute of African Studies, University of Nigeria, Nsukka, and at the Goethe Institut, Lagos. His work appeared in more than thirty-three group exhibitions, mostly in Nigeria, but also in foreign shows in Prague, East Lansing, Michigan (twice), Washington, D.C., Germany (four different exhibitions, two traveling to a number of sites), and Amsterdam. He frequently traveled abroad, as for an exhibit in Prague in 1972, a lecture tour of the United States in 1974, to Washington, D.C., at another time, to Budapest, Stuttgart, Paris, and Helsinki, trips for seminars, conferences, or exhibitions. Okeke had become internationally known as one of Africa's leading artists.

During his Uli Period, he organized a number of conferences and exhibitions, such as the 1976 International Symposium on Contemporary Nigerian Art at the university and the fourteenth annual meeting and exhibition of the Society of Nigerian Artists in 1978, also at Nsukka, and other exhibitions there and elsewhere. He was a member of the Visual Arts Committee for FESTAC '77, involved in planning its contemporary art exhibition. He participated in a TV production, *Nigerian Art—Kindred Spirits,* broadcast nationally in 1990 in the United States on public television channels, along with two University of Nigeria colleagues, Obiọra Udechukwu and El Anatsui, as well as other artists. In the program, Okeke is shown by his mother how to draw *uli* motifs on paper.[33]

In addition to the two important 1982 Minneapolis publications of Okeke, there were others as he continued to push for progress in contemporary art, for art education, and for government arts support.[34] Some of these reiterated his art principles and philosophy, and others showed his concern for the culture of the Nsukka area. He continued to publish poetry, though this had become secondary to his visual art and his writings on contemporary art. Most of his poetry also draws from Igbo themes, though at least one poem refers to the Yoruba.[35]

In the 1980s the Asele Institute began to sponsor a number of workshops (sometimes in cooperation with UNESCO), either at the Institute at Nimo or elsewhere in Nigeria.[36] A workshop in 1985 in Lagos was concerned with art for the young, a topic of great interest to both Okeke and his wife, for they felt that in Nigeria the creative potentials of youngsters and their future abilities to appreciate art were being stifled by the schools and the general attitude of some of the public toward art.[37] Okeke continued to promote his institutions through writing and occasionally to sponsor art exhibitions there, though some were also held at the Asele Art Gallery at Nsukka.[38]

The location of the Asele Institute, away from major urban and university centers, Okeke saw in a positive light, as his "contribution towards the further intellectual development of my hometown and place of birth."[39] There he attempted to create a major art center for research, for visiting artists and scholars to consult with him and his wife and to use his magnificent library, art collection, and archives and as a site for seminars, workshops, and exhibits in the arts. It succeeded in the 1980s, but the drying up of financial resources in Nigeria and elsewhere has caused a decline in its activities.[40]

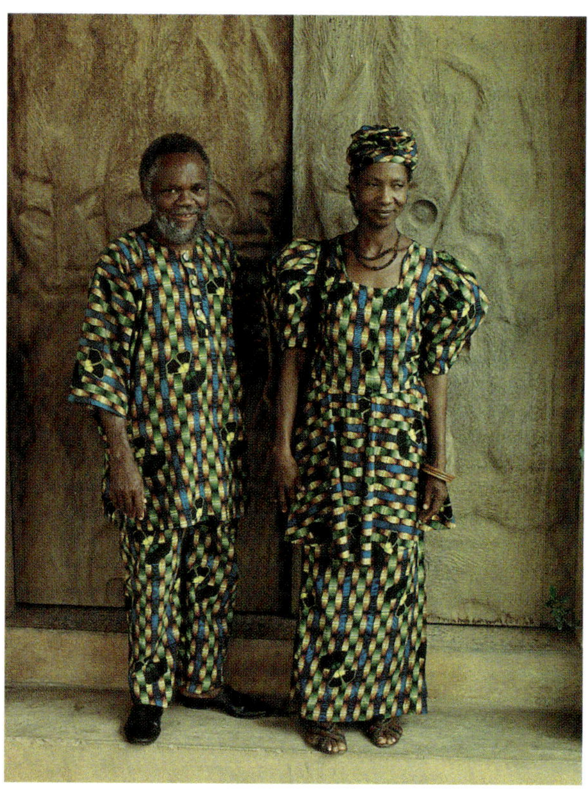

**56**. Uche Okeke and his wife, Kaego Uche-Okeke, standing before the front door of the Asele Institute, Nimo, 1994.

## THE NIMO PERIOD

Okeke's departure from the University of Nigeria in 1986 was not voluntary but forced by the university administration, who accused him of the mismanagement of research funds, although in 1987 the university's Council indicated that these charges were false. The matter is still in the Nigerian courts. In the 1986–87 academic year he was a visiting professor in the Department of Creative Arts at the University of Port Harcourt, where he worked to upgrade the program. Since then he and his wife have been living at the Asele Institute at Nimo, keeping in touch with the Nsukka artists, who frequently visit them (fig. 56). In April–May 1993 they organized a major retrospective of his work at the Goethe Institut, Lagos, as a sixtieth birthday celebration, for which nine of his former students each contributed a work.[41] Most of the art for the exhibition came from his collection; thus the exhibition did not always exhibit his best art, a good deal of which had been sold over the years and was dispersed throughout the globe. Yet the exhibition clearly indicated the development of his work and its range. At this time, art faculty and former students organized the Second International Symposium on Contemporary Nigerian Art, held at the University of Lagos, which was widely attended by Nigerian artists, art historians, and critics, as well as individuals from elsewhere.[42]

During his Nimo Period, Okeke continued to organize
seminars and workshops through his Asele Institute, including a 1988 exhibition in its honor.[43] His work was also present in the show *Uli Traditional Wall Paintings and Modern
Art,* at Iwalẹwa-Haus, Bayreuth, in 1989, at the Goethe Institut, Lagos, the next year, and also at Chinua Achebe's sixtieth birthday celebration at Nsukka. At Iwalẹwa-Haus in
1992, Okeke's friend Norbert Aas organized a solo exhibition of his work, *Uche Okeke: Auf dem Weg nach Kpaza.*[44]
Okeke's art continues to be of interest to others, even
though his productivity in recent years has been limited. He
has continued to organize art functions, including the First
and Second Christian Art Fairs of the Archdiocese of Ọnitsha (1987, 1989) and at the Holy Trinity Cathedral. He and
his wife have been associated with several conferences on
children and the arts.

For his 1993 retrospective he created five gouaches,
mostly on Igbo themes, with much of the qualities of his earlier work in gouache (fig. 57). There is a darkish, brooding
feel to these recent gouaches, a sense of seriousness. Despite
Okeke's evident pleasure in his mythic figures, they rarely
appear to be joyful or playful; rather, they possess an intense
quality.

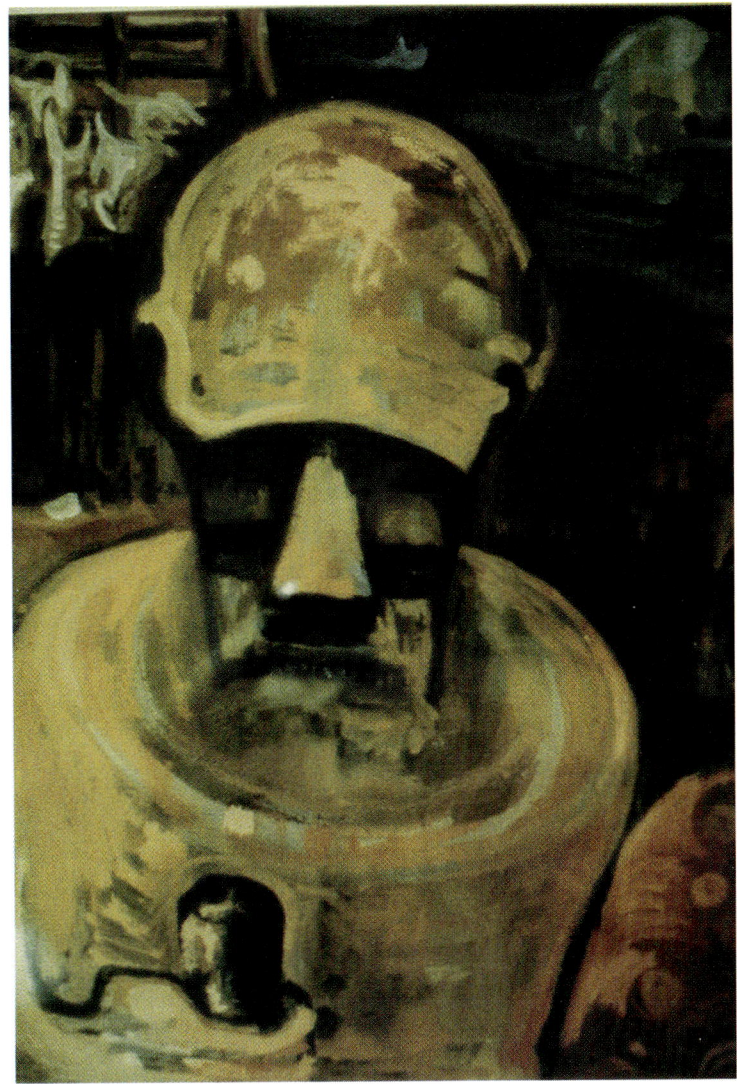

**57**. Uche Okeke, *Owẹllẹ of Ọwa,*
1993, gouache. 61 × 48 cm. Collection of
the Asele Institute.

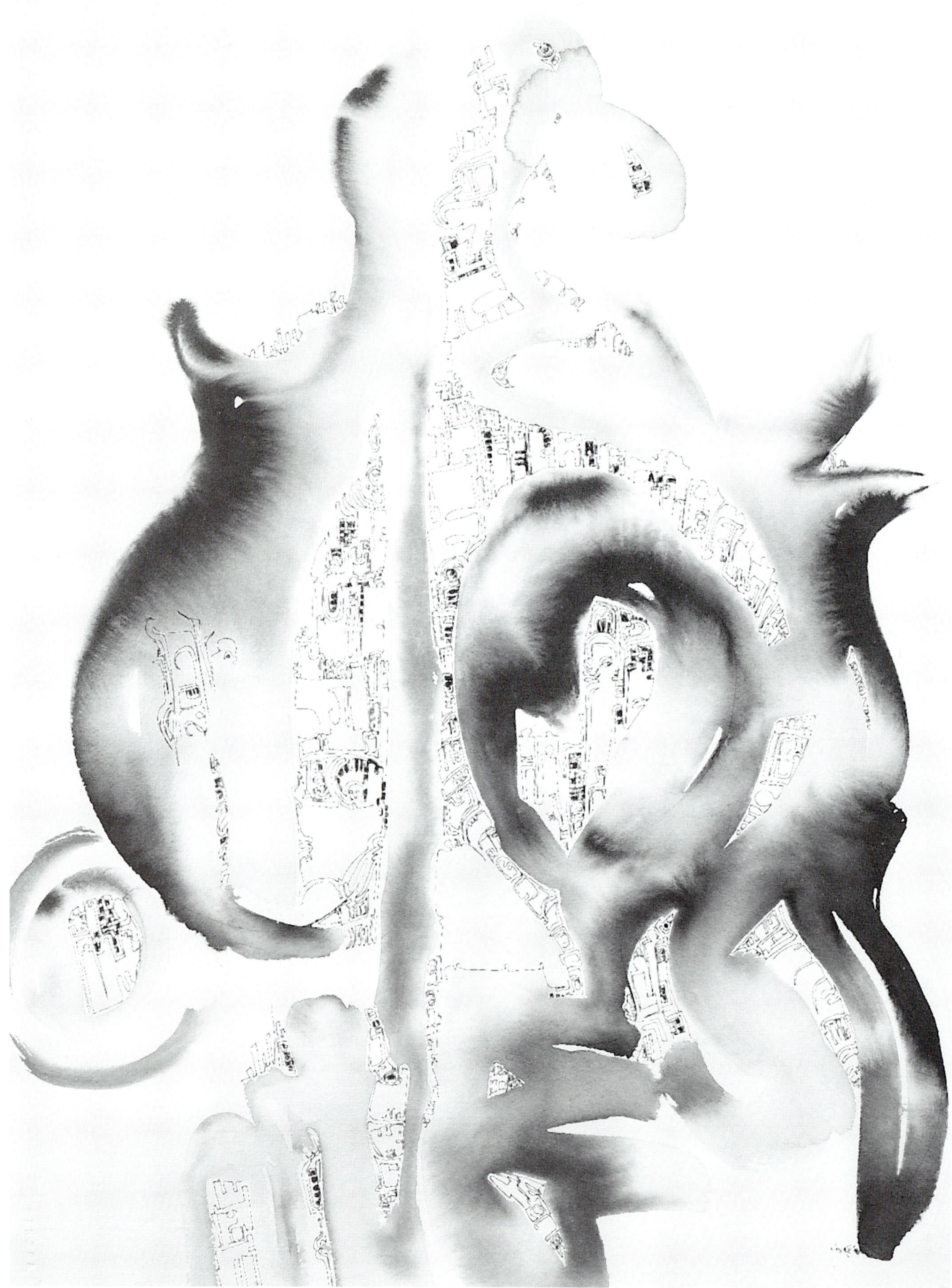

Detail of fig. 71.

# 5. CHIKE ANIAKỌR

## *ULI* ARTIST AND ART HISTORIAN

The artist must not only master the homestead, he must develop the eye of an eagle to see beyond it. That he does by becoming very conscious of his social environment of which he is a part.

CHIKE ANIAKỌR [1]

Born in 1939, Chike Aniakọr is six years younger than Uche Okeke, yet he is of the same artistic generation (fig. 58).[2] An artist and art historian who is a scholar of Igbo art and architecture, Aniakọr is also a poet and commentator on contemporary Nigerian art. While Okeke's links have mostly been with Germany, Aniakọr's are to the United States.

### THE EARLY YEARS, 1939–1970

Aniakọr was born in Abatete in Anambra State. His mother was an *uli* artist and one of his mother's brothers was a flutist and blacksmith. In grade school, Aniakọr was exposed to the usual teaching of crafts, but in Elementary II his teacher so liked a drawing of Aniakọr's that he copied it, which pleased the student. For the first time he thought of becoming an artist. Unusual for that time, in secondary school at New Bethel College, Ọnitsha, Aniakọr had an art teacher, Emmanuel A. J. Ulasi, who also moved other students toward contemporary art at this or other schools where he taught.[3] Under Ulasi's guidance, with art classes almost every year, Aniakọr created landscapes, still life drawings, and watercolors. During this unusually intensive art training for his age, and at the time in Nigeria, he determined to make art his career.

Unlike Uche Okeke, Aniakọr as a child experienced Igbo culture intensively at his home and was active in it. As a ten-year-old he led a dance group, and he has retained a strong interest in Igbo dance, music, ritual, art, and architecture since childhood. As with Okeke, Aniakọr's home village has been an important base.

After finishing secondary school, Aniakọr taught at Nnobi Community Secondary School in Anambra State,

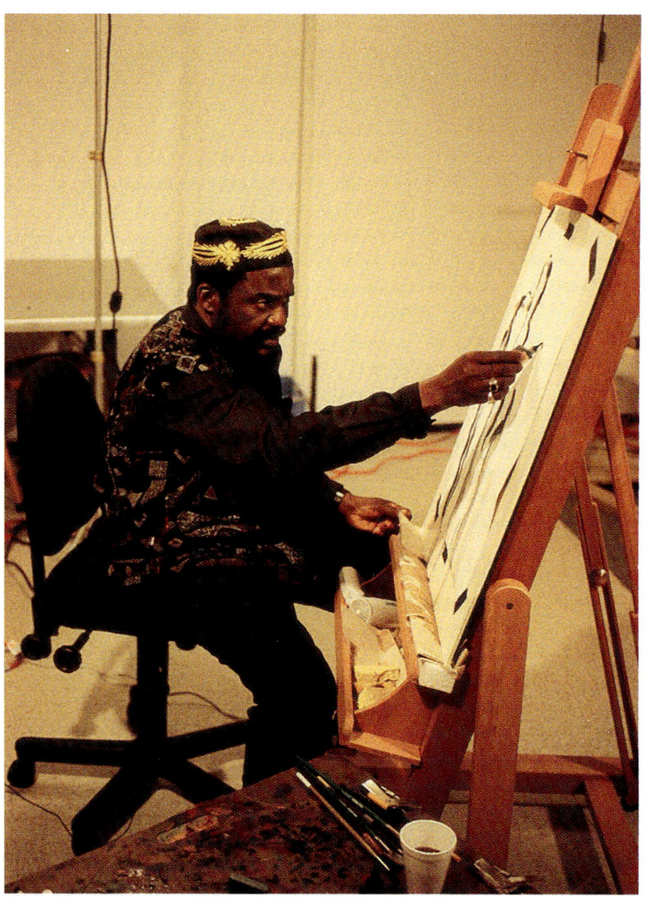



**58.** Chike Aniakọr creating *Changing Experiences,* National Museum of African Art, Washington, D.C., April 3, 1996.

not far from home. There the principal favored art but believed in teaching it by drawing on the board and having the students copy his work. Disapproving of this approach, Aniakọr had students reproduce designs from the village, which they enjoyed more. He remembers that in the 1950s and 1960s in his home town there were many wall and house murals; it was a visual delight. He perceived *uli* as being abstract yet related to many aspects of Igbo life.

Aniakọr studied at the Nigerian College of Arts, Science and Technology at Zaria from 1960 to 1964, graduating with a B.A. in painting and remaining for a year to take a postgraduate Art Teacher's Certificate. Though not a member of the Art Society, he says he attended several of its meetings, but did not perceive its members to be rebels nor as discussing any art ideology. Possibly he was excluded from this aspect of the society's activities; its members were protective of their interests. Ulli Beier's visits to Zaria, Aniakọr believes, encouraged the Art Society members to go on their own in their art, and Beier's influence later led to the formation of the Enugu Mbari center. These views minimize Okeke's role in the contemporary art movement. It is difficult to evaluate Aniakọr's claims; they need to be seen in the context of some rivalry between him and Okeke, with Aniakọr feeling that his role in the development of contemporary *uli* art has not been fully appreciated. He believes he developed his *uli* interests separately from Okeke and that the story of those involved in the start of contemporary *uli* art has not been written.[4] In any case, among Nsukka artists and others in Nigeria, Okeke is generally considered the founder.

During most of Aniakọr's schooling at Zaria, he had conventional art training as I have described it. However, in his 1963–64 year, a British art teacher, Charles Argent, encouraged the students to use colors other than the usual brown to paint a human model, and Aniakọr moved away from tonal moderation, employing a range of colors and departing from photo-realism.[5] It was an exciting experimental period for Aniakọr. He wrote a B.A. thesis on Igbo carved doors, which took him directly to the designs on them, not generally considered *uli*. Yet in a later work he argues that some of them are similar, such as *isi nwaọji* (head of the kola nut), *ọkala ọnwa* (crescent moon), and *akaraka* (spiral).[6] Aniakọr's thesis experience undoubtedly reinforced his belief that students at the University of Nigeria, Nsukka, where he later taught, should do field research theses, as he had previously seen its value for his art students at Nnobi.[7] After his Zaria training, Aniakọr returned to teach for a year at Nnobi, trying to work *uli* designs into his own art and taking students to the villages to explore the art.

When the war came, Aniakọr first took a management position in a refugee camp for about a year, then he was with the Publicity Division of the Ministry of Information in Orlu as art editor of its government newsletter, later moving from place to place. For the ministry he wrote publicity materials and information. He produced some art during the war, on refugees and related matters; unlike Okeke, he remained in Biafra through the conflict and was exposed to the brutal side of war. He made drawings—there was little time for more elaborate work—but much of his wartime art was destroyed by termites after the conflict. His war art included the employment of *uli*.

Aniakọr's war experiences contributed to his view of art as an element of social reconstruction—the artist in the service of society. The war was a psychic shock to him, he has told me; its emotional effects were great. Even seven years after the war, while pursuing graduate work at Indiana University, he created a pen and ink work entitled *Exodus I: The Refugees* (see fig. 62), referring to the conflict, and another work made in 1984 referring to refugees.[8] The war made him retreat into his culture, to appreciate better what he had always taken for granted. Because little of Aniakọr's wartime art or that from his time at Zaria survives, it is difficult to judge his early creations. Unlike Okeke who has kept good records of his work, Aniakọr has not.

In his early period of creative endeavors, Aniakọr was not involved with groups of artists to the extent that Okeke was. He was not a member of the Art Society in Zaria, nor involved with Okeke's Cultural Centre or the Mbari center in Enugu. During the war there were groups of artists working together in propaganda units, as we have seen, but Aniakọr seems to have remained largely separate.

## THE LATER YEARS, 1971 TO THE PRESENT

Aniakọr was a crucial member, as we have seen, along with Okeke and Amaefunah, in the formative years of the art program at the University of Nigeria, Nsukka. He has continued to play a major role there as a teacher of painting, drawing, and mixed media, and he has developed a course on the history of traditional African art. His classes are popular; one former student called him a "wonderful teacher," and he has done much to bring an African perspective to art history at the university.[9] In his course on the history of traditional African art, some principles of *uli* design are taught, which supplement the indirect teaching in studio courses, the students' observations of their teacher's *uli*-derived art and that of other artists and students, and the reading of articles on *uli* as well as theses in the university library on these motifs.

Aniakọr went to Indiana University in 1973, where he finished an M.A. in art history in 1974, returning to Nsukka for a year to carry out Ph.D. research. He then went back to Indiana where he wrote a pioneer study of Igbo architecture as his dissertation, unfortunately still largely unpublished, receiving his Ph.D. in art history in 1978.[10] He then taught briefly at Southern University, New Orleans, before returning to Nsukka. He was a consultant and research associate at the University of California, Los Angeles, in 1984, which resulted in a comprehensive book and exhibition surveying Igbo art, co-authored and co-curated with Herbert M. Cole; the book is now the standard reference on indigenous Igbo art.[11] At Nsukka he was director of the Institute of African Studies in 1986–88 and head of the art department for three years beginning in 1989. In 1988 Aniakọr traveled briefly to the United States under the United States Information Service International Visitors' Program; in the 1994–95 academic year he was a research fellow at the Metropolitan Museum of Art in New York, and the following year he held a fellowship in oral literature at the African Studies Center, Howard University, Washington, D.C. Despite his years in the United States, the content of his art is firmly rooted in Nigeria. I once asked him why he did not employ American images in his art when at Indiana, where he made drawings and paintings. He replied: "You play what you know. Maybe its the social experience at work. Experience is tied to an idiom, not an idiom to experience." And to C. Krydz Ikwuemesi he has said:

> If you saw the things I exhibited, you wouldn't believe that I did not create them in Nigeria. They were not American, at all, by virtue of the fact that I do not force subject matter. I didn't have to paint what I saw, just because I was in the U.S. Until my mind is engaged in such a way that I can reflect on something, only then can I make an entry.[12]

The tendency to create Nigerian images while abroad is characteristic of much of the art of the Nsukka artists.

Aniakọr's ties to his Abatete home remain firm. He still returns home for rituals. He has been a traditional dancer through much of his life, taking part in home events. Aniakọr has told me: "I see a vision of a day when art exhibitions should take place in the villages. We can move them around and people can see and react and know that this is also their art."[13] He has no difficulty bridging the community life with his urban and university experiences. Ikwuemesi writes that Aniakọr is someone "who believes in Igbo cosmology and yet is quite at home with contemporary modernisation."[14]

## ANIAKỌR'S ART

Aniakọr's creations, like those of Uche Okeke, have always had a strong linear quality, whether in wash and ink, pen and ink, oil, mixed media, or in his occasional prints. The art tends to be two-dimensional and quite vertical in style, with elongated human images and lines. Several Nigerian artists and critics argue that Aniakọr's earlier work is emulative of Okeke's and that it also draws heavily on Igbo tales and myths. But until 1970 Aniakọr had virtually no contact with Okeke, although he had seen some of his art. The similarity in their art may be because both draw on *uli* and Igbo life from neighboring areas of Anambra State. At any rate, Aniakọr is an original contemporary *uli* artist. Characteristic of *uli* creators, his art exhibits simplicity (though sometimes at first glance appearing complex), formal restraint, economy of creative means, but not necessarily economy of emotional content.[15]

Adenaike sees 1972 as the time of maturation of Aniakọr's art, the earlier years being experimental in form and subject.[16] In that year he held his first solo exhibition, *Visions of My Ikenga*.[17] I do not think a precise year can be set for his maturation. There was a gradual evolution after the war, so that his art is divisible into two periods. Into the 1970s, he drew heavily on Igbo tales, myth, and

**59**. Chike Aniakọr, *The Leader and Us*, 1994, pen, ink, and watercolor on glossy paper, dimensions unknown. Collection of the artist.

ritual, though he never has seen a return to the Igbo past as possible. Igbo life and culture are simply a part of him. It naturally appears as he creates: "I mean, I can't forget Igbo dance. I can't forget the masquerade. Body painting, wall painting, these are one of the finest textures of Igbo art. So need I forget them? Of course they can't be forgotten. The appeal is enduring."[18]

Although Aniakọr's use of *uli* linearity is retained, the Igbo content in his work continues to this day in lessened quantity.[19] Since the Biafran war he has increasingly been making visual social and political statements. "I live in a society where you turn to your left and you find people hungry. You turn to your right, you find the suffering and the helpless. It is no longer an issue of I want to create out of my social conditions, as if you are making a decision. No. You become a part of the decision; it becomes real and not that it's no longer a question."[20]

From the late 1980s, as the general Nigerian situation has deteriorated, the second type of content has dominated much of his art. In recent years, images of a powerful leader or leaders, in human form or metaphorically, dominate his work. The eagle as leader occurs, for example, with huddled and often helpless human masses below, patient but downtrodden by the leader (fig. 59). Aniakọr is depressed by the current Nigerian situation, not an uncommon emotion in Nigeria today. The content of this art does not depend on Igbo tradition except through employing *uli* linear qualities, yet because Igbos, as others in Nigeria, are seriously affected by social conditions in the country, even this art has an Igbo association.

Aniakọr's early oils generally have mild and gentle colors; more recently he has employed bolder ones, but has made fewer oils. He produced interesting mixed media in the 1970s and again for a time in the 1980s, but he has largely given up this medium.[21] His early mixed-media art has a surreal quality to it.[22] Since about 1989 much of his watercolor and ink work in

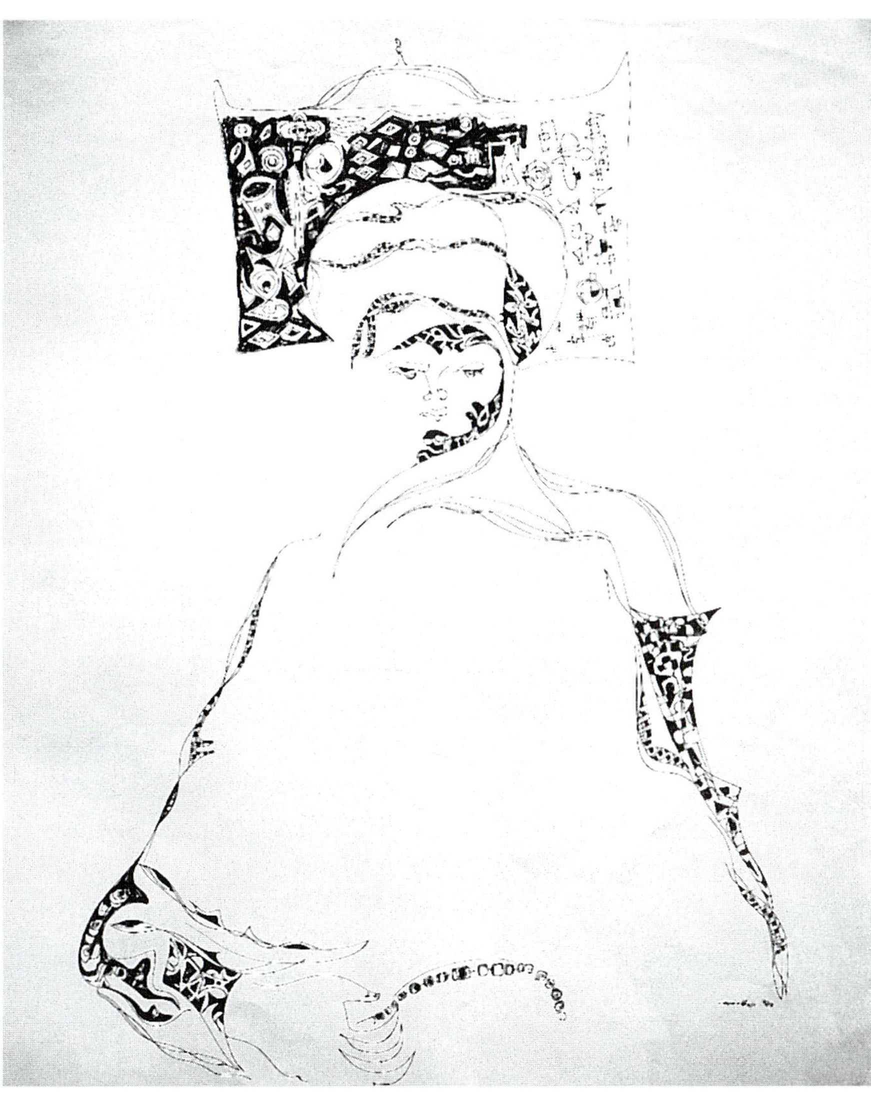

**60**. Chike Aniakọr, *Of Masque and Prayer*, 1994, pen and ink on paper, dimensions unknown. Collection of the artist.

Nigeria has been on large sheets of thick, glossy paper, which some viewers find a disturbing background, but which others feel enhances the art.

Aniakọr sees his social and political work as an attempt to reach the masses, as he hopes that his Igbo themes will, believing that all his art should. But he is aware of the difficulties, given that artists are part of an educated Nigerian elite, although not of the power elite. However, he has not taken the steps that Bruce Onobrakpẹya and a few other Nigerian artists have, to make available low-priced photolithographic copies of his art, although his pen and ink works have been reproduced in scholarly journals. He has also made prints as a member of the third and fourth Nsukka Printmaking Workshops in 1987 and 1990.[23]

Of his art, Aniakọr writes:

> My painting ideas are carried over months in the antipodes of the mind, undergoing creative mutation, occasionally surfacing to be synthesized—just in the way a goat sits under the shade to chew its cud. These ideas mature with time like the sprouts of yam seedlings. It is during this period that I feel like the traditional carver who says that "to carve a mask you must be the mask." [24]

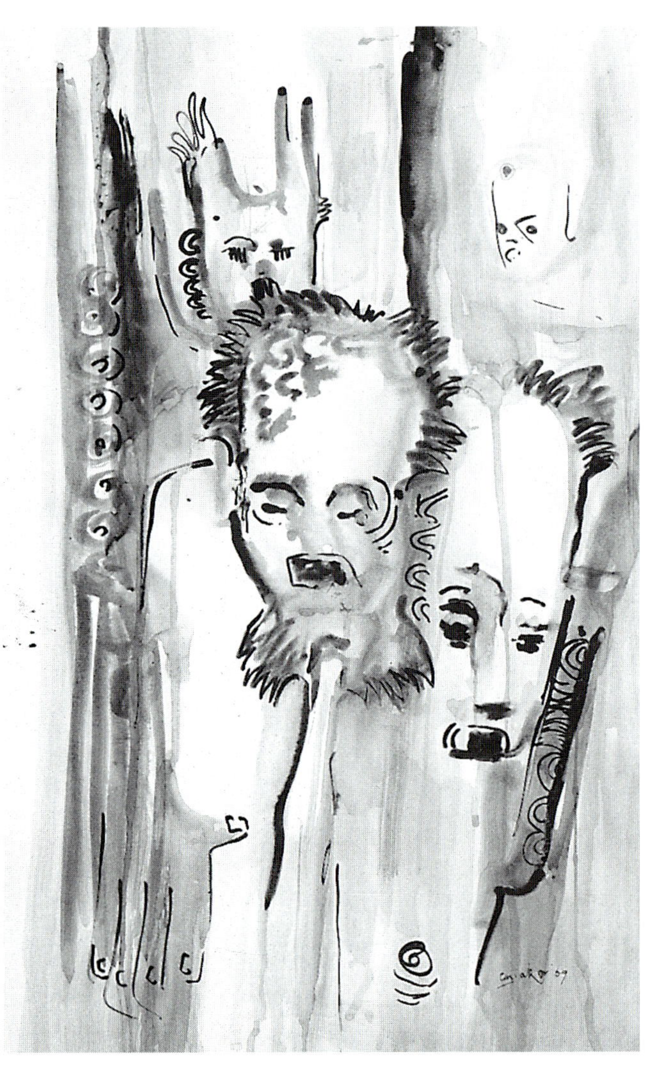

61. Chike Aniakọr, *The Elders,* 1967, pen, ink, and wash on paper, dimensions unknown. Collection of the artist.

There are a number of references here to tradition which suggest that Aniakọr draws heavily on Igbo culture even when the content of his art is current social issues. Christian themes are only rarely present; Aniakọr is not involved in balancing Christian and indigenous themes and beliefs in his art as is Okeke.

Aniakọr's employment of *uli* is sometimes as covert as Okeke's. This has allowed him to instill a sense of movement in his work that might be absent if he used many specific *uli* motifs. But Adenaike points out that sometimes Aniakọr employs *uli* directly, as in his *Spirit Land,* where a series of joined *isi nwaọji* (head of the kola nut) appear.[25] The yam tendril (*agwọlagwọ*) appears in women's hair in other works. As Ikwuemesi notes, along with Aniakọr's sweeping lines and curves there are often bits or suggestions of specific *uli*.[26] Yet much of the linear quality of Aniakọr's work is free-form (fig. 60). His pen and ink and brush and ink works employ broken lines, and there are empty areas in major images, leaving the viewer to fill them in by his or her own imagination.[27]

Sometimes, especially in his ink drawings, the whole is a shape suggesting an *uli* design, and then there are shapes within this that hint at other motifs.

In Aniakọr's recent pen and ink work, the center of the picture may be empty and the outside borders of the picture may be free. These empty spaces isolate and heighten the focus on the image. At times two major images appear with a space between them. Empty space is clearly a characteristic of his work. Sometimes the empty space implies a political void, a failure of social policy; at other times, particularly if it is at the center of the picture, it creates a focus for the neighboring images. In his writings on architecture, Aniakọr stresses the importance of the center in the Igbo community; perhaps there is a carryover to his visual art. He also equates the horns of the Igbo *ikenga* carvings with outstretched hands, which often appear in his art. Complex forms of *ikenga* are related to the high status of the owner, he believes, and perhaps link to Aniakọr's search for status through the multiple figures in much of his art.[28]

However, Aniakọr's oils generally fill the canvas or board; image and color together create the focus. In his ink and even his ink and watercolor work, the black ink tends to dominate; the watercolors—often yellows, blues, and greens—are frequently light, forming gentle contrasts to the dark lines.

A good example of an early work is the pen, ink, and wash *The Elders* of 1967 (fig. 61). Broad vertical ink strokes contrast with the oval qualities of the two faces and what appear to be two masks in the top background; the piece suggests the wisdom of Igbo elders. In Aniakọr's use of lines and in its general appearance, *the Elders* has the feel of some of Uche Okeke's art.

**62**. Chike Aniakọr, *Exodus I (The Refugees)*, 1977, ink drawing on paper. 32.7 × 27.9 cm. Collection of the National Museum of African Art. Photo: Franko Khoury.

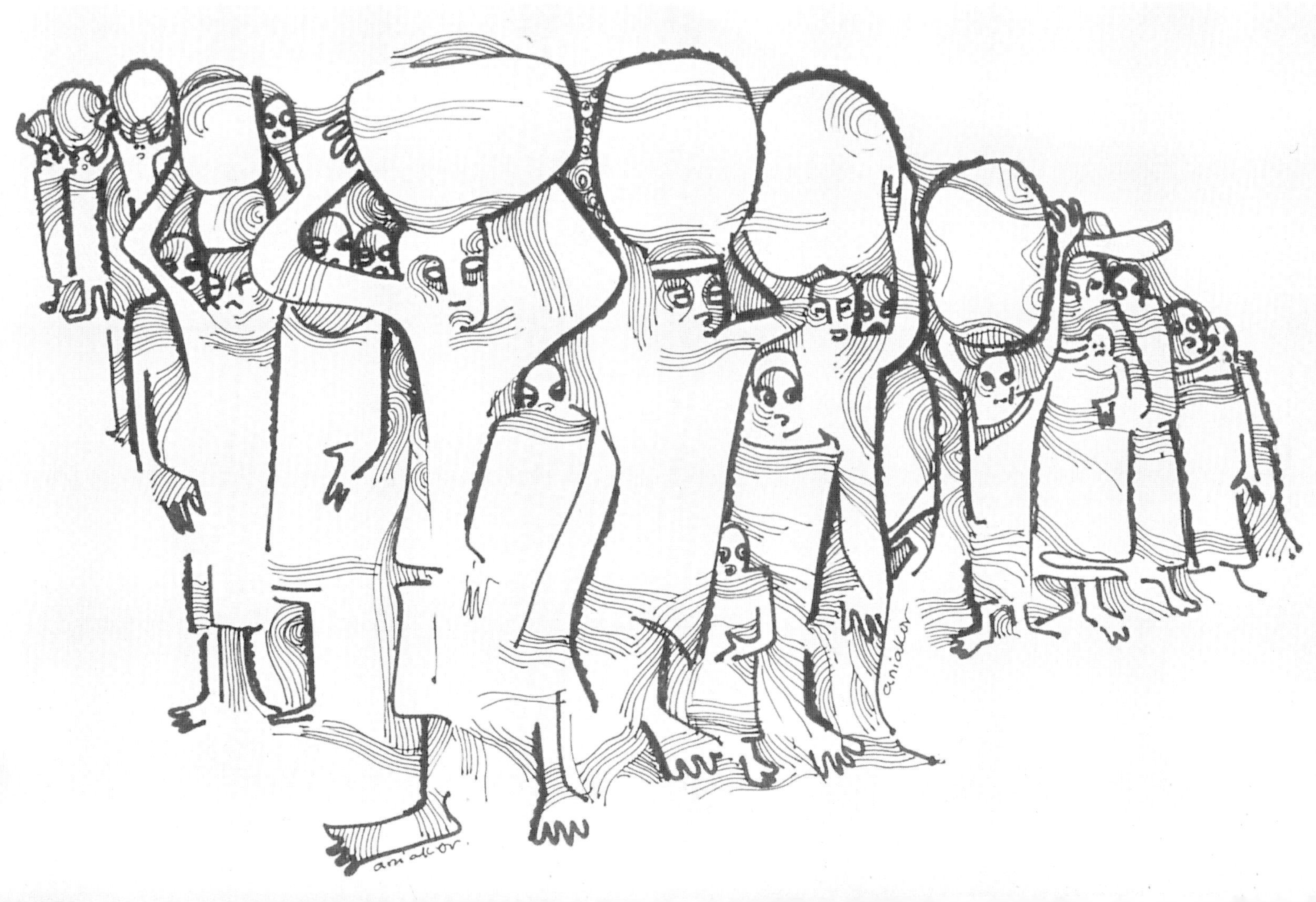

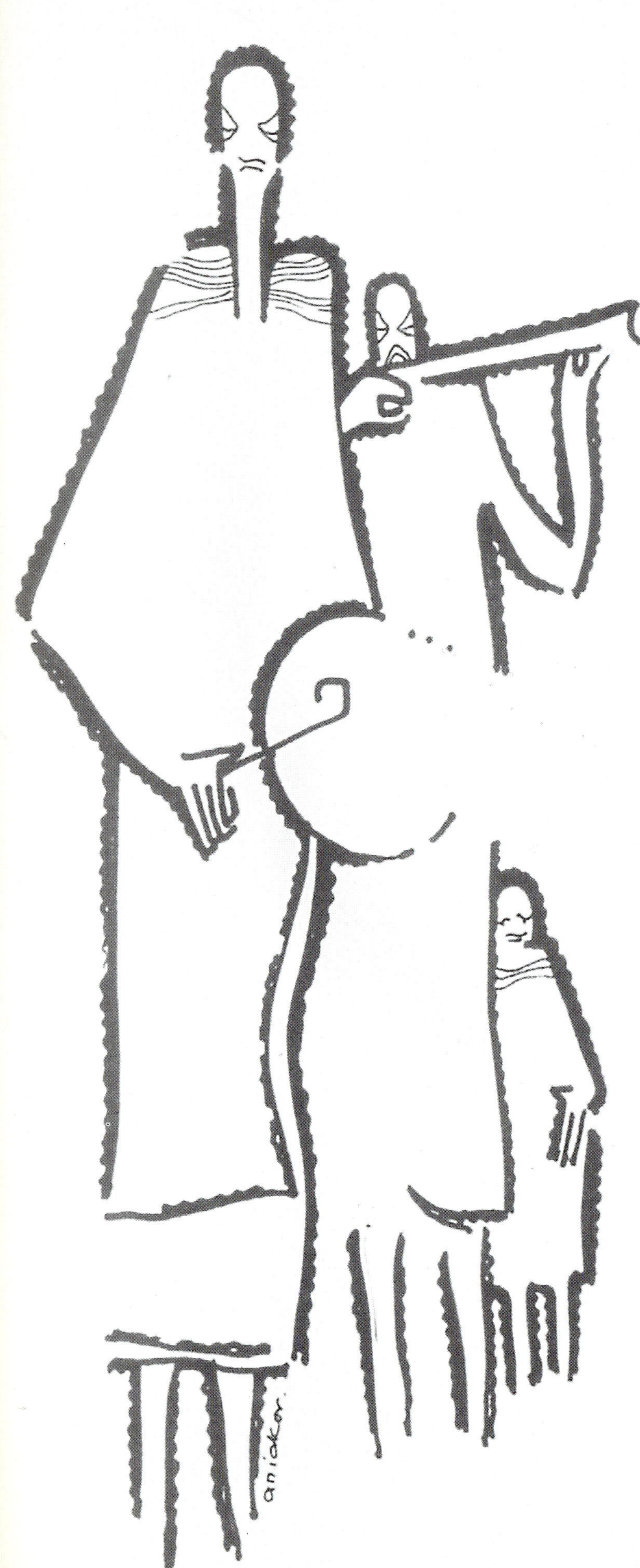

*Ritual Conversation,* a pen and ink piece, produced sometime before the war, with numerous vertical figures and three horizontal ones toward the right side, is a play on positive and negative space, with some figures associated with internal and external black lines, others in white and only outlined in black. Either the positive or the negative space could be the foreground, creating ambiguity, suggesting the multivocality of ritual. The whole image is compact and fully lined, leaving generous space around it.

Ikwuemesi sees Aniakọr's work as consisting of composite images that are "subjects of a major plot."[29] Aniakọr rarely employs a single figure in his art. He has told Ikwuemesi: "When you place a figure in it on its own it becomes static, it doesn't move," a view consistent with the strong quality of Igbo sociability.[30]

This use of multiple human figures, sometimes crowded together, sometimes arranged in interesting design patterns, characterizes Aniakọr's pen and ink work, such as his 1977 *Exodus I (The Refugees)* (fig. 62). In this medium he often employs short groupings of parallel lines to highlight or to shadow human features and clothing, as in his 1977 *Mother and Child.*[31] These two pen and ink drawings and a third, *Music Makers* (fig. 63), created the same year, illustrate Aniakọr's ability to develop images with a minimum of line. Of *Mother and Child,* he comments that he sees womanhood as being related to cosmic realization, the mainstream of human and Igbo life. This is in contrast to politics. "The other side is the voice of love and intimacy, a counter to the rudeness of politics," he tells me. In his later pen and ink art he often employs watercolors, as in *Falcon Descent on the People* (1992; fig. 64) on glossy paper: here he has filled out the body of the work, which includes numerous standing persons,

**63**. Chike Aniakọr, *Music Makers,* 1977, ink drawing on paper. 27.9 × 24.2 cm. Collection of the National Museum of African Art. Photo: Franko Khoury.

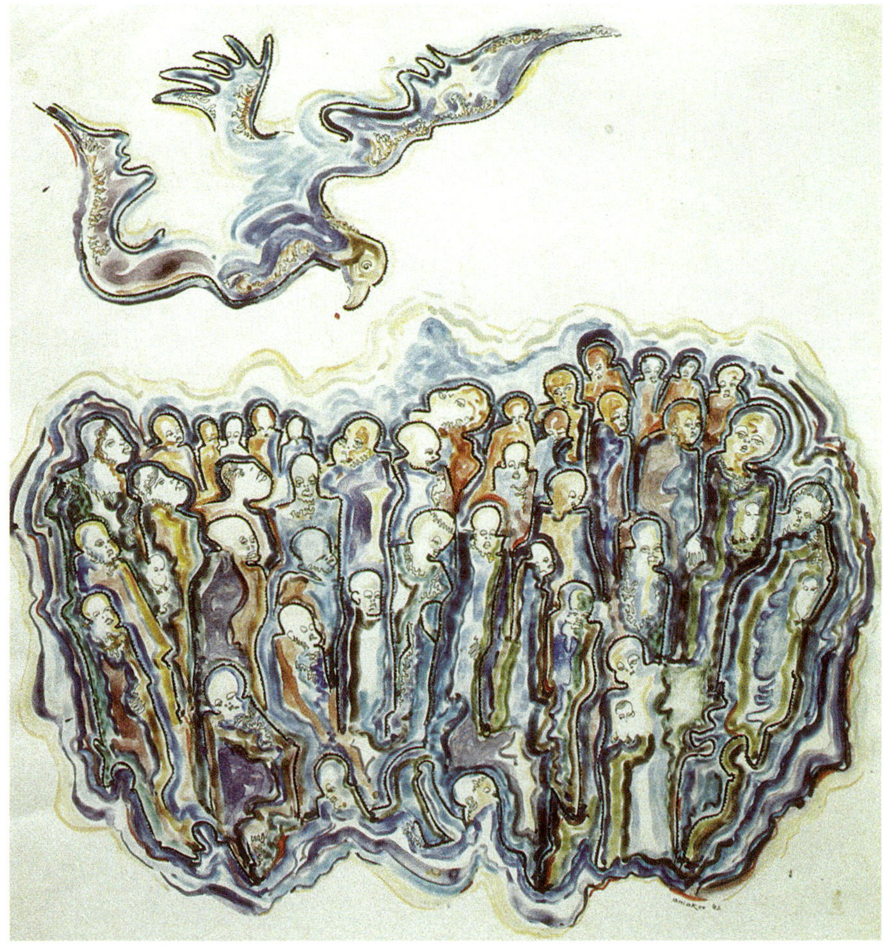

64. Chike Aniakọr, *Falcon Descent on the People,* 1992, pen, ink, and watercolor on paper, dimensions unknown. Collection of the artist.

with color and multiple short black lines. This is true of the falcon flying overhead, which has traces of blood on its mouth. This is typical Aniakọr, with the falcon, a common metaphor, representing a government that has the freedom to do what it wants, while the people are tightly packed together, as if in a container, controlled by the leader.

Aniakọr's oils, often linked to Igbo tradition, may employ large wavy brush strokes. If these are in the background, they are generally in contrasting colors to the central images, as in *Maiden.*[32] In *Ọgbanje* (1976; fig. 65), surely a favorite topic of some of the Nsukka artists, the lower foreground figures are almost dominated by the strong wavy upward, flamelike oil work on both sides of the painting. This in turn contrasts with an upper central dark vertical column within which ovals and a variety of linear designs in gray seem to move in different directions. The background suggests a powerful unknown spirit world, with helpless-looking standing human figures at bottom foreground. Aniakọr's oils seem rarely to deal with current social and political issues but to be linked to Igbo tradition.

In the oil *Sacrifice* (1974; fig. 66), produced while Aniakọr was at Indiana University, two men move forward, carrying large bowls for a ritual. The hair of the woman behind them has pointlike rays like a star. This design is duplicated at the back of the head of the lead sacrificer, as if to suggest a halo, emphasizing his sacredness. This design also appears in different colors in three background areas of the work, and it either suggests the *uli* sun (*anyanwu*) or the kola nut head (*isi nwaọji*), in the latter case with rays additional to those normally found. The design ties the painting together, suggesting either the peaceful quality of the kola nut or the strong power of the sun. In the painting the faces are grim, almost deathly, as in some of Aniakọr's other oils.

Given his strong knowledge of Igbo culture and art, it is not surprising that Aniakọr's more traditionally oriented art not only draws on *uli* motifs but on Igbo ritual scenes, masquerades, title taking, sculpture such as *ikenga* wood figures, and other elements. He is much immersed in Igbo ways, despite residing at a university.

Human beings dominate Aniakọr's work, even more than for most other Nsukka artists; animals occur only occasionally. His figures tend to face forward (fig. 67), as if to say: "Here we are and this is our condition." It is the way a good deal of traditional Igbo art was meant to be observed. Occasionally a human figure is quite stylized, as in the oil *Maiden,* mentioned above, where the female figure resembles an Aşante *akuaba* from Ghana. But generally his figures are looser, more naturalistic.

Aniakọr's pen and ink work has been reproduced in journals and books, though rarely associated directly to the text, which is often by other hands.[33] These black and white illustrations are suitable to accompany poetry and scholarly work in African humanities and arts. Published illustrations particularly appeared in the late 1970s,

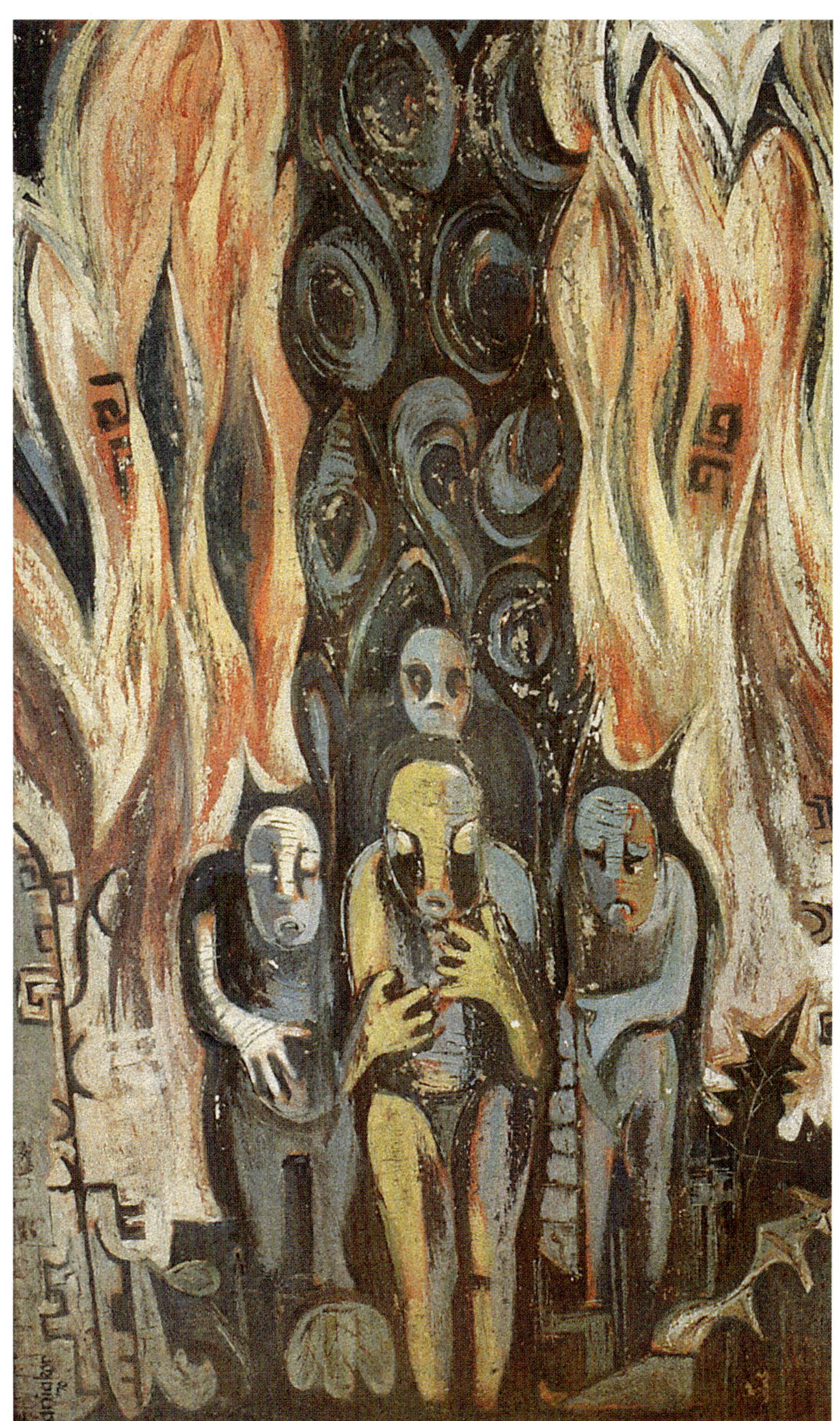

**65**. Chike Aniakọr, *Ọgbanje*, 1976, oil, dimensions unknown. Collection of the artist.

apparently associated with his stays in the United States. Strong black lines tend to outline the main figures or features, with thinner parallel lines that are straight or curved inside and outside these, providing shading and contrast. Internal and external white spaces make the black lines stand out. Arms are sometimes long and outstretched, adding an elegance to the figures, and hands are accentuated, as if Aniakọr was creating messages with them. He has told Ikwuemesi that upraised hands in some of his art symbolize innocence.[34] Faces in his illustrations are usually barely suggested and rarely smile. Sometimes figures are filled in with unorganized dots or rows of them, *ntukpọ* in *uli* parlance, but it is not always clear whether Aniakọr is consciously drawing from *uli* or whether they simply represent dots, or even dots in some European art tradition. This, of course, is always a difficulty with some *uli* designs that are found universally in the world. To me, some of Aniakọr's art has a "busy" quality.[35]

While Aniakọr's ink drawings and his ink and watercolors are generally two-dimensional, a few of his oils, such as *Sacrifice*, show three-dimensional qualities, particularly in the contrast of foreground figures and background designs. But deep three-dimensionality is generally absent from his art.

On a fellowship in oral African literature at Howard University, Washington, D.C., in the 1995–96

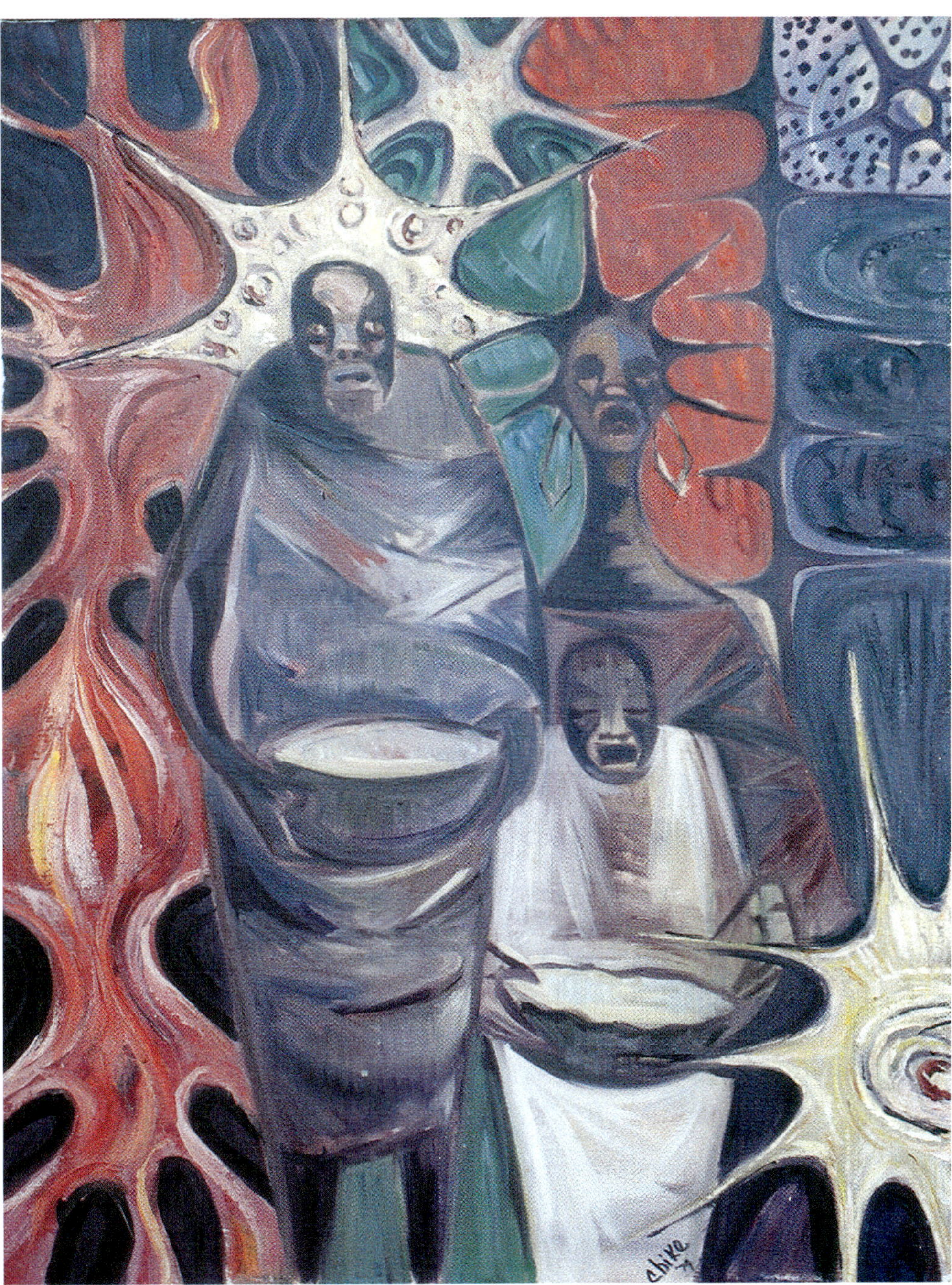

66. Chike Aniakọr, *Sacrifice*, 1974, oil on canvas. 101.6 × 77.5 cm. Collection of Simon Ottenberg.

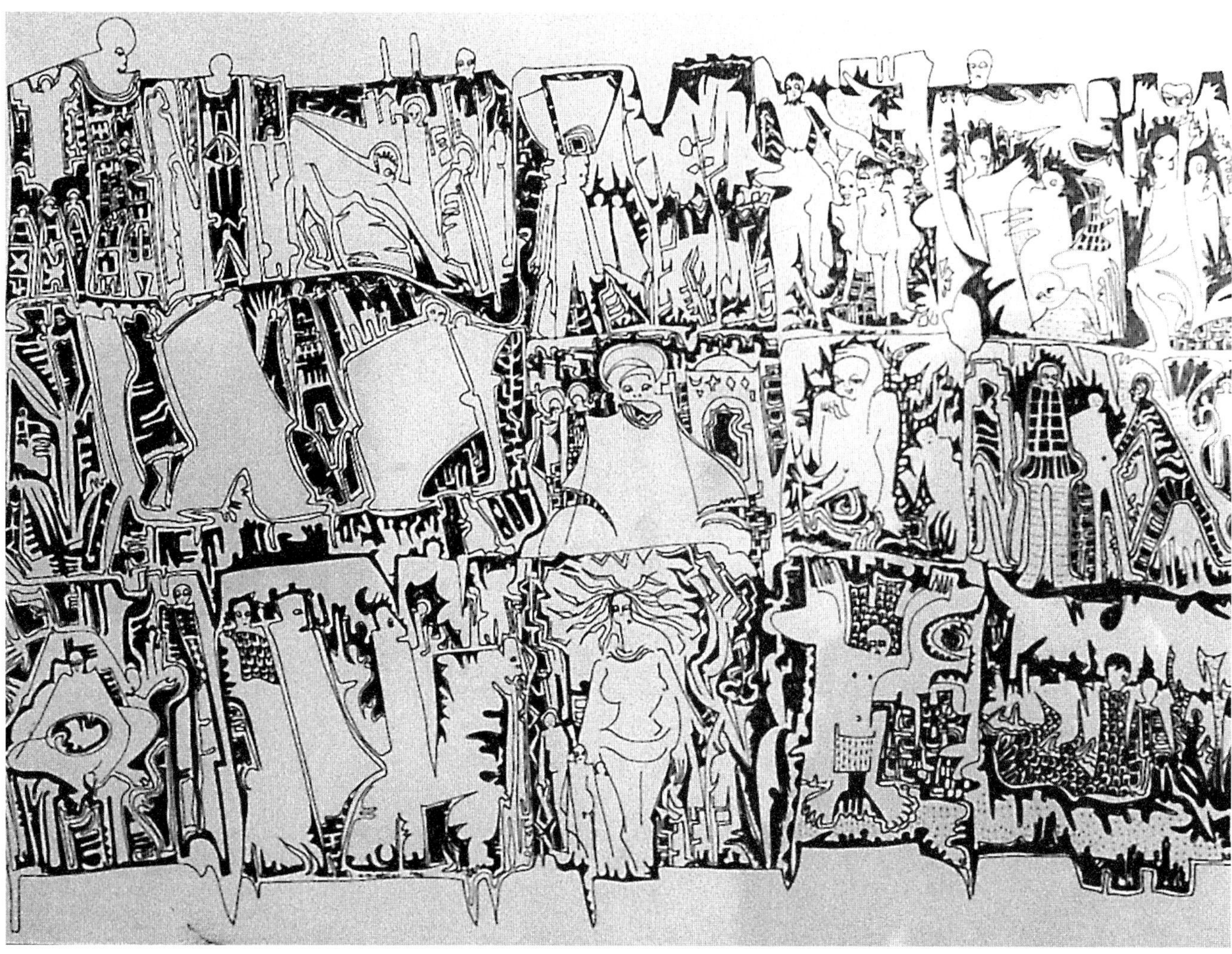

academic year, Aniakọr made associations between his visual art and African narratives, including Igbo minstrel songs. Here he sees his art as involving visual analogs of narratives. The lines in his work have become associated with sound. White areas are areas of no tension, no stress; the inked areas are stressed regions, as the tension-no tension contrast occurs in narratives (figs. 68–71). He calls his current art "visual epitaphs." This refers to the general idea of African narrative, not to specific ones, and, unlike some postmodern art, there are no actual written words in his art, although it has elements of what he calls "visual sound." The analogy goes further. He creates sections of a work with heavy black ink wash lines, then filling each one in with pen and black ink, creating linear elements, outlined human faces and figures, buildings, and other elements, perhaps leaving part of a section empty. He sees a section as equivalent to several stanzas, as stanzas are grouped into narrative sections by African minstrels. He calls his sections "visual containers" and notes that *uli* wall murals are often divided into sections. Even the larger wash lines sometimes form figures, with the pen and ink work within them. The human figures in a work are like narrative characters, like a visual theater in which each player depends on the others. As we have seen, making interconnections between different art forms is not unusual for Igbo and other African artists.

**67**. Chike Aniakọr, *Reminiscences,* 1974, pen and ink on paper, dimensions unknown. Collection of the artist.

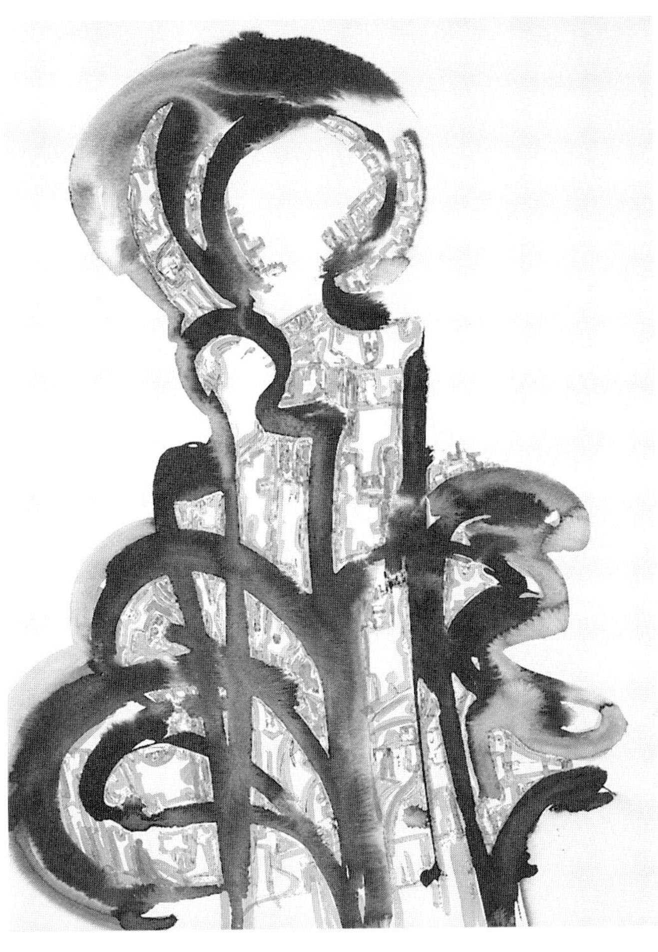

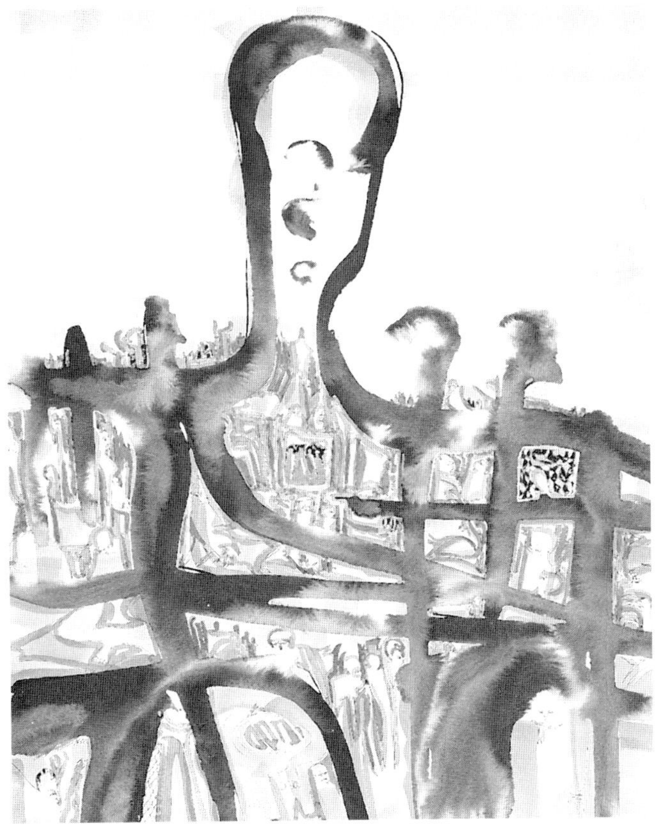

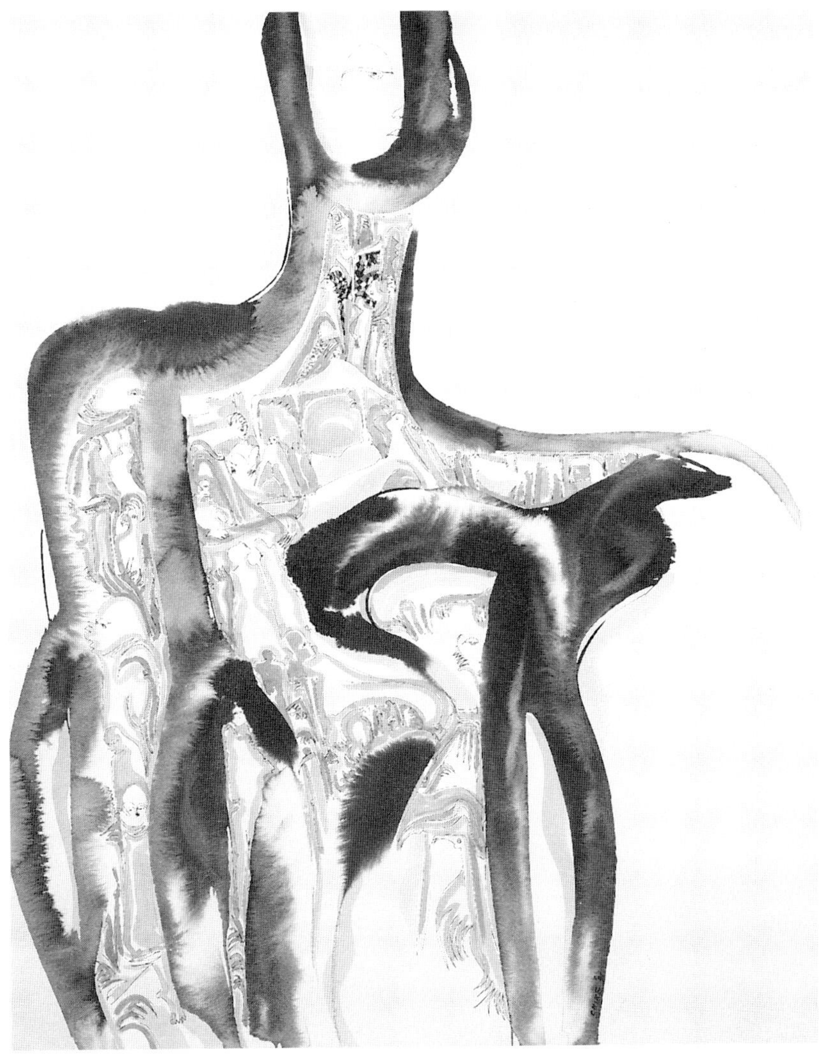

**68** (**TOP LEFT**). Chike Aniakọr, *Of Collective Memory*, 1996, pen, ink, and wash on paper. 60.8 × 45.7 cm. Collection of the National Museum of African Art. Photo: Franko Khoury.

**69** (**TOP RIGHT**). Chike Aniakọr, *Allegory of Power*, 1996, pen, ink, wash, and watercolor on paper. 61 × 45.7 cm. Collection of the National Museum of African Art. Photo: Franko Khoury.

**70** (**BOTTOM LEFT**). Chike Aniakọr, *Reminiscences Revisited,* 1996, pen, ink, and wash on paper. 60.9 × 45.7 cm. Collection of the National Museum of African Art. Photo: Franko Khoury.

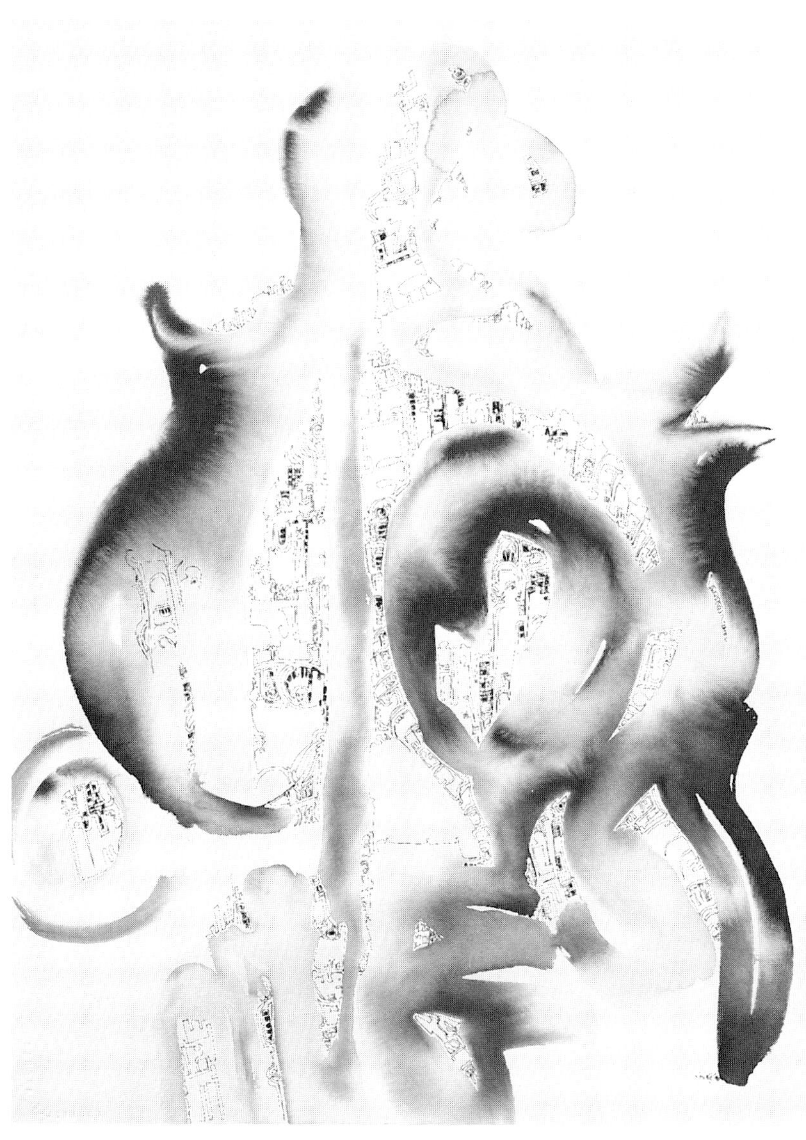



## EXHIBITIONS

Aniakọr has not exhibited as widely as Uche Okeke, yet his work, particularly his drawings, are not unknown. He has had at least five solo exhibitions: three in the United States, one in Lagos, and another in Port Harcourt in Nigeria. He frequently takes part in group exhibitions at the University of Nigeria, Nsukka, and in Enugu and Lagos.[36] He has regularly exhibited as a member of a group of thirteen artists (up to fifteen by 1996), who comprise the AKA Circle of Exhibiting Artists, showing annually in Enugu and Lagos, beginning in 1986.[37] The AKA artists do not all share a single art style or philosophy, although a number of them have or have had an association with the University of Nigeria, Nsukka. Among the seven artists in this book, not only Chike Aniakọr, but Tayọ Adenaike, El Anatsui, and Obiọra Udechukwu are members. This is a popular group with the public, and Aniakọr, as well as the other artists, receives good exposure.

## ANIAKỌR'S WRITINGS

Aniakọr's frequent introductions to the annual catalogues of the AKA Circle of Exhibiting Artists form part of a larger commentary of his on contemporary Nigerian art.[38] While not the political promoter of this art that Uche Okeke is, he has written a response to the Nigerian government's 1988 statement on cultural policy. In this response he indicates the importance of government art policy for developing countries, yet is critical that policy often does not end in results.[39] There are useful comments on issues in the relationships of artists and government and on government manipulation of the arts.

In another paper, Aniakọr raises the question of the relationship between traditional and contemporary art.[40] Opting for the selective use of tradition combined with elements from contemporary society, he notes that there are as many responses to tradition as there are contemporary Nigerian artists. In another paper, he reviews the art of El Anatsui, the Nsukka wood sculptor.[41] In the 1995 Skoto Gallery catalogue, Aniakọr discusses traditional *uli* designs and their relationships to contemporary art in a thoughtful and sensitive manner.[42] His AKA exhibition introductions raise questions as to the importance and uses of the artist's social vision. He asks: "Can art serve as visual markers in the creative rhythm of time?" and what kind of reality does art construct?[43] The importance of good craft as well as good themes in art is stressed, and he asks why there is such a continued reliance on tradition in much of the AKA artists' work if they do not live in traditional worlds? Aniakọr's writings on contemporary Nigerian art do not show him to have been influenced by postmodern thought, despite his years in the United States, and they are jargon-free and thoughtful works.

His writings on traditional Igbo arts are substantial. He does not suffer from the tendency to employ an Igbo subcultural parochialism, and his knowledge of the variations in the arts of different Igbo areas is considerable. He made very substantial contributions to the major work on Igbo art that he co-authored with Herbert M. Cole, which accompanied a comprehensive exhibition.[44] His article on Igbo aesthetics discusses Igbo concepts of beauty and the way Igbo aesthetic referents are drawn from animal and plant forms.[45] He sees correlations between skill, the time it takes to produce a work of art, the wealth and social status involved in the art, and the size of the material employed. These correlations are hardly absent elsewhere, but he shows their application to Igbo art. His comments in the Skoto Gallery brochure on traditional *uli*, mentioned above, form a beautifully condensed interpretation. Aniakọr's writings on Igbo architecture have already been mentioned. He has also written on Igbo masquerades, carved doors, and *ikenga* wood figures and has published a useful survey of the state of Igbo art studies.[46]

Like Okeke, Aniakọr is also a poet, having written a small body of work, much of it published in the United States as an outgrowth of his time there, as in the case of his illustrations.[47] It is not surprising that he is also poetic; I have already indicated the importance of poetry to the Nsukka artists. Much of his poetry refers to traditional Igbo life, objects, and experience, for example, the poems published in *African Arts*, where there are references to yams, the *iroko* tree, the market, dancers, and spiritual figures.[48] A number of poems relate to modern experience, particularly his later ones, so that images of a street newspaper hawker appear: "You / that hawks gossips / from street to street, / How many words did you spit out today?"[49] There is a poem referring to being at Heathrow Airport, another to flying in an airplane, yet another to boarding an aircraft in Nigeria. There is a cynical one about Nigerian university life, ending: "Who said that the ivory / tower / was part of God's creation? / If it was, then / God created the Tower, / took away the Ivory / to complete his other / Projects."[50]

Other poems refer to the decline of tradition, such as "What Happened": "Do you now prefer / the tingle of accordions / to the drumbeat of / the village gongs?"[51] There are poems of personal hope, such as "Heavensgate," yet others indicate despair.[52] In contrast to his recent visual art, there are few political references in the poetry.

Aniakọr's poetry reveals a man firmly embedded in everyday Nigerian and Igbo life, occasionally expressing nostalgia for the past and often reveling in Igbo culture. I have a better sense of him as a person from his poetry, as complexities of thought and ideas are more easily conveyed in this form than in visual art through metaphor, metonymy, and other tropes. I have little emotional reaction to his visual art, except for a few of his oils; the art seems a bit distant, yet to the point. But his poems evoke in me various feelings.


## CONCLUSION

Aniakọr's visual art is consistent with much of the work of the Nsukka artists, including his strong emphasis on drawing. He makes use of *uli* principles of linearity and space, employing specific *uli* motifs at times. He draws on Igbo cultural life in his art and on urban life and the condition of the Nigerian nation. To some extent his early work resembles that of Okeke, but his art shows the growth of independent styles, and it is more concerned with current affairs than Okeke's. Aniakọr's preoccupation with Igbo art historical scholarship and teaching and his association with his hometown of Abatete inform his art. He is also consistent with other Nsukka artists in his interest in writing poetry. As in the case of Okeke, his art is deeply embedded in the Nigerian world.

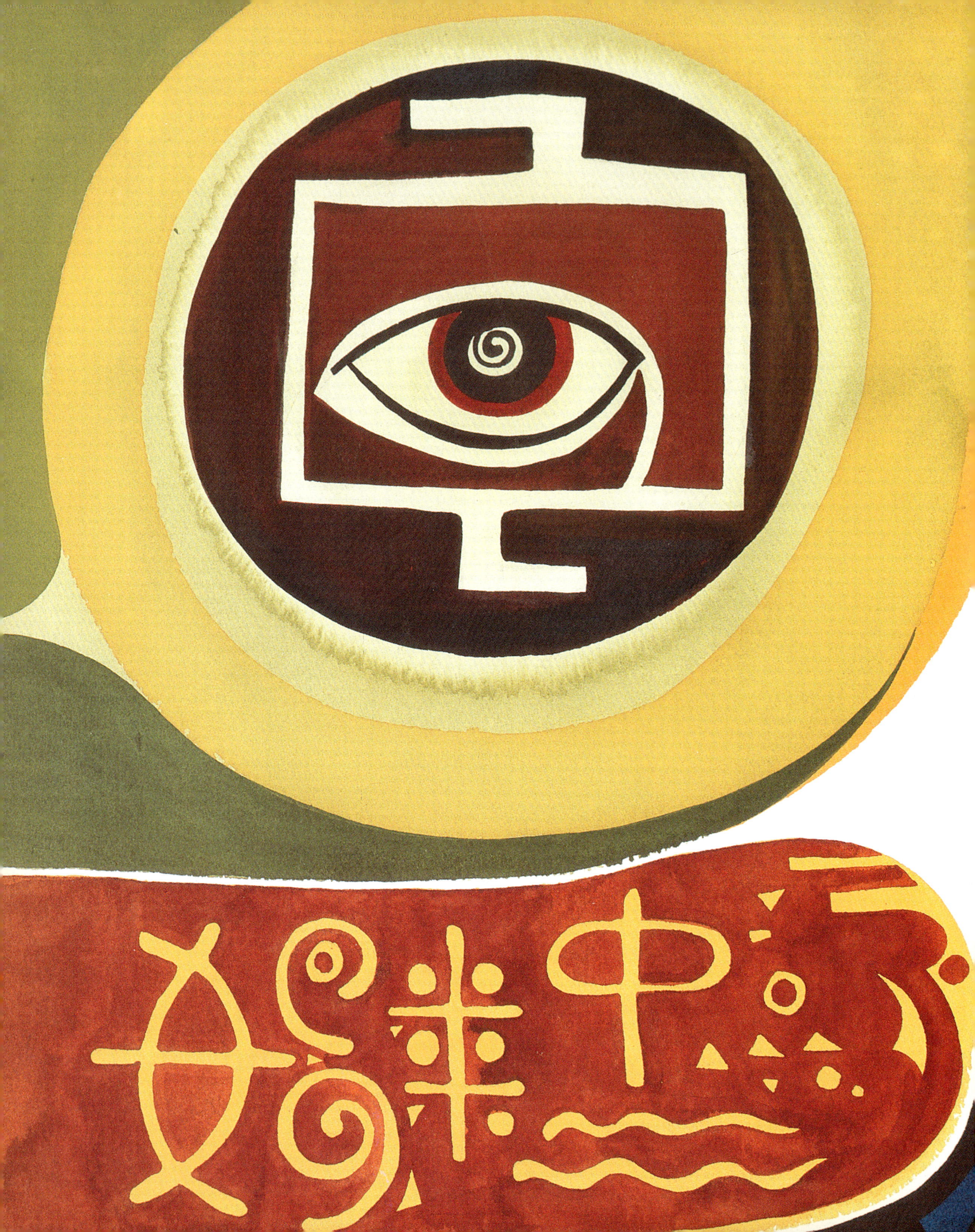

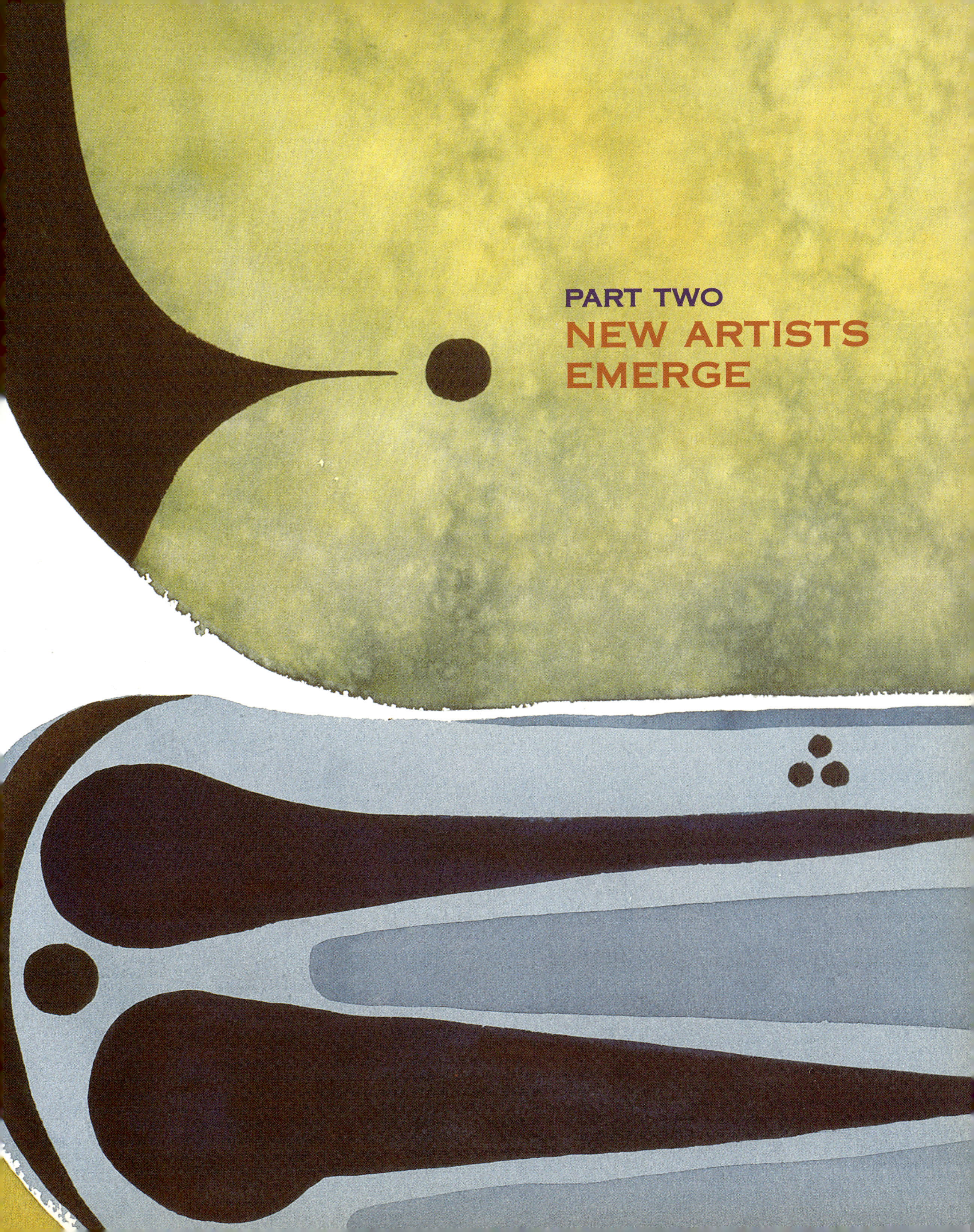

PART TWO
NEW ARTISTS
EMERGE

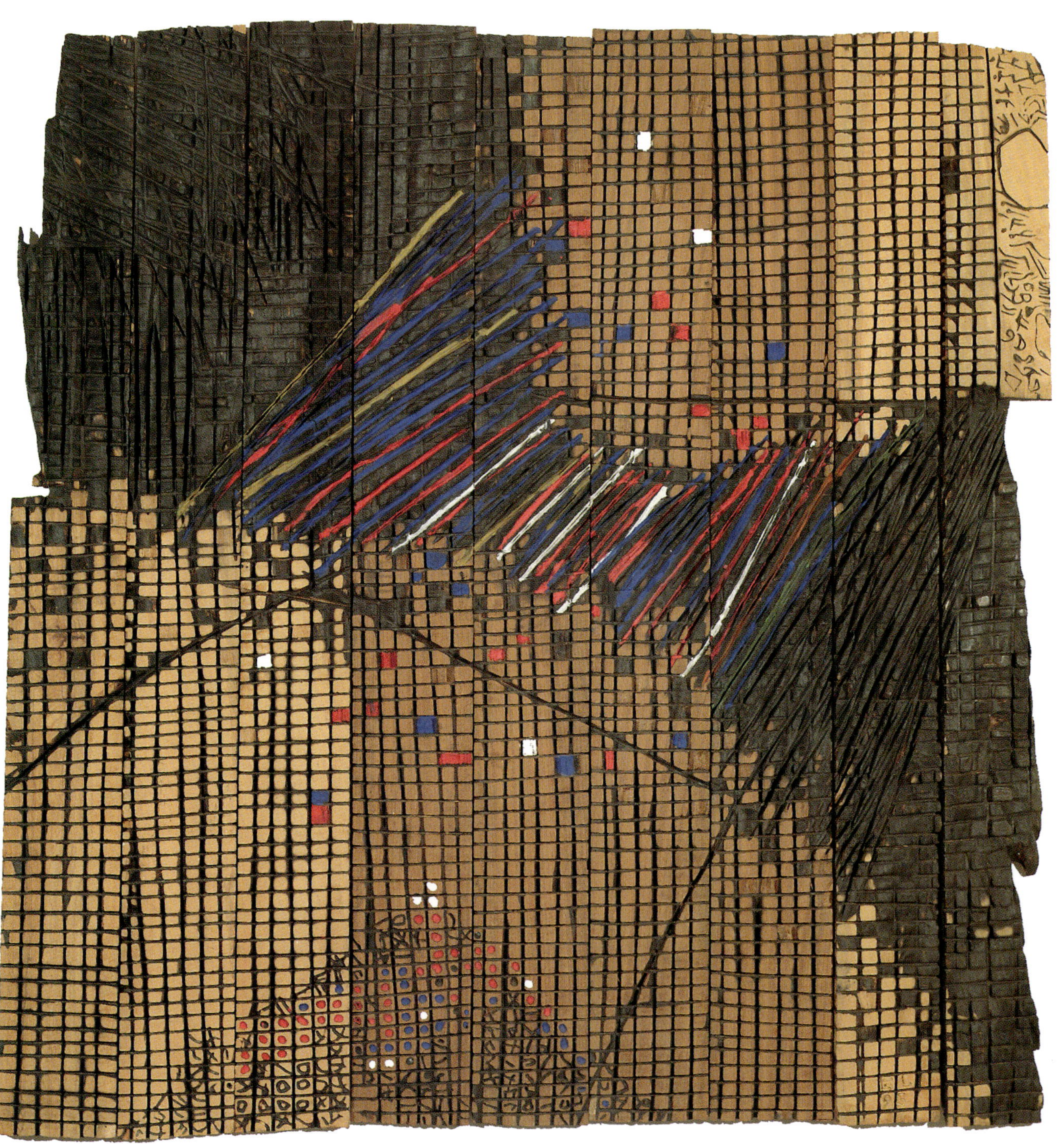

# 6. NIGERIAN CONTEMPORARY ART

## 1970 TO THE PRESENT

Despite the overwhelming reality of economic decline, despite unimaginable poverty, despite wars, malnutrition, disease and political instability, African cultural production grows apace: popular literature, oral narratives and poetry, dance, drama, music and visual art all thrive.

KWAME ANTHONY APPIAH [1]

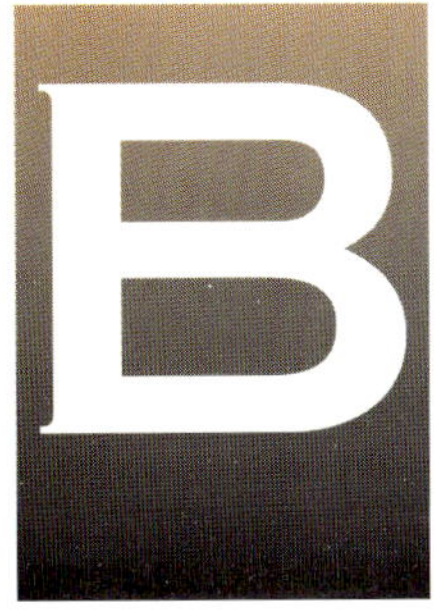

**B**efore discussing the remaining five artists, it is important to indicate the major features of Nigerian contemporary art from the 1970s to the present—the milieu in which they have lived and created.[2] The seeds sown by the contemporary artists trained in the 1950s and 1960s bore fruit as the Zaria artists spread out in the country, especially in the south, to teach, create, and exhibit art and to put pressure on the government to support the arts.

### INCREASING NUMBERS AND GROWING GENERATIONS

By the mid-1990s there were probably some two thousand individuals trained in contemporary art in Nigeria, many attempting to practice either full- or part-time, an impressive number compared to earlier times, though not particularly striking in a Nigerian population of more than 80 million. By this time, contemporary art had become an accepted profession for men, and women were appearing in it in slowly growing numbers.

The increase in art professionals relates to the growth of existing art departments, as at Nsukka, Ile-Ifẹ, Yaba, Zaria, as well as the development of new programs at the University of Benin, Auchi Polytechnic, the Institute of Management and Technology, Enugu, and Abraka in Bendel State and at some colleges of education.[3] Increased student interest has been fueled by an expansion of art teaching in secondary schools and the enlistment efforts of postsecondary institutions. The decline in the Nigerian economy does not appear to have slowed the numbers. A new generation of contemporary artists, largely trained in the 1970s, became known by the 1980s, including the late Gani Odutokun at Ahmadu Bello University, Zaria, Kolade Ọshinọwọ at Yaba College of Technology, Obiọra Udechukwu at the University of Nigeria, Nsukka, David Dale at Lagos, Dele Jẹgẹdẹ at the University of Lagos (now at Indiana State University), Mọyọ Okediji at Ọbafemi Awolowo University (now at Wellesley College), and Nsikak Essien at the Institute of Management and Technology, Enugu (now painting privately). El Anatsui of Ghana, trained at Kumasi in the late 1960s, has been at the University of Nigeria, Nsukka, since 1975. These artists each developed their own style, increasing the diversity of contemporary Nigerian art.

Some of these artists were involved in training the next group of artists in the 1980s, who include Bọlaji Campbell at Ọbafemi Awolowo University, Ile-Ifẹ, Tayọ Adenaike in advertising at Enugu, Jerry Buhari at Zaria, Ọlu Ọguibe at the University of South Florida, Tampa, Sokari Douglas Camp in London, Ndidi Dike at Owerri and Lagos, and Lara Ige and Olu Amoda at Yaba College of Technology. Again, these artists have moved in new directions, intensifying the already complex picture of Nigerian contemporary art, and a fourth generation now begins to make its mark. A fascinating general history of these artists awaits exploration. Most of the artists trained since the 1950s are still alive, making for fruitful interactions between members of different generations.

The art of most artists from the early 1970s on continues to draw from indigenous cultures, their own or others, sometimes blended with art about the contemporary scene. Past cultures are still powerful strings pulling on contemporary Nigerian artists, though what an individual artist chooses to draw from in the past and how this is done vary immensely. Purely abstract or abstract impressionist art is rare. Tradition still exists—strong in some areas, weak in others, but reworked and reinvented everywhere. It is part of the experience of virtually all artists; few do not have ties to their more traditional world and their home communities. That Nigerian languages are still actively spoken in Nigeria is another indication of the continuing value of the past. Yet contemporary art media are largely of Euro/American origin, as are exhibition styles and rituals of gallery openings and the considerable use of English by artists. Even the cartoon format draws from Euro/America, though the topics are local.[4]

## INCREASING ART MARKETS AND PATRONAGE

By the 1990s there were at least fifteen private contemporary art galleries in Lagos and several others in Ibadan, Oṣogbo, and Enugu. The National Museum, Onikan, Lagos, the center for exhibitions and collections of traditional art, has allocated two gallery spaces for contemporary art. However, Ọlọidi cautions that the increase in galleries and artists has led to some mediocre exhibits, something that I have observed myself.[5]

The federal government's involvement in contemporary art has increased as a result of the recognition of its value. In 1988 the government issued a report on cultural policy for Nigeria (see Chapter 5).[6] This did not lead to major changes, but it did direct discussion to the role of the government in the arts. The Federal Department of Culture began collecting contemporary art in the 1950s, which it exhibited at the First Economic Summit of the Organization of African States in Lagos in 1980 at the National Theatre, a huge arts complex constructed for FESTAC '77.[7] The collection was reorganized in 1981 as the National Gallery of Modern Art (now the National Gallery of Art); it has been on display there ever since, albeit, until recently, it has been much neglected.[8] The government's involvement has also been channeled through its National Council for Arts and Culture, which controls the National Gallery of Craft and Design, an institution that for many years has shown exhibitions of contemporary work near the National Theatre. Some  contemporary artists, including Bisi Fakẹyẹ, have had workshops under government auspices at the nearby National Studios of Modern Art. Yet the government has never played the strong role in directing the arts as occurred in Senegal, especially under Léopold Senghor between 1960 and 1980.[9] Contemporary art started  later in Senegal than in Nigeria, grew rapidly with Senghor's support, but has suffered from government overdirection. Due to the lack of a specific art policy in Nigeria, no reaction against government policy has occurred, as it has among Dakar artists. Rather, Nigerian artists, art historians, and others plead for greater government aid. The Nigerian pattern is that of a number of government agencies that operate rather independently, creating a diffuse general policy toward contemporary art.[10]

An important addition to the Lagos art scene is the Didi Museum begun in 1983.[11] Led by prominent chiefs, businessmen, and professionals, it regularly holds exhibitions of contemporary art and has a small collection of its own. Such a private museum is unusual in Africa, where most museums are government institutions.

With the growing number of artists, it is not surprising that the number of group exhibitions relative to solo exhibitions is increasing, though retrospective shows of well-established artists occur, such as those for Bruce Onobrakpẹya, Uche Okeke, and Obiọra Udechukwu, all in 1993 in Lagos. Yet young artists still occasionally have solo exhibitions.

Among foreign cultural centers, the Goethe Institut, as early as 1964, and the Italian Cultural Institute in Lagos, which closed in 1994, have been most active in displaying contemporary Nigerian art, increasingly to African audiences.[12] Others, such as Alliance Française, have held important exhibitions, while the British Council remains active in contemporary art in upcountry cities. Some state government centers sponsor exhibitions of contemporary art, as, for example, the Lagos State Council for Arts and Culture and the Imo State Mbari Centre at Owerri. Arts festivals, which began at regional levels in the 1950s, continue with the reorganization of Nigeria from regions to more than forty states. One has been held at Enugu almost every year since the early 1950s (except for the war period).[13] National Arts Festivals were held in Lagos in 1970, Ibadan in 1971, and Kaduna in 1972. The creation of government buildings and roads for the new states has led to new public art. This replaces the federal impetus of the 1950s and 1960s, now declined, though the ongoing move of the federal capital from Lagos to Abuja has developed a need for new public art there.

In the 1980s and 1990s, with the increase in the number of artists, a variety of private art organizations have arisen to supplement the Society of Nigerian Artists and its chapters. The best established is the AKA Circle of Exhibiting Artists; others include the Committee on Relevant Art (CORA), Visual Orchestra, Coalition of Nigerian Artists (CONA), the Pan-African Circle of Artists (PACA), The Eye, Okanga (in Enugu State), and the Ifẹ artists. Annual national prize competitions in painting and other media occur in Lagos through the private Art and Arts Conference Forum (AACF), with awards provided by senior Nigerian artists, chiefs, and businesses. And New Currents: Avant Garde Nigerian Art has held an annual exhibition of selected artists in Lagos from 1993, although the art is rarely avant-garde.

The expansion in contemporary art is associated with changes in patronage. According to the judgment of artists I have talked to, about 50 percent of Nigerian contemporary art is now sold within the country to Nigerians. The percentage sold to expatriates in Nigeria has decreased from about 90 percent in the 1960s, although, because of the greater volume of art sold today, the quantity has probably increased. The Nsukka artists are pleased with the growing Nigerian market. At the same time, the Nigerian artists' overseas markets in Europe and America are increasing, particularly in Germany, Britain, and the United States.[14] The increase in domestic sales over the past twenty-five years has come about through the patronage of wealthy Nigerian chiefs, professionals, business persons, government workers, and some military personnel. University academics have acquired collections through artist friends and students. Despite the economic problems, there is an impressive number of wealthy individuals, both the cause and the beneficiaries of the economic difficulties. It is becoming fashionable to collect contemporary art, as it has been for years to purchase Mercedes automobiles and to build elegant homes in Lagos and in one's hometown. Some Nigerian collectors are quite knowledgeable about the art they collect, while others collect principally for status. Art advisors have arisen in Lagos to advise collectors and assist artists to arrange exhibitions at galleries.[15] Ọlọidi writes that by the 1980s the salon for art sales at private homes had come back again, directed by Nigerians, and not as in the 1960s by expatriates.[16] By 1990 corporate sponsorship of the arts was also increasing. Prices continue to risedue to both inflation and an increasing demand for the work of better-known artists.[17] These features are similar, on a small scale, to the Euro/American art market experience, except for the lack of auction houses, whether arising primarily from internal evolution or from diffusion of outside models; probably both are involved. The growing contemporary Nigerian art market seems to take form to meet needs that are universal in the art world.

## ART CRITICISM

There is increasing art criticism, reviews of exhibits, and discussions of art in newspapers in Nigeria, particularly in Lagos, though some publications that regularly carried reviews, being liberal, have been suppressed by the government. The level of art criticism remains poor, though increased journalistic attention to contemporary art has brought more interest in and some prestige to the arts and has resulted in greater sales.[18]

## SPECIAL EXHIBITIONS AND ART EVENTS

The growth of contemporary art in Nigeria has been stimulated by some special events, such as FESTAC '77 in Lagos, which included an exhibition by more than seventy-five contemporary Nigerian artists as well as those from other African countries.[19] Some artistic events or festivals have also been held elsewhere in the country. The twenty-fifth anniversary of Nigeria's independence in 1985 involved an exhibition of contemporary Nigerian art in Lagos, Owerri, and Kaduna.[20] In 1989 the Society of Nigerian Artists held an extensive exhibition in Lagos to celebrate the organization's twenty-fifth anniversary.[21] Other significant exhibitions were held in the 1970–95 period.

In 1993 the Second International Symposium on Contemporary Nigerian Art was held in Lagos, like the first in 1976, arranged by artists at Nsukka.[22] In 1978 a conference on "The Interrelationships of the Arts" took place at the University of Lagos.[23] Both events brought together artists, critics, art historians, educationists, and other scholars in Nigeria and a few from elsewhere. They were notable in the history of contemporary art in stimulating discussion and interaction.

## ART CENTERS

The centers of contemporary art in Nigeria outside of the Lagos gallery scene are now at Nigerian universities, colleges of education, and technical colleges, where the majority of the artists are located, though there are notable exceptions, such as Bruce Onobrakpẹya in Lagos and the Oṣogbo artists. While the setting is academic, what the artists create is not necessarily academic art in the Euro/American sense of the term. The existence of art training at postsecondary schools focuses differing art styles around different establishments, as has occurred at the University of Nigeria, Nsukka. Art departments at these teaching institutions have tended to hire their own graduates, a practice that reinforces artistic distinctions among programs. The question "Is there a Nigerian art?"—which occupied artists, scholars, and art critics in the 1950–70 period—is no longer of much interest today, with the acceptance of different styles and "schools" of artists in the country.

One interesting multidisciplinary art center in the style of the former Mbari centers existed at Ile-Ifẹ between 1968 and 1976. Sponsored by the Institute of African Studies at the then University of Ifẹ, with financial support from the Rockefeller Foundation, it was led by the artist Solomon Irein Wangboje of that university and was called Ori Olokun.[24] It closed in 1976. The ethnomusicologist Akin Euba was in charge of music, Peggy Harper of dance-drama, Wangboje of art and design, and Michael Crowder was an advisor. It held art exhibitions, put on dramas and musical events, and attracted well-established artists such as Bruce Onobrakpẹya and some Oṣogbo artists such as Rufus Ogundele and Jimoh Buraimoh. Ori Olokun helped lead to the development of new artists, including Ademọla Williams and Tijani Mayakiri. Artists were encouraged to employ local materials and to draw from traditional culture, which in that area is Yoruba. The center was particularly innovative in printmaking and batik.

This project was followed in the 1980s by an art program at Ọbafemi Awolowo University (formerly the University of Ifẹ) that parallels the *uli* concerns of the Nsukka artists. Called Ọnaism, a term based on the Yoruba concept of *ọna*, referring to design, motif, or decoration, Ọnaism became a focus of the art of some Yoruba of southwestern Nigeria, especially those trained or teaching at Ile-Ifẹ. A leading devotee of Ọnaism and its founder has been the artist Moyọ Okediji.[25] It is not surprising that other contemporary African artists, in addition to those that employ *uli*, draw from their own culture's design system.

The University of Nigeria at Nsukka continues in the *uli* tradition to this day, broadening it with the use of designs from *nsibidi, mbari,* and elsewhere, without a radical change in its orientation to art. At Ahmadu Bello University, Zaria, the art program, with a faculty of diverse Nigerian cultural backgrounds, since the mid-1970s has emphasized individual expression, not collective cultural inheritance. The personality of the artists is to be reflected beyond cultural and national influences, "the global artist, making universalistic art."[26] The Yaba College of Technology, Lagos, on the other hand, developed a sophisticated genre style, which, however, is not a direct descendant of Kenneth Murray's genre artists.[27] The Auchi Polytechnic art program has become strong in the use of color in painting, particularly in acrylic and watercolor. The students, faculty, and graduates in each of these programs have a somewhat different language of art discourse, frequently with differing artistic interests. Yet all make use of basic European categories of art forms and most employ Euro/American media.

## SOCIAL AND POLITICAL CRITICISM

Although there is now a considerable amount of contemporary art in Nigeria that is critical of federal policies, practices, and the behavior of its military politicians, and the Nsukka artists are involved in this genre, the visual arts have not generally suffered from direct oppressive government tactics, as Nigerian writers, journalists, newspapers, and magazines increasingly have in recent years. But visual artists have less popularity and are less well known than some Nigerian writers, such as Wọle Ṣoyinka, the late Ken Saro-Wiwa, and the musician Fẹla. Musicians and writers reach a wider audience in Nigeria and overseas. Nigerian visual artists create social and political works on various themes, which sell along with their other art, but without much impact on the political process. Yet the artists often remain hopeful that they will have influence in the Nigerian world; they clearly have a need to express their feelings of frustration over conditions in their country.

Much contemporary Nigerian art remains in a nonmodernism period, if we employ Western art historical terms; only a little of it has been influenced by Euro/American modernism. And few Nigerian contemporary artists are moving into the postmodernist stage. This is partly an issue of center-periphery relationships in the larger world, but it is also a matter of the interest that Nigerian contemporary artists hold in their traditional culture and art and in working out of art fields on their own ground without reference to Euro/America. They are sometimes hesitant to take giant experimental leaps, especially into postmodernism, so much a Euro/American creation, seemingly foreign to much of Nigerian experience. Many Nigerian artists do not know much about postmodernism and have been little exposed to its art and theory. When they go abroad they may be preoccupied with creating their own art, free from teaching and other Nigerian distractions.

The conservatism of contemporary Nigerian art, from a Euro/American viewpoint, suggests a determination of these artists to find their own way within the context of national and local experience, and not simply to follow Euro/America. The general negative reactions of many Nigerians, including its artists, to Structural Adjustment and other foreign programs, through which some of them have suffered economically along with other Nigerians, do not encourage the acceptance of grand theories from Euro/America. As Ọlọidi writes:

> The fact that Nigeria seems to be about twenty years behind these [Euro/American] artistic currents should not be seen as evidence of creative insensitivity or artistic incapability. Simply, the necessary constraint of culture, the socio-cultural values as well as the economic realities, among some humanistic factors, have not really prepared Nigeria for such art.[28]

Rather, contemporary Nigerian art may best be seen, not in the context of Euro/American postmodernism, but in the framework of third and fourth world contemporary artistic experience, where issues of the role of traditional art and aesthetics vis-à-vis current sociopolitical conditions are major, where economic restraints limit the resources of artists trying to gain knowledge of Euro/American art and theory, and where the market for their art is largely a premodernist market.

## ECONOMIC AND POLITICAL DECLINE AND THE ARTS

Since independence in 1960, Nigeria has gone through a number of coups, having had a democratic government at the federal level for only some eight years; the remaining time the country has been ruled by the military. Since the decline of the Nigerian oil boom by the mid-1980s, before which Nigeria foolishly put most of its efforts into oil, destroying a mixed export and agricultural economy, Nigeria has increasingly suffered from a declining economy, increasing inflation and poverty, corruption of monumental proportions, gangsterism, and a declining infrastructure of roads, water supplies, electricity, communications, health services, and gasoline supplies, in a country that should have been one of the richest and most influential in Africa. There has been a major decrease in government scholarships and support for other forms of foreign travel. The artists, including the Nsukka ones, live daily in this climate of black pessimism in their land, struggling to survive as creators. Their daily lives and their art are continually influenced by the world around them and the immediate factors of low salaries, the scarcity of art supplies, library books, and journals, faculty, student, or staff strikes that close the universities, and so on.

In addition, many of the scholarly journals of the 1970s and early 1980s that had carried articles on contemporary art have gradually ceased publication or publish only irregularly because of high costs and decreasing morale. Even the government-owned *Nigeria Magazine,* almost since its inception a major source for contemporary art, publishes only occasionally and, due to the cost of postage, rarely sends copies overseas. Yet a serious new contemporary art journal, *The Eye,* published at Ahmadu Bello University, began in 1992, associated with The Eye Society of artists.[29] The same year a less scholarly art journal started in Lagos, *Artifacts,* aimed at collectors and the general public. The National Gallery of Art, Lagos, with its new director, Paul Chike Dike, as editor, in 1995 launched *USO: Nigerian Journal of Art,* which contains some articles on contemporary art. *Kurio Africana: Journal of African Art and Criticism,* which several years ago published two excellent issues, largely on contemporary art, but could not arrange to continue, has now been revived. The National Council for Arts and Culture, Lagos, has published books on culture and the economy and decision making in Nigeria, although they appear to have had little impact.[30] Bọlaji Campbell has, with others, edited an interesting collection of papers on the diversity of creativity in Nigeria,[31] and the artist and art historian Moyọ Okediji edited a useful work on what is meant by tradition in African art.[32] The increase in art teaching has led to the publication of a number of new texts for school use, for example, one by the well-known contemporary artist Irein Wangboje.[33]

Recurrent periods of political crises in Nigeria have led exhibitors to cancel or postpone exhibitions, or, if they went on, there have been low domestic sales, as everyone holds onto their money at times of crisis, leading to a cyclical pattern of good and bad times in the contemporary art market correlated with the rise and fall of political tensions. Art teachers' salaries at all educational levels are extremely low, in line with teachers' salaries as a whole. Government interest in the arts is overshadowed by problems in the political and economic spheres.

## OVERSEAS INTERESTS

There is an old pattern of contemporary Nigerian artists leaving Nigeria for Europe, particularly Britain, such as Uzọ Egọnu, Taiwo Jẹgẹdẹ and Sokari Douglas Camp in London. Greg Odo, associated with the Nsukka art group, though not trained in it, is there, and Ọlu Ọguibe lived there for six years before moving to the United States. Other Nigerian artists now teaching in the United States include Moyọ Okediji at Wellesley College, Dele Jẹgẹdẹ at Indiana State University, E. Okechukwu Ọdita at Ohio State University, and Barthosa Nkurumeh at Cheney State University in Pennsylvania. The general situation in Nigeria encourages other artists to leave. The movement of artists out of the country is part of a more general movement, especially to Europe, of artists from many parts of Africa, for increased opportunities and political reasons. *Third Text* in London and *NKA: Journal of Contemporary African Art* in New York have become centers for the interests of overseas Africans, whose contacts with postmodernism and other art theories provide them with perspectives different from those living at home. Overseas Nigerian artists help bring contemporary African art to Euro/America while being spokespersons for artists at home. Even artists living in Nigeria increasingly exhibit in Britain, Germany, the United States, and occasionally in countries such as Cuba, Japan, and South Korea. Despite some Euro/American resistance to their work that decries it as being derivative of Euro/American art, or overly linked to tradition, or not sufficiently linked to the past, or being modern and not postmodern, African artists are slowly having an impact abroad, including those from Nigeria, finding a niche in the Euro/American art world.

## HOPEFUL SIGNS

Surprisingly, despite the negative factors in Nigeria, sales of artworks in the country have been good in recent years, mature artists do have opportunities to go abroad, exhibitions are held, works sold help to supplement teaching and other salaries, and the contemporary art world appears to be still expanding. How much better it might be if political and economic conditions in Nigeria were to improve!

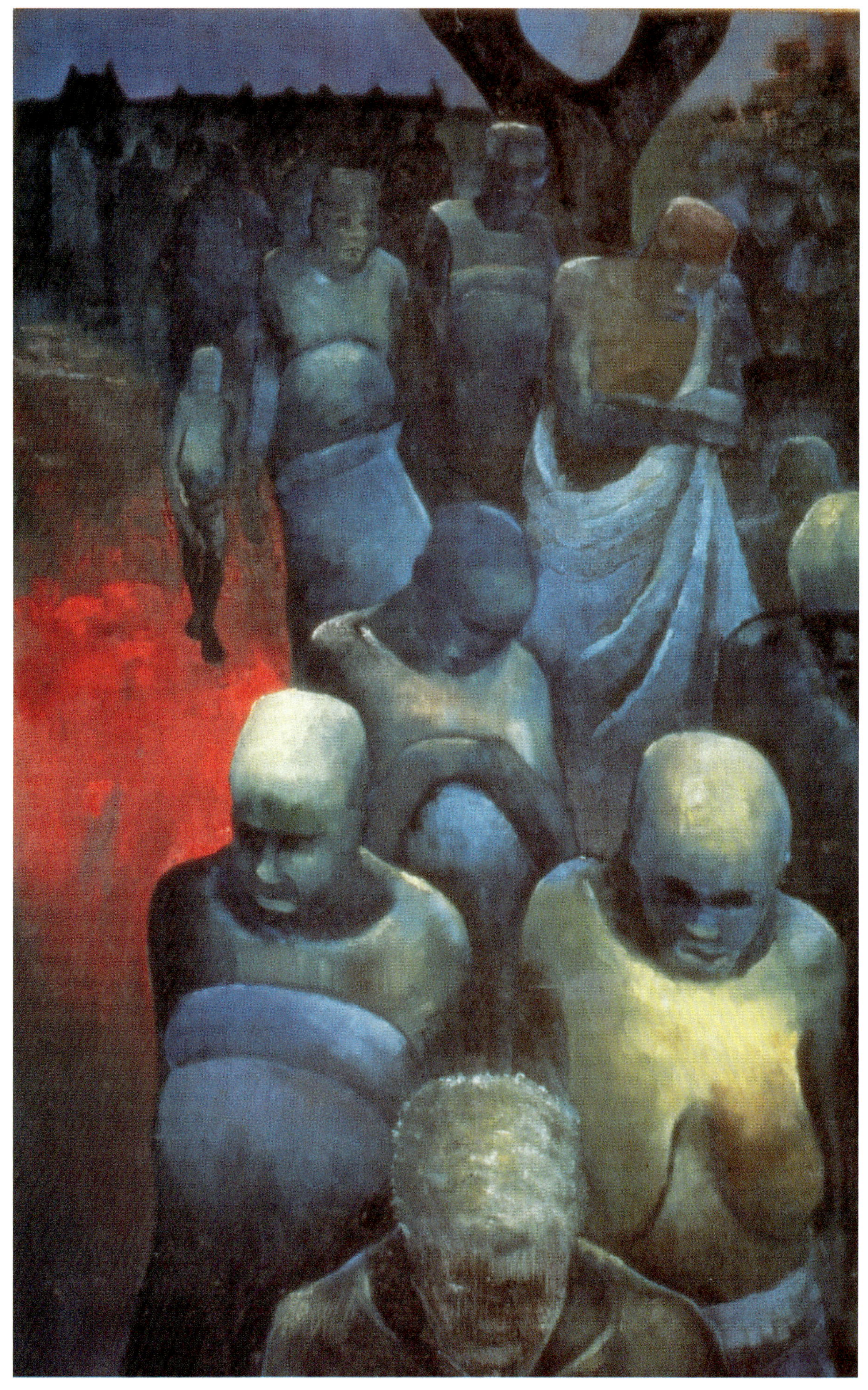

# 7. OBIỌRA UDECHUKWU

## I: GROWTH, LYRICAL SYMBOLISM, AND WAR

An analysis of Igbo drawing and painting reveals that space, line, pattern, brevity and spontaneity seem to be the pillars on which the whole tradition rests. It is these same qualities that I strive, both intuitively and intellectually, to assimilate in my work.

OBIỌRA UDECHUKWU [1]

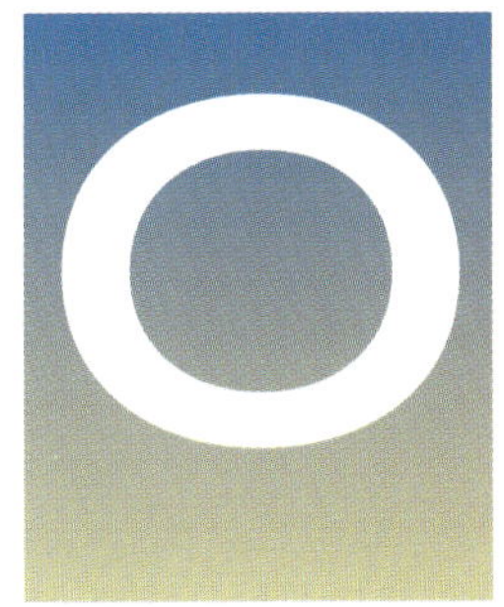

biọra Udechukwu has inherited the mantle of his teacher Uche Okeke.[2] He is a dominant figure today among the Nsukka artists and, with El Anatsui, the best known internationally (fig. 72). Udechukwu is a highly regarded Nigerian artist who creates in a range of two-dimensional media, with a rich background of experience in drawing. Highly productive, he frequently exhibits in solo and group exhibitions, writes critiques and commentaries on contemporary Nigerian arts, has substantial gifts as a poet, and is a person of wide scholarly interests. A strong advocate of the employment of *uli*, he makes more and more use of *nsibidi* motifs, employing these two in creating commentaries on Nigerian life that are satiric and pointed. In recent years his work has become more philosophical, and he has become frustrated and disillusioned over the Nigerian scene.

### EARLY DAYS

Born in 1946 in the Igbo market city of Ọnitsha, where his mother still has a flat, Udechukwu's home is at Agulu, where he, his mother, and his siblings have a home. Agulu, not far from Ọnitsha, nor from Nimo where Uche Okeke lives, shares cultural features with Nimo. Udechukwu lived and studied in Ọnitsha, but he has maintained ties with the more rural Agulu. Knowing both the modernity of Ọnitsha and rural Agulu has shaped his life and art.

Though his parents were not artists, Udechukwu's father was a role model in terms of his son's taking on

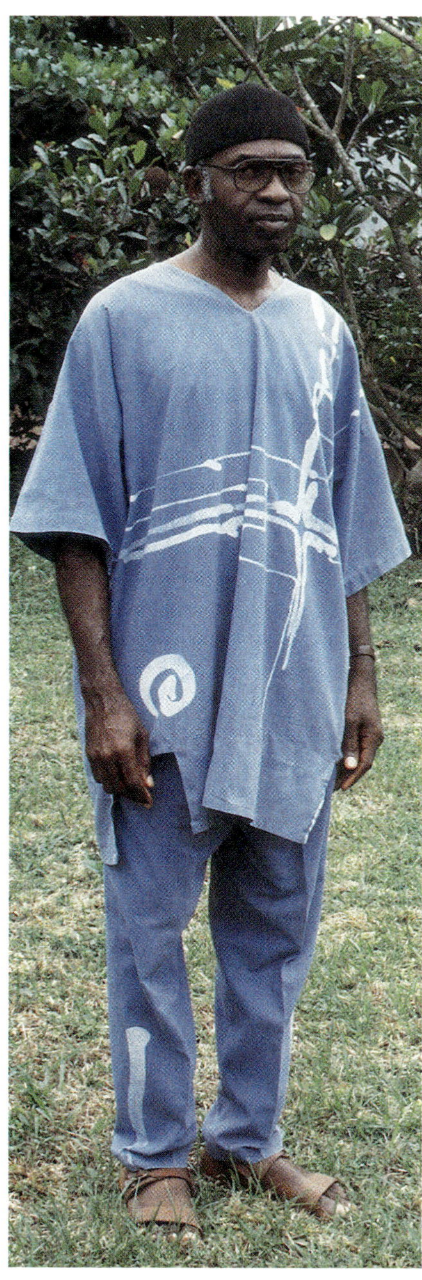

**72.** Obiọra Udechukwu in the garden of his Nsukka home, June 1995.

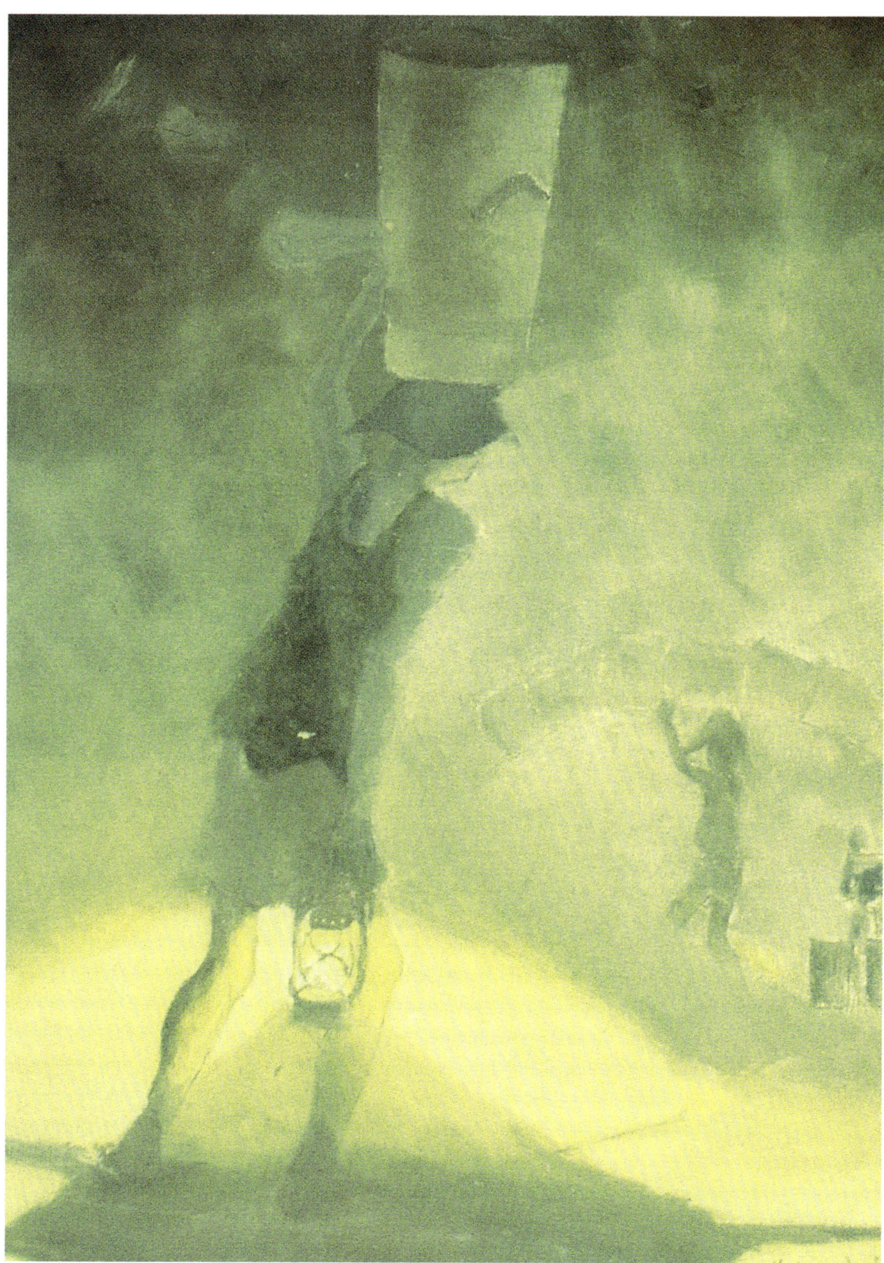

**73.** Obiọra Udechukwu, *Nightsoilman,* 1964, oil on board. 43 × 33.8 cm.

Collection and photo: the artist.

responsibilities and acting maturely. He was fortunate to have had art teachers in both primary and secondary school, unusual for contemporary Nigerian artists of his generation. His primary school teacher, Joseph Eze, at Central School, Ọnitsha, an Anglican institution, was trained to teach art in Nigeria.[3] Udechukwu drew and also created objects out of crepe and plywood; he copied published illustrations and Eze's drawings. His urge to draw, he has told me, "came from nature"; he held drawing competitions in the sand with other children.

He attended another Ọnitsha Anglican institution between 1958 and 1964, Dennis Memorial Grammar School, one of the oldest and best secondary schools in Nigeria. There he had a remarkable Nigerian art teacher, Rowland Ndefo, who studied sculpture at Camberwell School of Arts and Crafts in England in 1956–58 and furniture design at Central School of Arts and Crafts, London, in 1958–60.[4] Udechukwu studied with him in 1962–64, as his only art student, after his teacher's return from England in 1960. Ndefo also taught part-time at two nearby communities, stimulating other students who later became artists: Demas Nwoko, Emmanuel Okechukwu Ọdita, Oseloka Osadebe, Chukwuanugo Okeke, Benjo Igwilo, and Paul Igboanugo, a remarkable record.[5]

Ndefo's "class" with Udechukwu attracted nonregistered students to it with his tales of life and art in England; his was a magnetic personality. Udechukwu painted in oil and studied graphic design with him, drawing and painting objects around the house, festivals, market scenes, and food sellers (fig. 73). He wrote an article for the student newspaper, "Why Paint When You Can Photograph?" explaining that the artist creates beyond what the camera can accomplish. He studied art history much on his own, as Ndefo had little familiarity with it. Expatriate teachers helped him acquire European art books; primarily an artist today, Udechukwu has an impressive knowledge of art history.

At secondary school he produced and acted in plays by both European and Nigerian authors and created and painted sets. He did calligraphy for citations with decorated borders for distinguished visitors. He had seen body *uli* when young, though he did not incorporate it into his art; he did not see wall *uli* until later. He thought of becoming a commercial artist, wrote poetry and stories at a school strong in literature, and took part in sports. While at this school he saw a reproduction of a sunflower painting by Van Gogh at a teacher's home; he did not realize its importance until later. Graduating in late 1964, he served as art teacher at St. John's School, Fegge, Ọnitsha, from February to April 1965.


## ENUGU

After his teaching position ended and before university training, Udechukwu spent several periods in Enugu. There he met Uche Okeke and others in the various arts at the Mbari Centre. He was impressed that Okeke was able to be an independent, professional artist and was struck by the originality of his art, including his folktale drawings and his paintings.

Through his Mbari Enugu contacts, Udechukwu came to know the poetry of the late Christopher Okigbo, a dynamic Igbo writer whose complex, lyrical free verse and thought have influenced him and others in the arts. Okigbo's *Heavensgate* spoke directly to Udechukwu, whose poetry he has drawn on in his visual art.[6] Udechukwu's secondary school experience with poetry had been with European romantic poets, but Okigbo's verse was very modern, concerned with his relationship to tradition and the dilemmas of the modern African intellectual.

Udechukwu became a close friend of the budding artist Uzọ Ndubisi, who was involved with the Mbari Centre, and they went out sketching together. From April 1965 until he went to the university, he worked in

Enugu as an assistant commercial artist in the Agricultural Information Sector, Ministry of Agriculture, under Ogbonnaya Nwagbara, who had been one of the Zaria Art Society members and who was involved in Mbari Enugu. Udechukwu won a trophy in 1965 in painting at the Eastern Nigerian Festival of the Arts, and the year before in commercial art.

Udechukwu's brief Enugu experience exposed him to a lively art scene, opened his eyes to new frontiers in art and poetry, and stimulated him to be an artist. In 1966, with a friend, he founded the Nkisi Theatre Group in Ọnitsha, and he created the set and costumes for Wọle Ṣoyinka's *The Trials of Brother Jero.*

## ZARIA

Udechukwu studied art at Ahmadu Bello University in Zaria during the 1965–66 academic year, then transferred to the University of Nigeria, Nsukka, because of the pogroms against southerners in the north. While there was deep trouble in Zaria, it was not at the university, but he saw the destruction of the southerners' quarters in the city. After the academic year, he and other southern Nigerian students left to study elsewhere, fearing for their safety.

At Zaria he took a newly developed art foundation course in basic design and pursued other studies in drawing, painting, textile design, and ceramics, with some silkscreen training. Despite the earlier presence of Uche Okeke and the Zaria Art Society, the teaching remained conventionally British; there was only one Nigerian art teacher there, S. Suleiman (then known as Salmonu), at the junior level. Yet the new design course moved toward experimentation, allowing students to play with form, to explore and solve basic design problems, using shapes and found objects, before going on to human figures and still lifes. Udechukwu, as in Uche Okeke's day, sketched landscapes (he was impressed with the scenery around Zaria), rocks, rural villages and villagers, and domestic animals. He learned technical art skills and was exposed to Muslim culture more than at Ọnitsha, though there were Muslim traders, beggars, and others there. He has, over the years, created some images of Muslims. Udechukwu's school and university art was in a realistic style, in pencil, pen and ink, watercolor, gouache, oil, and linocut; he won a prize for his 1964 oil, *Landscape with Bridge.*[7] Already he showed an inclination to create images of ordinary people—blind beggars, palm wine tappers, dry grass collectors, a nightsoilman, people in a third-class train coach, a boy reading—as well as images from traditional culture and landscapes, all concerns that mark his artistic career.[8] From his early days he showed a serious interest in the visual, dramatic, and literary arts and in reading that continues to this day.

## NSUKKA

The art program at the University of Nigeria, Nsukka, in the 1966–67 academic year was another period of artistic stimulation for Udechukwu. The artistic activities in nearby Enugu flourished much of this time, and Udechukwu took part in a group exhibition there in 1967.[9] Not only did fellow eastern Nigerian students from Zaria come to Nsukka when he did, but Igbo students and faculty from elsewhere joined the art department. Udechukwu met the student Paul Igboanugo, who later became a teacher and a major printmaker, and Chuka Amaefunah, who after a few years became an expert at *uli* in mixed media.[10] Akinọla Laṣekan was head; I have previously noted that the program at that time was conventional, emphasizing realism (see Chapter 3). There was tension between the generally better students from Zaria and those already at Nsukka.

At school Udechukwu created scenes of people fleeing from the north, the Nsukka market, landscapes, and images drawn from Christopher Okigbo's poetry, using oils (but not acrylic until after the war), gouache, pastel, and ink and creating some watercolors and linocuts.[11] He has written that in his earlier work he was "concerned with the reproduction of objective reality."[12] Udechukwu describes how he became familiar with *uli*:

> My first contact with traditional uli by Igbo women came in 1966 when I came to Nsukka and had to write a term paper for the Humanities General Studies Course. We had a number of topics and one of them was Traditional Wall Painting. So, for the first time, I went to the village [Agulu] and took colour photographs of wall paintings and spoke to the artists and came back and wrote the essay. By that time, I did not even know that Uche Okeke's drawings, which I had seen, were influenced by those same paintings.[13]

He also saw *uli* body paintings at Agulu, though he did not employ *uli* in his art until later. In 1972, after the war, he turned the research into his B.A. thesis.[14] He was moving toward an *uli* commitment, reinforced when he later studied with Uche Okeke. At the end of his Nsukka university year he returned to Agulu to await developments; the fighting began on the sixth of July.

## WAR

At home at Agulu for some months, Udechukwu came to know Igbo village culture more than before.[15] Its festivals, music, musicians, and funerals are all reflected in his later art. In February 1968 he received a call to join the Audio Visual Unit of the Directorate of Propaganda, organized out of the Biafran Ministry of Information at Aba in southern Biafra. There, with other artists from his Nsukka university days, including Paul Igboanugo, Bons Nwabiani, Okechukwu Uchegbu, and Anthony John-Kamen as their head, he designed posters, magazine layouts, and single and strip cartoons, all for the war effort. He created a cartoon on Generals Ojukwu and Gowon, the two opposing war leaders. Two women artists, Ngọzi Ejiogu and Chinwe Oreki, some self-taught artists, and others who had been taught by popular artists were there—a friendly, cooperative artists organization. Udechukwu joined a poetry group formed to read their members' works. As he later wrote: "Poetry provided a survival tonic for some of us during the Nigerian Civil War."[16] He also created visual art privately. As the front shrunk, the artists moved north to Umuahia, where Udechukwu designed clothing to distinguish Biafrans' from federal uniforms. Then they moved westward to Umuaka Ọrlu as Umuahia fell, and again to Alaenyi-Ọgwa near Owerri as Umuaka Ọrlu gave way, where he was assistant art organizer. There he found himself in a period of intensive multi-art activity such as had occurred at prewar Enugu, but in a declining military situation. In order to improve morale and to raise funds, the Biafran government created a Cultural Affairs Division there to entertain the troops, refugees in the camps, and civilians through cultural workshops, such as the Armed Forces Theatre Group, Armed Forces Entertainment Band for dance music and musical plays, and a writer's workshop in which Udechukwu was involved. He also took part in the group *Biafran Cultural Workshop Exhibition*. Again, this was a village situation where he became better acquainted with indigenous Igbo life.

He played a leading role in the founding of the Ọdunke Community of Artists, a select group from the theater, music, literary, and visual arts.[17] They created and produced a play, *Veneration to Udo*, written by a number of them; Udechukwu wrote the first part. It dealt with the considerable suffering caused by the war, but also with corruption in Biafra.[18] He was involved in writing other plays and acting in them. A poetry group met once a week to read the members' work, both popular and serious.[19] The bombing in the war was terrible, and many poems were written about it. Some artists painted scenes of it, and Udechukwu created drawings on the theme. It is ironic that toward the end of a losing war, with little help from outside, isolated and faced with a diminishing war front in the midst of bombing and major refugee problems, the Alaenyi-Ọgwa artists were able to form a co-operative, stimulating, and creative group.[20] Chukwuma Azuonye has recently written concerning Ọdunke:

> It was by no means a form of escapism; each and every one of us was deeply involved in one way or another with the knitty-gritty of the war effort; but we found poetry, drama and the visual arts an appropriate avenue not only for the canalization of pent-up energies but also for the compensation of dreams and aspirations which the politics of the day had so rudely frustrated.[21]

Of the war, Udechukwu has stated:

> I as a person had to move from one town to the other with virtually no property, just a coat and a bag, occasionally sleeping in the open. So I know first hand what it is to suffer. I have known hunger. I have also seen people suffering. I have seen air raids where human beings are dismembered in under two seconds. So this has left a big mark on my psyche and over the years, I find that images of pathos that one associates with Biafra, keep surfacing from time to time. And this has been reinforced by this lack of direction in the country.[22]

Much of Udechukwu's art was lost during the war, especially some sketches and drawings. But more than ten works, mainly oils, were saved by being taken to Germany, along with the works of other Biafrans, for the Biafran exhibitions that Uche Okeke led.

## WARTIME ART

Udechukwu's art during the pogroms and the conflict that followed, not unexpectedly, is frequently associated with these events: the plight of refugees, the loss of family members, including children, hunger, wounded soldiers, the destruction of the landscape.[23] A 1968 *Self-Portrait* in chalk depicts a young, lean, serious face, expressing his determination to get on with matters.[24] Two pictures entitled *Refugees,* a work called *Study of Refugees,* and *Kwashiakor Family,*[25] all in felt pen, and many of his oils, such as *The Only Son* (1968; fig. 74), *Blue Figures (Refugees)* (1968; fig. 75), and *"Silent Faces at a Crossroads"* (1967; fig. 76), include elongated, distraught and hungry-looking, skeletal figures.[26] The elongation of the human figure in his work stresses the ideas of depletion and suffering.

In *The Only Son,* an anguished mother kneeling with arms outstretched is depicted in harsh yellow and greens as she wails over the body of her starved dead son with a swollen belly. In *Blue Figures,* the standing, emaciated mother and son are in strong blues. In *"Silent Faces at a Crossroads,"* the bodies and heads are highlighted in yellow with blues; there are greens and reds on other bodies. A like color scheme occurs in the 1970 oil, *Refugee Children.* The 1967 oil, *Lament of the Unsilenced,* reverses *The Only Son,* with the boy standing next to his dead mother lying on the ground. In these wartime oils, the contrasting background is sometimes dark and somber, suggesting that there is nothing left but death, or the background is red, bringing to mind blood and fire. Ọguibe points out how consistently Udechukwu pictured women during the war, and that after the conflict he continued to create images of widowed, begging, or otherwise suffering females.[27]

In *Exile Train* (1968, linocut), the heads of the refugees are elongated. In Udechukwu's 1966 oil, *The Aftermath* (fig. 77), an anguished man, whose family has been killed in a northern pogrom, holds his longish head in sorrow with his elongated arms. In much of Udechukwu's wartime art, distortion of the human body is equated with that of the social world. These and other of his wartime works were privately created and not for propaganda purposes.

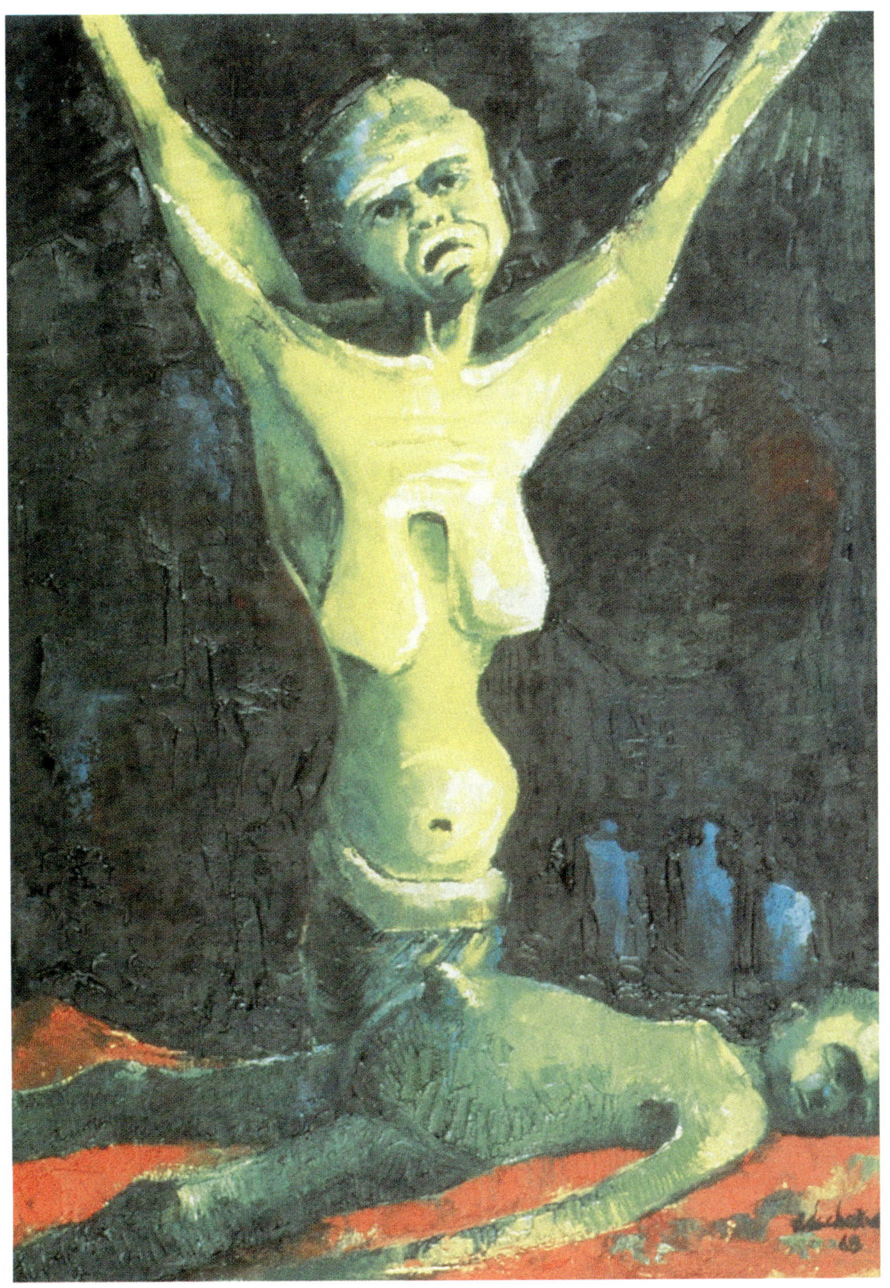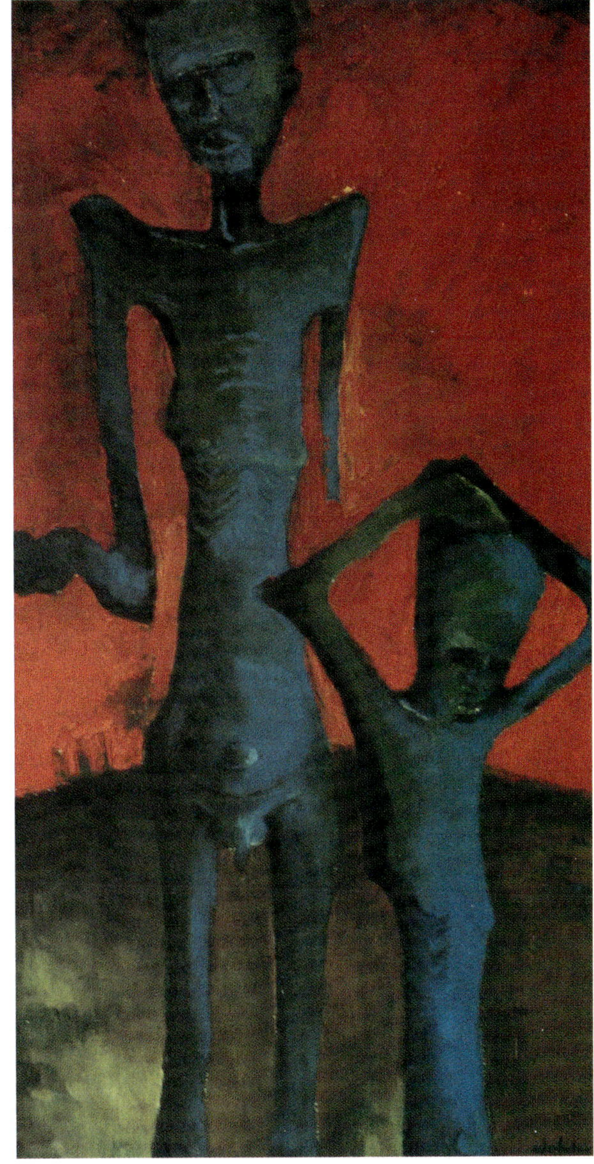

**74 (LEFT).** Obiọra Udechukwu, *The Only Son,* 1968, oil on plywood. 60 × 42 cm. Collection of the artist.

**75 (RIGHT).** Obiọra Udechukwu, *Blue Figures (Refugees),* 1968, oil on plywood. 89 × 47 cm. Collection of the artist.

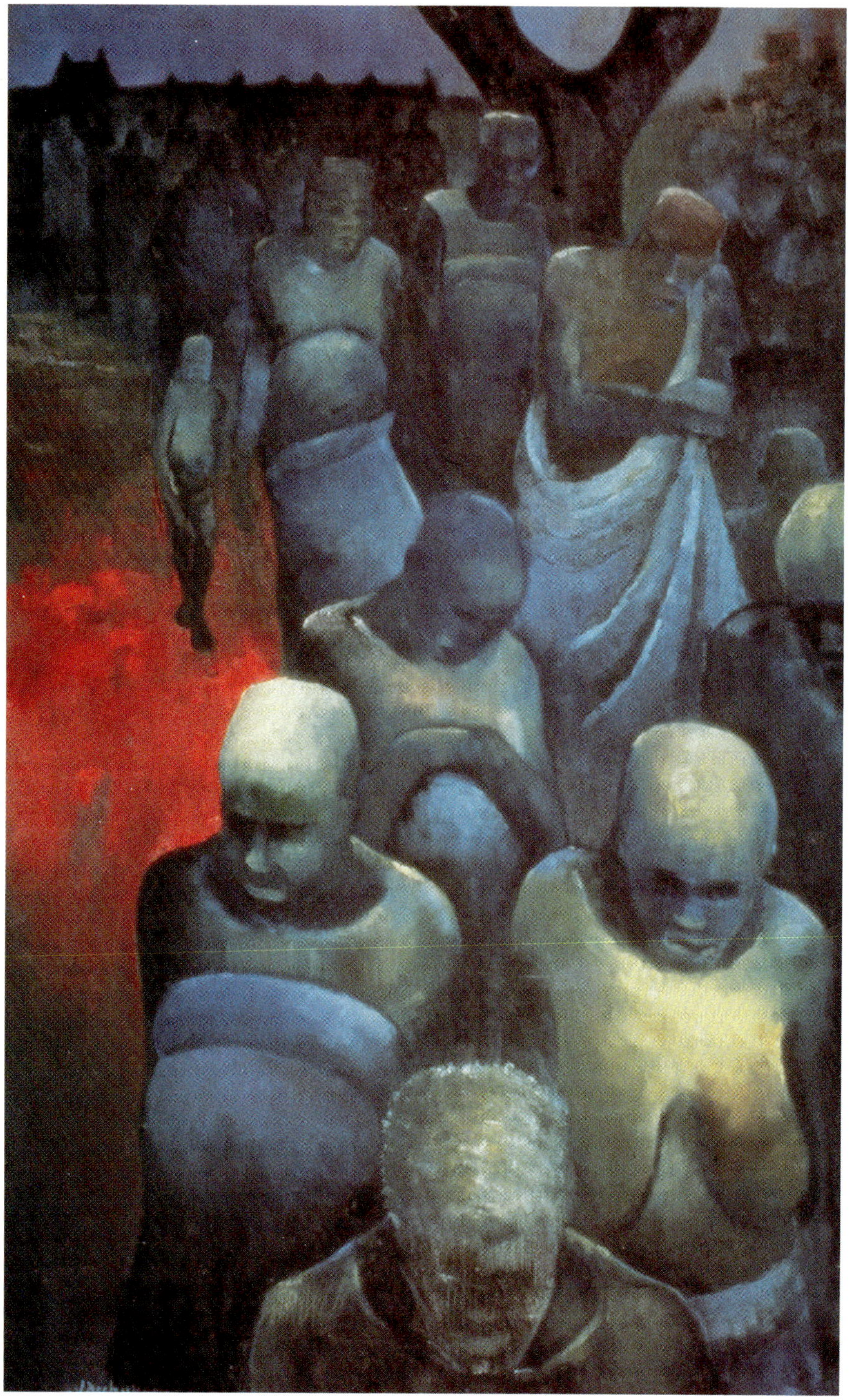

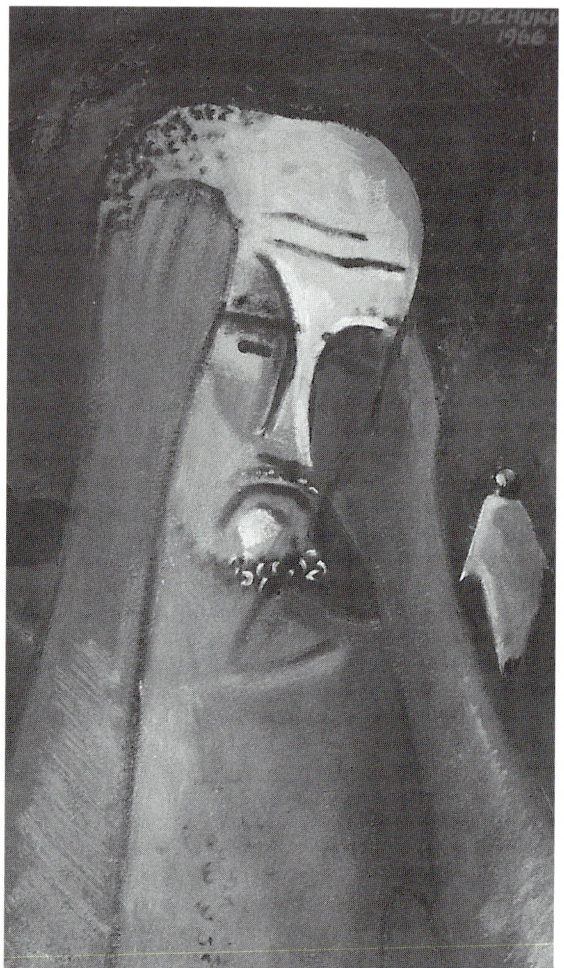

**76 (LEFT).** Obiọra Udechukwu, *"Silent Faces at a Crossroads,"* 1967, oil on board. 121.5 × 73.5 cm. Collection and photo: the artist.

**77 (RIGHT).** Obiọra Udechukwu, *The Aftermath,* 1966, oil, dimensions unknown. Collection and photo: the artist.

Udechukwu's prewar artistic realism changed in the war to a dramatic, emotional realism, often with intense coloration in his oils. After the conflict, he continued to create elongation in some of his human figures, but also other distortions of the human body that he had only very occasionally expressed before. These came to characterize much of his work. The conflict sensitized him to issues of suffering, poverty, and economic distinctions that have never left him, granted that before the war he had frequently depicted ordinary people.

He was occasionally to continue creating war-related images for at least fifteen years after the war.[28] As his former student Chika Okeke has written: "Like many artists in Biafra at the time the horrors of war catalysed Udechukwu's fecundity."[29] For him in art and poetry, as well as for other artists and poets, the wartime conflict shifted the emphases of the prewar years at the universities at Zaria, Nsukka, and at Enugu, from focusing on aesthetic forms and qualities, with a generally pleasant and peaceful thrust, to blending social concerns with aesthetic interests and experimentation. The war hardened them to express the harsh realities of everyday life in their work. When they came to teach, they passed this view on to their students. Aesthetics merged with the social message, without eliminating the significance of aesthetics. For Udechukwu, this earlier, more gentle period has occasionally returned in his landscapes, Igbo scenes, Igbo minstrels, musicians, and in some most recent work, mostly done in Germany away from the cares of Nigerian life.

Moved by the death of Christopher Okigbo on the northern war front near Nsukka in August 1967 at the age of thirty-five, Udechukwu wrote in his memory what he considers to be his first serious poem, "Lament of the Silenced Flute."[30] He was to write other serious verse in developing a mature poetic style, as he was to depict serious images in his visual art. Art and poetry, since the war, have been complementary, interrelated aspects of Udechukwu's life.


## TRAINING AND SUBSTANTIAL ARTISTIC DEVELOPMENT, 1970–1977

Between 1970 and 1977 Udechukwu's art altered in style, though not always in content. During this time he studied at the University of Nigeria, Nsukka, taking his B.A. degree in painting in 1972 and his M.F.A. in the same field in 1977, two periods separated by the academic year of 1972–73 as art master at Metropolitan College, Ọnitsha. After the war he had returned to the university as a junior fellow, ostensibly a research position, though he did some instructing. He went to Nsukka rather than returning to Zaria, because many of his artistic colleagues in various art fields at Alaenyi-Ọgwa were going there, allowing the attractive Ọdunke arts group to continue. And he has stated that "somehow I couldn't get myself to return to Zaria because of the intensity of feelings I had about the problems [the prewar pogroms]. I just couldn't see myself living in Zaria."[31] Uche Okeke, whose work at Enugu had earlier interested Udechukwu, came to the university at Nsukka to revamp the art department. In this 1970–77 period, Udechukwu traveled to Europe twice, in 1972 and 1976, the second time also to the United States. He held solo exhibitions in Ọnitsha, Enugu, and Lagos, and by the end of 1977, some months after graduation, he had taken part in nine group shows, in Enugu, Nsukka, Ibadan, and Lagos, including the prestigious Lagos FESTAC '77 exhibition. He established a pattern of frequent exhibitions that he maintains to this day, matching his high level of productivity.

*Uli* was a great influence on Udechukwu's art at this time, stimulated by his research at Agulu and elsewhere in Igboland. This also came about through Uche Okeke's influence and through that of Chike Aniakọr, also his teacher. Udechukwu became a confirmed Uliist without totally abandoning, in this period, other art interests. In an interview with me he has stated:

> When I became conscious of returning to my roots, *uli* became the thing that was immediately available. So for me
> it's a means of understanding myself, understanding my tradition, and using that as a basis for encountering other

traditions. . . . Masquerading I would see more as a total art in the sense that you are dealing with costuming, sculpture, with singing, with dancing, time-based and spaced-based art all coming together. But with painting, you are dealing with the two-dimensional surface.[32]

So while Udechukwu has created masquerade and mask images, his art has been largely directed and informed by *uli* aesthetic principles. It does not bother him at all that *uli* has moved from the female body and murals to its contemporary situation. The world changes, and this  is accepted in his art. "We cannot recreate it, we can modernize and make it part of our contemporary life; that is all we are saying," he has told me.[33] He stresses the importance of bringing to the modern world an indigenous medium that has been neglected by scholars in the past. It is a correction, a balancing of the value of African sculpture with those of two-dimensional work.

At this time he was greatly impressed by the Sudanese artist Ibrahim el Salahi, whose work Ulli Beier had arranged to exhibit at Mbari Ibadan in 1962. Udechukwu did not see this show, but he saw his art in the catalogue and was impressed with Salahi's linear and calligraphic style, which had affinities to the linear *uli*.[34] Salahi's art also expressed the quality of natural synthesis that Uche Okeke was imbuing in his students. Udechukwu claims that Okeke and Salahi were the two greatest influences on his development after the war; later he was impressed by Chinese *Li* drawing and another eastern Nigerian design system, *nsibidi*.[35]

Udechukwu's B.A. thesis, a study of wall *uli* at Agulu, where he commissioned two senior female artists to paint murals at his family compound and analyzed the art of two others, gained him a firsthand understanding of *igwa ife n'aja*—painting on the wall.[36] This was probably the first detailed study of *uli* in a single small area of Igboland; it may still remain the best one. He discusses how a known form is reduced to a simple design, the spontaneity of the artistic process, and the variety of effects gained from a few motifs and colors. The *uli* paintings "oscillate between ideomorphic or stylization and abstraction but are clearly on the symbolic side," he writes.[37] "The Agulu artist does not try to reproduce the illusion of what she *sees* but summarises what she *knows* is" (italics his).[38] Udechukwu uses the words "lyrical symbolism" with reference to *uli*; he has continued to refer to lyricism as a major quality of these motifs, for its rhythmic, flowing features and its balanced qualities of positive and negative space.

By 1975 Udechukwu's *uli* style was well developed, although it later became more complex. In that year he held an exhibition in Enugu, remounted the next year in Lagos, in memory of the poet Christopher Okigbo, that indicated that he had developed his own sophisticated style of *uli*, differing from that of Okeke or Aniakọr.[39] In his pen and ink art, in addition to employing the sinuous lines that the other two artists used, he made direct use of *uli*, such as the kola nut head, *isi nwaọji*, and the spiral, *agwọlagwọ*.[40] He also extended their lines and modified the motifs as he wished; they were not sacred emblems never to be changed. He created some motifs, and he sometimes drew lines that were unrelated to any motifs, although in *uli* they could be considered to be *akpala*, meaning "line." There is a sense of great freedom to explore *uli*'s linear qualities and to employ the line as a basic element. Sharp angles sometimes appear, in contrast to or at the ends of curved lines—the gentleness of curves counterpoised by a certain sharpness.

Many of his ink drawings seemed to float in a sea of white, with images sometimes suggested by a partial or broken outline, leaving the viewer to fill in the form. Ikwuemesi claims that his art "deals with frugality and moderation."[41] What became characteristic of his art—not only drawings but other works as well—was that the viewer often had to work hard to understand what it was all about. The faces and bodies of humans were often distorted, sometimes in anguish; they are striking rather than beautiful.[42] Bodies were not filled in with details, only faces, and *uli* was employed either as an integral part of the image, as in *Right On, Brother* (1975, pen and ink), where the saxophone body of the playing musician is mainly composed of a variety of *uli* forms, or as decorative effect or fill-in, as in *Tree Spirit* (1975, pen and ink).[43] Udechukwu's interests were moving strongly to pen and ink and pen and brush, and some print work, frequently in black on white paper, not at all resembling his prewar art and differing from much of his wartime efforts.

Another influence on Udechukwu's art was Christopher Okigbo's poetry, which Udechukwu honored in the exhibition mentioned above.[44] It is evident that Udechukwu aspired, and still does, to be a visual Okigbo, paralleling the latter's poetry with two-dimensional art, creating images that are as lyrical visually, and sometimes as complex and ambiguous, requiring work on the part of the viewer to appreciate them fully, with references not always easily understood. Udechukwu's fellow artist and friend Paul S. Igboanugo writes that "Obiọra does not readily give away the deeper meaning of his drawings. Many will certainly find his seriousness and sophistication difficult to comprehend."[45] There is a sense in some of Udechukwu's art of lack of a single focal point in the picture, of a need to let the eyes roam about here and there to its numerous elements before grasping it as a whole, as in Okigbo's poetry one needs to go back to separate parts to reread and think about them. In both cases, there may be matters that are not fully understood; one simply flows with the work, taking it in unconsciously and emotionally. With both creators one does not need to know all in order to appreciate the work. Note that Udechukwu has stated that Okigbo's poetry is very musical: "In fact you could almost say it is the equivalent to uli painting."[46] Okigbo was a master of the written line and its complex relationship to other lines, and Udechukwu became so for visual lines. In both cases there is a sense of a freedom to create. Udechukwu created some simpler images as well, as the 1975 pen and ink *At the Mirror,* but his richer work is often in his more complex drawings.[47] Despite complexity, many appear to have been executed spontaneously, as indigenous body and wall *uli* had been.[48] Yet they often consist of forms that appear again and again in his art. Many of his pen and ink or brush and ink works of this period and later are of one or two human figures or faces, occasionally more. People have been the focus of much of Udechukwu's art, especially his drawings.

Udechukwu's oils, his other major 1970–77 medium, often employ masses of somewhat muted colors contrasting with highlighted ones. They tend to have a lesser sense of linearity than his drawings (as might be expected for oils) and fewer evident *uli* motifs but do use the *uli* wall mural *akika* background and have circular and angular elements contrasting with rounded forms. These features occur in his *Girl and Ibibio Doll* (1977), *Nightsoilman* (1971), and *Through the High Arched Gate* (1971).[49] Curvilinear qualities also occur in other media, as in his 1977 Conté crayon, *Iya Ibeji,* where much of the composition is based on circles and ovals, probably drawing from *uli.*[50]

Already in this period, Udechukwu refers to his work as "cerebral art."[51] Other artists I have talked to have called it "intellectualistic" and "academic." I do not believe that Udechukwu has ever clarified what he means by "cerebral art," but while the thought element in his art is extremely important (as it is in Okigbo's poetry), he also aims for emotional content and for beauty, though the emotional aspect is perhaps less evident in his 1970–77 art than during the war. The affective side becomes strong again in the 1980s and 1990s, when his art spells out social, political, and economic issues affecting the common man, over which he has become angry, whether this is done in satiric form or not, wishing to pass on to the viewer feelings as well as thoughts.

Udechukwu became interested in *Li* drawings of the Chinese in the 1975–77 period when he was taking his M.F.A. degree.[52] In 1976, on his second trip abroad, he was greatly stimulated by viewing original *Li* art at the British Museum in London, the Walker Art Gallery in Minneapolis, and the Art Institute in Chicago. *Li* has striking resemblances to *uli* in its balancing of positive and negative space, its linear qualities involving rhythm and movement, its drawing from nature, and its apparent spontaneity. Further, some *Li* artists have been poets, and

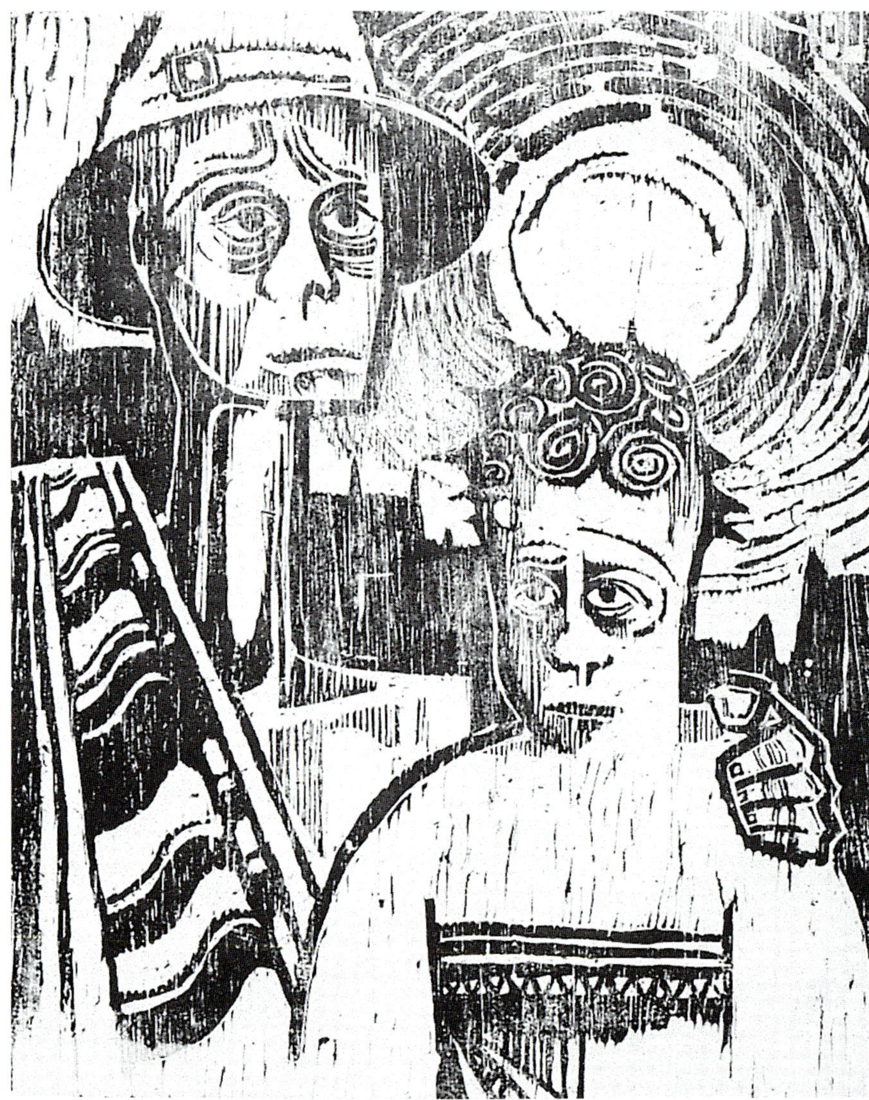



both *Li* and *uli* are old traditions, though the past history of *Li* is known and that of *uli* is not. As Udechukwu stated to Ulli Beier: "I found that there were areas of correspondence between Igbo and Chinese traditions. So that more or less confirmed me in what I was doing."[53] In commenting on the universality of some aesthetic principles, no matter what its history in particular cultures, this was clearly helpful to him in exploring new artistic areas in the relatively isolated Nigerian setting. Despite the influence of *Li*, he wrote in 1980 that "by and large my frame of reference has remained Igbo Uli."[54]

The Chinese, Sudanese, and Igbo similarities suggested to Udechukwu that there was something worldwide about what he was doing; outward differences between the three cultures masked important artistic similarities. *Li* delighted him, and he felt close sympathy with faraway artists whom he had never met. If *Li* did not influence Udechukwu at the very beginning of his *uli* work, as Okeke's and Salahi's art did, it reinforced his move to linear art. It was not an ideology of third world artists against the artistic hegemony of Euro/America that drew him to *Li* and to Salahi's art, as another Nsukka artist, Ọlu Ọguibe, might phrase it in more recent times, but simply Udechukwu's discovery of artists working elsewhere in styles similar to his art.[55]

In 1975–77 Udechukwu also became involved with Nigerian tales and myths, writing an M.F.A. thesis on this aspect of Uche Okeke's art and that of two other Nigerian artists, Bruce Onobrakpẹya, of Urhobo background, who also draws from Benin and Yoruba oral literature, and the Yoruba Oṣogbo artist Twins Seven Seven.[56] While this thesis did not lead Udechukwu to move in their direction in his own work, it showed his ability to evaluate other contemporary artists' work. The thesis, however, directly relates to Udechukwu's interest in Igbo minstrels, who recite songs and poetry, often to music. Already by 1975 Udechukwu had created a picture of a famous Igbo minstrel, Ezigbo Obiligbo, and in his career he has returned to images of him and other minstrels.[57] It is the performer of myths, as well as the myths, that intrigue him. Igbo minstrels are also social critics, which probably attracted Udechukwu to them. But he never had an Igbo tale period in his art as Uche Okeke did.

In the 1970–77 period, Udechukwu, profoundly affected by the war and the postwar problems of reconstruction and resettlement, still created war images (fig. 78). He did not shift a great deal to other social, economic, and political conditions, as he was to do in the 1980s. Rather, his work was diverse, drawing from Igbo culture, rituals, and dances, from Okigbo, from self-portraits, landscapes, nightsoilmen, from *uli, Li,* and other sources, gradually losing focus on the war.

Udechukwu illustrated the covers and the contents of some publications, especially a number of magazines that were emerging or reestablishing themselves after the war in southeastern Nigeria: *The Muse, Okike, Omabe,* and *Nsukkascope.* He also did eight drawings for a book of short stories in Igbo.[58] His attachment to Igbo life and language has been evident over the years in his writing in Igbo: poetry, occasional articles, co-authoring a book, and his involvement with an Igbo magazine.[59] He is thoroughly familiar with Igbo culture and language, despite his time at the university. While not an Igbo chauvinist, he moves effectively in Igbo culture and at the university, and these two experiences sometimes merge.

In this 1970–77 period, Udechukwu developed the ability to create in a variety of media. He had begun to employ acrylic, and he was creating in pen and ink, ink and wash, charcoal, colored pencil, Conté crayon, pastel, watercolor, pencil and oil, as well as in woodcuts, linocuts, and silkscreen. Some of this media diversity was due to the demands of his university training, but it also characterizes his later work. In addition, in 1974 he designed costumes for four plays and a set for one of them, and he continued to write poetry, with Okigbo as one model, and also through the stimulation of Chinua Achebe's literary endeavors. In a larger sense, Udechukwu's diversity of visual art media has been mirrored by his diversity of artistic forms and interests: visual art, book and magazine illustrations, poetry, theater, indigenous Igbo myth and minstrels, war, Salahi, Okigbo, *uli, Li*—all forming strands of his creativity. Udechukwu early came to believe that the various arts were integrated (as they often have been in Igbo culture), though some matters are better expressed in one medium or form than in others.[60]

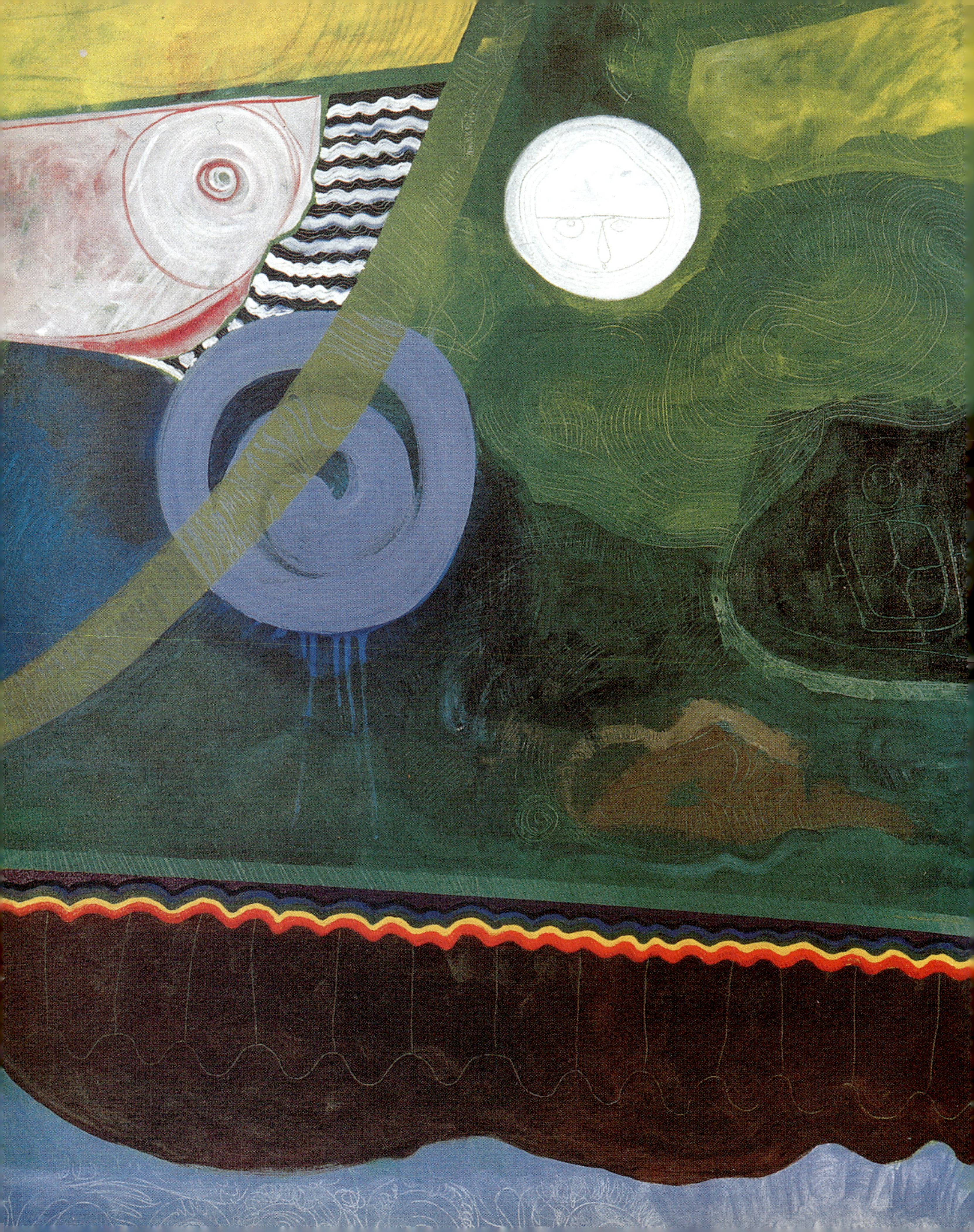

# 8. OBIǫRA UDECHUKWU

## II: MATURITY AND INCREASING DIVERSITY

*We were once poor but wealthy*

*We are now rich but poor*

OBIǪRA UDECHUKWU [1]

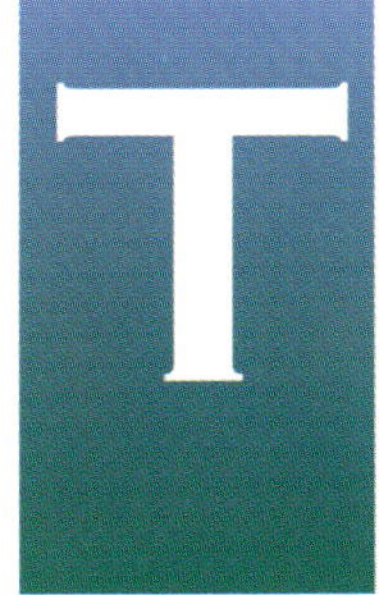

The period from 1977 on has been a rewarding one for Obiǫra Udechukwu. He has explored a second indigenous design system, *nsibidi,* showed an expanded skill in printmaking, further developed his abilities in ink and watercolor, and focused strongly on Nigerian social and political issues while still considering other visual interests. He has made acrylic a potent art tool, and his art has become more philosophical. He has also developed his poetic style and his skills as a commentator on Igbo tradition.

### NSIBIDI

Udechukwu began using *nsibidi* motifs in 1977, and he has increasingly used that design system either with *uli* or alone. He first learned of it in 1976 from his friend Chukwuma Azuonye, who was studying at the University of London for his doctorate. Then Udechukwu acquired copies of some of the basic publications.[2]

*Nsibidi* originally derived from the Ejagham (Ekoi) east of the Igbo, spreading southwestward to the Efik, the Ibibio, and the southeastern Igbo. Associated with men's secret societies, especially Ekpe, it is found on ceremonial cloth (*ukara*), walls of shrines and secret society houses, masks and masquerade dress, and various secret society objects. Unlike *uli, nsibidi* motifs can be communicated to the initiated through hand, arm, and body movements; while many of its motifs are viewed publicly, their meanings may be known only to secret society members. Like *uli, nsibidi* may differ in meaning from area to area. It is more directly concerned with social relationships

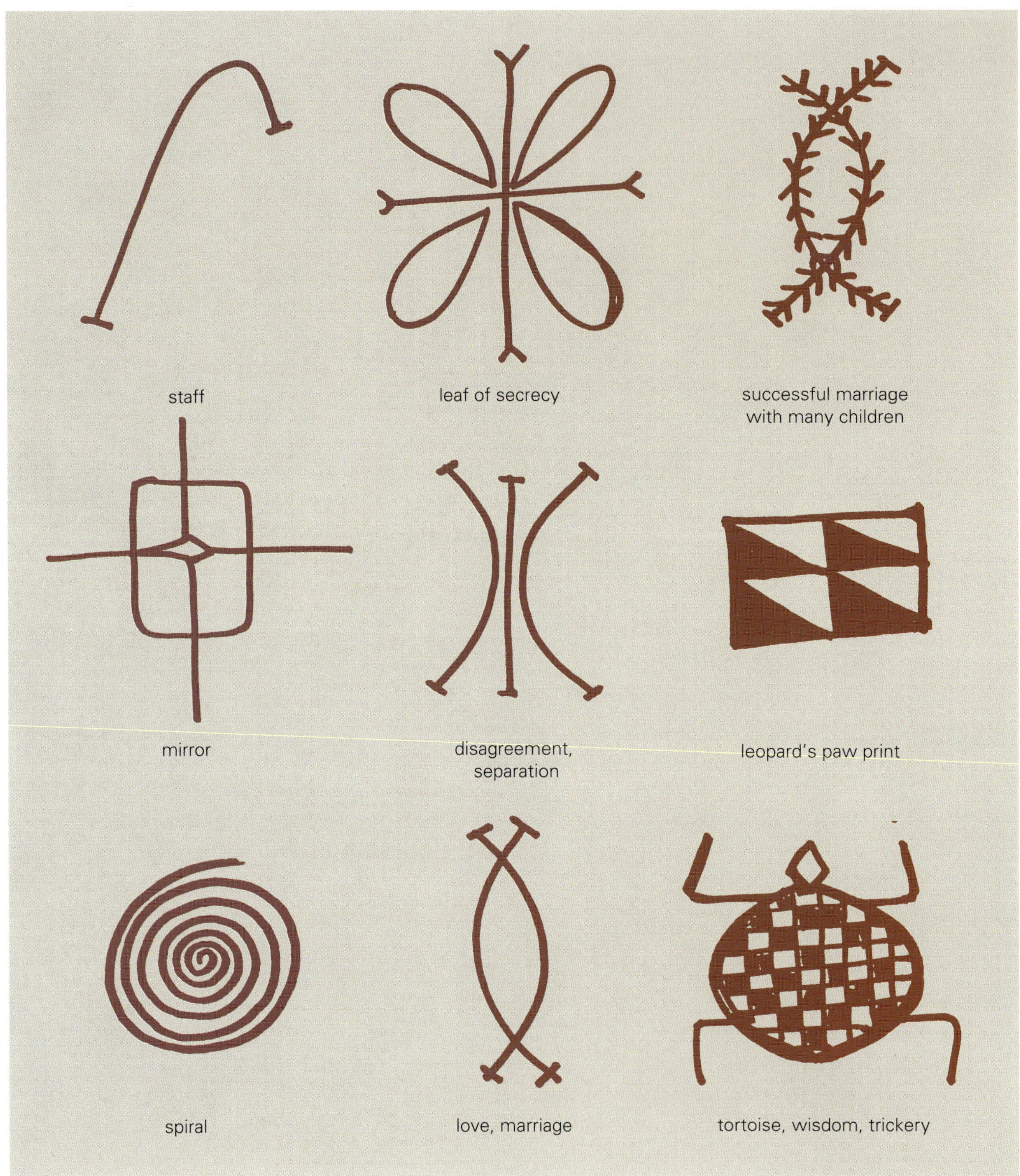


**FIG. B.** Nsibidi motifs. Drawn by Sylvester Ogbechiẹ.

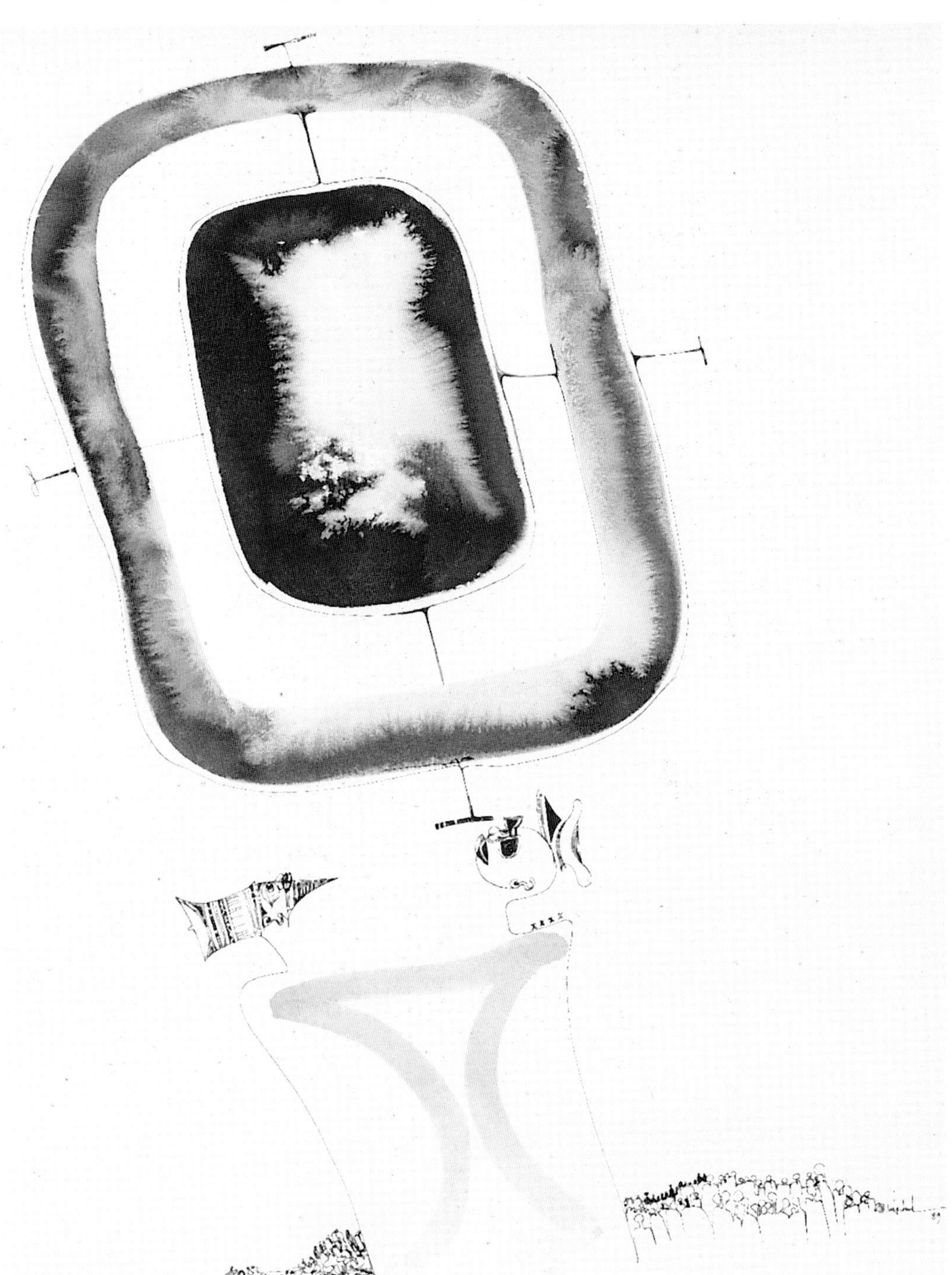

**79**. Obiọra Udechukwu, *Mirror Mirror,*
1989, ink drawing on paper. 49.9 × 36
cm. Private collection. Photo: Franko Khoury.

and emotions—love, hate, marriage, divorce, adultery, argument—than *uli* is. However, the majority of its motifs, as with *uli*, derive from manmade or natural objects. *Nsibidi* is closer to a written language than *uli* is (fig. B).

Despite its ritual attributes and secrecy, *nsibidi*, as does *uli*, has a strong aesthetic aspect, pleasurable decoration that expresses artistic skill. The designs are well created because of their ritual importance and for their aesthetic appeal. *Nsibidi* places less emphasis on negative space than *uli*; its images may be crowded together, as on *ukara* cloth, and they may be systematically arranged in parallel rows, unlike most *uli*.

As is true of a number of his students who have followed his lead, Udechukwu does not come from an Igbo area that employs *nsibidi*; his familiarity with it has come mainly from published writings and is not as extensive

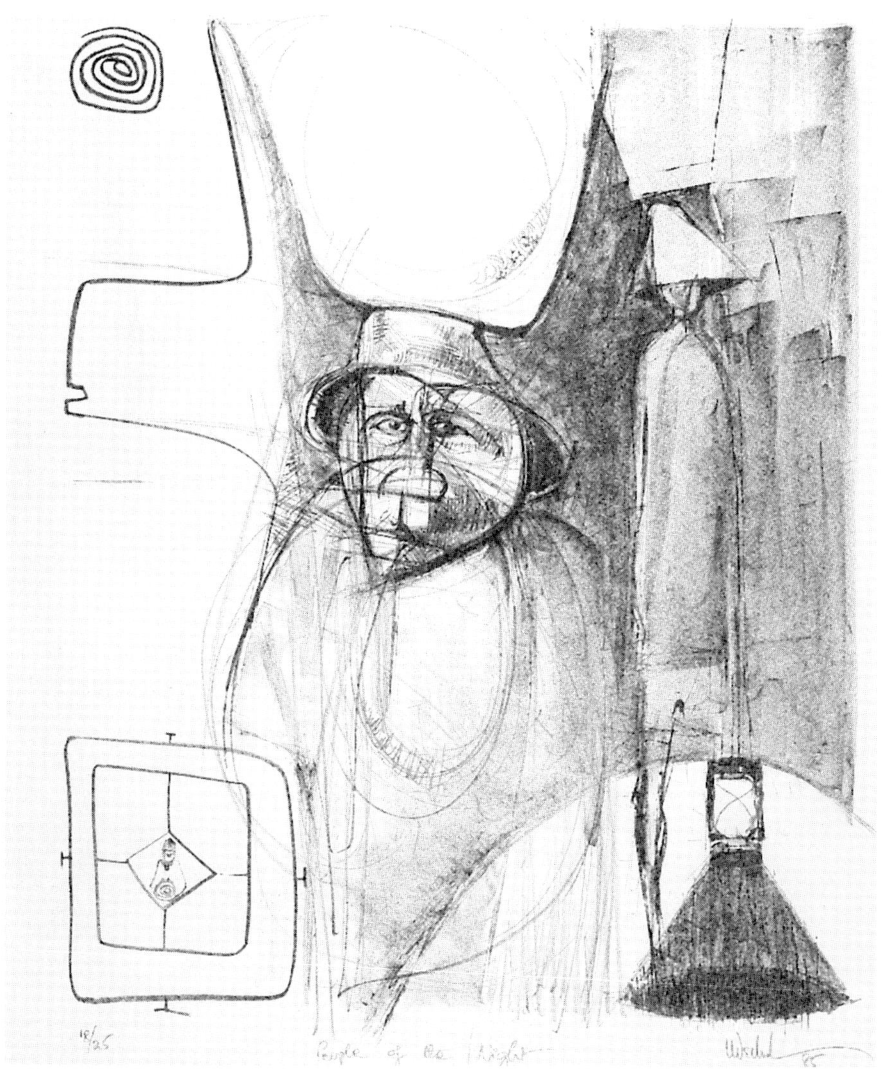

as his knowledge of *uli.* Yet *nsibidi* is considered an Igbo form by him and by others who employ it, regardless of its origin, because it occurs in some Igbo areas. I doubt whether Udechukwu is much concerned as to whether it is Igbo or not, rather that it is an indigerous two-dimensional motif system with appealing designs, strong symbolism, and interesting meanings.

The *nsibidi* love sign appears frequently in Udechukwu's work, but perhaps the mirror motif is the most common (figs. 79, 80). Of the latter he has written:

> My answer to those who ask of me pictures of more pleasant subjects is "The Mirror." The mirror enables us to see ourselves as we really are. We can only confront ourselves in a mirror: our blemishes are not hidden or painted over. It is only by keeping in view the issues of inequities in the world, the human condition in general, by asking our mirror how much we have contributed to alleviating suffering and improving the system (not who is the most beautiful!), that we can even begin to make progress.[3]

As with his *uli* motifs, Udechukwu may employ *nsibidi* as a decoration, to manipulate negative space, or for very specific reasons. In his 1985 lithograph, *People of the Night* (fig. 80), of men carrying pails on their head, either with water or human excrement (nightsoilmen), there is an *nsibidi* mirror at the lower left, perhaps reflecting the hard and somber labor that the men perform. An *uli* spiral (*agwǫlagwǫ*) at the upper left conveys the sense of the endless labor of these men.

## PRINTMAKING

Udechukwu had been producing prints for many years—block prints, linocuts, silkscreens, aquatints, and engravings—when in 1985 he had the opportunity to spend five months as artist-in-residence at Ulli Beier's Iwalęwa-Haus at the University of Bayreuth in that city, where he trained with and produced cooperatively with the German printmaker Dr. Winfried Schmidt. He also spent several weeks in Salzburg, Austria, making lithographs. The result was an outpouring of prints employing a variety of techniques, which led to an exhibition at Bayreuth and Lagos.[4] Udechukwu advanced his skills in printmaking in Europe.

Udechukwu's 1985 prints do not show much difference in subject matter from his other work to that time. Some are political, for example, *The Chameleon* (softground etching; see below, fig. 84) and *Faces and the Faceless* (lithograph; fig. 81), which depicts a politician, a chief, and a businessman, above whom are an anonymous mass of people and a nightsoilman. Some works refer to the Biafran war, as *Refugee Mother and Child* (aquatint) and *Refugee Family* (drypoint). Others have to do with ordinary laborers, as *People of the Night* (lithograph) and *Dreams of a Cattle Boy* (also known as *Dreams of a Shepherd Boy*, line etching), and some refer to indigenous culture, as *River Queen* (softground etching), probably representing the river spirit Mamiwata, and *Iri Aha* (drypoint), an Ǫhafia Igbo war dancer. *Iwalęwa* (linocut; fig. 82) has the image of a beautiful woman with neck rings (symbolizing her elegance), who is helping an old woman carry firewood; she is more beautiful for doing so, according to Udechukwu. Iwalęwa is the name of the place in Bayreuth where Udechukwu worked and means "character is beauty" in Yoruba.

## ARTISTIC CONNECTIONS

Udechukwu's 1985 experience at Bayreuth, including two exhibitions, was not only a springboard to further printmaking but also contributed to an increasing association for him and other Nsukka artists with Germany. He was at Iwalęwa-Haus again in 1989, where for an *uli* exhibition he painted a substantial-sized traditional *uli* mural in acrylic on board. Uche Okeke was in Germany in the early 1960s and during the Biafran war, and Udechukwu had been there briefly in 1972. Uche Okeke's 1993 retrospective exhibition was held at the Goethe Institut in Lagos. The German artist Gerd von Stokar had taught at Nsukka for a number of years after the Biafran war. Udechukwu took part in an exhibition of contemporary African art in Mainz and Bayreuth in Germany and in Wogl, Austria, in 1980.[5] He had also been at Bayreuth in 1982 for an exhibition of his drawings at Iwalęwa-Haus.[6] A sculpture workshop had been held at the university at Nsukka about 1981 under the auspices of the German artist Barbara Haeger. A few months after Udechukwu's return from Germany in 1985, a print workshop was organized at Nsukka under Dr. Schmidt, and again in 1986, and in 1987 with Schmidt and Thomas Gosebruch. While a 1988 workshop was developed by the British Council, the next two, in 1990 and 1991, were again under German leadership at Nsukka.[7] A metal sculpture workshop was held at the university in

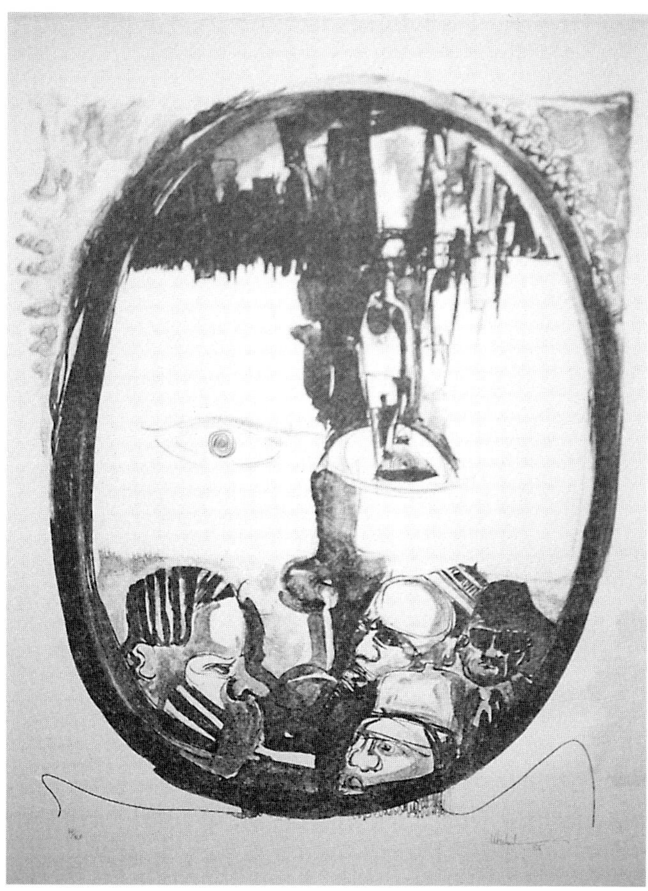

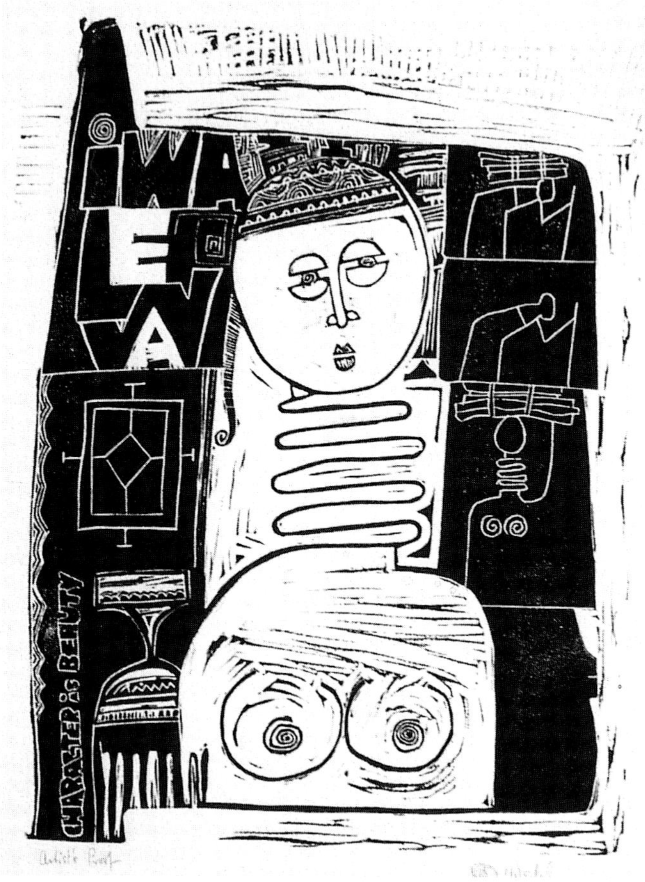


**81**. Obiọra Udechukwu, *Faces and the Faceless,* 1985, lithograph on paper. 42.5 × 32 cm. Collection of Simon Ottenberg.

**82**. Obiọra Udechukwu, *Iwalẹwa,* 1985, linocut. 27.2 × 19.5 cm. Collection of the artist.

1995, directed by the Hungarian-born German artist Sandro Antal. These workshops, generally lasting more than a week and open not only to faculty and students at the university but to other artists as well, were followed by an exhibition of the art produced. Udechukwu took part in some of the exhibitions and was involved in organizing some; there is no doubt that their presence on campus continued to influence his interest in printmaking. They were generally sponsored through the Goethe Institut, Lagos, which has held numerous exhibitions of Nsukka artists, including Udechukwu.

Thus since 1985 there has been an increasing association between the artists at Nsukka, the Goethe Institut in Lagos, and Iwalẹwa-Haus at the University of Bayreuth in Germany, largely through Dr. Schmidt,[8] Ulli Beier, its director, and in more recent years Norbert Aas, at one time at Iwalẹwa-Haus and now through his own organization in Bayreuth, art/arc.[9] Iwalẹwa-Haus has held exhibitions of Nsukka artists and owns a contemporary African art collection that includes works of Udechukwu. He has developed valuable access to the Nsukka-Lagos-Bayreuth axis, which has allowed his art to expand. It also allows him free time to create in peace away from

Nigeria and teaching duties, to meet and discuss art with German artists, and to learn about European art theories and view its art. This is not the only foreign connection he has made; over the years he has exhibited at the Italian Cultural Institute in Lagos, with which he has had close contact, having had his 1993 retrospective exhibition there. He has also been involved in traveling and exhibiting in Zimbabwe in 1988, Washington, D.C., in 1990, and New York in 1995.[10]

Another expansion of Udechukwu's activities has been through the AKA Circle of Exhibiting Artists. He played a major role in its foundation in 1986, and he has continued to be an important member. The group began about the time the Ọdunke Community of Artists effectively ended, though AKA exhibits only visual art, while Ọdunke also organized other art activities. Each member generally chooses three works not previously exhibited for its annual Lagos and Enugu shows. AKA, simply a collection of artists familiar with one another who live in the same general region and enjoy exhibiting together, includes some of Nigeria's top artists. It guarantees the appearance of some of Udechukwu's art in Enugu and Lagos every year. AKA exemplifies Udechukwu's interests in cooperative artistic groupings, a concern that grew from his wartime associations with other artists. In recent years he has been involved with other art exhibiting groups, in organizing art conferences, and in publishing. Udechukwu has taken over the mantle of leadership at Nsukka from Uche Okeke since the latter's retirement.

## SOCIAL AND POLITICAL ISSUES

Udechukwu's war-related art continued into the 1980s, while at the same time his interest in current social and political issues grew and turned to all of Nigeria, even to Africa in general. His social art remains important to this day.

With a growing reputation as an artist, at the height of the Nigerian oil boom in the early 1980s, he questioned why there was so much suffering, poverty, and unequal distribution of wealth in Nigeria, issues that still concern him today in post–oil boom Nigeria. In a 1980 exhibition, *Five Themes: Fifty-Five Works,* one theme refers to "refugees, the oppressed, the suffering and the struggling anonymous masses, who know little or nothing about politics and economics, but who in times of adversity and crisis bear the brunt, who usually show up only as numbers on the pages of newspapers and history books."[11] There are uprooted masses in the cities who are "herded into rented squalid lodgings and move about like cattle."[12] Another theme is the contrast between ordinary citizens and the wealthy, "the nouveau riches with their craze for power," the tycoons.[13] A further theme is the relationship between gifted individuals and people in power. Only one theme moves away from these issues and toward art relating to Igbo sayings and proverbs.

At about this time Udechukwu painted *The Exile Train* (1980, oil), in which huddled masses approach the viewer with agonized faces. The phrase "exile train" is taken from a poem by the Nigerian poet Okogbule Wonodi, a title that Udechukwu also employed later.[14] In the 1980 oil, *Shortage of Water,* two distraught women carry empty head pails, with a pile of empty pails and containers at their side; other water carriers are in silhouette in the right background. A third 1980 oil, *Tycoon and Stevedores,* shows men struggling to carry large, heavy bags forward on their shoulders, with the face of a tycoon in dark glasses and smoking a cigar eyeing them from behind, and with ships in the distance on the water.[15] Udechukwu has sometimes used a lighted cigar in a man's mouth as a symbol of ruthless power.

In 1981 Udechukwu mounted an exhibition, *No Water,* at Nsukka and Lagos, which thrust him into some popularity for the skill of his art and the exhibition's theme.[16] He asks why, if there is so much wealth in the country (from the oil boom), do so many persons have trouble finding sufficient water (a problem by no means solved today). Of course, the lack of water is a metaphor for poverty, for the uneven distribution of wealth, and for suffering. Pictures abound of people lined up with their empty pails and containers waiting for water, of political leaders unwilling or unable to solve the problem, of women with pails on their head, of people searching for and fighting over water. Udechukwu, in the exhibition catalogue, has a poem, "We Were Once Poor But Wealthy," from which I quote in part (italics his):

If thirst catches you in Uwani
If thirst catches you in Ogui
I say
If thirst catches you in Enugu
There are many gutters for free
Police will not arrest you

*We were once poor but rich*
*We are now rich but poor*

. . . . . . . . . . . . . . . . . . . . . .

They stole the people's money
Lent it back to them
At 1000% interest
And they talk of philanthropy
      and chieftaincy
      and status
    they talk of tradition
      of age and youth

If you shackle my feet
Have you manacled my ears?
If you pinion my arms
Have you manacled my tongue?

*We were once poor but happy*
*We are now rich but hungry* [17]

In a 1980 pen and ink, *No Water,* we see the arrogant head of a man looking away to his left, while in the lower right lie empty containers and pails. [18]

No better work depicts the artist's interest in social issues than his pen and ink *Road to Abuja* (fig. 83), with many people in movement to the planned new capital of Nigeria, hoping to gain from it; everyone needs to go there now. There are businessmen and women, workers, perhaps from a wharf, being transported in a trailer; there is a dead person in the foreground, fallen on the way. The work depicts the two sides of Nigeria, the affluent and the poor.

In his 1985 London exhibition *Rhythm of Hunger,* Udechukwu again plays on the themes of hunger and suffering, mostly in ink wash and watercolor. [19] A popular softground etching exhibited there, *Chameleon* (fig. 84), shows three faces in the lower foreground, dressed to represent the three main cultural and political blocs in Nigeria. [20] With an *akika*-like background derived from *uli* wall murals, there is a chameleon above the men's heads, an animal depicted in *uli* art and occasionally by Nigerian contemporary artists. As the chameleon changes its colors, so politicians change their beliefs and actions. Udechukwu explains that this is a necessary art for a politician to meet changing conditions, but of course it can also be hypocritical.

In 1985 Udechukwu held a solo exhibition in Lagos, *Onye Ndidi* ("patient person"). In the catalogue he states the theme:

> We seem to be caught in a new cult of easy money, embezzlement of public funds, exploitation of the weak and extortion. A nation that cannot feed her people is in trouble, and that is putting it mildly. Many years ago, Obiligbo [a famous Igbo minstrel] warned that hunger was around the corner and advised that one set of Nigerians should go to school while another set went to the farm. Was the voice of the poet, the prophet heeded? [21]

The works on exhibit are about everyday life: the birth of a baby, the theme of waiting, a master palm wine tapper, cars, and life in the city. The moral theme is the need for patience, as in planting food crops and waiting for them to grow. A 1985 linocut, *Fisherbird* (fig. 85), with a fish at the lower left with little fish inside, a dangling fishhook, an *nsibidi* mirror motif with fish inside, and a bird at the top of the print, refers to the idea that it is only a patient person who catches the fish. [22]

Since these exhibitions, Udechukwu has created other works of art in this vein, such as *Politician* (1989, pen

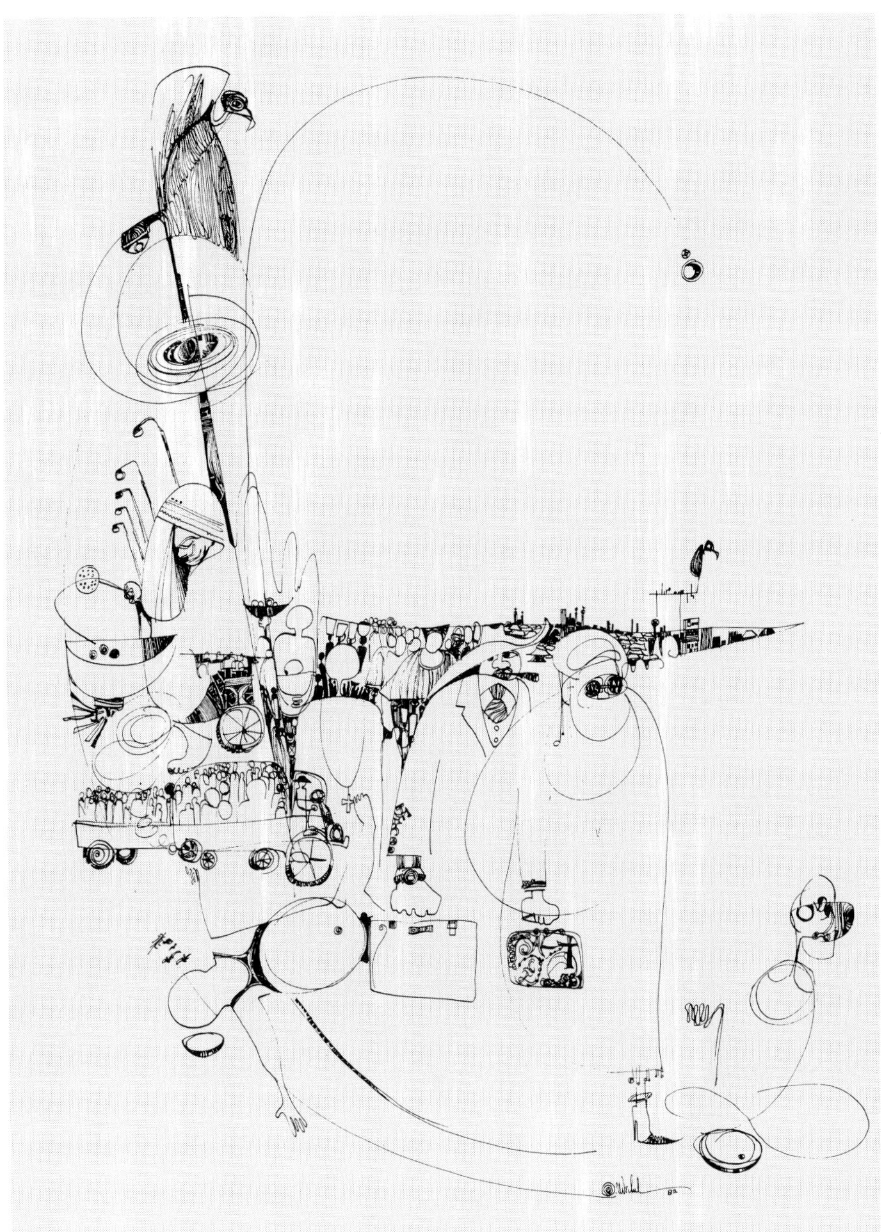

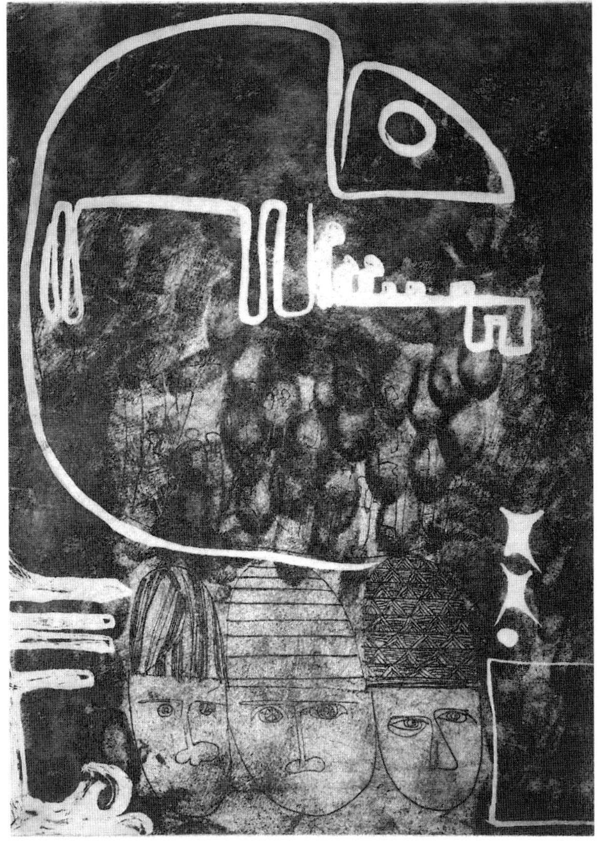

**83 (LEFT)**. Obịọra Udechukwu, *Road to Abuja*, 1982, pen and ink. 39.8 × 29.7 cm. Collection of the artist. Photo: Franko Khoury.

**84 (RIGHT)**. Obịọra Udechukwu, *Chameleon*, 1985, softground etching. 29.7 × 20.7 cm. Collection of Janet L. Stanley. Photo: Franko Khoury.

and ink), depicting a smug, cigar-smoking man looking over his shoulder.[23] *The General Is Up* (1987, ink and wash) shows the giant, looming figure of a military leader hovering over tiny silhouetted masses below.[24] *Writing in the Sky* (1989, silkscreen; fig. 86) has numerous silhouetted standing people in the foreground with their backs toward the viewer, looking into the sky, where a moon is crossed by a horizontal band holding a variety of *uli* and *nsibidi* images, such as star cluster, star, kola nut head, leopard's claw, love, mirror, and scorpion.[25] Udechukwu tells me that the print refers to the phrase from the Bible (Book of Daniel 5): "Mene Mene Teqel Upharsin," the handwriting on the wall at King Belshazzar's banquet. The Nsukka hills lie below the sky and above the masses

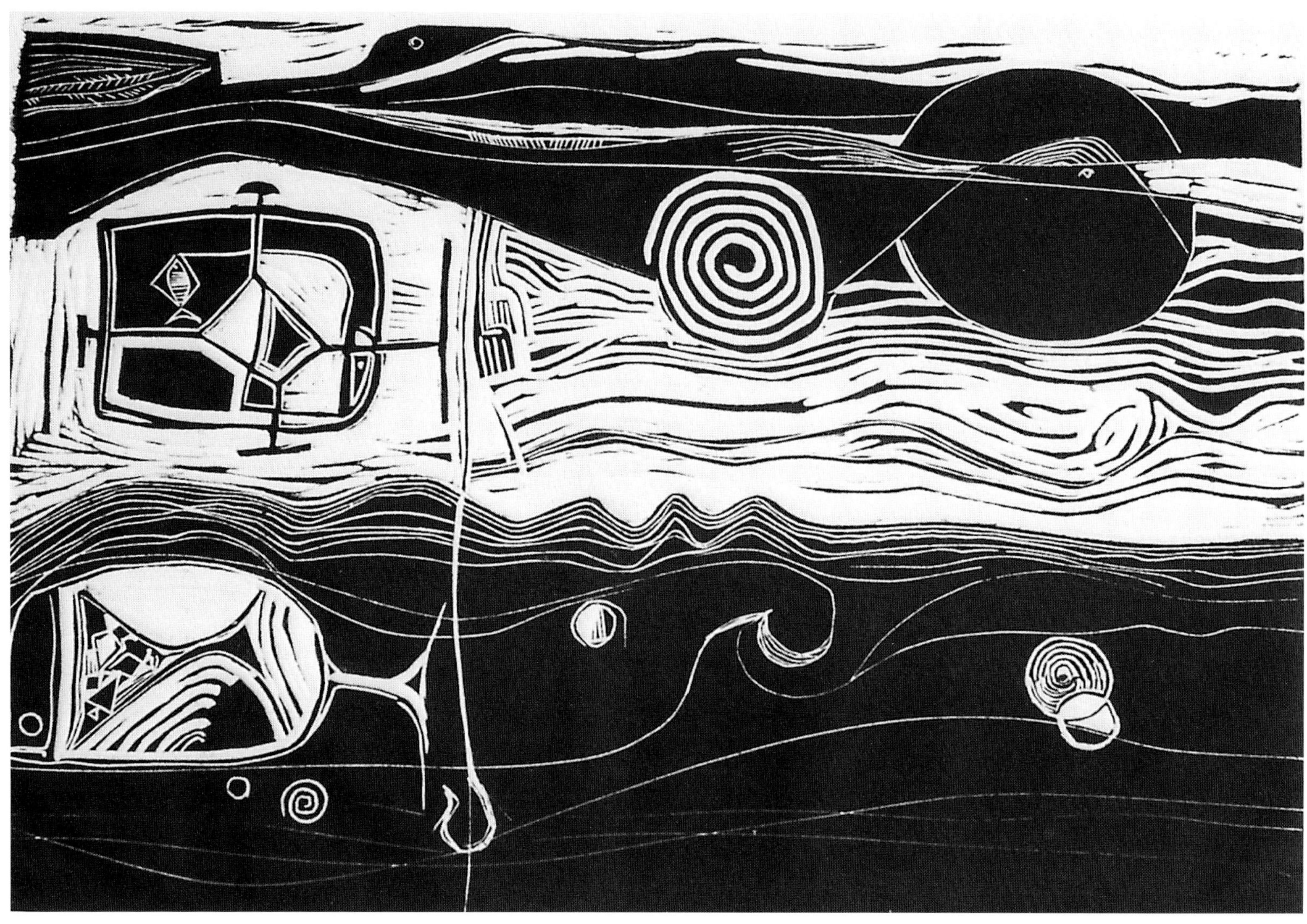

on the ground. Udechukwu says that Igbo minstrels claim that they look into the clouds and see signs, which they take and sing. So the print refers to minstrels, but also to people looking for a hopeful sign; it is also a political picture. We see how the artist integrates the past and present in one work.

Udechukwu's captions for some of his art, poetry, and prose are in Igbo and draw much from Igbo culture. Yet apart from his Biafran war art, his social and political messages have rarely been specifically about Igbo life. Rather they express a deep concern over conditions in Nigeria (and sometimes elsewhere in Africa). He moves widely and freely in the country with many friends and colleagues of various cultural backgrounds. Concerned about Igbo culture and life, like other Nsukka artists he does not wish to return to an idealized Igbo past, but rather is anxious for the future of both Nigeria and the Igbo people.

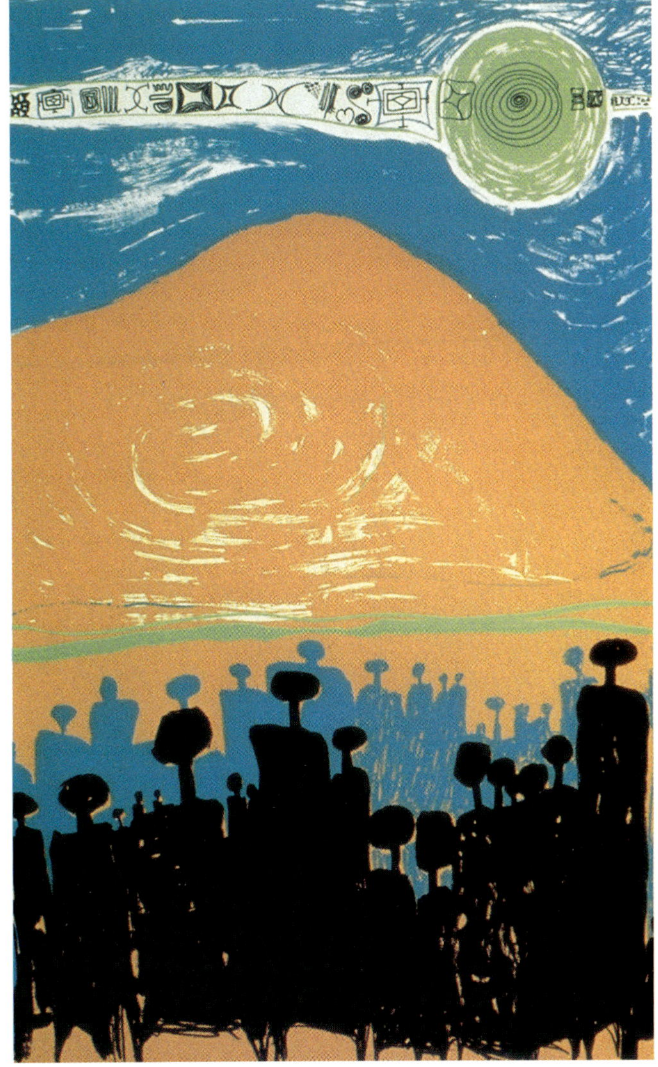

## LANDSCAPES

Another major theme in Udechukwu's art, present since the beginning of his career, has been landscapes. Since coming to Nsukka he has been stimulated by its lovely, largely bare, grassy rolling hills and the sometimes wondrous skies.[26] These contrast with views of destruction that he created during the war, for example, his 1968 oil, *Desolate Landscape* (fig. 87), showing a destroyed landscape. He expressed his love of the Nsukka landscape in a eulogy written for the catalogue of his 1989 Lagos exhibition *Nsukka Landscape,* many of whose works were created in the 1987–88 period, for example, *The Road to Nsukka* (fig. 88).[27] While there are several etchings, having something of the linear quality of his pen and ink or ink and wash work, such as *The Return of Ọmabe* (1987) and *Nsukka Landscape: Cornfield* (1987), which is quite realistic, most of the others are in other media and have different qualities.[28] There is less of a specific placing of *uli* motifs in the pictures, and he draws little on *nsibidi* motifs. Rather there are often broad linear swirls of color, ovals, circles, other large color masses, and a general absence of humans, as if the artist had returned to a primeval, prehuman world because of his dissatisfaction with social and political conditions and environmental damage.[29] The landscapes vary from those with a static quality to those containing swirling lines and forms that suggest powerful natural movements at work, as in *The Sky and the Earth* (1988, gouache) and *When the Bush Burns* (1986, watercolor).[30] The linear quality of *uli* is still there, but it takes a different form than in his ink work, and the roundish masses of colors are suggestive of the background *akika* of *uli* wall painting. Udechukwu sometimes uses this *akika* quality not only as background but also within key images. These postwar landscapes are not obviously political; however, they express a hope for a world respectful of nature. As many Nsukka artists, Udechukwu is sensitive to the unchecked environmental destruction that goes on in Nigeria.

Udechukwu moves back and forth between his sociopolitical images, with their often strong, satiric quality,

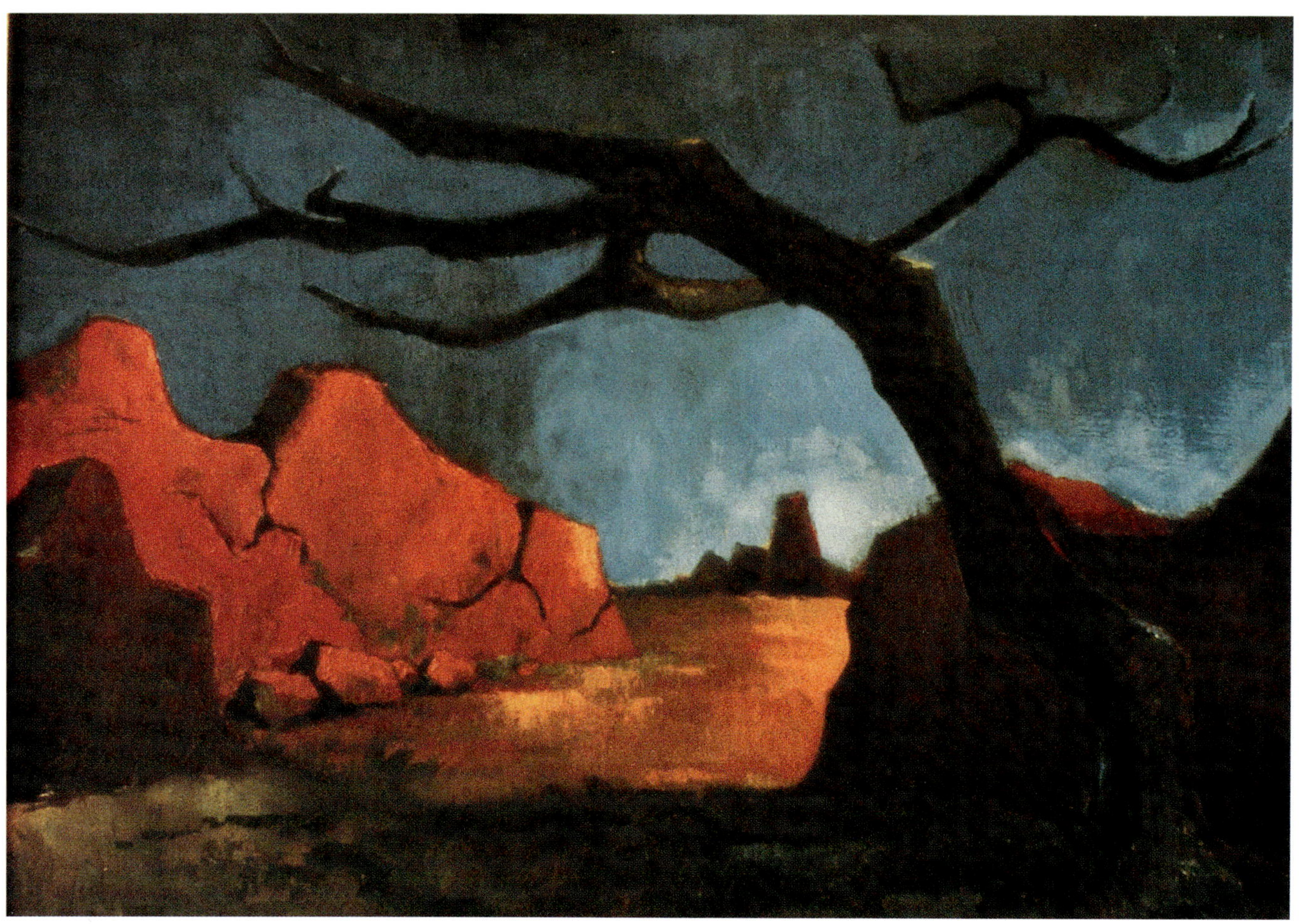

**87**. Obiọra Udechukwu, *Desolate Landscape,* 1968, oil on canvas. 48.2 × 65.5 cm. Collection and photo: the artist.

occasionally bordering on cartoons (if it were not for his considerable artistic skill), and his more peaceful, though occasionally quite powerful and turbulent landscapes. It is as if each kind of image is a change, perhaps a relief, from the other, representing two sides of Udechukwu's artistic interests and personality, the wish for a beautiful, peaceful, natural world, undestroyed by humans, and the need to point up and combat the evils of his country's social and political world.

## OTHER IMAGES

In addition to his sociopolitical and landscape themes, often quite pointed when Udechukwu has a solo exhibition, there are other themes that appear in his work, sometimes as early as the 1960s, which reflect continuing interests and concerns.

He frequently depicts ordinary persons. We have seen his portrayal of masses of people in his silkscreen, *Writ-*

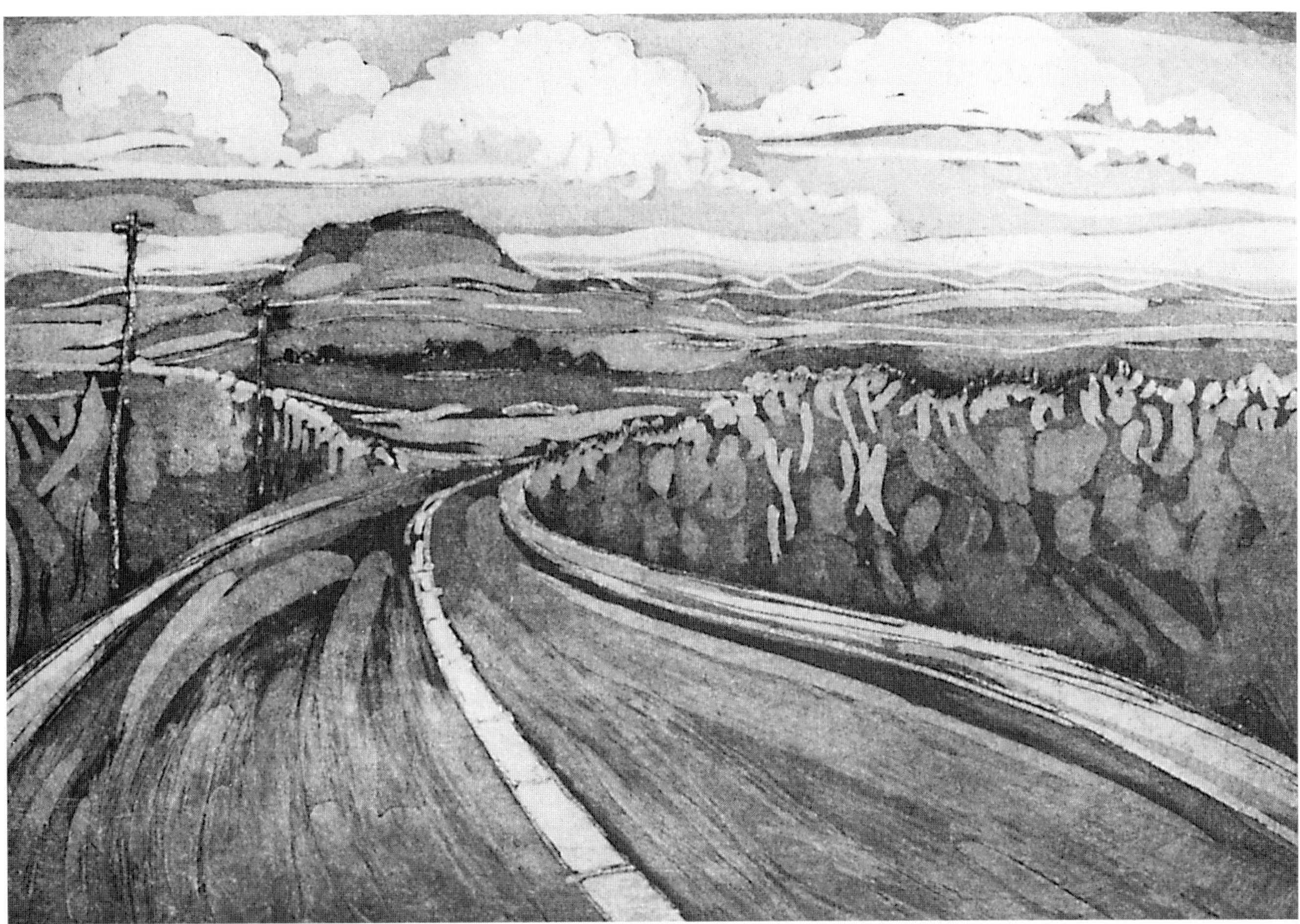

**88**. Obiọra Udechukwu, *The Road to Nsukka,* 1987, aquatint, dimensions unknown. Collection and photo: the artist.

*ing in the Sky;* they also occur in other works, as in some of his wartime art concerning refugees, which may be where he developed an interest in depicting groups of people. He has also created images of laborers, such as of water carriers in the 1980 oil, *Mai Ruwa.*[31] There are several works concerning stevedores, as his 1980 oil, *Tycoon and Stevedores.*[32] Nightsoilmen are also found, as in his effective and affective 1964 oil, *Nightsoilman* (see fig. 73), and his 1971 oil of the same title.[33] In the 1960s and 1970s he produced a number of images of beggars, beginning as early as 1963 with the oil, *Kpabiala,* depicting a blind Muslim beggar, and in 1978 the pen and ink, *Alien Beggars.*[34] Other images of the common man include a long-faced and grotesque visage in a 1967 gouache, entitled *Kepkanly,* a real-life character, referred to in Christopher Okigbo's *Heavensgate* as a half-serious, half-comical primary school teacher, alive in the late 1930s.[35] Other images of ordinary people include tailors, fishermen, and cattle herders. There is a class scale to Udechukwu's male images. The lower social levels are treated sympathetically; they are patient, hardworking, decent, suffering, incorruptible and are also favored in his poetry. At society's upper levels are the wealthy businessmen, senior politicians, and generals, who are portrayed critically

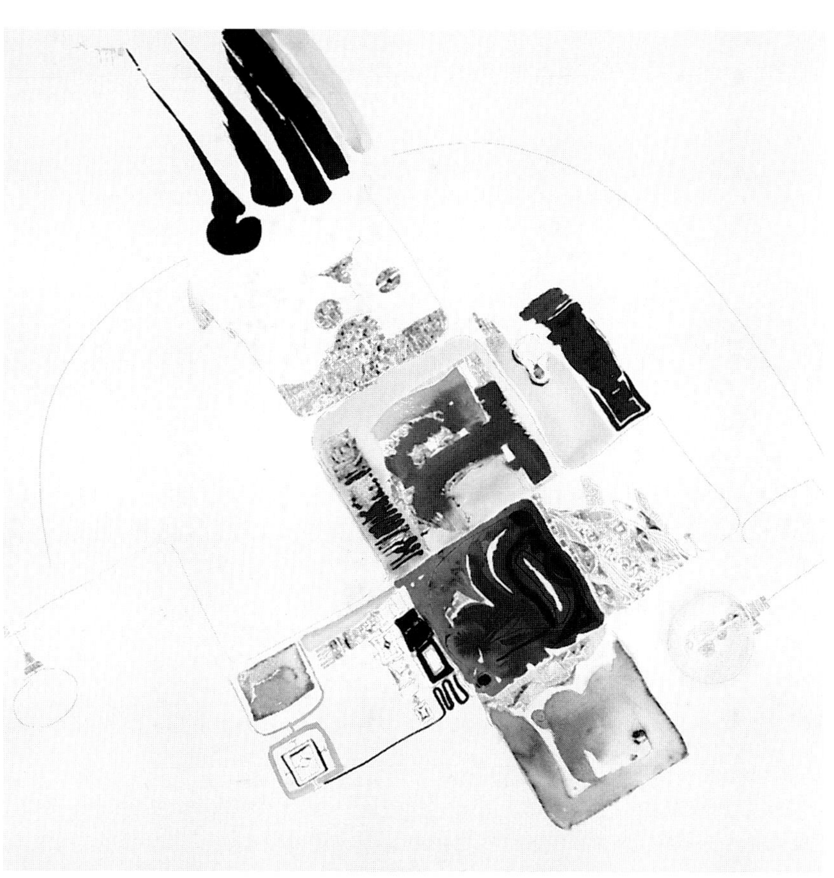

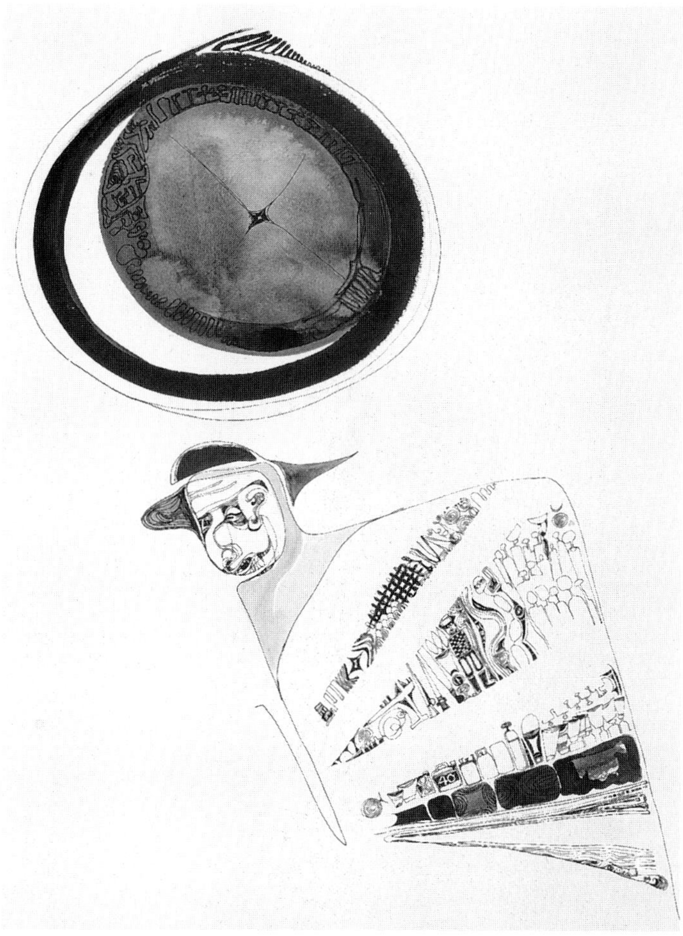

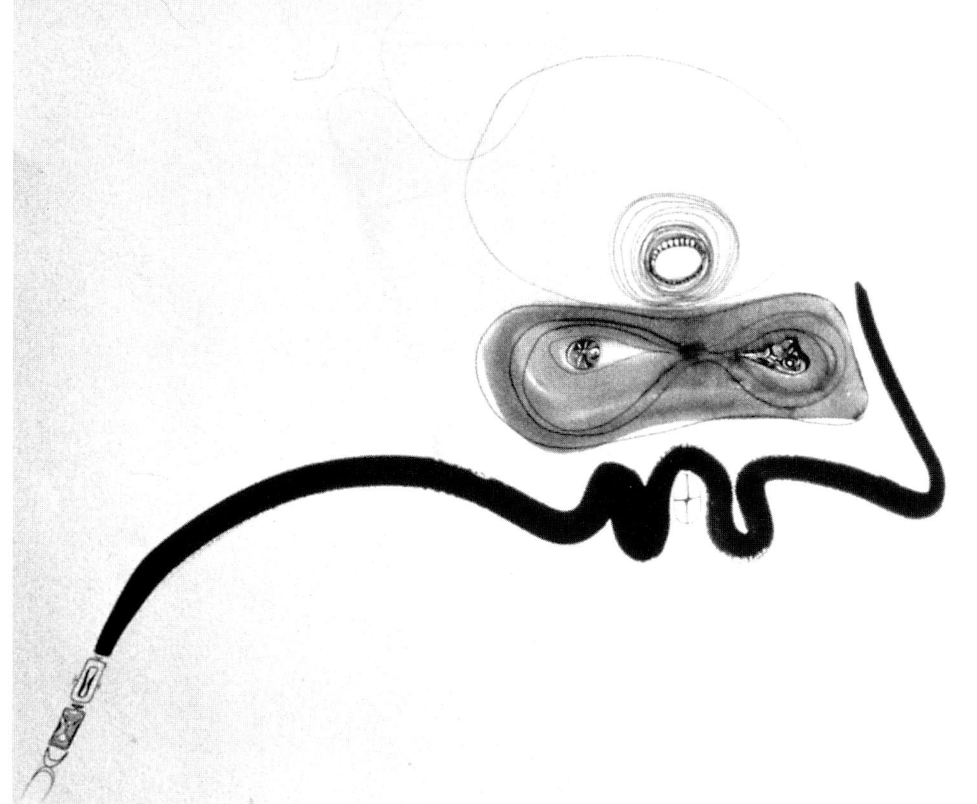

**89 (TOP LEFT).** Obiọra Udechukwu, *Magnificent Masquerade,* 1991, ink, wash, drybrush, pencil on paper. 57.2 × 77.5 cm. Collection of the artist. Photo: Franko Khoury.

**90 (BOTTOM LEFT).** Obiọra Udechukwu, *Behind the Mask,* 1989, ink and gouache on paper. 36 × 48 cm. Private collection.

**91 (RIGHT).** Obiọra Udechukwu, *Journey into the Unknown,* 1989, pen and ink. 48 × 36 cm. Gift of Bernice M. Kelly to the National Museum of African Art. Photo: Franko Khoury.

and satirically as corrupt, self-centered, greedy, and controlling, although a few leaders are praised. Muslims in his art occupy a range of images, from beggars to persons of substance; some of the leaders that Udechukwu depicts with scorn are of that faith.

Women in Udechukwu's art vary, not simply on a class basis. In his war and postwar art, they are seen as distressed mothers, a metaphor for human suffering, as they try to protect their children, the wounded, the ill, and the old, having patience and being custodians of society's values.[36] He has depicted them with political power in his 1967 pen and ink, *Woman of Giant Breasts,* referring to the mythical female figure of the 1929 Aba riots, which Uche Okeke painted in oil.[37] He has depicted them as stolid and determined in his 1969 oil pastel, *Nne (Ochie).*[38]

Udechukwu's depictions of women since the war have moved in various directions. For example, *Alien Beggars* shows a Muslim woman begging from a well-dressed man with a briefcase who is passing by, ignoring her. Udechukwu writes that his work "captures the exploitation of women and children in the name of religion; children and women beg aggressively on the roads while their fathers and husbands play cards under the flyovers."[39] On the other hand, *At the Mirror* (1975, pen and ink) and *Girl at the Mirror* (1985, aquatint/etching) show females preoccupied with beauty and self-appearance, as does *Iwalẹwa* (1985, linocut), which stresses beauty and character.[40] Since Udechukwu's wartime art, males predominate over females in the frequency of appearance; I am not certain why.

An occasional subject is that of musicians. The range is wide, from traditional Igbo playing the lamellaphone (*ubọ*),[41] as in the undated *Ubọ* in colored pencil, to modern musicians in *Homage to Rex Lawson* (1984, ink and wash).[42] Udechukwu's musical interest is not surprising; as already noted, he appreciates various art forms. It is also not unexpected in someone who talks and writes of *uli*'s lyricism, which he endeavors to emulate in his art.[43] His musical interests include his love for performances by Igbo minstrels. The minstrels chant and sing long epics, myths, and shorter poems, often playing the *ubọ*.[44] Udechukwu sees their work as being creative and original; he is more attracted to it than to the tales that entrance Uche Okeke; each artist draws from different aspects of Igbo culture. Udechukwu has created some dozen images of minstrels, and he has heard and sketched them, as he did Ezigbo Obiligbo in 1967 at Nsukka.[45] He has created images of Jadum, a well-known eccentric, sometime minstrel, mentioned in Christopher Okigbo's poem *Heavensgate,* for example, *Jadum* (1979, watercolor) and *"Jadum-Rockland Minstrel"* (1981, watercolor).[46]

Igbo tradition is not forgotten. In the highly stylized ink, wash, drybrush, and pencil on paper, *Magnificent Masquerade* (1991; fig. 89), whose title is taken from a song by the famous Igbo minstrel Obiligbo, there are various *uli* and an *nsibidi* mirror. Here politics and social issues are put aside, as in his ink and gouache, *Behind the Mask* (1989; fig. 90) with its kola nut *uli* mouth, where he moves to another level, that of the personal. Udechukwu has indicated to me that we do not know what is behind a face; this is true even for the artist.

Udechukwu has created few anticolonial works, perhaps because he began his serious artistic life after independence. However, he feels that colonialism did great damage to Igbo and Nigerian life and culture and that, in the politics of the postindependence era, these wrongs have never been righted and have even worsened.

Some works of the 1970s and 1980s have "exile" or "unknown" (or both) in the title. Udechukwu's 1980 oil, *Exile Train,* and a 1981 brush and ink of the same title[47] resulted from viewing Biafran war refugees, who faced an unknown future, as did the 1973 woodcut, *The Exiles (Facing the Unknown).*[48] At least ten of his works have the word "unknown" in their titles, and some four are called *Journey into the Unknown* (fig. 91). One of them, a 1989 pen and ink on paper, contains a male figure wearing a wrapper on which there are drawings of figures alluding to the war. This work also includes *uli* images, a rifle, a sword, a machete, a nightsoilman, and a group of people; a complexity of ideas is involved. There are several works titled *Facing the Unknown,* for example, a 1986 aquatint.[49] Recent art with the word "unknown" in the title no longer refers to the war but to present-day life, over which there is much uncertainty in the artist's mind and in that of others. The question of where Nigeria is heading today is a serious preoccupation for many Nsukka artists. The uncertainties of a past war and of the present situation in Nigeria have become linked in Udechukwu's art.

Other images in his work include self-portraits, several works entitled *Up There, Down Here,* and several called *The Spirit in Ascent.* Udechukwu's main areas of concentration are clear, but he is not an artist who sticks with one or two subjects over time, as he is not one to employ only one or two media. Diversity characterizes both subject and media.

## WRITINGS

As Udechukwu turned from depicting scenes of the war in the 1980s to those associated with the Nigerian condition, so he has done in his poetry. In his collected poems, *What the Madman Said,* published in 1990, the first half contains his war-related poetry and the second his current social and political poems, making for interesting contrasts.[50] This book, which contains thirteen of his finest drawings, won him the Association of Nigerian Authors Cadbury Poetry Prize for 1990, suggesting the degree of recognition that his poetry has gained in Nigeria. In the book's second half, his poems have the same satiric bitterness as his visual art. Referring to the rain in "Recessional," he writes:

| | |
|---|---|
| If it comes down | Will the lightning strike them with leprosy |
| Will the rain cleanse the land? | The rogues in resplendent robes? |
| Clear the constipated gutters | The swindlers with golden smiles? |
| And bury the stench? | Will the thunder de-shit their pot-belly |
| Can the flood clear the rotting garbage? | The saviours with bottomless pockets?[51] |

The drawings, rarely specifically related to his poems (some were created after they were written), have similar satiric qualities, for example, the three portraits of military leaders.[52] There is a superb integration of *uli* and occasional *nsibidi* motifs in the drawings. One of his best-known poems, "We Were Once Poor But Wealthy," quoted earlier in connection with his *No Water* exhibition, is included in this collection. The "madman" in the book's title refers to the author who, as a poet, speaks for the voiceless masses and sees himself as an alien on the fringes of society, one who can speak freely as a "madman," and with a certain wisdom, whereas the ordinary citizen is unable to do so.[53]

Udechukwu continues to write on Igbo culture, especially on *uli* and its relation to contemporary art.[54] Among his most interesting work on *uli* is a detailed study of wall murals.[55] He writes on political cartoons in Nigeria in the 1970s, perhaps of interest to him because some of his drawings reflect something of the cartoon spirit, though in finer aesthetic form.[56] He has also published a useful commentary on art criticism in Nigeria, a topic that continues to interest him.[57]

Udechukwu's reflective article, "Toward Essence and Clarity," explores his own art.[58] While there are international and universal qualities in good art, "qualities that are formal and technical, nevertheless, there are other equally important aspects that reflect not only individual personality but also period vision and cultural or national peculiarities."[59] Thus he places his art within the current Nigerian scene, a view modified a little by trips to Germany and the United States. He muses on the importance of the line in his art, which he sees as an extended dot or a moving point, delighting in his own work in the interrupted line, "to break the normal line defining a form of object with the salutary effect of creating surprise, novelty and interest."[60] Again, he writes: "There is something about the spontaneously executed work, a breath-taking vitality and freshness that defies description or repetition."[61] There "is no question of erasing or cleaning."[62] No better statements concerning Udechukwu's drawings exist than these. Writing about *uli* and the importance of the line with eloquence, he builds and extends on Okeke's concepts of *uli*'s linear qualities.

## RECENT ART AND ACTIVITIES

In the 1990–95 period Udechukwu continued to work in a range of images.[63] Yet this has also been a time of major change. He has increasingly turned to acrylics. And more and more he uses sgraffito in acrylics and watercolors, perhaps scratching parallel lines with a plastic fork, or creating wavy or circular lines, or scratching in *nsibidi* or *uli* motifs rather than, or as well as, painting them. These marks may cut across painting lines or follow them. These sgraffiti are often small and detailed, requiring close inspection to observe. Looking at the art from a distance does not always reveal them; they become almost secret, to be observed by closing in on the picture. This is consistent with what I have noted about Udechukwu's art, that it may take a range of observations to appreciate it fully.

Sgraffito increases the quality of abstraction in his recent art, but it is also becoming more abstract in watercolor, gouache, and acrylic, more philosophical and less concrete, as Norbert Aas has suggested to me. Chika Okeke writes that in the 1990s Udechukwu "reintroduced opaque pigments—mostly acrylics, in his furtherance of the interpretation of line as outline of a shape and texture. In these pictures, he would, on thin glazes, either drag his brushes creating patterns suggestive of the 'python's trail,' or he would scratch linear designs, both in the manner of traditional Uli wall painters."[64]

In recent years Udechukwu has become increasingly interested in nature, especially the Nigerian seasons, perhaps stemming from his late 1980s landscapes.[65] Political and social images continue to occur in various media, though not much in acrylic, as if this medium has presented other possibilities to him. He has also continued to move more and more toward an emphasis on *nsibidi,* though *uli* is still there. His colors, sometimes muted in the past, have become stronger and richer, although he continues to create his drawings in black. He began creating some quite large acrylic works in this period.

In the 1990s he expanded his German connections, visiting the country a number of times with fruitful results, despite the caution of Norbert Aas that Germany has not shown a great deal of interest in contemporary African art.[66] The peak experience has been his three-month stay there in 1993, mostly living at Merten, near Bonn, but also with a short stay at Bayreuth. In that year, his creativity exploded; he completed more than seventy works, almost all in Germany. Since his return to Nigeria he has been much involved in teaching, organizing exhibitions, taking part in numerous shows, and co-editing a book (with a related conference) in honor of fellow artist/architect Demas Nwoko.

Udechukwu's exhibition schedule during the 1990–95 period was formidable, indicating increasing recognition. He had some solo exhibitions and took part in at least fourteen group shows in Lagos, Enugu, Germany, Johannesburg, London, New York, and Washington, D.C. While these activities have been draining of his creative time, they have also been a stimulus to work.

In Udechukwu's Lagos 1993 retrospective of more than a hundred works created from 1963 to 1993, his recent acrylics show something of his new directions.[67] *What the Weaver Wove* (1992, acrylic on board; fig. 92), a

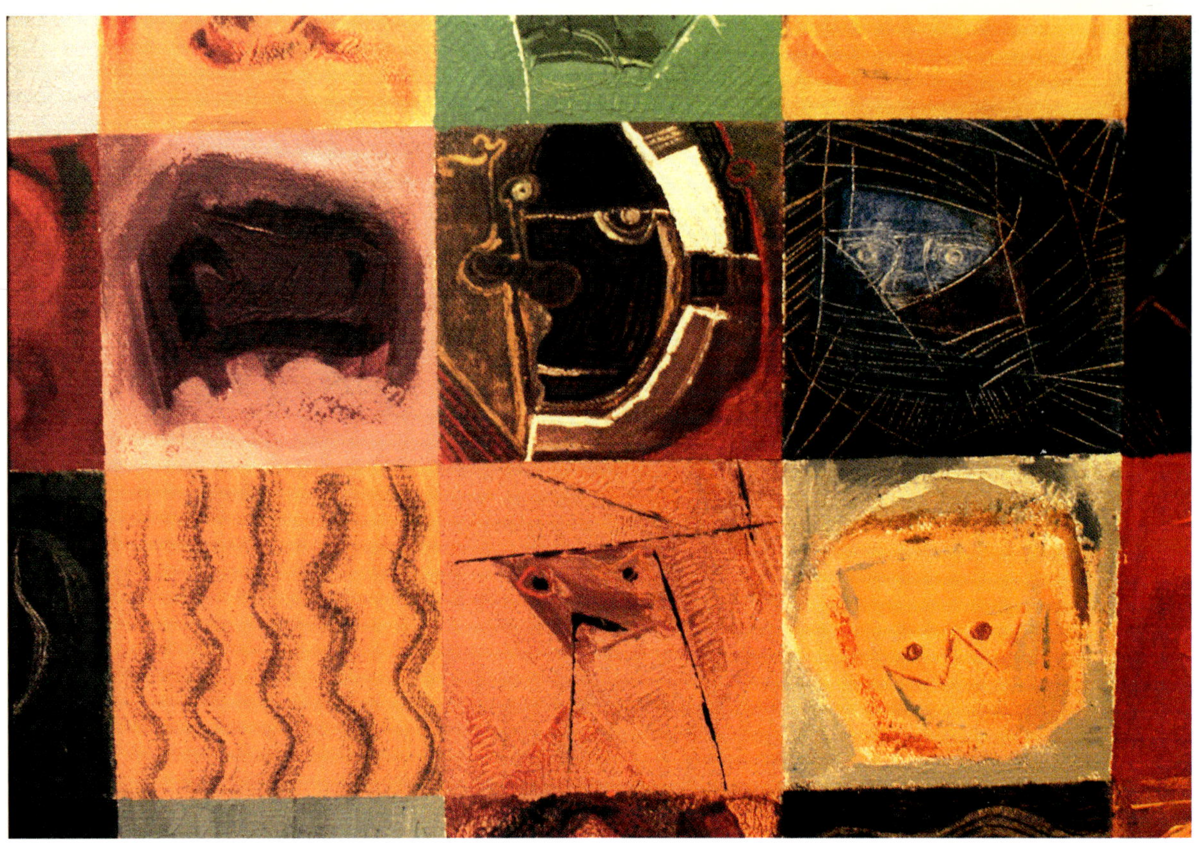

**92 (ABOVE).** Obịọra Udechukwu, detail from *What the Weaver Wove,* 1992, acrylic on board. 122 × 91 cm. Collection of the artist.

**93 (LEFT).** Obịọra Udechukwu, *Spirit in Ascent,* 1992, acrylic on board. 61.3 × 60.8 cm. Private collection.

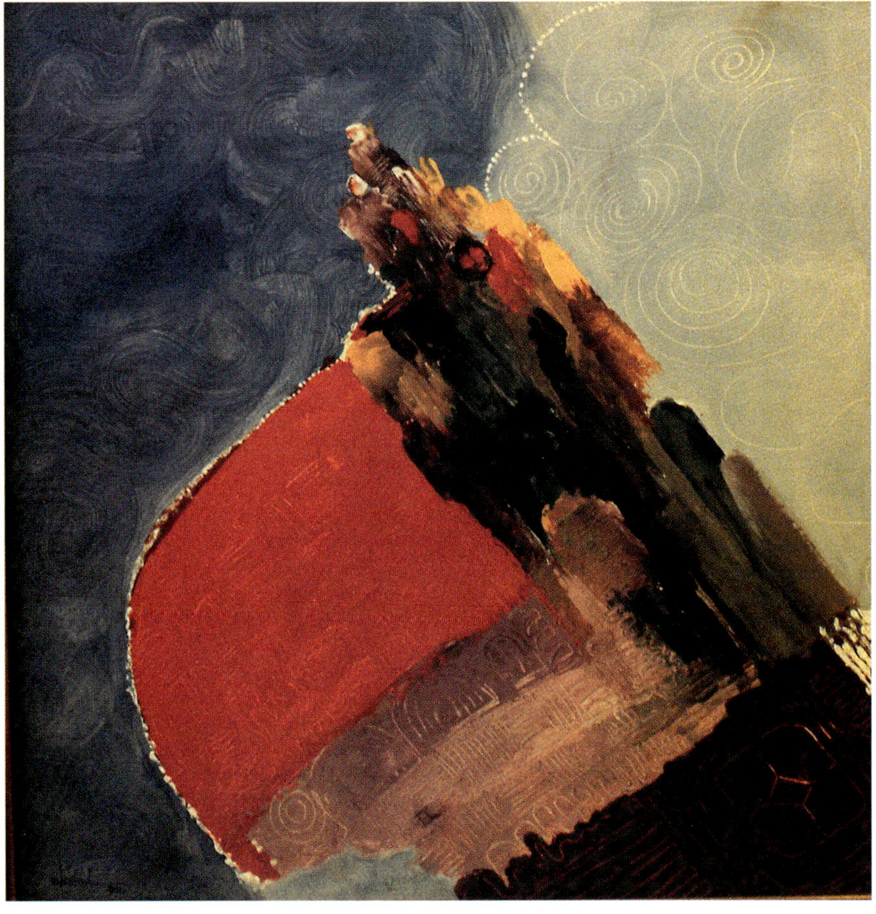

larger work than usual, consists of forty-eight squares arranged eight squares in six contiguous vertical rows.[68] Each square has one or more images within it: a face, a moon, an *nsibidi* mirror, parallel wavy lines, a number of pots, a group of people. The images in different squares seem unconnected but together represent aspects of the life of yesterday and today. The work is quite colorful; there is sgraffito in many squares. When one looks closely, the images seem somewhat realistic, but drawing back, the work as a whole has an abstract quality. It is as if Udechukwu's aim was to create a fine multicolored African cloth, which like exquisite African textiles, demands both close inspection and a distant view.

In the same retrospective, Udechukwu's *Spirit in Ascent* (1992, acrylic on board; fig. 93) shows extensive employment of sgraffito in a variety of parallel line patterns, an *nsibidi* mirror, and numerous *uli* spirals, these scratched into a variety of colors, but especially blue, red, and violet.[69] Going upward from right to left is a mixture of colors, as if a projectile was moving up out of a dark red ground into the blue. This is an unusually abstract work for Udechukwu.

In his three-month stay in Germany in 1993, Udechukwu greatly expanded his acrylic art under the aegis of Norbert Aas and Ulli Beier, with the aid of a fellowship from the Heinrich Boll Foundation. He was in a studio with six artists who were there on a regular basis; Udechukwu occupied a guest studio. As in other trips abroad, the art he produced was largely drawn from Nigerian culture and social issues, although he created some German scenes and a delightful ink and wash *Cat* based on one that sat at his kitchen window at Merten. Although he has produced some fine acrylics, he says he is still experimenting with the medium: "I am beginning to break away from black and white and moving back to painting and exploring other things, especially color as color, almost as an end in itself." [70]

During his German months, he created three related works on the Nigerian seasons, each 140 × 100 cm.[71] In *Ǫkǫchi (Dry Season)* (1993, acrylic and ink on canvas; fig. 94), there is a vague image of an Igbo maiden spirit mask (*agbǫghǫ mmuǫ*) and a moon with dancing figures and musical instruments; these represent the dry season festivals. Bold white lines, perhaps symbolizing life's journey, are filled with tightly packed black ink images of abstract designs and *uli* and *nsibidi* in tiny, simplified form, reminding this viewer of the artist's ink drawings. Red predominates, representing the earth in the dry season. Again there are various sgraffito marks, as well as *akika* swirls.

*Ugǔlǔ (Harmattan)* (1993, acrylic on canvas; fig. 95) has a blue-gray quality appropriate for that season, when the sky is filled with fine dust from the Sahara and strong winds blow. The swirling quality of the art suggests winds, with bits of abstract stuff tossed about in the sky. The use of sgraffito is extensive and easily visible, even from a distance, as in the parallel rows of horizontal, wavy scratch lines in the increasingly dark sky, as one goes to the top of the picture, and the irregular crisscrossing scratch lines below. Horizontal wavy brush strokes in the sky are common. At the work's bottom is a field of light gray with vertical cracks in it, suggesting the cracks in the earth and on humans' skin and lips that occur in this season.

The third work on the seasons, *Udummili (Rainy Season)* (1993, acrylic on canvas; fig. 96), is dominated by massive greens of various shades, appropriate for this fertile time, with suggestions of the Nsukka hills, and with blue at the bottom—the water brought by rain. Sgraffito occurs in the greens, including the ubiquitous *nsibidi* mirror, and in the blue. Mounds of dark earth, outlined in simple scratch lines above the water, represent earth mounds for growing yams, a favorite southern Nigerian food.[72] Above the earth there is a rainbow—a wavy horizontal band of blue, yellow, and red. A moonlike white circle toward the upper right contains a thoughtful face, as if observing the scene of nature at work, and a large fish appears to its left, with a thick-lined blue spiral below it. Without knowledge of the painting's topic, the work would appear to have an abstract quality. Over the years

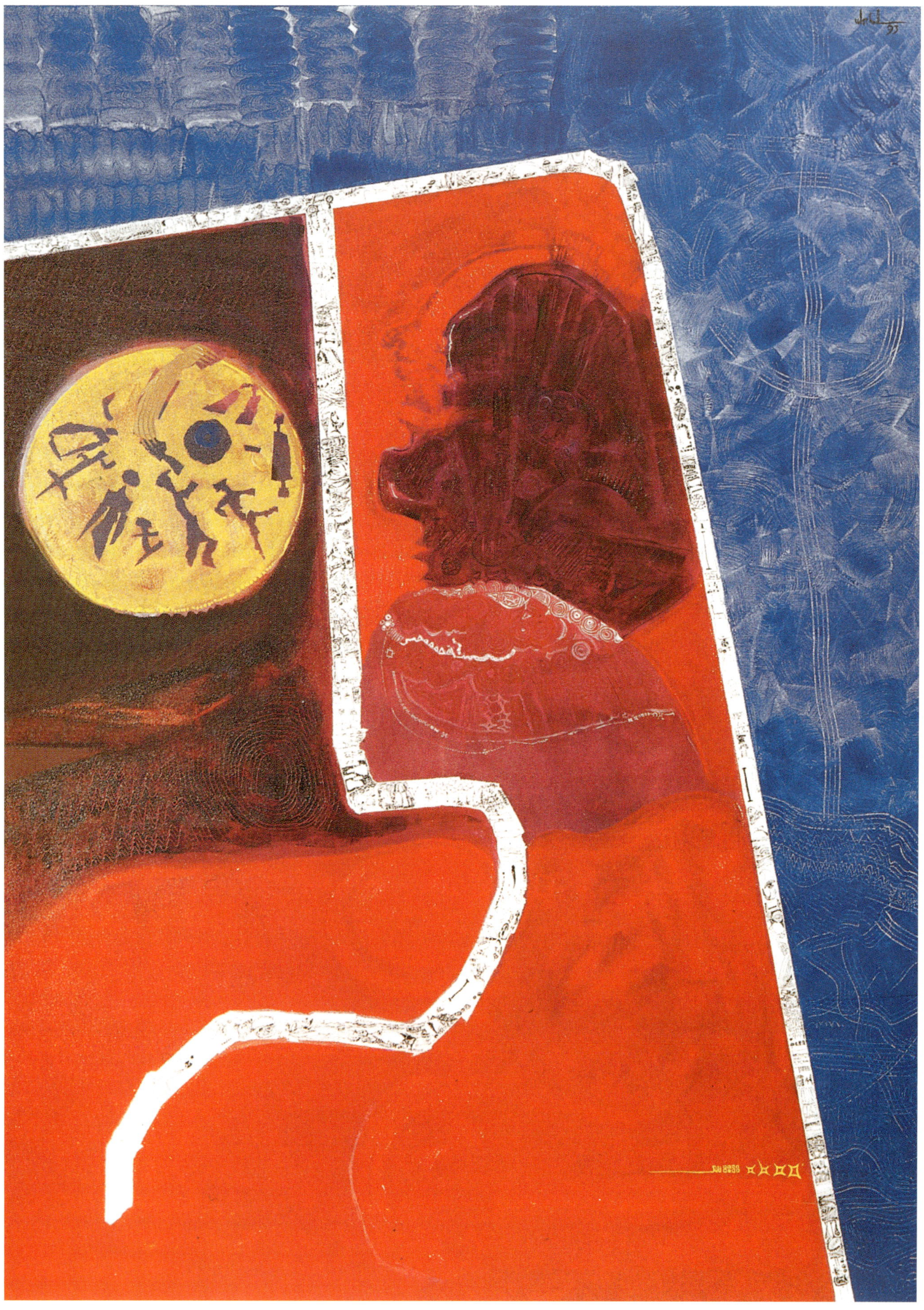

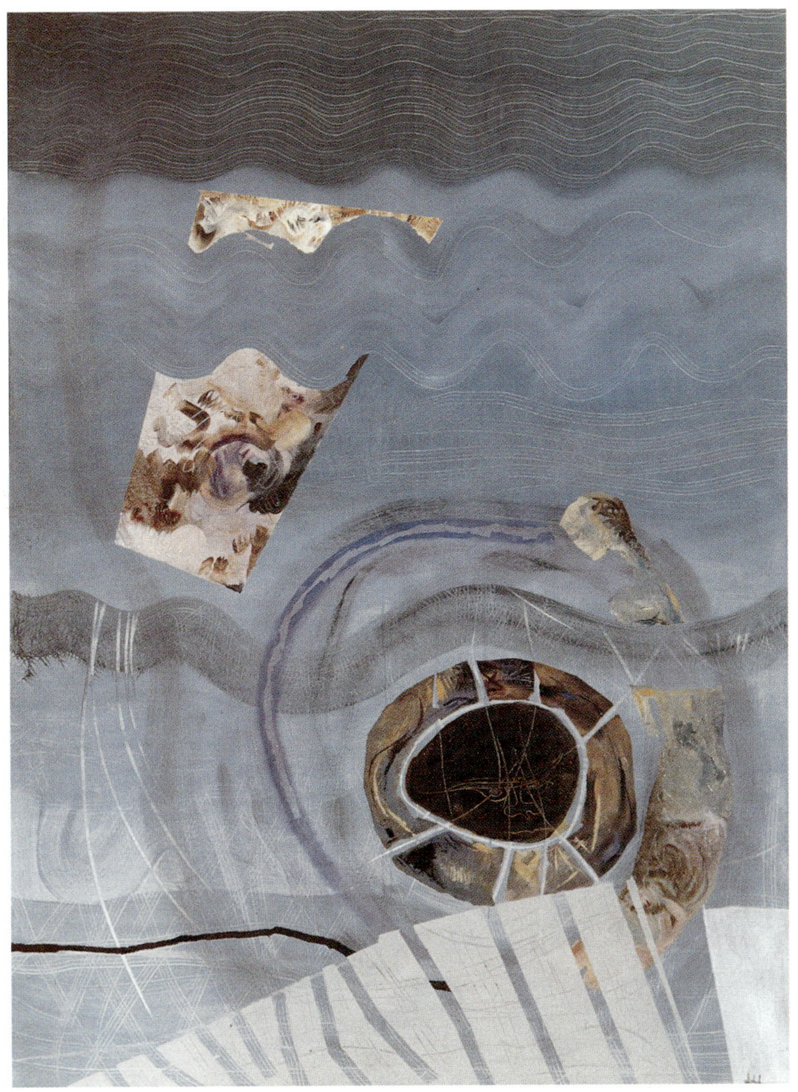

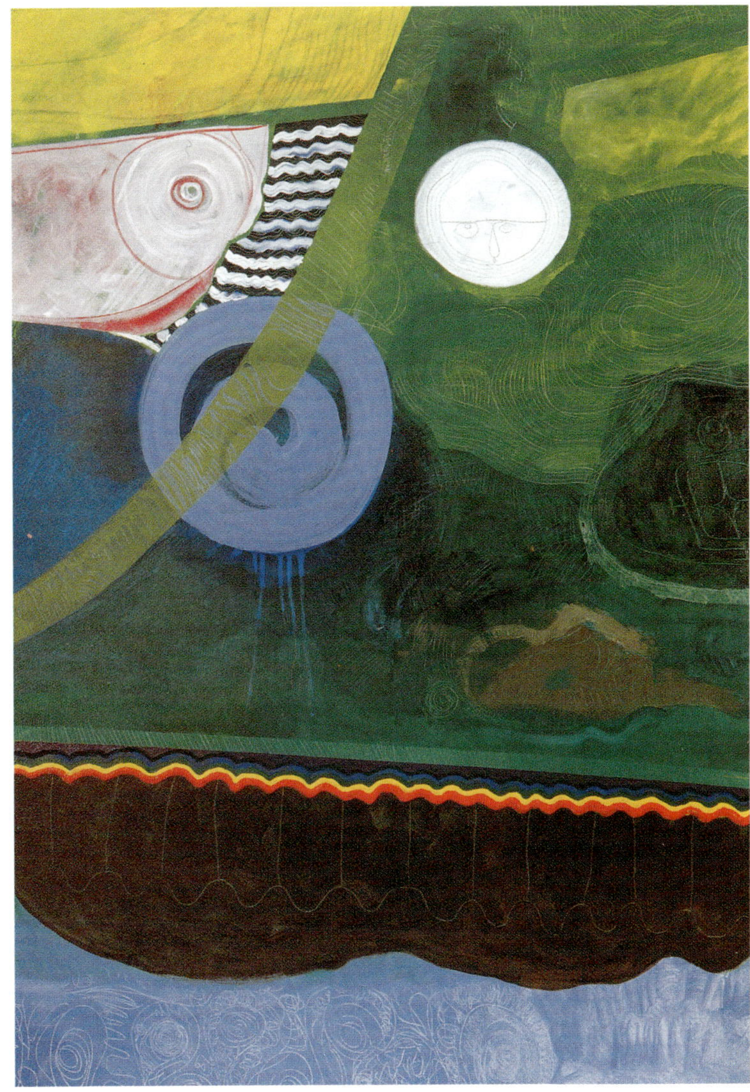

**94 (FACING PAGE).** Obịọra Udechukwu, *Ọkọchi (Dry Season)*, 1993, acrylic and ink on canvas. 140 × 100 cm. Collection of the artist.

**95 (LEFT).** Obịọra Udechukwu, *Ugụlụ (Harmattan)*, 1993, acrylic on canvas. 140 × 100 cm. Collection of the artist.

**96 (RIGHT).** Obịọra Udechukwu, *Udummili (Rainy Season)*, 1993, acrylic on canvas. 140 × 100 cm. Collection of the artist.

Udechukwu has produced a number of works on the seasons. These three represent the annual round of climate in southeastern Nigeria.

*Our Journey* (1993, acrylic on canvas; figs. 97–100), Udechukwu's largest two-dimensional work, consists of four side-by-side panels, each 200 × 160 cm. Weaving through all four panels is a broad yellow band representing the sacred Igbo python and also the road of life. The band curls into a spiral in the right panel and in wavy fashion moves across the panels through the left one. The band contains numerous black lined images. In the right panel it has an *nsibidi* mirror and a few traditional Igbo designs but is largely empty, as if representing the journey's birth, that of the Nigerian and Igbo people. The band in the second panel from the right has traditional elements: combs, a mask, mirrors, a couple, and seemingly an image of a Benin bronze head of antiquity. The next band to the left

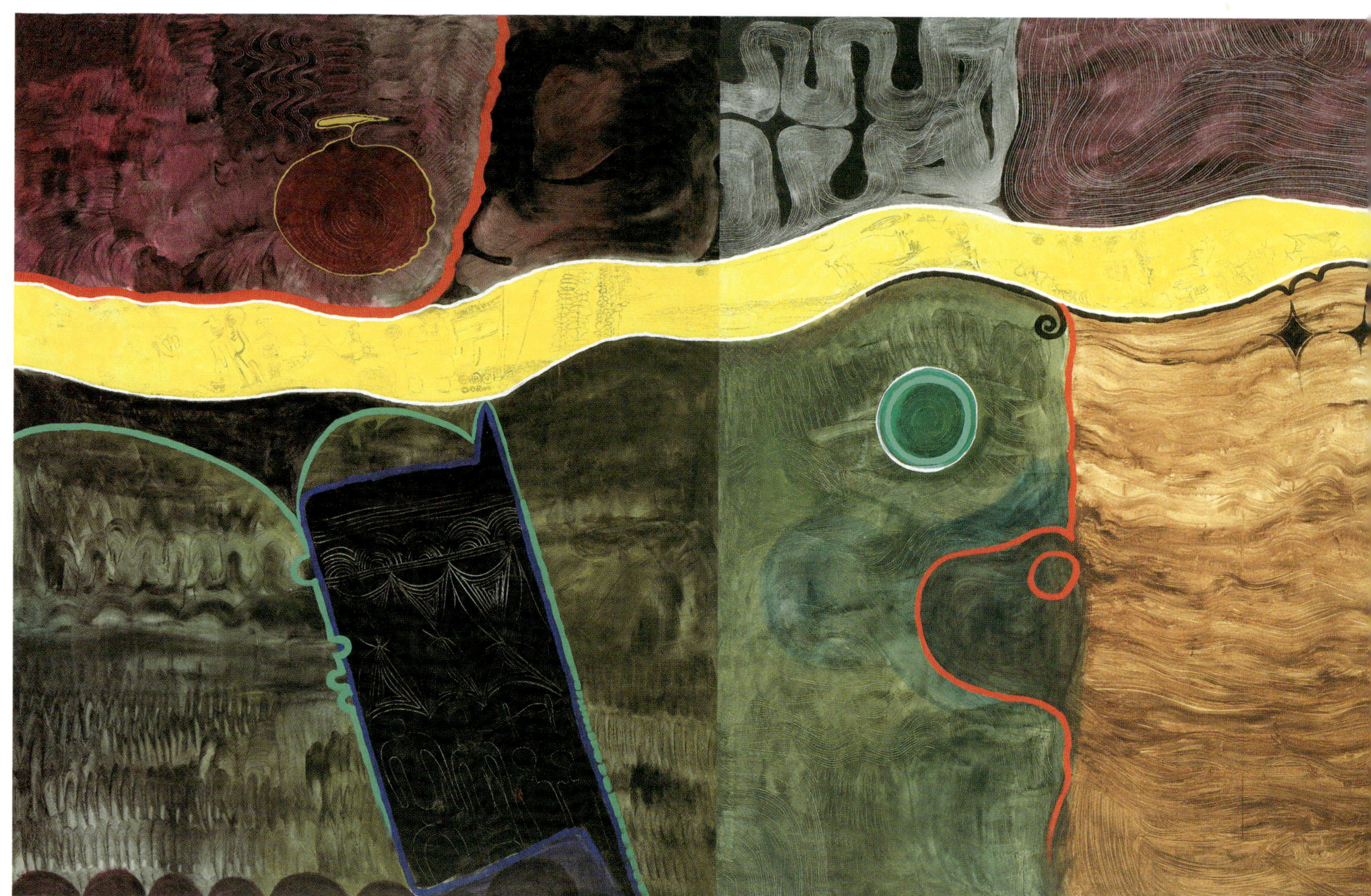

**97**. Obiọra Udechukwu, *Our Journey*, 1993, acrylic and ink on canvas, 200 × 640 cm. in four panels, each 200 × 160 cm. Collection of the artist. Photo: Franko Khoury.

draws on the Biafran war with the theme of patience, a chameleon, refugees, images of lack of water, and numerous *uli*, such as the crescent moon, the lizard, and the leopard's claw (fig. 99). The leftmost band shows people sitting, a woman with a mirror, a military man pointing a gun, a minstrel with his *ubọ* instrument, a lady with long breasts, destitute people with skulls and bones. This panel generally represents recent times. Many motifs and images in the four panels are found in Udechukwu's earlier work, as if *Our Journey* is a summation of his life so far, employing elements that have intrigued him over the years. The remainder of the work consists of masses of color, with a variety of sgraffiti in them, and numerous circular brush images. Udechukwu produced other significant acrylics during this period in Germany, including *"Eyes Open . . ."* (fig. 101), smaller in size, and three large works that stand side by side called *Isinwaọji* (fig. 102a, b, c), with the theme of the kola nut head.

In this 1990–95 period, the artist produced a substantial number of watercolors, a medium he has long em-

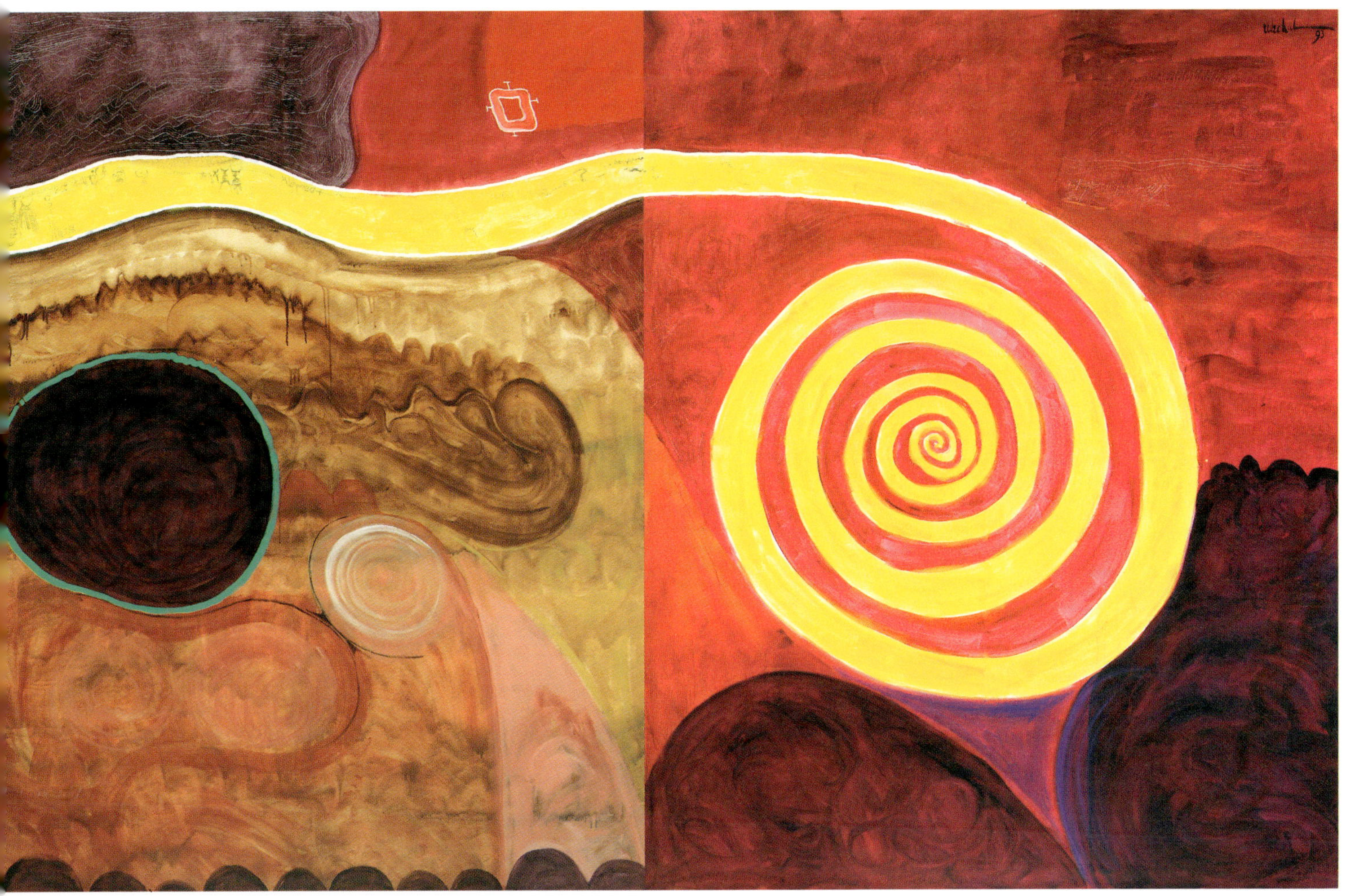

ployed. Some of these tend toward the abstract, as in his watercolor with ink, wash, and pencil, *The Road, the General and the Noose* (1993; fig. 103), and his 1994 watercolor, *The Prisoner* (fig. 104), both works making strong political statements. His watercolors are more muted and blended than his acrylics, with many strokes of swirls, circles, and ovals, often providing a sense of motion, even of turbulence, as in his watercolor and ink, *Landscape with Moon and Music* (1993; fig. 105). These watercolors have the appearance of being produced rapidly, yet with clear intent, having the suggested, not fully filled in, quality of his drawings. Sgraffito occurs in some of his recent watercolors, not differing much from that in his acrylics. Udechukwu's watercolors in this period show growth in depth, subtlety, and maturity over earlier ones.

In the summer of 1995 Udechukwu took part in a large-scale postmodern art project, *Configura 2*, in Erfurt, Germany, involving artists from nine countries working within the scope of six possible themes.[73] Obiọra Udechukwu, El Anatsui (see Chapter 9), and Buraimọh Gbadamọsi were the Nigerian artists, with Ulli Beier as their curator. The artists' work was produced throughout the city's streets.

Udechukwu worked with the theme of The Altar of Culture. He rejected as out of place, in terms of the city's architecture, and as too limiting, the use of one of the large modern white cement boxes within which the artists were to construct their work, with windows for the public to look into. Instead, Udechukwu created, in an old

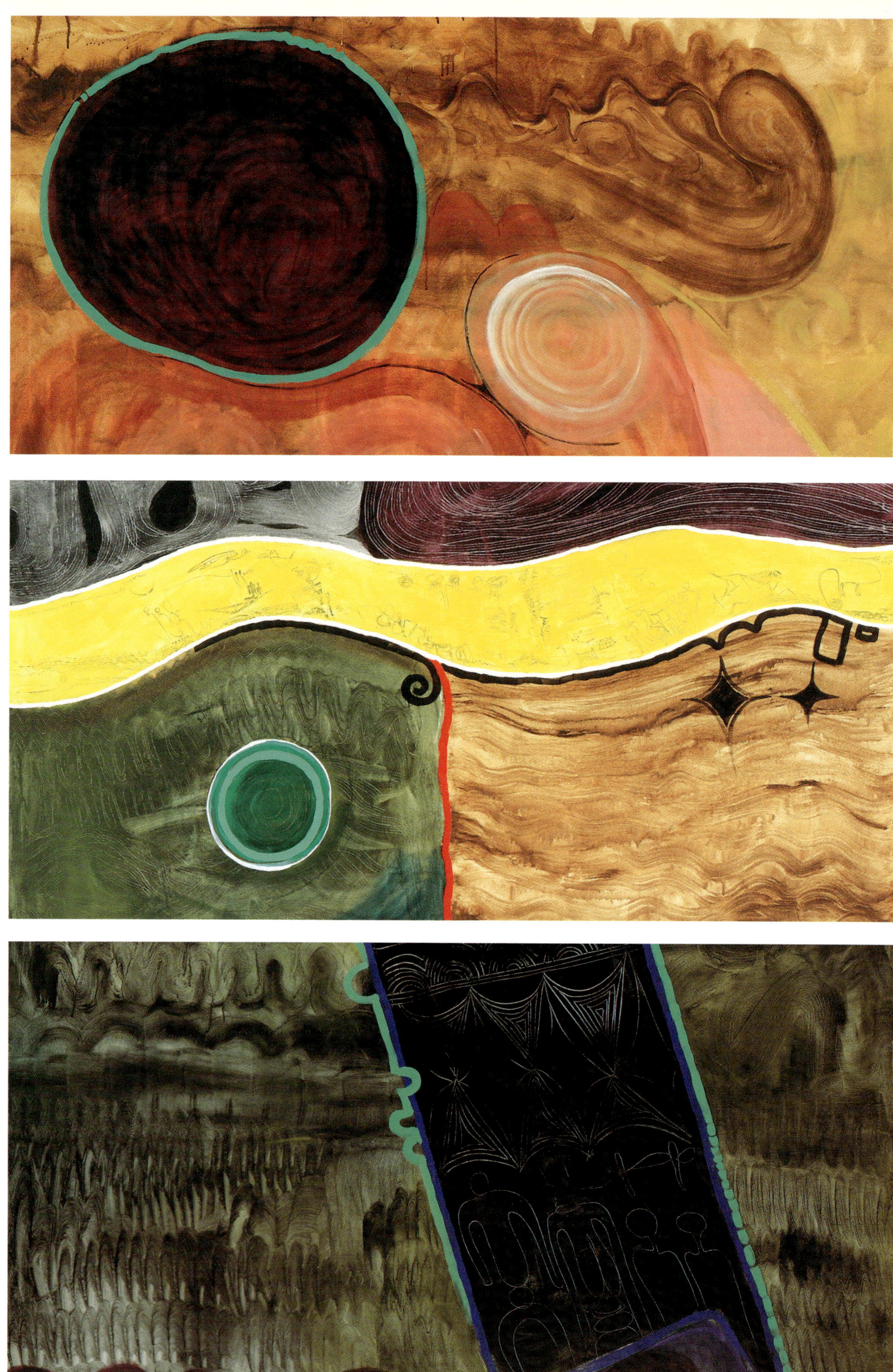

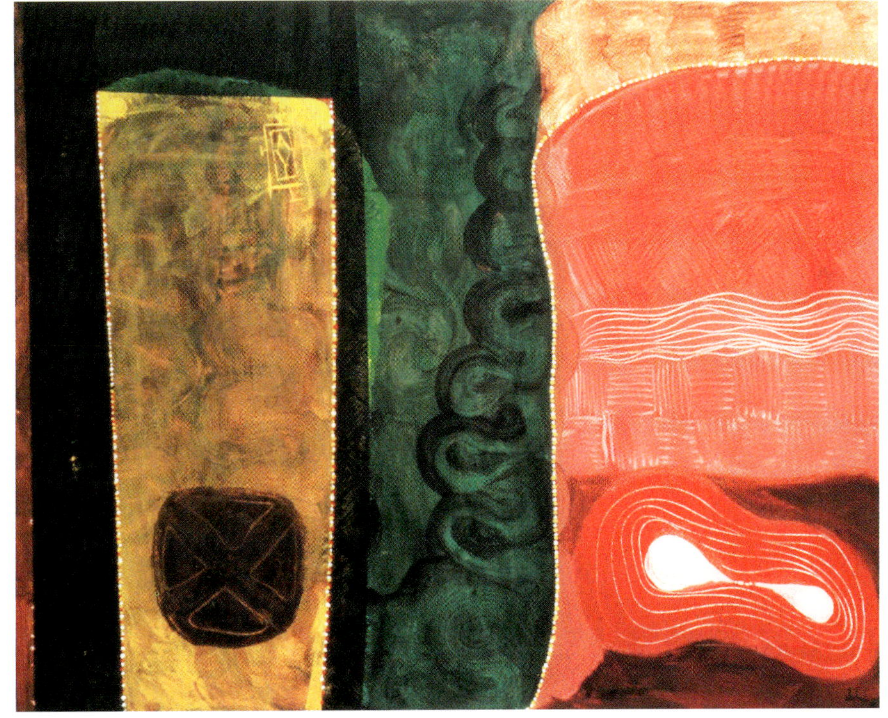

courtyard, a mud structure with chestnut trees at the edges, thus bringing Igbo culture to Germany (fig. 106). He developed a miniature, symbolic outer section of the Igbo *obi* meeting places for friends, with an inner family living area. The back wall and sides of the structure were composed of mud-covered insulating bricks, a meter high with rounded mud balls piled against their fronts. Jute was stretched upward from the back and sides of these walls and was painted in acrylic in *uli* mural style. The artist employed the four traditional Igbo wall mural colors and blue, a fifth color introduced in Igboland when washing blue became available. The *Altar of Culture* installation exhibited a characteristic sometimes found in traditional Igbo murals—a row of painted dots of another color, such as red, separating two color masses, such as black and white. The *nsibidi* marriage and mirror motifs were prominent, although the painting's general quality was more in keeping with *uli*. The wide areas of color indicated a dialogue of cultures, according to Udechukwu. The mud balls were continued to the outside of the side walls; the center inside balls were incised with a variety of linear decorations, occasionally a face, qualities familiar in Udechukwu's other art. A reed fence delineated the front borders and a Plexiglas ceiling protected the still soft mud from washing away, certainly not a traditional feature.[74]

Udechukwu has written concerning this work:

So there are two levels of response to the work: the general statement which you can perceive when you merely pass by; the other one is the more intimate one which you can only read when you really get close to the building. Then you begin to see figures and signs that relate to human relations; love and hatred; then there are statements about agriculture and transport—again this relates to people coming together here from so many different parts of the world. We have different cultures and we want to make statements about these differences, but we also have to remember that we have some basic things in common. Remember the Igbo proverb: *People in different parts of the world speak different languages but they cough—it is the same!* [italics his][75]

This was not a traditional Igbo compound; it was too small, the mud walls would have been smoothed, and there

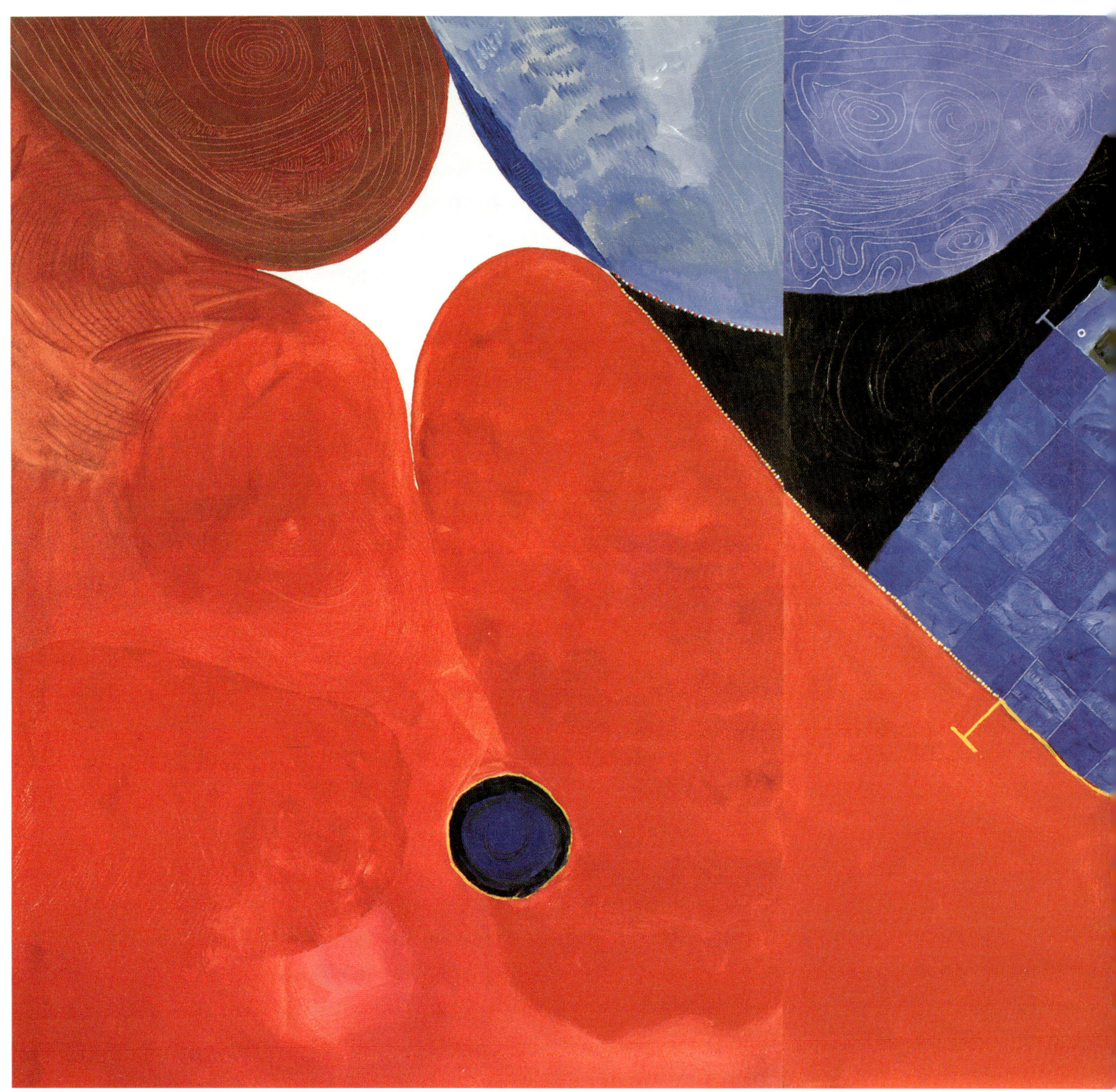

102 **A**, **B**, and **C**. Obịọra Udechukwu, *Isinwaoji,* 1993, acrylic on canvas, triptych, each panel 100 × 70 cm. Collection of the artist. Photo: Franko Khoury.

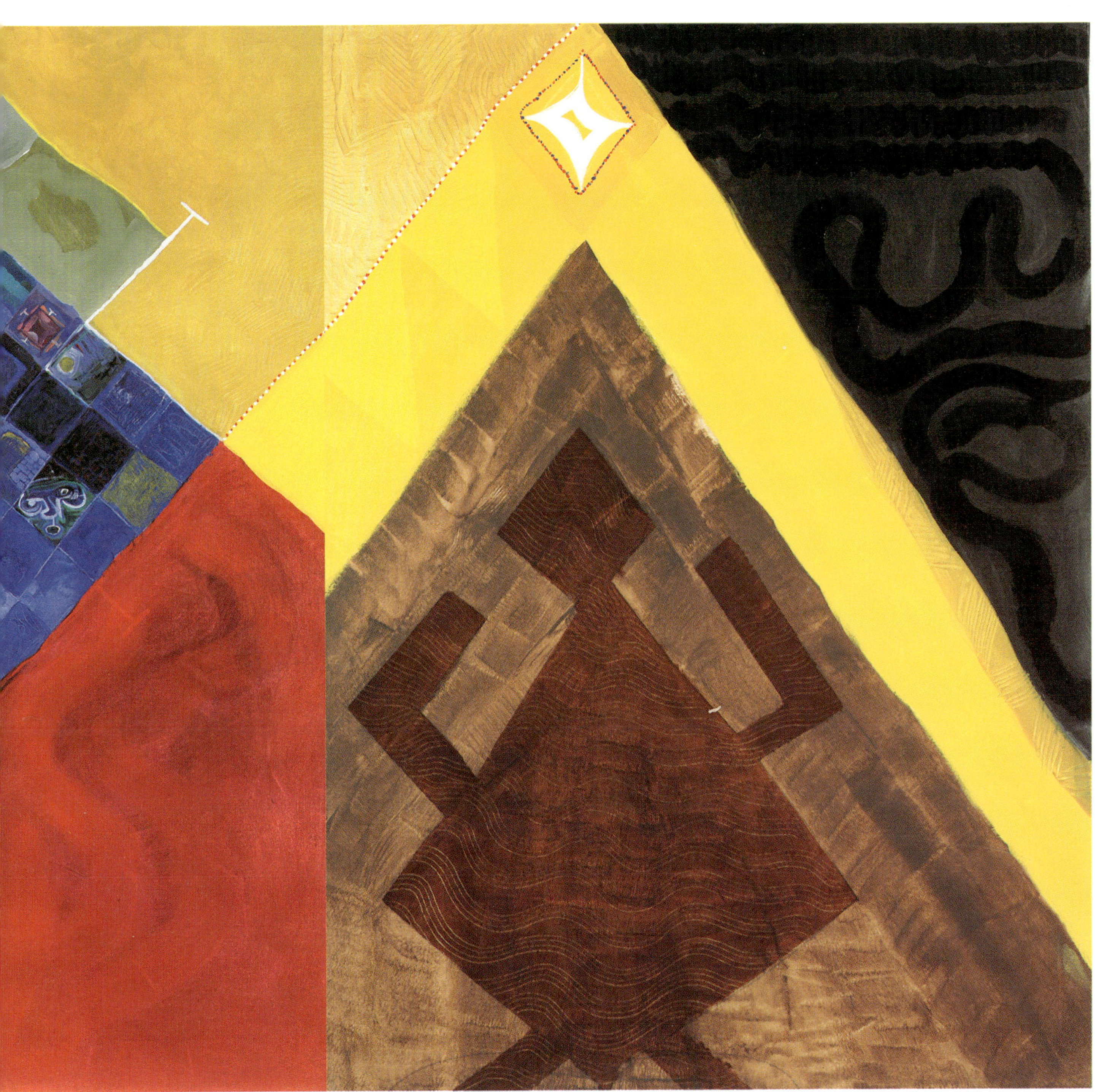

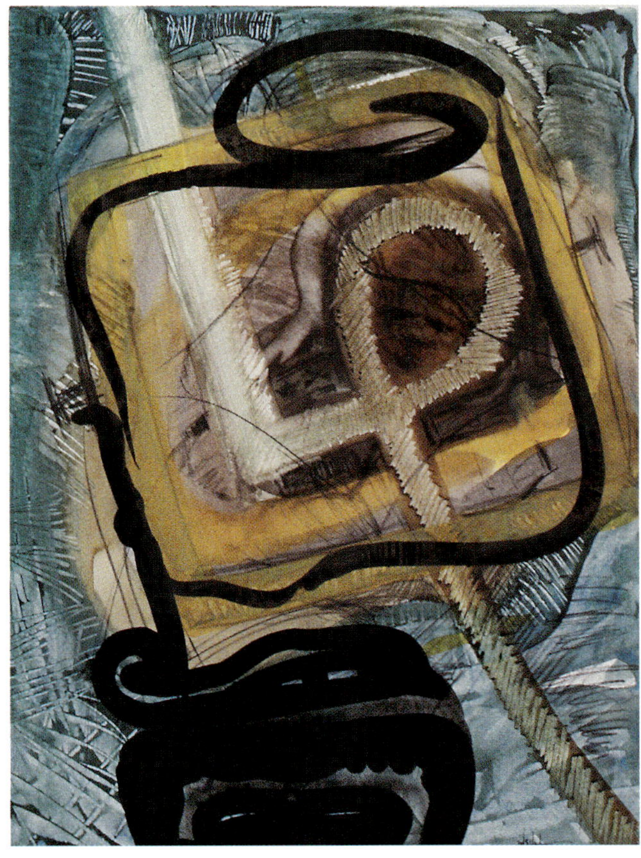

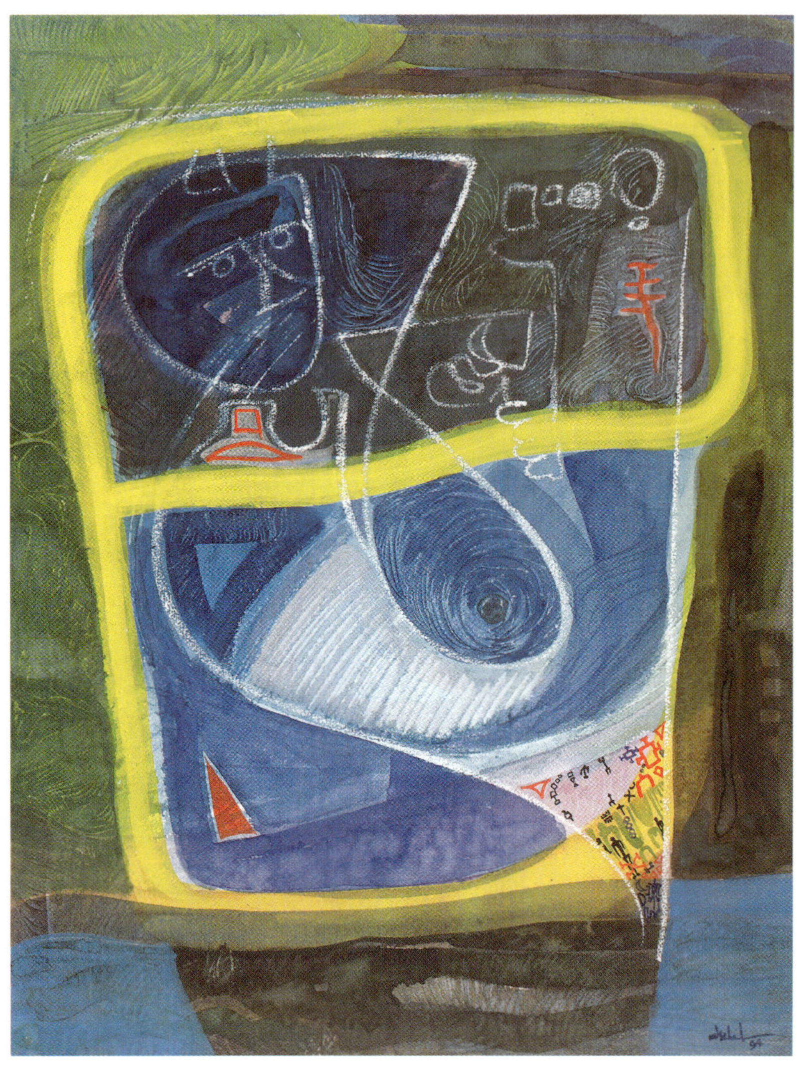

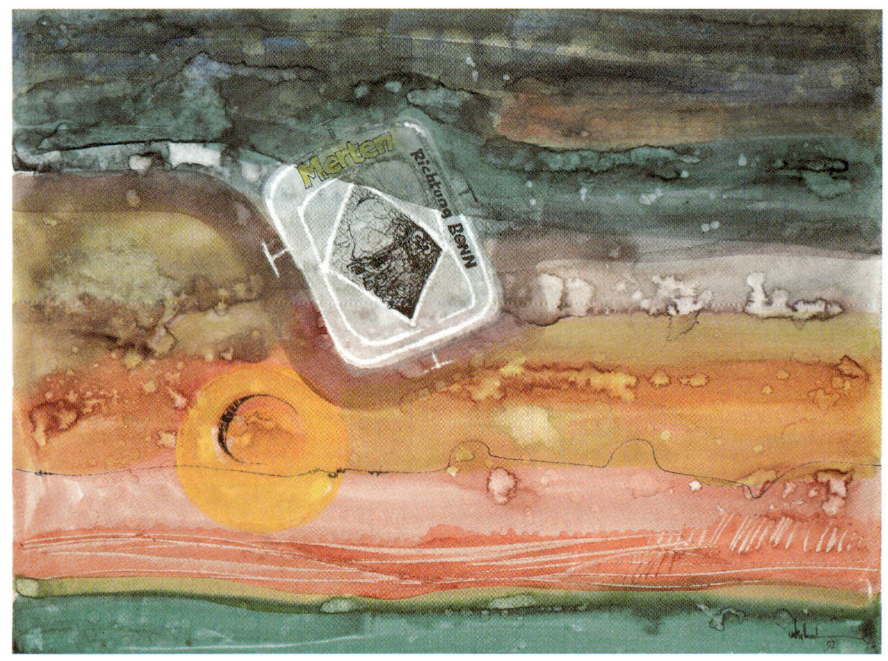

**103 (TOP LEFT)**. Obịọra Udechukwu, *The Road, the General and the Noose,* 1993, ink, wash, pencil, and watercolor, dimensions unknown. Collection of Eva and Klaus Häfner. Photo: Norbert Aas.

**104 (TOP RIGHT)**. Obịọra Udechukwu, *The Prisoner,* 1994, watercolor. 56 × 41.7 cm. Collection of Simon Ottenberg. Photo: Franko Khoury.

**105 (BOTTOM RIGHT)**. Obịọra Udechukwu, *Landscape with Moon and Music,* 1993, watercolor and ink. 31 × 41 cm. Collection of the artist. Photo: Franko Khoury.

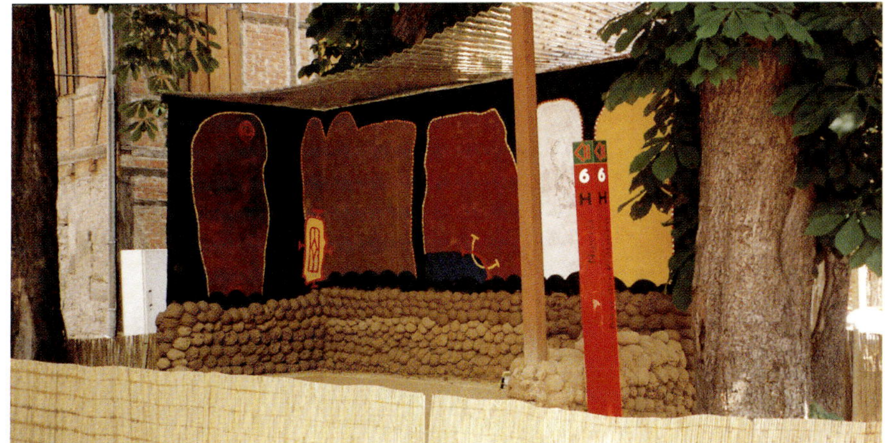

106. Obịọra Udechukwu, *Altar of Culture,* 1995, mixed-media installation at *Configura 2,* Erfurt, Germany. Photographer unknown.

would be no Plexiglas. Rather it was "natural synthesis," with traditional and modern materials (and the assistance of several young Germans), a symbolic Igbo residence in the midst of another culture. Udechukwu feels he is at home with postmodernism, having knowledge of it, but that does not preclude his rooting his art in his own culture, yet being sensitive to the environment of other people in which it may be placed.

## STUDENTS

Udechukwu's legacy also lies with his students, for he has trained many of them, a few who have followed close to his style and others who have not. Among them are Tayọ Adenaike (see Chapter 10), Ọlu Ọguibe (Chapter 12), Chinwe Uwatse, Barthosa Nkurumeh, C. Krydz Ikwuemesi, Sylvester Ogbechiẹ, Chika Okeke, Marcia Kure, and Blaise Gbaden. He has influenced others, including Ray Ọbeta, Obịọra Anidi, Chris Afuba, and Tony Nwachukwu. These artists have all been involved in exhibitions, and some teach art. They have helped spread his artistic ideas, the value of *uli* and *nsibidi,* and how a professional artist should act. He has been a healthy role model for them.

## CONCLUSION

One reason Udechukwu is interesting as an artist is that he keeps growing, moving in new directions, yet retaining certain persistent traits: the diversity of his media, a wide range of subjects, and his use of *uli* and *nsibidi.* He expresses serious social concerns and consistency in integrating past and present; he views written and oral poetry and visual art—and, at times, music, dance, and theater—as integrated elements, despite their differing expressive forms. His interest in visual art is broad. He has modeled his art and, to some extent, his poetry on Christopher Okigbo's verse. Udechukwu has become a modern-day minstrel in visual art and poetry, emulating the traditional Igbo bards, of whom he is so fond. In addition to his own art, there is his teaching, his participation in and organizing of exhibitions and conferences, and his writing on indigenous Igbo art and culture and contemporary Nigerian art. Unlike some artists, he is well organized and makes good use of his time, whether in creating works or in other activities. He is a major figure in contemporary Nigerian art and one who is slowly achieving international attention.

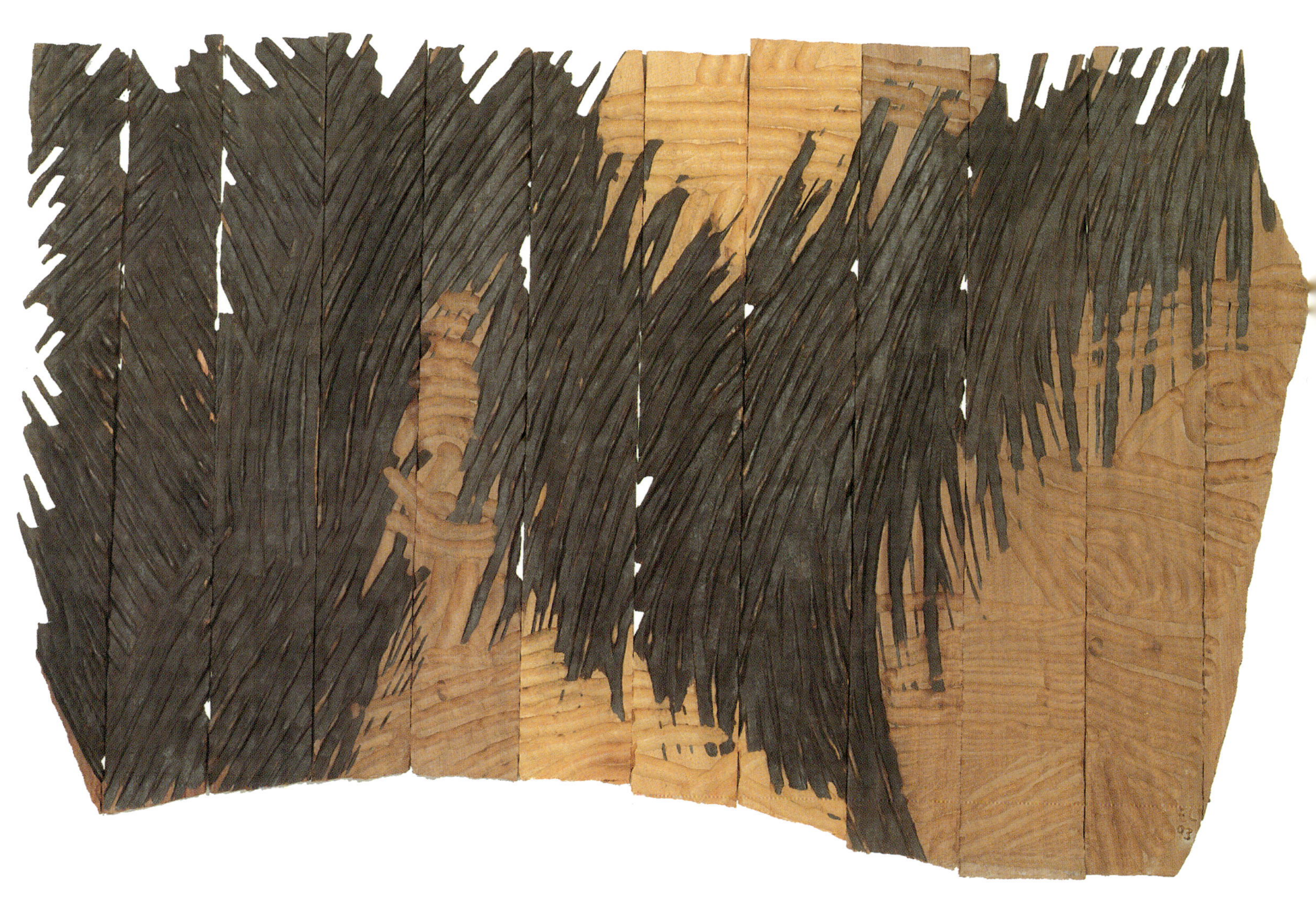

# 9. EL ANATSUI

## COLORFUL WOODS AND DARK LINES

New wood has poetry locked in it,

Old wood is poetry itself, time

Having worn off its prose

EL ANATSUI[1]

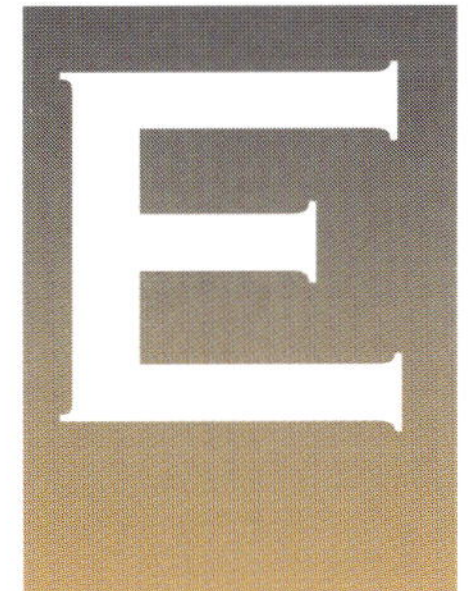

l Anatsui, born in 1944 at Anyako in southeastern Ghana and of Ewe background, moved to the university at Nsukka in 1975 and has made his home there ever since (fig. 107).[2] Igbo and Ewe social groupings have much in common. They have traditionally been composed of noncentralized, largely patrilineally organized communities and towns, with strong traditions of individualism and enterprise and proximity to large-scale traditional states. The transition to Igbo society must not have been a difficult one for Anatsui.

### CHILDHOOD

When young, Anatsui lived in a mission compound at coastal Anloga in Ewe country, isolated from the culture and social life of the town and under the influence of an uncle who was a Presbyterian minister. He attended primary and middle Presbyterian mission schools, learning little of Ewe or other African cultures.

His uncle wished him to be an engineer, lawyer, physician, or teacher—top careers for an aspiring Western-educated child in Ghana in the 1950s. At Keta Secondary School, in coastal Ewe country, he decided to be an artist. His art teacher taught European style, as demanded by the school curriculum. Lacking the opportunity to explore indigenous cultural sources, he drew pineapples, oranges, and other still lifes in the English grammar school tradition. Of his pre-university schooling he has written that "whatever artistic stimuli, images or model I was exposed to were limited to what these two institutions provided which were not only from foreign sources but were bland examples from such sources."[3]

This was a different form of cultural isolation from that experienced by Uche Okeke. Although Okeke was brought up in a foreign cultural area, his parents extolled Igbo culture, while Anatsui's mission seniors lived surrounded by Ewe life, art, music, and rituals but rejected much of it. As Okeke developed a strong curiosity about Igbo culture as a consequence of his childhood cultural isolation, Anatsui developed strong curiosities about Ewe and other Ghanaian cultures, later to extend to other African peoples. Cultural inquisitiveness has made Anatsui's art rich.

Anatsui's political ideas developed early. After secondary school, he took a local teaching position but refused to take part in an annual Ghana independence day celebration, much to the anger of his uncle and others, and he was fired. He felt that local leadership had become corrupt and mismanaged after only some six years of the country's independence. He was later to express strong political ideas through his art.

## UNIVERSITY DAYS: THE WORLD OPENS UP

Undaunted by his childhood experiences, Anatsui soon entered the College of Art at the University of Science and Technology, Kumasi, one of the oldest and most distinguished African art schools. He left the broad beaches and fishing communities of the coast for the tropical forests of inland southern Ghana, and one language, Ewe, for another, Twi. Here he earned a bachelor's degree in sculpture in 1968 and obtained a postgraduate diploma in art education the following year. Away from the mission world, his curiosity could develop, and he thrived. Kumasi, the capital and cultural center of a confederation of traditional Aşante states, had a rich cultural tradition in cloth, bronze, gold work, woodcarving, and all kinds of chiefly regalia.[4] At the National Cultural Centre at Kumasi, with its various craft workshops from Ghanaian cultures, Anatsui had the opportunity to meet artisans and examine their works and to listen to a variety of Ghanaian music. The rich *kente* cloth designs of the Aşante intrigued him, as did the *adinkra* black-stamped ones, where each symbol stands for a saying or a proverb. Through Anatsui's B.A. thesis on chieftaincy regalia, he acquired knowledge of Ewe designs.[5]

These experiences contrasted with the European-oriented art courses at the university. Anatsui made little use of indigenous designs or other cultural materials while at Kumasi, though several of the African faculty had begun to consider their own roots. There was no Zaria Art Society, as there had been for Uche Okeke. After taking course work in life-studies, anatomy, and portraiture, he moved into freer explorations. A modeling he made of a figure in typical Graeco-Roman contrapposto left him unsatisfied, though it pleased his teachers. As he has written:

It somehow started dawning on me that there was something inadequate and superficial about this way of looking at the world. As I became more aware of art as a way of re-ordering, re-interpreting, re-creating the world rather than copying it, my understanding and rapport with African traditional sculpture, which I encountered only in a few books, then began.[6]

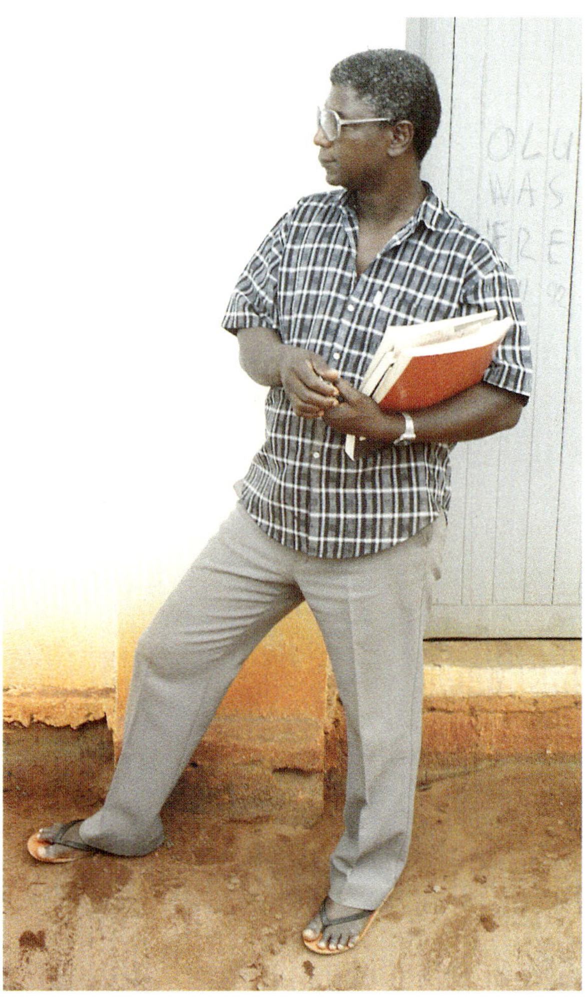

107. El Anatsui outside his Nsukka studio, October 1993.

Quickly gaining a mastery of figure studies, he was soon bored with them and began playing with pure lines and shapes.[7]

## THE TRAYS OF WINNEBA

Anatsui lectured in the Art Education Department of the Specialist Training College at Winneba in Ghana for five years between 1969 and 1975. This teacher's training college was located in another Ghanaian coastal town in the Fante area, a cultural group that Anatsui seems little to have drawn upon, albeit its members belong to the same language group as the Aşante. He came there as a prominent Ghanaian sculptor, Vincent Kofi, left to teach at Kumasi. Oguibe thinks that Anatsui was influenced by his particular artistic qualities, though he largely worked in bronze at the time, which Anatsui did not do.[8]

Anatsui, attracted to the market at Winneba, noticed the wooden trays on which the market women displayed their wares. Wanting his art to have strong links to social life, he contacted the tray carvers, who were delighted to talk with him, and he spent whole days traveling with them as they cut trees and shaped trays. On commission, they would carve fifteen to twenty trays a day for him, from the soft *sese* wood that did not easily warp. Some were circular, some oval, some irregular in shape, but they had a slightly recessed central section and were generally small, about 43–50 cm in diameter. He burned designs into the upper surface of the central portion and the raised rim, often drawing from *adinkra* motifs. Anatsui used a hot knife or hot rods of various thicknesses, even shaping the rods into a variety of forms so that he could create repeat patterns with them. As Anatsui was aware, burnt designs were an old African technique. One possible model was the designs on the numerous fishing canoes in the Winneba area, sometimes partially burned. Working with fire and heat, hardening the object, has become an important part of Anatsui's art, whether in wood or clay. On these trays he also placed some color, sometimes using poster paint, and occasionally flat metal, such as copper plate or aluminum foil. The trays went through a transformation from utilitarian horizontal objects to artistic vertical wall hangings or plaques. In Anatsui's art, the idea of transformation of some sort seems always at work.

Anatsui created rich designs on these wooden trays, varnished and burnished to create a soft, shiny surface. The lines stand out clearly, contrasting with the wood, paint, and metal. The key images are generally in the central portion, with the rim often completely filled with parallel lines pointed toward the center, concentric squares, circles, or ovals of some sort; sometimes these are broken up with contrasting motifs. Colors tend to be derivative of *kente* cloth,[9] simulating the cloth's "gay primary harmonics."[10] With the employment of *adinkra*, mostly in the center of the work, of *kente* colors and sometimes designs, of burned lines, and of indigenous style market trays, Anatsui made a sharp break from his art training at the university at Kumasi. As O. Udechukwu writes: "By burning designs into, adding some colour and varnishing them, the 'common' trays were transformed into vibrant plaques for interiors."[11] Cloth designs and cloth as metaphor play a seminal role in Anatsui's art at Nsukka in later years as well. Oguibe states: "By introducing Adinkra motifs into his form he was not only defining a cultural location for his work, but also defining an attitude to form by emphasizing that the graphic is integral rather than peripheral to sculpture."[12] This became a basic principle of much of his sculptural work from then on.

The content of the wall plaques varies greatly but largely reflects indigenous themes.[13] *Yaw Berko: Stand Up and Say No!*, an irregularly shaped plaque, refers to a legendary Ghanaian who worked hard in many Ghanaian towns for forty years and was not able to save up to forty *cedis* at the end of it all.[14] The center depicts a bent-over man, face down with arms crossed. His body, appearing exhausted, is simply outlined. On the rim there are

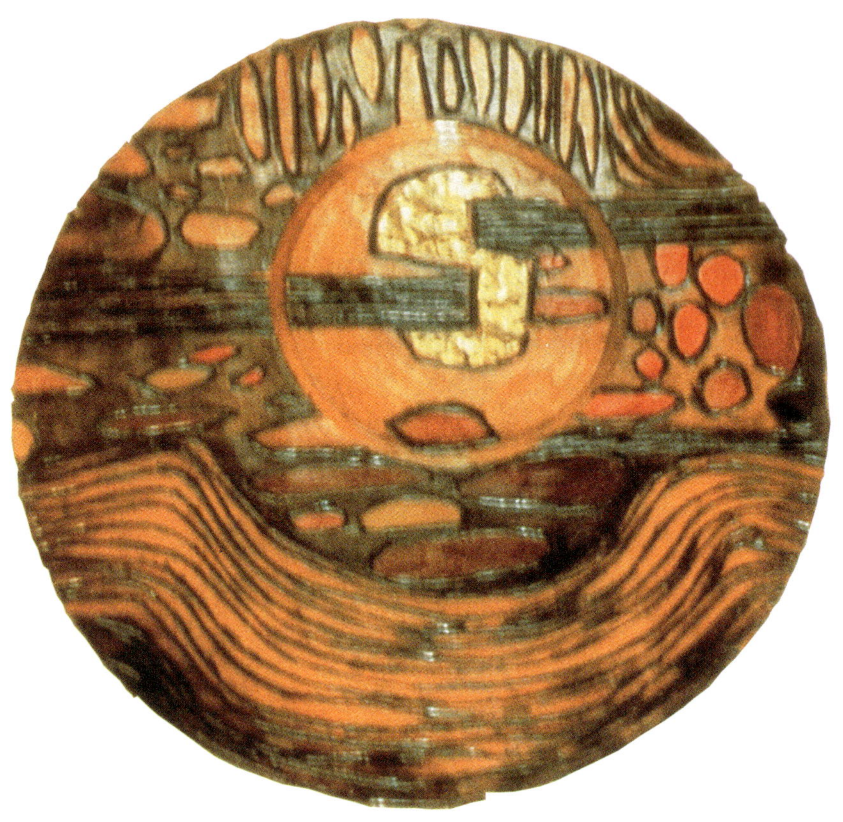

angular lines, boxes within boxes and parallel lines, perhaps suggesting the loads he has had to bear, and there are touches of white and other colors in the work for relief. But the dark patches that immediately surround the figure, add to the sense of depression.

The title of the circular *Blood of Your Sweat* (1974, wood, poster paint, aluminum sheet; fig. 108) is from the work of an African poet whose name Anatsui could not immediately recall to me, but is probably David Diop. The design and title refer to the days of colonial slavery. History, especially African history and the impact of Euro/America on Africa, has been a major theme in Anatsui's art through the years. The center of this plaque is unusually small and somewhat off center, apparently made that way for Anatsui. The black horizontal lines toward the middle contrast with the vertical lines at the top and the broad, wavy, and colorful lines at the bottom. The shining metal reminds one of the gold that, from pre-European days, has been mined in Ghana.

Other plaques have specific references to Aşante symbols, such as crossed lizards with a common stomach found on Aşante gold weights, referring to the need of cooperation. There is the *adinkra* symbol of the soul, *Gye Name*. Other works draw designs directly from proverbs, such as "Because of death we shouldn't sleep?" and "No one is born with all his teeth." This is not surprising, as many traditional designs in southern Ghana are linked to proverbs. An occasional crucifixion scene is found. Other works have titles such as *Wisdom*, *Versatility*, and *Fanatics*. In these plaques, the art on the rim often frames the work and contrasts with what is in the center, creating a balance of elements, even though the artist, as if being playful, violates this distinction in some pieces by using elements that cross both regions, such as in *Blood of Your Sweat*, *Crucifixion*, and *Versatility*. One does not have to know the meanings of these works to enjoy them as abstract or semi-abstract expressions.

While teaching at Winneba, Anatsui took part in five group exhibitions, there or at Accra, and in 1976, the year after coming to Nsukka, he had his first solo exhibition based on his plaques at Uche Okeke's Asele Art Gallery.[15] At Winneba in 1972, Anatsui designed and created a giant ceremonial chair, mace, and crest for the University of Cape Coast, but he is better known for the plaques from his Winneba days.

The beginning of Anatsui's professional career was modest, but he showed skill, had a willingness to explore indigenous cultures with a sensitivity to traditional materials, and had a desire to experiment technically.

## BROKEN POTS, *SANKOFA*, AND HISTORY

In 1974 Gerd von Stokar, then head of the Department of Fine and Applied Arts at the University of Nigeria, Nsukka, who had previously taught Anatsui at Kumasi, asked him to apply for a teaching position at Nsukka. By the time the appointment was confirmed in 1975, von Stokar had left and Uche Okeke had again taken over as head. Anatsui was impressed by Okeke and his orientation to art. Both shared a strong interest in indigenous symbols and design. Anatsui liked to refer to the Ghanaian Twi term *sankofa,* meaning "go back and pick," that is, to draw from indigenous Ghanaian life and not Europe. As he states:

> Sankofa syndrome was a reaction to a conscious and forcible attempt to denigrate a people's culture and replace it with an extraneous one. As in all situations of this kind, it is recognised also that there are always elements of an invading culture which stay behind; you cannot obliterate it completely because every culture has its positive aspects. Thus the essence was neither a wholesale return to the past nor a total exclusion of external influence. The thrust was inward orientation and selectivity.[16]

The Nsukka art department was a stimulating one not only because of its interest in indigenous cultures but because its members, such as Obiọra Udechukwu, Chike Aniakọr, and Uko Akpaide, were willing to go to the villages to get to know people and their designs and art; this very much fit Anatsui's interests.[17] *Uli* designs intrigued Anatsui, as well as their linearity, also present in some Ghanaian symbols, and he began to incorporate these into his art.

The wood tray plaque period was over, except for exhibiting them. Anatsui went on to work in clay from 1976 to 1982. He had the opportunity to travel and see Nigerian antiquities: the bronzes of Ile-Ifẹ, the Cross River Akwanshi carved stone monuments at the National Museum in Lagos, the ancient Nok terra-cotta sculptures at the Jos Museum, and the Awka carved doors of the Igbo, among other arts. A rich new world to draw upon opened up. Already used to absorbing ideas into his art from other cultures in Ghana, he had no difficulty in doing so in Nigeria, without setting aside his interests in the former. But now he did so through clay rather than wood.

With this earthy substance, with grog composed of crushed potsherds and using manganese tailings, sometimes melting in pieces of glass, he created terra-cotta works, dark gray and blackish in color as a rule. These ceramics resulted in the well-known exhibition at Enugu and Nsukka, *Broken Pots,* and a 1982 exhibition at the Goethe Institut in Lagos.[18] Anatsui took to the idea of "the inevitability of destruction and continuity, death and immortality, hate and love. Although a broken pot does not return to its original shape, it is not negated. It passed on to another level of existence." [19]

As with the tray plaques, there is transformation, though of a different nature: the old potsherds, ground up as grog, take on a new life in the new ceramic object, serving to harden it. There is continuity. This is a metaphor for human ancestors, perhaps for reincarnation. The transformation is spiritual, Anatsui believes, which relates to its positive outcome in his art. Clay has spiritual qualities associated with the earth, with fertility, growth, and regeneration.[20] In these ceramics we see the increasing development of Anatsui's ideas.

The *Broken Pots* series also contains political and social associations, referring to what Anatsui calls the "Chambers of Memory." As he has written:

> All of Africa is undergoing a period of turmoil. There is despondency, despair, bewilderment and frustration all over. It is to this predicament that my attempt in these works to use decadence and destruction as elements of creation, addresses a message. I hasten however to reiterate that regeneration and growth are not automatically consequent upon break-down.[21]

Conscious effort is necessary to regroup. Broken pots represent broken African societies. But as with broken peoples and shattered cultures, they can be rebuilt. Oguibe feels that "memory and remembrance have remained the preoccupying themes of Anatsui's work since the beginning of the 1980s."[22] This is clearly linked with Anatsui's interest in African history and in the African cultural past. Yet he does not wish to return to the past, but to incorporate it into the present.

The artist draws upon the significance of pottery in indigenous life in Ghana and later in Nigeria. Ceramics, formerly widespread in Africa, have had many uses—in rites, at shrines, in sacrifices, and as funerary objects in Ghana. They carry water, palm wine, and other elements and are employed in cooking. While nowadays they are largely replaced by plastic and metal containers, the many uses of the clay forms suggest to Anatsui a variety of ceramic metaphors.

He believes that clay represents the earth, "and the earth is recognized as the source of life, or creativity in most places I have lived."[23] Clay also relates to a well-known Ewe historical account in which an oppressive king once asked the Ewe to weave a rope of clay, an impossible task. They were able to extricate themselves by diplo-

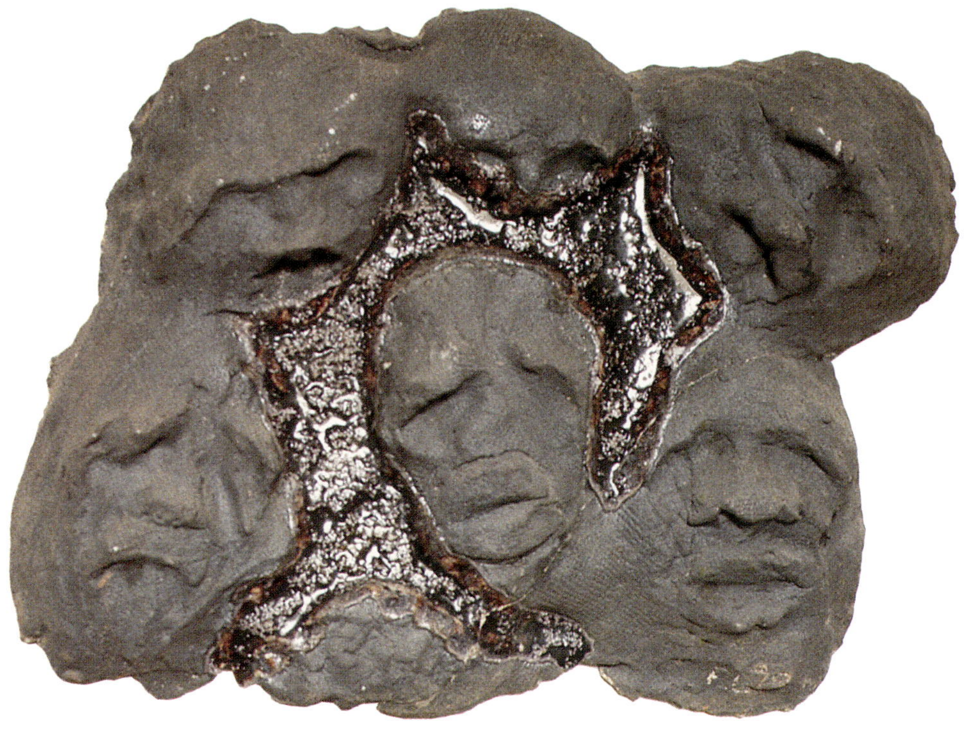

**109 (LEFT).** El Anatsui, *Sinking Men,* 1979, manganese with clay and glass. 38.1 × 48.3 × 4 cm. Collection of the artist.

**110 (FACING PAGE, TOP).** El Anatsui, *Chambers of Memory,* 1977, manganese body. 40 × 29.3 × 7 cm. Collection of the artist.

**111 (FACING PAGE, BOTTOM).** El Anatsui, *Gbeze,* 1976, manganese body. 40.7 × 45.7 × 35.6 cm. Collection of the artist.

matically asking the king for a sample clay rope
to guide them. So "working with clay enables
me to re-enact the essence and challenges of,
or, to fantasize with this period in the history
of my people." [24]

For Anatsui the pots are symbolic containers, as were the tray plaques, and as would be
old Igbo palm oil mortars that Anatsui later
made artistic use of, suggesting that the theme
of containers is a major one in his work. [25]

Manganese tailings came from a mine in
Ghana; the clay came from near Enugu in
Nigeria. The electric kiln he used was at the
University at Nsukka and was fired to at least
1,100 degrees centigrade to fuse the manganese
to the clay. Manganese bits were mixed with
clay and the grog of potsherds and sometimes
with glass pieces. The manganese gave the objects a spotted dark quality, with black representing African people. [26] Glass, when used,
provided a twinkling quality. A work had an
antique appearance, as the Nok and Yoruba
Esie terra-cottas, yet was also modern and
fresh, with irregular shapes and openings. [27]
Past and present are joined—clearly the artist's
intent. By controlling the percentage of manganese in the clay, Anatsui regulated the tonal
values of a work. The ceramic's texture was
mostly created by rolling the clay on pieces of
jute fabric during the forming process.

Anatsui developed two ceramic forms, a
flat one meant to be laid on the table or hung
on a wall and a freestanding form; only the latter belongs to his *Broken Pot* series. In either
case, there is no correct way of viewing any of
these works; it's up to the viewer, Anatsui says.
As with the wood plaques, their themes range
widely. Some have to do with suffering, as *Vic-
tim, Sinking Men* (fig. 109), and *Kwashiorkor.*
Some draw from Igbo culture, as *Nsukka
Shrine,* or Ewe pottery, as *Gbeze;* some relate

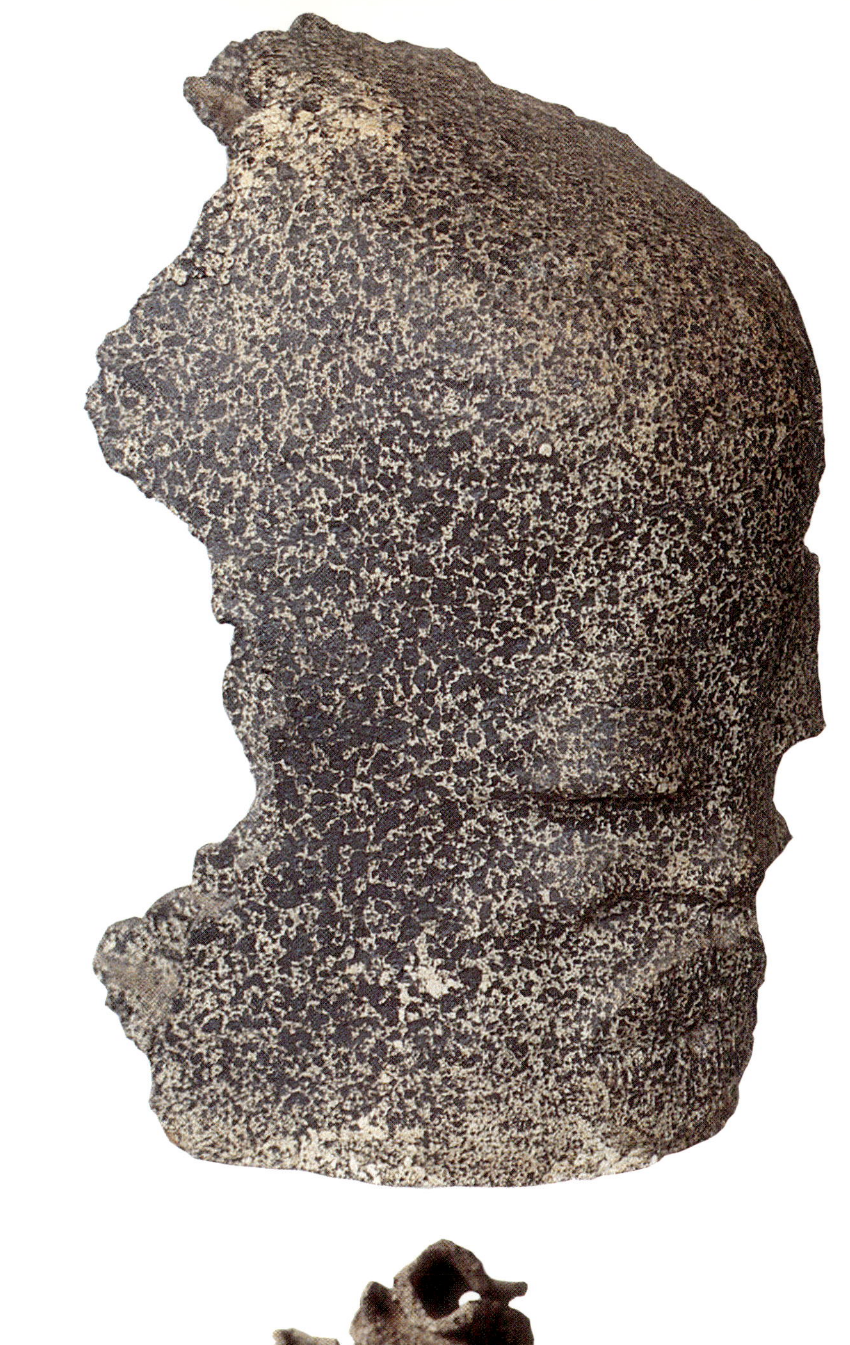

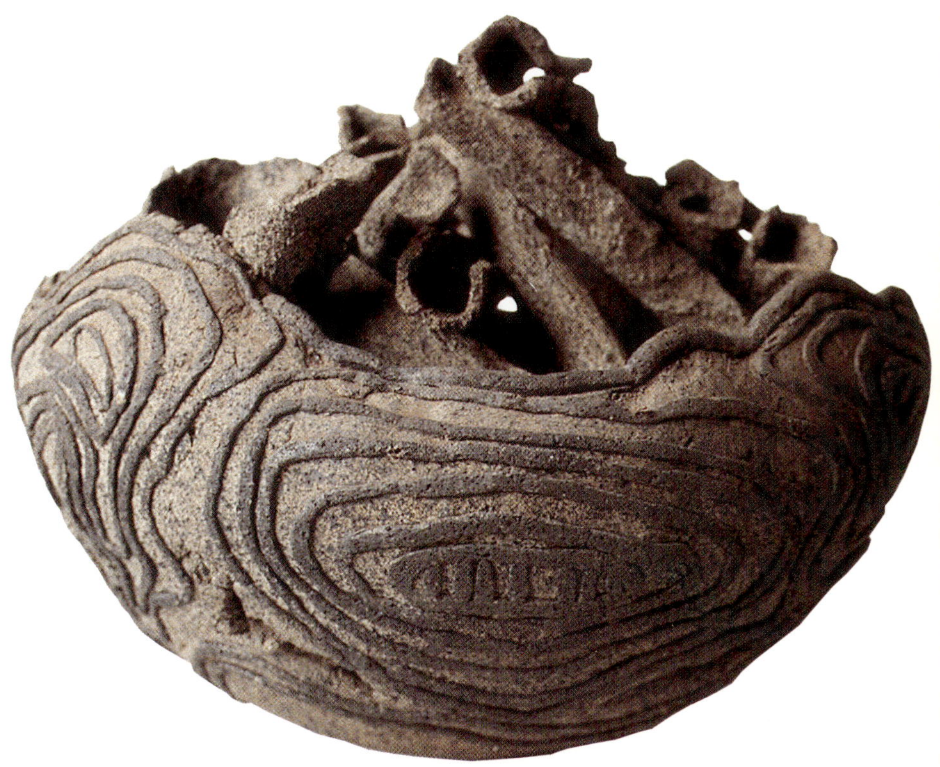

to the past and history, as *Chambers of Memory*. A human head or figure may occur, yet human elements are not frequent. Several works refer to a popular modern male dress, *agbada*. There is an occasional hint of *adinkra* design, and some pieces exhibit *uli* features.

Symmetry is rare. Almost all of the standing forms show marked contrast between a relatively complete side and an open opposite one, the former regular, the latter highly irregular and full of holes and cavities. It is as if there is a dark side and a positive side to a work. Because of incompleteness, empty spaces and places, there is a sense of never being finished, the process of regeneration never complete.

One of the best known of Anatsui's ceramics is *Chambers of Memory* (1977, manganese body; fig. 110). Anatsui draped a clay slab on wood; when it hardened the next day it looked like a Nok terra-cotta piece, so he developed it along that line. It is a strong but quiet face, and in the back there are a number of irregular chambers that contain nothing. "In most of Africa we keep making the same mistakes," he tells me; "we do not remember anything, the chambers of memory seem to store nothing. Those who follow never learn from history." The reference to Nok is to a collective memory. He seems to hold an idealized picture of these ancient northern Nigerian peoples as being at peace. The idea of peace is suggested to him because the shadows in the work are soft and not deep, he says. This is the only Nok-style work he has made.

*Gbeze* (1976, manganese body; fig. 111) is named after an Ewe herbal pot that holds potent herbs and is not to be left uncovered.[28] Anatsui tells me that in his piece the potent forces are let loose; he has left the pot uncovered. "They will have to look for what is wrong and do whatever they can," he says. Linear incisions on it, some carved and some irregularly straight, show *uli* influence. A second *Gbeze* work (1979, manganese body and slip) has numerous curvilinear lines of dark manganese slip on a lighter manganese body.

*Broken Pot Series* (1976, manganese body) is another example of a work with incised lines, including a number of designs of a circle within a circle with a dot center, relating to *adinkra*. *Sinking Men* (1979, manganese slip with clay and glass; fig. 109), one of his mural ceramics, depicts six dark male faces sinking in a quagmire, a rather ghostly view. Unlike some of his other ceramics, there is no sense of regeneration here.

Anatsui ceased working in ceramics in 1982 as the facilities at the university deteriorated, but in 1985 he went through a second pottery period as a visiting artist at the Faculty of Art and Design, Cornwall College of Further and Higher Education, Redruth, England. He was there for two months, during the vacation period, so that he concentrated on his ceramics. The result was an exhibition of his work there in 1987 entitled *Venovize*, the term referring to Ewe twins' pots.[29] The art was

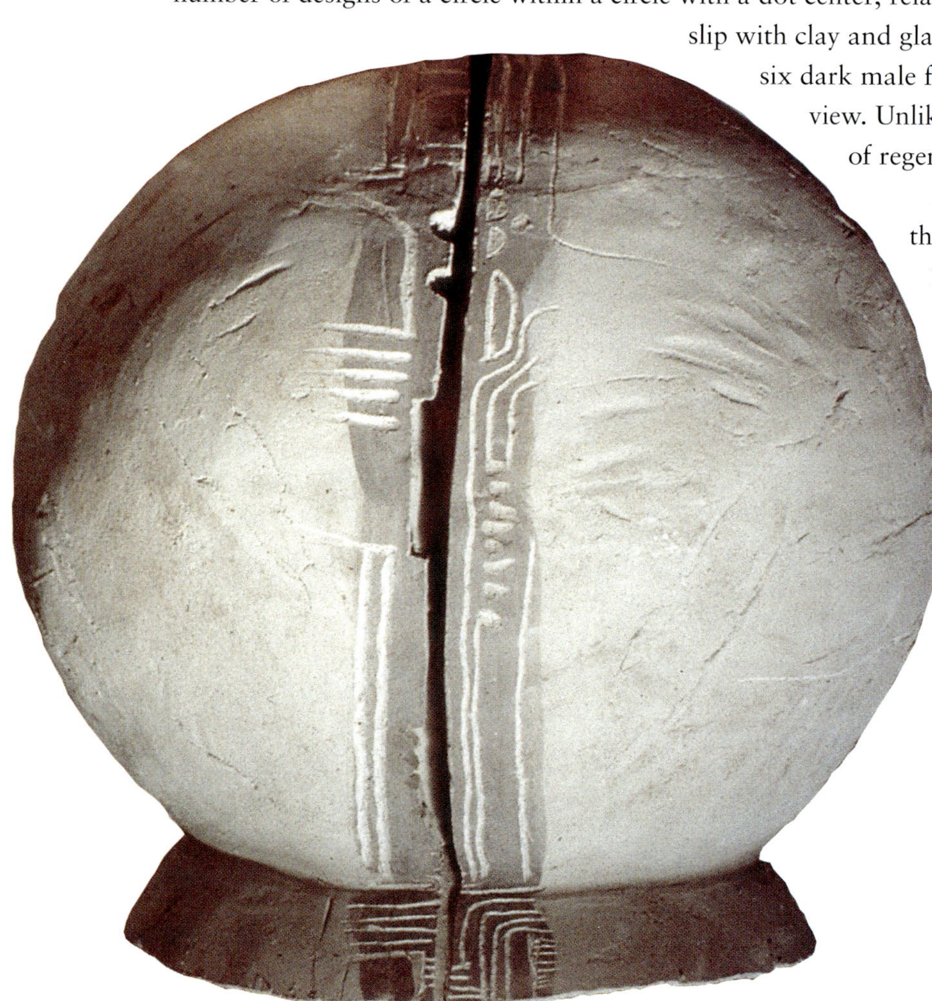

**112**. El Anatsui, from the *Venovize Series*, 1985, ceramic. 38 × 18 × 40 cm. Collection and photo: the artist.

devoted to the issue of divided personalities. It refers to the failure of acculturation process which is not voluntary. The process which has led to the dilemma in which most Africans (especially the formally educated ones) find ourselves, torn between two worlds, belonging to none. In real life, Venovize consists of two little pots used in ritual ceremonies for twins in my part of Ghana. My personal conception fuses these two individual and parallel consciousnesses into one, split up by either horizontal or vertical fissures or by employing two differently coloured clays, the different aspects and colours that create the twin or split personalities in one individual. My formative years lived between the quasi-western world of the church and school on one hand, and that of the indigenous society has left quite an imprint.[30]

Again Anatsui, as other Nsukka artists, synthesizes Africa's past with current issues in imaginative ways. He views *Venovize* as a continuation of the *Broken Pot* series, though they differ in theme (figs. 112, 113). He says of the Cornwall experience that "a lot of things from home kept coming to me more intensely. When you are separated from a place, an event, and you long for them, that nostalgia for an artist, can translate into more meaningful work."[31]

## WOOD RELIEF WALL PANELS AND VISUAL METAPHORS

Between Anatsui's two ceramic experiences he spent several months in 1980 at the Community of Arts, Cummington, Massachusetts, attracted there by, among other things, a plentiful supply of wood. This led him in new directions. He had used the chain saw at annual wood gathering expeditions for students' use while at Winneba and to reduce blocks of wood in the studio preparatory to carving, but at Cummington he discovered that he could easily use it to cut rough designs into wood. The rough edges of cuts could then be smoothed and blackened by burning with a torch.[32]

From this experience Anatsui developed many metaphors around gouging and burning wood. A basic one is the chain saw, or power saw as it is also called, destroying, cutting, and tearing arbitrarily as he dictates, as the European colonialists once cut up Africa arbitrarily. Another is that the "powersaw tearing rough-shod through organic wood at devastating speed, to me, constitutes a metaphor of the hassling, rat-racing hypertensive pace of present day living."[33] Again, there is the idea of decay and regeneration; the power saw destroys the old form of the wood and creates a new one. Wood, for Anatsui, has a spiritual quality that he sees embedded in his own creations. Trees in Africa are sometimes believed to have souls and thus must be propitiated with prayer and ritual before cutting.

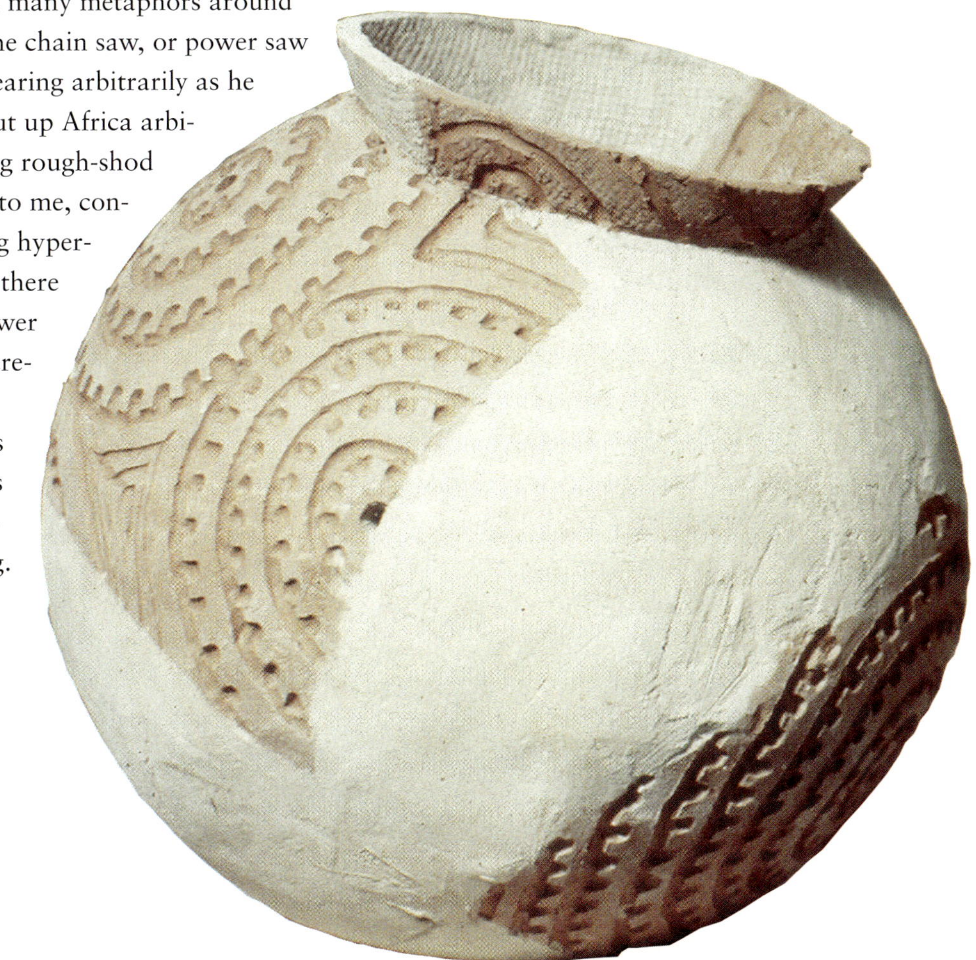

**113**. El Anatsui, *Patched Pot*, from the *Venovize Series*, 1985, ceramic. 36 × 36 × 38 cm. Collection and photo: the artist.

Anatsui's respect for his woods is considerable. As Ọlọidi writes of him: "Whether or not the artist is at work, he sees wood, thinks wood and feels wood, because he has already developed that spiritual attachment to wood forms." [34]

Back at Nsukka, it took time for Anatsui to develop the potential of the chain saw and torch, discovering that the saw was useful in creating designs on flat pieces of wood. He developed a form of wood relief wall hanging that he has continued to make until recently, over a period of some fifteen years, though now his attention turns more and more to standing objects.

The basic style of a wall hanging consists of five to fifteen vertical slat pieces, about 3 cm thick or slightly more, generally of even thickness. The width of each piece of wood in a hanging may be the same, about 8–13 cm wide, though they may vary in both width and length, lengths being in the neighborhood of 50–75 cm. The slat pieces hang tightly side by side on the wall, with cut and burnt lines, further scorching to create masses of plain black areas, and cut nonburned lines made with a router. Often the pieces show partial use of paint, the whole finished with a lacquer. There is generally continuity between the designs on one piece of wood and its neighbors, so that the whole is coherent, and there may be repetition of the same design elements on a number of the pieces. Different African woods, as many as five or six, may be employed in a work; their color variations add to the interest of the piece. Their selection, done before cutting into the woods, is an aspect of Anatsui's creativity. Wood pieces are generally cut to proper size by him or by an assistant using a chain saw.

With a nail as a hook in back of each piece, they are easily hung on a horizontal wall bar. Each piece is numbered so that its owner can readily assemble the work; Anatsui may do this before starting to work on them. However, he does not mind, and even encourages, the owner to reassemble the pieces, even to change their relative height position, as another artist, Tayọ Adenaike, has done with a work of Anatsui's at his Enugu office. Anatsui occasionally likes the reassembled version better than his own. However, he says that so far mainly artists and architects have had the courage to reorder his art. His view is that, once a finished work of art has left his hands, it is up to its owner to interpret it as he or she chooses; the owner takes over. The idea, he says, is to awaken the artist in everyone.

Ọguibe argues that Anatsui has been fascinated with multiples from his seashore childhood, for "his was an environment that in several respects involved a paradox of multiples, the mass of fishing boats on the banks, the bustle of the fish market in the morning as the fishermen return from the waters, the tumble of catches which, nevertheless, had to be sorted and separated." [35]

Anatsui sees the edges of the rough chain saw cuts in the wood as "savage," which are "civilized" by scorching with fire, smoothing them. So fire is also associated with colonization in his mind. Fire also imparts strength and hardness to his woods, he says. The chain saw is to him the modern equivalent of colonial firearms. The different-colored woods represent the different African colonies, and I believe they also stand for different cultures in an African country or in Africa. [36] The burnt lines cutting across the different-colored woods, and the repeat of similar burnt patterns on different pieces of a work, provide unity to the variety of colored woods used in the wall hanging.

Some time after beginning these wall panels, Anatsui saw what he thinks was in his unconscious, that the panels are analogous to cloth, for each wood piece is about the width of African woven strip cloth, strips sewn together side by side to form cloth. He still employs *adinkra* and *kente* cloth symbols on some of his panel work, and now he also uses southern Igbo *akwete* cloth motifs. The whole wall panel is a metaphor for cloth, also suggested by a number of his pieces' titles having cloth associations.

The designs on the pieces have increasingly come from a wide African scope. He not only draws from the three types mentioned above but also from *uli, nsibidi,* and Igbo *mbari* motifs, and recently from Bamun and Njoya scripts from the Cameroun, Yoruba Aroko symbols, and the East African Bolange script. Anatsui is convinced that there have been many more traditions of writing in Africa than is generally realized: he searches for these elements to use in his own art, what Aniakor calls "visual calligraphy." [37]

Anatsui suggests that Euro/American art's preference for three-dimensional art relates to the tendency to

conceive of these categories of art in terms of manipulating various light reflecting capacities of planes; in African art traditions, one sees, in addition to this, the practice of defining forms on the flat plane by sheer use of texture. Awka carved wood panels of the Igbo for instance provide a good example of this. My works are closer to this attitude. [38]

Anatsui seeks an African artistic view with its own qualities.

Similar themes to Anatsui's earlier ceramics and wall tray plaques occur here: the impact of colonialism, slavery, and history; the selecting of elements from indigenous cultures to be retained, used, and manipulated; the idea of destruction and regeneration; the value of indigenous motifs. His *Migration Series* refers to the days of slavery, the recent movement of Africans out of Africa to Euro/America in search of a better life, and the many migrations within Africa, including, he points out, the Ewe to their present home at some time in the past. Of course, Anatsui himself migrated from Ghana to Nigeria, where he is quite at home, fully integrated into the Nsukka art scene, without rejecting his Ghanaian past and experience.

His themes characteristically have a broad sweep; there is little of his art that does not have this characteristic, whether the theme arises before or during his preliminary sketches, if he employs these at all. Considerable travel in Europe and the New World in recent years has not diminished his African thematic orientation. If anything, his travel experiences have enlarged it, and he has found non-Africans receptive to it (fig. 114).

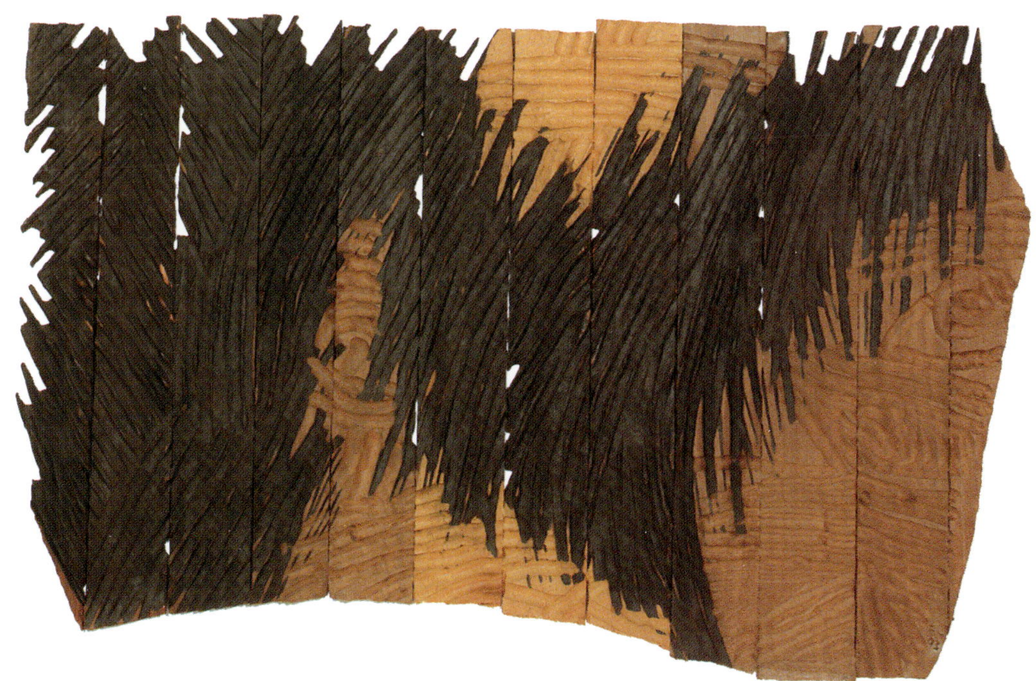

**114**. El Anatsui, *Undercurrents*, 1993, wood relief, *opepe, oyili-oji,* camwood, twelve pieces. 76 × 118 × 3 cm.

Collection of the artist, courtesy of the October Gallery. Photo: Franko Khoury.

At first Anatsui did not use much paint on his wall panels, but he has increasingly employed it, particularly red, blue, white, and black, which he views as major colors for shrines and rituals. He began with acrylics but found that they did not bind well with the wood and now employs water-based paints—tempera, gouache, and the almost similar poster color—which are absorbed. He used to fix a work with lacquer but felt this left the piece too glossy; now after painting he sprays with lacquer and then repaints to create a more matte-like finish. Other changes have occurred over time. He has changed from a blowtorch to an acetylene one, which burns more finely and effectively. He has learned the limitations of the chain saw, and he also employs a gouge, a plumber's hole saw, and wood routers of various thicknesses. He began by employing only two woods, mahogany and *iroko*, but now selects from at least nine others as well: *akparata, afara, oke ǫfǫ, oyili-ǫji, okpo-ǫcha,* ebony, *ufie* (camwood), *opope,* and *mansonia.* Fortunately he lives where a wide variety of woods are available. He sees these various-colored woods as being in interaction in his work and as metaphors for people of different skin color in interrelationships. Yet he feels that each piece of wood, with its designs in a wall hanging, also has an independent existence.

The wood colors also relate to history in Anatsui's mind:

> I look at the textures of my work in process
> And I think about the texture and grain of Africa's history;
> I look at the authentic colours of the different types of wood
> And they remind me of the real colours of history . . .[39]

As Anatsui's skills in creating wall hangings developed, he began to vary his work and play with it. Some pieces of wood in a work are arranged in nonparallel fashion, as in *Crumbling Ancestral Fence.*[40] Some are deliberately arranged to be reset in different yet coherent patterns; *Zuma* occurs in three forms, *Conceiving Moon* in two.[41] He occasionally employs numerous round wooden knobs or spools—custom-made for him—as in *Mahogany Face* or in *Beckon . . . distance . . . beckoner.*[42] Sometimes he cuts through a panel so that the background wall appears. Recently he has created more rounded and irregular pieces in a wall hanging, separated by some space, as in *The Ancestors Converged Again* (see fig. 120).[43]

*Adinkra* symbols are traditionally bunched together on cloth; *uli* motifs use space between them. Similarly there is variation in the use of empty space in Anatsui's panels. Generally the upper portions of the individual pieces are full, with human forms or figures, or cloth designs or other elements. The middle and lower parts may or may not be filled; there is variation here. I find my eyes going first to the top of a work, then to the rest. He often creates his own motifs as well as drawing from indigenous sources.

Ǫguibe has indicated how Anatsui creates these panels:

> El works like the traditional sculptor of his roots. He works straight on his wood, making rough, bold outlines in charcoal or chalk. Then he descends on the pieces of wood with the powersaw, working freely without any additional sketches, paying due respect to both material and tool, each a living force. He lets these forces direct his hand, follows their reverie with the anxiety of a diviner. To suggest that he is totally reduced in this process to the position of a medium may not be accurate, but it is no less the truth to say that, like the traditional sculptor, he is only a part, contributing to, and at the same time discovering the independent existence of the creation.[44]

His titles are intriguing, whimsical, sometimes drawing from Pidgin English, as . . . *long before the chief executive told us the only way to get water is prayers,* referring to the endemic shortage of piped water in Nigeria; *Began wall but abandoned; Dey patch; The travelers have returned, carrying burdens of debt;* or:

*When I last wrote to you about Africa*
*I used a letterheaded parchment paper,*
*There were many blank slots in the letter . . . . . . . . .*
*. . . . . . . . . . . . . . . . . . . . . . . . . . . . . . . . . . . . . .*
*. . . . I can now fill some of these slots because . . . . .*
*I have grown older.*

The last title is for a work with its panels hung horizontally, containing some twenty panels that curl something like a scroll.[45]

## EXAMPLES OF WALL HANGINGS

*Coins on Grandma's Cloth* (c. 1993; fig. 115) concerns the past and the present.[46] The circles, mostly on the right half, represent coins, the left and darker side, the cloth. The reference is to the way African material treasures and antiquities are sold off for barely a few coins. People come and buy them, crate them away to sell elsewhere at high prices in Euro/America. Anatsui says the same thing is happening with contemporary art. People buy it for practically nothing in Africa and sell it for high prices; the artist gets virtually nothing. There is no good system of marketing controls in Africa.

This is typical of much of Anatsui's work in its references to cloth and history, and to the negative influence of Euro/America on Africa and its heritage. A linked work is *Remnant of Grandma's Cloth*, characterized by jagged edges at both top and bottom and angular cuts through some pieces, much of it in black.[47] There are,

**115.** El Anatsui, *Coins on Grandma's Cloth*, c. 1993, wood relief, *akparata*, *oyili-ọji*, camwood, *oke-ọfọ* woods, fourteen pieces. 58 × 127 × 3 cm. Collection of the artist. Photo: Franko Khoury.

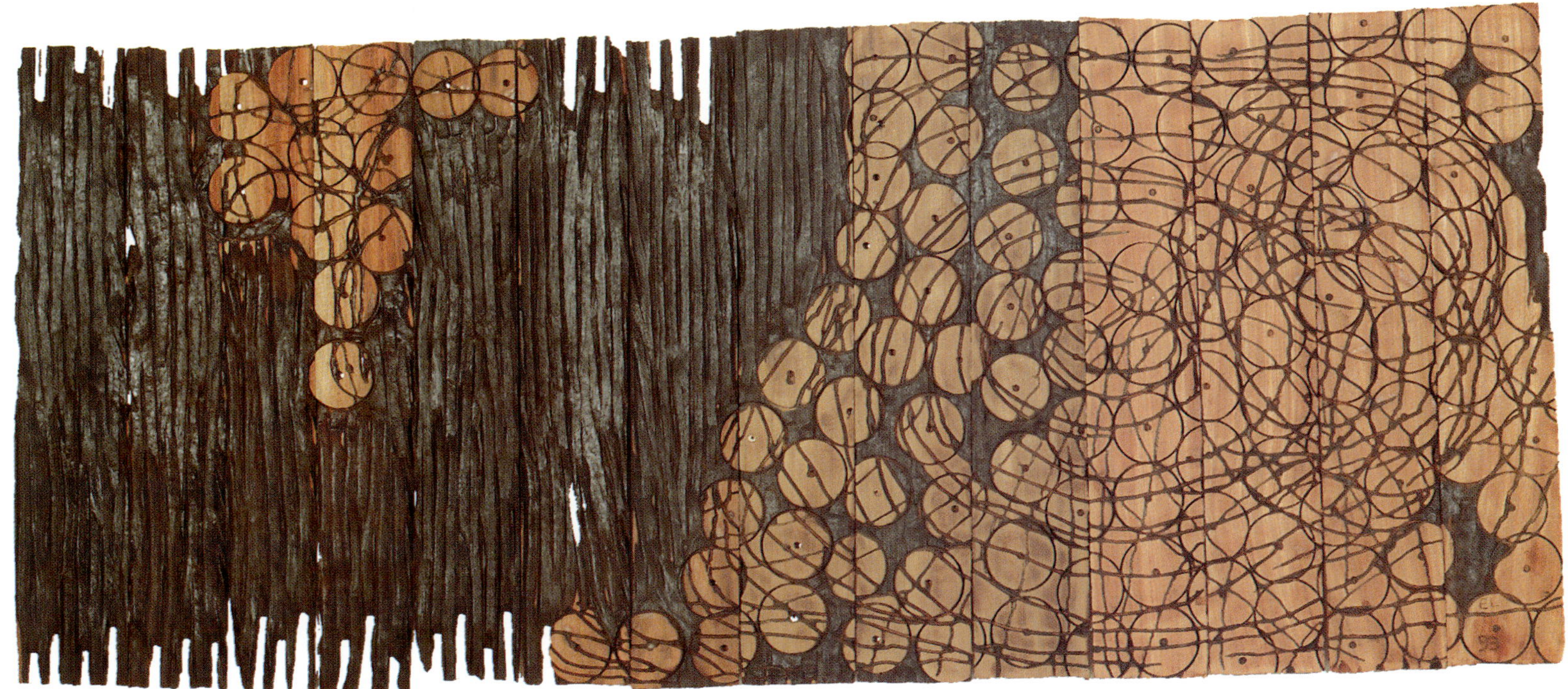

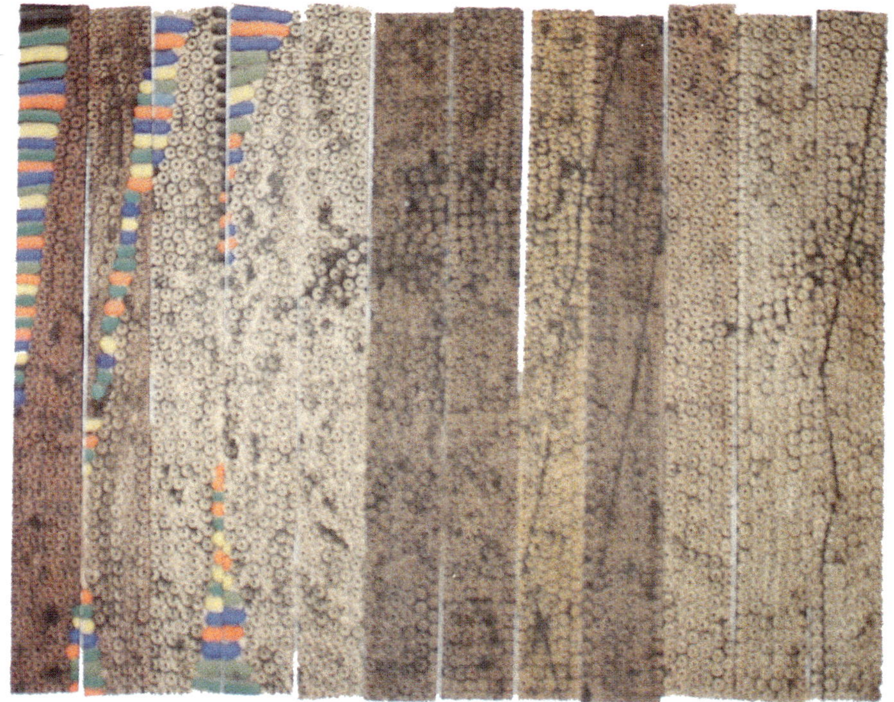

**116 (LEFT)**. El Anatsui, *Lace and Kente*, c. 1993, wood relief, *okpo-ọcha, oyili-ọji, akparata* woods, tempera, twelve pieces. 94 × 116.9 × 2.5 cm. Collection of the artist.

**117 (BOTTOM)**. El Anatsui, untitled, 1989, wood relief, *afara, oke-ọfọ,* and other woods, acrylic, thirteen pieces. 55.9 × 146.7 × 2.5 cm. Collection of Nkiru Nzegwu.

**118 (FACING PAGE)**. El Anatsui, *Earth-Moon Connexion,* 1993, wood relief, *okpo-ọcha, oyili-ọji,* tempera, nine pieces. 90 × 84.4 × 3 cm. Collection of the National Museum of African Art. Photo: Franko Khoury.

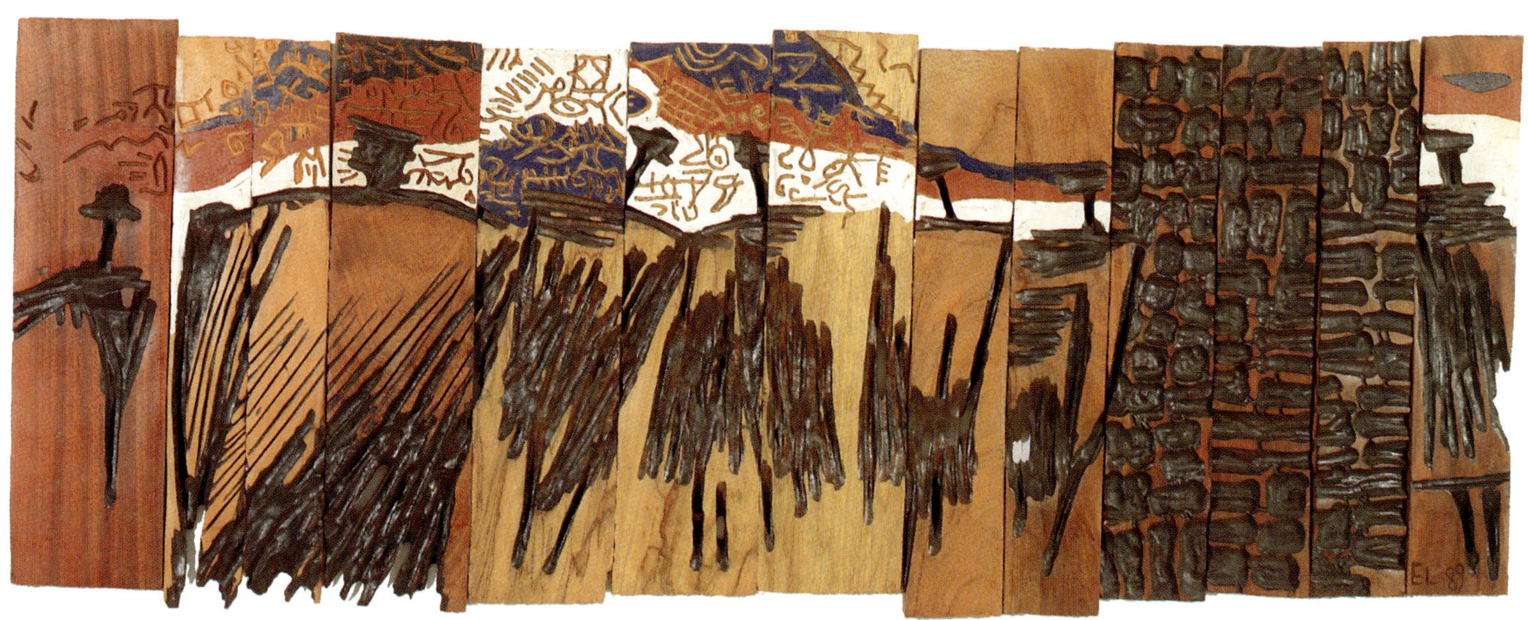

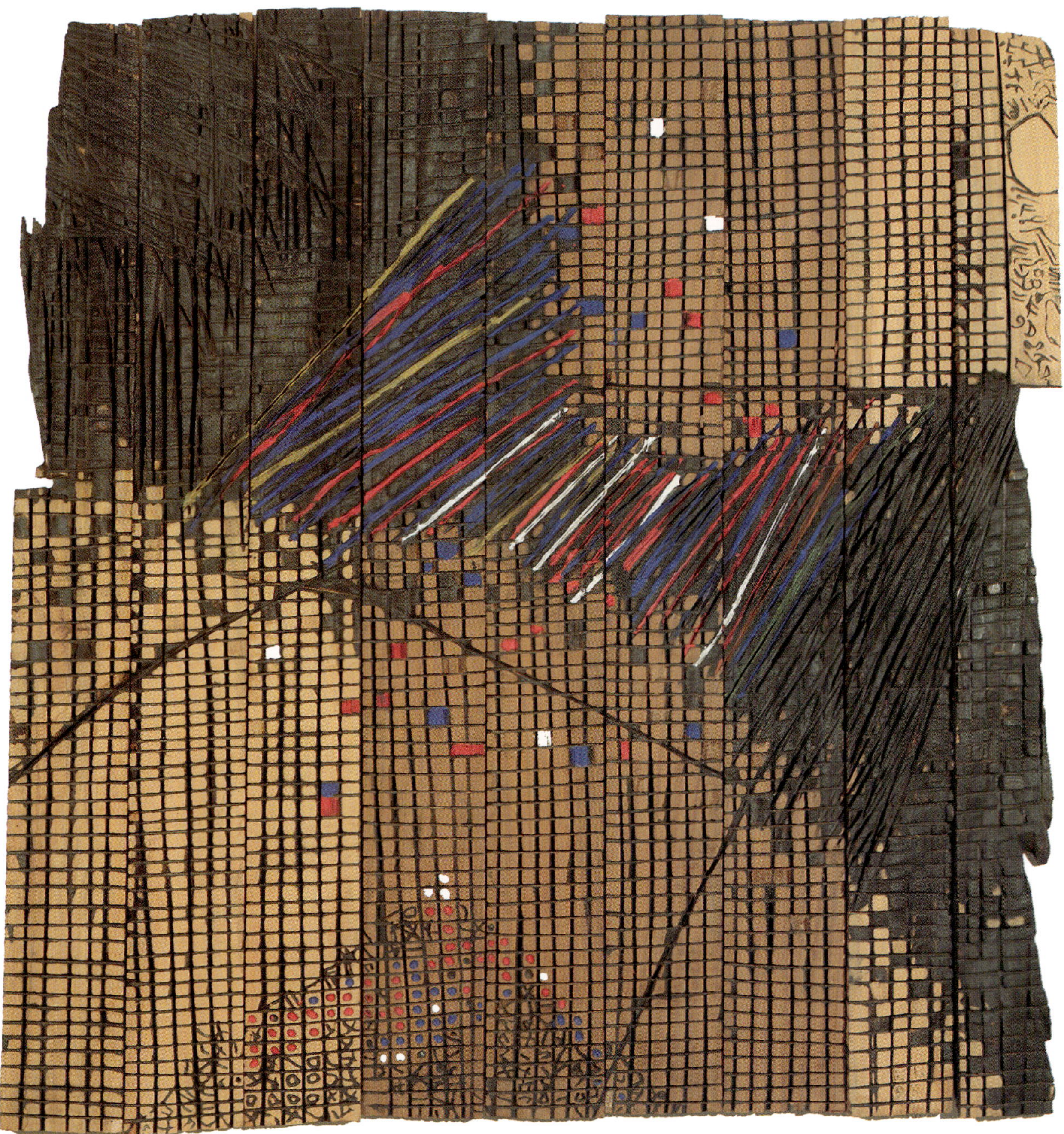

however, two sections composed of small squares in yellow, red, blue, and green, which are the remnants. In fact, the work looks like a burned cloth remnant.

In *Lace and Kente* (c. 1993; fig. 116), the tempera colors of blue, orange, yellow, and green represent the *kente* cloth colors of Ghana.[48] The many circles, made with a hole saw, represent lace, a popular and fashionable contemporary cloth in Nigeria. To Anatsui these are the cloths of the two countries he has lived in, linking the past and present in his life.

A work with no title (1989; fig. 117) represents roughly sketched people with their heads in a white sky.[49] They are going out of control, estranged from realities, concerned with ideals. Anatsui says the work is a jab at African universities, and maybe even those elsewhere, which are static and not producing manpower for immediate

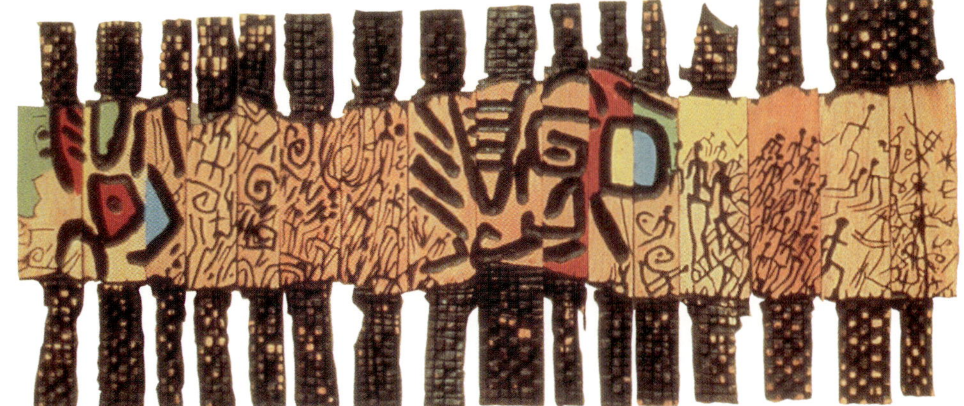

**119 (TOP RIGHT).** El Anatsui, *Unfolding the Scroll of History*, 1995, wood relief, *oke-ọfọ, oyili-ọji, akparata, okpo-ọcha* woods, tempera, sixteen pieces. 61 × 141 × 4 cm. Collection of the artist, courtesy of the October Gallery.

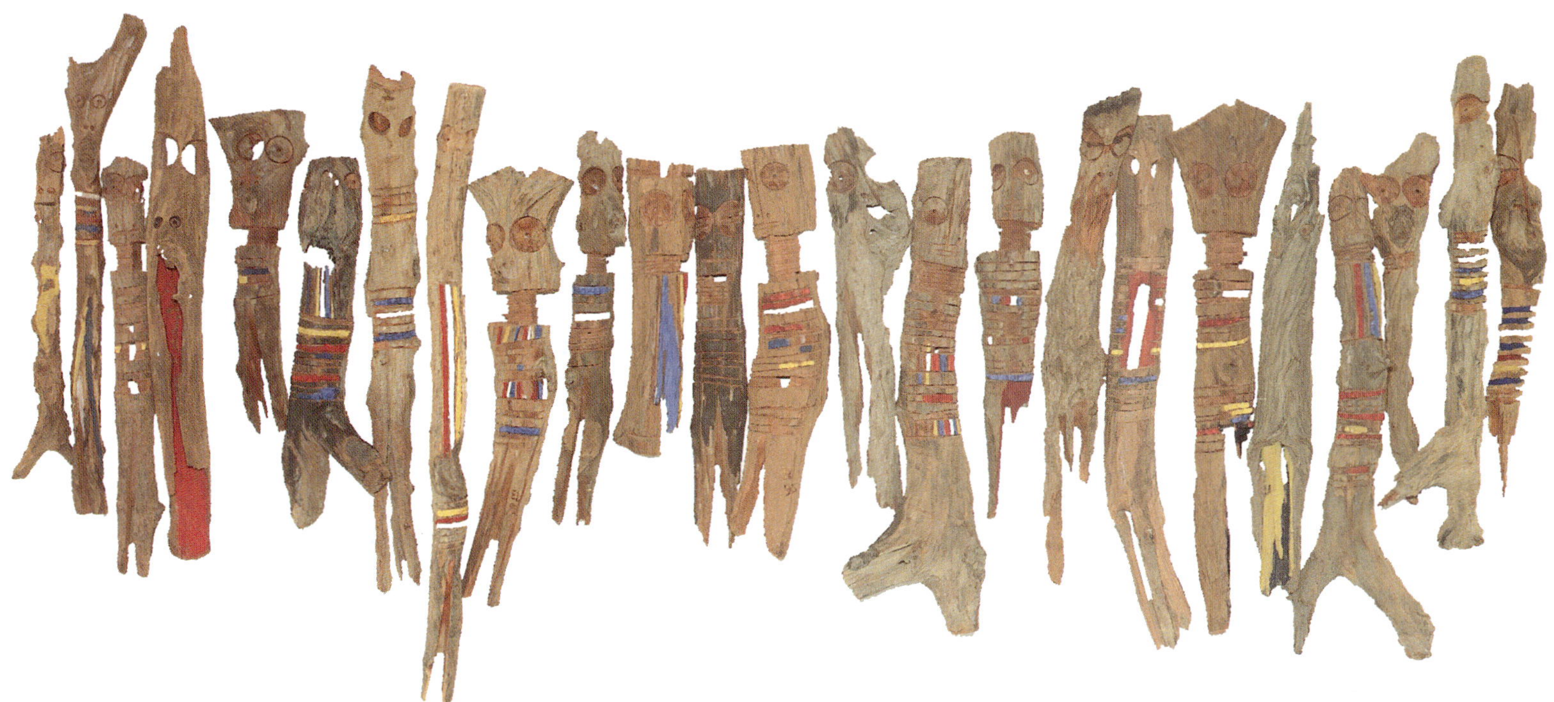

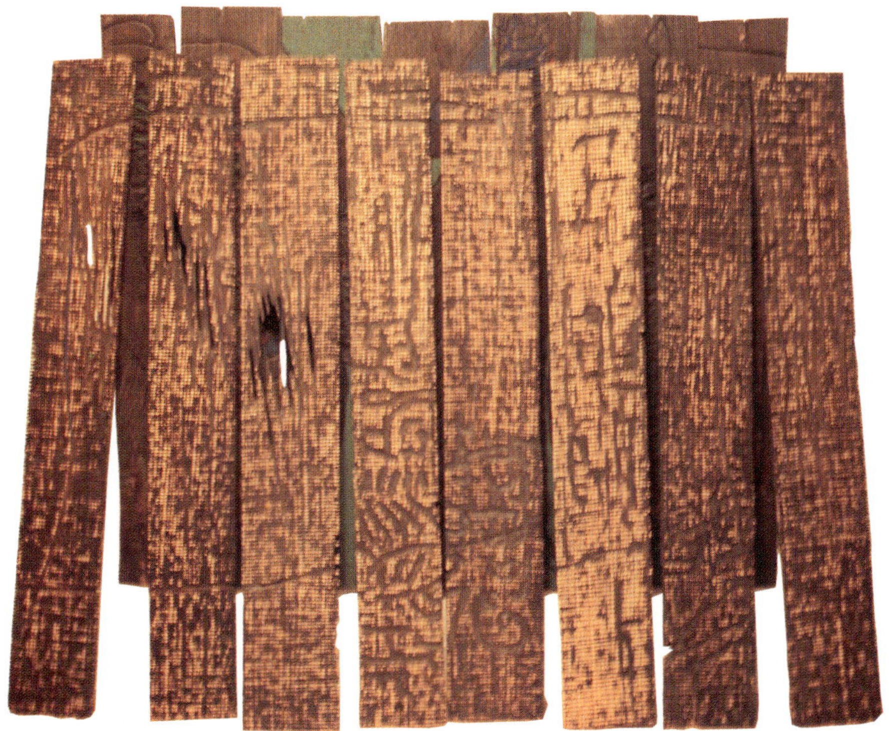

**120 (CENTER).** El Anatsui, *The Ancestors Converged Again,* 1995, *okpeye,* tempera, twenty-four pieces. 98 × 150 × 15 cm (variable). Collection of the artist, courtesy of the October Gallery. Photo: Franko Khoury.

**121 (BOTTOM RIGHT).** El Anatsui, *Invitation into History*, 1995, wood relief, *iroko, oyili-ọji,* tempera, fifteen pieces, dimensions unknown. Collection of the artist.

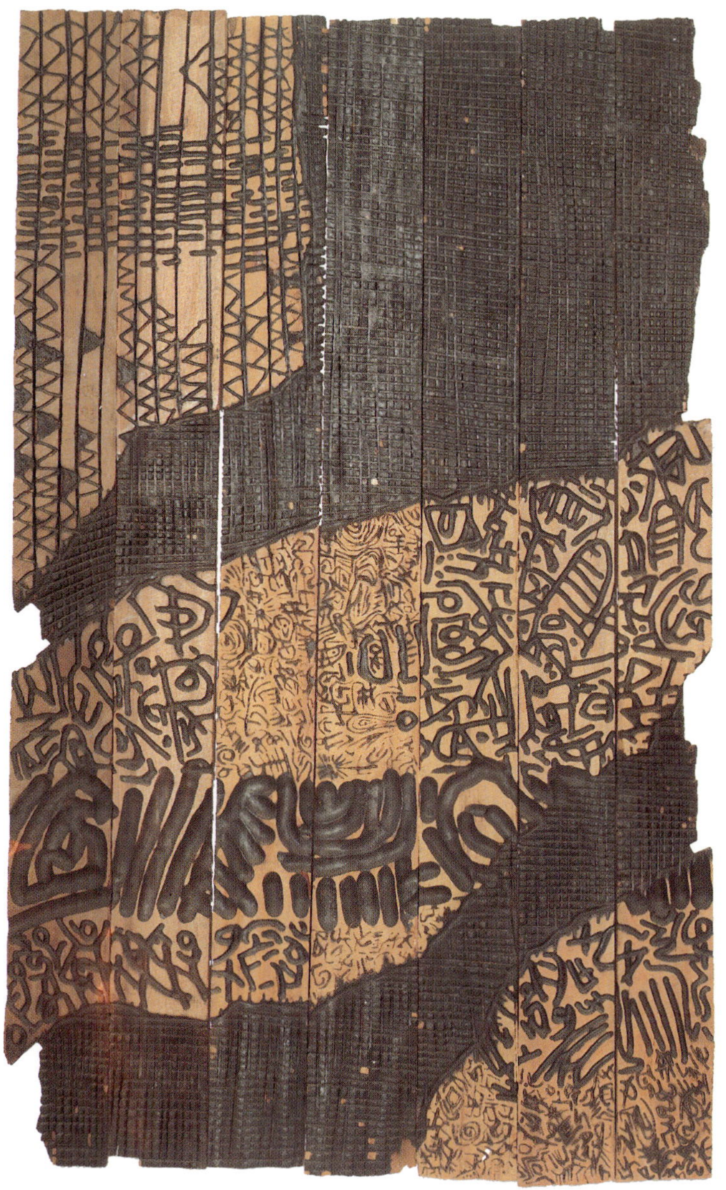



needs. There is ivory tower reasoning going on. In the white areas a variety of different motifs are drawn from different cultures, including an *nsibidi* mirror.

*Earth-Moon Connexion* (1993; fig. 118) is more squarish in shape than most of Anatsui's other panels.[50] It gives the sense of two strong visual sections, at lower left and upper right, connected by more or less parallel lines that hold the work together, with darkness in the upper left and lower right, as if setting the earth and moon in space. *Unfolding the Scroll of History* (1995; fig. 119) shows the artist's tendency in some works to use strong tempera colors.[51] The rich designs gouged out and blackened and those in tempera suggest a scroll, some form of writing.

*The Ancestors Converged Again* (fig. 120), in Anatsui's more rounded, irregular piece form, with spaces between most of them, rep-resents a meeting of ancestors to discuss present conditions.[52] The heads, mouths, and eyes of the ancestors are large compared to their bodies (not unusual in traditional African culture), and they appear unworldly, as if as-tonished as to what has happened to earth in recent times. There is an appearance of antiquity about them. Groups of people or crowds appear in other panels, such as *Mammoth Crowd I* (1993) and *One out of a Crowd* (1993).

*Invitation into History* (1995; fig. 121) is at least twice the size of most of Anatsui's wall hangings.[53] Transi-tional between a wall piece and a standing work, being both, it has eight long, wide, brown outer panels that rest on the floor with their tops leaning on seven darker inner panels hung on the wall. The outer panels represent Euro/American conceptions of African history, the inner panels African history as Africans see it. Both sets of panels contain irregular, unsystematic black gouges in the wood that appear to stand for the writing of history. The meaning of the work is clear: true African history has been hidden and is not well known, being misrepre-sented by Euro/America. This is only one of Anatsui's works that relate to history; others include *Patches of His-tory III* (1993; fig. 122)[54] and the already mentioned *Unfolding the Scroll of History*.

By the early 1980s Anatsui was creating standing wood figures. This work in wood has increased over time, until he now feels he is ready to put wall hangings aside for these generally larger pieces, a few of which are wall leaning pieces, such as *Invitation into History*. In 1984–85 he produced some acrylic paintings and considered moving in that direction, but his woodwork has proved more attractive to him.

He has created a variety of standing forms, generally creating works for the indoors. Nevertheless, in 1983, he designed two outdoor sculptures at the University of Nigeria, Nsukka, in concrete with terrazzo finish, which he prefers to metal.[55] In *The Ambivalent Hold*, in black (also entitled *The Goddess*), a huge humanlike figure holds some form of creature in its giant hands. The work refers to science—its potential for destruction or for the improvement of mankind. *For the Upliftment of Man*, in white, rests off the ground on a number of poles, having "a ruggedness befitting its theme of tenacity and ascent." [56] The title of this work refers to the motto of the University of Nigeria: "To restore the dignity of man." Both works show Anatsui's ability to create strong public sculpture.

A characteristic standing form of Anatsui's involves flat pieces of wood, horizontally stacked upon one another, some about the thickness of his wall hanging panels but others 7–10 cm or more deep. With these, in various shapes, he creates human figures or other images; their outsides are often scored with burnt lines. One example of this type of work is the couple, *Mr. and Mrs. Nyanga* (1988).[57] A similar work, *Couple* (1990; fig. 123), is composed of blocks of wood of different sizes for each figure, partially worked on the outside with burnt lines, the woman with a small face, the man's quite large.[58] The man's body is darkish brown, the woman's is light brown with burn marks that provide contrast. Anatsui once spent some time rearranging the pieces for me in different poses, a characteristic of many of his standing works. In one pose the couple faced forward and seemed detached and somber; in another they slightly faced each other, appearing cheerful and communicative.

He has produced three *Wonder Masquerade* figures. The second (1990; fig. 124) is again composed of numerous pieces that are cleverly arranged.[59] There is little sense of a face mask, rather more of a total body costume. In another work, *Back of Front* (1990, 186 cm high), the upper

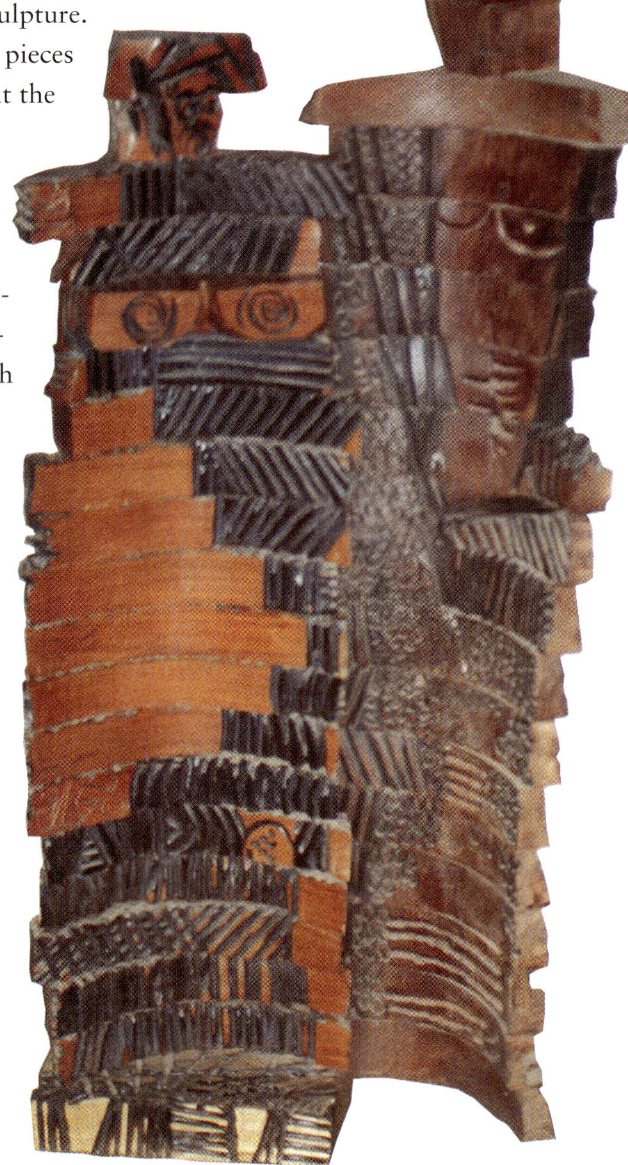

**123**. El Anatsui, *Couple,* 1990, standing figure, *oyili-ọji* and other woods, c. 172 cm high. Collection of the artist.

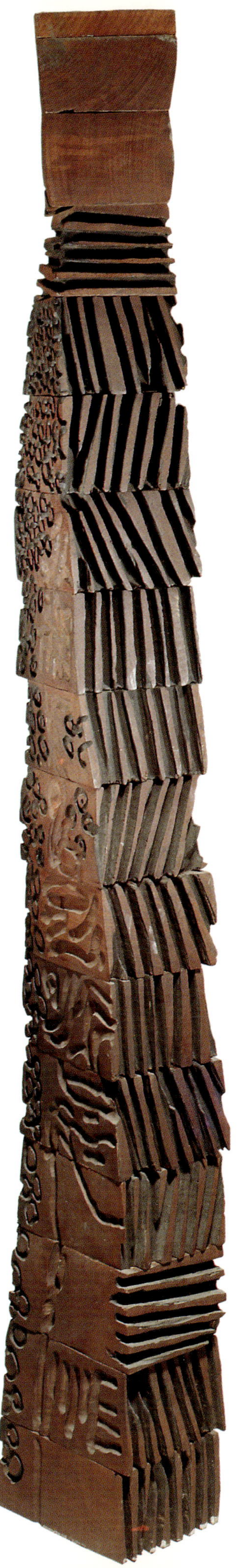

**124** (LEFT). El Anatsui, *Wonder Masquerade II*, 1990, standing figure, oak. 159 × 20 × 14 cm. Collection of the artist. Photo: Franko Khoury.

**125** (BOTTOM MIDDLE). El Anatsui, *Erosion,* 1992, installation, *piqua, marfin,* tempera. 300 cm high. Collection of the National Museum of African Art. Photo: Franko Khoury.

**126** (BOTTOM RIGHT). El Anatsui, detail from *Erosion,* 1992.

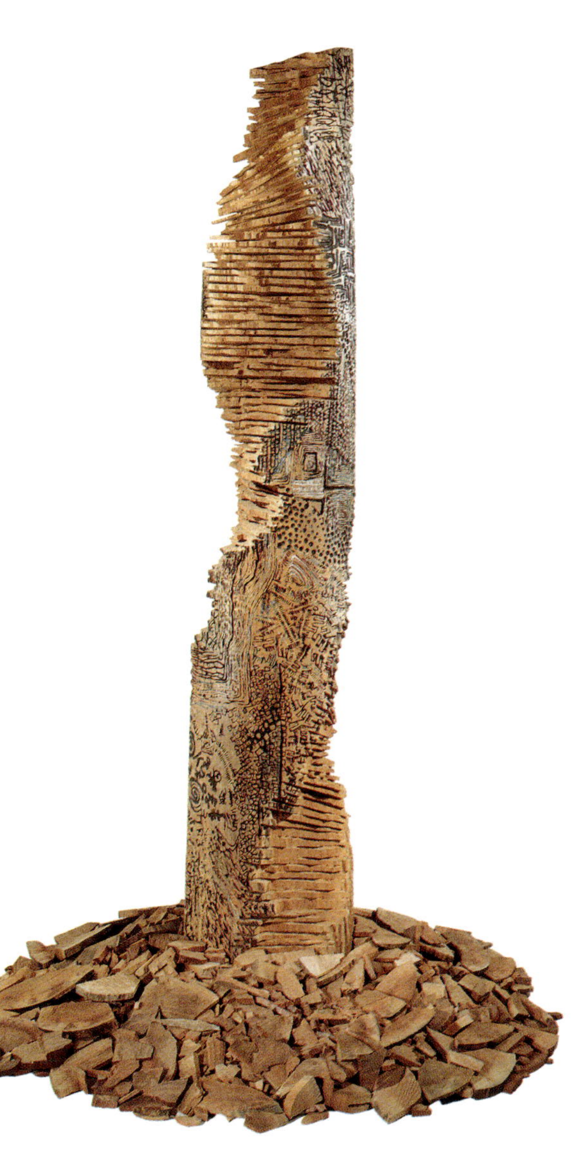

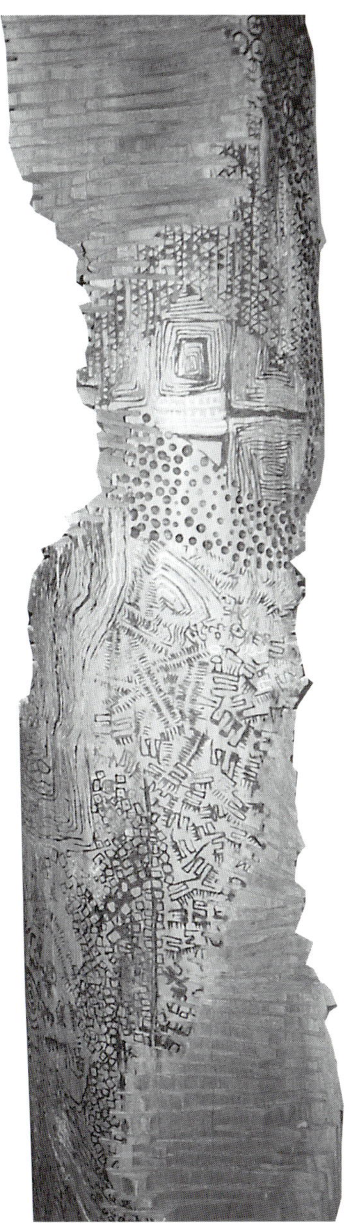

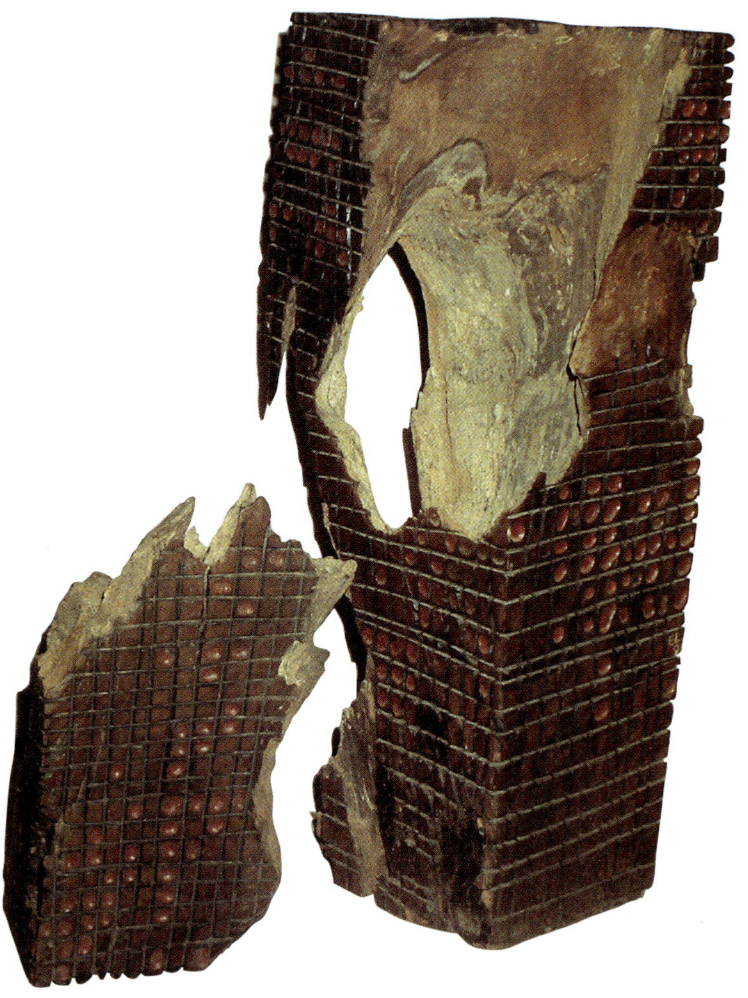

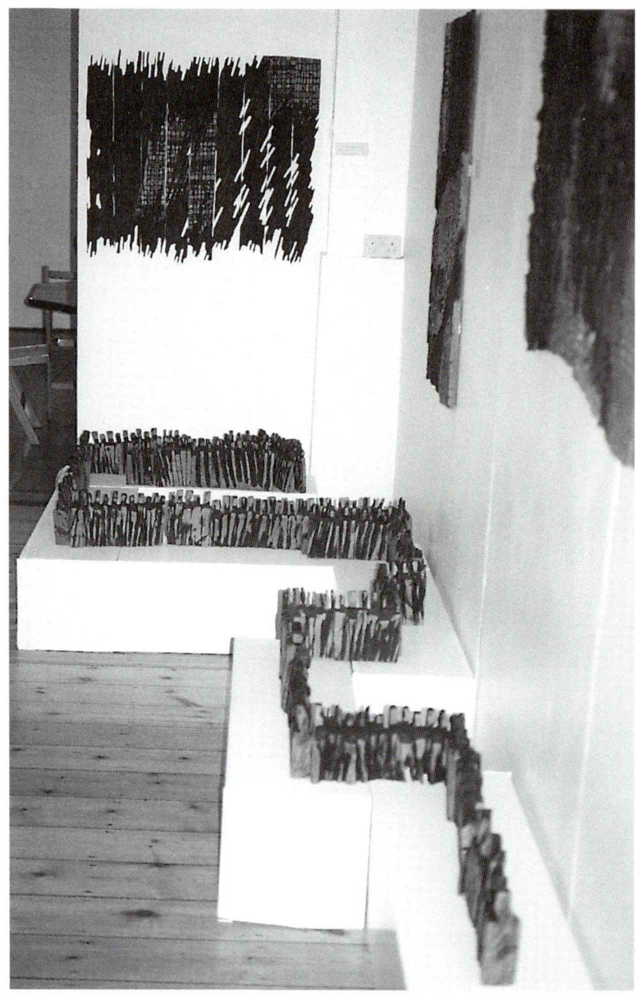

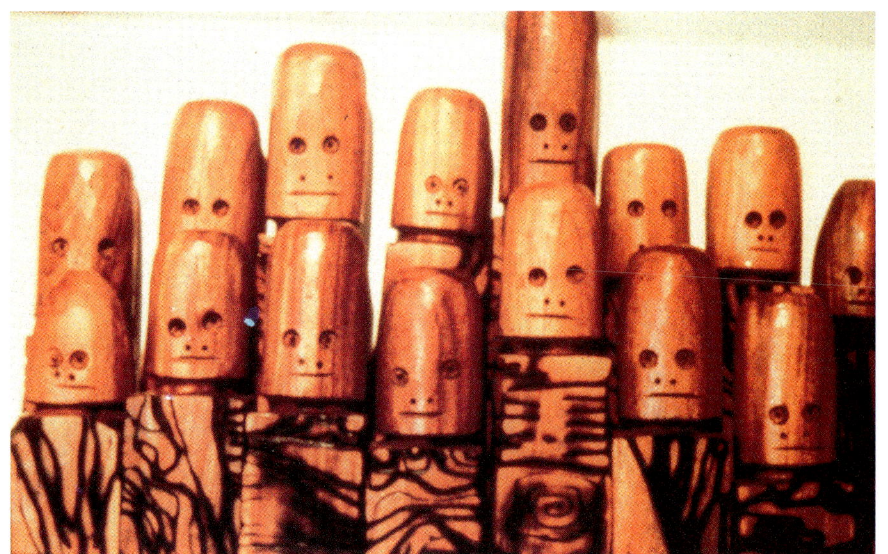

**127 (TOP LEFT)**. El Anatsui, *Chip off the Old Block*, 1991, two standing figures, *iroko* wood. 125 × 45 × 32 cm. Collection of the artist.

**128 (TOP RIGHT)**. El Anatsui, *Visa Queue*, 1992, installation, tropical hardwoods, numerous standing figures, dimensions unknown. Collection of the artist, courtesy of the October Gallery.

**129 (BOTTOM LEFT)**. El Anatsui, *Group Photograph*, 1988, standing figures, oak. 39 × 60 × 15 cm (variable). Collection and photo: the artist.

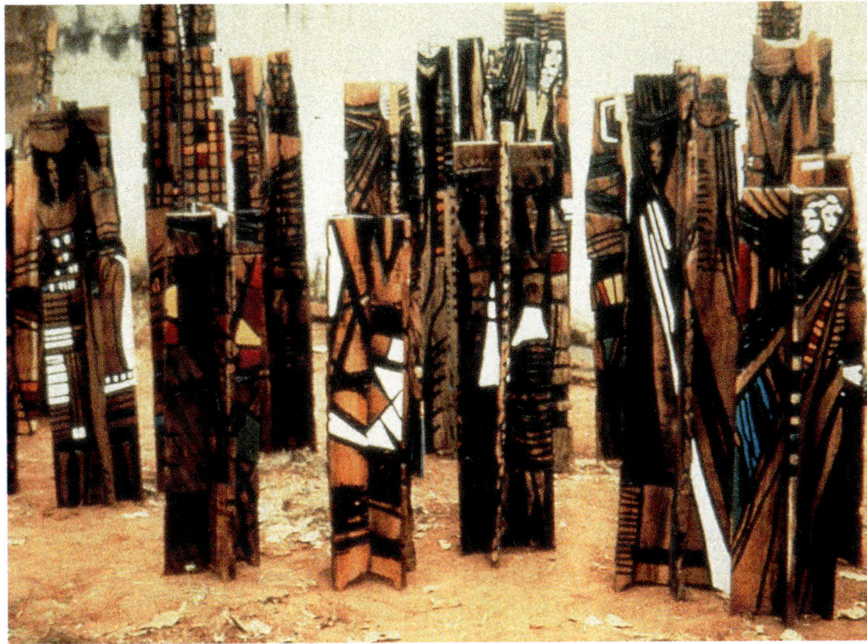



part opens up like a flower. One side is composed of numerous vertical burn marks, contrasting with a second side of irregular unburned cuts that look much like those in some of his history pieces.

In these wood standing sculpture works the individual pieces are numbered. While generally assembled in the same order, the way individual pieces lie on top of one another can be altered to change the overall impression. Again, we see Anatsui's belief that the owner of the work should feel free to interpret it.

In 1992, for an international artists' workshop, Arte Amazonas, in Manuas, Brazil, which preceded the Earth Summit in Rio de Janeiro, Anatsui created a tall wood piece entitled *Erosion* (figs. 125, 126).[60] Here there were no serious restrictions on size, materials, or other facilities. The workshop's theme was "Environment and Development"; the results were exhibited at the Modern Art Museum in Rio, touring to Berlin and Aachen, Germany. In 1995, *Erosion* was also shown as part of Anatsui's 1995 solo exhibition at the October Gallery, London. Anatsui says he delighted in the freedom to create in the workshop, with all its facilities:

> I indulged in the extravagance. The result or effect was that when I felt about for a theme, what I ended up with was something with monumental implications. Or it could be that the freedom engendered monumental concepts. . . .
> I was not thinking of soil erosion as you suggested earlier, but something more basic to that, something which is at the root of it, but which is more monumental, more epochal—the erosion of cultures.[61]

This is one of his larger works. Composed of a central single piece of wood with some complex surface designs, it has separate flat wood pieces that appear to have fallen from it to its base, indicating deterioration. The midpoint is narrow, as if wasted, and there is a general sense of decay about the work, with intricate cuttings on the surface of the lower half.

The pattern of Anatsui's creations has gone from smaller to larger over time, from tray plaques and ceramics to wall hangings to standing figures. Partly this reflects accessibility of materials, but it is also due to his increasing skill and willingness to move toward postmodern giganticism, which he has certainly seen in his world travels, but without giving up his African ties and fundamental themes. His standing art exemplifies the continuity of his imaginative creativity with his past work.

A different style is found in Anatsui's *Untrimmed Art Exhibition Catalogue,* which consists of three vertical boards linked by rope. There are pages of illustrations of art—animals, a snake, a human figure, a ladder—in wood relief on light brown panels with black surrounding the panels.[62] Anatsui says it is "untrimmed" because the concept is unfinished—he might add more pages. To him an exhibition catalogue is like a scroll that is open-ended. An artist's life is a series of catalogues, he adds.

Another style is in *Chip off the Old Block* (1991; fig. 127), created from an old wood block that once was in one piece with a crack in it and that split when he put something in the crack.[63] Placing burnt cross-lines on its flat outer surfaces, he created many small squares; as with some of his other works, the two pieces can be arranged in a variety of ways.

He has created works involving numerous small standing pieces. *Visa Queue* (1992, assorted tropical hardwoods; fig. 128) consists of dozens of simply fashioned figures waiting in what seems like an endless line to obtain visas to leave Africa because of conditions there.[64] Other works with a number of small pieces include *Devotees* and *Group Photograph* (1988; fig. 129) and *Africa: Internal Rhythms* (1988; fig. 130).

On the lookout for pieces of old wood, Anatsui visits the villages around Nsukka and gets to know the people there, which he enjoys. He purchases some wood from shrines of priests. He is on the lookout for old palm oil mortars, which somewhat resemble small shallow wooden canoes. Women use these mortars to thresh palm fruit with their feet to extract the edible oil. When he obtains a mortar, he rolls it down a hill; this breaks off the weaker parts and makes for a stronger object (fig. 131). He then uses them in standing sculptures, generally only working the inside. Again we see the idea of rebirth, of regeneration. He is thinking of using some mortars and found objects in an assemblage without working them at all.

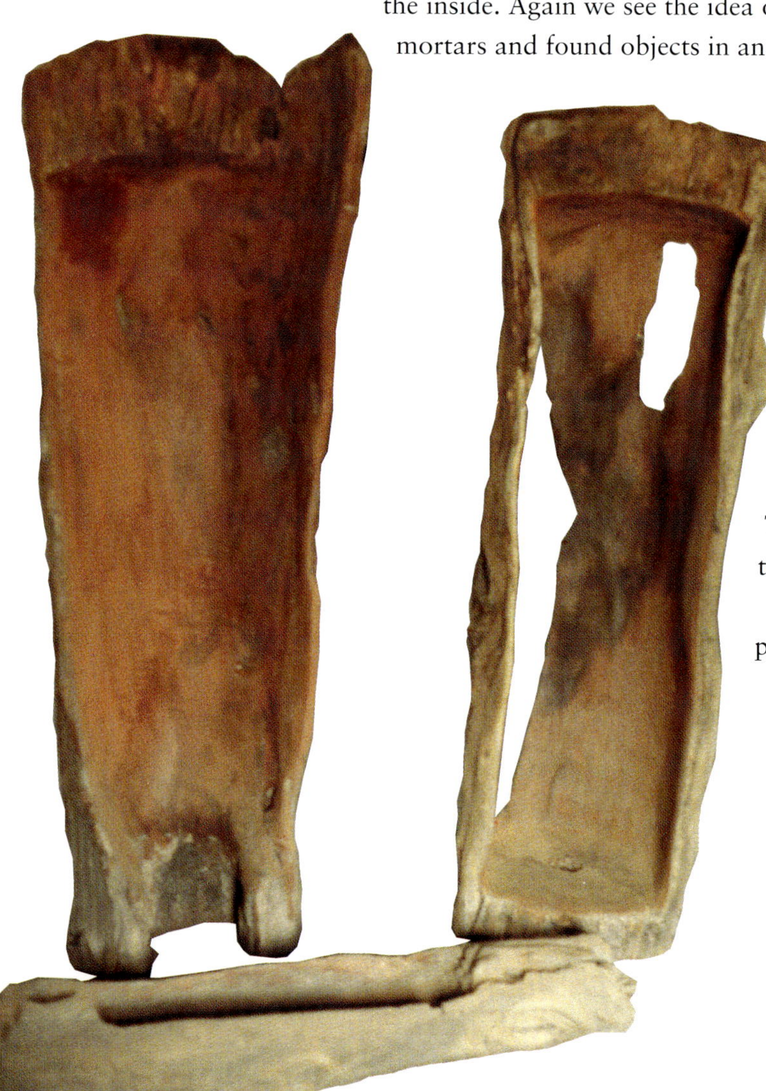

In *Tapper* (1995; fig. 132), an upended mortar forms the body of a palm wine tapper, with his raffia palm fiber belt of the type actually used in tree climbing and a cloth hat.[65] On his right shoulder, the tapper carries firewood that he found along the way. The arms and other parts of the figure can be adjusted to give the tapper different poses. *Man with Flying Tie,* based on an old mortar, was created for the 1995 *Osaka Triennial Sixth Contemporary Art Exhibition* at the Osaka Festival of Culture. This work won him the Kansai Telecasting Corporation Prize for sculpture.[66] These mortar-based works are intriguing to me as well as to others.

Anatsui's interest in mortars and other old wood is part of his desire to keep in touch with ordinary people

**131**. Old and worn village mortars used to pound palm fruits, in El Anatsui's studio, c. 123 cm high. Collection of the artist.

outside the university. We have seen this with the market women
and their trays and the woodcutters in the Winneba area of
Ghana; it continues in Nigeria in his search for a range of
woods in the markets. These nonacademic contacts undoubtedly stimulate his creative skills and provide
him with new ideas for his art. He may have been
critical of the university's "ivory tower" (in his untitled wood panel discussed earlier), but he successfully
moves between academia and the external world. His
wood standing figures show his ability to experiment, to
try different forms, and to do so with humor.

## MOVING ON AND OUT

Anatsui frequently exhibits in Nigeria, where his work is popular. His work appears most often in group shows, such as with
the AKA Circle of Exhibiting Artists, in which he played an important founding role along with Obiọra Udechukwu. In a 1982
exhibition at Lagos, he showed drawings and photographs of his
work as well as ceramics.[67] His line drawings appeared in
*Okike* (numbers 18, 19, and 20, 1981), mostly preliminary
sketches for sculpture. He also exhibited in *New Currents:
Avant Garde Nigerian Art* (1993, Lagos) as one of eight
selected Nigerian artists.

In the last fifteen years Anatsui has moved into the international world. I have already mentioned his 1995 London,
October Gallery solo exhibition, his prize-winning work in
Osaka the same year, and his 1992 Brazilian workshop. He also
exhibited in New York at the Studio Museum in Harlem with eight
other African artists in 1990—the exhibition toured four other
American cities—and in a group *uli* show in New York in 1995.[68]
He took part in the 1995 *Configura 2* exhibition in Erfurt along
with Obiọra Udechukwu; unlike the latter, Anatsui sent work rather
than creating it on the spot.[69] He also joined in an exhibition of contemporary Nigerian art in three German cities in 1989. He took part

**132**. El Anatsui, *Tapper,* 1995, mixed
media: wood, raffia, palm fiber, cloth,
c. 183 cm high. Collection of the artist.

in 1990 with four other African artists in the first Venice Biennale to exhibit contemporary African art, and he participated in the 1994 Fifth Havana Biennale, which he enjoyed more than the Venice exhibition.[70] Matters were arranged so that the artists had a better opportunity to get together, in this case, largely third and fourth world artists whom Anatsui was eager to meet. He was one of four Nigerians in the first South African Biennale in 1995.[71] There were other exhibitions abroad as well.

One of Anatsui's most unusual artistic experiences was in 1984 at Cuxhaven, Germany, at the Zweites Symposion Nordseeküste, where nine artists each created separate works relating to the weather at a sandy North Sea estuary. Anatsui was the only African among the artists, most of them being German, with others from Korea, Yugoslavia, and the United States. His public sculpture was a huge mound of earth on top of which he placed a large self-produced black pot, calling the whole *Altar*. Then with the help of six other artists dressed in white shawls, he developed and carried out a ritual to the weather spirits, casting himself as priest, calling it an "Offering to the Weather" (fig. 133).[72] He had taken the weather for granted in Africa, so at Cuxhaven he had to consider what to do. As the area was flat, he felt he had to break the horizon, which he did with the help of an earth-moving tractor. This is an excellent example of Anatsui's ability to innovate; it is one of his most postmodern works.

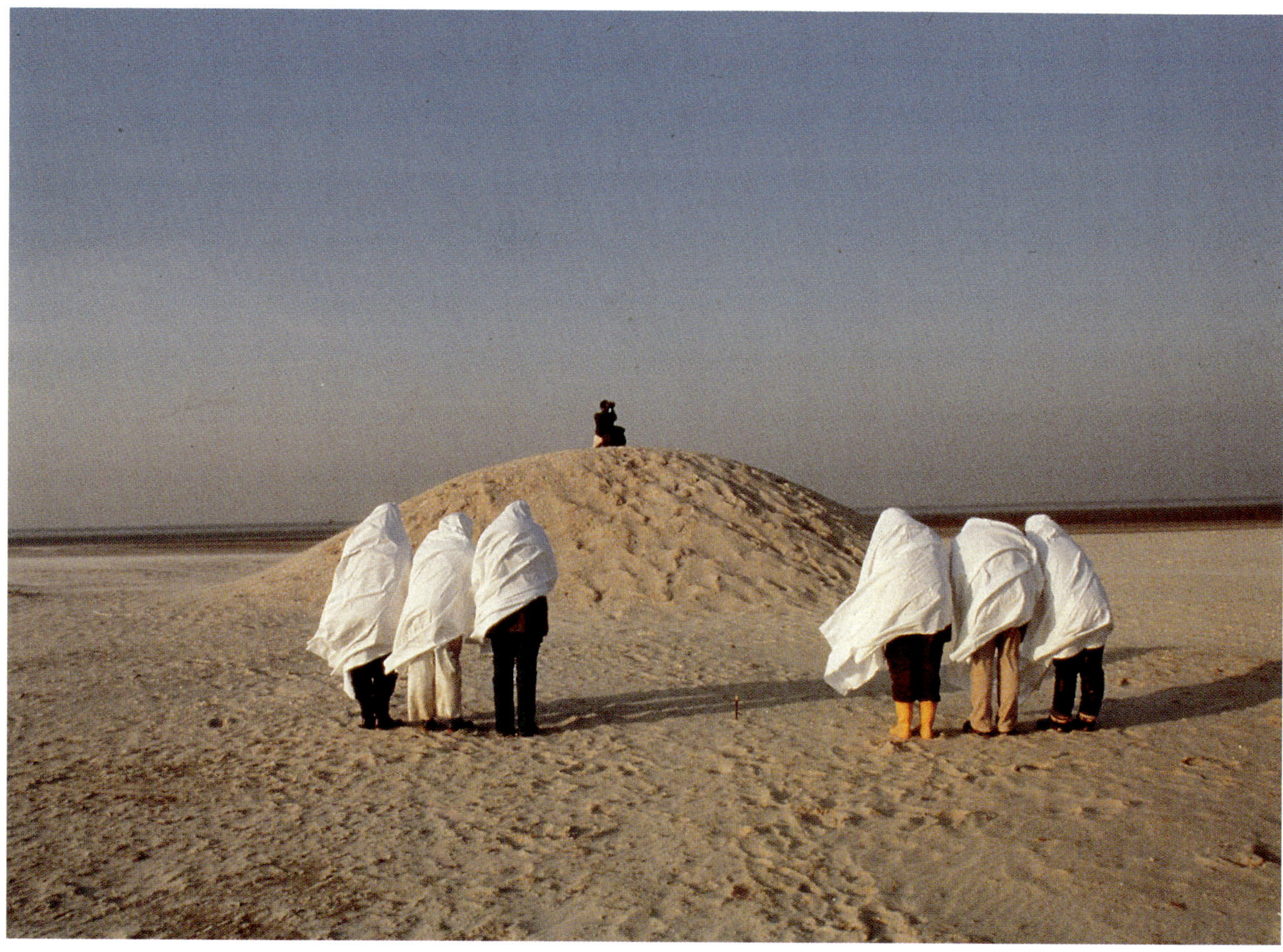

Though the ritual pot and associated rites were very African, the ritual mound is more Middle Eastern and Mediterranean, and the white clothes of the participants suggest Christian rites.[73]

In 1996 for two months Anatsui participated in two events at Copenhagen in the third Images of Africa Festival, *96 Containers: Art across Oceans* and *Images of Africa*.[74] For the latter he worked in an old hammermill that had produced Dane guns used in slave raids in the Gold Coast many years ago, his work commenting on slavery. In *96 Containers*, these were stacked up into a little "city" at the port of Copenhagen, with each serving as a space for an artist's installation. The recent work of Anatsui, particularly away from home, shows an ability to move toward postmodernism and to installations without giving up his strong interests in Africa.

Anatsui's increasing international recognition as an artist has given him the opportunity to meet many contemporary artists, postmodern and otherwise, from Europe but also from third and fourth world regions. He has the recognition to exhibit internationally and is becoming a world artist, moving beyond the *kente, adinkra, uli,* and *nsibidi* design traditions of Ghana and Nigeria. Though many of his themes are still African, for example, his deep concern with African history and the erosion of African cultures, some of his art takes on a more universal character, as his Brazilian *Erosion* and his North Sea *Altar.* The contrast with Uche Okeke, and even Obiọra Udechukwu, strongly rooted in Nigerian culture, is clear. Anatsui has moved further into the international scene. He will, I believe, continue to move out, experiment, and go in new directions. His career is characterized by change and development.

**133 (FACING PAGE).** El Anatsui's acolytes before the *Altar,* 1984, installation and performance, earth and ceramic pot, dimensions unknown.
Photo: El Anatsui.

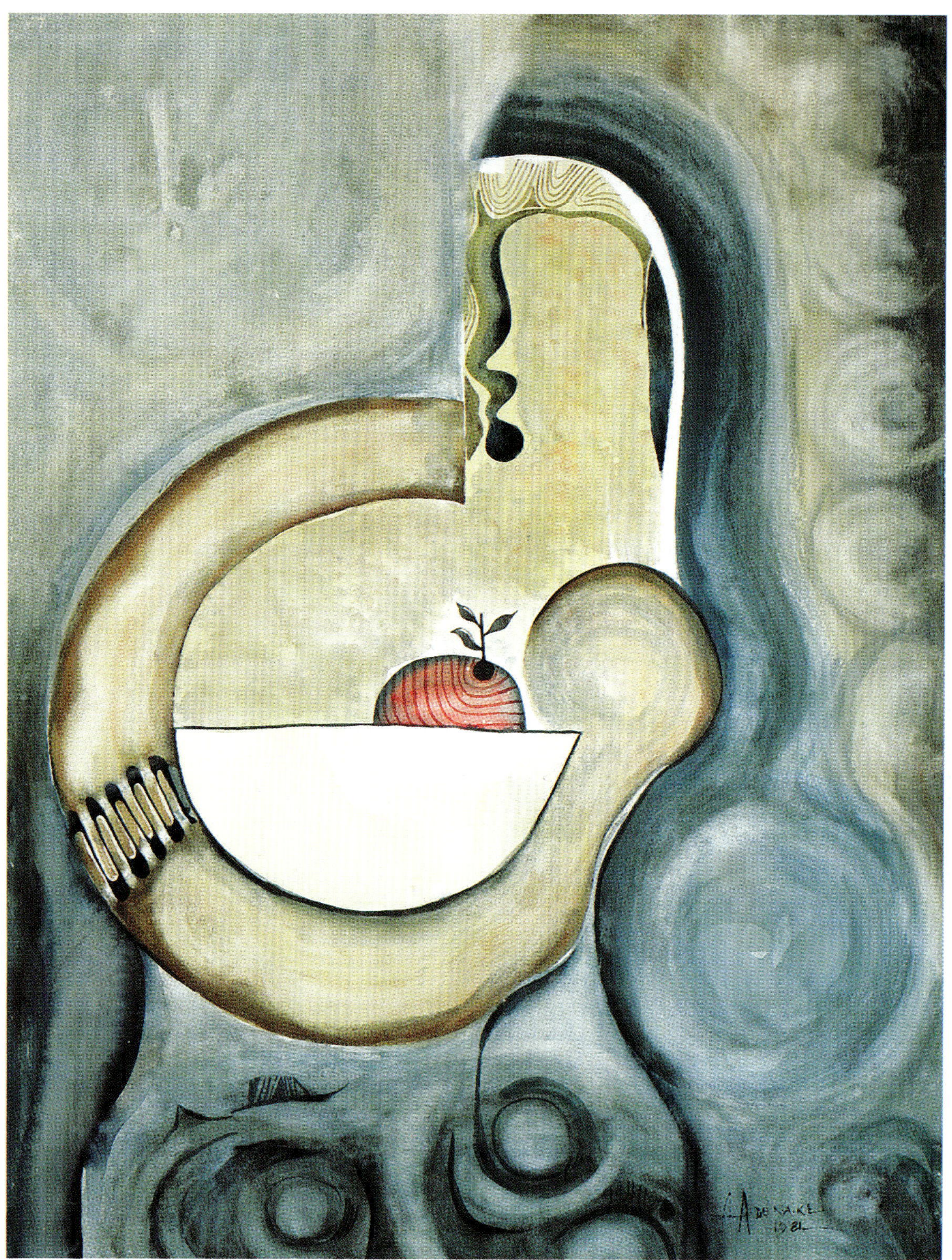

Fig. 136.

# 10. TAYỌ ADENAIKE

## WATERCOLORIST OF FACES AND FIGURES

I like watercolors. For now, I am not sure I will be in a position to express my inner feelings better using any other materials or any other medium.

TAYỌ ADENAIKE[1]

Tayọ Adenaike, born in 1954 at Idanre, Ijebu-Imushin, Ogun State in Yoruba country, southwestern Nigeria, of Catholic and Yoruba background, was given the name Augustine Ọmọtayọ Adenaike, Ọmọtayọ meaning "a child is enough to make you happy" in Yoruba (fig. 134). His childhood was apparently pleasant; like many African children, he drew on wet ground and on sand and, as an older child, created works on paper based on Yoruba tales. After attending primary school in Ibadan, he studied at Federal Government College, Warri, a secondary school outside Yorubaland, near the Nigerian coast, where he had his first art course in 1967. Except for three months during the Biafran war, when the school moved to Kings College, Lagos, he studied at Warri between 1966 and 1972. He had a good art teacher, and art materials were plentiful; the students worked in acrylics, chalk pastels, oil pastels, and other media. He loved music, especially that of James Brown, and enjoyed singing and playing the drums.

Toward the end of his secondary school training, he decided to become an artist rather than a geographer or musician, and despite a strong interest in literature. At first his father was not happy, expecting a son he was educating to go into one of the prestigious professions such as medicine or law. But the father was not antagonistic, and the parents supported Tayọ's further schooling financially and in other ways.

In 1972 Adenaike won second prize in painting at an All Nigeria Secondary School National Art Workshop at Ahmadu Bello University; this encouraged him to go into art. He sold his first painting that year in Lagos, an image of a Fulani cattle herder; he subsequently sold other works. In 1974 he gained admission to the University of Nigeria, Nsukka, meanwhile working as a clerk and then as a designer in an advertising agency and continuing to develop his art interests. By that year he claims that he had mainly seen only popular art, the work of roadside

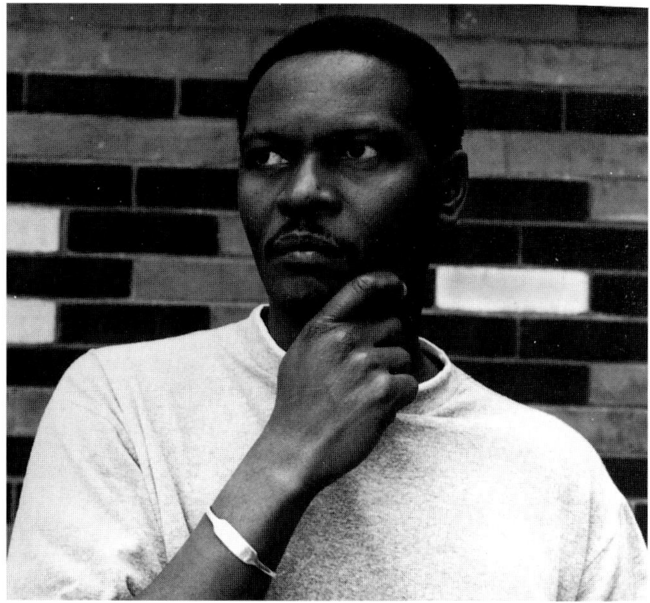

134. Tayọ Adenaike, Washington, D.C., 1995. Photo: Amy Staples.

artists, with their posters and barber signs, and that this was largely what he was doing when he entered the university on government scholarships. He did not move to southeastern Nigeria because of any particular attraction to its cultures but pragmatically, because he was admitted to the university there. However, he was to become absorbed into Igbo culture and modern social life, to become an excellent speaker of Igbo, and to make use of *uli* motifs and linearity in his art.

## UNIVERSITY ART TRAINING

Although since 1970 the art program at the University of Nigeria, Nsukka, has had an Igbo and *uli* focus to it, it is a federal university and has attracted students and staff from elsewhere, not only El Anatsui from Ghana but at various times the teachers Kokoroko, Isaac Ọhene, Uko Akpaide of Ibibio Nigerian background, and Ọla Ọlọidi of Yoruba heritage.[2] Students come not only from Igbo areas but from Yoruba, Ibibio, Tiv, Hausa, Benin, and Warri regions and other parts of Nigeria; the program has never discouraged faculty and students from drawing on their own or other cultural backgrounds. So it is no surprise that Adenaike attended the art program between 1974 and 1979 and again from 1980 to 1982. He has lived in the Igbo area ever since.

Adenaike obtained his B.A. degree in 1979, then taught for a year at the Institute of Management and Technology, Enugu, returning to the university to complete his M.F.A. in 1982, both degrees in painting. For his B.A. degree he wrote a thoughtful thesis on Oṣogbo artists, with useful insights on that Yoruba art group.[3] For the second degree he developed an interesting and wide-ranging thesis on the role of *uli* in contemporary Nsukka artists' painting, published in part in *Nigeria Magazine*.[4] By the time of his graduation, Adenaike, although still developing his own style, had mastered the principles of *uli,* not so much through direct teaching as through contact with Uche Okeke, Chike Aniakọr, and especially Obiọra Udechukwu, who became his mentor and remains a close personal friend. Udechukwu gave him books to read and at times allowed him to watch him paint, not a usual privilege for students at that time. It is not surprising that some of Adenaike's early artwork resembles Udechukwu's in its linearity, the use of a few lines to depict an image, its rounded, curvilinear qualities, and its use of negative and positive space.[5] Adenaike later followed Udechukwu in moving toward the use of *nsibidi* motifs. Adenaike had seen *uli* wall murals in Nnobi and the surrounding regions, which reinforced his interest in this design form. He found *uli* of interest rather than Yoruba designs and images, though there has never been an overt rejection of his Yoruba background. Yet Adenaike is not a clone of Udechukwu; he has found his own way, and he has said to me that he has been influenced by the Sudanese painter Ibrahim el Salahi (as was Obiọra Udechukwu), as well as by Andrew Wyeth and Vincent van Gogh (particularly the latter's strong colors—Adenaike has become a noted colorist).

Adenaike took the standard range of university art courses; as a student, he created a large mural in enamel paint in the recreation room of the University Staff Club as part of his M.F.A. degree. Oils were his favorite medium, but in January 1979 Obịọra Udechukwu suggested that he try watercolors, providing him with professional quality watercolors, brushes, and paper.[6] This led to his first exhibition in this medium in December of that year.[7] Uche Okeke also encouraged him in the direction of watercolors.[8] Adenaike has essentially been a watercolorist since that year, although in 1986 he switched to oils for a time and in 1994–95 to acrylics, as if on each occasion he needed to change. Adenaike has never been interested in creating prints, though he recognizes the advantage of having multiple copies of a work. But he senses the importance of a single original work of art: "It is my wish that such a work should outlive me, and I want to be very, very careful about what I do. I go for the tested materials. If one buys the work, I can go back home, rest, and tell myself I've given whosoever has it the best that is available in the market in terms of material used."[9]

Although Joseph Mallord William Turner was a famous watercolorist, one could argue that watercolor is not a strong painting medium compared to oil and acrylic. Yet, through the years, Adenaike has created powerful images in this medium, generally of human faces and figures. His faces are often distorted, sometimes agonized, at times more so than in Obịọra Udechukwu's art. Adenaike tells me that it is only through seeing a person's face that he can tell what is going on with someone he is interacting with; thus its importance to him. His art is pre-eminently social. Facial distortion is not typical of *uli* images; human faces and figures are not common in it, yet Adenaike employs *uli*'s linear qualities to create them.

On watercolors, Adenaike has said:

> Watercolor as a medium is rather delicate. You know, when you think of the level of transparencies that one could achieve with watercolors, you know it is very, very *subtle*. And one would expect that perhaps with watercolors the best that one could do is landscape paintings, market scenes, where you just put little dabs here and there and then the entire picture is made. But I am different. I don't do landscapes, for example. I don't paint market scenes, what I call genre. I do things that are more intuitive.[10] [italics his]

Early in his career, Adenaike was impressed by seeing Obịọra Udechukwu's art, reproductions of Uche Okeke's work and an occasional original, and Chike Aniakọr's drawings. By 1976 he began to employ the *uli* style from which came his 1980 and 1982 solo exhibitions at the Goethe Institut, Lagos, *Childhood Fears* and *Distorted Souls*, and his 1981 solo show at the Africa Centre, London, *Homage to Uli*.[11] In his university days he began a pattern of frequent exhibitions, both solo and group, which continues until now. By the time he had finished training in 1982, he had taken part in some thirteen group exhibitions, including two in Germany, as well as three solo ones.[12] His art sells well and is in collections in many countries.

Adenaike sees himself, and others see him, as belonging to a third generation of Nsukka artists, with Uche Okeke and Chike Aniakọr in the first, Obịọra Udechukwu, Bons Nwabiani, and others in the second, and in the third the former musician and now furniture designer and wood sculptor Gbubemi Amanoritsewọr Amas, the painter Oseha Ajọkpaezi, and the sculptor/painter Samson Uchendu at the Institute of Management and Technology, Enugu.[13]

Some of Adenaike's art came to express sociopolitical issues. He painted social themes, thinking he could change politicians. But while he still does these, he sees that his art has had little influence on social and political matters and now feels that he paints from within. In fact, much of his art has had a deeply personal, even a subconscious, element, more so than the work of Uche Okeke and Chike Aniakọr, though matched by some of Obịọra Udechukwu's art.

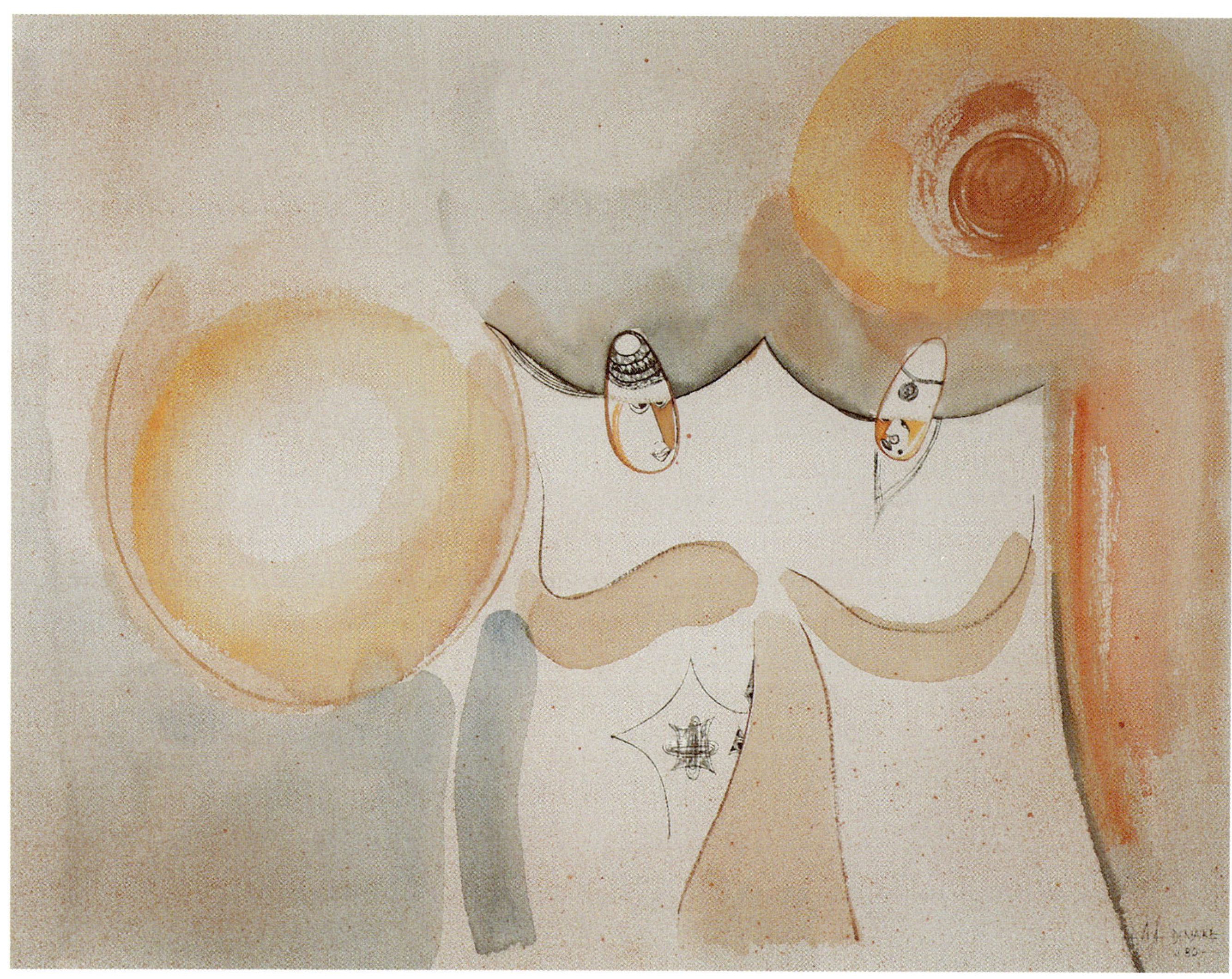

135. Tayọ Adenaike, *Alhaji Takes the Floor*, 1980, watercolor on paper. 45.5 × 60.6 cm. Collection of Simon Ottenberg. Photo: Franko Khoury.

## ADENAIKE'S EARLY ART

Adenaike's first solo watercolor exhibition, *Childhood Fears*, containing twenty-two works, begins on a personal note.

> Once, I was told not to draw lines on brown-earth, or I stood the chance of having my "mother's breasts crawling on the ground for eternity . . . should any housefly perch on the lines." I never could go near old people because "they have the powers to make one laugh, even when the need doesn't arise." On lonely roads, I have had to kick sandgrains for fear that any approaching figure might be a witch or wizard. I was made to believe "witches and wizards walk with their heads down and legs up," and that by my action I could go past them unnoticed. Usually, the stories ended with my being advised to desist from whatever might expose me to the invincible forces.
>
> Strange as these may sound, to deny the impacts that they had on me, would mean denying the very essence of what has today molded my being—my ability to decipher the good from the bad, and more importantly the sources of inspirations for the works on show.[14]

Through much of Adenaike's art, the rational side—from school, university, and life—intersects with the world of emotions, fears, and the subconscious. In this first exhibition the focus is on the emotions. There are images of Yoruba spirits and related matters: *abiku,* the Yoruba equivalent of the Igbo *ọgbanje, oju ajẹ* (witches), *iroko* spirits, and a possessed goat. The human figures, as in *They Are Coming, Vigilantes,* and *Death,* are simply outlined, with elongated bodies and distorted, sometimes elongated faces, which appear anxious, frightened, or ghostly. Obvious *uli* motifs are generally absent, but their linear qualities are there. Appropriate for these themes, there is often a sense of nighttime. The art combines Adenaike's growing skills in technique, *uli* influence, and his Yoruba past.

Concerned with his childhood days at the time of his university training in the face of Euro/American-influenced life and Igbo culture, Adenaike was able to create in watercolor his childhood anxieties, as if working them through helped him to come to a better understanding of their place in his life.

In 1981 Adenaike held an exhibition at the Africa Centre, London, whose small and poorly designed gallery has served for many years as a European starting point for African artists. *Homage to Uli,* more to the rational than the emotional side, consisted of forty-one works in watercolor, watercolor and ink, pen and ink, and ink and wash, representing Adenaike's tribute to the influence of *uli* on his work and also that of his teachers.[15] He has come to see his use of *uli* as helping sustain it for the future. Many specific *uli* symbols appear that were becoming popular with the Nsukka artists, such as the kola nut head, lizard, spiral, and python. An ink work with the exhibition's title (1981) contains these and others and could pass for a segment of an *uli* mural, except that it is in black.[16] Some works display circular swirls of watercolor at the periphery of the main image, suggestive of the *akika* sweeps and swirls of *uli* murals. This occurs in *Alhaji Takes the Floor* (1980, watercolor; fig. 135), where there are images of two northern Nigerian Muslims, with small *uli*-like designs incorporated into the clothes of one figure and the faces of both, a bicultural blend different from that in his *Childhood Fears* show.[17] Muslims, not rare in Yoruba country, are more generally associated with the north of Nigeria, and not with *uli*. The joined outline of the Muslims' garments suggests a half kola nut head *uli* motif, so that in this work *uli* plays both a decorative and an integral role in the main images. This work, and some of his pieces in the National Gallery of Art, Lagos, including *How Time Flies* and *Giant Strides* (1980, both oils), display figures and elements barely delineated by thin lines, surrounded by major swirls and circles of soft and muted colors.[18]

Adenaike, in the exhibition's catalogue, writes: "I presume that they [his teachers] will be happier when someday I am able to make of my Yoruba tradition what they have done to their Igbo tradition."[19] But other than his 1980 *Childhood Fears* exhibition and *Story-Telling* ten years later, in which he makes use of Yoruba tales, albeit in an *uli* style, Adenaike does not draw heavily on Yoruba culture.

In his third solo exhibition, *Distorted Souls* (1982), combining rationality with emotionality, Adenaike follows Obiọra Udechukwu and Chike Aniakọr in employing *uli* to look at social issues, namely, the plight of beggars, who by this time were becoming endemic in Nigeria.[20]

> The anxiety, anger, torment, anguish and disgust one sees on the faces in the streets, serve as pointers to the disparities that exist within our society. At every creative stage these realities had a mark in my mind. . . . Distorted Souls therefore cannot be a glorification of the down-trodden, neither is it a way of saying there are better prospects for the numerous unfortunate ones among us in the near future. Essentially, it only seeks to make the present more obvious.[21]

The exhibition contains images of street people, who are common in urban Nigeria today and whose presence is reinforced by the Muslim practice of almsgiving, as in his watercolor, *Fruit of Life* (1981; fig. 136). In these works the faces are generally larger, more delineated than in his *Childhood Fears* exhibition, but often distorted, showing pain, patience, or hunger. The theme of beggars, occurring here, is close to some of Obiọra Udechukwu's

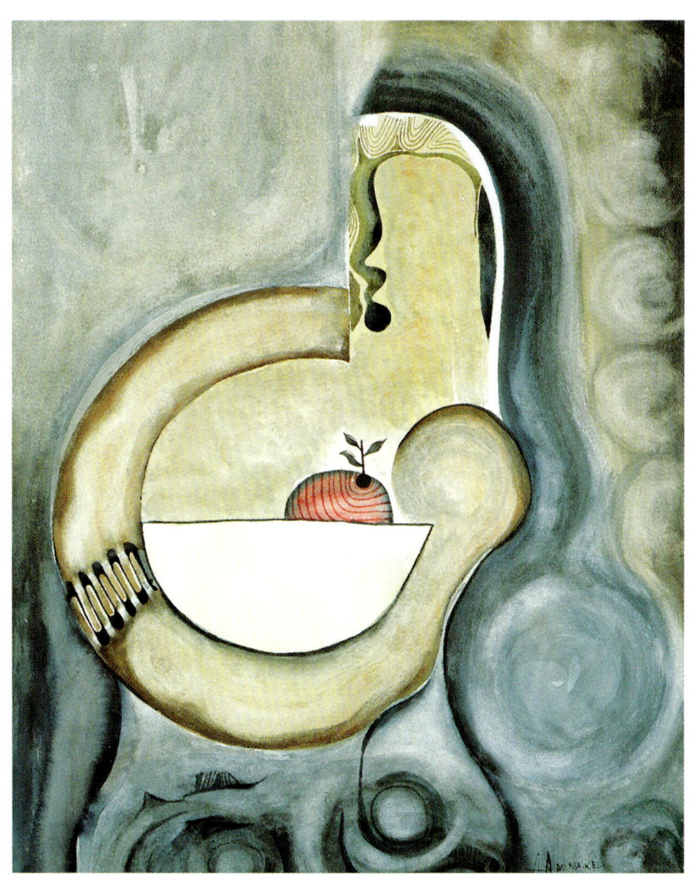

**136 (LEFT).** Tayọ Adenaike, *Fruit of Life,* 1981, watercolor on paper. 57 × 40 cm. Collection of the artist. Photo: Franko Khoury.

**137 (BOTTOM).** Tayọ Adenaike, *Friends on the Street,* 1982, watercolor on paper. 45 × 61 cm. Collection of the artist. Photo: Franko Khoury.

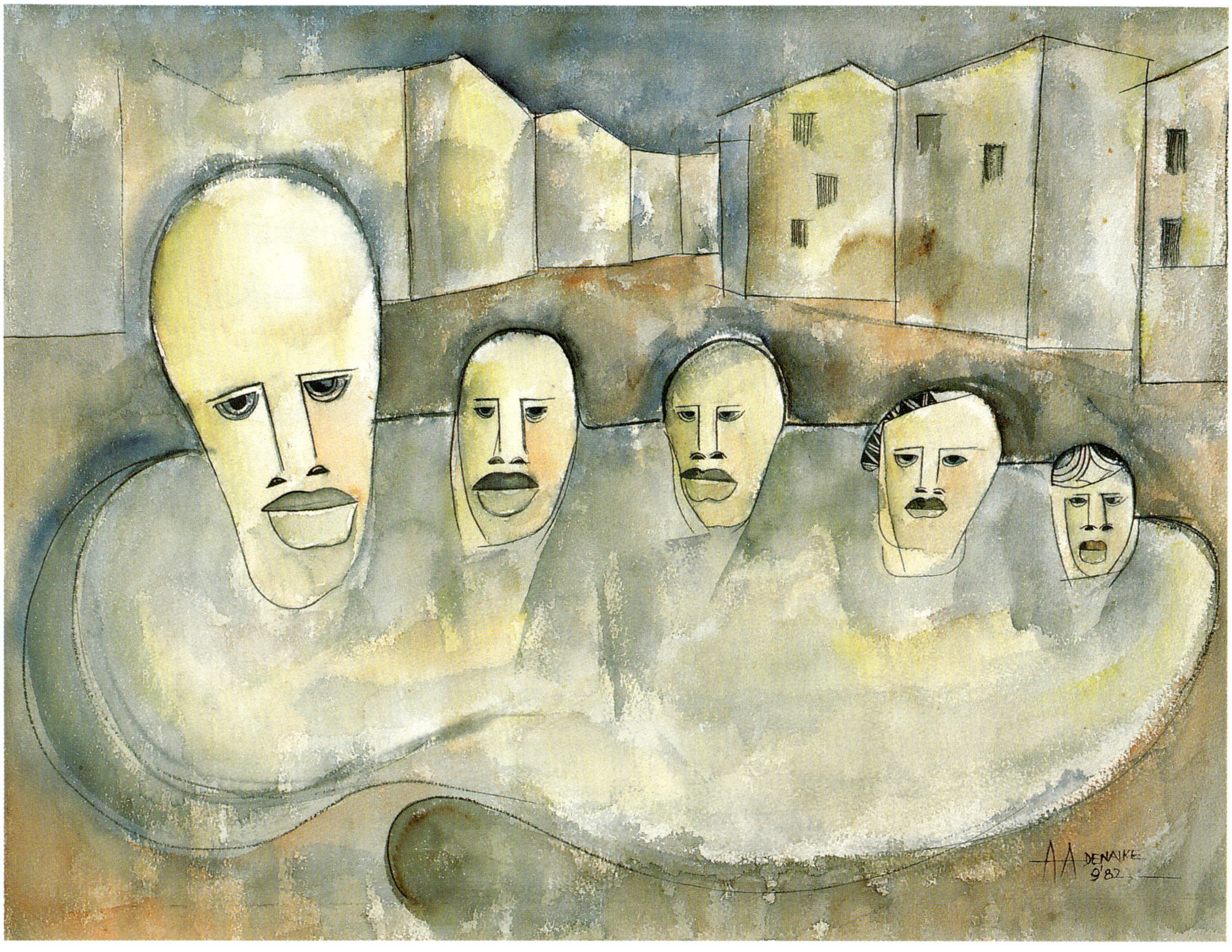

work. In another watercolor from this time, though not in the exhibition, *Friends on the Street* (fig. 137), ghostly heads face forward in a row, with two- and three-story buildings on an empty street in the background, as if the five heads are bound together by the lack of other people elsewhere. As in Adenaike's earlier art, his ink drawings are often more detailed than his watercolors, but his art is becoming more abstract, freer, and with greater control of technique over time.

## AFTER TRAINING, 1982–1990

In Adenaike's first solo exhibition after graduation, *Faces of Time,* held in Lagos in 1983, his depiction of faces and heads becomes stronger, more grotesque, especially the upper eyelids, and the prominent mouths and lips, as well as the nose, strongly dividing the face, and the penetrating eyes.[22] He has told me that he used to think of Nigerian faces as being happy, but changing conditions in the country have altered this perspective. The faces, with the important exception of facial distortion and a lack of facial serenity, seem to draw on indigenous Yoruba facial wood carving, whether on figures or masks, whether Adenaike is aware of this association or not. It is almost as if they are Yoruba faces, but angry, intense, or sorrowful. The head in Yoruba culture is an important seat of spiritual power; Adenaike has turned the face into a powerful tool. As usual with his work, there are one to three faces per painting, rarely more, and they occupy the main portion of the work. In contrast, Obiọra Udechukwu often presents social and emotional issues through figures.

In Adenaike's exhibition, the works have titles such as *Confused Lady, Two in Agony, Comfort from Tears, Insufficiency,* and *The Face of a Lost and Found.* From the art and the artist's statement in the catalogue, the theme of the exhibition is clear: the disparity between Nigeria's wealthy and the many poor, unemployed, and hungry: "This exhibition is my protest against the injustices that have eaten deep into our social fabric, and a call for a stronger apprehension of the bitter experiences that have informed these works."[23] Ironically, this was at the height of the oil boom in Nigeria; the wealth it produced went to enrich only a few.

The colors in his watercolors are still relatively soft, sometimes with watery backgrounds, as if to contrast with the disturbing or shocking faces. *Uli* forms are sometimes built into the faces in the heavy upper eyelids that become half-moons, the eyes stylized cowrie shells (in some indigenous African carvings, they are actual shells). A face may be framed by a half kola nut head or a whole one. The *uli* motifs are so much a part of the construction of the face as not to have a separate life. As Frank Aig-Imoukhuede writes in the exhibition catalogue: "Tayọ's métier lies in his ability to convert *uli* ideas into organic forms which attain remarkable fluidity in his water colours."[24]

Adenaike's 1984 solo exhibition, *The Subconscious: Watercolours and Drawings,* continues his fascination with faces.[25] But the themes are more varied, not necessarily related to poverty and social issues, but to a wide variety of concepts: a pregnant woman, Christian and Muslim matters, music, a dancer. A bulbous forehead and lack of head hair are common; the triangular face comes to a point at the chin. All these features were seen in his art before this exhibition, but they are more prevalent here. Adenaike's colors become darker; the anomaly between his previously gentle colors and his images disappears. Yet even here the dark colors are soft and not intense.

Adenaike already had the habit of avoiding preliminary sketches, painting directly on paper. He continues to use this method, emphasizing the importance of spontaneity in his work, common with the *uli* body and wall painters. Sometimes he has an idea in mind when he begins to paint; on other occasions it develops as he goes along. In this 1984 exhibition, he is still concerned with the impact of his work: "Nobody eats a painting or any other work of art. Art is not an end unto itself. More often than not, the belief is that for any work of art to be meaningful, it should be a means to an end." [26]

Two seemingly opposing qualities come out of this exhibition and the previous one. There is a desire to deal with issues of social reality, to protest gross inequalities. The other quality is what Adenaike calls the "subconscious," the communication, largely through the medium of the face, of unconscious feelings and states. Here inner thoughts are projected in the art. Adenaike does not come out favoring either view. What one senses is that there is a lot of passion, a lot of anger, idealism, and frustration in the young artist at this time, feelings supported by, rather than contradictory to, those of other Nsukka group artists.

In February 1986 Adenaike went to Germany on a Goethe Institut scholarship, traveling to and exhibiting his work in nine cities. This was an important year for him, for he also held two solo exhibitions in Nigeria, and he became a founding member of the AKA Circle of Exhibiting Artists.

His 1986 Goethe Institut exhibition in Lagos, *We Live in the Deep* included twenty watercolors and twelve ink drawings.[27] The watercolors have the familiar faces, but there is a simplification of detail, creating softer features, even if often irregular and contorted. Cutting down the number and intensity of lines creates a dramatic change.

The drawings, in ink and in ink and wash, are where detailed presentation of the face occurs. In *The Philosopher* (1986; fig. 138), the frontal face is not only made up of the facial outline but contains within it a complex of segments of small circles and parallel lines within triangles, ovals, and circles, some elements looking like seashells or snail shells. Despite the complexity of linear details, one can virtually see the man thinking. In his *Young Hawker* (1986), we have a sense of a young person determined to make good in a highly competitive Nigerian street business.[28] Both works are strong, relying on *uli* linear qualities, but the strengths are of a different quality than in Adenaike's watercolors. The intensity of the black lines and designs is impressive in the drawings. Adenaike had been producing and exhibiting art in ink and in ink and wash beginning at the university, but after this exhibition he seems to have created few works in these media.[29] These drawings were usually not preliminary sketches but works in their own right, in the tradition of the significance of drawing to the Nsukka artists. Adenaike has also created a number of book cover illustrations.

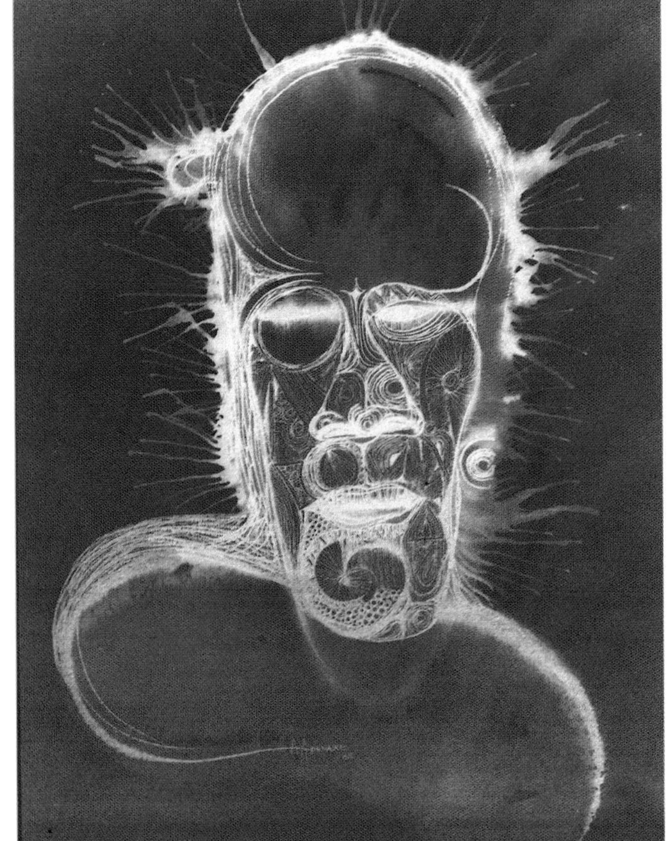

**138**. Tayọ Adenaike, *The Philosopher*, 1986, ink and wash on paper. 61 × 45.8 cm. Collection and photo: the artist.

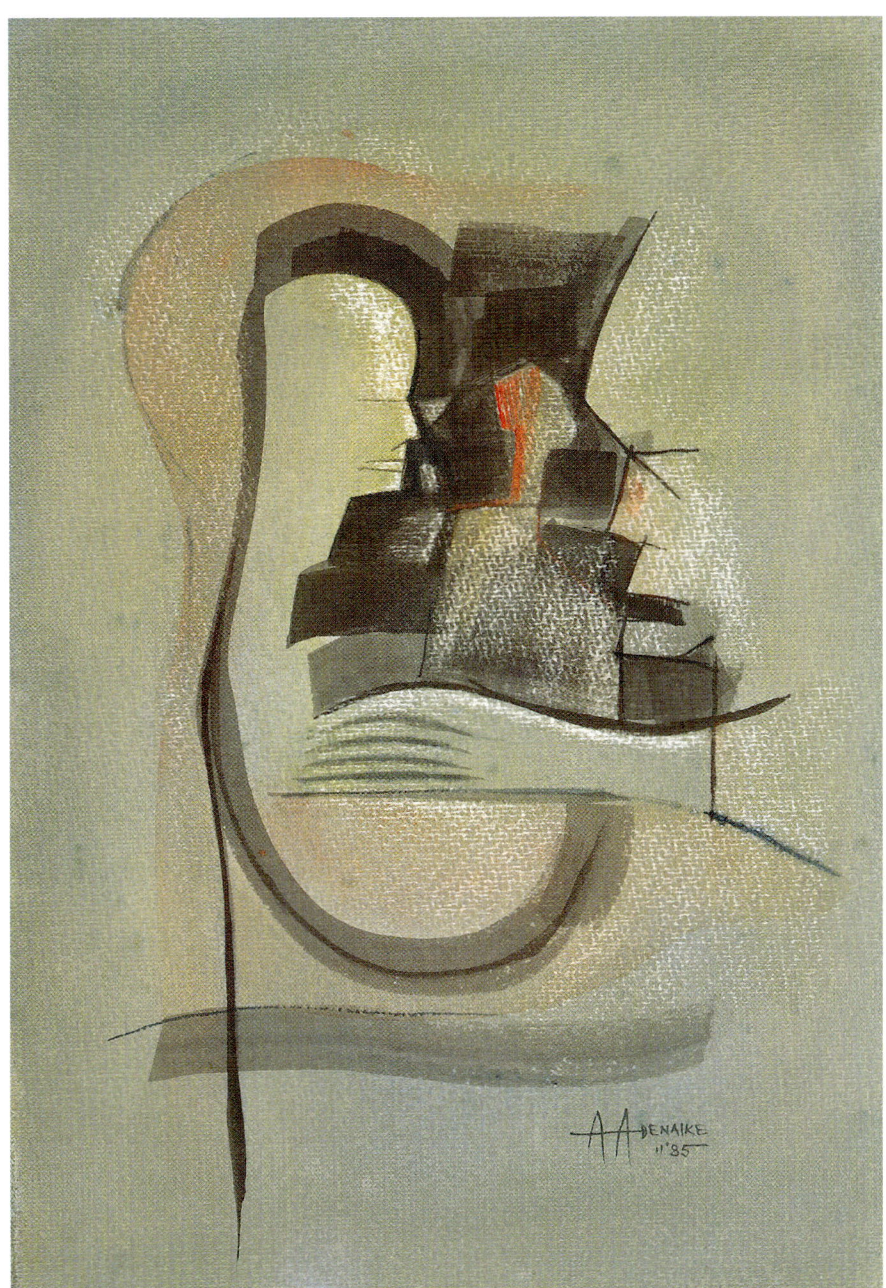

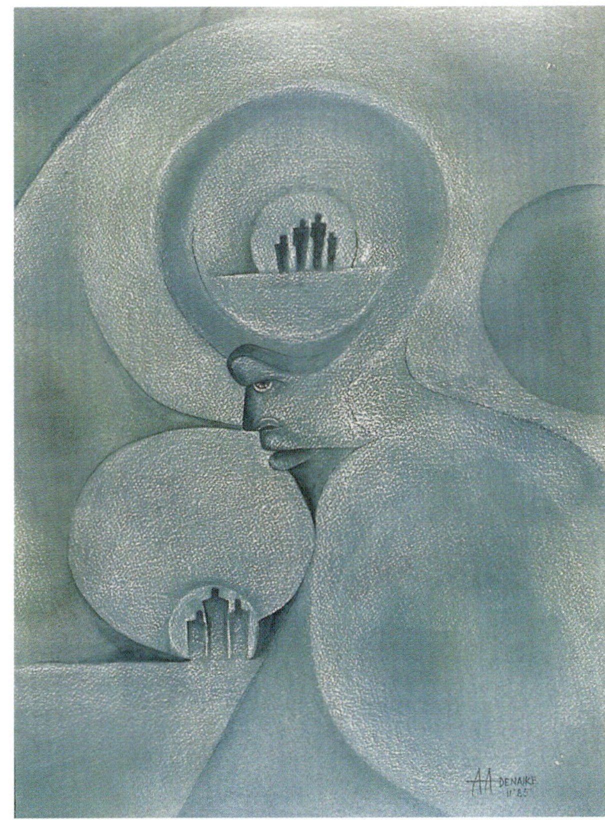

**139 (ABOVE).** Tayọ Adenaike, *Up There, Down Here,* 1985, watercolor on paper. 61 × 45.8 cm. Collection and photo: the artist.

**140 (LEFT).** Tayọ Adenaike, *Shadows of the Past,* 1985, watercolor on paper. 47.5 × 32.5 cm. Collection of the artist. Photo: Franko Khoury.

The watercolors in this exhibition represent a quite different approach, with large *uli* elements and spiraling *akika*-like forms, the latter particularly noticeable in *Up There, Down Here* (1985; fig. 139), where a large face appears between two small groups of standing figures, as if mediating between them. And in *Shadows of the Past* (1985; fig. 140), where the watercolors are also soft, the work has a dreamlike quality, with a large, mysterious hand, perhaps representing time, reaching toward the main human figure. In the exhibition catalogue, Adenaike writes of the subconscious and the social, explaining the exhibition title.

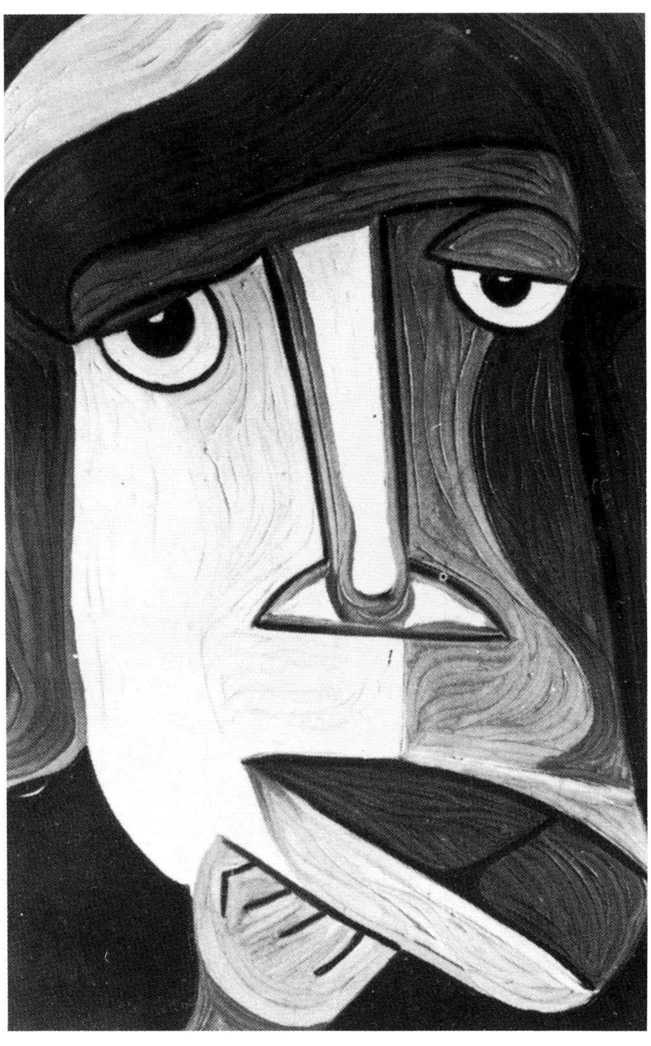



Do we not live in the deep when with our eyes wide-open we consistently hit our heads on the wrong door?

Do we not live in the deep when we can only manage to keep afloat in an ocean of uncertainty? *Should* the artist not go back to his subconscious dictates in search of new creative ideas when it has become clear that no single individual can change his society? [italics his] [30]

Here we see social and political idealism tempered with realism. The signature work in this exhibition, *We Live in the Deep*, is described by Joni Akpederi as being "more obscure. 'The deep' is represented by a spiral that swirls around three heads swallowing and sucking them into a vortex. The idea is got from nature's perpetual effort to submerge man and man's struggle to keep from its powerful forces." [31]

For Adenaike's other 1986 solo Nigerian exhibition, *Dialogue*, he returned to oils, which he had not worked in much since his university days, showing twenty-eight of them, five from his student days, the remainder created the year of the exhibition. [32] He felt that he had had enough of watercolors for a while and desired a change, returning to the favorite medium of his university days. Perhaps this was for the last time, for he soon returned to watercolors. The oils appear more direct, less subtle than his watercolors, as in *Thinker: Our Thoughts Differ* (1986; fig. 141) and in *We Call Them Refugees*. [33] A number of these works have the angular quality of some of his drawings, and works such as *The Arrival of the Masquerades* use more intensive color than his often muted watercolors. [34] A few of the works look as if the artist was trying to create similar effects with oil as he had with watercolor. He has written: "Horizontal and vertical brush strokes do not give the same flat visual effect [as in watercolor] even when the colour consistency and tonality remain the same." [35] Some of his oils, such as *The Arrival of the Masquerades*, have a three-dimensional quality to them.

It is not clear why Adenaike abandoned oils, other than his obvious love of watercolors. In 1992 he told me he was not dissatisfied with his oils: "I just went back to watercolor." Time may have become a factor. After graduating in 1982, he became art director for an advertising agency, Maan Limited, Enugu; and in 1984 he became creative director and co-owner of Dawn Functions Nigeria Limited, another advertising concern, also in

Enugu, with another office in Lagos. This is a major Nigerian advertising company, and he is particularly busy in the latter half of the calendar year, when plans for the following year have to be developed and calendars produced (sometimes employing his own art). So he paints late at night, putting in the final touches in the daytime and on weekends, producing intensively for a time but sometimes not creating for months. In recent years he has also used trips to the United States as periods in which he is free to create.

In 1986 in an interview with Alfons Hug, director of the Goethe Institut, Lagos, Adenaike was asked:

> *Your family background is Yoruba but you have received most of your formal training in Eastern Nigeria. Do you consider yourself as [a] Yoruba or an Igbo artist?* [italics in the original]

To which he replied:

> Well, I am of course, a Yoruba, but I see myself not primarily as a Yoruba artist, neither am I an Igbo artist. I'd put myself in between. Most of my themes I derive from Yoruba mythology or Yoruba stories and folklore. On the other hand the style I use in my painting is derived from the traditional Igbo artistic heritage. This is why I am saying that I am in-between.[36]

Except for his 1980 *Childhood Fears* exhibition, already discussed, I do not feel that by 1986 most of his themes and stories were Yoruba derived, though I have suggested that he sometimes draws from Yoruba carving. Rather, they have been from Igbo culture, current social and political issues, and from what he calls his "subconscious," his personal self.[37]

However, in 1990 Adenaike exhibited fourteen ink and wash works and twenty-six watercolors at the Italian Cultural Institute, Lagos, in *Story-Telling,* pieces created in 1989 and 1990 employing images relating to Yoruba tales told to him as a child by his grandmother.[38] Yet he himself says that he drew stylistically from *uli*. Unlike his earlier return to Yoruba materials in his 1980 *Childhood Fears* show, these images, while sometimes having a fantastic quality, only occasionally display fear and anxiety. Rather they are reflective, sometimes gentle, even amusing.

> Mama Alagbafọ—Grandma, was a washerwoman. With the non-availability of pipe-borne water, it was always such a delight going with her to the Yemọja River twice weekly and returning home, to sit close to the fire on which her irons were subjected to the sudden change from cold to hot. Then the stories would come, and it was only while eating or when the gods of sleep descended on me that the questions to her stopped pouring in. Her answers, true or false, frightening, or convincingly conclusive, left me with some indelible impressions that roam in my mind till this date.[39]

If Obiọra Udechukwu turned to minstrel songs within his culture, Adenaike turned to tales from his background, as did Uche Okeke.

The watercolors in the *Story-Telling* exhibition have a diffuse, abstract quality. Obvious *uli* elements are few; when they occur, they are sometimes large in size. Objects and images seem to float, a characteristic of Adenaike's watercolors noted by Ikwuemesi.[40] There are often large areas of what seem to be watercolor washes, not clearly defined, but now rarely of swirling circles, as previously found. There are fewer faces. There is an element of mystery, of fantasy appropriate for the tales. Social issues are absent, though morals and behavior are linked to some images. It is as if Adenaike, in 1980, had to clear himself by relating to the past in his *Childhood Fears* exhibition, before going on toward artistic development and maturity. Then, in 1986, he felt the need to refresh himself by experimenting briefly in oil; and in 1990, in artistic maturity, felt comfortable enough to look back in whimsical amusement and reverence to his childhood life, blending Igbo design with his Yoruba heritage, a sign he had successfully integrated two cultures in his life.

The 1990s has been a period of extensive activities for Adenaike. He held a major Nigerian exhibition, *Statements*, at the Italian Cultural Institute, Lagos, in 1994, with the sculptor Obiọra Anidi, who also employs *uli* in his art.[41] This was the fourth major exhibition for Adenaike at the institute, which has also exhibited work of Obiọra Udechukwu and other Nsukka artists.[42] Adenaike has also shown elsewhere, including as a member of the AKA Circle of Exhibiting Artists. In Nigeria he sells some 60 percent of his art to Nigerians, the rest to expatriates.

Adenaike has also expanded his contacts with the United States, holding an annual solo exhibition there every year, beginning in 1990. These have occurred in Washington, D.C.; Greensboro, North Carolina; New Orleans, Louisiana; Charleston, South Carolina; Denver, Colorado; and Seattle, Washington. He also took part in the *uli* group exhibition at Skoto Gallery in New York in 1995 and had another exhibition in Denver in 1996.[43]

The year 1996 marks his seventh trip to the United States, a country he finds interesting and its people likable. Although he has yet to exhibit in a major urban gallery in New York City, Chicago, or Los Angeles (rare, in any case, for contemporary African artists), his art sells, and he has found supportive individuals and collectors. This differs from his experience in Britain. Although he has been there a number of times since his 1981 *Homage to Uli* exhibition in London, he does not feel at home with British people or society, a not uncommon experience for African artists, especially in contrast to the United States, France, and Germany. He also uses his U.S. trips to purchase art supplies and equipment for his advertising agency, generally coming in the spring, when agency business is slack.

## CHANGING STYLES

Adenaike's art has been changing in the 1990s. He sees himself as wishing to be bolder than previously in his art. This comes less from the strong faces he has created in the past (though he still produces some of these) than from bright and dark colors, less watery-looking use of watercolor, and more solid color areas, often strongly demarcated from one another. In addition, beginning about 1992, he began to add *nsibidi* designs in his work, sometimes in conjunction with *uli*, sometimes without, though he still does work only with *uli*. When Adenaike employs *nsibidi*, it is not usually in an organic way, as he sometimes does with an *uli* half-moon as an upper human eyelid, but generally as a separate, decorative element or sometimes with a number of *nsibidi* together for aesthetic effect. But in *Three Statements* (1996, watercolor; fig. 142), Adenaike uses an *uli* and an *nsibidi* motif and an Arabic inscription. Obiọra Udechukwu influenced Adenaike to take up *nsibidi* through his own use of it. Adenaike also saw Robert Farris Thompson's *Flash of the Spirit,* and he finds this symbol system stimulating and exciting.[44] He wrote of his 1993 *Impulses in 27 Watercolors* exhibition: "In this exhibition, an attempt is being made to infuse *uli* with *nsibidi*—a pictographic system of the Ekpo [Ekpe] cult of southeastern Nigeria—purely for artistic purposes, in the hope that my works will begin to have new meaning."[45]

Adenaike's 1990s exhibitions each seem to have a mixture of themes, sometimes drawing from personal life, experience, and emotions, sometimes from social and political matters, and occasionally from Yoruba or Igbo culture. Despite his tendency not to produce landscapes, he has created an impressive, imagined one in watercolor, *Desolate Landscape* (1992), and another watercolor landscape, *Trouble Above,* in 1996. An important watercolor reflection on early life is *Childhood Innocence* (1994); there is an acrylic of the same title, but the images are different (1995; fig. 143). A number of works depict animals: a bird, cow, lizard, or fish, such as *Day of the Hook* (1996; fig. 144). There are more human figures and somewhat fewer faces. He uses more and more

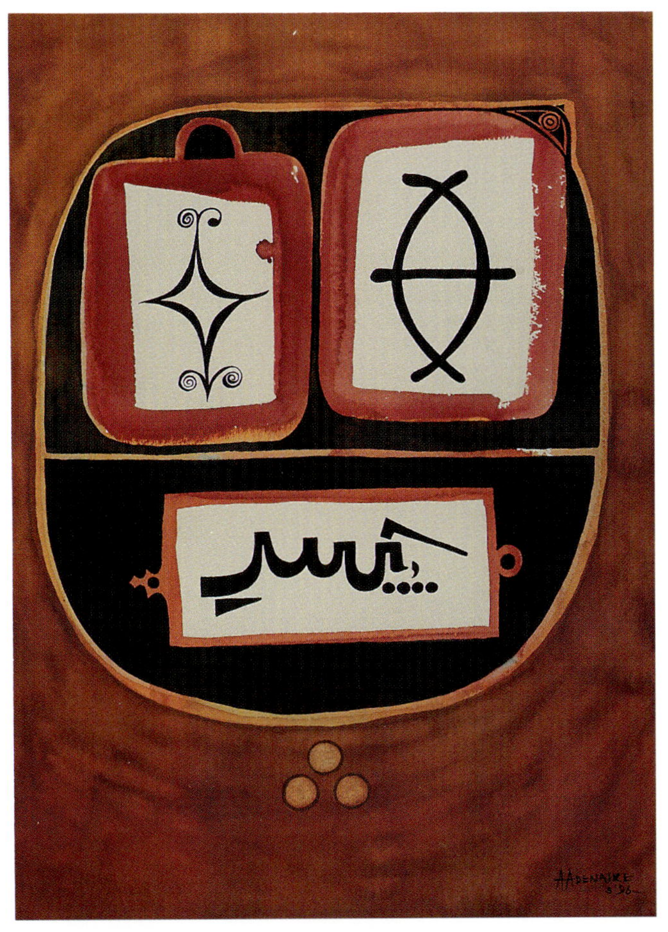

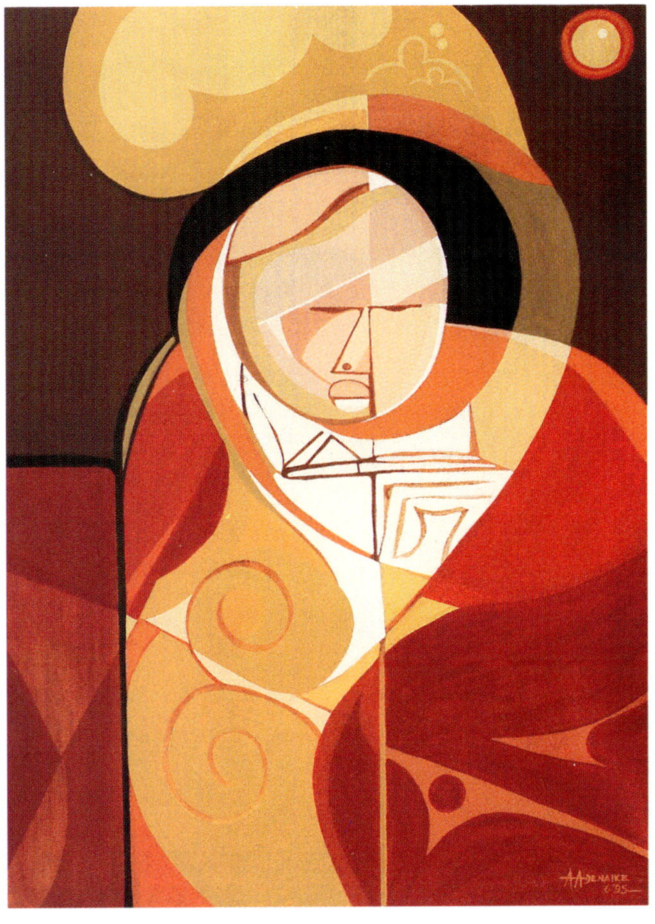

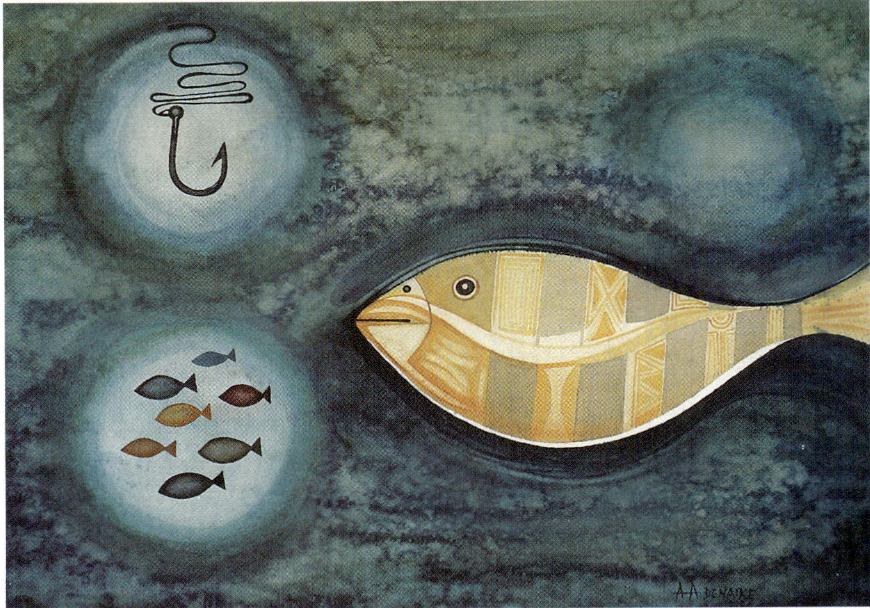

**142 (TOP LEFT).** Tayọ Adenaike, *Three Statements,* 1996, watercolor on paper. 61 × 45 cm. Collection of Simon Ottenberg.

**143 (TOP RIGHT).** Tayọ Adenaike, *Childhood Innocence,* 1995, acrylic on canvas. 91.4 × 66 cm. Collection of the artist.

**144 (BOTTOM LEFT).** Tayọ Adenaike, *Day of the Hook,* 1996, watercolor on paper. 61 × 45 cm. Collection and photo: the artist.

white in his work, but it is the white of empty paper, not of watercolors, for he says that white watercolor turns dull or yellow in time.

Stylistically there is variation in the present watercolors of Adenaike. In *Caged Within* (1994; fig. 145), small, standing, white-outlined figures appear imprisoned in an *uli* kola nut head design, with a larger seated figure in control, an apparent political reference. *Rejuvenation* (1994; fig. 146) depicts a large face with numerous *uli, nsibidi,* and unidentified designs, as if the designs were rejuvenating the person or perhaps are an expression of the person rejuvenated. *Cow at Rest* (1994; fig. 147) shows a highly schematized Nigerian cow with piercing eyes, resting from the long journey from the north of Nigeria to the south, going to eventual slaughter. *What the Eye Saw through the Tablet* (1994; fig. 148) has a central kola nut head design in white in somewhat distorted fashion, as is sometimes the case with the Nsukka artists. There is an eye at the upper left but no other human features. *Through the Broken Wall We Saw the Chameleon Change Its Colors* (1990; fig. 149) is rich in small designs and in *akika*-like watercolor swirls surrounding the central image; the work probably relates to politicians changing their views as they see fit.

Adenaike sees himself as a pioneer in employing watercolors in Nigeria, which are not popular as other media there. However, others among the Nsukka artists sometimes use it, including Obiọra Udechukwu, Ada Udechukwu, and Chike Aniakọr. Despite overseas exhibitions and visits, Adenaike has not drawn images from America or Europe. His explanation, at least with regard to the United States, is that he simply is not familiar enough with the culture to do so, suggesting how deeply embedded he, and probably some other Nigerian artists who act similarly, such as Chike Aniakọr, need to be in order to draw images from another culture. There is also

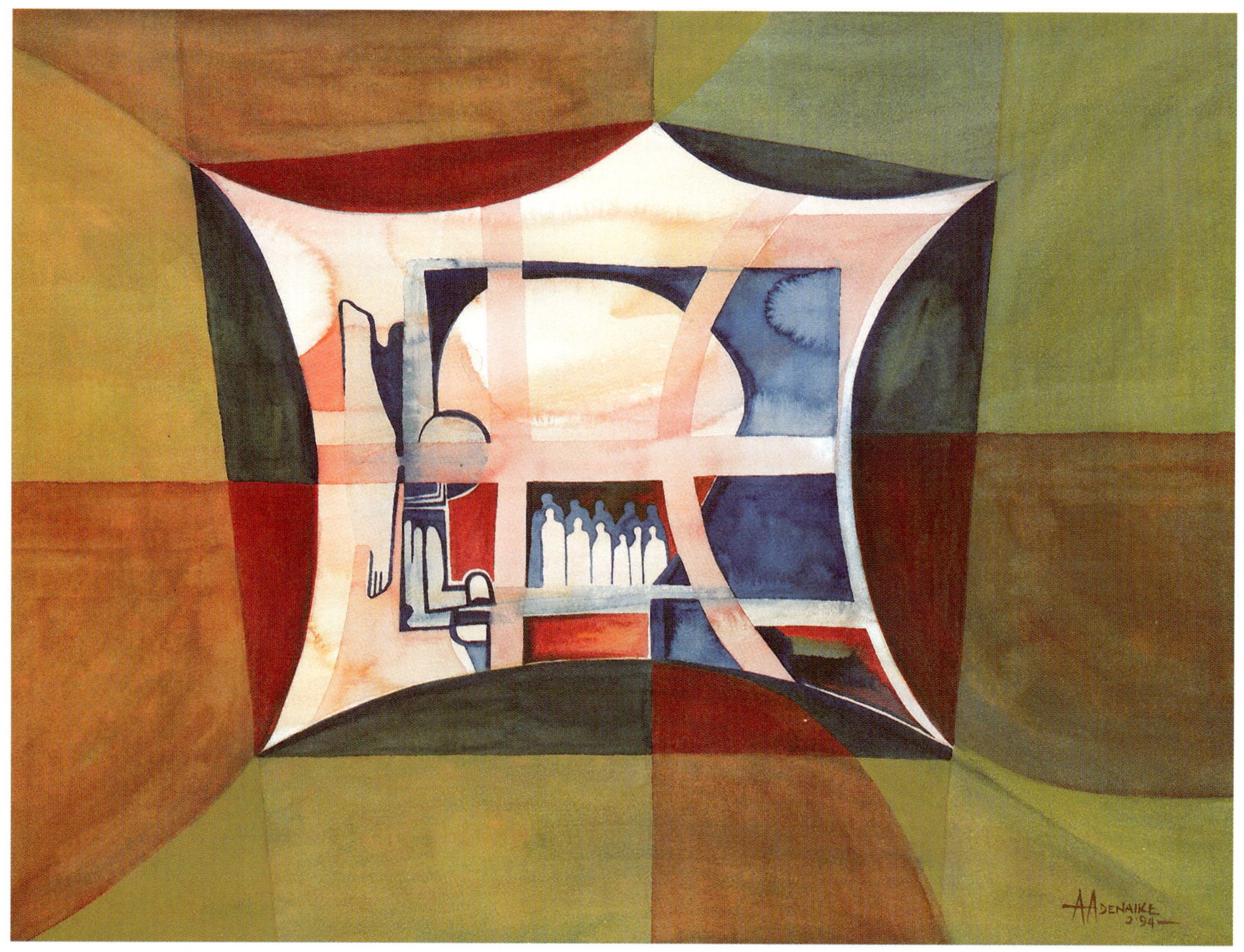

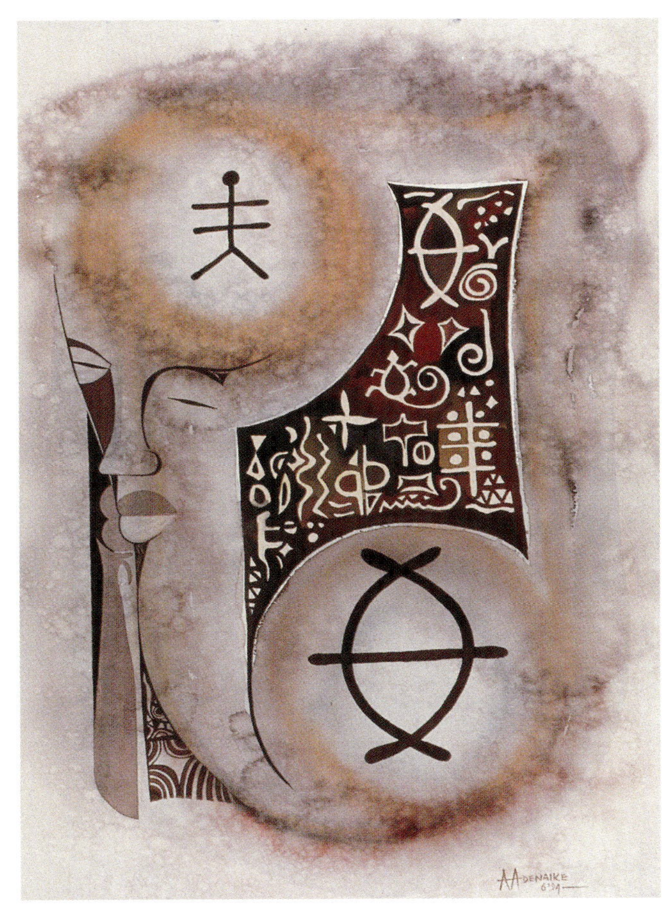

**145 (FACING PAGE).** Tayọ Adenaike, *Caged Within,* 1994, watercolor on paper. 45.7 × 61 cm. Collection of the artist. Photo: Franko Khoury.

**146 (RIGHT).** Tayọ Adenaike, *Rejuvenation,* 1994, watercolor on paper. 61 × 45.7 cm. Collection of Janet L. Stanley. Photo: the artist.

**147 (BELOW).** Tayọ Adenaike, *Cow at Rest,* 1994, watercolor on paper. 45.7 × 61 cm. Private collection. Photo: the artist.

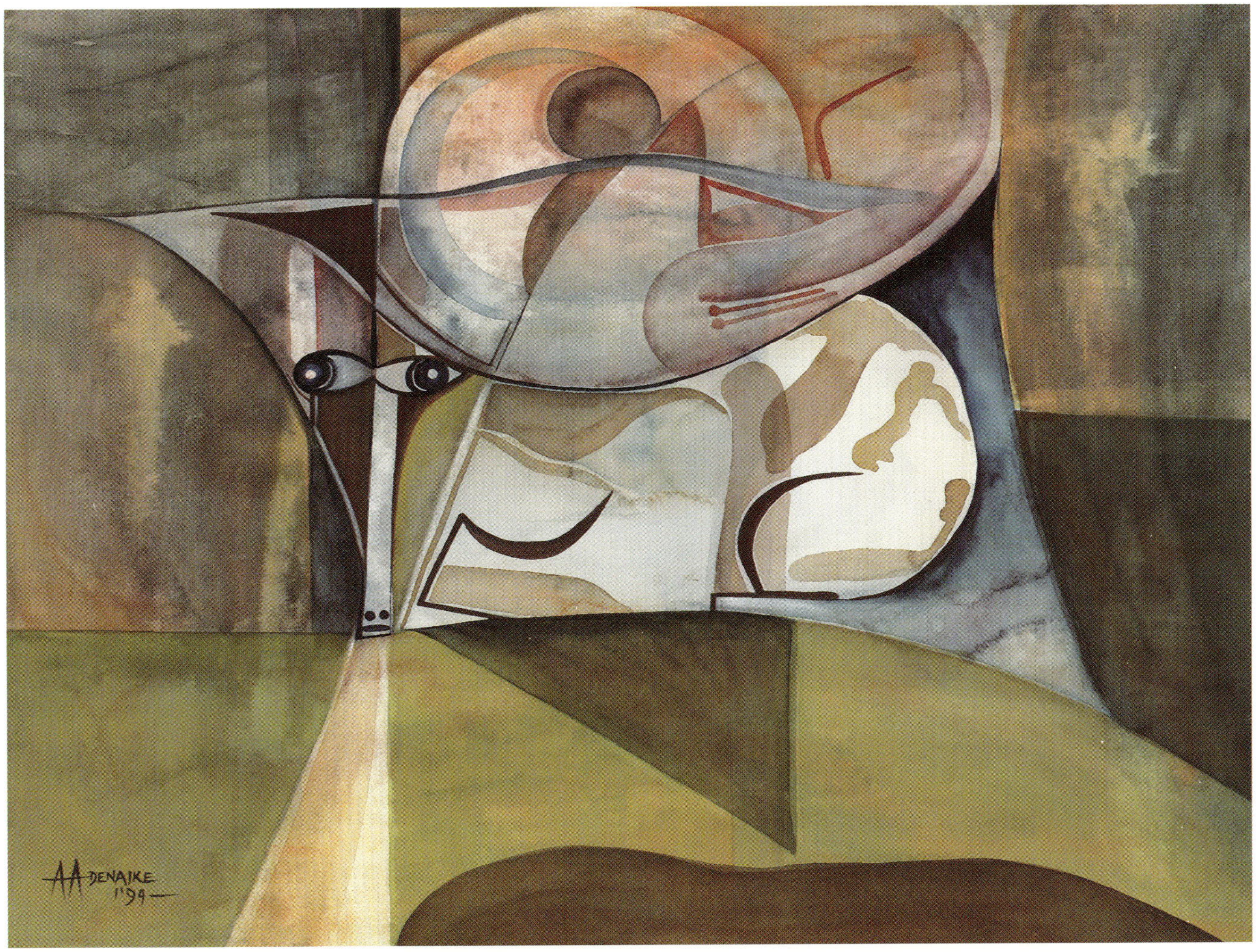

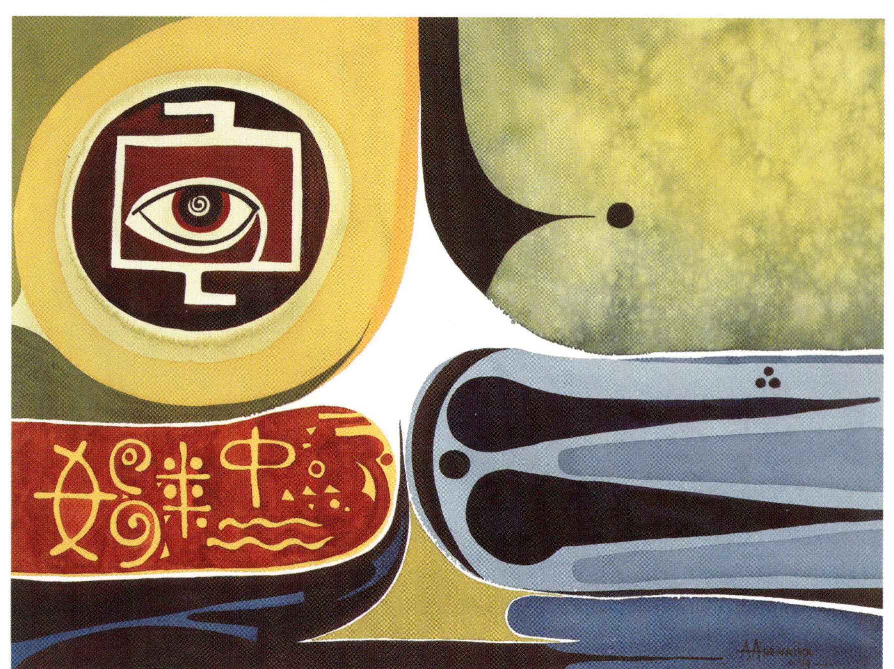

**148 (TOP)**. Tayọ Adenaike, *What the Eye Saw through the Tablet,* 1994, watercolor on paper. 45.7 × 61 cm.

Collection of Earnest Bonner. Photo: the artist.

**149 (BOTTOM)**. Tayọ Adenaike, *Through the Broken Wall We Saw the Chameleon Change Its Colors,* 1990, watercolor on paper. 76.8 × 61.6 cm.

Collection of the National Museum of African Art. Photo: Franko Khoury.

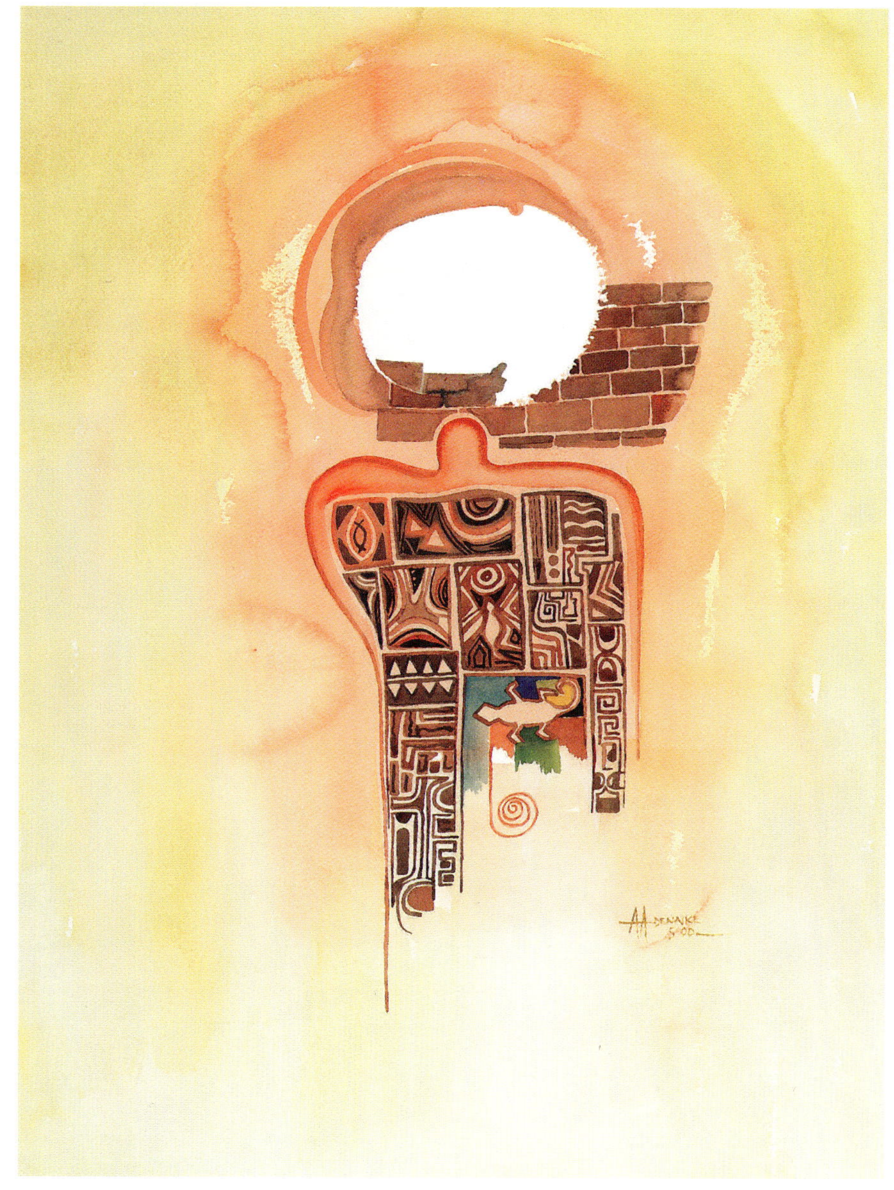

the unstated issue of the art market. To present oneself as an African artist creating Africanlike themes (which may also be universal, such as sorrow or poverty) relates to a specialized market niche in the Euro/American art world, in the face of difficulties in getting into major art markets.

Adenaike thinks that a good deal of modern and contemporary Euro/American art, including Minimalism and Abstract Expressionism, is escapist, not relating to social reality, and that art should have a message. It should communicate interpersonally. Any art should have a leaning toward the understanding of man, and it should be relevant. It should tell a story, he told me in 1992, placing himself within a conventional tradition, but one that has considerable relevance in Nigeria. Adenaike's art is usually message oriented.

Although familiar with some Nigerian writing, Adenaike does not draw much from it in his art, in contrast to Obiọra Udechukwu. Nor does he publish poetry or other forms of writing, other than in art exhibition catalogues and in his previously mentioned 1982 *Nigeria Magazine* article on *uli* in contemporary Nigerian art.

## ART AND ADVERTISEMENTS

Interesting contrasts and possible links exist between Adenaike's art and his advertising. He tells me that advertising is all about products for business customers and his art about relationships among people. His business does not bring him the same kind of excitement as his art, which is joyful work, though he may become sad to see it sold, unlike his advertising. He paints what he wants, to please himself, but the advertisements are created to please clients. He does not like to take commissions in art, but the advertising business is based on contracts. He tells me that he does not sell much of his art to corporations, despite his contacts with them (although Agip and at least one other Nigerian business have bought work from him), for these are not usually the kind of people that purchase contemporary art. But it does not bother him to design advertisements for a client and to reach the client's target group. He did study graphic design for a while at the university, which relates to both art and advertising, but basically Adenaike sees these as distinct aspects of his life. Moving back and forth between them seems to be refreshing to him. He is one of the very few individuals in Nigeria that I know of who has been able to maintain strong careers in both fields. Two former Nsukka artists, Bons Nwabiani and Uzọ Ndubisi, are now working full-time in advertising.

Yet advertising also has artistic aspects. Adenaike designs newspaper and magazine advertisements, product labels, posters, and calendars with the help of assistants, employing computers. Do his design styles in advertising influence his watercolors and other artwork? I suggest that advertising experience may now do so, insofar as his work has moved from a more watery style to the use of solid colors with clear definitions between them and increasing boldness. This is not suggested as negative criticism but as an observation. I have not investigated the reverse possibility, only being aware that his art sometimes appears on business calendars he prepares for clients.

## ACRYLICS

Adenaike largely switched from watercolors to acrylics and to somewhat larger sized works after returning to Nigeria from his 1994 visit to the United States, continuing to work in acrylics upon his brief return to the States the following year.[46] The shift was, I think, part of his attempt to create bolder and stronger works, a direction in which he was already moving in his watercolors. The move may also have been influenced by his artist friend Obiọra Udechukwu's 1993 concentration on acrylics in Germany. The acrylics that Adenaike produced in Nigeria are on canvas on board, those in the United States only on canvas, although he used a temporary board backing in painting them; canvas alone was easier to transport.

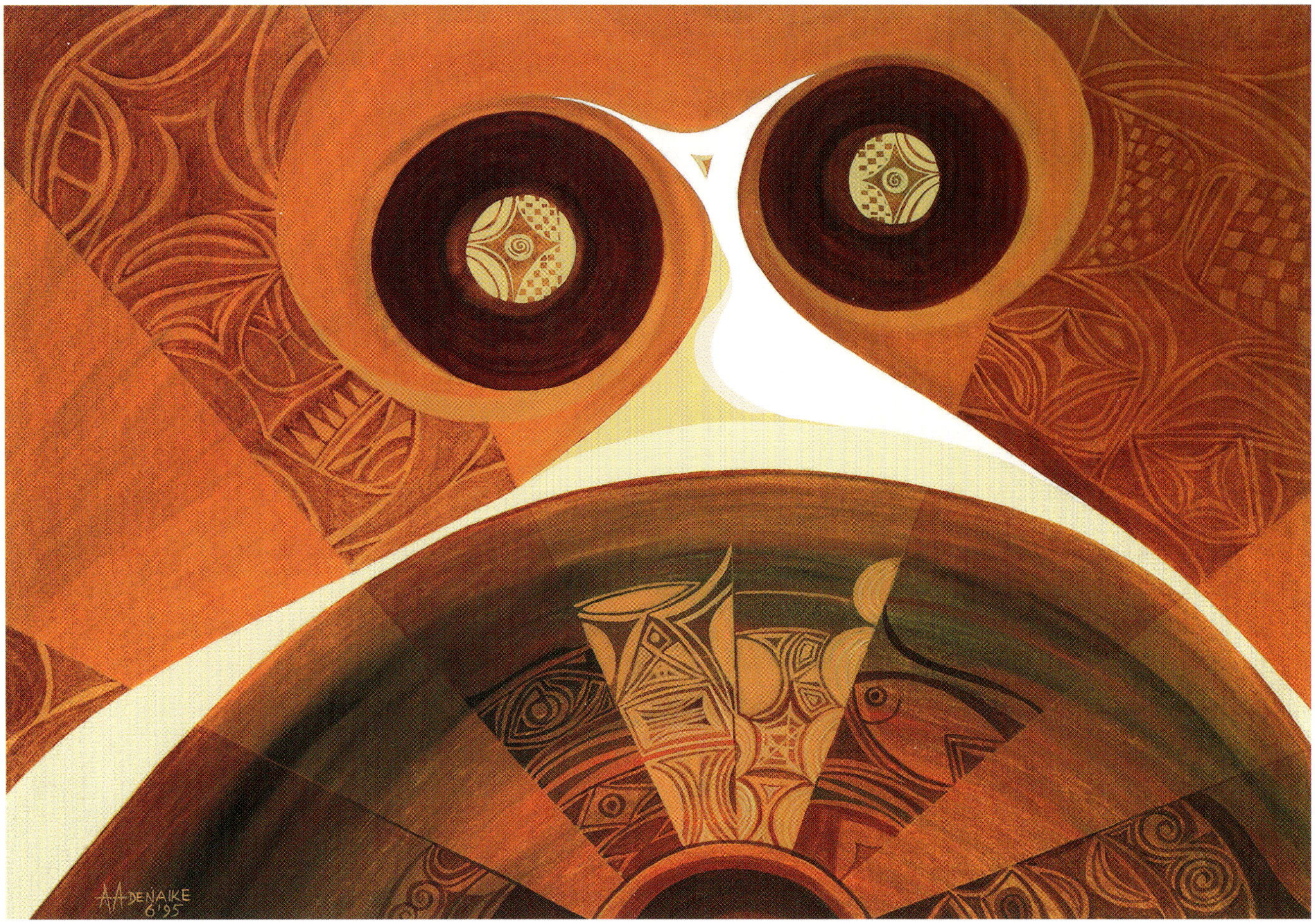

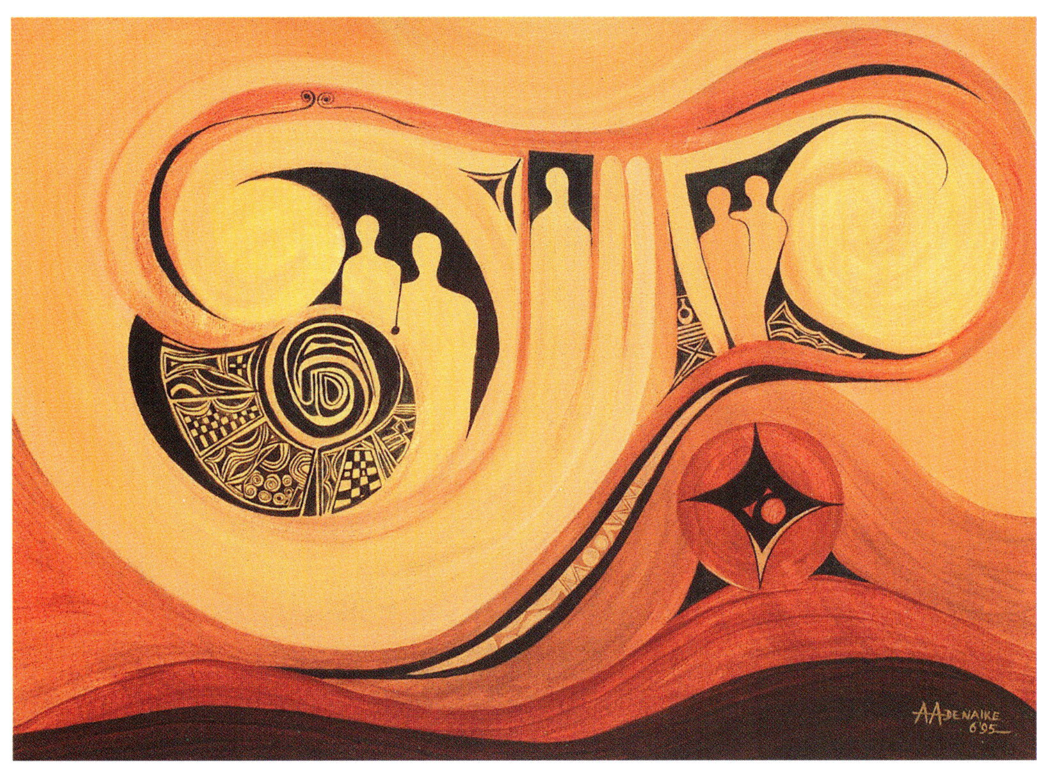

**150 (TOP)**. Tayọ Adenaike, *Pots,* 1995, acrylic on canvas. 82.2 × 114 cm. Collection of Simon Ottenberg. Photo: Franko Khoury.

**151 (LEFT)**. Tayọ Adenaike, *Between the Couples,* 1995, acrylic on canvas. 67.3 × 91.4 cm. Collection of the artist.

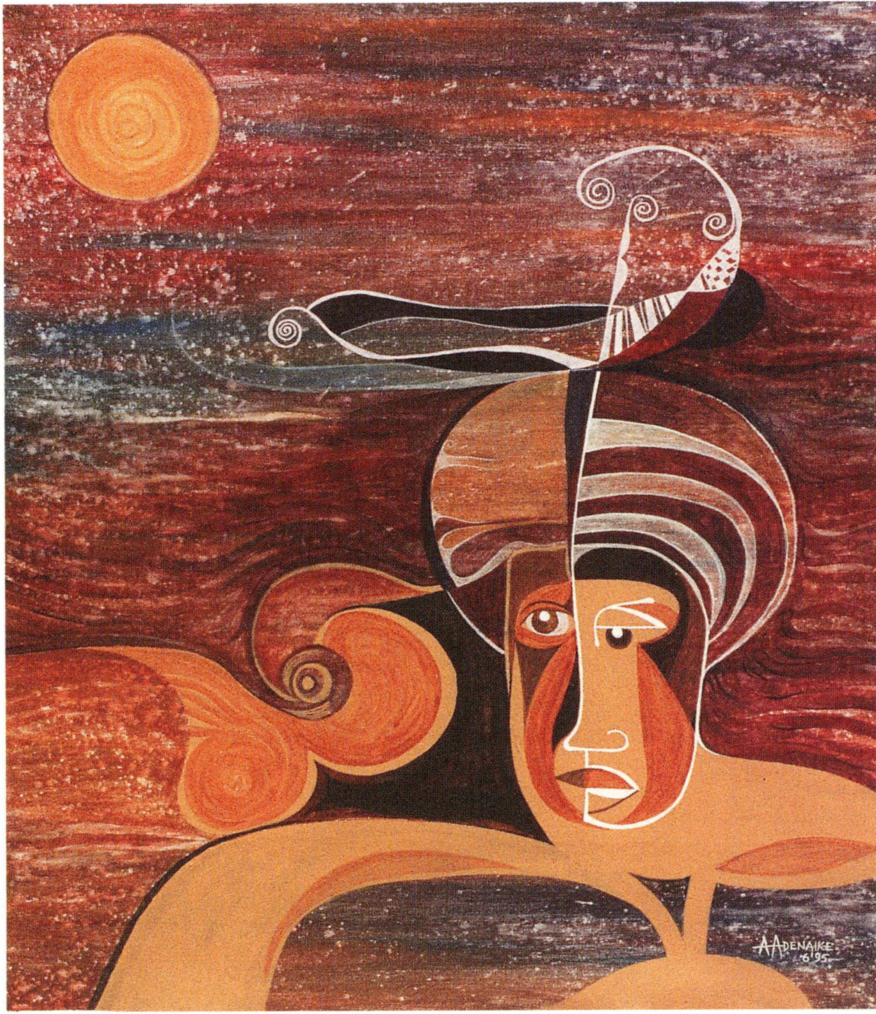



**152**. Tayọ Adenaike, *Nwanyi Ọcha,* 1995, acrylic on canvas. 85.1 × 69.2 cm. Collection of the artist.

A few of the acrylics evoke watercolors, such as *Pots, Between the Couples,* and *Nwanyi Ọcha* (figs. 150–152). All these 1995 works have relatively muted earthy colors and backgrounds suggestive of *akika* wash.[47] *Pots* is rich in *uli,* which might be seen as decoration on the ceramics. There is a suggestion of a face in this work, with two strongly depicted eyes, perhaps an overinterpretation on my part, though works by Adenaike without a face are not common. *Between the Couples* depicts two standing couples in outline, as his figures often are, with a third standing figure between them, as if some domestic drama was in progress. *Nwanyi Ọcha* depicts a depressed-looking white woman with a turban or head tie.

Most of Adenaike's acrylics have strong colors, sharply bounded in relation to one another. *It Happened behind Me* (1995; fig. 153) grew out of his experience of setting out to paint with the light behind him and seeing his shadow on the canvas. So he drew it, filling in his shadow head with the side view of a woman's face and head, wearing an elaborate earring. Eleven standing figures are simply outlined at the back of her head and neck (and his shadow head and neck), as if waiting. He sees the work as having the sense of people behind him watching. The background of light gray reminds me of his watercolor wash efforts, so the work seems transitional between his watercolor style and an emerging acrylic mode. The latter is seen in *Burden of Leadership* (1995;

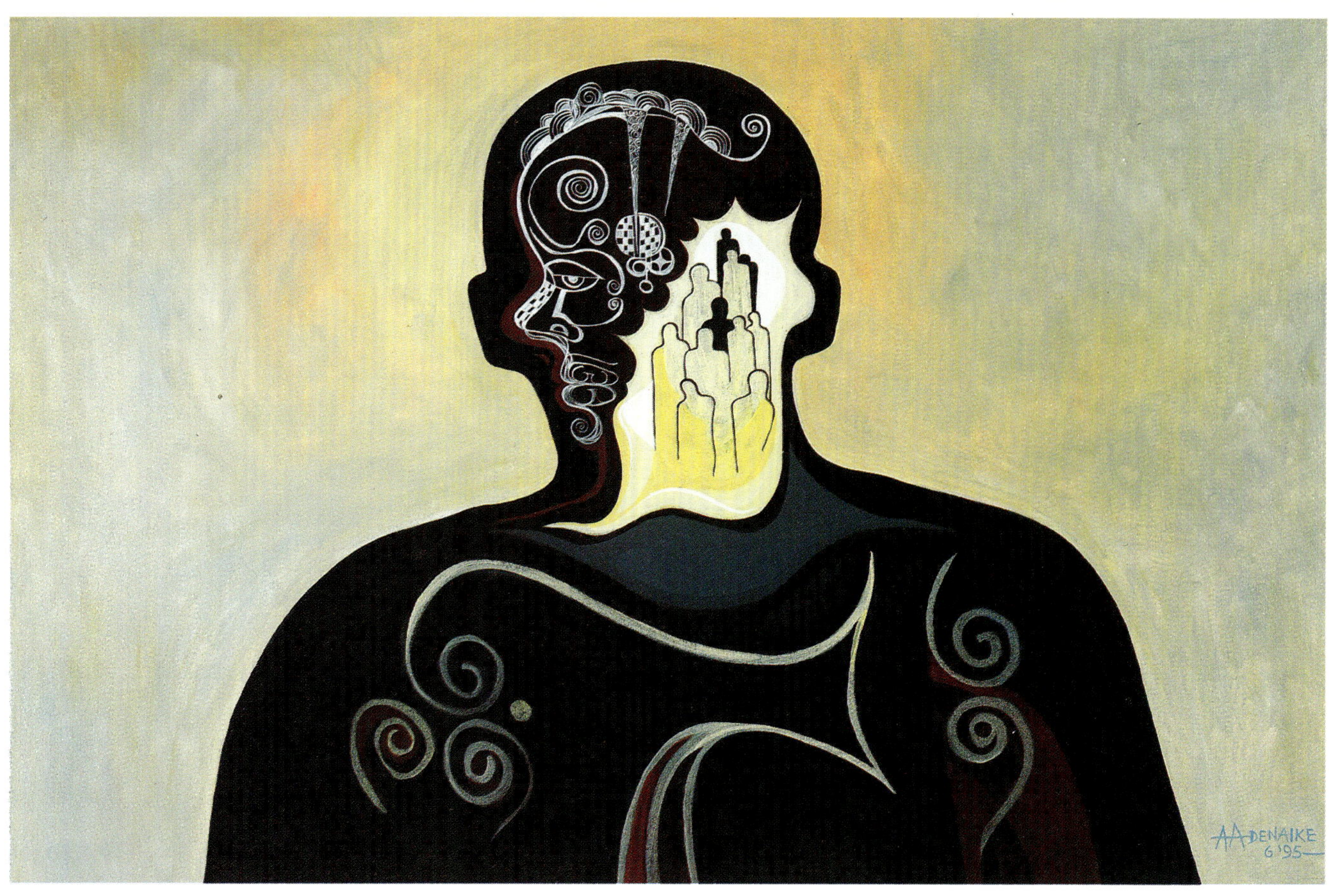

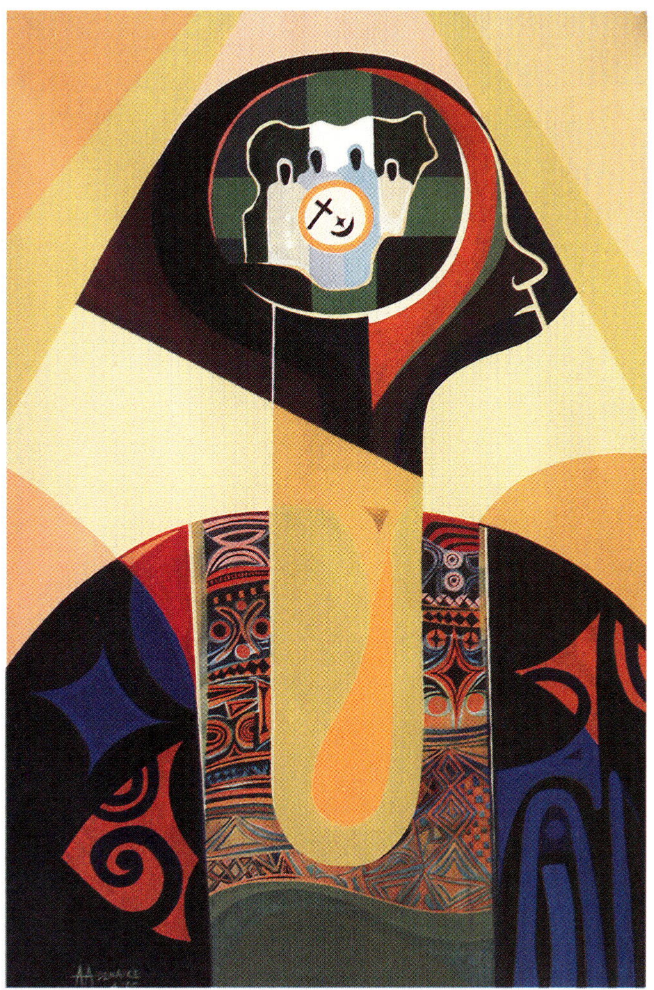

**153.** Tayọ Adenaike, *It Happened behind Me,* 1995, acrylic on canvas. 78 × 113.5 cm. Collection of Simon Ottenberg. Photo: Franko Khoury.

**154.** Tayọ Adenaike, *Burden of Leadership,* 1995. acrylic on canvas. 108. × 71.1 cm. Collection of the artist.

fig. 154), with strong colors through much of the work. Here the face and head include an outline of Nigeria's borders, the colors of the Nigerian flag (green and white), the Muslim crescent and star, a Christian cross, and four figures, representing the four major Nigerian cultural groups: Yoruba, Igbo, Hausa, and Fulani. The figure of a leader, with richly decorated clothing containing numerous *uli* elements, suggests someone quite well off. The work is not so much a satiric statement on Nigerian politics, according to Adenaike, as it is a summing up of Nigeria's problems, with four major ethnic groups, two major religions, and wealthy leaders. Although the work has a good deal of black, Adenaike does not use black pigment, as he feels it deadens the work. Rather, he mixes blue and brown with some red to create a near-black color.

*Uli* motifs, both specific and modified, occur in his acrylics; they work well in this medium, as Obiọra Udechukwu has earlier shown. But there is virtually no *nsibidi*—Adenaike is not certain why. When working in this medium, he employs white acrylic, although he does not use white watercolor. As with his watercolors, he makes no preliminary sketches.

Returning to watercolors, in the latter half of 1995 and into 1996, a medium that he says he feels more comfortable with than acrylics, his trends continue toward darker and brighter colors, sharp lines distinguishing color changes, increase in the use of *nsibidi* motifs, and somewhat lesser emphasis on faces, though there is the powerful *The Stare* (1996). The growing mixture of themes in his works continues. Some very strong images occur in intense colors, such as *Dry Earth, Dark Cloud* and *Labyrinth* (both 1996). The acrylic period should not be seen as an isolated incident in his overall watercolor progression but as an aspect of it (except for its lack of *nsibidi* motifs and often the lack of a watery effect and *akika*-like wash). In fact, some of the most recent watercolors resemble his stronger acrylics in style, form, and color.

## CONCLUSION

Adenaike's art, despite the predominance of a single medium, watercolor, exhibits development and change, with brief periods of oils and acrylics. His style and type of images have altered somewhat, as has the audience for his work, with his increasing attention in the United States. He seems more distant from his Yoruba background since his 1990 *Story-Telling* exhibition, but looking at his work as a whole, one can discern important dual cultural influences. Compared to El Anatsui, who has explored cultural designs in numerous African cultures, or Chike Aniakọr and Obiọra Udechukwu, who draw mainly from Igbo culture, Adenaike is in between, taking from both Yoruba and Igbo but moving toward the second position. He is an atypical Nsukka group artist not being in the academic world (except occasionally as an external examiner) but rather in business, thus not having students of his own and a line of followers, as do Obiọra Udechukwu and others. Adenaike keeps in contact with other Nsukka group members through his friendships with Obiọra Udechukwu and his wife, Ada, and through members of the AKA Circle of Exhibiting Artists. He is an artist who has created his own independent niche, developing a unique watercolor style for Nigeria and Africa.

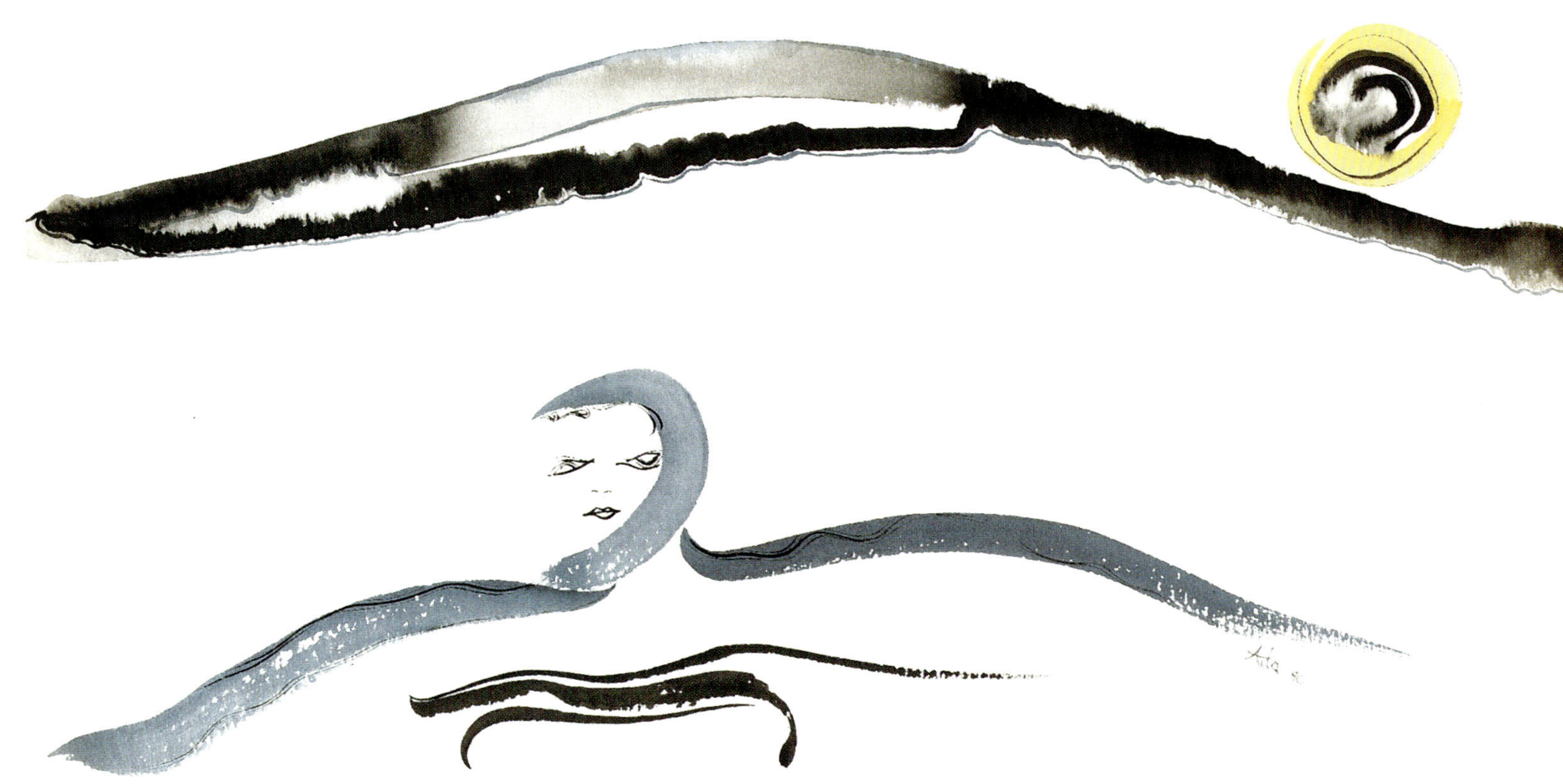

Fig. 172.

# 11. ADA UDECHUKWU

## POETIC AND PERSONAL LINES

Yes, my poetry is private in the sense that each poem is literally a monologue by my inner self, an inner self that needs to be listened to. This "listening to self" is, for me, the essence of my art. It is this that gives rise to and sustains my art, be it literary or visual.

ADA UDECHUKWU [1]

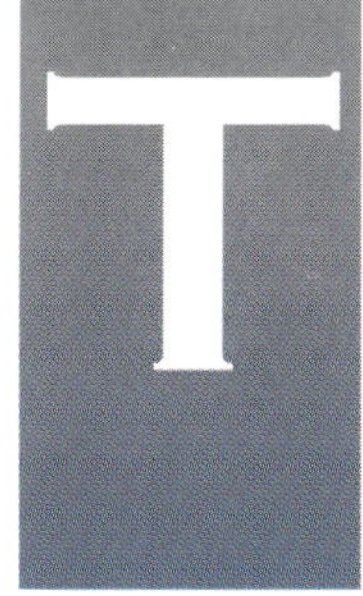

The art and life of Ada Udechukwu present new aspects to an understanding of the seven Nsukka artists (fig. 155). Her art raises gender issues among these artists. She is the only one working in textiles as well as on paper, the only one not to have studied art at a university. She has an urban background, and she is the only one whose poetry plays as dominant a role in her creativity as her visual art. Of the seven artists, both her visual and her written work are the most internal and personal.

### CHILDHOOD

Born Ada Dorothy Obi in 1960 in Enugu, of a Nigerian father who died in 1996 and an American mother who is still living, Ada Udechukwu comes from a well-established and educated middle-class family, which includes two brothers and a sister.[2] Her father was for many years a Nigerian civil servant. Her mother, with a B.A. degree from Berea College in the United States and a master's degree in library science from Columbia University, worked for many years as a librarian at the University of Nigeria, Enugu, and now obtains locally published materials for the U.S. Library of Congress; she is also a poet and a visual artist.[3] Udechukwu's father was not artistic, but he did not discourage Ada's interests. She was influenced in the direction of poetry and the visual arts by her mother's talents in those areas.

Ada Udechukwu attended All Saints School in Enugu in 1966–67, then, between the ages of seven and eleven, she and her family lived in the United States because of the Biafran war and her American-born mother.

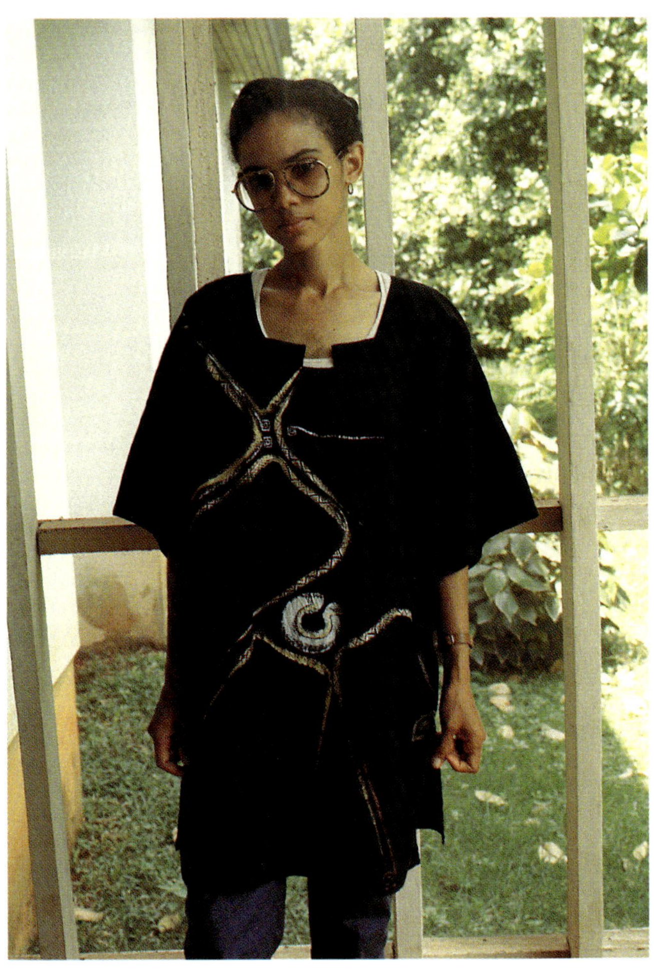

**155.** Ada Udechukwu wearing unisex shirt she designed and painted, 1993.

The family remained there until the end of the war in 1970, during which time she went to a school in East Lansing, Michigan, and two different schools in Pittsburgh, Pennsylvania. Although it was disturbing to pull up roots in Nigeria for a time, she found her U.S. experience an interesting one. She has always retained an attraction for the United States, where one of her brothers and her sister now live. Thus she did not directly experience the war, unlike some of the other Nsukka artists; neither her visual art nor her poetry reflects it, as does the work of some of the other artists, including her husband, Obiọra Udechukwu. Nevertheless, her family was concerned about the fate of relatives, friends, and others on the Biafran side.

Her U.S. experience familiarized Udechukwu with a culture different from her Nigerian one, which has been reinforced by later occasional trips to the States. This has led to an enrichment of both her life and her art, but also to conflicts over her cultural identity. In the United States she visited museums and galleries, but this art had little impact upon her as a young child.

Returning with her family to Enugu after the war, she attended secondary school at Queen's School there. It was a traumatic return for her. She was with older students and in a different culture, and she only wanted to go back to America. As a result, she withdrew into herself. There was "an outside and an inside me," she has told me, and she did a lot of reading, especially literature. This phase lasted into her twenties, and swings from the "outside" to the "inside" and back again have continued to this day; they relate especially to her visual art and her poetry, which often expresses her "inside" aspect. But the secondary school years were also times that aroused her interest in visual art, through her mother's concerns; the two of them went to any art exhibitions that were held in Enugu. These influences were reinforced by taking classes in visual art at school during a good deal of her time there, when she really became interested in it. During those days she continued to experiment with writing poetry, as she had in earlier childhood. In 1977 she began studying at the University of Nigeria, Nsukka, majoring in English and literature and earning her B.A. degree in 1981.

## UNIVERSITY DAYS

Immersed in English and literature studies, she wrote her B.A. thesis, "The Art of Regeneration," on Ngugi wa Thiong'o, the well-known Kenyan writer. She continued to write poetry, some of which was published in *The Muse: Literary Journal of the English Association at Nsukka*[4] and in *Omabe: Journal of Poetry at Nsukka.*[5] Her verse was, and remains, generally brief in the number and shortness of lines. It has been personal, about feelings, sometimes love, other times despair and endlessness, agony and dreams, free-flowing like a stream.

> A Journey
> A hollow step
>     resounds through the corridors
>     of an anguished soul,
> And halts at the final exit.
>   Down,
>     step by step,
>       its beat echoes
>         fleeting
>       dazzling
>         spiraling
>           dreams –
> Dreams of wishes faraway.[6]

She became associate editor of *The Muse* for the 1979–80 academic year and art editor the following year. During her university days she continued to experiment with drawing and painting, especially in pen and ink, drawings to accompany stories and poems in *The Muse* (nos. 12–13, 1980–81), where she felt somewhat constrained by the nature of the writing she was illustrating. She also continued to draw for herself.

Her published pen and ink drawings from this time are very linear (fig. 156). Empty spaces abound, and there is economy of line. Faces and heads are more suggested than detailed, simply outlined as squares with rounded edges and with eyes, but few other facial features or none. There are curvilinear elements and spirals, and there are not a great deal of thick ink lines or dark ink areas. The art has a light quality, an implied spontaneity, and appears joyous. In some ways, particularly in its linearity, use of space, apparent spontaneity, simplification of images, and curvilinear qualities, her work from this time appears to draw on *uli.* Yet I believe it arose independently, even though she had met Obiọra Udechukwu at the university and was to marry him in 1982. In briefness and sparsity of statement, her drawings of this period resembled her poetry and still do.

After graduation she fulfilled her National Youth Service

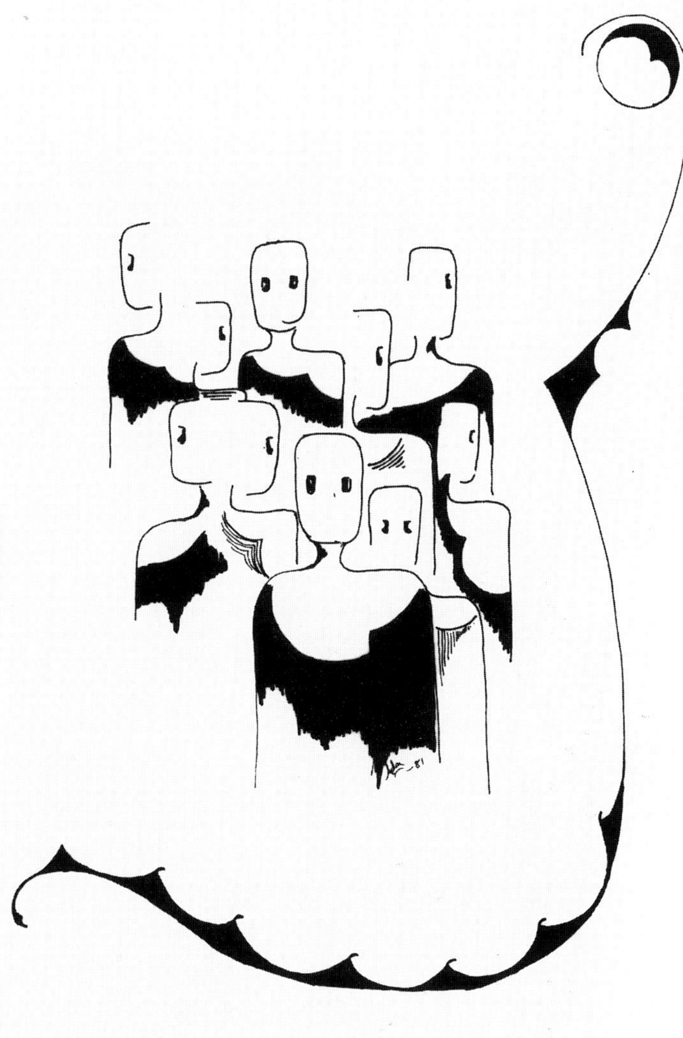

**156**. Ada Udechukwu, untitled, ink on paper drawing from *The Muse: Literary Journal of the English Association at Nsukka* 13 (May 1981), 49.

Corps post-university degree requirement by teaching English and literature for a year at Ansar Ud-Deen Teachers Training College, at Ọta, Ogun State, not far from Lagos. There she continued to write but stopped creating visual art. She was accepted for library school at Columbia University for a master's degree but did not go because of lack of funds, and also because she was by then planning to marry Obiọra Udechukwu.

## TEXTILES

After her youth service, Ada Udechukwu worked as a librarian in 1982 and 1983 at the Medical Library, University of Nigeria Teaching Hospital, Enugu, and then at the Nnamdi Azikiwe Library, University of Nigeria, Nsukka. Her library interests, shared with her mother, reflect her deep love of books and literature, which continues to this day.

Following her marriage, two important events occurred in her life. For one thing, the couple had their first child, Ije. Udechukwu was not quite prepared for the event emotionally, being young and still settling into marriage. It was as if she had not quite caught her breath, feeling enveloped, a sense that has occurred to her a number of times since then; this relates directly to some of her visual art and poetry.

The other event was that, about 1983, she obtained from her husband a fabric paint tube with a ball point. Working with Mary Ezewuzie, a student in textile arts at the university, she experimented in the medium. Together they held an exhibition in 1984 at the university's Ana Gallery of the Department of Fine and Applied Arts, *An Exhibition of Marada Design*. The two then exhibited with other artists in the same year at the National Gallery of Crafts and Design in Lagos.[7]

Udechukwu worked in hand-painted cotton cloth, batik, and appliqué. Her art of this time shows *uli* influence in the painted cloth work, in depicting motifs, and in its linear qualities; undoubtedly she was now acquiring knowledge of *uli* from her husband and their artistic friends. Some of her designs involved specific *uli* motifs. Their linear quality can be attributed to *uli* influence, the use of the pen, which directs the art toward linearity, and her previous inclinations in this direction in her drawings on paper (fig. 157). There was little emphasis on fancy tailoring of garments; rather, they were loose men and women's shirts and women's dresses. She later broke from the specific employment of *uli* motifs to their essence, experimenting with modifying designs and developing her own lines. She also turned to using brushes with fabric paint, which has given her greater design fluidity.

**157**. Ada Udechukwu wearing unisex shirt she designed and painted, 1993.

Udechukwu did little further textile work until 1990, being involved with children and the home. Then in that year she took part in two exhibitions. In the first, a solo one at the university, she still largely employed the pen, with only a little brushwork, as well as some specific *uli* motifs among the linear elements.[8] There is economy of style, which marks her painted fabrics, even in the chest and stomach area, where it usually is most abundant. Much of the cloth remains undecorated, which focuses interest on the portions that are. Sylvester Ogbechię, the art historian and artist, himself a product of the Nsukka art program, writes of her work in this exhibition:

> The idea behind her creations is unobtrusive presence, sublime yet arresting. And so, in her patterns, which are basically linear designs making effective use of space and analogous colour schemes, we see her manipulating Uli symbols not transferred in their purest forms but adapted as purely decorative elements which reflect a greater concern with aesthetics.[9]

Later the same year she held an exhibition at the Zodiac Hotel, Enugu, with Elizabeth Ọhene, a graduate of the university's art program.[10] Udechukwu displayed brush-painted cloth, batik, and appliqué work and a piece on East African bark, obtained from her parents, painting on it and adding white backcloth. In the catalogue, she wrote:

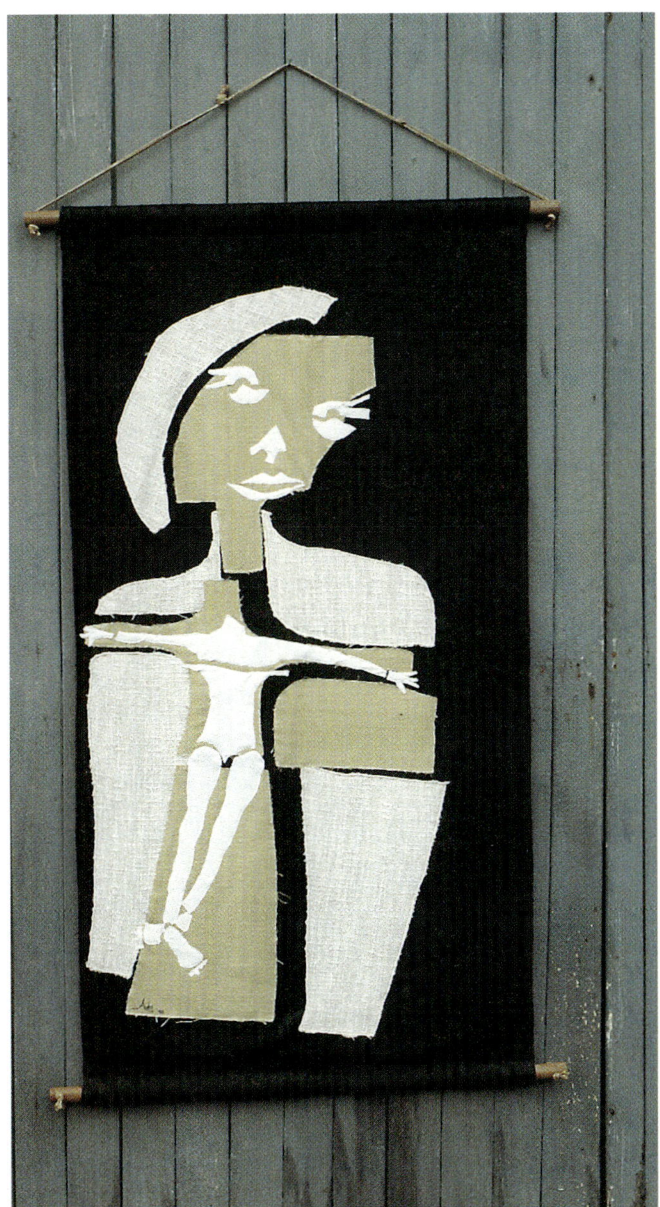

The search for form, for medium to contain and yet maintain, as it were, the vibrancy and intrinsic fluidity of the design, is my major preoccupation. . . . To restrain the design within boundaries and at the same time to create the illusion of unrestrained motion, the merging of garment with body as a total continuous marriage of statics and dynamics—these are the essence of my art.[11]

The hand-painted work included men's and women's trouser suits, shirts, and other clothing. Using brushwork on cloth rather than pen provided for stronger designs and greater variation in line quality, aesthetically pleasing to the eye. Two of the four appliqués in the exhibition were abstract; the other two were of human forms. One of the latter, untitled, reveals the darker side of the artist's nature (fig. 158).[12] A human figure stands, somewhat dismembered; upon its front lies a smaller, white, headless figure, with its arms outstretched, as if on a cross. Ada Udechukwu tells me that at that time, and for a while, she felt dismembered herself, trying to balance her own expectations of herself with the reality of her life as she saw it—mother-

**158.** Ada Udechukwu, untitled, appliqué, c. 1990. 130 × 68 cm.
Collection of the artist.

hood and family and the creative artistic aspects of her poetry and visual art. It has often been in her periods of moodiness, and sometimes withdrawal, that she has done her most creative work. Her painted cloth work shows none of her dark side; if it is there, it is well hidden.

In 1992 she organized an exhibition of seven women artists, *Uli: Different Hands, Different Times,* at the university.[13] Five of the artists in the show had studied there, and one, Mgbadunnwa Okanumee, was a traditional *uli* artist. Udechukwu exhibited drawings, appliqués, batiks, and hand-painted garments at this celebration of traditional and contemporary *uli* by three generations of women artists who were among the few, under-recognized women artists currently or formerly associated with the university. Her role in the exhibition indicated the strength of her involvement with *uli,* and she writes glowingly of it in her catalogue introduction.[14] She stresses ideas relating to her own creative work—the importance of individuality in the *uli* art of the indigenous body and mural painters but also their evident cooperation in artistic creativity, an "individualism that recognizes the boundaries of the very idea of individuality."[15] Through this exhibition she symbolically declares that she is a member of the *uli* group, though not trained in it, and yet has her own creative qualities, experience, and background that differ from others.

She also exhibited her textiles in 1993 in Lagos with a Yoruba textile artist and a silversmith from Niger.[16] By then her style was well developed; she had moved toward even looser-fitting garments with open sleeves. She writes in the catalogue:

> My approach to fashion designing *per se* is essentially two-fold in that I create contemporary designs which involve working with a basically fitted style of clothing, as well as creating designs that make use of a more fundamental and traditional response to clothing, one that makes use of as few fitted seams as possible and relies on the body as the prime "shaper" of the garment. Increasingly I have found myself leaning toward the latter approach as it lends itself more readily to what I might call the "poetics" of *Uli.* More significantly, it provides the scope to create a garment in which structure and surface design are able to blend subtly, providing a "stage" as it were, that creates the illusion of unrestrained motion.[17]

Thus the artist recreates body *uli* on the human form with his or her modern "skin." And the loose nature of the garments allows the designs on the cloth to dance about as the wearer moves, easy to note as the cloth is not overwhelmed with patterns.

Udechukwu's textile work has continued in this vein. Aesthetically pleasing, with no other messages, she employs *uli* symbols, generally quite modified, and her own linear designs for their effect on the eye rather than for their meaning. She has abstracted the already abstract *uli* motifs further. There is economy of line, fine linear flourishes; the colors tend to black, white, and browns rather than bright reds or oranges, subdued though clear and easily seen. Her work shows a good sense of color, generally using black, gray, white, and beige commercial cloth. The painting tends to be located on the front of the garment, with occasional touches on a sleeve or lower back. The designs on men's clothing do not appear particularly different from those on the women's garments. There are areas of open space; her art is never busy. On the matter of space, she has told me: "Silence has always meant a lot to me. And I think I say a lot by my silences in my work and as a person, the way I operate. And I would hesitate to say that it has anything to do with being a woman because I am sure there are men who are like that as well."[18]

Udechukwu has recently been painting silk scarves, which she says has made her more aware of color and interests her in working with watercolors on paper more fully (see below). One scarf, which I observed her working on in 1995 in silk fabric paint, was rich in turquoise, aquamarine, gold, and white.

Udechukwu did not return to works on paper until 1988. A friend and fellow painter and poet, Greg Odo, had seen her work in *The Muse* and encouraged her to begin again. She had not been creating works on paper nor writing much poetry since her days at the university. She began with watercolors, but did not feel comfortable with them and went back to ink, but now with brush instead of pen. Her earlier work had been on plain white paper, but she was now using watercolor blockpaper and handmade paper, where the surface was a little rough, so that a brush was more free-flowing than a pen.

Since 1988 she has produced a number of works on paper, mainly in black ink, sometimes combined with white ink or watercolor; occasionally watercolor occurs alone. Sgraffito is sometimes employed, using a knife or fork, a technique she came to use independently of her artist husband. Much of her work on paper has been created spontaneously and has many of the hallmarks of her textile painting. There are often considerable empty spaces; there is economy of line, strong linear qualities, as if she is employing the brush as a pen. There is often a flowing quality to the art.

The works on paper generally involve human faces or figures, often

159. Ada Udechukwu, *Self-Portrait,* 1991, ink and brush on paper. 38.1 × 51 cm. Collection of the artist. Photo: Franko Khoury.

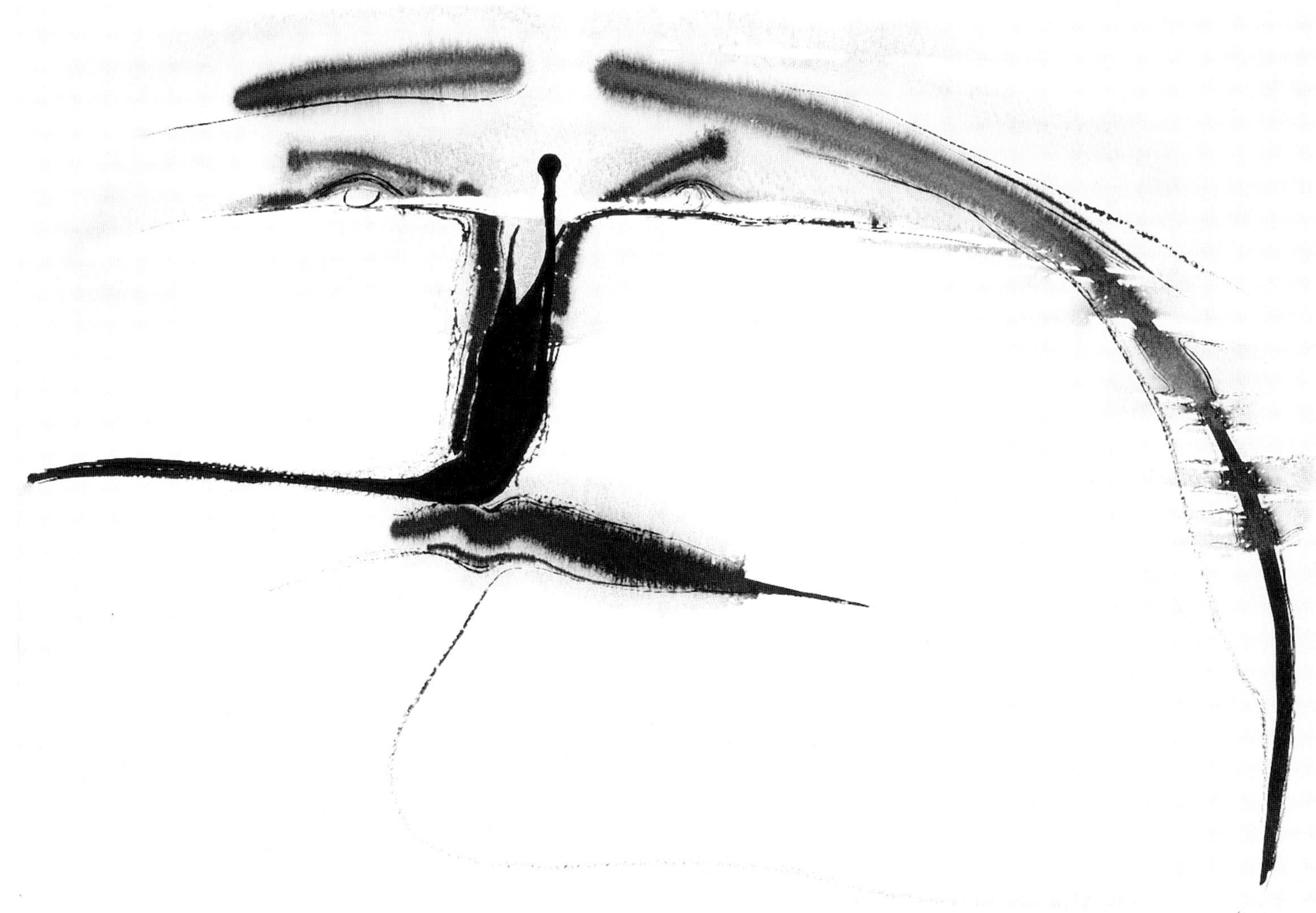

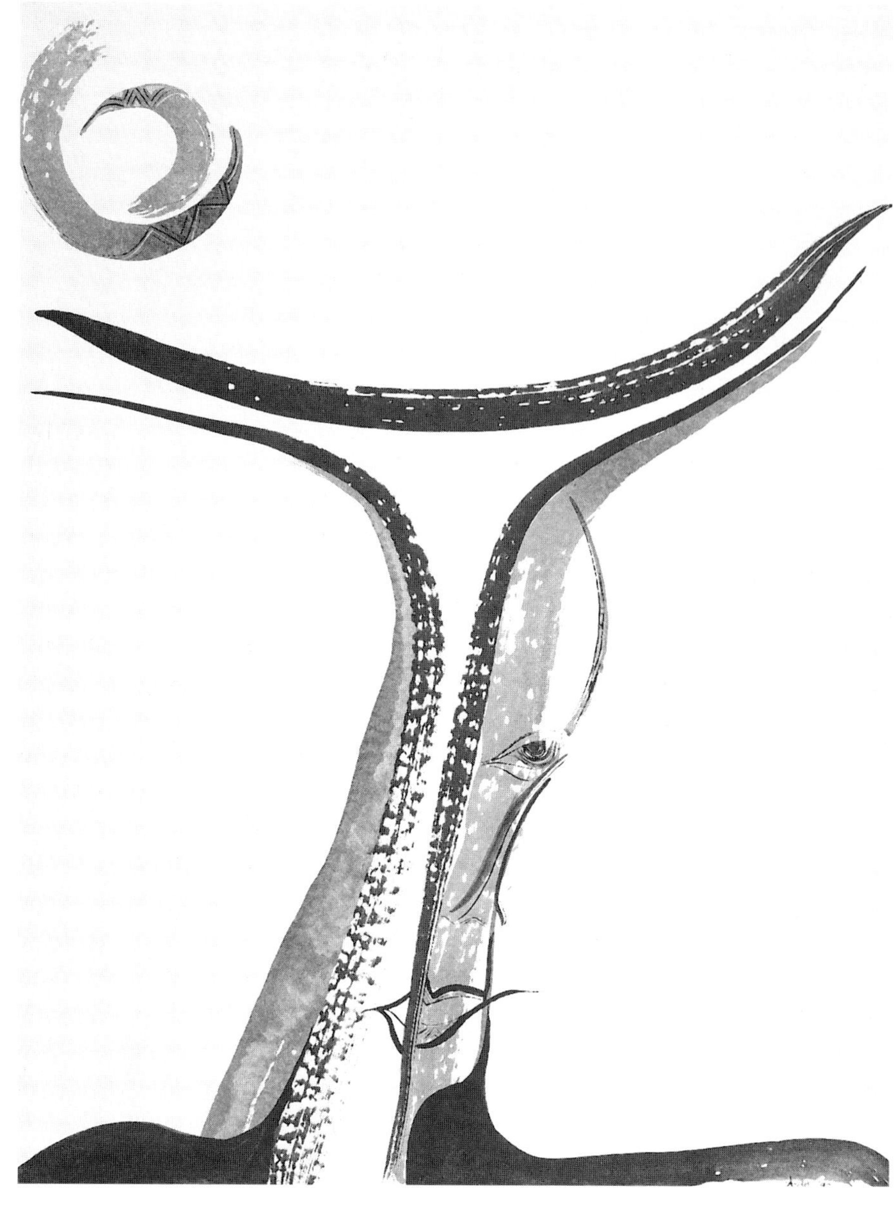

160. Ada Udechukwu, *"In the Temple of My Familiar,"* 1990, ink and brush on paper. 39.8 × 30 cm. Collection of Simon Ottenberg. Photo: Franko Khoury.

that of a female representing the artist. When a male face does occur, it is balanced by a female one. There are usually only one or two persons in the work, unlike some of Chike Aniakọr's, where many figures occur. While the textile art is abstract, her art on paper tells a story, reflects a mood or a personal conflict. These works are concerned with personal relationships and their difficulties. Many of the works are untitled, and Udechukwu has told me that she does not like to talk about them, though she has graciously done so for me at times. Her reluctance to do so is natural given their content. This is the other side of the artist, contrasting with the joyful, outgoing, socially inter-acting one of her textile arts. She is very critical of her own work on pa-per and has rarely exhibited it, occasionally selling it privately and sometimes giving it to friends.

*Self-Portrait* (1991, brush and ink; fig. 159), produced spontaneously, she tells me, is "a visual interpretation of an emotional state of mind." [19] There is a brooding face, suggested rather than detailed, a picture that clearly remains close to her for it hangs in the living room of the Udechukwu home. The heavy lines of the nose and mouth, the arc sweeping above, the sense of a face compressed from top to bottom, all suggest pain. The work, perhaps, is concerned with questions of the artist's personal identity. Another work (untitled, 1994, brush and ink) involves three human figures. She says she has tried to create in the work the experience of existence. Here she sees herself as a loner (which she really is not at all). People are not what society thinks, although it controls much of one's life. The three figures represent the watchdogs of society. There are heavy masses of black ink in the work, unusual for her, which suggests the idea of oppression. The title of *"In the Temple of My Familiar"* (1990, brush and ink; fig. 160) is taken from a book by Alice Walker, an African-American writer whose name she could not remember, though the work has had an impact on her. The central image is a three-part kola nut *uli* motif, which reminds her, she tells me, of where the human ovaries are attached, the core of womanhood. Conjoined are

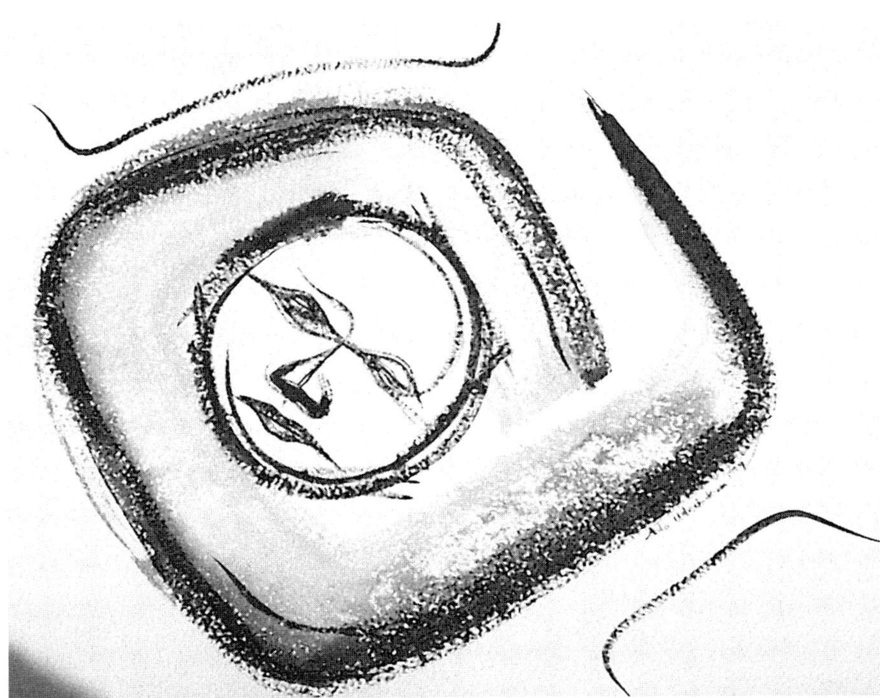

**161** (TOP). Ada Udechukwu, *In Between,* 1994, ink and brush on paper. 22.8 × 30.5 cm. Collection of the artist.

**162** (BOTTOM). Ada Udechukwu, *Watching the Game,* 1994, ink and brush on paper. 60 × 48.2 cm. Collection of the artist. Photo: Franko Khoury.

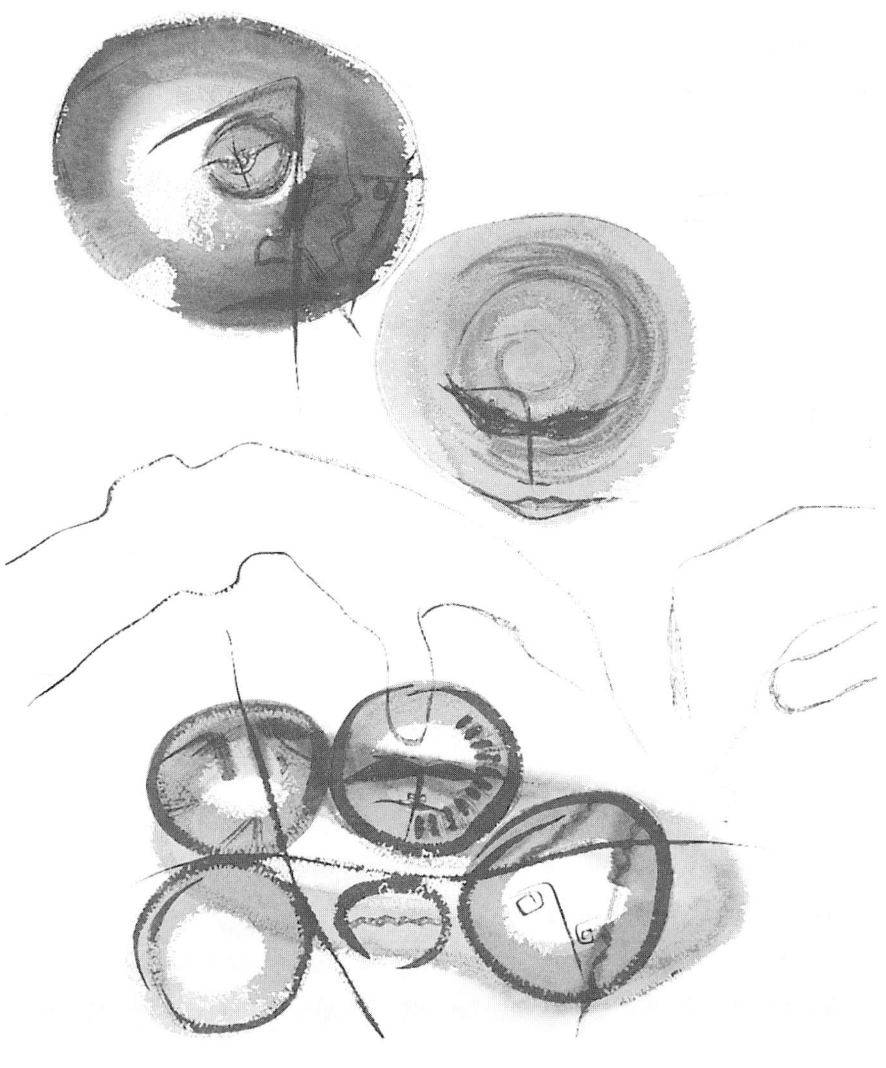

the African-American experience, in which literature she has read widely, Igbo women's art, and female fertility. Further, the artist indicates that the picture is autobiographical, concerned with the issue of personal identity. This suggests the complexity of her art, which at first appears quite simple.

Many of Udechukwu's works on paper represent conflicts, the kinds that one might expect from her life experience. There is the cultural one stemming from having an American-born mother and a Nigerian father, from having lived most of her life in Nigeria but with a crucial period of her childhood spent in the United States. Perhaps the conflict is reinforced by her physical appearance, which is more light skinned than many Nigerians. There is the conflict of being a mother, a wife and a person in charge of the household, where she has a strong sense of skillfully caring for its members, as against her wishes to have more time to herself—reflective time, time to write poetry, to create visual art. That women artists and writers have these conflicts is not rare, though it does not make matters less difficult to be aware of that.

There is the gender conflict of being a female visual artist in a modern society that has not been very accepting of women creators, however favorably society may have regarded them in the traditional past. The situation is better for women novelists, but perhaps not so enlightened for female poets. That *uli* art was originally a woman's art does not necessarily improve the status of the female visual artist today; contemporary female *uli* artists are only gradually emerging, as well as other women artists in Nigeria. Even now, there is sometimes a sense that working with textiles is the acceptable art form for them, so that Ada Udechukwu's exploration of this form should come as no surprise. She has exhibited primarily with other women artists, a reflection of gender differences in modern Nigeria, and there is a sense that she shares some solidarity with other women creators, particularly evident, perhaps, in the 1992 *uli* exhibition she helped arrange.[20] She needs quiet and time to reflect and create, be it visual art or poetry.

There is a lot of conflict, but not really in a negative sense. There are the positive sides as well. I must say that my marriage to an artist has certainly stimulated me in a lot of ways, and we share a lot of interests, and I've grown really through this relationship. But there is certainly no doubt that it is difficult for any woman to combine roles. For instance, I don't produce as much work as I would like to. Not because I don't want to, but because there really isn't time or the solitude to do this.

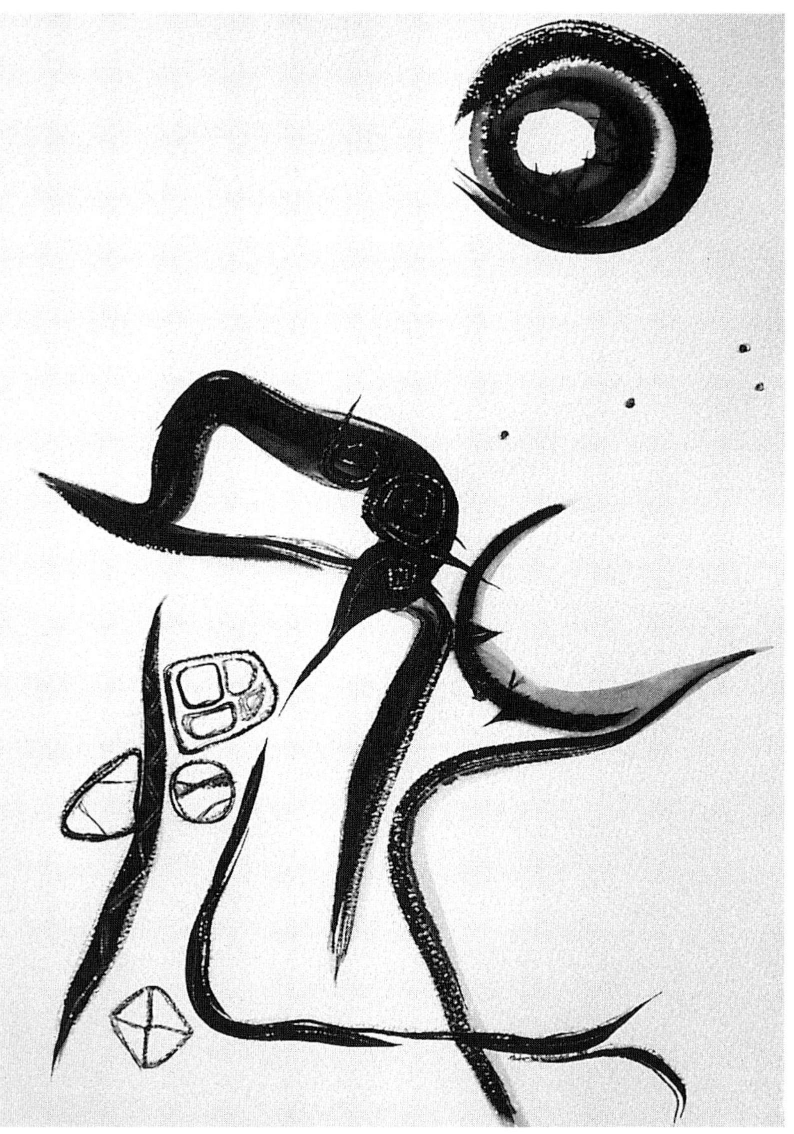

**163**. Ada Udechukwu, *Companions,* 1994, ink and brush on paper. 71.1 × 38.1 cm. Collection of the artist.

I am somebody who really needs solitude to create. It's difficult to try and create and handle housework and run back to creating, something which is basically what I have to do. I do things in bursts of energy really or I decide, okay, the house is going to suffer for today and I tackle this or that.[21]

I am not so sure that this differs from the older Igbo culture, where women worked long hours on the farm and on household duties and child care, with only brief periods available for artistic activities. Yet in these brief moments they created wonderful art. Of course, other artists discussed in this book have time constraints, such as Tayọ Adenaike with his business interests and Obiọra Udechukwu, Chike Aniakọr, and El Anatsui with their teaching.

*In Between* (1994, brush and ink; fig. 161) is one of several of her works that expresses the artist's sense of being of two cultures. Here she sees it in a negative sense rather than as a positive experience. Both cultures are literally pressing in on her in the drawing, one from above, the other from below. The face is typical of some of her work on paper, unsmiling and enclosed, almost like that of a resentful child. The lines around her head suggest that the face is quite locked in. As she has said to me:

I was in the United States for a length of time. I was very young and in the formative stages of my life really. But what that tie probably did for me was to give me another culture. It's true that I am from a mixed marriage, and of course there are two cultures at work. And, in fact, I think it's slightly a bit of a handicap for me in a way, though I've always tried to handle it positively—this aspect of belonging to two cultures and perhaps not being fully in either one. And because of that I would put it in this way: I don't know either one very well.[22]

In *Watching the Game* (1994, brush and ink; fig. 162), a male face (left) and a female face (right) watch two hands playing with pebbles and stones. Udechukwu says: "Some action is being played out, and they are only watching it." There is a sense of family drama going on here, but exactly what is unclear, as if the mystery relates to her phrase, "they are only watching it."

Sometimes her art seems to reflect tensions between her and her very active and creative husband. In an untitled work (1994, brush and ink), there is a woman's face at the upper left and a male one at the lower right. He is looking at some dots and she is not, simply objects to observe in the picture; they are not of significance in themselves. Udechukwu interprets this scene as different ways of perceiving reality and that there is some division between them. The differences are reinforced by the angularity of the male face and the blackness around it, in contrast to the woman's rounded face, and the lighter black and gray about it. Perhaps the work relates to feelings about her marriage at the time; perhaps it reflects a sense that all people perceive reality differently and are basically isolated from one another. Or both views may be involved. The theme occurs in slightly different form in *Companions* (1994, brush and ink; fig. 163), which the artist indicates is concerned with relationships between men and women. The female form is on the right, the male on the left, the latter not well defined. The artist tells me of the work "that she does not see his face though there is a pose of intimacy. She doesn't really know him." Again we sense her message, that we are, each of us, basically alone, with differing perceptions of the world.

These various conflicts may crisscross one another; in any case, the artist sometimes questions her identity. Who is she, what can she be, given her commitment to her husband and family and living in Nigeria? Her spouse has been very supportive of her creativity and artistic interests; she has learned much from him, and they enjoy many activities together and with the children. It is not a question of her being sour on the world.

In addition to *In Between*, discussed above, a number of Ada Udechukwu's works on paper suggest a sense of being confined, enveloped, trapped with no exit possible. In *These Burdens I Bear* (1990, black and white ink on paper; fig. 164), the sense of being enveloped is strong. There is a bent-over woman with her hair hanging down. The three swirls near her head may represent her family or they may not. The dark black brush line at her backside

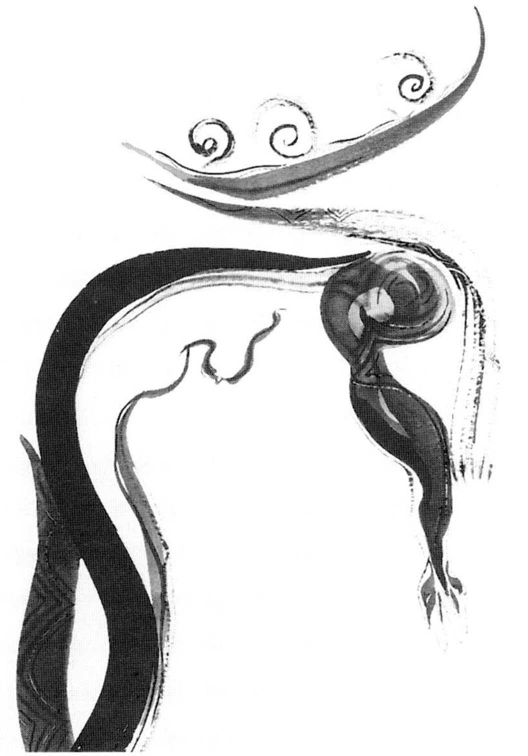

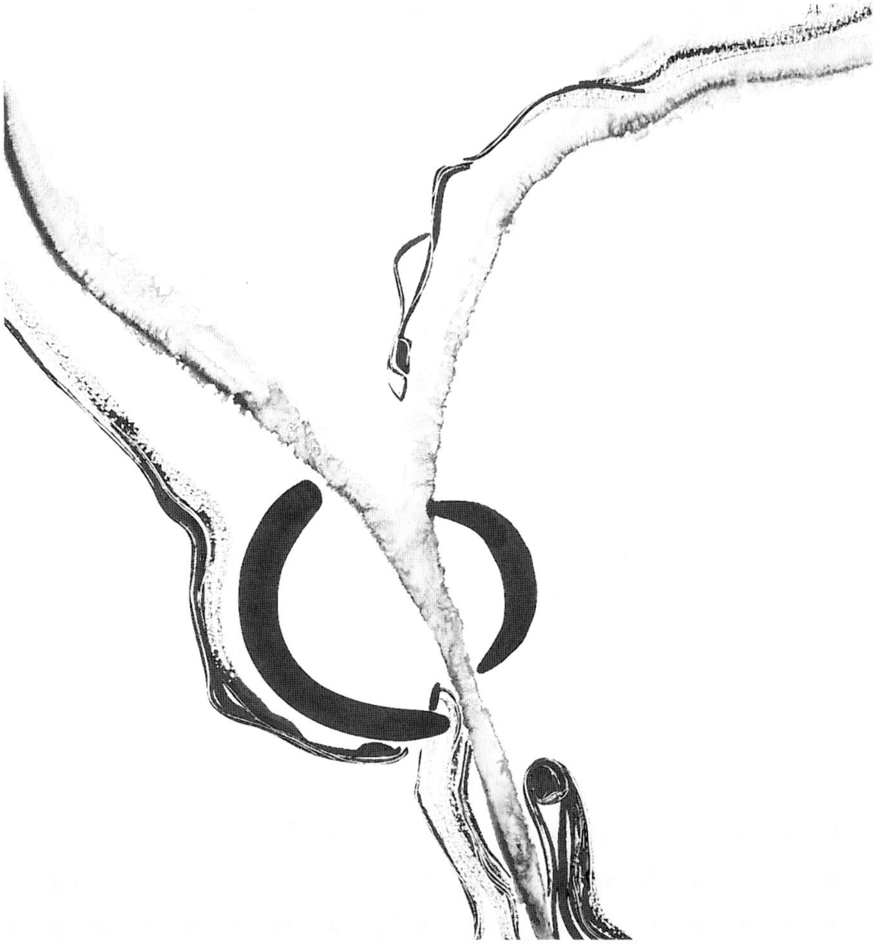

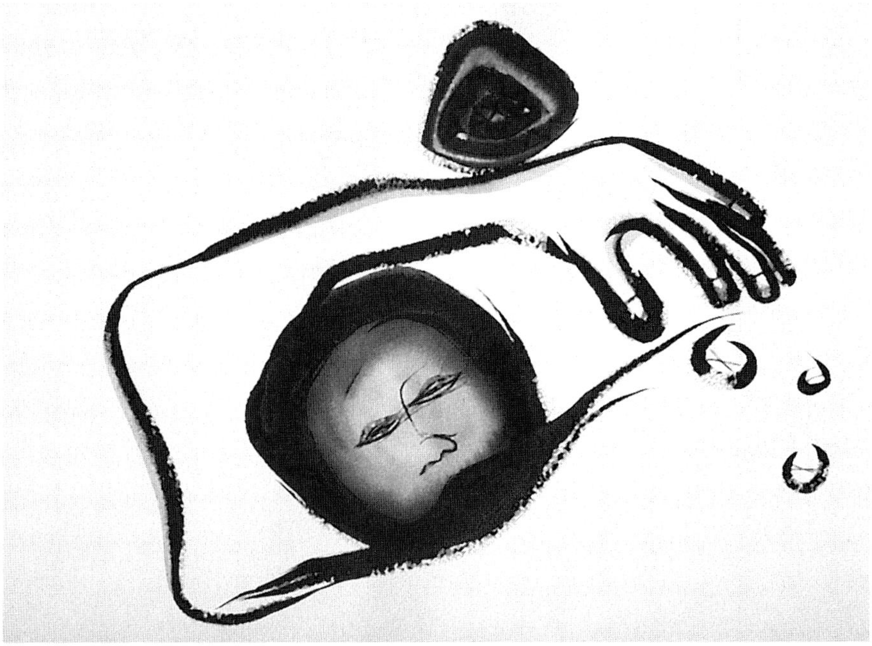

**164** (TOP LEFT). Ada Udechukwu, *These Burdens I Bear,* 1990, black and white ink on paper. 35.6 × 25.4 cm. Private collection. Photo: Franko Khoury.

**165** (TOP RIGHT). Ada Udechukwu, untitled, 1990, black and white ink on paper. 50.2 × 35.3 cm. Collection of the artist. Photo: Franko Khoury.

**166** (BOTTOM RIGHT). Ada Udechukwu, *Sleep,* 1994, ink and brush. 48.2 × 61 cm. Collection of the artist.

**167** (FACING PAGE). Ada Udechukwu, untitled, 1991, watercolor and ink on paper. 48.2 × 64 cm. Collection of the artist. Photo: Franko Khoury.

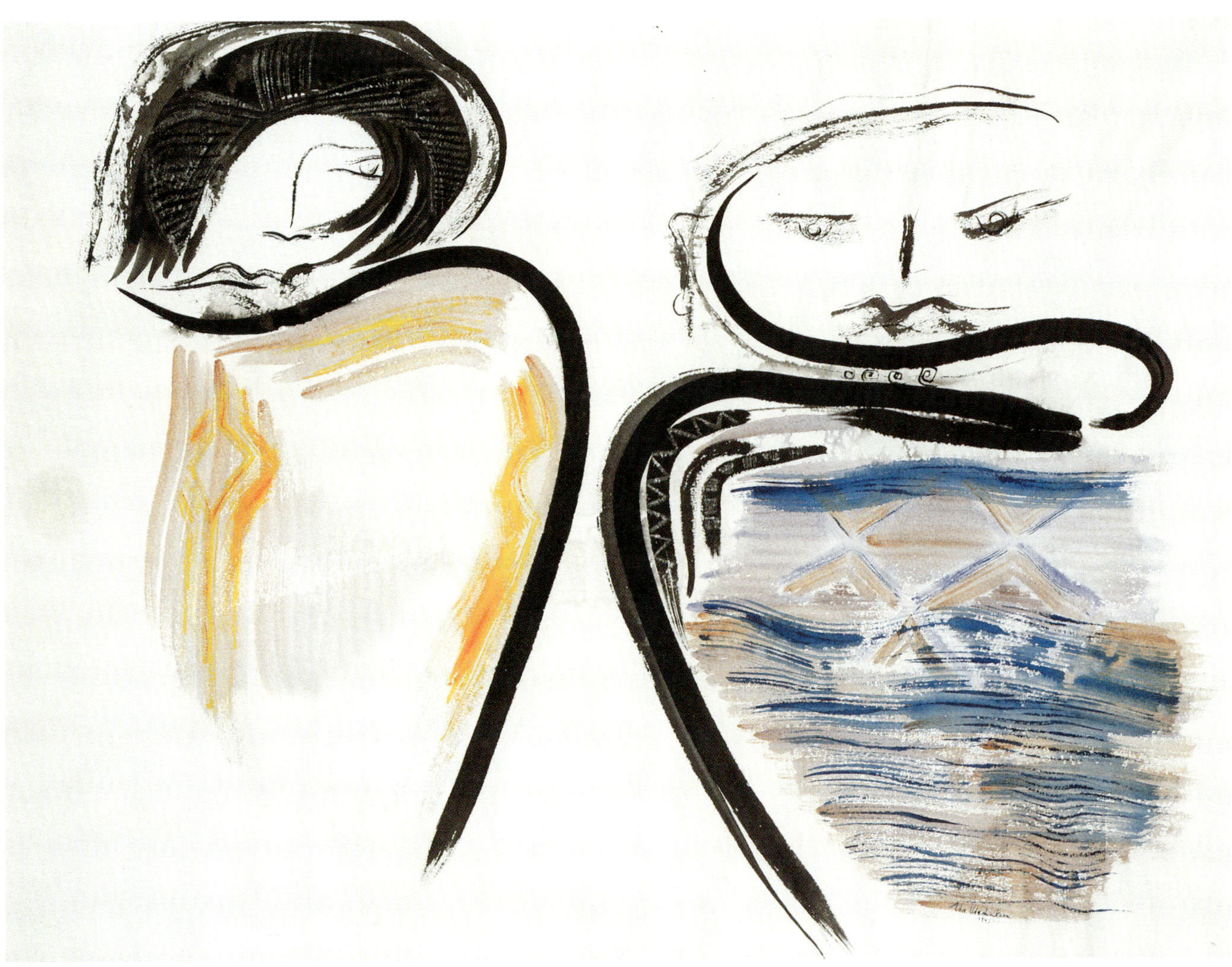

suggests borders. When I viewed the drawing with her, it reminded Udechukwu of the birth of her first child, when she felt she was still learning about and exploring her marriage; she felt in prison at that point, with no other life. She wasn't reading or thinking, she had no outside job, and she felt weighed down.

A number of Udechukwu's works on paper have the theme of grasping and reaching out, for example, an untitled 1990 piece (brush and ink; fig. 165). Here a black pincerlike hand seems to be grasping into something elegant, plantlike, and flowing. And there is *Sleep* (1994, brush and ink; fig. 166), where the face, unusually well detailed, suggests sleep, but an arm is reaching out trying to grasp some objects. The artist says that some burden above the wrist is pushing down on it, preventing this from occurring.

Another untitled work (1991, watercolor and ink; fig. 167) represents both the general and the specific. It is two aspects of the female, the brash and bold (right figure) and the retiring and watchful (left figure). In one sense, the work represents females in general, and in another the artist herself in her active and her retiring moods. The difference between the two figures in the piece is represented by the smaller head of the retiring female, the larger head of the brash one. The latter figure is more strongly delineated, the browns and blues are strong against the

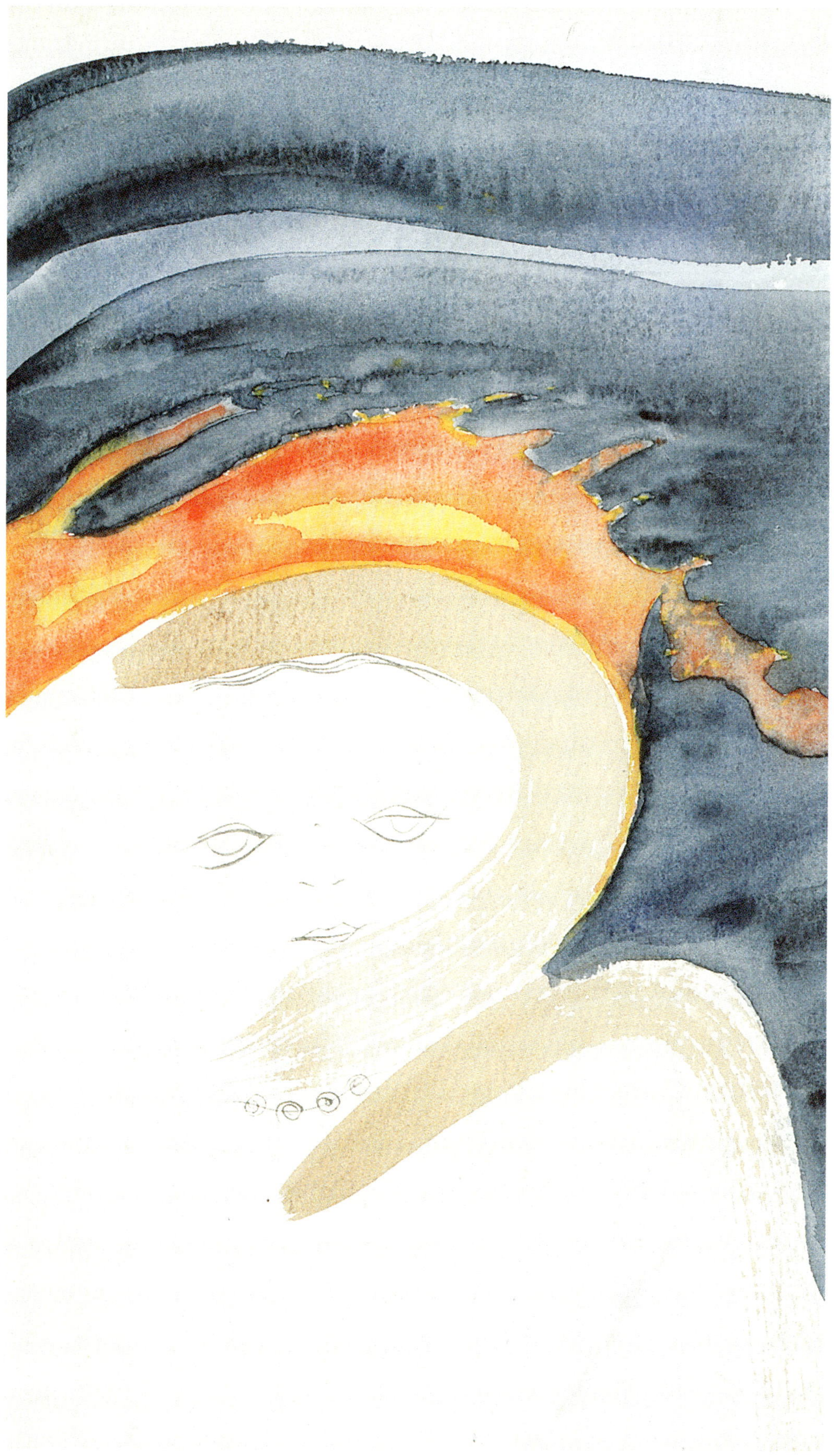

**168** (RIGHT). Ada Udechukwu, *Waiting*, 1988, watercolor and brush on paper. 28 × 15.2 cm. Collection of the artist. Photo: Franko Khoury.

**169** (FACING PAGE, LEFT). Ada Udechukwu, *Backward Looking Journey*, 1994, ink and brush. 51 × 36 cm. Collection of the artist.

**170** (FACING PAGE, RIGHT). Ada Udechukwu, untitled, 1994, ink and brush. 30.5 × 22.8 cm. Collection of the artist.

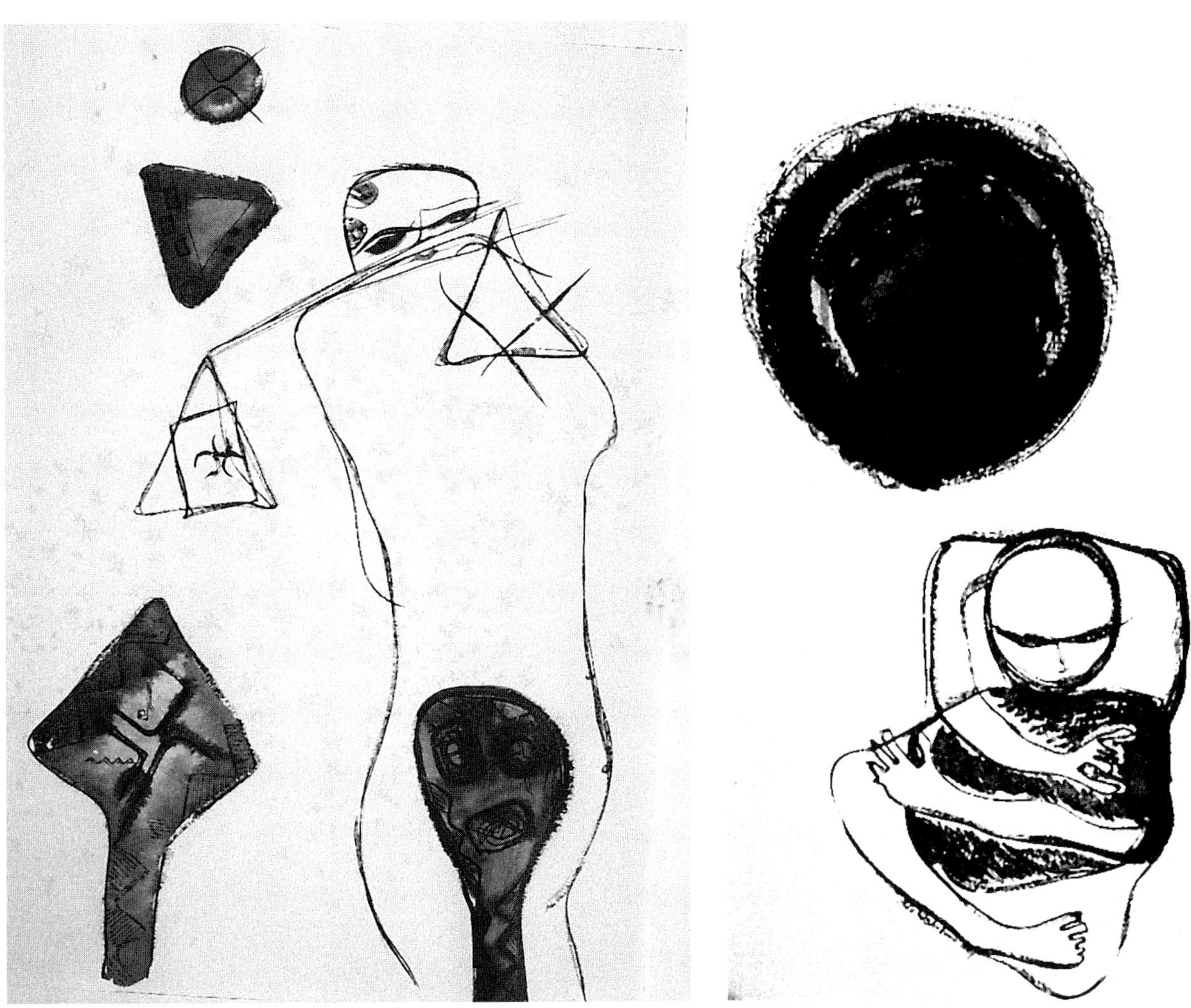

quieter brown of the retiring figure. The two images, physically separated by bold lines, are not facing each other, not talking to each other, suggesting the separateness of these two sides of a personality, as if there is no flow back and forth between them. The black shroud around the retiring figure suggests a sense of withdrawal; the face of the brash figure is not so enclosed. The facial features are simply drawn, characteristic of Udechukwu's work on paper. The paper itself is more than usually filled for the work of this artist.

Other works suggest other moods and feelings. In *Waiting* (1988, watercolor and brush; fig. 168), one of her first works after she began seriously to draw on paper again, she experimented in trying to create a personality and a mood through facial expression. The face, as often in her work, is pensive, unsmiling. The strong, wavy, background blue color suggests uncertainty, trouble, a brewing storm. The reddish brown above the figure's head implies action, perhaps danger. The empty lower portion of the picture may be because it is unfinished, or it may represent her waiting for something. The work, from its appearance, might also be entitled *Patience*.

*Backward Looking Journey* (1994, brush and ink; fig. 169) displays the linear form of a woman moving forward, carrying burdens on a stick on her shoulder, but her eyes are in the back of her head. As the artist explains:

**171 (TOP).** Ada Udechukwu, untitled, 1994, ink and brush. 49.5 × 27.9 cm. Collection of Katherine E. Adams. Photo: Franko Khoury.

**172 (BOTTOM).** Ada Udechukwu, untitled, 1990, watercolor, ink, and brush. 25.4 × 35.6 cm. Collection of Sharon C. and Larry L. Adams. Photo: Franko Khoury.

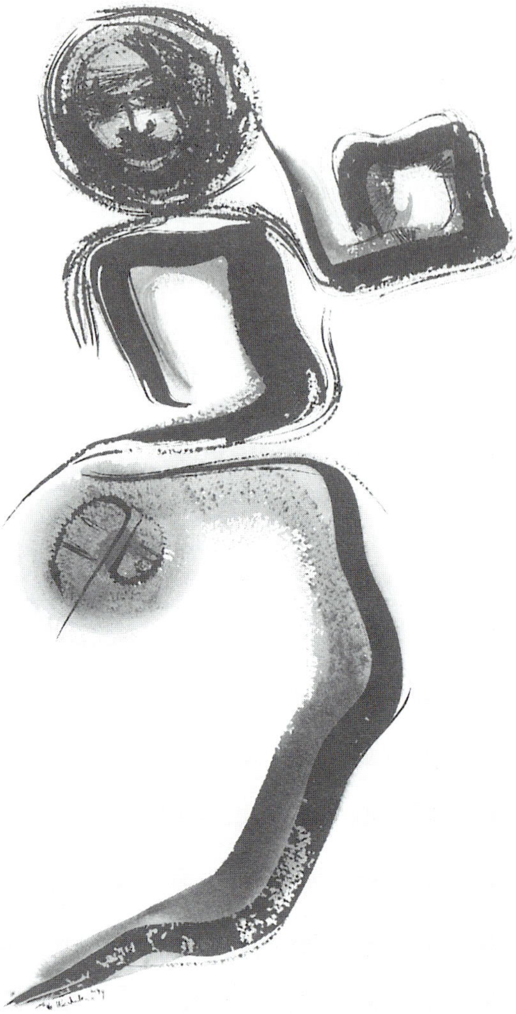

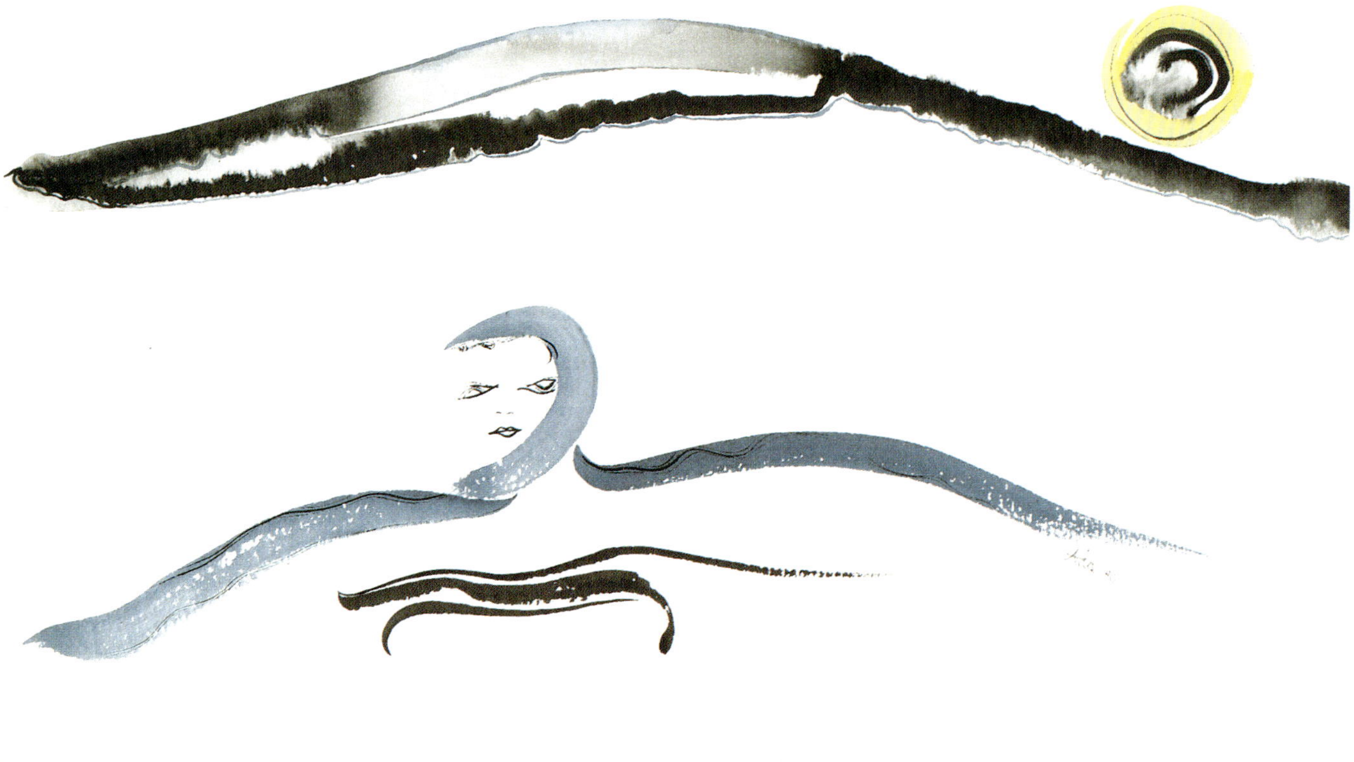

"The past is always with her. It pulls her down." The other elements in the picture represent the landscape of the journey. The image of burdens reminds one of Obiọra Udechukwu's lithograph, *People of the Night* (1985; see fig. 80).[23]

Another theme, having or holding, is expressed in an untitled work (1994, brush and ink; fig. 170), where a seated figure holds onto something that it is not really entitled to hold. The artist calls it an illusion of having something, but she made no further interpretation.

Ada Udechukwu's works on paper appear simple—just a few lines, sometimes white as well as black, a black ink area or two, perhaps some color. But the meanings behind them are deep in emotion and thought, and are sometimes complex. She does not always freely discuss the meanings or motivations behind her art, as in a 1994 untitled brush and ink of a human figure (fig. 171) and another untitled piece of a human figure with a mirrored landscape above her (fig. 172). Udechukwu is an Igbo artist by virtue of her ancestry through her father and by virtue of where she lives. She takes on the *uli* style, albeit with considerable modification and despite her much greater use of human images. Thus it is possible to identify her as a member of the Nsukka group of artists, one of its few females.

Yet her drawings and watercolors also depict universal human themes: questions of personal identity, cultural orientation and conflict, the role of women in male-dominated situations, family conflicts and tensions, reaching and trying to grasp that which may be difficult or impossible to obtain, and dealing with one's past. Perhaps precisely because she was never so much in touch with indigenous African culture as the other artists among the seven in this book, she has not drawn from Igbo myth, tales, minstrel songs, masquerades, dances, and musicians as other Nsukka artists have. She is the only one of Igbo background who has not talked to me of her village of identity, where some of her Igbo relatives live. Of the seven, she is one of the most urban by childhood life and adult experience, the most distant from indigenous culture, something reinforced by her years in the United States at a crucial developmental age, years also largely spent in urban situations.

She is also the visual artist who, of the seven, except for Ọlu Ọguibe, has been professionally active the shortest amount of time, since 1984 for her textile art and 1988 for her works on paper, and the only one untrained in visual art. The brief time of her work does not allow for a full picture of its development. I do note, however, an increasing tendency to fill up the space on the paper, growth in skill with her brushwork, a tendency to employ sgraffito to good effect, and greater use of color. One hopes that over the years she will find quiet and time to develop her considerable talents further.

She is not the only female artist who employs *uli* in her work. Chinwe Uwatse (née Ntephe) is another.[24] Graduating from the art program at Nsukka the same year that Tayọ Adenaike obtained his M.F.A degree, they shared studio space together at one time as students, and her work was apparently once influenced by his. She creates whole human forms and faces out of *uli* symbols with great care. Another female artist, well known in Nigeria and with a following outside the country, is Ndidi (Didi) Dike, who graduated from the art program at the university in 1984, specializing in painting, but prefers mixed media.[25] She has taken up wood sculpture, employing *uli* and other designs in wood panel work and other wood forms, often with attached elements, such as tiny brass Aṣante *akuaba* figures. She is one of the few women sculptors in Nigeria, an unusual transformation from past times, when males sculpted in wood. Marcia Kure, a painter who recently finished a B.A. degree in art at Nsukka and shows much promise, employs *uli* and other Nsukka artists' traits in her work, though her background is Christian Hausa.[26] Ada Udechukwu has had intermittent contact with all three of these artists, but her style is quite her own.

Ada Udechukwu's poetry is personal. She says that it does not reflect influences from other poets, except perhaps Emily Dickinson, for whom she feels "a sort of kinship." Both write short poems, often personal, reflective ones. Ada Udechukwu's poetry has attributes that relate it to her visual art. Both are brief, neither exist in large quantities, and space seems as important in the placement of written lines as in her art. Both forms are introspective and quiet, sometimes suggesting pain and suffering, and both can be haunting. Her poems are sometimes akin to her textile art in happiness, sometimes to her less joyful art on paper. Both poetry and visual art are generally created for herself; an external audience has been secondary. Only in her textile art is the external world primary. In answer to my query: "Do you see your poetry as relating to your visual art, or do you see it as being a separate experience," she replied:

> I think they are very similar and related to each other. It's just that one is visual and the other is literary, and the poetry served its own purpose at a particular time for me, just as my art serves its own purpose. They are both emotional outlets. I have to say that, first and foremost, I wasn't trained as an artist, and I never really took myself for an artist per se. I mean, in terms of this as a career and this is how I am going to earn my living, and so my art, literary and visual, has always first and foremost for me been a way of bringing out feelings, and that's why both are very emotional. They help me to deal with my life.[27]

Although she does not draw from Igbo minstrel poetry, her conjunction of poetry and visual art is not surprising from an Igbo viewpoint, where various art forms often join together. As Toyin Nduka writes of her poetry: "We see the painter in the poet, flicking with her paint brush, drawing upon earth colours to create scenarios that appear immediately reachable but like the mirage, we must keep seeking to find."[28]

Her book of poetry, *Woman, me*, came about through contacts of the Udechukwus with a German friend, Norbert Aas, who has an interest in the Nsukka artists. He had a publishing enterprise and published her poems.[29] Also printed in the book are some of her favorite works on paper, including *Self-Portrait* (fig. 159), "*In the Temple of My Familiar*" (fig. 160), and one of her untitled, grasping drawings (brush and black and white ink, 1990). The book's title poem, "Woman me," expresses something of the pain of her art on paper:

> Place me —
> greengold
> a haze of colors
> clinging to a beam
>
> Then lay me open
> shoulder bare
> hold me, hold me . . .
>
> Echo's hostage in driftwood memories
> ancient in scoured surface
> aching pain dashed against a shore,
> Woman, me.[30]

Yet there are also happy poems here, which more resemble the brightness, the positive qualities of her textiles, as "You came to me."

A splash
of color
on my palms implanted
with brush strokes fanning out
from radiating core,
you came to me.[31]

Her poetry and visual art fit together splendidly in this book.

Her verse derived quite independently from her husband, Obịọra Udechukwu's, and has probably not been influenced by his. His is only occasionally personal, much of it being concerned with social and political issues in Nigeria and Africa; while hers is oriented toward her own person and expresses a female viewpoint.[32] He is concerned with external pain—the suffering of others—while she, in poetry and visual art, is involved with her own pain, though not in a selfish manner. His concern with external sufferings expresses his internal anguish at the condition of the world about him, while hers is involved with the world within the person. Their creations complement each other.

## CONCLUSION

Ada Udechukwu is an unusually creative artist in textiles, works on paper, and poetry. Her art directly expresses her personal qualities: efficiency, economy of effort, considerable care in activity, quietness, doubt, and reflectivity. Two sides of her person are in her work, an outgoing one, desiring to pass on her aesthetic skills to others through her fabric painting, and an inner view in her visual art and in poetry, often created in an effort to deal with internal personal matters. Her life and art go back and forth between these two poles. Making a living from her art is not her main concern, rather it is expressing herself in ways that satisfy her. Her literary and visual outputs are slim, yet remarkably mature. Her art forms an interesting and lively contrast to that of the other Nsukka artists.

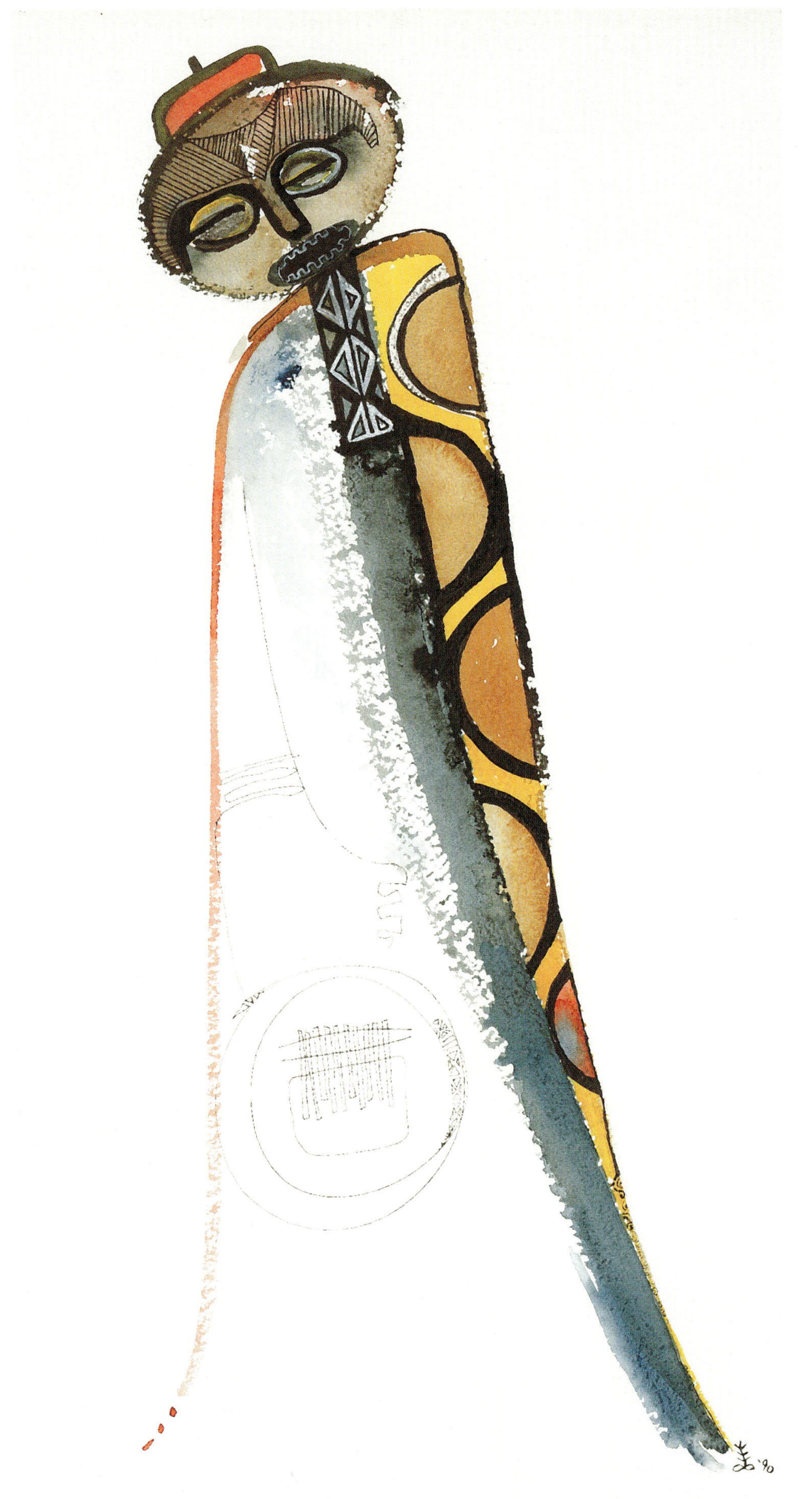

Fig. 180.

# 12. ǪLU ǪGUIBE

## ANGRY YOUNG MAN, ARTIST, AND POET

An artist as transitory as myself would not fit into a style. I have referenced Uli, Nsibidi, Adinkra, Adirẹ, Mbari, Dogon sculpture, Ndebele murals, San rock art, Maya and Inca textile art, European abstract expressionism, postmodernism, social realism and conceptualism, in addition to my own forms and ideas. Many of the works in my last show drew on the format of Fante flags, the very way Brancusi drew on Nordic totem sculpture. My show in Australia in September will draw on Aboriginal rock art and feature photography. In a recent letter Ulli Beier, asks "Who is Ǫlu Ǫguibe?" An artist! is the answer, not an Igbo or Uliist or whatever else. No one asks "who is Jeff Koons?" and David Hockney is not studied as a Cockney artist.

ǪLU ǪGUIBE[1]

Of the seven artists in this book, Ǫlu Ǫguibe's childhood is best known because he has written of it himself. In his childhood the links between early life and art are clear (fig. 173).[2] He was born in the large, bustling southern Igbo city of Aba, known for its market, an important railway station, and vehicular crossroads. His father was a preacher and former schoolteacher who had converted to the Church of Christ under American missionary influence. He was also a wood sculptor, creating Christian religious objects and Igbo masks, a graphic artist, and a sign painter. Ǫlu Ǫguibe's mother was trained as a stenographer but never practiced it; she acted as her husband's secretary and became a hairdresser. Through her, Ǫguibe learned plaiting as a child; Nigerian hairstyles are complex and require skill to create.

The Biafran war changed many things for the family, leaving a strong imprint on Ǫguibe. The family moved twice during the war, and he remembers cowering from air raids near Owerri, seeing the airplanes, viewing dead soldiers, fleeing from Aba on the crossbar of a bicycle, and later walking. There was great family anxiety toward

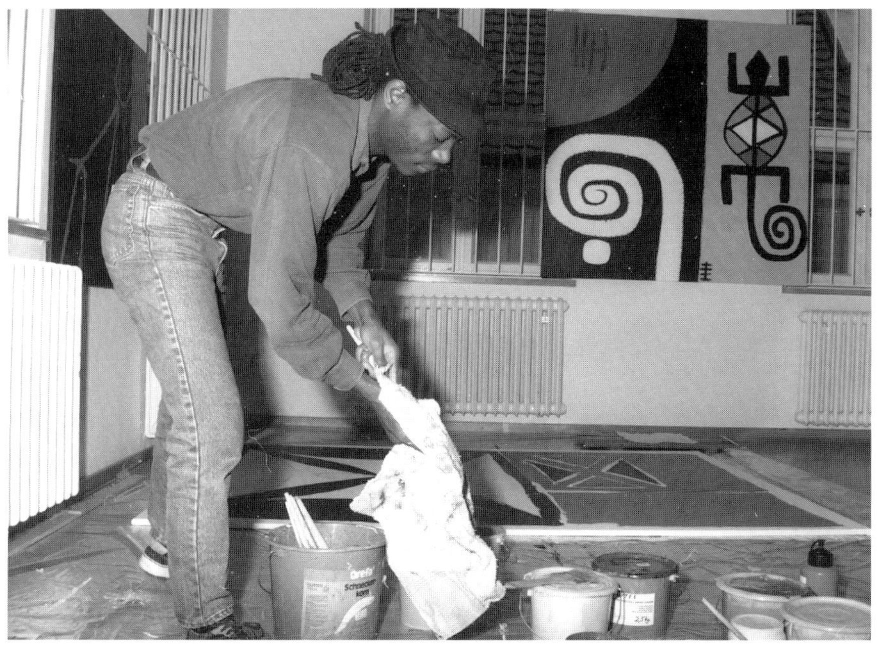

**173**. Olu Oguibe in the ArchivGaleria, Friedberg, Germany, 1994. Photo: ArchivGaleria.

the war's end in leaving a physically handicapped favorite aunt behind, at her request, as the Nigerian troops advanced, but she was later found to be safe. Oguibe says today that his family felt sadness and humiliation, having to paint "One Nigeria" on their home at Akpodim village in the present Imo State, before Nigerian troops arrived toward the war's end, so as to save it from destruction, though they did not then believe in one Nigeria. "The memory of that price of humiliation we had to pay will never leave me," Oguibe has said.[3] Today he still has nightmares about the war.

After the conflict the family settled at their Akpodim home, between Aba and Owerri. Oguibe went to schools in nearby Mbaise until he left for the University of Nigeria, Nsukka, in 1981. His father led a congregation in the village and was an itinerant preacher in neighboring areas. He had a large library, and his son read a great deal of religious literature at an early age; by the time he was sixteen, he was preaching. Beier comments: "The combination of school teacher and preacher made Olu's father a very strict disciplinarian, perhaps pushing his son into the anti-establishment, anti-authoritarian stance for which he was to become known in later life."[4] Oguibe himself states:

> But religion made me. It made me straight and trim and taciturn, completely ascetic. Or may be I got them from my father who, besides the ever looming giant figure of God, was the only dominating institution in my life. My childhood defined my view of life and it is this that guides my convictions and so my art. If there is little place for the purely pleasurable in my art, I think it goes back to my childhood which though it was pleasant, eschewed the "pleasures of the flesh."[5]

By the age of twenty-one he had quit preaching and his religion as well.

But there was another side to his father. In order to supplement his meager preacher's income, he sculpted in wood, creating religious figures and masks for local age-grade masquerades and other rites. At age six, Oguibe joined his father's workshop, scraping and sandpapering objects and doing odd jobs, gradually becoming involved in sculpting. He started drawing at about this time, and at age six drew a long train on the sand in his village with considerable detail, although he had not seen a train since he left Aba some years earlier. Despite his interest in art, for many years he wished to be a journalist. So he applied to the University of Nigeria, Nsukka, to study it but he was turned down; the next year he was accepted into the fine arts program. Visual art and writing were to become two of his three major interests.

In the 1970s Akpodim still carried out many traditional activities, and there was strong communal feeling. The future artist made masks as a boy, wore a white-faced mask of a European that his father carved for him, and joined in and led boys' masquerades, the lads beating bits of metal for music and collecting pennies for their performances. Despite the family's religious interests, both father and son were involved with masking. Oguibe heard elders' tales and took part in moonlight plays that reenacted stories in song, dance, and dialogue. He learned drumming and played the *ikoro,* the large village drum.

As a child, Oguibe studied art on his own, painting in the naturalistic mode. His parents brought him numerous books about British painters and an American series, the Walter Foster do-it-yourself books. He was fascinated with flags and copied pictures of them with delight. He visited a noted basket maker, Clem, in a nearby village, and learned to make baskets, which later connected to his art. At secondary school he had a well-known art teacher, and he learned about European art.

> I was taught that my father was actually a "carver" and somewhat different from a sculptor who, inevitably, had to be European. I was told that my master Clem was not an artist but "a mere craftsman." I learned that the greatest sculptors in history were Phidias, Michelangelo, Rodin and Moore and no mention was made of the sculptors of the Sphinx or the Great Zimbabwe. I was taught that there is Art, and then African art, which is something different from Art.[6]

At school he learned that African art was dying, which did not agree with his village experience. His classmates sometimes called him "Marcus Garvey," after the African-American political leader, for he was already interested in politics. He grew up with stories of justice and injustice in his family, which sharpened his social concerns—politics is Oguibe's third major interest.

## UNIVERSITY DAYS

Oguibe attended the University of Nigeria, Nsukka, in 1981–86 and 1987–89 and was active as an artist, poet, and in student politics, receiving his B.A. in painting summa cum laude in 1986. Then for a year he was in the National Youth Corps Service as a lecturer in drawing and painting at the Federal College of Education, Abeokuta. During the 1981–89 period he had two solo exhibitions in Nigeria and took part in at least five group exhibitions; it was a productive, developing time.

Oguibe studied painting at the university with the Ghanaian Seth Anku, who produced images of rituals and dances in stylized naturalism, using special graphites; however, this was not of interest to Oguibe. He then studied painting with Obiọra Udechukwu, whose artwork excited him, though he did not duplicate it; he later created some work stylistically like his teacher's but with different themes. Oguibe read widely in what was then a well-stocked university library and was influenced by Courbet, Kollwitz, Goya, nineteenth-century French artists, and the Mexican muralists. He became interested in social realism and created images of himself, Lenin, and Marx, but he was not attracted to the social realist art of the Soviet Union. He did no *uli* work in class, he has told me, as it was not taught; he claims that at the time it was not allowed in his courses, though El Anatsui did encourage students to look into it. Yet *uli* was in the air, and Oguibe saw exhibitions of Adenaike's work and that of other Nsukka artists.

Oguibe became aware of the Biafran war images of Obiọra Udechukwu and other artists, but

I never really related to it in that manner, because I was always very much a nationalist on the Nigerian level, and I was a believer in putting things in the past behind, and moving on and evolving a different country and society. Doting on the agony and anguish of the civil war was not part of my growing up at that stage, but over time it has come back to me and it's very much about my own personal experience.[7]

He studied drawing with El Anatsui, whose artistic ideas interested him; Anatsui allowed a bit of experimenting and introduced him to *adinkra* forms. But the greatest influence on him during his university days was probably seeing the art of the faculty and advanced students. Courses in art history with Ọla Ọlọidi, who had studied at Howard University, introduced to Oguibe the social context of art, which greatly interested him. Ọlọidi was familiar with the Black Art and Africobra movements in America, and Oguibe absorbed this, paying particular attention to the African-American social realist artist Charles White.

While at the university, Oguibe went back to his home area, conducting a study of *mbari* houses and designs. He has told me that "the books you read in the library did not give you the impression that what you found in your village was art, but the curriculum did, the courses did, the teachers did, and you could connect all of these things and it made sense."[8] He did his B.A. thesis on wall murals in Lagos and Kaduna, largely by university- and college-trained artists. For Oguibe, their art related to both modern times and village murals and to the Mexican muralists.

He also created assemblages and installations while at the university, something he has returned to in recent years. Some of these appeared in his graduate exhibition of 1986, which involved audience participation. He also went out with El Anatsui and experimented with arranging stones and rocks in natural settings and sketching them. Oguibe was already showing far-reaching interests and an inquiring mind.

On the whole, he felt that the university art training was that of European academy art of the 1960s, including life drawing, anatomy, and still life. After he left for England in 1989, he claims to have discarded much of this training, though not his art history studies.

While at the university he became secretary of the Students Union, fighting against the abolition of government subsidies for the students. He helped initiate a period of student activism against government actions and the sexual harassment of female students by senior faculty. He was very popular; whenever he spoke, students flocked to him. His early preaching experience undoubtedly translated into political oratory. He won the University Prize for Best Graduating Student in 1986 and was valedictorian and class president. His valedictory speech at the graduating convocation was strongly political and angered the university authorities and the government.

When Oguibe returned to work for his master's degree in 1987, on his way to a doctorate, the university authorities did not want him, but he reentered, took courses, and wrote his master's thesis. This, however, was never accepted because of disagreement between two of his faculty members. The university authorities also claimed that he had been involved in inciting a student riot at an earlier time, when, in fact, he was teaching at Abeokuta. He left for England, fortunately holding a British government fellowship. Later he discovered that there was a police warrant for his arrest in Nigeria. He returned only briefly to Nigeria some years later.

## EXHIBITIONS IN NIGERIA

Oguibe was involved in group print and graphic exhibitions in Nigeria in 1986, 1987, and 1988 and in exhibitions of various forms of his art with Jonathan Lessor, a fellow National Youth Corps Service lecturer at Abeokuta

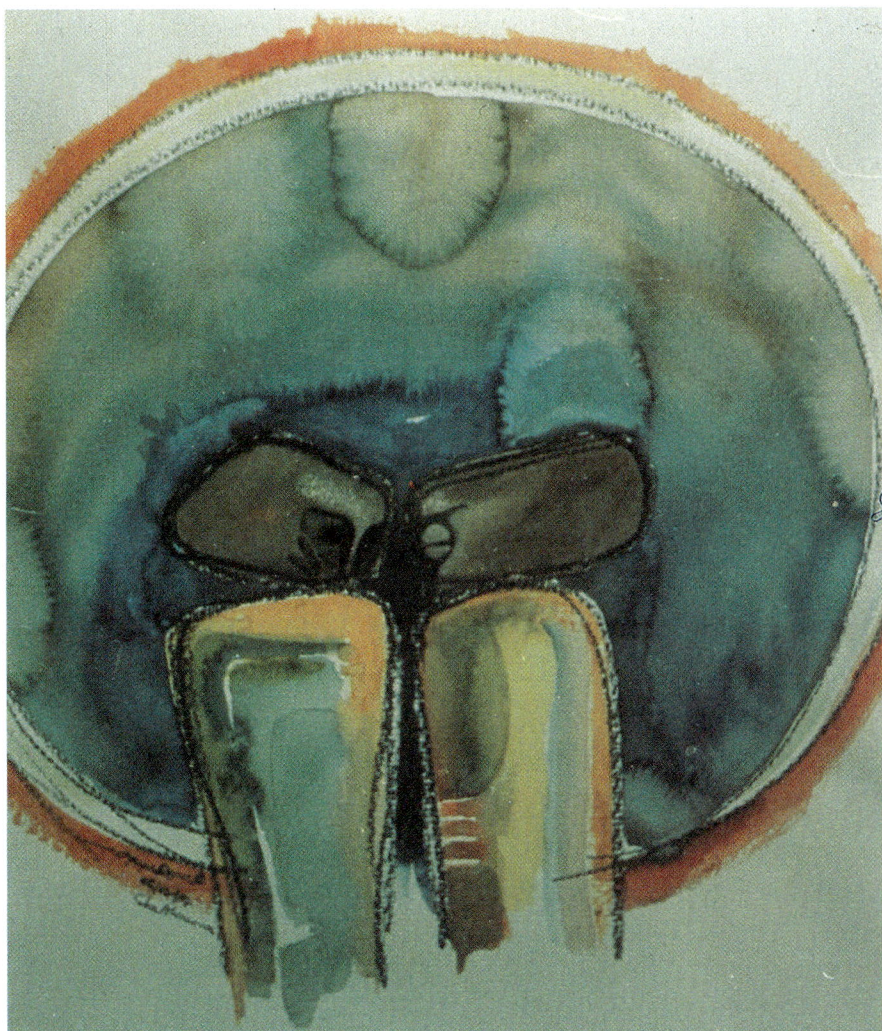



in 1987. Ọguibe's first major statement was a 1988 joint exhibition with Greg Odo, *Art on the Street*.[9] This was held on the main university thoroughfare and thus was seen by many students, as well as Nsukka townsmen and farmers who passed by the then unwalled campus. On this, Ọguibe writes:

> It is only the vain art of the artschool artist that has continued to delude itself by remaining in the weird setting of inaccessible halls with guards and carpeted floors that keep away the people for whom art should be meant. We feel ashamed to have continued to emasculate art by removing it from its rightful place and making specimens of it. We bring art back. No, we bring the art of the university artist back to the natural setting of all meaningful art.[10]

Not surprisingly, Ọguibe exhibited works of a political nature, such as the watercolor, *Image of the Beast*, concerning "graft, greed and corruption, with a rampaging beast as metaphor."[11] The beast, usually a bull, was to become a favorite image of Ọguibe's. Other works derived from the African-American writings of James Baldwin and others. Another watercolor, *The Present Is a Dangerous Place to Live* (1987; fig. 174), suggests Ọguibe's anxiety about life in Nigeria.

. . . *unbind me,* Ọguibe's first solo exhibition, was held at the nongovernment Didi Museum, Lagos, in 1988.[12] The title is from Christopher Okigbo's "Elegy for Alto," one of a group of poems published as *Path of Thunder* in 1968, which some think foretold the coming of Nigeria's war. The key lines are:

> O mother mother Earth, unbind me; let this be
> my last testament; let this be
> The ram's hidden wish to the sword the sword's
> secret prayer to the scabbard —

and later:

> Earth, unbind me: let me be the prodigal, let this be
> the ram's ultimate prayer to the tether . . .[13]

Probably Ọguibe was one who was wishing and trying to unbind, and perhaps he is suggesting that others do so as well.

The exhibition of some forty-eight works—line etchings, oils, aquatints, and watercolors—was held in front of the museum, again an "on the street" show.[14] Ọguibe felt that this arrangement took away the exhibition space's elitist atmosphere. Many works were of social protest, Ọguibe writes:

> People see roses and paint them. Others are even blessed with angels in their visions. But I see burden and pain. I walk the streets and I see men and women lonely and broken, groaning under giant loads. I walk up the hills for a sight of the rising sun and I see bodies limp, dangling in the horizon. I see processions of prisoners with their heads bowed. Dying mothers. Starving children. Men with a silent sob. Stevedores . . . Whoever shovels these images under is not an artist.[15]

As in his earlier exhibitions, his work depicts human and animal forms, but the artist has departed from naturalism to stylized figures, simply suggested, including several of hanging human beings. The line etching, *A Portrait of the Artist* (fig. 175), somewhat resembling Edvard Munch's *The Scream,* shows Ọguibe with big eyes, holding his head in his hands, looking like a caged bird, with a hangman's rope nearby.[16] Ọguibe writes here: "Colour means much to me. That is why I use a lot of brown. Brown. Yellow ochre. The colour of withered grass. Of dust. And a lot of blue and the colours of gloom. The bright colours are not of life. They are the colour of drought. The colour of brushfires . . . Green is for the new grass which will sprout tomorrow."[17] The beast and the butcherbird are

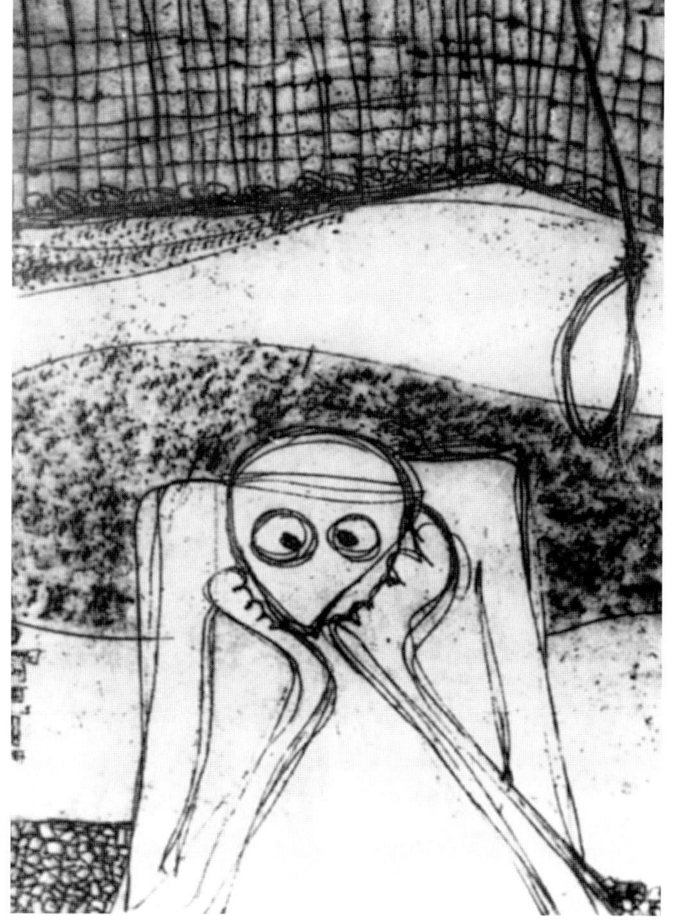

**175**. Ọlu Ọguibe, *A Portrait of the Artist*, 1989, line etching. Dimensions and collection unknown.
Photo: the artist.

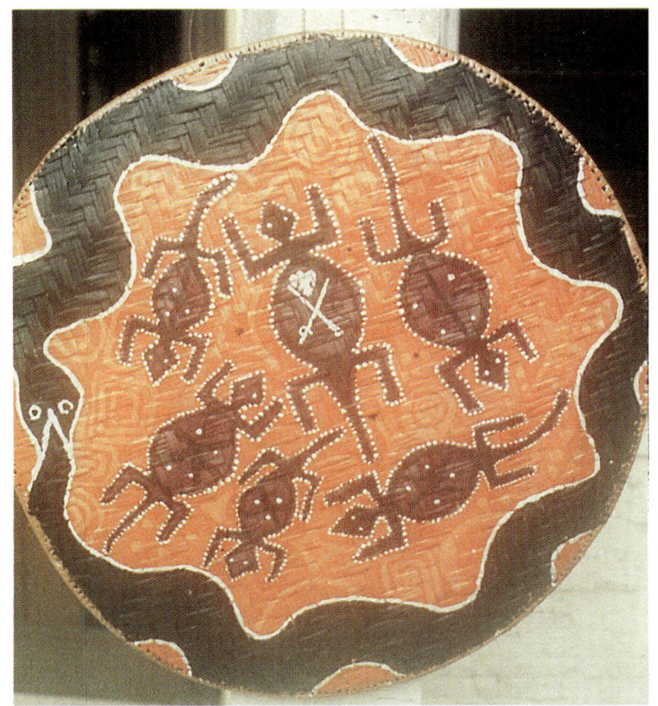

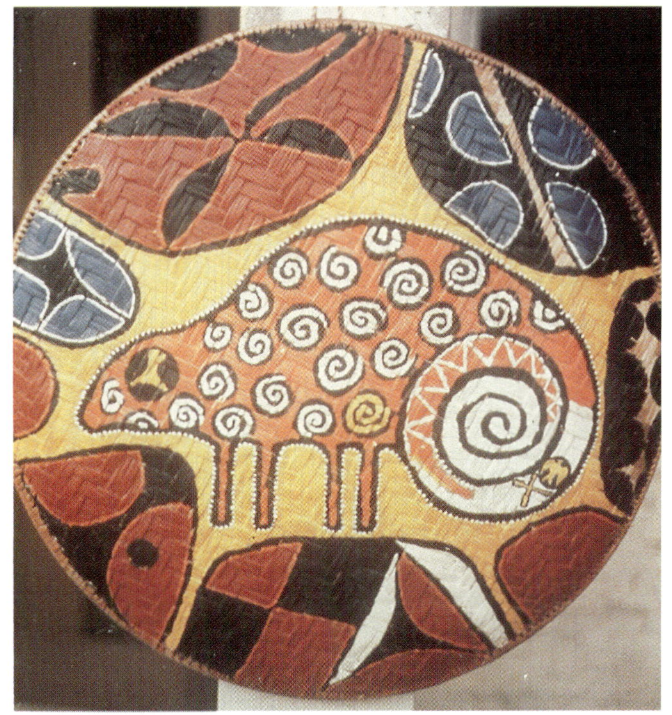

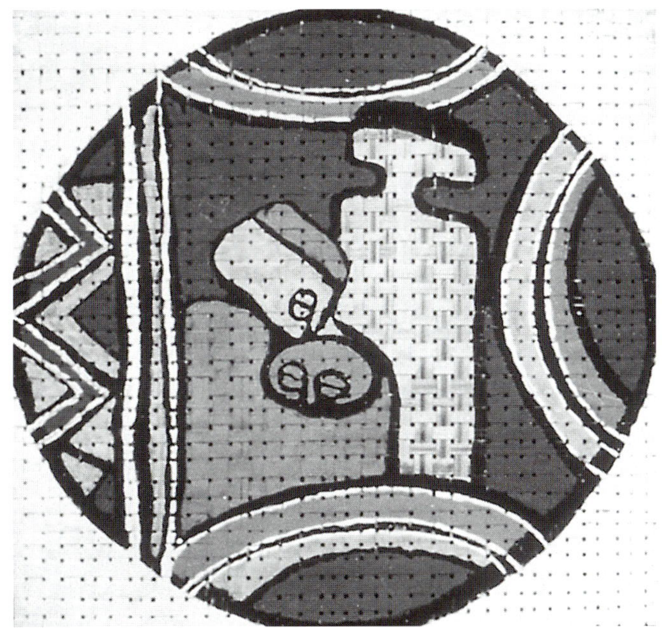

**176 (TOP LEFT).** Ọlu Ọguibe, *We are all lizards sprawling in the sun,* 1989, gouache on basket. Diameter c. 62 cm. Collection of Chinua Achebe. Photo: the artist.

**177 (TOP RIGHT).** Ọlu Ọguibe, *Tiger or Chameleon?* 1989, gouache on basket. Diameter c. 62 cm. Collection of Chinua Achebe. Photo: the artist.

**178 (CENTER).** Ọlu Ọguibe, *Widow and Child,* 1989, gouache on cane-mesh. 52 × 52 cm. Collection unknown. Photo: the artist.

**179 (BOTTOM).** Ọlu Ọguibe, panel from the *National Graffiti* series, 1989, enamel on mat, dimensions unknown. Collection and photo: the artist.

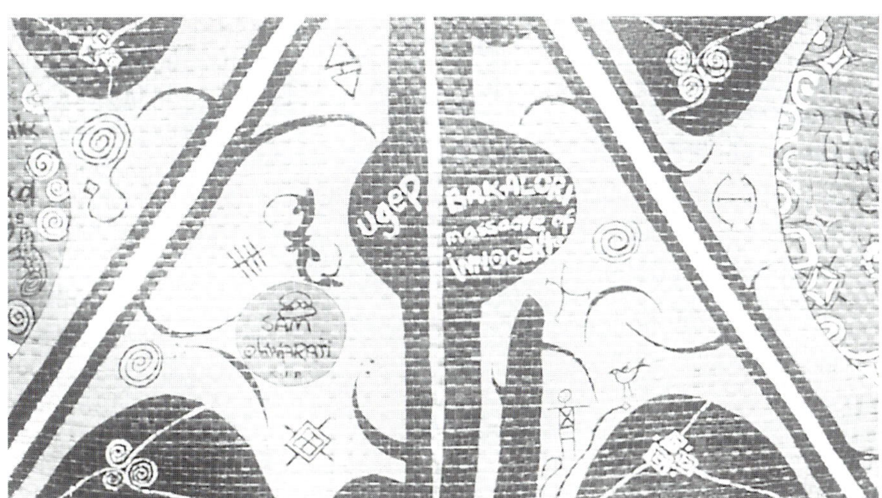

portrayed. Some works are untitled; Oguibe indicates that he does not wish to impose his vision on others, and titles may be pedestrian and lame. He seems later to have dropped this view. There are suggestions of *uli* and *mbari* influence in some of the art.

The exhibition was widely reviewed in Nigerian newspapers and was one of the most politically oriented art exhibitions of its time in Lagos, if not the most. Oguibe's anger and creative ability to employ art to develop social and political images, some of them metaphorical, were impressive, though his style itself was not unusual. That was soon to change.

In *Statements: Recent Art and Poetry,* at the Syrian Club, Lagos, in 1989, Oguibe turned to valuing Africa.

> My recent paintings are done on mats and baskets. My motifs draw from those age-long traditions of wall painting and decorative embellishment which turned every object into a work of art. Not only do these define an authentic identity for my vision, I also find them consistent with my yearning for the ultimate eloquence. Those who worship oil and canvas and ornate frames can walk straight into hell.[18]

In works in gouache on baskets and on cane mesh (for sifting cassava flour), and in enamel on sleeping mats, Oguibe moves away from European conventions (except for gouache and enamel), as El Anatsui earlier did with his decorated wooden market trays.[19] Much of the work is political, but Oguibe indicates that it is not anger that produces great works of art but passion.[20] By this time, Oguibe's hair was in dreadlocks, not common in Nigeria, and as an artist he was being referred to in the newspapers and elsewhere as the "angry young man" and the "angry young artist," phrases he rather came to cultivate in his later years in London as well, if for no other reason than to call attention to the ideas he embodied.

A basket work, *We are all lizards sprawling in the sun* (1989; fig. 176), depicts a central lizard with crossed sword and staff and a general's insignia surrounded by five smaller lizards, suggesting the hopelessness of the ordinary person under leadership. Another basket painting of the same year entitled *Tiger or Chameleon?* (fig. 177) depicts a chameleonlike animal surrounded by *uli*-like designs. The reference apparently is to the quality of leadership in Nigeria, though it could be a critique of the nature of the public's response to this leadership. Two cane-mesh works from 1989 with human figures have to do with loss and death, *Widow and Child* (fig. 178) and *The Bereaved*. By now Oguibe had developed a stylized and somewhat stultified human figure in simple outline with a rectangular or square head and rather square shoulders, an image he also employed in some of his paintings later in London.

At the Lagos exhibition, Oguibe showed ten enamel sleeping mat paintings, *National Graffiti* (1989; fig. 179), which reappeared at the 1995 *Seven Stories* exhibition in London.[21] Drawing strongly from *uli* and *mbari* wall designs, with some *nsibidi* and *adinkra* motifs, these works often have words or phrases on them, for example:

i ♥ My contri
i no go lie down
Afrika is the centre
of our foreign Police
grin-white-grin [22]

Phrases and words from Pidgin English and Nigerian popular songs abound in these ten works; the common person is intended. Chika Okeke writes that "the political protest develops into a cultural one as he rejects modern, western 'specifications and delineations.'" And "Graffiti gives the artist an opportunity to give vent to his gut feelings about his society. It is also the *vox populi* from which one can read the times: Oguibe continues a tradition that had long been established inside prison cells, public toilets and railway stations."[23] Even the Syrian Club in

Lagos, on Ribadu Road, which led to a major military barracks, was not the usual Lagos exhibition location.

In the exhibition catalogue, a long poem by the artist, "A Gathering Fear," portrays a dismal, corrupt, decaying Nigeria of 1989, with an uncaring elite. The poem contains much the same ideas as the *Graffiti* series and Oguibe's other sociopolitical works of the time, with familiar metaphors such as the beast. The verses are more powerful than his visual art, to my mind, as the mats and baskets, whatever the artist's intent in using this indigenous material, do not make a strong impact. Oguibe's sociopolitical commentaries in his visual art are more direct and sharper than those of Obiọra Udechukwu, whose work undoubtedly influenced Oguibe's, though the protest poetry of both is very strong. Oguibe has continued to join visual art and poetry. The writing of words and phrases on the enamel-painted mats is a blending of the two, not unusual in postmodern art.

## EARLY CRITICAL WRITINGS

Oguibe's master's thesis on the images of women in Nigerian art from 1970 to 1989 deals with the negative impact of colonialism on the females depicted in it, noting that even contemporary women artists are not free of this orientation.[24] Starting with the early Nigerian contemporary artist Aina Ọnabolu, Oguibe goes on to explore different images: portraits of notable women, nubile ones, milkmaids, the mother, and mythic woman. Grounded in the history and political evolution of Nigeria, the thesis links the images to the kind of society Nigeria has been. In a related article on Obiọra Udechukwu's presentation of women in his art, Oguibe concentrates on Udechukwu's Biafran war creations and the immediate postconflict period, examining a series of works dealing with bereaved women.[25] Udechukwu and Oguibe share a sympathetic eye for the ordinary person. Oguibe, in these writings, begins a very active career in art criticism. While his writing is not as decisive in 1989 as later on, it is a thoughtful beginning.

By the time Oguibe left for England in 1989, he had come a long way from his large childhood drawing of a railroad train in the ground at his home village. He had established himself as a passionate and angry young man, artist, and poet, anxious to break with many conventions, even in his critiques of Nigerian contemporary art, an artist who had gone through several transitions and was not afraid of the unorthodox and controversial. Given the political climate of Nigeria at the time he left, he would have had to depart sooner or later or be faced with jail. The situation is hardly better today.

## LONDON

In England, Oguibe met many of the problems that Africans without strong financial resources face, including artists. He had no studio and had to work in his flat. He spoke English fluently but missed any intensive use of the Igbo language. He discovered persistent British racism, which undoubtedly has influenced his view that racism is a major factor in Euro/American contemporary art.[26] He would not produce the sort of art he felt might be shown in London's Cork Street galleries, which set Britain's art fashions; as most third world artists, he was largely excluded from the center of the London art scene. He associated with the Savannah Gallery, which opened in 1992, specializing in African and black British art. Located in Bethnal Green, outside the London gallery areas, its Ghanaian owner never had the resources for proper publicity. It was one of only two galleries regularly exhibiting African art during much of Oguibe's time in London, the other being Westbourne Gallery. (Both have now closed.) A few other galleries in England did so intermittently, and Oguibe took advantage of these. Most of his sales were to Germans and Italians; the British were little interested in his art.

Although Oguibe had planned to go to Britain and had a grant in hand, his swift departure from Nigeria left him with a sense of lament and exile; this stopped him from creating for a time. When he began, he no longer had sources for Nigerian fiberware. He returned to watercolors on paper, which he did not much care for, and to ink and brush, then moved to acrylics on canvas and later also to mixed media. He has commented on these difficult early years in Britain and has published a book of poetry on this theme.[27] He writes about going to live in England: "In stealing into the overwhelming arena of the colonist culture, the dangers of a renewed loss of language were doubled, and the first year I spent dealing with this, more like 'a King fighting two battles.' In a sense, this has strengthened the vehemence of that striving to stay visible, under my own name, speaking my own language."[28]

Yet Oguibe's six years in Europe were highly productive. He met a wide range of persons interested in visual arts and literature; he was exposed to postmodernism and other artistic and political theories and to exiled third world and black British artists. He viewed a range of art, including art from other parts of Africa and other third world art he was unable to see in Nigeria. He held six solo exhibitions in England and Germany and took part in some twenty group shows in England, Germany, Northern Ireland, Sydney, Australia, and Italy. He traveled to Australia, Mexico, the United States, and Germany, whether exhibiting or not, meeting with other artists. He received a Ph.D. degree in art history from the University of London.

His early exhibitions in Europe focused on Nigeria and his exile, but in time he moved to other images.[29] He resented being considered an African or a Nigerian artist, as he was viewed in Britain, considering himself to be simply an artist. He moved from Nigerian themes to worldwide ones, in keeping with his growing postmodern interests, taking concepts not only from Africa, such as Fante flags of Ghana and Ndebele paintings of southern Africa, but from Near and Middle Eastern images, writers, and politics, from ancient Mexican art, Australian Aboriginal creations, Bavarian Catholic church steeples, and contemporary German politics. While still recognizing his African roots, he was free to absorb from anywhere. He changed orientation so much that two senior Nigerian contemporary artists commented to me that every artist must work from *some* single cultural root and that Oguibe had gone too far from that position. But Oguibe thrives, drawing from here and there, feeling that change is a good thing in his art—nowadays very postmodern views.

From about 1992 Oguibe began creating installation art, and at times he worked in photography, sculpted wood poles, and was less hostile to Euro/American media, such as acrylics on canvas, than he proclaimed in his Lagos *Statements* exhibition of 1989. Oguibe's training in art history went well at the Department of Art and Archaeology, School of Oriental and African Studies, University of London, and he absorbed knowledge of critical theory and postmodernist thought. He finished his doctoral dissertation in 1992 on a remarkable Nigerian artist, Uzo Egonu, who had been living in Europe from 1945 until his death in 1996, a man whom Nsukka artists, including Oguibe, consider to be a foremost contemporary African artist and who had a modest impact in Britain. The revised dissertation has been published.[30]

While in England, Oguibe published three collections of poetry, receiving the Christopher Okigbo All-Africa Prize for Literature in 1992 for his *A Gathering Fear,* which established him as a major African poet.[31] He edited a collection of poems by Africans in Britain, which includes his earlier published "A Song from Exile."[32] In the introduction, Oguibe discusses something of the history of Africans in Britain and their alienation there, certainly related to his own feelings. In England and in the United States, he published useful commentaries on the work of other artists and essays on art criticism, which reflect his transition from a rather angry young man in Nigeria to a more intellectually skillful one in Britain.[33] As he sharpened his artistic views, his own art became more sophisticated, although sometimes appearing to be simple. The connections between his postmodern thought and his visual art have been consistent; he is not an artist with one set of ideas in his head and another on canvas.

In Europe, Oguibe's art continued to be political; it is not surprising that he was also involved in matters relating to Nigeria and Africa. In London he was associated with the newsletter *Nigeria Now;* he was European editor of *African World,* 1993–94 (Amherst, Massachusetts), and research officer and project coordinator for the African Research and Information Bureau, 1991–93. He was guest editor of number 23 of *Third Text: Third World Perspectives on Contemporary Art and Culture,* an issue on Africa, and later a member of the magazine's advisory board and a writer for the journal.[34] He was arts and culture editor of *African World Review.* His publishing activities continue today.

Oguibe taught critical theory and postmodernism for a time in 1993–94 at Goldsmiths' College in London and conducted seminars on practice and identity in the art of the modern world. He organized a seminar series in 1991 on postcolonial African literature where he was studying.

Oguibe's original interest in returning to Nigeria after his schooling gradually faded as the Nigerian political condition worsened and new interests took hold, but he was never very comfortable in Britain. When in 1995 he had the opportunity to become an editor of *NKA: Journal of Contemporary African Art,* founded by Okwui Enwezor in New York City, he moved to the United States. He taught art history at the University of Illinois, Chicago campus, and then at the University of South Florida, Tampa.

In six years in London, Oguibe made the transition from a budding contemporary Nigerian artist to one actively engaged in a wider art scene, taking images and ideas from wherever he chose in postmodern style, though critical of postmodernism's Euro/American origins. He left behind the concepts and images of the Nsukka artists, employing *uli* and *mbari* less and less. Though he is included in this book as an Nsukka artist because of his artistic origins, he no longer considers himself a member, though he respects the work of some of its artists and recognizes that its art differs from his own. The substantial changes in his art while in England, however, should not be taken as typical of the younger Nsukka artists. Most of them have stayed closer to Nsukka art traditions. Yet Oguibe's way is a probable direction for some of them in the future. His movement out of the Nsukka style was not so much due to his spending more time abroad than the others, but rather because of his restless, inquisitive, exploratory qualities, his unwillingness to be stereotyped as any particular type of artist, and his willingness to take unpopular positions. It is never predictable as to what his next aesthetic direction will be. What is consistent are his interests in visual art, art theory and criticism, poetry, literature, and politics.

## OGUIBE'S EARLY EUROPEAN ART

Some of Oguibe's earliest European works, shown at an exhibition in 1990 at Iwalẹwa-Haus, Bayreuth, employ watercolor.[35] *The Poet* (1990, watercolor, pen, and ink on paper; fig. 180) is not a self-portrait but an interpretation of the personality of the Igbo poet/minstrel. In a style similar to

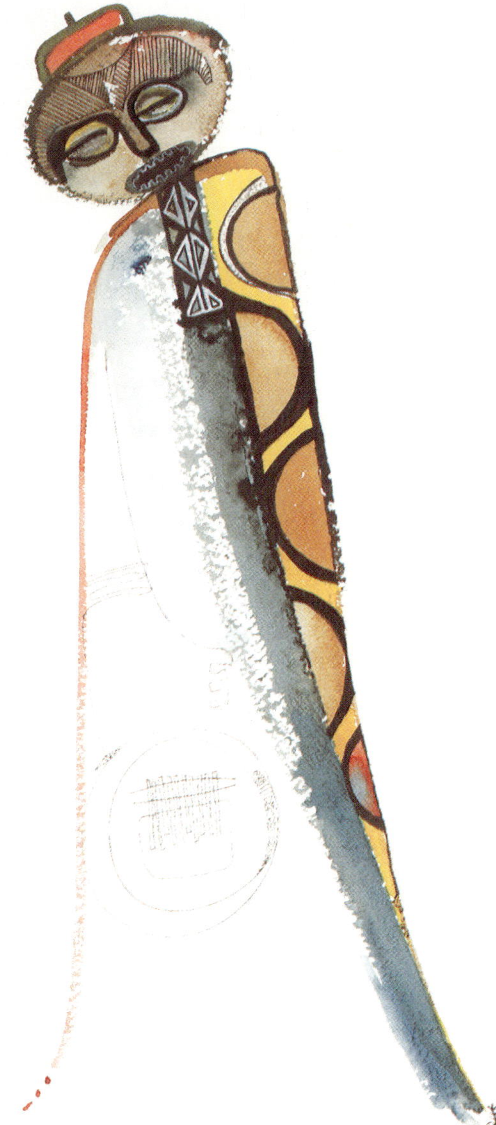

**180**. Olu Oguibe, *The Poet,* 1990, watercolor, pen, and ink on paper. 56 × 38 cm. Collection of Norbert and Hannelore Aas. Photo: Franko Khoury.

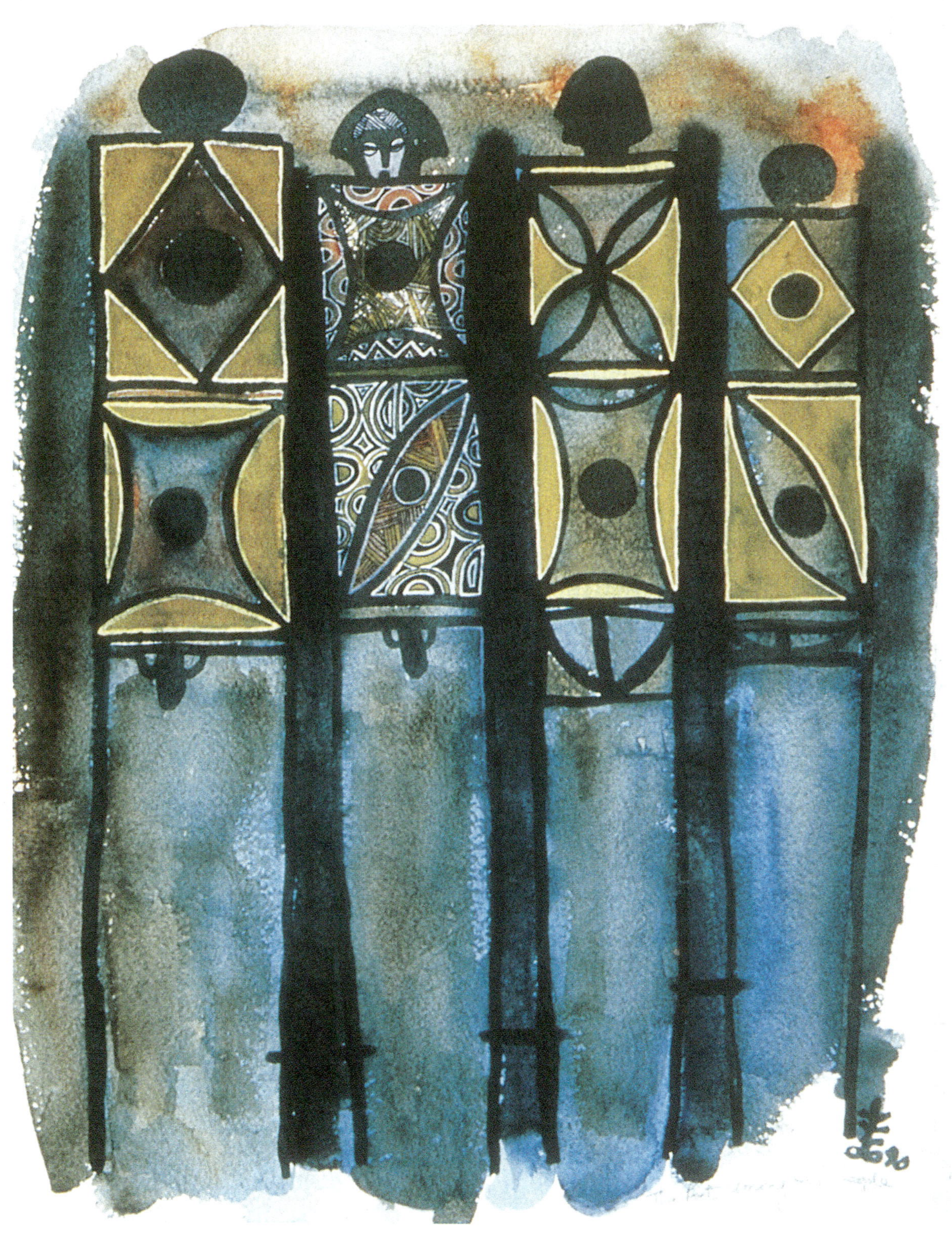

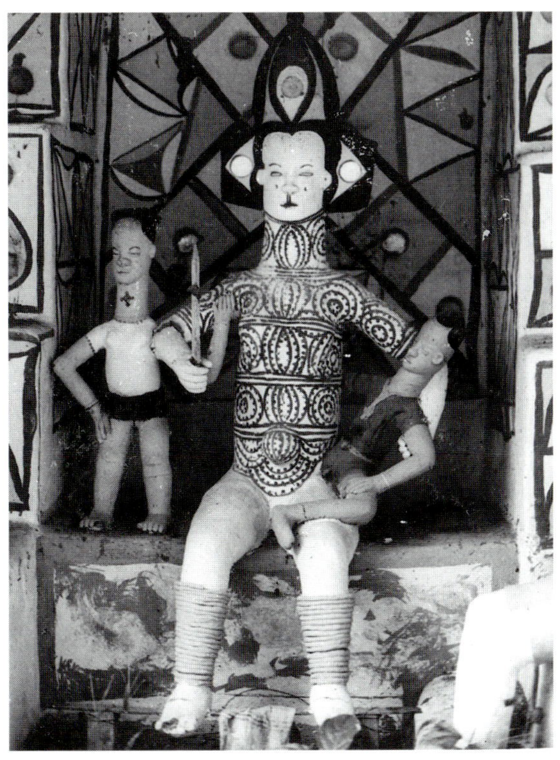

181 (**FACING PAGE**). Ọlu Ọguibe, *The Poet among His People,* 1990, watercolor on paper. 27.5 × 37.5 cm. Collection of Hiltrud Egọnu. Photo: the artist.

182 (**LEFT**). A section of an Igbo *mbari* house, c. 1967. Photo: Herbert M. Cole.

183 (**BELOW**). Ọlu Ọguibe, *The Emperor,* or *The Beast in Landscape,* 1990, watercolor on paper, dimensions unknown. Collection and photo: the artist.

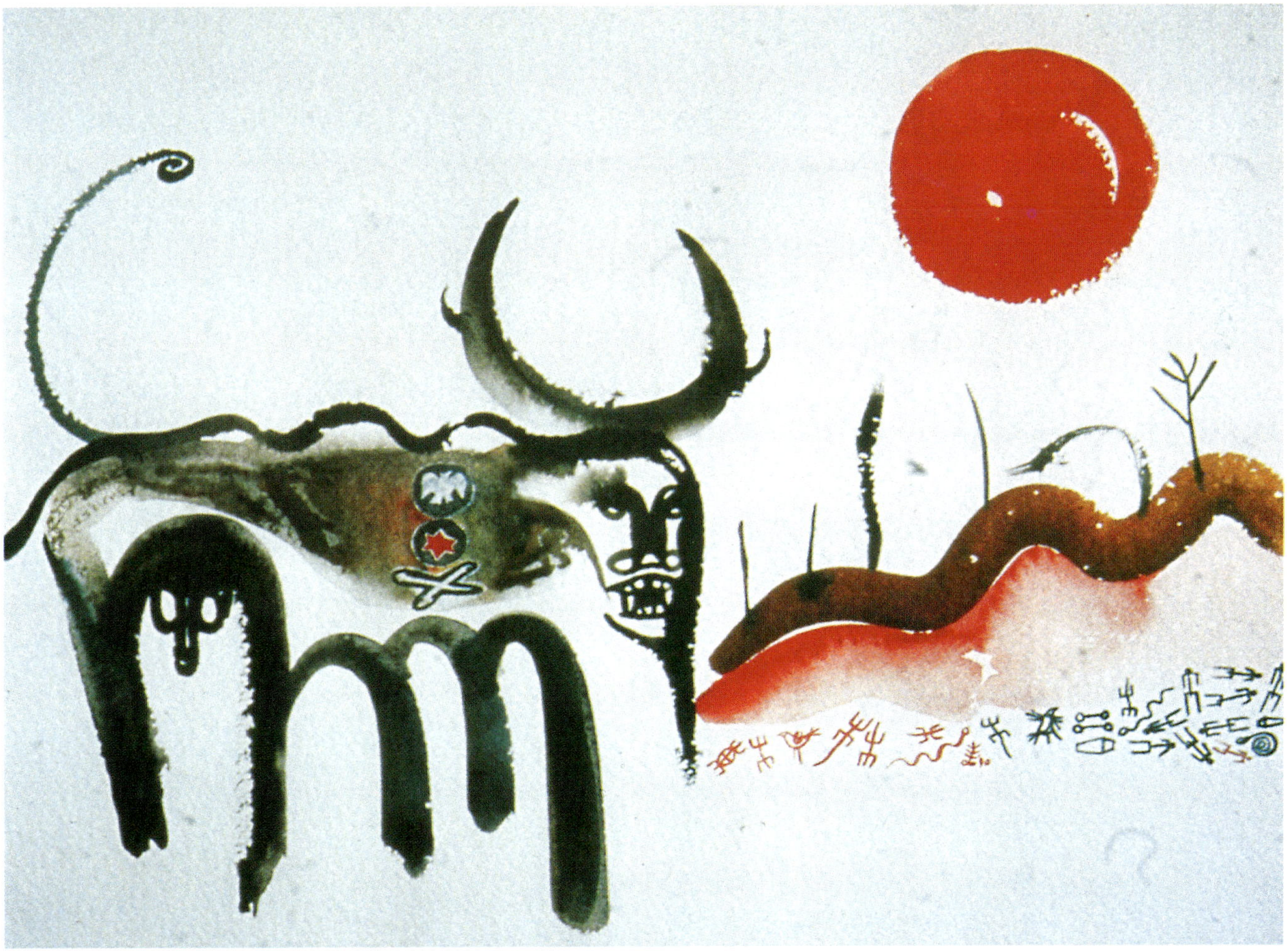

Obiọra Udechukwu's, the minstrel stands with his *ubọ* ("thumb piano" in popular parlance). The poet's dress expresses the flamboyance of these professionals, the red cap that he is well respected, the *ichi* facial scarification, found in central Igbo groups, that he is titled. The work shows delicate use of watercolor lines.

Another watercolor in the exhibition, *The Poet among His People* (1990; fig. 181), finds the poet standing second from the left among three standing figures. All four have variations of *mbari* wall designs on them; the poet's face is delineated in the style of a white-faced Igbo mask. As a child, Oguibe had seen ruined *mbari* houses, though not at home, and later visited the artist S. A. O. Chukueggu and his contemporary Mbari center at Mbaisẹ in Igbo country, which had *mbari* wall designs.[36] Oguibe was also familiar with Herbert M. Cole's book on *mbari* houses (fig. 182).[37] In this watercolor, Oguibe drew from designs painted on some *mbari* pillars; so he made his figures tall. The poet is not him, he told me, but all poets. The work relates to an earlier work of his of someone standing among his people, drawing from Christopher Okigbo's poetry. Oguibe later moved away from Okigbo's influence in his visual art.

Another watercolor in the exhibition, *The Emperor,* or *The Beast in Landscape* (1990; fig. 183), seems to be a bull trampling on a field, but he has the insignia of an army general on his body, and there is scorched earth at his right, below which, as if buried in the earth, are small animal and human figures and a casket. The painting's reference to Nigeria is generalizable to all military dictatorships, to death and deprivation through politics. In the artist's Igbo village, the bull, a smaller forest variety than the larger, more common savannah form in Nigeria's north, is a sacred totemic animal, allowed to roam freely. The picture thus plays on relationships between Nigerian politics and Igbo culture.

Oguibe's untitled, three-paneled work in mixed media (1990–91, acrylic on board, feathers, wood, plastic Catholic rosaries; fig. 184) has four wood *ikenga* figures bracketed by sticks in the center panel (*ikenga* is a popular male spirit sculpture found in Igboland).[38] The white center panel contrasts with two green side panels; together they represent the Nigerian flag. A rosary and four feathers in the central section—symbols of Christian and indigenous religions—signify the diversity of Nigeria's religious life. The work thus suggests unity and diversity in Nigeria rather than being a political critique—unusual for Oguibe. It is postmodern in its placing together of differing cultural and religious elements, foreshadowing Oguibe's moves in that direction.

An untitled, four-part watercolor on paper (1990; fig. 185) places an *adinkra* cross-lizard design at the lower left. Above it is a bull-like creature, to its right the sacred Igbo python, *eke*, which relates to intelligence and creativity, according to the artist. Beneath this is a motif of Oguibe's creation, standing for the Igbo market, traditionally occurring one day in the four-day week. The work, referring to African life, is signed in two places and can be viewed horizontally or vertically.

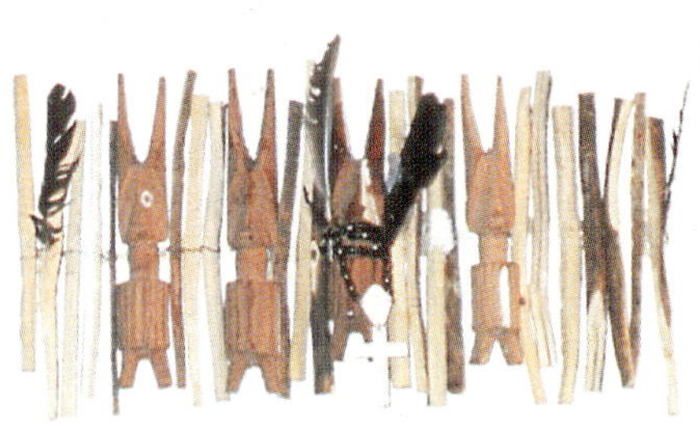

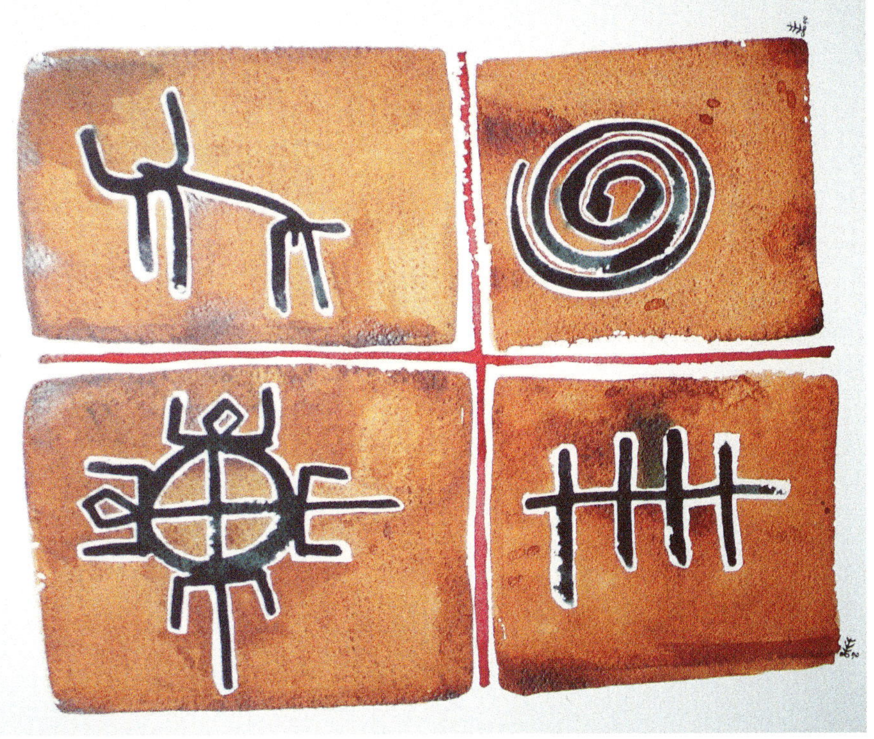

**184 (FACING PAGE)**. Ọlu Ọguibe, untitled, 1990–91, mixed media: wood, feathers, plastic Catholic rosaries, acrylic on board, dimensions unknown. Collection and photo: the artist.

**185.** Ọlu Ọguibe, from the *Totem Series,* 1990, watercolor. 57.2 × 63.5 cm. Collection of Simon Ottenberg.

**186.** Ọlu Ọguibe, from the *Totem Series,* 1991, acrylic on paper, dimensions unknown. Collection of Simon Ottenberg.

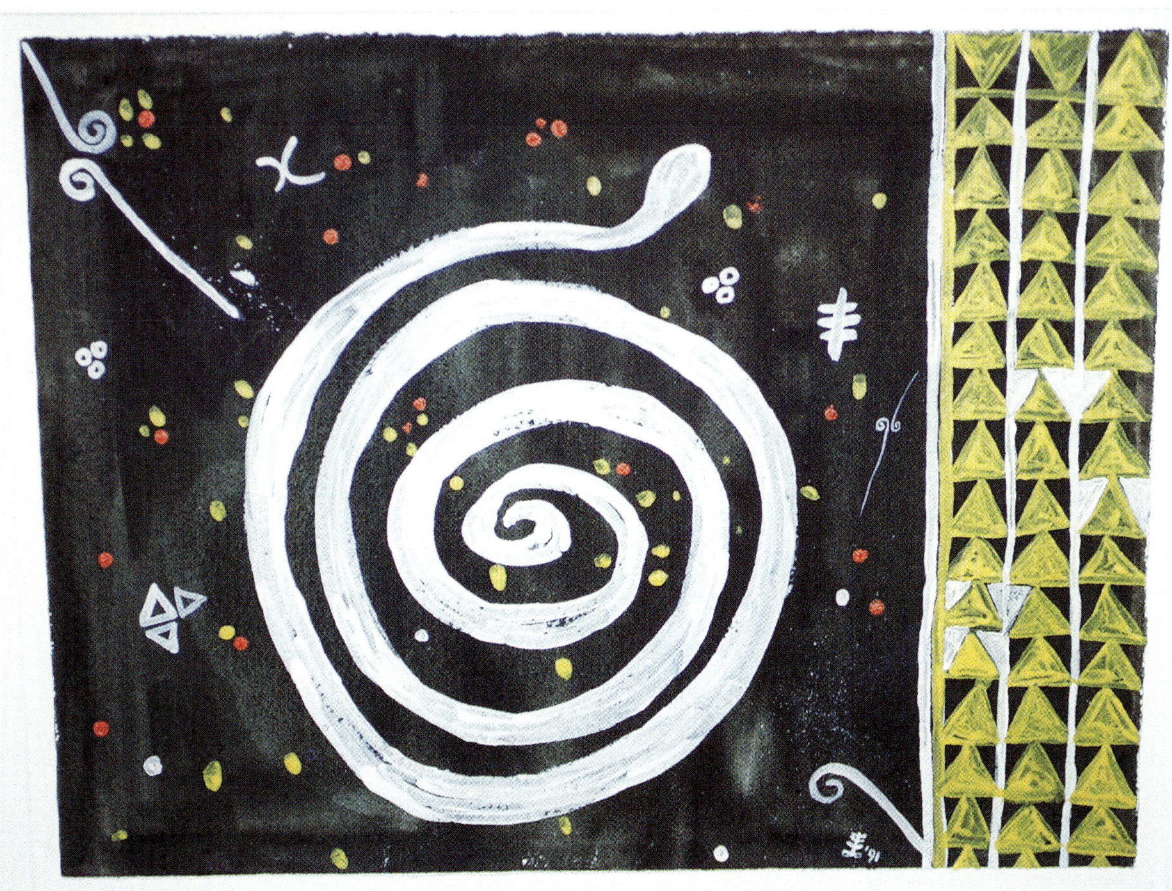

Another untitled work (1991, acrylic on paper; fig. 186) is part of Oguibe's *Totem Series,* whose images consist of sacred animals from Igbo and other cultures. We see another Igbo *eke* serpent, with *mbari* designs at the right, according to the artist (which could also stand for the *uli* leopard's claw, *mbọ agu*). He takes delight in the occasional reversal of *mbari* triangles in white or at times in yellow, relating this to jazz improvisation, where a musician suddenly "breaks off" and then returns. Conscious departures from a set design pattern are not rare in traditional African art. The stars surrounding the python provide a celestial quality to the work, reminding one of some *uli* murals, and there are three separate white lines with spiral ends that also have *uli* qualities, as well as a possible *nsibidi* motif. The python design, similar to an Asafo flag snake motif from Ghana, occurs in a number of Oguibe's works in the immediate years after 1991, and it is not always clear to the viewer when it relates to *uli* or Asafo or is simply a design element.[39] Oguibe continued to employ *mbari,* and occasionally *nsibidi,* during much of his time in Europe.

In the *Totem Series,* about 1990–92 (figs. 187, 188), each work involves a bird, a bull, or a python. Oguibe once told me that he likes to believe the snake is his totem—it has never bitten him. These are simple, two-dimensional forms, outlined or otherwise without much detail, generally against a monochromatic background. Totemic animals are common in Igbo country, often one to a village, particularly the python, which is not killed or eaten but left to roam. The works in the *Totem Series* are elemental and focused, without the busy quality of Oguibe's paintings on mats and baskets.

Many of Oguibe's early works in Europe, mostly in London, suggest his nostalgia for Nigeria, a looking back, a drawing on known cultural resources and artistic skills. Another artist told me that Oguibe "brought *uli* to London."

Some of the art discussed here was also exhibited in 1991 at the Commonwealth Institute's Bhownagree Gallery in London, where Oguibe also planned to show eight enamel on mat paintings he had made in Nigeria and exhibited in Lagos.[40] But a conflict arose, as the Institute refused to hang two of the eight pieces on the

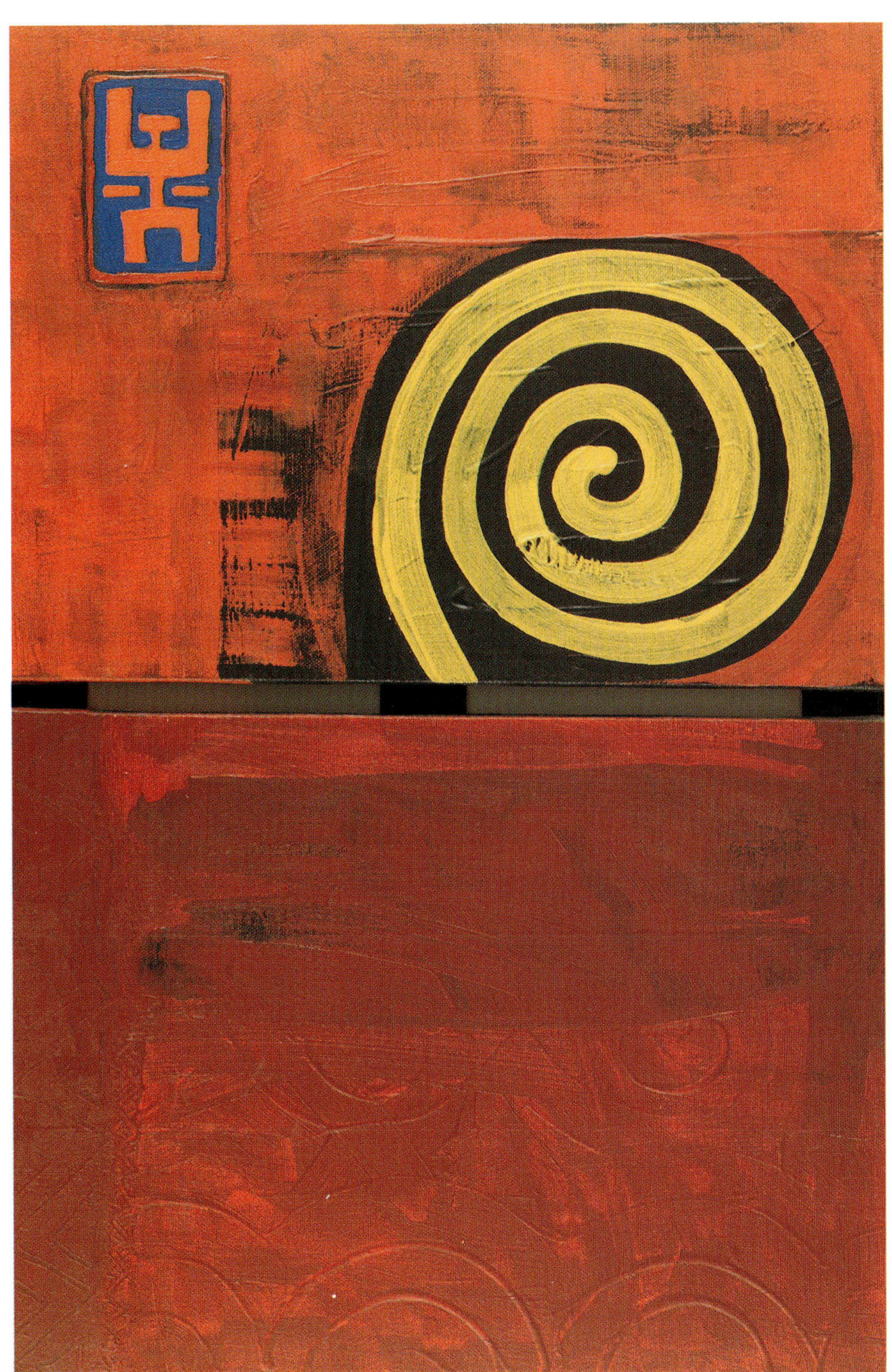

**187 (FACING PAGE).** Ọlu Ọguibe, *Totem Series 2,* c. 1990–92, acrylic on canvas. 190 × 150 cm. Collection of the artist. Photo: Franko Khoury.

**188 (LEFT).** Ọlu Ọguibe, *Totem Series 7,* c. 1990–92, acrylic on canvas, two panels. 76.2 × 61 cm each. Collection of the artist. Photo: Franko Khoury.

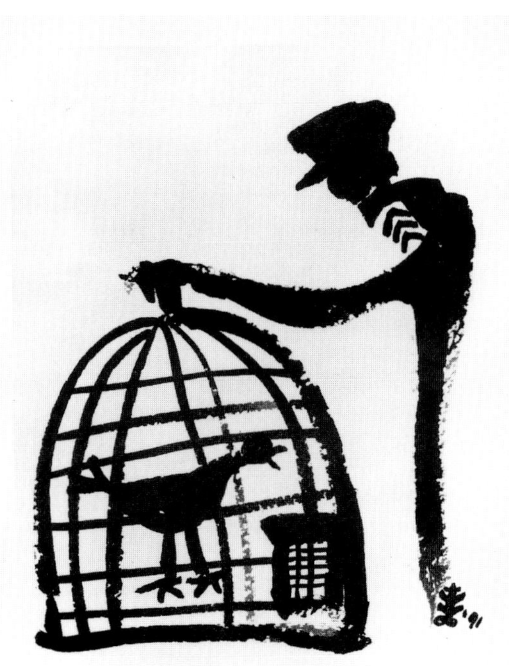

**189 (ABOVE).** Ọlu Ọguibe, untitled, 1991, ink and brush on paper, dimensions unknown. From Ọguibe 1992b, 32. Collection unknown.

**190 (RIGHT).** Ọlu Ọguibe, untitled, 1990, ink on paper, dimensions unknown. From Ọguibe 1990a, 12. Collection unknown.

grounds that they were improper for children to see. One contained the phrase "Fuck the President" and the other "Fuck Makontiri" (i.e., "My Country"), among numerous words and phrases on the paintings. Ọguibe objected and refused to let the other six pieces stand; to him, all eight formed a whole. As the gallery refused to relent, Ọguibe withdrew all eight paintings.[41] The row over the matter brought Ọguibe publicity; it did not detract from the view of some that he was an "angry young artist."

In 1992 Ọguibe held an exhibition at London's Savannah Gallery, *A Gathering Fear: Drawings,* along with the publication of his book of poems, *A Gathering Fear.* The art in brush and ink, some reproduced in the publication, largely consists of human figures.[42] There is a man in ankle irons linked to a ground stake, with a locked prison door nearby; he sits with head bowed, his elbows on his knees. Other drawings show three standing figures, each bound to a stake, a hanging human figure, a prisoner behind bars, a bird in a large cage held by a ghostly military figure (fig. 189), and a man with a long staff carrying a huge load on his back to a nearby town. The wide brush technique in the drawings makes for strong, simple figures, with a silhouette quality. They resonate with the mood of the poems, which are somber and mostly concerned with degeneration, cruelties, and iniquities in Nigeria. The qualities of the drawings and poetry reinforce each other.

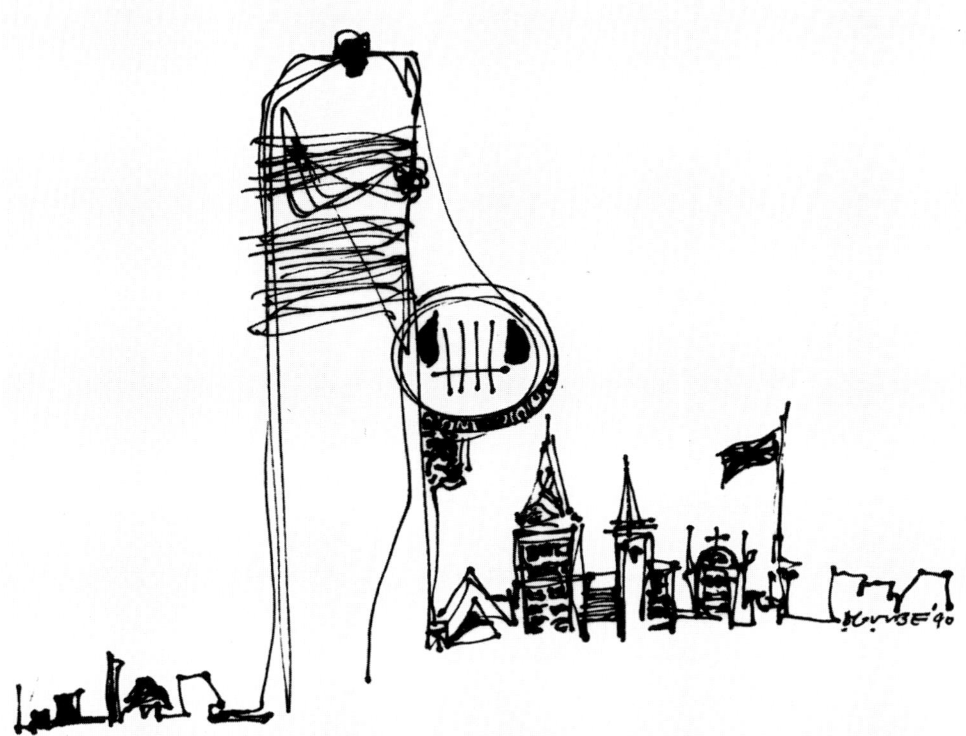

Ọguibe's briefer first poetry book, *A Song from Exile,* also contains drawings, some made before leaving Nigeria and some after, which express similar feelings in the verse on Nigerians in exile.[43] The drawings, mainly in thin-lined pen and ink, are nevertheless forceful, as is the poetry. Verse and visual art sometimes echo Obiọra Udechukwu. There is a fine drawing of an Igbo minstrel with his *ubọ* instrument, his arms and body bound in cords, with what seems to be a British flag and an English village at his side (fig. 190). Ọguibe's drawing skills in ink continue. In 1994 in Friedberg, Germany, he produced more than three hundred of them.

## LATER WORK IN EUROPE AND ELSEWHERE

Ọguibe has also created complex images. In his *Painter* (1993, mixed media: acrylic on canvas, trousers; fig. 191), he returns to employing writing in art. Here we see Arabic script from a poem, "The Wandering Guitar Player," by the major Palestinian poet and former PLO member Maḥmūd Darwīsh (from his *The Music of Human Flesh*), a man whose verse is as political as Ọguibe's.[44] "A Painter he was, but pictures . . ." is in Ọguibe's work, but the rest of the line, "normally open no doors," is not, the whole capturing Ọguibe's realism at that time. Ọguibe sees the painting as a transition; now his political art is about his status in Europe dealing with European issues. He feels that not finishing the sentence heightens the work (and perhaps, I think, Ọguibe's own sense of his ambiguity in Europe).

In interpreting the painting, Ọguibe suggests that the blue section is perhaps a reflection of mortality, and the red writing on the right side, which begins with "There is a great fire raging in my house," is associated with neo-fascist attitudes on German minorities and on Asians in Britain at the time, but it is also drawn from a line in a poem by Obiọra Udechukwu. The red footprint in the blue side is about immigration, emigration, and exile, refer-ring to the title of Darwīsh's poem (and undoubtedly to Ọguibe himself). The trousers astride the red and blue sec-tions suggest movement to Ọguibe, from the red as home to the blue as Europe, the pants on the two colors sym-bolize exile, something Ọguibe was still concerned about, though he had turned toward Europe in many ways. In the blue there is: "If Tomorrow/This/Heart/Stops Beating," and below it enclosed within lines: "EUROPE/WILL KILL ME YET." The triangles on the right derive from *uli* murals; Ọguibe is not specific as to what *uli* form they repre-sent. Ọguibe sees the work as both modernist and postmodernist—the trousers as reminiscent of American mod-ernism, the writing on the canvas as postmodernist. The eclecticism of sources stands out, though the central themes are exiles and minorities in a not very welcoming Europe.

About 1993, Ọguibe became attracted to the colorful appliqué and embroidered flags of the Asafo companies of the Fante of coastal Ghana.[45] He created a number of acrylics on canvas derived from these flags, with simply delineated images on a monochrome background, all or partially decorated with border designs—often different-colored squares or triangles.

One such work, *Martyr* (1993; fig. 192), refers to an unpublished poem by Ọguibe concerning peace in Jerusalem. The male figure with his hands raised in prayer appears to be a Muslim, Ọguibe tells me, but he could also be an Israeli. There is a dove and olive branch signifying peace. Ọguibe originally intended his poem to be in the work, but later he felt that would make the painting too specific. The artist is thinking of broad issues of peace. It is not clear whether the Asafo designs on the border of paintings like this one are meant as decorative contrast to the central images, whether they refer the work to Africa, or whether the artist is simply attracted by the border designs' aesthetic qualities. Ọguibe's signature in the upper left-hand corner is another Ghanaian refer-ent, an *adinkra* motif for resilience, derived from the perennial fern, from Aṣante culture north of the Fante. To Ọguibe, the motif is a sign and the insignia of military invincibility, a design he was using before going to Europe. Here he is not suggesting militarism but rather resilience.

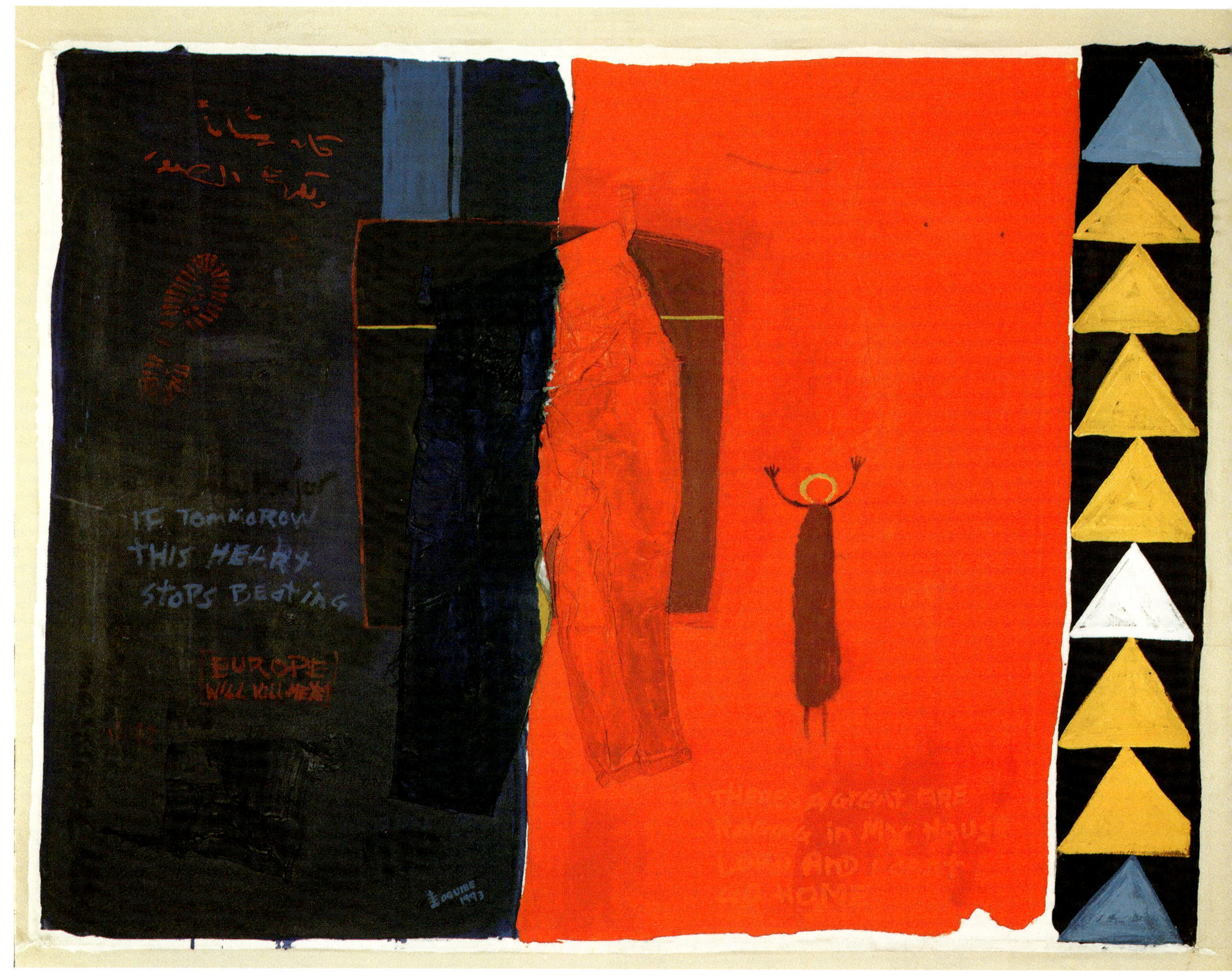


**191 (ABOVE).** Ọlu Ọguibe, *Painter,* 1993, mixed media: acrylic on canvas, trousers. 152 × 198 cm. Private collection. Photo: the artist.

**192 (FACING PAGE).** Ọlu Ọguibe, *Martyr,* 1993, acrylic on canvas. 190 × 190 cm. Collection and photo: the artist.

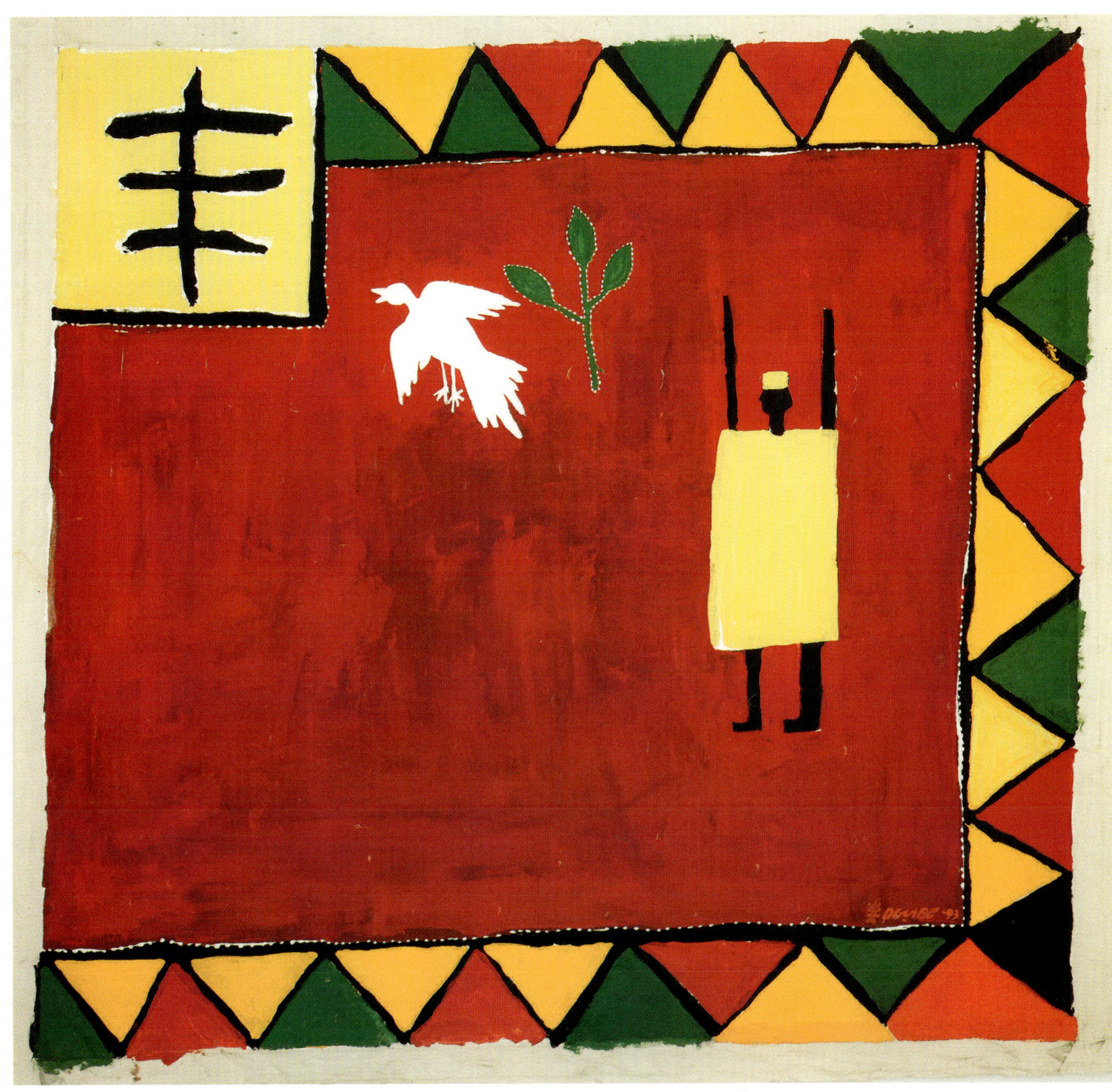

Ọguibe's several trips to Germany for workshops, to exhibit, present talks, and take part in video sessions interested him in German affairs. *Man Walking Dog* (1994, acrylic on canvas; fig. 193) has the bare images of a man and a dog, with Ọguibe's *adinkra* signature on the lower left and a Bavarian Catholic church steeple and red-roofed house at upper left. This is not a complex scene, though German men and dogs are hardly as thin as the work depicts. The work has the quality of his ink drawings.

More complex is *Mandela* (1994, mixed media: acrylic on canvas, photograph; fig. 194), created in Germany at the time of a major election. This large work (190 cm high and 250 cm wide) has a black-and-white photograph of Nelson Mandela at upper center. Mandela had become president of the Union of South Africa not long before the painting was made. The names of the two contesting German leaders, (Rudolf) Scharping and (Helmut) Kohl are on it, with question marks after them, suggesting to Ọguibe that many Germans could not tell the difference between them. There is reference to German racism through the words on the canvas, "Gegen Nazi" ("Down with the Nazis"), and a crossed-out swastika, invoking both the extreme German political right and opposition to it. There is a German sentence incorrectly written ("spreche sie deutch"), meaning "Do you speak German?" suggesting that it was written by an immigrant, a reference to the immigrant question in Germany. There is the name "Susu," the name of the daughter of Ọguibe's host at Friedberg, Germany, where the work was created. The name MANDELA occurs in good-sized letters, and "amigo" in smaller ones, and there is a bicycle, an airplane, and a soldier with a gun in the work. Another written reference is to a Bavarian soccer club. There is Ọguibe's *adinkra* signature and the popular West African saying found on lorries: "No Condition Is Permanent." Ọguibe has suggested to me that the only central theme of this work, where German, West African, and South African elements

193 (RIGHT). Ọlu Ọguibe, *Man Walking Dog,* 1994, acrylic on canvas, dimensions unknown. Collection of the artist.

194 (FACING PAGE). Ọlu Ọguibe, *Mandela,* 1994, mixed media. 190 × 250 cm. Collection of the artist. Photo: Norbert Aas.

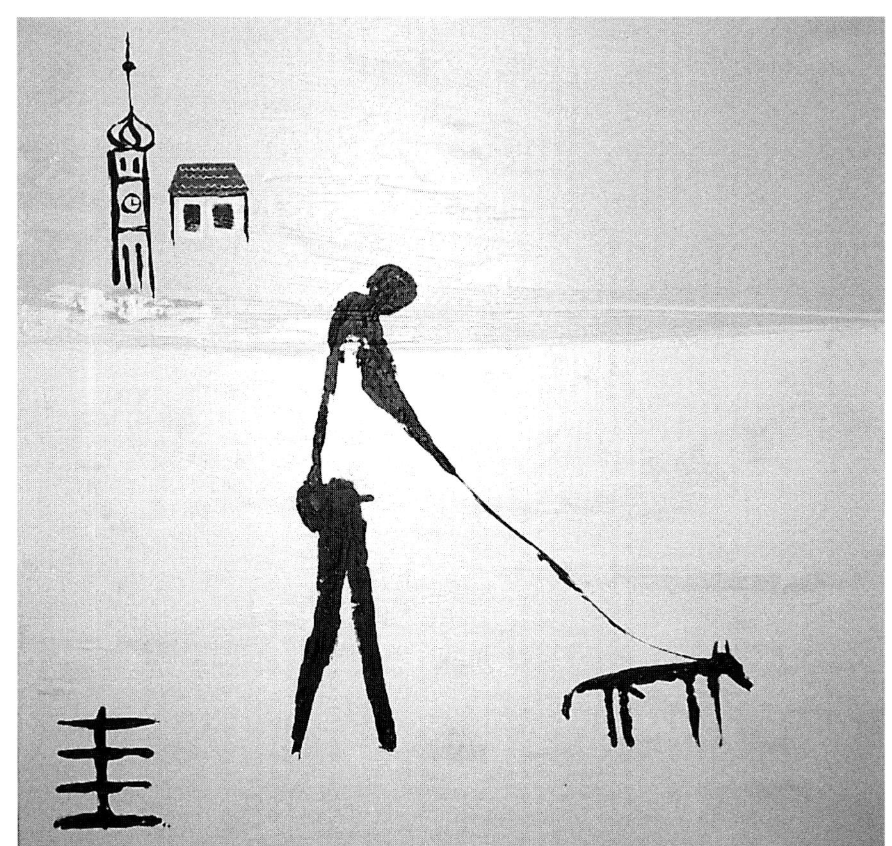

do not seem directly to connect, is the idea expressed in that African saying. To me, *Mandela* also represents Ọguibe's postmodern inclinations in a multicultural world, with rapid movement of people and materials, everything in contact with everything else.

Ọguibe's eclecticism in drawing from apparently unrelated sources, and his postmodernist inclination to employ writing to get his messages across, shows this work to be daring, but rather centerless, though perhaps Ọguibe would say that the world is centerless today. But the messages are so disparate that the work's aesthetic qualities suffer.[46] The large size of the canvas suggests Euro/American modernism rather than Nsukka art, where the pictures are generally smaller, perhaps because of economic factors. Ọguibe has continued to work in large format at times.

Visiting Mexico in 1993, he not only explored Mexican art but once met briefly a young Mexican, Catalina. This acted as a catalyst in Ọguibe's art and led to a book of poems, *Songs for Catalina*.[47] The book's poems are love verses; several of them also refer to the Biafran war, the Nigerian situation, or to persons mysteriously disappearing in Argentina. The large acrylic on canvas, *Two Lovers by the Rio Santa Catarina* (1994; fig. 195), shows an indistinctly portrayed pair standing side by side in semidarkness, a blue crescent moon overhead and a blue river running down the center from top to bottom. Against a swirling green background with colored specks, we see colored square borders of Asafo flags and an *adinkra* sign for love at the upper left. The colors are attractive to the eye. In sharp contrast to his 1994 *Mandela* painting, this work is highly focused. It and the love poems reflect another side of Ọguibe—passionate and unabashed affection. One misses the bite of his political art but cheers the very human feeling of love he projects.

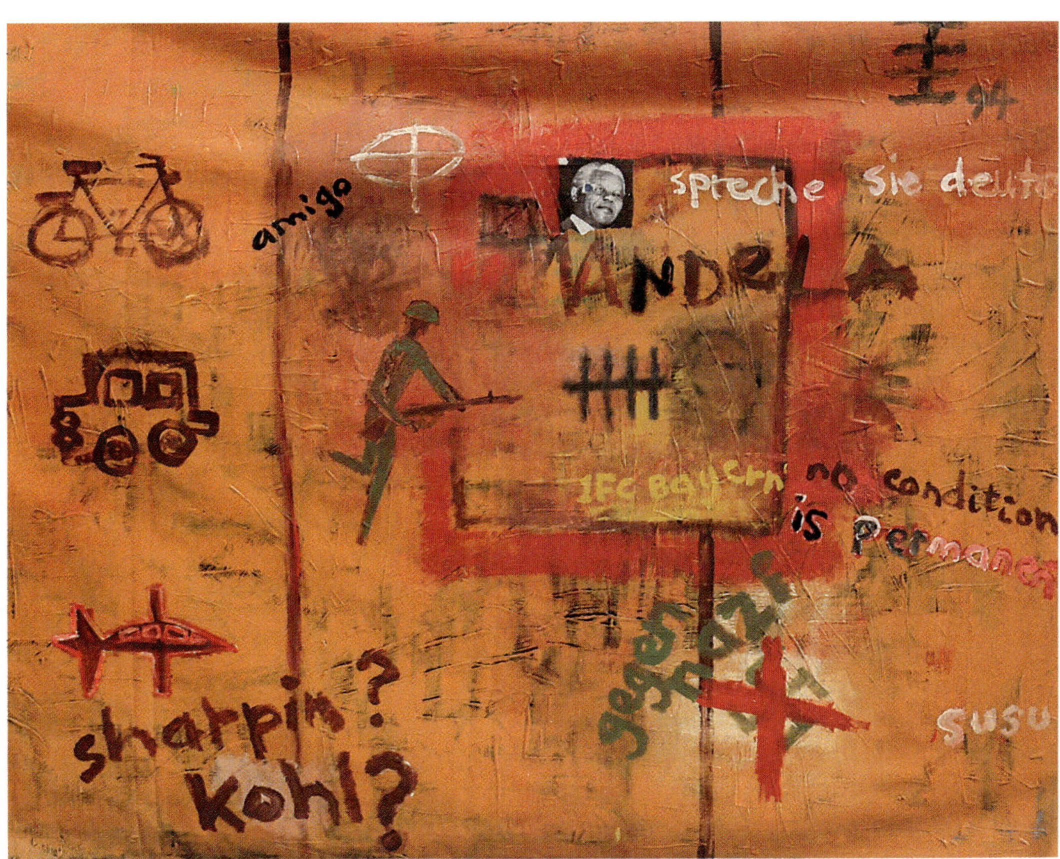

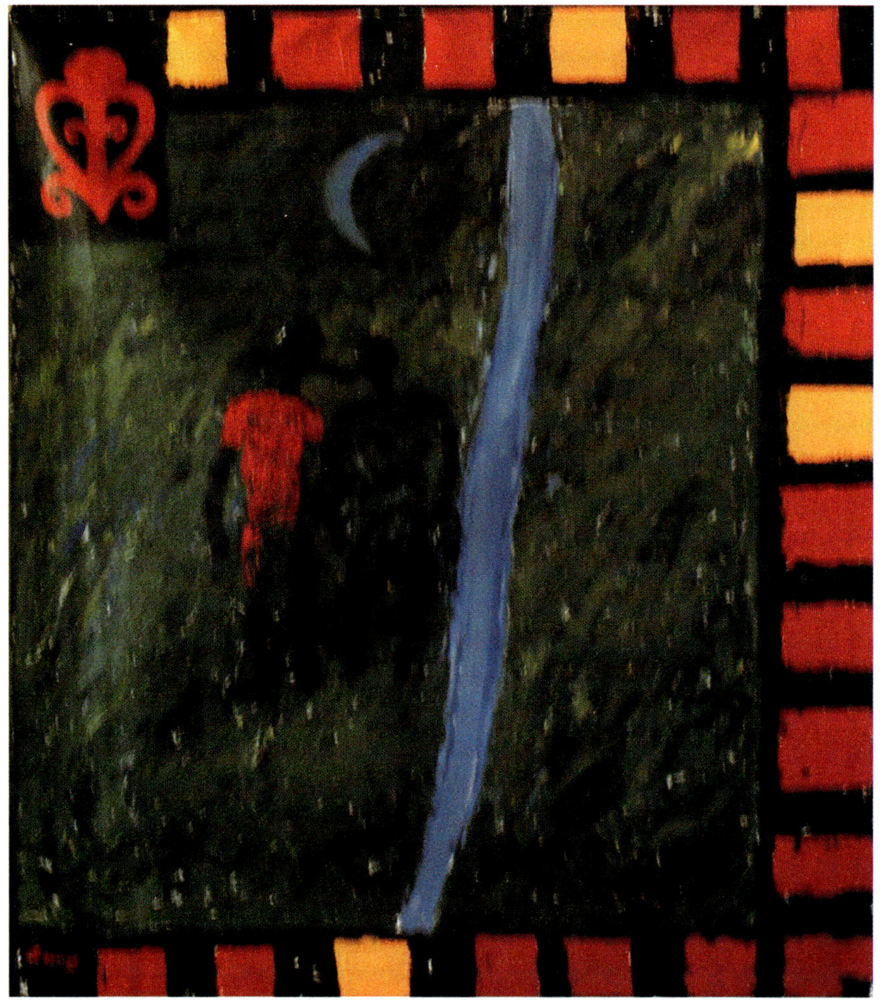

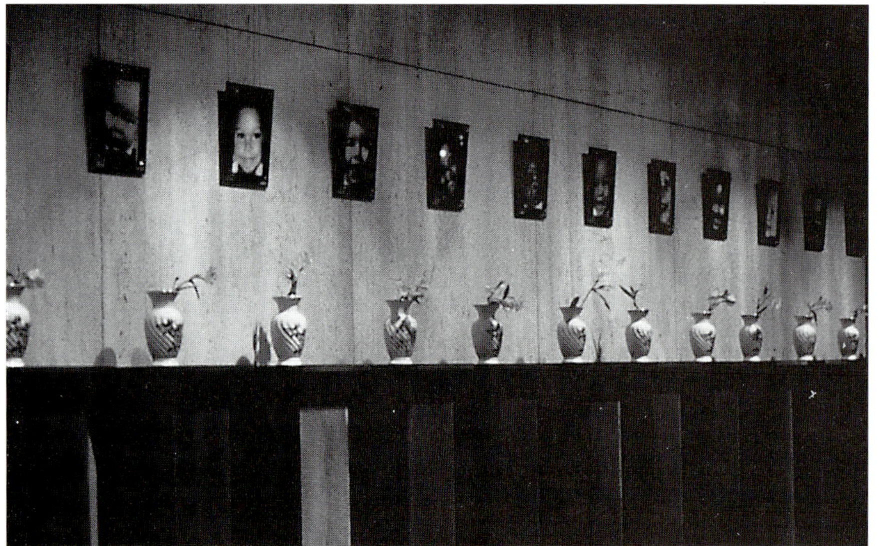

**195 (TOP LEFT).** Ọlu Ọguibe, *Two Lovers by the Rio Santa Catarina,* 1994, acrylic on canvas, dimensions unknown. Collection and photo: the artist.

**196 (TOP RIGHT).** Ọlu Ọguibe, *Requiem,* 1993, mixed-media installation. 152 cm high. Collection and photo: the artist.

**197 (BOTTOM LEFT).** Ọlu Ọguibe, large detail from *Oklahoma,* 1995, mixed-media installation, c. 4.8 m long. Collection and photo: the artist.

Another 1994 work, untitled and also large, in oil pastel, depicts Catalina's face in photocopy repeated twelve times in four rows of three, lightly washed over in differing colors. There is writing below this, lines from a Mexican poet:

> . . . Your eyes are like the sea
> Upon which my yearning crashes
> With the impatience of waves

This mixed-media work, which Oguibe considers minor compared to the one above, is in a contemporary Euro/American style of blending photography and painting, as the acrylic of the two lovers is in the style of earlier art forms.

In Sydney, Australia, in 1994, Oguibe prepared for an exhibition at the Roslyn Oxley9 Gallery by creating his works in a small basement studio in the city's Italian neighborhood. He was in contact with Aborigines, their ancient and current art, and he produced works that draw on their sacred art. In one small untitled sketch, he opposes a boomerang, which is also the head of a human, to an image of a television set. Oguibe indicates that the work is more or less in postmodern mode, with its collapse of history, its representations of the past and the present. Oguibe's interest in art criticism and art history intertwine in his art. It is not usually clear in his art whether theory or image come first; perhaps they come together.

Oguibe has produced installation art since 1992, without giving up other media.[48] A main theme is the worldwide suffering of children, which links to his childhood memories of the Biafran war. His installations are not specifically concerned with Nigeria but present a broader, sometimes worldwide stage, including Euro/America, and concern not only the impact of war on children but childhood abuse and neglect. In *Requiem* (1993, mixed media; fig. 196), on a black platform, 152 cm high, four dressed white dolls lie on their backs, feet toward the viewer, with a photograph above them, framed in black, of a white child. Anthony Ilona writes that the installation "is a memorial to a dead child. The daguerreotype texture of the sad-eyed portrait temporarily evokes the early part of this century and somehow suggests a war child."[49] The tall black box suggests a coffin and the dead.

In the fall of 1995, following the bombing in Oklahoma City that killed many children, Oguibe exhibited an installation, *Oklahoma* (mixed media: photographs, tall wood stands, ceramic vases with flowers; fig. 197), at the gallery of the *Economist* in London. This roughly 5 meter-long work, with twelve photographs of children killed in the explosion, had vases with stands beneath each one. And in 1996 in the United States, Oguibe developed an open cardboard container, 61 cm square, with four dressed dolls lying side by side in it, entitled *Mementos*. In these works he evokes issues of violence against children, the victims of war, crimes, deprivation, and famine.

These memorials to children, related to Oguibe's own childhood wartime experience, are focused and simple in design. He is not only thinking of Africa—Rwanda and Somalia—and other third world countries but also of Euro/American children who suffer in war and from abuse and neglect. Oguibe is now, as in part of his *Mandela* acrylic, able to aim his interest on Euro/America; Nigeria may form part of a total picture in some of his art, but it is no longer the major part.

## ART CRITICISM AND ART THEORY

Oguibe's writings on art differ considerably from those of most Nsukka artists, as he has located himself in terms of the art discourses of contemporary Euro/America (he prefers the term "West") as both an insider and an outsider. His views importantly relate to his artistic creations. I cannot fully summarize his writings, nor can I make use of more than a few points from his discussions and correspondence with me.[50]

Ọguibe is very aware of the power of Euro/America in determining the nature and direction of art discourse, as this is where the art market largely resides and where the academic interests and most art criticism of the theoreticians lie. He is an outsider critic of Euro/American views on art, particularly art beyond that geographic area. Skeptical of Western conceptions of history, which determine what the art history periods are and their categories of classifications for non-Euro/American art—such as primitive, popular, modern—he desires the discourses on art not to center on Euro/America but to have many centers in the world, each receiving equal treatment, with exchanges among them.[51] Euro/American writing locates African and other third and fourth world art in specific external spheres, which the artists and writers from these areas often succumb to, because of the power of Euro/America and its art market. But Ọguibe is skeptical of applying Euro/American notions of modernism to African art, rejecting its exoticization of this art and resisting Euro/Americans' speaking for the "native." "Otherization is unavoidable, and for every One, the Other is the Heart of Darkness. The West is as much the Heart of Darkness to the Rest as the latter is to the West."[52] He urges an equalization of discourse rather than its domination by Euro/America.

He is also critical of endless theorizing by Euro/Americans on art in general and African art, which prevents viewing the reality of what contemporary African art is about. While there is an interest in the rise of a new internationalism in the arts, and Ọguibe has interests here, he is suspicious of it as this began in Euro/America and is ultimately linked to its power and global politics.[53] Ọguibe sees himself as a postmodernist in theory and in art practice, but again he is suspicious of its Euro/American origins and the dominance of its art discourse. Ọguibe is much concerned with the often unstated racism in the arts, linked to a tendency to control art discourse. Thus there is a strong need to decenter discourse from Euro/America. Euro/American attitudes toward art and artists elsewhere can be patronizing and concerned with maintaining control, fitting the art and artists of the rest of the world into Euro/American concepts rather than reworking their ideas to fit realities.

Ọguibe argues that one cannot look at art alone; one has to look at the general attitudes and orientations of Euro/America—often self-serving—in maintaining their dominant position in the art world, as elsewhere, views that inform their artistic interests. He is critical of Euro/America's definitions of who are the interesting artists and its selections of which ones to exhibit, which, for Africa, tend to focus on the naive artists, the exotic, the folk-style contemporary artists, such as Cheri Samba of Zaire, Middle Art of Nigeria, and the Oṣogbo artists rather than more technically skilled artists, whether academically trained or not, such as Ibrahim el Salahi and Uzọ Egọnu.[54] The latter type of artist is largely unrecognized in Euro/America, and Ọguibe places himself in this category.

Euro/America pays low prices for contemporary African and other non-Euro/American art, reflecting its attitude toward it, its creators, and the cultures from which it derives. Euro/American art theorists do not recognize the existence of indigenous art theory in African contemporary art, as in Nigeria, the ideas of Aina Ọnabolu, those of the genre group, Ben Enwọnwu, the Zaria artists, the Nsukka, Ọna, and Oṣogbo artists.[55] The use of the term *ethnic,* formerly *tribe,* in reference to the arts of many people categorizes them in demeaning ways rather than recognizing the artists' individualities, their own histories and traditions in a positive light. He calls this "neo-primitivizing" African art. He sees Euro/American approaches to African art as pornographic. What is desired by Euro/America in contemporary African art is "the fantastic, the fetishistic and shamanist . . . a pornographic desire for the subnormative."[56] The elaborately carved burial caskets of Kane Kwei, which in their home in Ghana have quite specific relationships to death and burial, become a folk art in Euro/America. Euro/America tends to see contemporary African art as in a sort of no-man's land, either mimicking Europe's supposedly superior creations, thereby denying it its authenticity, or imitating its own past.

Oguibe has become a spokesperson to change Euro/American views of the art of the rest of the world, which requires changes in views of Euro/American art itself. He has sought the multiplicity of artistic discourse, visiting Mexico and Australia and drawing from their art but also from Ghana, the Near and Middle East and elsewhere. His horizons are wide.

**CONCLUSION**

In his visual art, Oguibe has put great distance between his Nsukka university days and the present, more so than other artists of the Nsukka group. Others will undoubtedly follow similar paths in the future. El Anatsui, while still living and teaching at Nsukka, though not trained there, follows a differing worldwide path. From an artist concerned with university and national Nigerian affairs, Oguibe has moved to worldwide interests. From Nsukka styles he has gone on to larger aesthetic concerns in the Euro/American postmodern world. He has moved from the Nsukka art theories to third world theoretical interests. He has gone from drawing on Igbo motifs and aesthetics to extracting from any culture, any nation, as he will. Traditional African art sometimes drew from elsewhere than from home, but the geographic area involved was often small; Oguibe's interests are worldwide.

Yet, in certain ways, Oguibe still retains commonality with Nsukka artists. This is so in expressing social and political matters through art. Other associations include his linking of poetry and visual art and his penchant for art criticism and writing about art. His work, as with Nsukka artists, carries a high level of symbolic content, even as Nigerian symbols are replaced by others. There is similarity in his acceptance of academia as a possible training and hosting place for the artist. Yet the major thrust of Oguibe's art has been away from the Nsukka group, with its emphasis on drawing skills and its links to the Igbo past.

He is intensely curious, mobile, and investigative, as his widespread travels indicate, willing to try the new, to experiment with what for him are new media and in differing styles. His art varies from the presentation of simple, focused works, such as his *Two Lovers by the Rio Santa Catarina*, to highly complex pieces with multiplex meanings, such as *Painter* and *Mandela*. The bull and the python, two sacred Igbo totems, appear a number of times in his art. Sacred beings, free to go wherever they want—this seems to fit Oguibe's sense of himself as an artist. Between Oguibe's political interests, his writing and editorial work, and his teaching, he cannot develop his visual art interests full-time, though this has not stopped him from moving along and changing artistically.

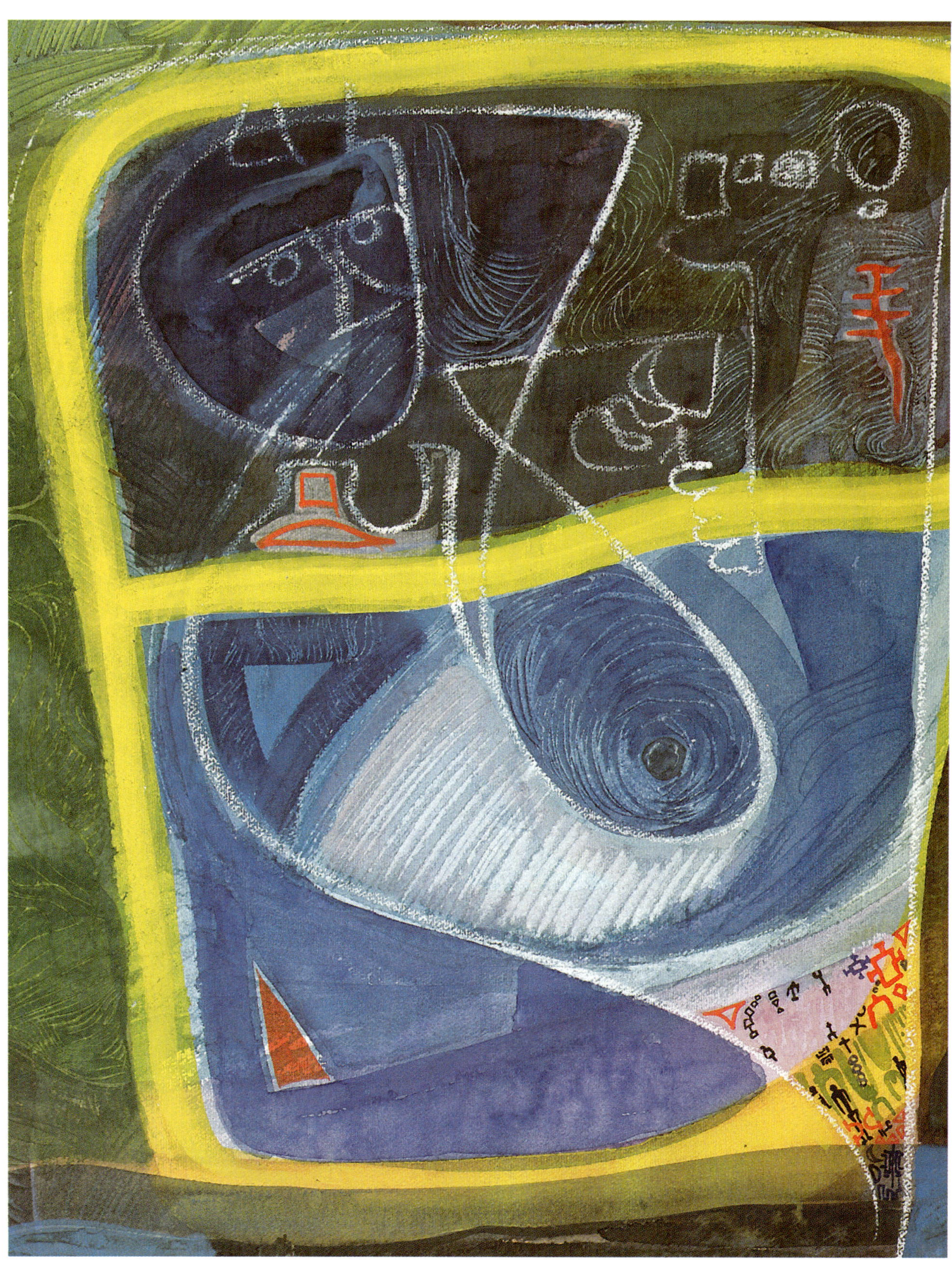

Detail of fig. 104.

# CONCLUSION

## PAST, PRESENT, AND FUTURE

The nineties will witness greater recognition and acceptance of serious contemporary Nigerian art abroad. Exhibitions of the works of Nigerian artists are increasingly featuring in the United States, Europe and Asia. It should not be long before the disdainful attitude which in the past characterised Euro-American perception of contemporary African art is replaced by a healthy appreciation.

FRANK AIG-IMOUKHUEDE[1]

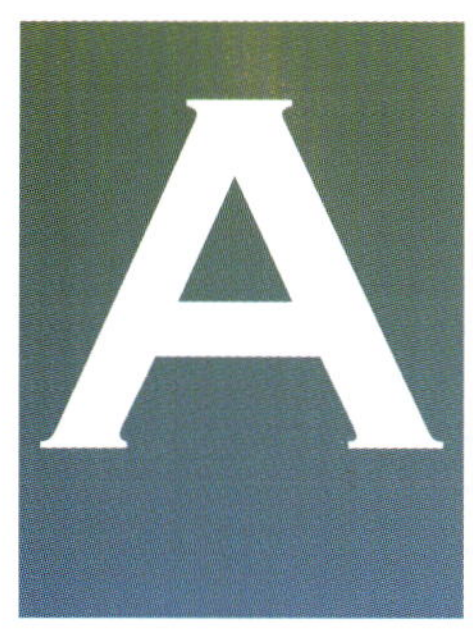

A s these seven artists live in today's Nigerian world and beyond it, they have made use of traditional cultures and art in crucial ways. It is not simply that they have drawn from indigenous cultures that continue in modified forms to the present and merge with it, but that the relationships of these artists to the past have changed over time. They have differing conceptions of what the past was and is and of those aspects that interest them today, varying senses of its significance in their art and lives, and of how the past relates to the present and the future.

## THE RELEVANCE OF THE PAST

These artists generally draw selectively from a past that existed in the first half of this century, whatever may have come before that. They have made use of published accounts, largely written by non-Africans, their own memories and those of relatives and others, and their own field research and those of their students. The artists rarely make specific claims that these indigenous elements—*uli, nsibidi, mbari, adinkra,* Ewe designs, masquerades and rituals, tales, minstrel songs, and others—are earlier than this century. It is primarily a relationship with their parents' and grandparents' days in cultures where family ties are quite strong. But there is an implied sense that some cultural elements are older, representing a deeper past, such as *uli* and *nsibidi,* a view encouraged by archaeological findings, such as at Igbo-Ukwu.[2] Whether past time is conceived of as short or long, it contrasts with the rapidly changing present in Nigeria, which has gone from colonialism to neocolonialism, to massive oil production and rapid development, and now to decline. The past is seen as an anchor of stable indigenous cultures, in contrast to an ever-changing present and an uncertain future, even if, in fact, the past went through numerous changes.

The past assists these seven artists to place themselves and to be identified by others, not only by their particular styles but by their cultural backgrounds, in a country where cultural identity is very important. This goes along with their various national, regional, and world identifications, with a sense of being African, and with identities associated with their profession, social class, education, place of residence, and religion. The Nsukka artists' uses of the past reinforce their relationships to one another and to the public. They know full well that African artists were esteemed and respected in the past; they hope for a like response today in a different world. Their middle-class, largely academic life provides them with respect as teachers, if not always as artists.

## INDIVIDUAL ARTISTS' INVOLVEMENT WITH THE PAST

Previous chapters have indicated differences among these seven artists, even if they may not be as individualistic as some Euro/American artists today. Complex relations of individualism and group activities characterize Igbo culture and certainly the Nsukka artists.[3] If there has been diversity in their art, as well as that of others associated with the University of Nigeria, Nsukka, they have arrived at their particular artistic viewpoints through experimentation over time. They sometimes use the term *experiment* to refer to their art. Their artistic positions vary as to how they integrate the past with the present and what styles and images they employ. Olu Oguibe has given up using *uli* and *nsibidi* motifs, but in recent work he has reflected on his childhood experiences during the Biafran war through installation art on the theme of childhood suffering everywhere. Obiora Udechukwu has minimized his use of specific *uli* and *nsibidi* elements in some of his 1993 acrylics created in Germany, but not their linear qualities. El Anatsui seeks new ideas for his sculpture through various African indigenous writing systems. There is a sense of freedom to explore and experiment, rather than a binding aesthetic. Experimentation has kept these artists from becoming stultified.

These seven artists make us aware of indigenous cultures in various ways, all forms of hybridity, the conscious or unconscious mixing of elements from different cultures. While all art is hybrid and all cultures are and have been, there is considerable interest today in this phenomenon.[4] Multiculturalism has become an important topic in postmodernist thought and in the social sciences, related to the increasing migration of peoples around the globe, the spreading movements of cultural revivalism, and the communications revolution. In this book it has been of interest to explore the particular experiences that have led to blendings of the present with the past. El Anatsui and Olu Oguibe explore and incorporate materials from non-Nigerian cultures in their art, Tayo Adenaike and El Anatsui have absorbed Igbo culture, though born elsewhere, and Tayo Adenaike and Obiora Udechukwu draw from *nsibidi*, which originated east of the Igbo. Uche Okeke and Chike Aniakor are the two artists most closely associated with Igbo culture; Ada Udechukwu draws from *uli* linear and spatial qualities, but her work is less markedly cultural than personal.

## UCHE OKEKE

For Uche Okeke, the past is an Igbo one. Though his Igbo interests are broad, they are focused on the Anambra area around his village of Nimo with its wonderful tales and mythical or spiritual figures. As with some of the other artists discussed in this book, Okeke only partially experienced Igbo culture in childhood, as he grew up away from home, though he also attended two secondary schools in Igbo country. His close attachment to his mother, his early exposure to a rich corpus of Igbo tales, and the early death of his father, which took away an important guide in his life and made him more self-propelled than he might otherwise have been, all directed his curiosity toward Igbo culture. He seriously explored it and then pressed his students to do likewise for their own cultures. In his adult life, Okeke developed his cultural center at his home at Nimo, after its start elsewhere, thus stating that his roots lay in Igboland as well as with the world of contemporary Nigerian art.

Okeke's art was and remains grounded in the past, reflecting Igbo culture, rather than current Nigerian social and political concerns, and focusing on Igbo tales, myths, and spiritual figures. Though he occasionally deals with Nigerian issues, such as in his oils, *The Conflict (After Achebe)* and *Aba Revolt,* he takes a historical view. Even in these works there is a component of tradition: the depiction of the masqueraders protesting against the mission in the first work, and the presence of a powerful, mythical Igbo female in the second. However, Okeke, as a university professor and a contemporary artist, has lived very much in the present. In the Nigerian contemporary art scene, he has, over time, persistently worked for the development of contemporary art and its teaching in schools. His retirement to Nimo in 1986 has blunted this effort, as Nimo is somewhat isolated and Okeke has lost the resources of an academic base.

Okeke's view is not to deny the past but to take it seriously, whatever one decides to do about it or however it is used. His conception of the past is idealized, yet it has led the Nsukka art students to pay attention to their own cultural backgrounds, whatever they do with this knowledge. In drawing from *uli* body painting and murals, Okeke modernized a style that fits well into contemporary art, particularly two-dimensional forms, which has readily been taken up by other Nsukka artists. Without proclaiming "We must save Igbo culture," he and his students and colleagues have helped to do just that through contemporary art. Okeke and other Nsukka artists and students also gave recognition to the importance of indigenous Igbo women's art, largely neglected by Euro/American scholars, and to the significance of female painting in traditional Igbo life, suggesting that it may have been neglected elsewhere in Africa. These uses of the past have been rewarding to Okeke, to other Nsukka artists, and to scholarship.

If Uche Okeke had not existed, would this trend to draw from the past among Nsukka artists have occurred? Probably it would have. The members of the Zaria Art Society, of which Okeke was only one, albeit a leader, held similar general ideas on the values of Nigerian cultures and spread them in the country, particularly in the south. Earlier, the work of Kenneth Murray's genre artists, and some of Akinọla Laṣekan's and Ben Enwọnwu's art, drew from indigenous cultures. The evidence from third and fourth world cultures, such as Native Americans and Australian Aborigines, is that similar uses of the past occur elsewhere.[5] Uche Okeke's orientation is an aspect of a world pattern, no matter how remarkable a development it has been within Nigeria and the effort it took to bring it about, nor how independently it arose. It is not denigrating the efforts of Okeke and others to say that the Nsukka art is part of a worldwide reaction to cultural suppression by the Euro/American world, taking different forms in different geographic and cultural areas. What is interesting about these artistic renaissances is why they occur at the time they do. What elements from the past do they draw upon, why these elements, and who makes the selection? In the case of Okeke and the Zaria Art Society artists, there is no doubt that the coming of independence in Nigeria stimulated their desire to draw from their cultures. Independence, despite the continual presence of European influence and of neocolonialism, created conditions for doing so. The fight for political freedom was mirrored by a fight for artistic freedom, not only in visual art but in literature, poetry, drama, and music.

Okeke might have moved with the "natural synthesis" concept toward depicting Igbo sculpture, rituals, *mbari* traditions, *nsibidi* motifs, everyday Igbo life, historic events, and the struggle of Igbos and other Nigerians against colonialism, but he did not do so to any extent. Those Igbo elements that he emphasized seem linked to his early life and his mother. He loves to draw, and this led him to Igbo women's painting rather than to Igbo sculpture.

The growth of the Nsukka artists is related *both* to social and political events in Nigeria in their time *and* to their personal life experiences. The particular blendings of these two form a basis of the Nsukka heritage. But there is a third factor. A fair number of the early Nsukka artists, including Uche Okeke, Chike Aniakọr, Obiọra Udechukwu, and Chuka Amaefunah, came from the Anambra area, inclining the Nsukka artists to draw from that Igbo subculture (even though it is not fully uniform), only later taking cultural elements more widely from other Igbo subregions, such as from the *nsibidi* area of southeast Igboland and the *mbari* region south of Anambra. That Anambra Igbo culture is strongly represented among Nsukka artists is not surprising. It has been exposed to intensive government and missionary European educational efforts during and after the colonial period, and its citizens have gone into professional fields of all sorts in substantial numbers, including the arts. So in addition to personal experiences and Nigerian sociopolitical factors, the shape of the work of the Nsukka artists has been influenced by a cultural/regional feature.

## CHIKE ANIAKỌR

Chike Aniakọr, only slightly younger than Uche Okeke, overlapped in time with him and the Zaria Art Society at Ahmadu Bello University. He was not a member, though developing in similar directions as Okeke toward Igbo culture, both independently and, though he might deny it, through Okeke's influence. But there are significant differences. Aniakọr did not have to move toward Igbo culture as Okeke did, who lived as a child in the north; Aniakọr was steeped in it from early childhood at home. Further, he has drawn more widely from Igbo culture outside the Anambra area in his art than has Okeke, as an art historian of the Igbo and a specialist on its architecture. Also, in recent years Aniakọr has been depicting political oppression and suffering in Nigeria, which Okeke has not greatly concerned himself with in his art.

Although also employing *uli,* Aniakọr's style differs from Okeke's, especially in Aniakọr's later work. While both artists employ *uli* linearity and spatial qualities, neither uses specific *uli* motifs to a large extent, even if Okeke's women's hair images have the quality of the *uli* yam tendrils motif and some of Aniakọr's lines refer to *uli* animal markings. Their images differ, too, for Aniakọr frequently employs numerous human figures with elongated bodies and limbs, features that do not characterize Okeke's work. Aniakọr's art also sometimes lacks the intensity of Okeke's.

## OBIỌRA UDECHUKWU

Obiọra Udechukwu, who was a student of Uche Okeke, reclaims from the past in differing ways than Okeke. Though his family home is in rural Anambra State, Udechukwu spent much of his childhood in Ọnitsha, not far away. This large, urban Igbo center has customs that differ somewhat from Agulu's, so he became bicultural within Igbo culture. Once committed to *uli* under Okeke's influence, Udechukwu has done much to explore its aesthetic qualities in his art and writings, building upon Okeke's knowledge. Udechukwu employs specific *uli* motifs in his art, such as the kola nut head and the crescent moon, more so than Okeke. He has been inspired by Igbo minstrels and poetry, rather than Igbo tales or spiritual figures as has Okeke, and by Christopher Okigbo's poetry. Udechukwu also introduced to Nsukka artists the use of *nsibidi* motifs, and he has explored the processes of varying and rearranging *uli* designs, stretching, extending, and modifying them, having a deep interest in *uli* and its aesthetics.

His art vigorously expresses social and political conditions in Nigeria and the suffering of ordinary people, sometimes in satiric form, building upon Igbo satire. These works are moral tales, each one telling a story, equivalent to traditional Igbo ones. Udechukwu, even more than Aniakọr, has moved the Nsukka artists toward a concern for current Nigerian conditions. He has shown students and others how to combine styles drawn from *uli* and *nsibidi* with commentaries on Nigerian life. He carries the natural synthesis idea further than Okeke, whose art remains closer to Igbo culture than to current Nigerian life; Udechukwu balances and integrates the two.

## EL ANATSUI

El Anatsui, from Ghana, does not always draw on *uli*. It is particularly present in the gouged and burnt lines of his wall panels. He also draws from other pasts—cloth designs from his Ewe culture, Ghanaian *adinkra* and *kente* cloth motifs, and other African designs. African cloths and their designs are basic to much of his art, important metaphors in his work. The other six Nsukka artists in this book occasionally draw from Igbo Akwete cloth patterns, but cloth is not a focus of their art. Anatsui also makes use of indigenous African written languages and languagelike systems. His constructed past is pan-African, not heavily focused on one culture. He has a strong interest in expressing in his art African views of African history and how these have been distorted by non-Africans. His art is sometimes concerned with the current Nigerian situation. The twin themes of destruction and regeneration are basic to his work. He has been technologically inventive in wood and ceramics.

## TAYỌ ADENAIKE

Tayọ Adenaike, though of Yoruba background, employs *uli* enthusiastically, using its motifs sometimes quite specifically. He has come to know *uli* design elements through his training at Nsukka and his close friendship with Obiọra and Ada Udechukwu. He has become particularly skilled in using *uli* in watercolors and in drawing from the background *akika* quality of its murals, as well as in using explicit *nsibidi* motifs. He explored his Yoruba background of tales and childhood experiences, and some of his numerous facial images suggest forms of Yoruba sculpture. He has also worked in acrylic and in oil. His art can be critical of Nigerian conditions. He is fully a member of the Nsukka artists' group; it is characteristic of the Nsukka artists to be welcoming to artists of other cultural backgrounds.

## ADA UDECHUKWU

Ada Udechukwu has been the least exposed of the seven artists to Igbo traditional culture, because of her mother's American background and her own urban Igbo and American upbringing. She draws from *uli* linearity, not so much to express Igbo culture, but her own personal themes of sadness, identity, sorrow, and conflict. Her politics is not that of the nation but of personal relations. Her use of *uli* linearity and its spatial concepts, but rarely its specific motifs, associates her with a traditional culture that she has only partially experienced, though this has not resolved questions of her identity. In fact, the *uli* emphasis in her work is an outgrowth of a pre-*uli* interest in line drawing. Her work on cloth and paper has a sparse but impressive aesthetic quality.

Ọlụ Ọguibe, involved with Igbo tradition and *uli* while an art student, has drawn from Fante flag designs of coastal Ghana, ancient Aztec art, Australian Aboriginal art, contemporary Near Eastern writers, and German politics, among other sources. He has moved the farthest from *uli* and Igbo traditions of the seven artists in this book, reinforced by six years in London and his present home in the United States; he does not employ *uli* nowadays. His past has been a springboard to a very different present than the other artists discussed here. The most intellectual of the seven artists, though all have high scholarly interests, his art is strong in social and political commentary, and now with reference to the world at large rather than to Nigeria. Ọguibe, a postmodernist, is critical of some postmodernist views as reflecting Euro/American biases toward Africa and the rest of the world. He has recently turned to installation art that connects with his childhood experiences and suffering in the Biafran war, work framed in terms of the abuse of children in the world.

## ART MATERIALS

The Nsukka artists' interest in the past has only occasionally involved indigenous art materials. However, there is a striking parallel between El Anatsui's use of Ghanaian wooden market trays early in his career and Ọlụ Ọguibe's early use of baskets, cane-meshes, and sleeping mats, both artists employing European paints. In each case, contemporary art became associated with ordinary objects and life, and both artists abandoned the practice when they moved and these materials became unavailable. They both would probably have moved on to using other materials in any case.

Some Nsukka artists, such as Tayọ Adenaike and Obiọra Udechukwu, have at times restricted their colors to those employed in *uli* murals. One is reminded of the soil paintings of Ọna, the Yoruba Ifẹ artists' group, especially Moyọ Okediji and Bọlaji Campbell, who have used traditional colored soils and plant dyes in contemporary art, but this has not occurred among the Nsukka artists. They have readily adopted Euro/American media, with which they are quite comfortable, blending these with non-Euro/American images.

## THE PLEASANTNESS OF THE PAST

The images of Igbo and other African cultures in the work of these artists are generally pleasing, including spiritual figures, masqueraders, *mamiwatas,* and minstrels. Exceptions are some of the grotesque Igbo and Yoruba tale figures, where being frightening is the point. The beauty and attractiveness of *uli* are evident—its flowing linear forms and its uses of space. Aesthetically delightful, *uli* is associated with positive traditional rituals such as marriage, title taking, and ascension to leadership roles. Other design systems, such as *mbari, nsibidi,* and *adinkra,* are also often put forth in a positive aesthetic light regardless of the images they depict. Yet these indigenous designs often occur in the contemporary art in conjunction with unhappy images of suffering, corruption, and hunger in present-day Nigeria. The contrast is striking between aesthetically pleasing designs and the associated commentaries on Nigerian conditions. The artists are skillful in using elegant styles to portray serious issues.

Rarely referred to in the work of these artists are the wars between African peoples and the sometimes destructive political conflicts of the precolonial past in Nigeria or other parts of Africa. When they are, as in El Anatsui's art, Euro/American slavery and the beginnings of colonialism are seen as the cause. The sufferings associated with past conquests of one African people by another, Africa's own fierce political competitiveness, are not disclosed in the art, granted that the slave trade and activities related to colonial conquests exacerbated these and that unhappy conditions in history are not the same as those today. The artists tend to idealize the past as a peaceful, aesthetically pleasant world, which of course does not totally agree with historical reality. This phenomenon in art often occurs during cultural revivals both in and outside Euro/America. For the artists, the believed past contrasts with the unhappy conditions of present-day Nigeria. The artists seem to be stating that people had a better life at an earlier time. Not that the artists wish to return to many of the cultural details of the past, for they live fully in the present. Rather, there is a desire to repossess the supposed quality of life of earlier times while living in the modern world. When these artists employ indigenous African cultures in their art, they are exploring its values in terms of present-day life—where and how it has and does not have meaning.

The distinctions between past and present that I employ are analytical categories, useful for an external analyst in writing and thinking about the artists and their art. But it is an exaggeration from the artists' viewpoint. They live in an integrated world where past and present are not often sharply distinct. Both are aspects of their daily lives, and they do not necessarily distinguish between them. Switching readily in speech between Igbo and English, between kola nut and coffee, and palm wine and commercial beer, the past and present are both resources to be used or discarded as the artists desire or according to the pressures of their art world and current Nigerian life.

There is no well worked out ideology of Igbo cultural revival among the artists today. Rather, there is a pragmatism over the use of traditional cultures that asks which cultural elements fit present needs, in what reinterpreted form, and when should they be employed. Why deny them as the British colonialists and missionaries often did? Cultural concerns do not have to take the form of a direct and explicit ideology, as occurred among some Native American and Australian Aboriginal groups, whose cultures were badly damaged in the face of the massive influx of hostile strangers and whose cultures are now partially reconstructed. That kind of cultural revival has not occurred with the Nsukka artists today, for in Igboland people are still living its culture in various forms and speaking its language, and there has never been a huge number of European settlers to take the land and kill off large portions of the population through conflict and disease.

However, there *was* an Igbo cultural revival from 1970 into the 1980s, after the Biafran war, when traditional shrines, sculptures, dress, and other items were recreated and rites were restarted, which could not be carried out during the war. The Nsukka artists' group, which began in 1970, shortly after the fighting ended, was part of that revival, a reconstruction of Igbo life and culture, although some of their interests in Igbo elements began before the war. The artists' embracing of *uli* and other Igbo aesthetic qualities, after the fighting, contributed to a general Igbo revival; the Nsukka artists thus played a historic part in this revival. Of course, there was no full return to prewar culture in the arts or elsewhere, but reinterpretations of it and some abandonment of prewar practices. Rituals altered, new sculptures and masquerades developed, and old ones were revised. Traditional kinship patterns adjusted to rapid urbanization and economic change. The use of *uli* and other Igbo images in contemporary art was part of this revival.

The war influenced the direction of some of the artists' work, particularly that of Obiọra Udechukwu. Even among younger Nsukka artists, such as Ọlu Ọguibe and Chika Okeke, who were children during the conflict, the war left its mark on their art. It sensitized the future Nsukka artists, as well as other Igbo, toward social and political issues and to the importance of maintaining their cultural institutions and identity. During the war, existing and future artists, such as Obiọra Udechukwu, Chike Aniakọr, Uche Okeke, and Ọlu Ọguibe, were thrust into Igbo village situations, away from school, university, and city life, which enriched their knowledge and experience of Igbo culture and life in ways that would not otherwise have occurred. Visual artists, poets, dramatists, and musicians were organized into active arts' groups that made patriotic presentations and extolled Igbo culture during the war; they thus learned a pattern of cooperation that they maintained after the war in Ọdunke, the AKA Circle of Exhibiting Artists, and other groups. The war not only threatened the lives of people in Biafra, it also threatened Igbo culture, although one recognizes that there were some non-Igbo involved on the Biafran side in the conflict. The sense of freedom to explore their own culture, which Uche Okeke and other artists felt at the time of Nigerian independence in 1960, was reinforced by the conflict and its consequences, leading to the Igbo-style art program at the University of Nigeria, Nsukka, beginning in 1970. Ada Udechukwu went as a child to the United States during the war and missed out on this wartime Igbo experience, perhaps one reason her art has turned toward exploring close personal relationships. El Anatsui and Tayọ Adenaike also missed the wartime experience, but all three depict suffering, Ada Udechukwu expressing an internal kind and the other two relating to Nigerian and African life.

Yet most of the Nsukka art that expresses social and political concerns is focused on conditions in Nigeria as a whole rather than being commentaries in particular on the Igbo condition in Nigeria or on Igbo suffering alone. The Igbo interest and the social and political concerns for Nigeria are two key aspects of the Nsukka art. The artists are nationalists and, at the same time, retain their Igbo identity as a base.

The Nsukka artists live in an uncertain Nigeria of today, with the possibility of cultural or religious conflict or both. A concern for Igbo culture is a defense against the potential destruction of, or harm to, the people associated with it, a rallying ground for them. Nigerians think much, these days, of the possibility of a breakdown in the country. Economic, social, and political conditions feed the survival of cultural distinctions for security and as a fallback position, which occurs in the arts as elsewhere. This prevents the development of a distinctive Nigerian national contemporary art.


## THE FUTURE

Rarely do the artists directly depict what the future might be, though insofar as their art criticizes and comments on present Nigerian conditions, it speaks indirectly of a hoped-for future. If their art condemns corruption, despotic leadership, poverty, hunger, and suffering, this expresses hope for the future, without representing what that future would be like in detail. It is clearly a future that includes important roles for indigenous cultures and languages, rather than total Europeanization. It is a future in which the artists would have greater ability to move about and to show and sell their art in Africa, Euro/America, even in Asia, with increased interest in their art at home, and in which university life would be drastically improved.


## CHILDHOOD AND ARTISTIC INTERESTS

Because of my interest in childhood experience and its relationship to adult life, I was curious about the early lives of the seven artists and what moved them into the arts, hoping to find general features.[6] I have located only a few. All but Ada Udechukwu, who studied English and literature, entered university fully committed to a career in art and to formal art training rather than by apprenticeship or on their own. All of them either had one or both parents as artists, or were exposed to art teachers and courses in primary or secondary school. Sometimes both parental and school factors were involved. Some of the seven had relatives who were in other art fields, such as music. All seven artists had at least one parent who had some schooling, and in some cases both did. The parents' schooling and occupations put them among those who accepted changing conditions, modern education, and new work roles, opening the way for their children to enter the new field of contemporary art. The extent of exposure as children to traditional visual art and other artistic forms, such as oral literature, music, masquerades, and rituals, varied considerably among the seven. None of their parents opposed their becoming artists for very long, and a few encouraged the artists to go ahead with it. Most of them studied in schools that were mission or church sponsored; Ọlu Ọguibe and El Anatsui were brought up in strong Christian environments. However, the relevance of a Christian upbringing to the development of an interest in contemporary art is not clear, but as something new vis-à-vis indigenous Igbo culture, it may have presented an opening view to other fields. For El Anatsui, art may have been a reaction to his childhood mission experience. Ọlu Ọguibe was taught art as a child by his fundamentalist Christian father and also became a child preacher; perhaps his art, which frequently carries strong messages, is a secular form of preaching.

The most important factors appear to be whether the person was exposed to art in school and/or through one or both parents or other close relatives who were artists of some kind; that at least one parent had some schooling; and that parental disapproval of an artistic career, if it existed, was temporary.

## LANGUAGE AND COMMUNICATION IN THE NSUKKA ART

The employment of *uli, nsibidi, mbari, adinkra,* and other indigenous elements in the contemporary art preserves African visual communication systems that have language qualities without being true languages as linguists view these.[7] Some of the Nsukka artists take pride in the existence of these graphic systems as African equivalents of true written languages elsewhere, seeing them as valuable to retain and to express artistically. This is a way of stating that through their use in visual art these artists have their own important means of communication. African words and phrases, especially Igbo, sometimes appear as part of the art or as titles. This is not surprising, as Nigerian tongues, including Igbo, are actively spoken in the country, though less commonly seen in printed form. (Obiọra Udechukwu publishes some poetry and texts in Igbo.) The artists clearly desire to retain African systems of communication, both true languages and graphic forms, and to employ European languages, especially English, which they also use in art titles, as well as in poetry, art criticism, and other writings. Ọlu Ọguibe has employed English, Pidgin English, German, and Arabic in his paintings, and Obiọra Udechukwu is now experimenting with Igbo and English in his art. Language issues therefore are important for the Nsukka artists.

## INTELLECTUAL ARTISTS

The German scholar Norbert Aas calls the Nsukka creators "intellectual artists."[8] They not only produce art but take part in discourse on it. It is a message-oriented art, whether in its social and political form or its expression of cultural elements. The art talks to the viewer. And the quality of art criticism that these artists engage in is well known in Nigeria, heightened by its contrast with the low level of art criticism often found in Nigerian newspapers and magazines. Although, until recent years, scholars have written little about Africans' own aesthetic criticism and judgment, these have certainly not been rare in indigenous cultures, albeit verbal rather than written, so that contemporary art evaluations have continuity with the past. Again, satiric political commentary has occurred among the Igbo and other Africans in masquerades, in other ritual, and through minstrels; a parallel exists with the Nsukka artists' interest in political satire in their visual art.

A variety of kinds of writing is common to these artists; print is a major avenue of communication about their art, their aesthetic viewpoints, and those of other artists. Their knowledge of African literature and poetry is often considerable. The intellectual aspects can also be seen through the poetry that some of them write, particularly Ada and Obiọra Udechukwu and Ọlu Ọguibe, and its interesting relationships to their visual art.

If their art is intellectual, this does not mean that it is cold or distant. It is often passionate, expressing strong feelings and sentiments, at times less calculated than spontaneous in its production. This contrasts with traditional *uli,* which, while frequently spontaneous, usually lacked the element of passion, aiming to be aesthetically pleasing and not directly communicating social and political messages, though its presence on walls and bodies does say something about Igbo social life.

The Nsukka artists often view poetry and visual art as allied fields, sometimes practicing both. They are minstrels of the written word as well as creating striking visual images, frequently developing similar themes in both fields. Each art medium complements the other and has its own particular impact. At least two of the seven artists, Uche Okeke and Obiọra Udechukwu, have had periods in their lives when they were involved in writing or producing drama or both.

It is simply incorrect to view these seven persons as only visual artists. Their visual art must be placed within the context of their other skills; these artists have a broad range of art media and artistic interests.

## SUPPORTERS AND PATRONS

When the Nsukka artists group began in the 1970s, they had little expatriate support, except for Uche Okeke, only later receiving help from non-Nigerian sources, even as Nigerian patronage gradually has grown to the significant level of today. The seven artists have had, and continue to have, their patrons and supporters, both Nigerian and expatriates, some of whom regularly buy work of one or more of the artists. But they have not had a single dominant patron, or even two or three of them, as in the Oṣogbo artists' case with the Beiers. True, for the Nsukka artists there has been the Goethe Institut at Lagos and support from persons and organizations in Germany, such as Ulli Beier and Norbert Aas. There has also been the Lagos Italian Cultural Institute and the British Council in Enugu, among others. The pattern of external support is more that of a number of persons and institutions, a diffuse arrangement. The Nsukka artists group—as was the case of some other artists and art groups in Nigeria—originally developed as a negative reaction to expatriate teachers at Zaria, from whom they did not receive support for their "natural synthesis" views. Since then, relationships with non-Nigerians have been much more positive, however.

Does the range of present support provided by non-Nigerians to the Nsukka artists represent a situation of dependency? It may appear so, although artists everywhere rely on patrons, gallery owners, art critics, entrepreneurs in the art market and museum curators. I do not believe that the Nsukka artists see themselves in a dependency situation of neocolonialism vis-à-vis expatriate patrons. These artists generally welcome and encourage external support, associating it with making positive foreign contacts, gaining sales and recognition. For artists who teach at Nigerian universities, the sale of their work—whether in or out of the country—has become a requirement for survival, given the meager purchasing power of their salaries today.

## WORLD CONTACTS

For these artists, increasing contact with the world outside Nigeria goes on, despite conditions within the country. Sometimes this contact is with other parts of Africa, as El Anatsui's participation in the 1995 Johannesburg Biennale and Obiọra Udechukwu's 1988 trip to Zimbabwe. But contacts have primarily been in Europe and the United States. It began with Uche Okeke's German trip in 1962, and the German connection continues to be important. Obiọra Udechukwu's numerous German visits and exhibitions; his wife's visits to the United States and

Germany; Ọlu Ọguibe's six years in London, showing at a number of galleries there and in Germany, and now his teaching in the United States; Tayọ Adenaike's six exhibitions in the United States in as many years and an earlier one in London; Chike Aniakọr's studies in art history at Indiana University and his recent two years on fellowships in the United States; and El Anatsui's association with the October Gallery in London, which now represents him, as well as his appearances in a number of other countries, are all evidence of the growing world mobility of the Nsukka artists.

There are a number of other young artists associated in some way with Nsukka with external experience, including Greg Odo, who formerly lived in London; Barthosa Nkurumeh, who teaches in Pennsylvania and exhibits in the United States; Sylvester Ogbechie, who is pursuing graduate studies in art history at Northwestern University and has had a year's fellowship at the National Museum of African Art in Washington, D.C.; and Chika Okeke, who curated and exhibited in the Nigerian section of the 1995 Johannesburg Biennale and the Nigerian section at the *Seven Stories* exhibition at London's Whitechapel Gallery in the same year. The sculptress Ndidi Dike, part of whose childhood was spent in England, has exhibited and taken part in workshops there and in the United States; and Benjo Igwilo, who teaches ceramics at Nsukka, studied art in the United States and recently spent a year in South Carolina. Age and artistic experience do not seem to be factors in whether Nsukka artists have external contacts or not. The base of training is still at Nsukka, but as contemporary African art becomes better known outside the country, artists from Nsukka, as other African creators, show increasing mobility; this in turn opens up further interest in their art.

We are no longer discussing a largely localized group of artists associated with training at Nsukka and living only in southeastern Nigeria, as existed to a considerable degree in the early 1970s when the Nsukka group began; they are now world travelers, and some have left Nigeria. This is not a pattern only for Nsukka artists but for others of African birth; for some countries, such as Ethiopia and the Sudan, the best artists are in exile. Traditional African artists sometimes traveled locally, and some ended up in the New World or other parts of Africa as slaves. But Nsukka artists, as well as other contemporary creators in Africa, are not heavily isolated, living only localized lives, although there are very serious financial and other problems in leaving Nigeria for exhibitions, workshops, and visits, and the artists are often preoccupied with conditions in their own country. True, of the seven artists in this book, only Ọlu Ọguibe sees himself as a postmodernist and is immersed in the Euro/American art world; however, some of the work of El Anatsui moves in that direction, and Obiọra Udechukwu's art is beginning to as well.

## THE PERSISTENCE OF AFRICAN THEMES

Yet, despite considerable overseas experience, these artists—with the notable exception of Ọlu Ọguibe's later art and occasional work by others—still largely draw on African images and styles, even after spending much time abroad. There is a preoccupation with Nigeria and Africa in their artistic images and often with Igbo culture. Several of the artists told me that, despite their trips abroad, they did not feel familiar enough with Euro/American culture to draw freely from it artistically, although they are comfortable with its media. The focus on African images in their art is reinforced by Euro/American art markets and dealers, who often consider their work as ethnically African no matter what the images are, as Ọlu Ọguibe discovered in his London years. In order to sell to Euro/America, there is pressure to create works with African themes. The artists are denied access to major Euro/American art galleries and markets, generally showing at specialized, often peripheral ones abroad, which regularly or irregularly exhibit African art. (In the United States, these are often galleries that specialize in contemporary African-American or traditional African art.) The artists from Nsukka find that, in order to identify themselves as distinctive from other artists in the world, even from other African artists, it is useful to use themes from home, an experience also familiar to Australian Aboriginal and Native American contemporary artists.

Nsukka artists (as well as others of African background) feel they have something important and unique to offer from their own cultures' perspectives, which they desire to present to the world for its appreciation and understanding, rather than emulating Euro/American modernism or postmodernism and drawing from their images. They want to present their unique offerings abroad as well as to members of their own and other cultures in Nigeria. The artists are proud of their contemporary artistic traditions and its links to the past and generally see little point in giving these up, except for Olu Oguibe. Thus there are a number of factors restraining these artists from exploring images and styles from elsewhere.

## GENDER ISSUES

A gender transformation of the artists involved in *uli* has occurred: in earlier days, body and wall paintings were female occupations; today these art forms are dominated by contemporary male artists who use *uli*, though a number of young women Nsukka artists, such as Ndidi Dike, Chinwe Uwatse, Ada Udechukwu, and Marcia Kure, are now active. (In Dike's case, there is also a reverse gender transformation; she is a sculptress, whereas in the past sculpture was a male occupation.) One reason for the male dominance among Nsukka artists is that, until recently, males made up the majority of students and faculty in Nigerian universities. This has been a consequence of patriarchalism in British colonialism and in Igbo culture and of colonial and missionary attitudes. The gender problem has been compounded by the decline of traditional *uli* artists, when females changed to wearing full clothing, thus eliminating body *uli,* and the disappearance of wall murals as a result of changes in rituals and in building structures. Thus there has been no training of contemporary women artists by traditional *uli* ones; that tradition is gone. Where there have been relationships between surviving senior traditional *uli* artists and contemporary women artists, the latter have often been Europeans, such as Elizabeth Willis and Doris Weller, who have lived in the Igbo area for periods of time and have worked with the traditional artists and who sometimes incorporate *uli* into their own art, or the American scholar Sarah Adams, who studies *uli* art.

These gender attitudes are slowly giving way, though women art teachers at Nigerian universities are rare.[9] The University of Nigeria, Nsukka, had none in its Department of Fine and Applied Arts at the time of writing, though there are female students and have been in the past. Nor does the AKA Circle of Exhibiting Artists, among its now enlarged membership of fifteen, include a female artist. Males largely developed the contemporary *uli* form through analyzing its traditional styles, meeting with the indigenous artists, making use of the published literature, and training other males to use it. *Uli* artistic continuity has occurred through gender transformation.

If males had not taken over *uli,* it probably would have disappeared temporarily, rather than thrive as it does today, only to reappear again during some future cultural revival. So it is a case of males rescuing a disappearing female art form, placing it in different art contexts, moving it from the village to the university, from ritual to largely secular life, to urban galleries and homes, and to the discourse of written texts.

*Nsibidi,* traditionally largely a male matter, has not involved gender transformation. While it is probably declining, as the secret societies associated with it lose some of their force, it is still a vital indigenous element.

There are differences of perspective among the Nsukka artists in Nigeria and Ọlu Ọguibe and other African artists and art historians residing in Euro/America. In Nigeria the artists are often preoccupied with Nigerian affairs, which are in serious disarray, certainly so at the University of Nigeria, Nsukka (the campus is frequently closed by strikes or government fiat, and there are serious administrative problems, as at other Nigerian universities). The Nsukka artists are preoccupied with questions of the role of indigenous cultures and motifs in their work, as well as with current Nigerian social and political conditions. They, as other Nigerian artists, struggle to receive recognition in their own country as members of a new professional field, not only as artists but as teachers, art critics, and art historians. At the same time they attempt to survive in a country where living conditions are difficult for many of them. Ideological issues of postmodernism, critical theory, and deconstruction, with which some of these artists are not yet very familiar, appear to have little relevance in the nitty-gritty of survival in Nigeria today, whether in fact they do or not. Postmodern theory is sometimes seen by them as a preoccupation of the art scene in the wealthy and powerful Euro/American capitalist world.

Yet some African artists and art historians regularly living in the Euro/American world speak for those in Nigeria and Africa, not only Ọlu Ọguibe, one of the seven in this book, but also the Nigerian Okwui Enwezor, founder of *NKA: Journal of Contemporary African Art* in New York, the Sudanese art historian Salah M. Hassan at Cornell University, the Tanzanian artist Everlyn Nicodemus, living in Belgium, and others.[10] These individuals living in Euro/America generally take a modified postmodern viewpoint and are familiar with current Euro/American art trends. They see the issue as how to obtain greater acceptance and understanding in Euro/America for contemporary African art; they view themselves as pioneers in bringing contemporary African art to the attention of Euro/America, which they are in numerous ways. As Africans concerned with this art and living in Euro/America, they are the spokespersons to Euro/America for contemporary African artists residing in Africa, rather than artists and art historians living in Africa itself. What they represent in viewpoints may seem to have little to do with the problems of artists living in Africa today, as those at home see them. Those away from Africa are often involved with issues such as the dominance of the art markets by Europeans and Americans, the distortion of understanding, the misrepresentation of contemporary African art by Euro/American scholars, pseudo-scholars, and collectors, and with issues related to postmodernism.

Compare, for example, the frequently postmodern-oriented articles in the New York-based *NKA: Journal of Contemporary African Art* with the Nigerian arts magazine *Glendora Review,* published in Lagos, both owned and operated by Nigerians, both new publications. The first presents views of how contemporary African art has been and should be viewed outside Africa and discusses African and African-American artists. The second, less theoretical and not usually postmodern, deals with Nigerian art conditions and art development, issues, patrons, and artists. It is not a question so much as to which view is right or wrong—they both are products of their settings in the world. Both speak for the contemporary African artist, from the social and political environment in which they presently reside, from their differing milieus within and without Africa. Uche Okeke represents the "at home" approach, while Ọlu Ọguibe lives in the Euro/American world of postmodernism, multiculturalism, and hybridity. El Anatsui and Obiọra Udechukwu are somewhere in between.[11] This may reflect generational factors, although some younger Nsukka artists might side with Uche Okeke.

Despite differences in perspective, the African artists in Euro/America do stimulate interest in contemporary Nigerian and African art through their creations, publications, speeches, exhibitions, and other activities and act as correctives to ignorance and misinformation about this art outside Africa. They also form useful links with artists in Nigeria and elsewhere in Africa.

## L'ENVOI

It has taken the Nsukka artists only a few years to master Euro/American media, and they have done it well. Artistic continuity with the past, merged with contemporary life and experience, is a reality. What has occurred is a series of transformations—of the gender of most of the artists, the separation of art from ritual, the much greater use of art for sociopolitical critiques, and different social settings for the art. The transition has been gradual and continuous. The newer contemporary art did not spring up wholly out of contemporary life but through a continuity with the past.

In this book I have tried to present a sense of the life experiences and viewpoints of these seven artists and to place them in sociopolitical settings. Fortunately I have been able to carry on discussions with them in person, through video, and by mail. I have provided much detail and offer little grand theory here, an approach that is consistent with much of my previous anthropological work, though not with the writings of some other anthropologists. I believe what is needed in the study of contemporary African art today is not so much large-scale theory or grand reviews of contemporary art of the continent—of which there have been plenty in recent years, often derived from not well thought through Euro/American backgrounds—but detailed studies that present the art in terms of African experience, history, and social life, with theory as orientation but not the dominating element. This is what I have endeavored to accomplish here.

# NOTES


**INTRODUCTION**

1. The university at Nsukka should not be confused with the University of Nigeria, Enugu, about an hour's drive south of Nsukka, which does not teach art.
2. In the older literature the term is spelled Ibo.
3. Imoagene 1990; Njọku 1990; Uchendu 1965.
4. Ottenberg 1959; Uchendu 1965.
5. Cole and Aniakọr 1984, 120–29.
6. Cole 1982; Ọkparọcha 1976.
7. Nicolls 1987.
8. Aronson 1980, 1989a, 1989b; Lamb and Holmes 1980, 237–50.
9. Willis 1986, 1987, 1989, 1997.
10. Aniakọr 1978, 1985, 1995b; Dmochowski 1990.
11. Jemkur 1992.
12. Shaw 1970.
13. Hackett 1987, 1989.
14. Ottenberg 1959; Uchendu 1965.
15. Ọguibe 1994a.
16. O. Udechukwu 1972.
17. I prefer the term *Euro/American* and *Euro/America* to the less awkward and more frequently employed *the West*. The latter implies an "East," which refers to the Near or Far East rather than Africa. Also, Europe is north of Nigeria, not west of it. *The West* implies dominance and, in the art world, control of much of the arts of those external to it; its hegemonic implications make it unsuitable. The terms *Euro/American* and *Euro/America*, being geographic designations, do not quite carry the value connotations of *the West*, though they are not completely free of them.
18. See, for example, Ottenberg n.d.
19. I was fortunate enough to conduct a brief interview with Chuka Amaefunah and to photograph some of his art before his death.
20. Ottenberg 1968, 1971, 1975, 1989a.
21. Ottenberg 1972, 1973, 1975, 1979, 1989b.
22. Ọguibe 1994a, 1994b.
23. See Fisher 1994 for papers discussing these issues.
24. Studio Museum in Harlem 1990; Centre Georges Pompidou 1989; Centro Atlantico de Arte Moderno 1991; Vogel 1991; Deliss 1995.
25. General books include Beier 1968; Eckhardt 1979; Fosu 1993; Gaudibert 1991; Kennedy 1992; Miller 1975; Mount 1989. Journals include *NKA: Journal of Contemporary African Art, Third Text,* and *Revue Noire.*
26. See, for example, *Africus: Johannesburg Biennale* 1995; *Art*

*from the Frontline* 1990; Campschreur and Divendal 1989; Museum of Modern Art, Oxford 1990; *Incroci del Sud* 1993; Younge 1988.

27. Savannah Gallery and Westbourne Gallery in London are now closed, but October Gallery exhibits this art. In New York, the Gallery of Contemporary African Art and Skoto Gallery show contemporary African art regularly; Eric Robertson Gallery is beginning to do so.

## 1. PIONEERS AND PREDECESSORS

1. Beier 1968, 14.
2. For detailed studies see Agoro 1980; Ogbechię 1993, 1994; Ọlọidi 1991a. See also Jęgędę 1983; Kelly and Stanley 1993, 406–7; U. Okeke 1979a; Ọlọidi 1980, 1986, and 1995b, 193; and D. Ọnabolu 1963. Photographs of his hard-to-locate art are in Agoro 1980; Federal Department of Culture 1981, 8; D. Ọnabolu 1963; Wangboje 1977, 102.
3. Ọlọidi 1991a, 40.
4. Ọlọidi 1980, 109–10; 1991a, 22, 36.
5. C. Anyakora 1975; Brown 1966, 69, 70, 74–75; Crowder 1978; Ibeto c. 1962; Kelly and Stanley 1993, 193–98, 232–33, 482–84; Murray 1938a, 1938b; *Nigerian Wood-Carvings* 1937; Nnachy (sometimes written Nnachi in the literature) 1940; J. Okeke 1993; U. Okeke 1979a, 106–10 and 1985, 13–17; Ọkpara 1993; Ọlọidi 1986. For photographs of their art, see, for Ibeto: Ahamba c. 1940; Meyerowitz 1937, 73; *Nigeria* 14, 1938, 121, 136; 39, 1952, 239, 249; and 42, 1953, 131; for Umana: *Nigeria* 14, 1938, 99; McClusky 1987, 22; Murray 1938b; for Ibrahim (sometimes incorrectly written as Ibrahim Uthman, as in Danford 1949): *Nigeria* 14, 1938, 88; for Enwọnwu's genre art see Meyerowitz 1937, 70, 71; *Nigeria* 14, 1938, 105; for Nnachy see twenty-three unmounted watercolors in the Library of Congress, Manuscript Division, Harmon Foundation File, and Nnachy 1940.
6. Born S. A. Ọladetimi, Laşekan changed his name in 1941. See Brown 1966; Kelly and Stanley 1993, 270–72; Murray 1938a; U. Okeke 1975, 37 and 1993a, 28–30; Ọlọidi 1986, 119; Oludare 1981; O. Udechukwu 1979a, 14–15. For examples of his art, see *Nigeria* 14, 1938, xxi, 164, and 33, 1958, 169; Federal Department of Culture 1981, 79–81; Oyelọla 1976, 89. Fourteen of his works are at the Carl Van Vechten Gallery of Fine Arts, Fisk University, Nashville, Tennessee; thirty others are at the Hampton University Museum, Hampton, Virginia.
7. Harry F. Hemmerich Collection, Washington, D.C. Hemmerich served as U.S. vice-consul in Lagos in 1944–45; his wife, Anne, taught art at the British Council, and some of her students were Africans.
8. See Kelly and Stanley 1993, 271, for a list of Laşekan's publications; see also Laşekan 1949 and Mbadugha 1958.
9. That a number of the early nontraditional artists were Yoruba is not surprising, as their region felt the impact of colonialism earlier than other Nigerian areas. Lagos, the capital of Nigeria until its recent move to Abuja, always the center of Nigerian contemporary art, is in the Yoruba area.
10. Bascom 1969, 118; Brown 1966, 67; Kelly and Stanley 1993, 79–80; U. Okeke 1993a, 29; "Our Authors and Performing Artists—II" 1966, 134–35; Poynor 1987, 61; Thompson 1971, chap. 17, p. 2; "Thorn Figure Carving" 1938; Willett 1986, 1989. For illustrations of his art, see *Nigeria* 14, 1938, 134–37 and 15, 1938, 216, 32, 1949, 86–97; *Nigeria Magazine* 75, 1982, 82; Willett 1986, 1989; National Archives and Records Administration n.d., slides 15–19.
11. Chukueggu's name is sometimes spelled Cukueggu, Chukego, Chukuegga, or Chukwuegu. See Cole 1988, 58; Kelly and Stanley 1993, 149–50; U. Okeke 1975, 41; *Exhibition of Sculptures* 1972; *Exhibition of Wood Carvings from Mbaişe* 1971; N. Eze 1978, 6–7. For photographs of his art, see Chukuegga 1952, 252; East Central States Art Council 1972, 31; *Exhibition of Sculptures* 1972, pls. 1, 2A, and 2B; *Nigeria Magazine* 115/116, 1975, 35 and 122/123, 1977, 121. Also see his ethnological article, Chukuegga 1952.
12. Ogbechię 1993, 5, note 8, believes that Enwọnwu may have been born three years earlier, if Enwọnwu's elder brother is correct. Kelly and Stanley 1993, 193–98 is the best bibliographic source, and Ogbechię 1988 the best description of his art. See also Beier 1960a, 9–10 and 1968, 48, 50; Enwọnwu 1956, 1963, 1969; Frankel 1958; Ogbechię and Nzegwu 1991; U. Okeke 1979a, 112–14; Oyelọla 1976, 93–95; Whiteman 1994. For photographs of his work, see Ogbechię and Nzegwu 1991; Beier 1960a, 9–10 and 1968, 49; Federal Department of Culture 1981, 64–65; Kennedy 1992, 32; *Nigeria* 14, 1938, 105, and 15, 1938, 243; Lehmann 1966; Malan 1973; Mount 1989, 176; C. Okeke 1995, 43–46; Oyelọla 1976, 93–95; Wangboje 1977, 106. For slides see National Archives and Records Administration n.d., slides 78–86.
13. Ebọng 1991; Jahn 1966, 239–76; Owomọyela 1979, 37–51; Senghor 1956, 1966, 1967.
14. Kennedy 1992, 32; Ogbechię 1994, 14; U. Okeke 1979a, 112–14; Ogbechię 1988, 35–36 calls it "a style of -emotion."
15. Adenaike 1982b, 41, although the genre artist C. C. Ibeto had used *uli* in his *Awka Dancers*, c. 1936.
16. *Guide to the Nigerian Museum* n.d., 2.
17. Aig-Imoukhuede 1991, 155–56; *Ifę Art School* 1984; Jęgędę 1983, 16–17; Ọlọidi 1986, 120; *Zaria Art School* 1990, 5, 7; Zerby and Zerby 1971.
18. These neotraditionalist artists are discussed in Kelly and Stanley 1993, Kennedy 1992, and Mount 1989. Benin, east of Yorubaland, had been a famous kingdom, strong in art, so that it is not surprising that contemporary artists came from there.
19. For Osawe see Ben Amos 1967; Highet 1969, 38–39; Kelly

and Stanley 1993, 428–29; Kennedy 1992, 39–40. For
Onobrakpẹya see Highet 1969, 40–41; Kelly and Stanley
1993, 410–21; Kennedy 1992, 43–46; O. Udechukwu
1977. For Emọkpae see Highet 1969, 39–41; Kennedy
1992, 40; Kelly and Stanley 1993, 190–92; Mount 1989,
184–86; and C. Okeke 1995b, 52–53, who writes that
Emọkpae drew "from such international 'rebel' art as surre-
alism and the biomorphic abstractions of contemporary
western sculpture" (52). For Egọnu see Ọguibe 1995a,
1995b, 1995g. For Fọlarin see Kelly and Stanley 1993,
223–26; Kennedy 1992, 40–41. For Eze see A. Eze 1989;
Kelly and Stanley 1993, 199–201; *Okpu Eze: New Dimensions* 1992.

20. For Ngu see Kelly and Stanley 1993, 290–91; Kure 1994,
28; C. Okeke 1992. For Ekọng see Kelly and Stanley 1993,
186–87; Kure 1994, 28–30; "Lagos Art Galleries" 1967, 7,
12, 24.

21. Kelly and Stanley 1993, 87–89; Highet 1969, 35–37;
Kennedy 1992, 52–53; Mount 1989, 133–35.

22. U. Okeke 1993a, 2.

23. Beier 1965 and 1968, 101, 103–7; Duerden 1961; Ekom
1966, 161. On Beier's impressions of Nigeria at this time, see
Beier 1993 and Ọbafemi 1993. On the indigenous *mbari*
structures, see Cole 1982 and Ọkparọcha 1976.

24. Adenaike 1979; Beier 1965, 1968, 89–130, and 1991; Critic
1963; Jẹgẹdẹ 1983, 53–81; Kennedy 1992, 67–81; U.
Okeke 1977a and 1978–79, 1–2, 13; Wewe 1989, 84–86.

25. For discussions of this and debates concerning the role of
Osogbo art in Nigeria, see Benson 1986, 37–38; Jẹgẹdẹ
1983, 88–96; Lawal 1977.

26. Good accounts of Mbari Mbayọ art occur in Adenaike 1979;
Beier 1968, 89–130, 1991; Jẹgẹdẹ 1983, 53–81; Kennedy
1992, 67–81. See also Beier 1965; Critic 1963; U. Okeke
1977a and 1978–79, 1–2, 13; Wẹwẹ 1989, 84–86.

27. For information on the Osogbo artists, see Beier 1968,
113–30 and 1991; Fosu 1993, 47–56; Kennedy 1992, 71–83;
and the appropriate references in Kelly and Stanley 1993.

28. Agberia 1988; Cardew 1971, 1988, 1993; Clark 1976;
Na'Allah 1980.

29. Beier 1968, 24–27; Carroll 1966; Mount 1989, 31–38.

30. Kelly and Stanley 1993, 214–17.

31. Arnot 1937, 1950; "Ibo Body Designs" 1946; McFarlan
1957, photograph opposite p. 94.

32. "Gallery Labac" 1967; "Lagos Art Galleries" 1967; Law
1969, 353.

33. Jẹgẹdẹ 1983, 229–30, 256, 264; Goethe Institut, Lagos 1979.

34. Duerden 1953; Ekwensi 1956, 1966; Enwọnwu 1956.

35. Akinosho 1985; "Exhibitions" 1964; Ọnwuzurọha 1980:
Society of Nigerian Artists 1964.

36. St. Jorre 1972 provides a useful general account. Akpan 1972;
Kirk-Greene 1971, 1975; Moore 1968; Tamuno and Ukpabi
1989 offer largely external accounts. For views from the Bi-

afran side, see Achebe et al. 1971; Azuonye 1991; Forsyth
1977; Ike 1976; Iroh 1979; Kalu 1991; Madiebo 1980; A.
Nwankwo 1972; O. Udechukwu 1991a; Wonodi 1971.

37. For the views on the conflict of a non-Igbo artist, Bruce
Onobrakpẹya, living outside Biafra but in Nigeria, who was
a friend of some of the Nsukka artists, see Darrah and Quel
1992, 211–23.

38. Afigbo (1992) feels that the reconciliation with Nigeria was
successful, but Chinua Achebe (1985), Nsukka Analyst
(1994), Igbokwe (1995), and some of the Nsukka artists to
whom I have talked disagree, arguing that the Igbos have
been seriously and deliberately left behind in national development through federal government actions. I myself was
surprised at how well reconciliation appeared to go at first,
but the longer-term picture has been much less positive.

### 2. UCHE OKEKE, I

1. Uche Okeke, video interview by Simon Ottenberg, May 26,
1994, at Asele Institute, Nimo.

2. Okeke's full name is Christopher Uchefuna Okeke. See Kelly
and Stanley 1993, 361–68 and U. Okeke 1993b, for basic
information on his life and art.

3. Jos was not far to the northeast, and Zaria could be reached
by rail or road via Kaduna.

4. For this section see Chidume 1973, 15–17; Ndubisi 1991;
C. Okeke 1995, 47–48; U. Okeke 1971a, x, xi–xiii; 1982a,
14; 1988, 5; 1993b, 3–5. See also U. Okeke and Uche-
Okeke 1978, 2–10, 13–16; *Programme for the Funeral Ceremonies* 1994; Uche-Okeke 1975; O. Udechukwu 1977, 65.

5. Chinwe Achebe 1986

6. Ekwensi n.d. The illustrator's name is not indicated, but at
this time it would probably not have been a Nigerian. In this
publication the author called himself C. O. D. Ekwensi. In
his later and better-known works of fiction, he used the
name Cyprian Ekwensi.

7. For his early efforts see U. Okeke and Uche-Okeke 1978,
9–10.

8. U. Okeke 1993b, 3–4.

9. Ndubisi 1991, 104.

10. Ndubisi 1991, 105.

11. U. Okeke and Uche-Okeke 1978, 11.

12. Ndubisi 1991, 105.

13. Adenaike 1982a, 11.

14. U. Okeke and Uche-Okeke 1978, 11.

15. U. Okeke 1982a, 41.

16. C. Okeke 1993a, 39. Asele refers to a female Igbo deity in
Okeke's home area who is associated with art and creativity.
See below.

17. This section draws on Akinosho 1993; N. Eze 1978; Ndubisi
1991, 21, 23; Ogbechiẹ 1993; U. Okeke 1978a and 1993b,
4–6; Onobrakpẹya 1995; Umegakwe 1967; as well as other
references cited below.

18. In addition to Uche Okeke and Simon Okeke, the members included Yusuf C. Grillo, William Ọlaosebikan, Bruce Onobrakpẹya, Demas Nwoko, F. N. Ekeada, E. O. Ọdita, O. O. Osadebe, and E. O. Nwagbara. Jimọ Akolo is sometimes considered to have been a member (see N. Eze 1978, 12, 71, 72), but Uche Okeke does not consider him one (personal interview), nor do his records from that time. Akolo has indicated to me that he found the group too militant and dogmatic, although he was in basic sympathy with its ideas.

    N. Eze (1978, 17–18) indicates that the Art Society was formally organized, with a constitution, bylaws, membership cards, letterheads, patrons, and patronesses including the sole Nigerian art teacher there, Clara Ugbodaga Ngu, and P. George, head of the Department of Fine Arts. The society had a president, financial secretary, treasurer, and auditor and held monthly and special meetings. Organizations like this were common in Nigeria for student and cultural groups and for professional people. The society may have rebelled against British art teaching, but it accepted British private organizational structure.

19. Onobrakpẹya 1995, 196; *Simon Obiekezię Okeke* 1976, 9.

20. U. Okeke, 1982a, 2 and 1995a. Okeke's speech to fellow members, "Natural Synthesis: Art Society, Zaria, 1960," became the society's manifesto. See also his talk to them the year before: U. Okeke 1982a, 1 and 1995b.

21. Letter from Uche Okeke, Kafanchan, to Evelyn Brown, Harmon Foundation, New York, Jan. 5, 1962, p. 3. This and subsequent letters of Okeke to the Harmon Foundation cited in the notes are in the Manuscript Division, Library of Congress, Washington, D.C. See Ottenberg n.d. on the topic of Okeke's Christian interests. The views of the Art Society did not involve a rejection of Christian beliefs; society members created Christian art images and were to do so in the future. However, the members were critical of missionary attitudes toward tradition.

22. Ottenberg n.d.

23. N. Eze 1978, 104–5.

24. Ogbechiẹ 1993, 4–5, 14–15.

25. Brook 1958 offers a critique of the Zaria training, questioning why the government authorities did not obtain advice from Nigerian artists before planning to site the art department at Zaria, as most of the students would be coming from the south. On the other hand, one could argue that, in the long run, the artists' exposure to cultures quite different from their own experience was beneficial to them.

26. Ọnwuzurọha 1980, 9.

27. C. Okeke 1993a, 40.

28. Chinua Achebe 1962a (originally published 1958).

29. In 1965 Okeke produced an oil painting, *The Conflict (After Achebe),* which refers to the church burning scene. See below and fig. 42..

30. U. Okeke 1977a.

31. U. Okeke 1982a, 55.

32. U. Okeke 1977a, 60; *Simon Obiekezię Okeke* 1976.

33. Onobrakpẹya 1995, 195.

34. Odutokun 1993a, 4.

35. Ọlọidi 1986, 121–22; Ogbechiẹ 1992, 25–27.

36. *Zaria Art School* 1990, 5. What little is known of the teachers' viewpoint suggests that some of them were not uninterested in Nigerian indigenous art, but were also not used to teaching students with so little previous art training. See V. Butler 1963, 1964; Ogedengbe (possibly a pseudonym) 1963.

37. U. Okeke 1993b, 5.

38. Grillo, Ọlaosebikan, and Simon Okeke finished their training in 1960; Uche Okeke, Nwoko, and Onobrakpẹya in 1961; and Ekeada, Nwagbara, Ọdita, and Osadebe in 1962.

39. U. Okeke 1961. A few of his drawings, as well as some of the Igbo tales that he had collected, were published in issues of *NIGERCOL* between 1958 and 1961, the student publication of the Nigerian College of Arts, Science and Technology, Zaria. Seven of the drawings were made in Lagos, before Okeke moved to Zaria for schooling (U. Okeke 1982c, 2).

40. A. Eze 1995; Lindfors 1973; O. Udechukwu 1977.

41. O. Udechukwu 1977, 18.

42. Kennedy 1992, 46.

43. Beier 1968, 46–47.

44. Beier 1961c, no pagination.

45. Letter from Uche Okeke, Kafanchan, to Evelyn Brown, Harmon Foundation, New York, Jan. 5, 1962, p. 2.

46. O. Udechukwu 1977, 75.

47. O. Udechukwu 1984a, 84.

48. O. Udechukwu 1984a, 84, 85.

49. O. Udechukwu 1984a, 84; Beier 1961c, no pagination.

50. For published examples of Okeke's Igbo tale art, see Beier 1961a, 48 and 1968, 45–46; Kennedy 1992, 45; Mount 1989, 139; U. Okeke 1961; *Research in African Literatures* 6:2, 1975, front cover and 236, 252, 264, and back cover. A portfolio of reproductions of thirty-five works, including thirteen from his 1958–59 Igbo tale series, are included in a 1982 issue that appeared in Minneapolis (U. Okeke 1982c). Photographs of some tale figures are in the Harmon Collection at the United States National Archives and Records Administration, Still Picture Branch, College Park, Maryland.

51. United States National Archives and Records Administration, Still Picture Branch, College Park, Maryland, Harmon Collection, numbers 9E-4, 11 and 12.

52. See C. Okeke 1993a, 15 for *Self-Contemplation* and *Beggar—Jos.* Terra-cotta pieces were in the Nok archaeological sites in northern Nigeria; Okeke apparently saw an association between them and his work.

53. C. Okeke 1993a, 19.

54. In U. Okeke 1982a, 13, he writes that "the new Nigerian man has fashioned himself into a gorgeously attired being

with calabash bowl in hand." Here he means government handouts as well.

55. C. Okeke 1993a, 17; Ottenberg n.d.

56. Uche Okeke, video interview, May 26, 1994.

57. Beier 1961a, 30; U. Okeke and Uche-Okeke 1978, 42; U. Okeke 1988, 7.

58. Aragbabalu 1960 and *Demas Nwoko* 1961, respectively.

59. Letter from Uche Okeke, Kafanchan, to Evelyn Brown, Harmon Foundation, New York, Jan. 5, 1962, p. 1.

60. Beier 1960b, 1961a; Crowder 1962a.

61. U. Okeke 1988, 6; 1993a, 5; 1993b, 2–3.

62. Letter from Uche Okeke, Ibadan, to Evelyn Brown, Harmon Foundation, New York, July 23, 1961, p. 4.

63. Chidume 1973, 16; Kelly and Stanley 1993, 362.

64. Beier 1962b, 26; Kelly and Stanley 1993, 362. Letters from Uche Okeke, Kafanchan, to Evelyn Brown, Harmon Foundation, New York, Feb. 7 and July 16, 1962, p. 1.

65. Kelly and Stanley 1993, 363.

66. Letter from Uche Okeke, Kafanchan, to Evelyn Brown, Harmon Foundation, New York, Sept. 11, 1961.

67. Letter from Uche Okeke to Evelyn Brown, Harmon Foundation, New York, Jan. 5, 1962, p. 1.

68. This section is based on Aas 1993; Kelly and Stanley 1993, 362; U. Okeke 1988, 7–9, 1993a, 3–4, 1993b, 6–7; and letters from Okeke in Germany to Evelyn Brown, Harmon Foundation, New York.

69. C. Okeke 1995, 48. Ọja refers to an area of Lagos, Abule Ọja, where he largely produced these works. *Ọja* is also the Igbo word for "flute."

70. Aas 1993.

71. Letter from Uche Okeke, Munich, to Evelyn Brown, Harmon Foundation, New York, Dec. 12, 1962.

72. U. Okeke 1982a, 2.

73. The stained glass window was actually produced by the Franz Mayer workshop, which later created a second one that remains with the *14 Stations of the Cross* mosaics at the factory today.

### 3. UCHE OKEKE, II

1. Uche Okeke, video interview by Simon Ottenberg, May 26, 1994, at Asele Institute, Nimo.

2. U. Okeke 1993a, 5.

3. It was subsidized by the Society for Cultural Freedom, Paris. Its Executive Committee included Okeke, the British Council director at Enugu, a writer, a musician, a dramatist, and a librarian.

4. The clearest description of these events at Enugu is found in U. Okeke 1985, 21–22.

5. Letter from U. Okeke, Enugu, to Evelyn Brown, Harmon Foundation, New York, March 29, 1965.

6. Adenaike 1982a, 19; Kelly and Stanley 1993, 284.

7. He was also artistic director and designer for two operas produced by the Enugu Musical Society, the plays and operas being performed at the British Council. See Chidume 1973, 15; U. Okeke and Uche-Okeke 1978, 42–44.

8. Chinua Achebe 1962a; Munonye 1966.

9. Kelly and Stanley 1993, 362–63; U. Okeke 1993b, 7–8.

10. Kelly and Stanley 1993, 364.

11. Called "Art in Nigeria"; see U. Okeke 1963.

12. In Uche-Okeke 1975, 63.

13. Kelly and Stanley 1993, 470–71.

14. The name was changed to the Department of Fine and Applied Arts in 1971 after the Biafran war. Before the conflict, all university departments were named for prominent persons in their fields, at the suggestion of Nnamdi Azikiwe. He had much to do with the founding of the university and wanted it to have a sense of history. The name was transferred after the war to the building in which the art department was housed. See Ukpabi 1971 for cultural background data on the Nsukka area; Ọfọmata 1978 and Zerby and Zerby 1971 for other information on the area and the university.

15. This section is largely based on interviews with the artist Obiọra Udechukwu, October 24 and 27, 1993, at Nsukka, who studied at Nsukka in the 1966–67 academic year, and the art historian Babatunde Lawal, in New York City, April 19, 1995, who was also a student there in 1962–65, studying graphics, and was a cartoonist for the student paper, *The Arrow*. See also N. Anyakora 1991; Ọdita 1966; U. Okeke 1985, 21; Ọlọidi 1985, 3–4.

16. Kelly and Stanley 1993, 260–62.

17. Kelly and Stanley 1993, 427–28.

18. Ọlọidi 1985, 4; see also U. Okeke 1979a, 23.

19. N. Anyakora 1991, 6.

20. Kelly and Stanley 1993, 242–44.

21. U. Okeke 1982a, 26.

22. U. Okeke 1985, 28.

23. Kelly and Stanley 1993, 97–100.

24. The dark body dye is also called *uli;* to paint with it is *ide uli* (to write *uli*) or *ise uli* (to draw *uli*). Mural designs are *akika aja* or *uli aja,* and in some areas they are called *upa*. See U. Okeke 1982b, 4.

25. Adenaike 1982a, 38–52; Aniakọr 1995a; Cole and Aniakọr 1984, 39–46; U. Okeke 1976a, 1977b, 25–35, 1982b; O. Udechukwu 1972, 1980a, 1981b, 1984b.

26. Willis 1989, 62.

27. Egbo 1994; Uchendu 1964.

28. Willis 1986, 20.

29. Willis 1986, 7–8.

30. Willis 1989, 63–64. The most comprehensive survey of *uli* is in Willis 1997.

31. O. Udechukwu 1972, 1981b, 1991b; Willis 1989, 67.

32. Willis 1989, 64.

33. Cole and Aniakọr 1984, 34–38, 46; U. Okeke 1982b, 11–12.

34. P. Nwoko 1973, 1–2.

35. Ubagu 1984.
36. See various photographs in Cole 1982 for some striking *uli* body designs on the *mbari* figures.
37. U. Okeke 1976a, 1977b, 25–35, 1982b.
38. Willis 1986, 1987, 1989, 1997.
39. Onwuejeọgwu 1981.
40. Hobsbawm and Ranger 1984.
41. See front and back covers of Weller 1992; see also Weller 1994; Nzewi 1994; and *Upa Paint-Drawing* 1995. For other relatively recent *uli* wall murals, see *Configura 2* 1995; Courtney-Clarke 1990; C. Okeke 1995; Smith 1986; A. Udechukwu 1992, 4, 6, 7; O. Udechukwu, 1984b. Scholarly interest in *uli* has also been stimulated in recent years by the largely unpublished research of Elizabeth Willis (see the Bibliography), Norbert Aas, Sarah Adams, and this writer, but of course mainly by the numerous creations, publications, and exhibitions of the contemporary Nsukka artists.
42. U. Okeke 1982b, 4–8.
43. Willis 1989, 64–65.
44. Cole and Aniakọr 1984, 46.
45. U. Okeke 1982b, 10–12; Willis 1987, 92.
46. U. Okeke 1982b, 6–9; O. Udechukwu 1972, 18; Willis 1986, 1987.
47. Willis 1986, 26 and fig. 32.
48. Lévi-Strauss 1971, 233–35.
49. Willis 1986, 30.
50. U. Okeke 1977b, 25, 28–29, 1982b, 10; Willis 1986, 28.
51. O. Udechukwu 1972.
52. U. Okeke 1982b, 10, agrees: "Uli lines are lyrical and songs of outstanding poetic quality have been inspired by this art form and by the mythical *uli* artist, Asele."
53. O. Udechukwu 1981b.
54. Willis 1986, 27. I am following Ọlọidi 1979, 9: "Abstraction in its ordinary meaning can be defined as a summary, simpler, or less elaborate form of anything. It can also be a smaller, but representative form of a larger entity. . . . Abstraction . . . is simply any pictorial or sculptural representation whose formal or conceptual characters show, no matter how slight, a departure from nature." The work of Okeke and other Nsukka artists is very rarely abstract in the Western sense of not apparently relating to any object or figure at all. It is close to Ọlọidi's sense of abstraction, as is traditional *uli*. Traditional Nigerian art, particularly sculpture, is rarely abstract in a total sense, although textile design and some painting is. See also Egonwa 1986.
55. O. Udechukwu 1972, 21.
56. Aniakọr 1995a, 2. However, Aradeon 1987, 9, argues for some perspective, for example, in Okeke's 1961 *The Orphan* and in his *Drawings* 1961.
57. U. Okeke 1982b, 4.
58. Willis 1986, 7.

59. Ikwuemesi 1992a, 9.
60. Shaw 1970. For an early photograph of *uli* wall painting, see fig. 2. Aniakọr (1978, 27) refers to late nineteenth-century missionaries passing through Awka, who noted of the chief's house: "The walls were beautifully smooth, and painted with all sorts of queer designs." Unfortunately no reference is given.
61. See O. Udechukwu 1972 for an excellent discussion of wall *uli* in one Igbo town, Agulu.
62. Willis 1986, 32.
63. Smith 1986, 58.
64. U. Okeke 1982b, 15–16; Willis 1986, 31–32.
65. O. Udechukwu 1972, 8.
66. U. Okeke 1976a, 114–15.
67. U. Okeke 1982b, 21.
68. See U. Okeke 1977b, 13–15, 1982b, 1–2, 1985, 1–4, 1993a, 14–15, 16–17. See also O. Udechukwu 1984a, 85.
69. I distinguish Igbo tales from Igbo myths, in that the myths relate to powerful spiritual forces that are often associated with shrines and to beliefs as to how the spirits in the myths affect humans. These myths often have a sense of the faraway past. Tale characters, on the other hand, are often humorously eccentric; duplicity and intrigue are rampant in the tales, and the setting is timeless. I have tried to avoid the term *folk,* as in *folktale,* because it implies simplicity of the culture associated with the tales, in this case tending to deny the sophistication and complexity of Igbo culture.
70. Okeke 1985, 1–4.
71. Ottenberg n.d.
72. U. Okeke n.d., 30.
73. For a photograph of *Ọgbanje,* see Wangboje 1977, 123. For a listing of some of these oils, see C. Okeke 1993a, 39.
74. Adenaike 1982b, 22.
75. The title *Efuru* may be related to Efuru in Flora Nwapa's novel with the same title. See Nwapa 1966.
76. Cole and Aniakọr 1984, 38–39.
77. Chinwe Achebe 1986 contains an excellent discussion of *ọgbanje.* Some of the repeated deaths may be due to genetic factors relating to a severe form of sickle cell anemia or to a persistent illness of the mother, such as dysentery.
78. For a photograph of the painting, see C. Okeke 1993a, 25.
79. On the Aba riots, as they are frequently called, see Coleman 1958, 174; Gailey 1970; Meek 1937, ix–xvi, 325–56; Perham 1937, 206–20; and, from more recent feminist viewpoints, see Bastian 1993; Van Allen 1976; Whipper 1982.
80. O. Udechukwu 1984a, 83.
81. U. Okeke and Uche-Okeke 1978, 29–30.
82. See C. Okeke 1993a, 26 for photographs of *Refugee Family* and *The Return.*
83. U. Okeke 1988, 13.
84. N. Nwankwọ 1964.
85. U. Okeke 1993a, 6.

86. Okereke 1979, 26, 131–35. See Okeke's 1968 poems, "War-Time Dishes" and "War Front," 132–33 in this publication. See *Werbung für Biafra* 1985, between pp. 10 and 12 for photographs of two wartime posters.

87. U. Okeke 1982a, 15–16 and 1988, 12.

88. U. Okeke 1982a, 16.

89. Azuonye 1972, 1. See also the novel by Ike 1976 and Chapter 7, note 18.

90. U. Okeke 1969a. Another publication relating to Biafra, a history of Igbo art, was U. Okeke 1970. See also Aas 1993.

91. Most of the art in the German exhibitions was not returned to Nigeria until 1992. It was stored in a castle in the south of Germany for some years and then transferred, through the efforts of Ulli Beier and others, to Iwalẹwa-Haus, Bayreuth. An exhibition of seventy-seven of the pieces was held there in 1985. See *Werbung für Biafra* 1985, which reflects back upon the war and the role of art in it.

92. Okereke 1979, 132. The first two movements (as Okeke called the acts) of *Ekeama* appear in Okeke 1973, the fourth movement in Okeke 1972b. In 1971 he won an All-African Drama Award from the African Studies Center, University of California, Los Angeles, for this dance drama. In 1971 he designed a tall wood sculpture, *Ekeama* (see below and C. Okeke 1993a, 29, 39).

93. U. Okeke 1971a.

94. U. Okeke 1971b.

95. U. Okeke 1969b.

96. U. Okeke 1982a, 17. Also in U. Okeke and Uche-Okeke 1978, 31.

97. U. Okeke 1971a. See also the portfolio of reprographs, Okeke 1982c, and the photographs of "A Trial of Strength" and of "Ọnalu" in C. Okeke 1993a, 28. Not all of his gouaches of Igbo tales appeared in his book.

98. O. Udechukwu 1977, 76.

99. O. Udechukwu 1977, 77.

100. O. Udechukwu 1977, 77–78.

101. O. Udechukwu 1977, 18.

102. For photographs of all three of these war works, see C. Okeke 1993a, 27.

103. U. Okeke and Uche-Okeke 1978, 36.

## 4. UCHE OKEKE, III

1. Uche Okeke, video interview by Simon Ottenberg, May 26, 1994, at Asele Institute, Nimo.

2. Kalu 1991 discusses the reconstruction period after the war. See also Chinua Achebe 1985, 45–50; Igbokwe 1995; Nsukka Analyst 1994. Adiele Afigbo, the well-known Nigerian historian, recounts how the war turned him from eastern Nigerian and African history research to that on Igbo history (1992, 13–15), and he notes a tendency among African historians to change from the study of the com-forted to the discomforted (1992, 21–22), a move paralleling that of the Nsukka artists after the war.

3. Uche Okeke, video interview, May 26, 1994.

4. Kelly and Stanley 1993, 106–9.

5. U. Okeke indicates to me that the name "Fine Art" as used at the Ahmadu Bello University, Zaria, is British usage, while "Fine Arts" is American usage. Okeke added "and Applied" to make for a plural conception of art and to make it possible for two departments to be created in the future for budgetary purposes. This has not occurred.

6. Kelly and Stanley 1993, 97–100; Ọlọidi 1993a. His name is sometimes spelled in the published literature without the final "h."

7. Willis' 1986 M.F.A. thesis summarizes much of the information gathered in the student theses on *uli* motifs: their names, what they looked like, and where they were located. See also Willis 1987, 1997.

8. Alaneme 1971.

9. U. Okeke 1972a, 2.

10. U. Okeke 1982a, 53. For his cultural politics writings, see U. Okeke 1982a, 11, 26–27, 29–32, 33–35, 41–47.

11. U. Okeke 1993a, 58–72. Nnah William Udosen, in textiles, actually came a month before Okeke. Uko Akpaide, of Ibibio background, began teaching sculpture in 1974; El Anatsui, who came from Ghana in 1975, is a sculptor and has worked in ceramics; George A. Adams, from Vienna and Britain, taught graphic design in 1973; P. H. David-West, from Nigeria, taught graphic design in 1975–76; C. S. Okeke began teaching textiles in 1975; Benjo N. Igwilo, ceramics in 1973.

12. Ọlọidi 1984, unfortunately never published, although sections of it have appeared as articles in journals and books.

13. Ọlọidi 1978b.

14. Ekekwe 1994; Nkurumeh 1992; Sibigam 1987.

15. Unfortunately the symposium was never published, though a few individual papers were. Copies of some papers are in the library, National Museum of African Art, Smithsonian Institution, Washington, D.C.

16. U. Okeke 1976b, 1977a.

17. An exhibition of the art of students and former students covering the years 1970–84 surveys the accomplishments of the art program during much of Okeke's time at the university. See *Echo* 1985.

18. C. Okeke 1993a, 18, 20.

19. U. Okeke and Uche-Okeke 1978, 36.

20. C. Okeke 1993a, 30, contains photographs of two of these wood reliefs.

21. *Christian Arts in Nigeria* 1979; see pp. 33–34 for two photographs of portal designs.

22. C. Okeke 1993a, 29, 39; Afuba n.d. Afuba eventually took a diploma in art at the Institute of Management and Technol-

ogy, Enugu, and now teaches there. For his record see Kelly and Stanley 1993, 56–57.

23. "Nigerian Master Artists" 1979, 34, 36. In 1972 Okeke had made a gouache painting of the design, from which he produced a smaller work to employ as a model for the weaving.

24. Nsukka artists exhibited as well, including Paul Igboanugo, Chuka Amaefunah, Chike Aniakọr, Ego Uche-Okeke (Okeke's wife), and Obiọra Udechukwu. See *Nigerian National Exhibition* 1977. For a catalogue of the festival, see *FESTAC '77* 1977.

25. Ekekwe 1994, 28.

26. Federal Department of Culture 1981. The gallery has been badly run down, with the air conditioning out of operation and its works deteriorating. New works have rarely been added for exhibition. Now, however, under its new name, the National Gallery of Art, and a new director, Dr. Paul Chike Dike, it is being revitalized, and major art conferences are planned to be held there in the future. Part of the collection has been moved to Abuja, the new capital of Nigeria, for eventual exhibition there.

27. The solo exhibitions were *Contemporary Nigerian Prints, Drawings and Paintings*, Katherine E. Nash Gallery, University of Minnesota; *Homage to Asele, Exhibition of Prints, Drawings and Paintings*, organized by the African American Cultural Center, Minneapolis; *Uche Okeke, a Retrospective*, University Gallery, University of Minnesota; *Contemporary African Painting and Drawings by Uche Okeke*, Dolly Fiterman Gallery, Minneapolis. The Detroit exhibition, *Magie Noire*, was held at the Jazzonia Gallery and included five other West African artists.

28. U. Okeke 1982a, 1982b, 1982c.

29. Dolly Fiterman Gallery n.d. For two of his etchings from this time, *Ana, Asele and Badunka* and *Flowers of the Primeval Forest*, see C. Okeke 1993a, 31, where their titles are reversed.

30. C. Okeke 1993a, 32–33, 39.

31. See *Research in African Literatures* 6:2, 1975; *Okike* 1 and 2, 1971; *Nimo* 1:1, 1973; *New Culture* 1:9, 1979, 49; *Ufahamu* 6:3, 1976. In addition, Okeke issued a number of postcards of his art at the Asele Institute.

32. Good general sources for this section are U. Okeke 1993b, 10–18; Kelly and Stanley 1993, 363–64.

33. 1990, produced by WETA-TV and Smithsonian World.

34. U. Okeke 1977a, 1978b, 1978–79, 1982a, 20–25, 1988; U. Okeke and Okechukwu 1978. For a series of essays on the Nsukka area by various authors in eastern Nigeria, see Ọfọmata 1978.

35. "The House of Images," *Okike* 1, 1971, 26. For some of Okeke's poetry, see *Nimo* 1:1, 1973, 30–32; *Okike* 1, 1971, 26–29; *Okike* 17, 1980, 50–51, C. Okeke 1993a, 40.

36. U. Okeke 1988, 19, 21.

37. U. Okeke 1993a, 73–94.

38. For his writings see U. Okeke 1982a, 53–55, 1988, 1993a, 2–20, 43–44, 124–26.

39. U. Okeke 1982a, 53.

40. U. Okeke 1982a, 53–55, 1988, 19, 21.

41. C. Okeke 1993a.

42. It is hoped that the symposium papers will be published. The library, National Museum of African Art, Smithsonian Institution, Washington, D.C., holds many of them.

43. U. Okeke 1988.

44. Aas 1992.

### 5. CHIKE ANIAKỌR

1. Chike Aniakọr, video interview by Simon Ottenberg, June 7, 1994, at his home at the University of Nigeria, Nsukka.

2. For general information on Chike Aniakọr, see Kelly and Stanley 1993, 106–9; Ikwuemesi 1991, 1992b.

3. Including Anthony Morah, Osita Njelita, Benjo Igwilo, and Oseloka Osadebe.

4. Ikwuemesi 1992b, 96, 106–7, and personal discussion with Aniakọr and others.

5. Ikwuemesi 1991, 12; 1992b, 94. Argent also influenced the late Gani Odutokun in the matter of color. See C. Okeke 1995, 59–61.

6. Aniakọr 1978, 204–14.

7. Ikwuemesi 1992b, 96.

8. The first, dated 1977, is in the collection of the National Museum of African Art, Smithsonian Institution, Washington, D.C. For the latter see AKA Circle of Exhibiting Artists 1986, 30.

9. However, Aniakọr has had students who felt that he unnecessarily held up their theses or other work; he can be a hard taskmaster.

10. Aniakọr 1978. See also Kelly and Stanley 1993, 108–9 and Aniakọr 1995b for further references to his architecture writings.

11. Cole and Aniakọr 1984.

12. Ikwuemesi 1992b, 106.

13. Chike Aniakọr, video interview, June 7, 1994.

14. Ikwuemesi 1992b, 88.

15. Ikwuemesi 1992b, 39–56.

16. Adenaike 1982b, 25–26 and pls. 25–28.

17. Aniakọr 1972.

18. Chike Aniakọr, video interview, June 7, 1994.

19. However, Aniakọr recently published a traditional Igbo tale that he has illustrated in color; see Aniakọr 1992.

20. Chike Aniakọr, video interview, June 7, 1994.

21. See *Propitiation* on the cover of his 1972 solo exhibition (Aniakọr 1972), and Ikwuemesi 1992b, 50, figs. 28 and 29.

22. Ikwuemesi 1992b, 52.

23. *Original Prints from the Third Nsukka Workshop 1987* 1987, and *Prints from Nsukka 4th Printmaking Workshop 1990* 1990.

24. Aniakǫr 1972, "Artist's Background," no pagination. This statement appears again in Aniakǫr 1975, 42.
25. Adenaike 1982b, 16, 21.
26. Ikwuemesi 1992b, 10.
27. Adenaike 1982a, 44.
28. See Aniakǫr 1972, 1978, 1992. 1995b.
29. Ikwuemesi 1992b, 97.
30. Ikwuemesi 1992b, 103–4.
31. Aniakǫr (1978, 207, and fig. 55, item 21) notes that parallel stripes "may refer to the beautiful stripes of the bush rat (*ǫgini*). Hence they are known as *agwa ǫgini* which the Igbo cite as an example of beauty in the bush." This is close to the form that Aniakǫr employs in his art.
32. Federal Department of Culture 1981, 40. See also "The Triumph," in Aniakǫr 1980, 55.
33. See *Research in African Literatures* 10:1 and 10:3, 1979; *Black American Literature Forum* 13:3, 1979; *Obsidian: Black Literature in Review* 5, 1979; *Ufahamu* 8:1, 1977 and 9:1, 1979; *New Culture* 1:7 and 1:8, 1979; *Greenfield Review* 8:1/2, 1979; *African Arts* 8:4, 1975; *Okike* 9, 1975; 10, 1976; and 12, 1978.
34. Ikwuemesi 1992b, 52.
35. Ikwuemesi (1992b, 61) calls it "flowery."
36. For Aniakǫr's detailed exhibition record, see Kelly and Stanley 1993, 107–8.
37. *Aka* means "hand" in Igbo, referring to the importance of the hand in art, the necessary cooperation of the differently shaped fingers of the hand, and also in Igbo culture for the hand's use in sacrifice and its links to destiny. For catalogues of the various years of its exhibitions, see AKA Circle of Exhibiting Artists; see also Ogbechie 1992 and Ottenberg 1994.
38. AKA Circle of Exhibiting Artists 1986, 1987, 1988, 1989, 1991, 1993, and 1995.
39. Aniakǫr 1990a; Nigeria 1988.
40. Aniakǫr 1980.
41. Aniakǫr 1991.
42. Aniakǫr 1995a.
43. AKA Circle of Exhibiting Artists 1989, 9.
44. Cole and Aniakǫr 1984.
45. Aniakǫr 1982.
46. Aniakǫr 1973, 1984, 1986.
47. See *Obsidian: Black Literature in Review* 5:1/2, 1979, 94–105; *Greenfield Review* 8:1/2, 1979, 81–84; *African Arts* 8:4, 1975, 42–43; *Okike* 16, 1979, 33; *Ufahamu* 8:1, 1977, 4, 106 and 9:1, 1979, 81, 173; *Black American Literature Forum* 13:3, 1979, 96–99; Achebe and Udechukwu 1982; Aniakǫr n.d. Some of his published poetry is accompanied by his illustrations, though the latter are not necessarily linked to specific verses.
48. Aniakǫr 1975.
49. "Newspaper Vendor," in Aniakǫr, n.d., no pagination.
50. Aniakǫr n.d.
51. Aniakǫr n.d.
52. For "Heavensgate," see *Obsidian: Black Literature in Review* 5:1/2, 1979, 98.

## 6. NIGERIAN CONTEMPORARY ART

1. Appiah 1992, 157.
2. For general comments on the state of contemporary Nigerian art in the 1970–95 period, see Akolo 1987; Aradeon 1987; Crowder 1978, 1981; Fǫlarin 1987; J̣ẹgẹdẹ 1981 (reprinted 1983), 1983, 1984, 1988, 1994, n.d.; Ǫlǫidi 1981, 1995a; Oyebǫla [Oyelǫla] 1981.
3. Aig-Imoukhuede 1991, 155–56; Ǫlǫidi 1995a; Ruprecht 1988.
4. There is a clear relationship between the modern Nigerian cartoon and traditional satire in masquerades, song, poetry, and other indigenous forms. A useful general source on Nigerian cartoons is Udechukwu 1979a. See also Asuquo and Ǫnuǫha 1985; Azuru 1980; Iloaputaife 1976; Ngerem 1986; Ǫnwudinjǫ 1987; Ǫrjih 1985. On indigenous Igbo satire, see Egudu 1972; Nwǫga 1971; Ottenberg 1975.
5. Ǫlǫidi 1995a, 71–72.
6. Nigeria 1988.
7. Ashiwaju et al. 1977.
8. Federal Department of Culture 1981.
9. Ebǫng 1991; Harney 1996.
10. Yet the federal government, as well as Nigeria's states, support university and college art programs, thus playing indirect roles.
11. "Didi Museum: A Leader in Private Museums" 1990.
12. Goethe Institut 1979.
13. East Central State 1971, 1; Reed 1996.
14. France, always an art-acquiring country, draws heavily on Francophone artists, but rarely is interested in work from the English-speaking African areas—a leftover of colonial attachments. The same is true of Britain with regard to the French-speaking areas of the continent.
15. Akantu and Ǫlanipekun 1991.
16. Ǫlǫidi 1995a, 70.
17. Ishaka 1990; Ojukwu 1989.
18. C. Okeke 1991; Egonwa 1986; O. Udechukwu 1995.
19. *Nigerian National Exhibition* 1977; *FESTAC '77* 1977; *Pageants of the African World* 1980.
20. *Silver Jubilee National Art Exhibition* 1985.
21. Jẹgẹdẹ 1990.
22. Copies of some of the papers from each conference are on file at the library, National Museum of African Art, Smithsonian Institution, Washington, D.C.
23. Ǫlǫidi 1995a, 68.
24. Ukhuegbe 1986; Brokensha 1969.
25. Okediji 1989. See also B. Campbell 1993; *Ifẹ Art School* 1984; Harris 1992, 1994.
26. C. Okeke 1995, 42; Jari 1995a, 1995b; Ruprecht 1988,

75–79; *Zaria Art School* 1990.

27. C. Okeke 1995, 43.

28. Ọlọidi 1995, 72.

29. Jari 1995a, 1995b.

30. Bello 1991a, 1991b; Bello and Nasidi 1991.

31. Campbell et al. 1993.

32. Okediji 1992.

33. Wangboje 1982. See also Ajayi 1985; Olorukoọba 1991.

## 7. OBIỌRA UDECHUKWU, I

1. O. Udechukwu 1980a, 44.

2. On Udechukwu see Kelly and Stanley 1993, 474–80; O. Udechukwu 1993; Beier 1980, 1981a; "*The Muse* Interviews Obiọra Udechukwu" 1993.

3. See O. Udechukwu 1993, 4, for a photograph of Eze.

4. Okafọr 1980; Ifeọma Madumere 1993. Ndefo's photograph is in O. Udechukwu 1993, 4.

5. Examples of Ndefo's drawings are in *The Sacrificial Egg and Other Short Stories* by Chinua Achebe (1962b). Before the Biafran war he had a furniture factory in Ọnitsha, and he has also created bas-reliefs and other wood sculptures, largely of a Christian religious nature.

6. Okigbo 1962, 1971, 3–19; "*The Muse* Interviews Obiọra Udechukwu" 1993, 21. Much has been written about this remarkable poet, killed on the northern front in August 1967, during the Biafran war, who has been a major influence on Udechukwu. See Aas 1995; Chinua Achebe and Okafọr 1978; Anafulu 1978; Egudu 1977, 3–22; Lindfors 1982, 155–63; Nwọga 1984; Obiechina 1980; Okigbo 1971; Pieterse and Duerden 1972, 132–47; P. Thomas 1968; O. Udechukwu 1975.

7. O. Udechukwu 1993, 65. For photographs of his art in the 1963–66 period, see O. Udechukwu 1993, pls. 5–20.

8. A nightsoilman is a person who collects human excrement from bucket latrines and disposes of it. One of Udechukwu's best works from this early period is his *Nightsoilman* (1964, oil; fig. 73). See O. Udechukwu 1993, pl. 64.

9. With fellow artists Uzọ Ndubisi, Bons Nwabiani, Okechukwu Uchegbu, and Ifeanyi Madu.

10. See Kelly and Stanley 1993, 242–44 for information on Igboanugo, and Kelly and Stanley 1993, 97–100 on Amaefunah.

11. For the Nsukka market, see O. Udechukwu 1993, fig. 21.

12. O. Udechukwu 1980a, 43.

13. O. Udechukwu 1981a, 7.

14. Ogbechiẹ 1992, 110; O. Udechukwu 1972.

15. The best general accounts of artists during the Biafran war are Azuonye 1991; Okereke 1979; and O. Udechukwu 1991a.

16. O. Udechukwu 1990a, back cover.

17. This group was mostly based on persons who had been in the various arts at the University of Nigeria, Nsukka, before

the war. "Ọdunke" refers to a major festival held every ten years in a number of communities in the central Igbo area.

18. *Veneration to Udo,* the play's official title, has also been called *Veneration to Peace.* Udo is the Igbo goddess of peace. A feeling existed among some artists in the war, as well as others, that the corruption in leadership that existed in Nigeria before the conflict, had occurred again in Biafra, in the allocation of relief supplies and in other ways. The play, which was by the Ọdunke artists, contained such a critique. See also Azuonye 1972, 1; Ike 1976; Iroh 1979; and the story "Girls at War" in Chinua Achebe 1973.

19. Eight of Udechukwu's war poems are in Azuonye 1972, 5–9; poems are concerned with much the same topics as his visual art at that time.

20. Ọdunke survived at Nsukka after the war, as a good number of its members went to the University of Nigeria. It has been intermittently active since then, producing interesting plays, art exhibitions, and publications. For example, a play some of its members wrote in 1973, *Ọjaadili,* was produced at the Nigerian Festival of the Arts in Lagos. Udechukwu designed the costumes for it. See *Ọjaadili* 1979. A collection of war poems was published by Ọdunke, edited by Azuonye (1972). See also Azuonye 1991, 25.

21. Azuonye 1991, 20.

22. *Nigerian Art—Kindred Spirits* 1990, from the text of reel 12, pp. 4–5.

23. O. Udechukwu 1993, pls. 38, 40, 68, 69, and p. 14.

24. O. Udechukwu 1993, pl. 32.

25. Okereke 1979, figs. 30–33.

26. O. Udechukwu 1993, pls. 69, 70, and 68, respectively.

27. Ọguibe 1989a.

28. For example, *The Exiles (Facing the Unknown)* (1973, linocut; fig. 78); *Flight* (1977, oil); *Exile Train* (1980, oil); *Refugee Mother and Child* (1985, aquatint); *Refugee Family* (1985, drypoint); *Rhythm of Hunger* (1985, ink and wash). *The Exiles, Refugee Mother and Child,* and *Refugee Family* are illustrated in O. Udechukwu 1993, pls. 44, 60, and 61 respectively.

29. C. Okeke 1993b, 5.

30. Azuonye 1972, 5–6; O. Udechukwu 1990a, 16–18.

31. Obiọra Udechukwu, video interview by Simon Ottenberg, June 4, 1994, at his studio at Nsukka.

32. Obiọra Udechukwu, video interview, June 4, 1994.

33. Obiọra Udechukwu, video interview, June 4, 1994.

34. Beier 1962c. See also Beier 1961b, 1968, 29–34, 1990; Kennedy 1992, 109–13; Mount 1989, 108–12. Salahi no longer uses the "el" in his name.

35. The Nsukka-trained artist and friend of Udechukwu, Tayọ Adenaike (1982b, 48), believes he may also have been stimulated by the linear art of Ben Shahn.

36. O. Udechukwu 1972.

37. O. Udechukwu 1972, 19.

38. O. Udechukwu 1972, 20.

39. O. Udechukwu 1975; Igboanugo 1976.

40. Odutokun (1993b, 10) suggests that Udechukwu's art assumed "such a sinuous character" because it was a celebration of the end of the war. Perhaps so, perhaps not, but certainly he draws strongly from mural *uli*. He saw little body *uli* during his Agulu research.

41. Ikwuemesi 1992b, 52.

42. An exception is *The Dancer* (1974, pen and ink), a beautiful drawing reminiscent of some of Ben Enwọnwu's Négritude style art. It is reproduced in *Research in African Literatures* 7:1, 1976, 52, and in O. Udechukwu 1975, no pagination.

43. Both in O. Udechukwu 1975.

44. Okigbo's major poems were already available in Nigeria by 1971. See Okigbo 1971.

45. Igboanugo 1976, 25. Norbert Aas believes that there is an intended or an accepted ambiguity in Udechukwu's art (personal communication).

46. Beier 1981, 65.

47. C. Okeke 1993b, pl. 46; O. Udechukwu 1993, pl. 46.

48. For reproductions of some of Udechukwu's pen and ink drawings of the time, see *Research in African Literatures* 7:1, 1976, front cover, 52, 60, 63, 138; 7:2, 1976, front cover, 161, 210, 232, 234, 311; *Ufahamu* 6:2, 1976, 4, 63, 133, 168; *Greenfield Review* 8:1/2, 1979, 70, 73, 78. See also the list in O. Udechukwu 1993, 84 for other reproductions.

49. For the last two works, see O. Udechukwu 1993, pls. 70 and 71.

50. O. Udechukwu 1984c, pl. 22.

51. Igboanugo 1976, 26.

52. O. Udechukwu 1981b. On *Li* traditions see Goepper 1963, 31, 51, 140; Sze 1963, vol. 1, 30–32, 48, 50, 98–99, vol. 2, 628.

53. Beier 1981, 64.

54. O. Udechukwu 1980a, 43.

55. While admitting that some of his art shows similarities to that of Paul Klee, Udechukwu does not consider him to have been an influence. Norbert Aas (personal communication) has suggested that the idea of Klee's influence on Udechukwu is an often expressed Eurocentric opinion about Udechukwu's work.

56. O. Udechukwu 1977.

57. *Ufahamu* 6:2, 1976, 62.

58. Ọgbalu 1965. See also O. Udechukwu 1993, 82–83 for a list of his illustrations.

59. The magazine *Ụwa Ndi Igbo* (1984–) is a cultural journal in Igbo and English, of which two numbers have appeared so far. The book in Igbo, by Chinua Achebe and Udechukwu (1982), consists of contemporary poetry, to which Udechukwu contributed three poems.

60. Beier 1981, 66.

## 8. OBIỌRA UDECHUKWU, II

1. From the poem "We Were Once Poor but Wealthy," by Udechukwu. See O. Udechukwu 1990a, 53.

2. Macgregor 1909; Thompson 1982. Other key references to *nsibidi* are Battestini 1991; K. Campbell 1983; Chikamnele 1994; Cole and Aniakọr 1984, 59–61; Dayrell, 1910, 1911; Kalu 1978a, 1978b; Kubik 1986; Irene Madumere 1988; Oji 1994; Talbot 1912, 447–61; Thompson 1978.

3. O. Udechukwu 1985a, no pagination.

4. The German exhibition, entitled *Dialog mit Grafik*, was held at Iwalẹwa-Haus, Bayreuth, July 18–August 15, 1985. For the Lagos exhibition, see Schmidt and O. Udechukwu 1985.

5. Beier 1980.

6. The exhibition *Zeichnungen* was held there May 14–July 1, 1982. See O. Udechukwu 1982a. The same year he also exhibited in a Nigerian exhibition at Bonn. See *Nigerian Art Exhibition* 1982.

7. *Nigerian-German Prints Exhibition* 1986; *Original Prints from the Third Nsukka Workshop 1987* 1987; *Prints from Nsukka: 4th Printmaking Workshop* 1990; Ekekwe 1994; Nkurumeh 1992; Sibigam 1987.

8. See Schmidt 1988 for his interpretation of the Nsukka artists and their work.

9. They met when Udechukwu was in Germany in 1982. Aas later published Udechukwu's collection of poetry, *What the Madman Said* (1990a), and his wife Ada's poetry, *Woman, me* (1993), at his Boomerang Press. Aas has also mounted exhibitions of Udechukwu's and other Nigerian artists' works in Germany.

10. See O. Udechukwu 1988, 1990b; *Uli Art: Master Works, Recent Works* 1995.

11. O. Udechukwu 1980b, 3.

12. O. Udechukwu 1980b, 4.

13. O. Udechukwu 1980b, 4.

14. Wonodi 1971, in the poem "Dusts of Exile," Part V: "A man stood by a deep gorge. He was of the exile train/ that moved from town to town."

15. All three oils belong to the National Gallery of Art, Lagos. The last two mentioned are pictured in Federal Department of Culture 1981, 103.

16. O. Udechukwu 1981a.

17. O. Udechukwu 1981a, 45. Reprinted in his *What the Madman Said* 1990a, 53–55 and *Okike* 18, 1981, 16–17.

18. O. Udechukwu 1984c, pl. 75.

19. O. Udechukwu 1985a.   The prints from this exhibition were also exhibited at Iwalẹwa-Haus, University of Bayreuth, July 18–August 15, 1985.

20. O. Udechukwu 1993, pl. 77.

21. O. Udechukwu 1985b, 4–5.

22. See O. Udechukwu 1993, pl. 77.

23. O. Udechukwu 1993, pl. 85.

24. AKA Circle of Exhibiting Artists 1987, 60. There are also three reproductions of ink drawings of generals in his *What the Madman Said* 1990a, 35–37.

25. O. Udechukwu 1993, pl. 83.

26. The German scholar Norbert Aas (personal communication) believes that Udechukwu's interest in landscapes grew out of his conventional training at Zaria.

27. See O. Udechukwu 1989a, 3–4, where he lovingly extols the beauty of nature but laments that humans have spoiled it. In addition to photographs from this exhibition in the catalogue, see also AKA Circle of Exhibiting Artists 1988, 60–64.

28. O. Udechukwu 1989b, 14–16.

29. Animals rarely occur in any of Udechukwu's art; there is only an occasional sheep, cat, chameleon, bird, or some domestic cattle. The focus of his art is either on humans or landscapes and, as we shall see, the seasons.

30. O. Udechukwu 1989b, 12 and 20 respectively.

31. O. Udechukwu 1993, pl. 72. *Mai Ruwa* is a Hausa term for water carrier.

32. Federal Department of Culture 1981, 103.

33. O. Udechukwu 1993, pls. 64 and 70.

34. O. Udechukwu 1993, pls. 5, 53.

35. O. Udechukwu 1993, pl. 26; Okigbo 1971, 6–7.

36. Oguibe 1989c.

37. O. Udechukwu 1993, pl. 23.

38. O. Udechukwu 1993, pl. 35.

39. O. Udechukwu 1980b, 4. Flyovers are elevated motor roads crossing over other roads below them.

40. These three works are depicted in O. Udechukwu 1993, especially pls. 46, 75, and 74.

41. Popularly known, especially in Euro/America, as the "African piano," an incorrect designation in ethnomusicological terms.

42. O. Udechukwu 1984c, pl. 32; 1993, pl. 78.

43. It is interesting to note that the poet Christopher Okigbo, whose writings Udechukwu so much admires and from whom he draws inspiration for his visual art, was himself heavily influenced by music in his poetry. His later writing has been called "choral poetry." See Pieterse and Duerden 1972, 137–38, 143–44.

44. For discussions of Igbo minstrels and examples of their verse, see Chinua Achebe and O. Udechukwu 1982; Azuonye 1984, 1985a, 1985b, 1990; Azuonye and Udechukwu 1984; O. Udechukwu 1984d.

45. See the sketches entitled *Obiligbo in Concert* (1967, blue ball pen), in O. Udechukwu 1984c, pl. 6, and the ink and wash, *Obiligbo* (n.d.), pl. 7 in the same work. See also Chinua Achebe and O. Udechukwu 1982, 9–14, for examples of

Obiligbo's verses in Igbo, as well as that of other minstrels elsewhere in the book.

46. O. Udechukwu 1993, pls. 54 and 55. On Jadum see Okigbo 1971, 8; Ekwueme 1993, 175–79. Jadum, from Aguata in Anambra State, was not a true minstrel but one who chanted like one, wandering about the Awka and Onitsha areas. He was known for his bold and witty statements and for taking the law into his own hands, "oblivious of the British colonial administration, whose authority he sometimes challenged" (Ekwueme 1993, 175). He was a popular anticolonial figure in Igboland.

47. The title *Exile Train*, as already noted, derives from Okogbule Wonodi's *Dusts of Exile* (1971). The first work is in the collection of the National Gallery of Art, Lagos. For a photograph of the second one, see O. Udechukwu 1984c, pl. 50.

48. O. Udechukwu 1993, pl. 44.

49. Aka Circle of Exhibiting Artists 1989, 61, and O. Udechukwu 1993, pl. 80, respectively.

50. O. Udechukwu 1990a. See also *Okike* 16, 1979, 53, and 18, 1981, 16–17.

51. O. Udechukwu 1990a, 65.

52. O. Udechukwu 1990a, 35–37.

53. C. Okeke 1990.

54. O. Udechukwu 1979b, 1981a, 1981b, 1981c, 1984d, 1984e, 1989b, 1991b.

55. O. Udechukwu 1991b.

56. O. Udechukwu 1979a.

57. O. Udechukwu 1978. See also his unpublished paper, 1995.

58. O. Udechukwu 1980a.

59. O. Udechukwu 1980a, 227.

60. O. Udechukwu 1980a, 45.

61. O. Udechukwu 1980a, 45–46.

62. O. Udechukwu 1980a, 45.

63. For a thoughtful analysis of a 1993 Udechukwu aquatint, *Watermaid*, see Aas 1995.

64. C. Okeke 1993b, 6. For a discussion of Udechukwu's recent art, see Aas 1994a.

65. Aas 1994a, 61.

66. Aas 1994b.

67. O. Udechukwu 1993.

68. O. Udechukwu 1993, front cover.

69. O. Udechukwu 1993, pl. 66.

70. Obiora Udechukwu, video interview by Simon Ottenberg, June 4, 1994, at his studio at Nsukka.

71. For photographs of the cat and the three seasons paintings, see Aas and Vierke 1993.

72. A different root crop than the American yam.

73. *Configura 2* 1995. The countries were Brazil, China, Egypt, Greece, India, Nigeria, Mexico, Russia, and the United States, and the themes were The Image of Man, Secure Values, The Altar of Culture, The Laid Table, The Magic of Objects, and Signs of Life.

74. See *Configura 2* 1995, for photographs of this project.

75. *Configura 2* 1995, 9, 12.

## 9. EL ANATSUI

1. Anatsui 1991, 7; Anatsui and Oguibe 1993, 42.

2. General information on Anatsui's life and work is to be found in Anatsui 1992; Anatsui and Oguibe 1993; Aniakọr 1990b, 1991; Kelly and Stanley 1993, 102–6; Oguibe n.d.; C. Okeke 1994.

3. Anatsui 1992, 4–5.

4. Aṣante was formerly spelled Ashanti. See Rattray 1923, 1927; Wilks 1975, 1993.

5. See Lamb 1975, chap. 3 on Aṣante cloth and chap. 4 on Ewe textiles.

6. Anatsui 1992, 6.

7. Aniakọr 1990b, 14–15. For a somewhat different account of Anatsui and his work by Aniakọr, see Aniakọr 1991.

8. Oguibe n.d., 1–2.

9. Anatsui 1992, 10.

10. Akpaide 1976, 2.

11. Udechukwu 1982b, 1.

12. Oguibe n.d., 3.

13. See Anatsui 1976, 3; 1982, 8–10.

14. Anatsui 1992, 9–10.

15. Anatsui 1976.

16. Anatsui and Oguibe 1993, 50–51.

17. Oguibe n.d., 3–4.

18. Anatsui 1979, 1982.

19. Anatsui 1979, 2.

20. For the best discussion of Anatsui's ceramics, see Oguibe n.d., 5–8.

21. Anatsui 1982, 5.

22. Oguibe n.d., 14.

23. Anatsui 1992, 22.

24. Anatsui 1992, 23.

25. Anatsui 1992, 26.

26. Anatsui 1992, 45.

27. Aniakọr 1990, 15.

28. See the front cover of Anatsui 1982.

29. Anatsui 1987a; see also the front book cover in Nwọga 1982.

30. Anatsui 1992, 14.

31. C. Okeke 1994, 35.

32. C. Okeke 1994, 37.

33. Anatsui 1987b, 10.

34. Ọlọidi 1991b. See also Anatsui 1992, 23.

35. Oguibe n.d., 1.

36. Anatsui 1992, 16, 25.

37. Aniakọr 1990b, 15; C. Okeke 1994, 35. On these various African scripts and design systems, see Amaeshi 1977; Kubik 1986.

38. C. Okeke 1994, 37–38.

39. Arinze 1991, 3.

40. Anatsui 1987b, 38–39.

41. Anatsui 1987b, 21–23, 29–30.

42. Anatsui 1987b, 19 and 1988, 15.

43. Anatsui 1995, front cover.

44. Oguibe 1987, 663.

45. Anatsui 1987b, 19; C. Okeke 1995, 59. See Oguibe 1987, 664, for some other titles, as well as in Anatsui's various catalogues.

46. *Akparata, oyili-ọji*, camwood, *oke-ọfọ*, 1993, 58 × 127 cm, fourteen panels.

47. *Okpo-ọcha, oyili-ọji*, 1993, 90 × 84 cm, nine panels.

48. *Okpo-ọcha, oyili-ọji, akparata*, tempera, 94 × 116.9 × 2.5 cm, twelve panels.

49. *Afara, oke-ọfọ*, and other woods, acrylic, 55.9 × 146.7 × 2.5 cm, thirteen panels.

50. *Okpo-ọcha* and *oyili-ọji* woods, tempera, 90 × 84.4 × 3 cm, nine panels.

51. *Oke-ọfo, oyili-ọji, akparata, okpo-ọcha* woods, tempera, 61 × 141 × 4 cm, sixteen panels.

52. *Okpeye*, tempera, 98 × 150 × 15 cm (variable), twenty-four pieces.

53. *Iroko, oyili-ọji*, tempera, dimensions unknown, fifteen panels.

54. *Opepe, oyili-ọji*, camwood, 114 × 69 × 3 cm.

55. See Oguibe 1996, n.d., 20–22; Fosu 1993, 201.

56. Oguibe n.d., 21. Both sculptures are given a more detailed reading in Oguibe 1996.

57. Oak and resin; *Mr. Nyanga*: 175.3 × 49.5 × 34.3 cm; *Mrs. Nyanga*: 170.4 × 49.5 × 44.5 cm. See Studio Museum in Harlem 1990, front cover.

58. Mostly *oyili-ọji*, each about 172 cm high, eighteen and nineteen pieces.

59. Oak, 159 × 20 × 14 cm.

60. Piqua and marfin woods and tempera, 300 cm high.

61. C. Okeke 1994, 40.

62. *Iroko* and rope, 1992, 199 × 61 cm.

63. *Iroko*, 125 × 45 × 32 cm (variable). See AKA Circle of Exhibiting Artists 1991, 22; C. Okeke 1994, 40.

64. Assorted woods, 1992, 18 cm high. See Ogunwa 1995, 1576; Anatsui 1995; C. Okeke 1994, 34.

65. Wood, cloth, raffia, palm fiber, c. 183 cm high.

66. "Sculptor Wins Japanese Prize" 1995.

67. Anatsui 1982.

68. Studio Museum in Harlem 1990; *Uli Art: Master Works, Recent Works* 1995.

69. *Configura 2* 1995.

70. Gervasoni 1990; *Arte—Sociedad—Reflexión* 1994.

71. *Africus: Johannesburg Biennale* 1995. Sometimes Anatsui is included in international exhibitions as a Ghanaian, at other times as a Nigerian. He is both, in a sense.

72. Dwyer 1985; *Zweites Symposion Nordseeküste* 1984; Oguibe 1996 and n.d., 22–23.

73. Oguibe 1996, 76; n.d., 22.

74. "News from Denmark" 1996 and personal communication.

## 10. TAYỌ ADENAIKE

1. Tayọ Adenaike, video interview by Simon Ottenberg, Washington, D.C., June 13, 1994.
2. In addition, Kim Kimmerlin from the United States was there in the early 1980s, Anna Rospond from Poland briefly taught during the same period, and George Adams and Paul Champman from Britain were there in the middle 1970s.
3. Adenaike 1979, printed in part in Adenaike 1995a.
4. Adenaike 1982b, 1982c.
5. Aradeon 1987.
6. Adenaike 1980, 1–2.
7. *Diversity* 1979.
8. Adenaike 1993a, 5, pays tribute to Uche Okeke in the latter's Lagos retrospective catalogue. "My salute to a great teacher, the teacher of my teacher [Obiọra Udechukwu] and I bow in appreciation." He also had a watercolor in Uche Okeke's 1993 retrospective exhibition in Lagos in his honor, entitled *Homage to Uche Okeke* (see C. Okeke 1993a, 36). Adenaike studied less with Uche Okeke than with Obiọra Udechukwu, as was true of some other students, yet the former was also an important influence on him.
9. Tayọ Adenaike, video interview by Simon Ottenberg, June 30, 1995, at the National Museum of African Art, Smithsonian Institution.
10. Tayọ Adenaike, video interview, June 30, 1995.
11. Adenaike 1980, 1981, 1982a.
12. Kelly and Stanley 1993, 38–39.
13. See Aniakọr 1995a for a different classification of the Nsukka artists' generations.
14. Adenaike 1980, 1.
15. Adenaike 1981.
16. Adenaike 1981, 10.
17. Adenaike 1981, 14.
18. Federal Department of Culture 1981, 10, 25.
19. Adenaike 1981, 4.
20. Adenaike 1982a.
21. Adenaike 1982a, 4.
22. Adenaike 1983; Aradeon 1987, 5–6. The exhibition consisted of twenty watercolors, seven works in ink, and three in ink and wash.
23. Adenaike 1983, 5.
24. Aig-Imoukhuede 1983.
25. Adenaike 1984. The exhibition contained twenty watercolors and nine ink works. See also Akinosho 1984.
26. Adenaike 1984, 4.
27. Adenaike 1986a.
28. Adenaike 1986a, 14.
29. For his other ink and ink and wash work, see Adenaike 1981, 1982c, 1983, 1984, 1990a, 1994a; AKA Circle of Exhibiting Artists 1986, 1989, 1990, as well as illustrations in *Okike* 18, 1981, 64; 19, 1981, 100; 20, 1981, 78, 97; 23, 1983, 27, 96, 104, 122, 126, 144; 24, 1983, 23, 46, 56, 70, 76, 104.
30. Adenaike 1986a, 5.
31. Akpederi 1986; see also Adenaike 1986a, 17.
32. Adenaike 1986b.
33. Adenaike 1986b, 15, 13 respectively, both created in 1986.
34. Adenaike 1986b, front cover.
35. Adenaike 1986b, 4.
36. Adenaike 1986a, 6.
37. Okediji (1989, 93, 99) feels that Adenaike's art exhibits both Yoruba *ọna* style, as he calls it, and *uli* influence, though he is not specific as to what Yoruba art Adenaike is drawing from. He considers that virtually all Yoruba indigenous art displays *ọnaism*, particularly sculpture and metalwork. He suggests that some of Adenaike's art, specifically the 1980 oil, *Giant Strides* (see Federal Department of Culture 1981, 25), displays *ọnaism* but provides no details. As there has been a tendency to describe all Igbo art as drawing from *uli* design, so there is a tendency to say that all Yoruba art fits into the category of *ọnaism*. Both are overgeneralizations.
38. Adenaike 1990a.
39. Adenaike 1990a, 4.
40. Ikwuemesi 1992a, 10.
41. Adenaike 1994a.
42. Unfortunately, with the retirement of its director, Dr. Gabriele Tombini, in 1994 at the end of the exhibition, the Italian Cultural Institute in Lagos closed.
43. Adenaike 1990b, 1991, 1992, 1993b, 1994b, 1995b; *Uli Art: Master Works, Recent Works* 1995.
44. Thompson 1982.
45. Adenaike 1993b, 1.
46. Adenaike 1995b. He can create in the United States and at his home at Enugu, but he cannot (he says) while at Lagos, as it is too disturbing and messy a place.
47. *Nwanyi Ọcha* means literally "White Woman," which Adenaike translates as "light African lady," referring to a common belief in Nigeria that Igbo women are somewhat lighter skinned than other African women. See Ardener 1954.

## 11. ADA UDECHUKWU

1. A. Udechukwu 1993, no pagination.
2. "Ada" means first-born daughter of a woman in the Igbo language.
3. See her poems "Biafra" in *The Muse* 13:12, 1981, and also "Winds of Africa," *Black Orpheus* 1:10, 1961, 10, and in Bankier and Lashgari 1983, 288.
4. *The Muse* 12:5, 1980, 34; 13:8, 1981, 9.
5. Originally *Omaba. Omabe* is the name of an extensive Igbo

ritual in terms of the number of people involved, the length
of time over which it occurs, and its expenses.

6. *The Muse* 13:8, 1981; A. Udechukwu 1993.

7. The first event was *An Exhibition of Marada Design* 1984.
The word "Marada" is a union of the first names of the two
artists and not an Igbo word. The second exhibition was entitled *Textile and Clothing* 1984.

8. A. Udechukwu 1990. The exhibition was in conjunction
with a celebration to honor the well-known Nigerian writer
Chinua Achebe.

9. Ogbechie̩ 1990, no pagination.

10. *Fabric Dimensions* 1990.

11. *Fabric Dimensions* 1990, 4.

12. *Fabric Dimensions* 1990, 9.

13. A. Udechukwu 1992.

14. A. Udechukwu 1992, 3–5.

15. A. Udechukwu 1992, 3.

16. *Celebrating Africa* 1993.

17. *Celebrating Africa* 1993, 9.

18. Ada Udechukwu, video interview by Simon Ottenberg, Nov.
11, 1995, at her home on the Nsukka campus.

19. A. Udechukwu 1993, front cover.

20. A. Udechukwu 1992.

21. Ada Udechukwu, video interview by Simon Ottenberg, May
22, 1994, at her home on the Nsukka campus.

22. Ada Udechukwu, video Interview, May 22, 1994.

23. See Chapter 8.

24. Kelly and Stanley 1993, 485–86.

25. Kelly and Stanley 1993, 163–65.

26. A. Udechukwu 1994, 2, comments on Kure's work in an in-
telligent analytical manner that suggests that she has a good
eye for the art of other artists.

27. Ada Udechukwu, video interview, May 22, 1994.

28. Nduka 1994.

29. A. Udechukwu 1993. Her poems have also appeared in
*Anthill Annual* 1, 1988, 85–86; *The Muse* 12:5, 1980,
24 and 13:8, 1981, 9; *Celebrating Africa* 1993, 1, and in
several issues of *Omabe*.

30. A. Udechukwu 1993.

31. A. Udechukwu 1993.

32. Nduka 1994.


## 12. O̩LU O̩GUIBE

1. O̩lu O̩guibe, letter to Simon Ottenberg, Jan. 9, 1994, London.

2. Oguibe and Beier 1994, 5–6, 13, 15; Oguibe and Lessor
1987, 6; Oguibe 1989b, 2–3, 6–7, 12; O̩lu O̩guibe, video
interview by Simon Ottenberg, March 24, 1996, at Oguibe's
Chicago apartment.

3. Oguibe and Beier 1994, 6.

4. Oguibe and Beier 1994, 5.

5. Oguibe 1989b, 6–7.

6. Oguibe 1989b, 3.

7. O̩lu O̩guibe, video interview, March 24, 1996. On Oguibe's
awareness of Udechukwu's war art, see Oguibe 1989a.

8. O̩lu O̩guibe, video interview, March 24, 1996.

9. See Kelly and Stanley 1993, 331, for the print and graphics
exhibitions; Oguibe and Lessor 1987 for the Abeokuta show,
and Oguibe and Odo 1988, Okonta 1988, for the *Art on the
Street* exhibition.

10. Oguibe and Odo 1988, 1.

11. Okonta 1988, 44.

12. Oguibe 1988.

13. Okigbo 1971, 71–72.

14. Oguibe and Beier 1994, 16.

15. Oguibe 1988, no pagination.

16. Oguibe 1988.

17. Oguibe 1988.

18. Oguibe 1989b.

19. Oguibe's fellow artist, Greg Odo, claims to have previously
introduced the idea of painting on traditional baskets.

20. Oguibe 1989b, 7.

21. C. Okeke 1995, 70, 72.

22. C. Okeke 1995, 72.

23. C. Okeke 1995, 70.

24. Oguibe 1989c.

25. Oguibe 1989a.

26. Oguibe 1994a, 27–28, 1994b.

27. Oguibe 1990a, 1990c, 1991a, 6–7, 9.

28. Oguibe 1991a, 7.

29. Oguibe 1990c, 1991a.

30. Oguibe 1995b.

31. Oguibe 1990a, 1992b, 1992c, 1994d.

32. Oguibe 1994e.

33. For the commentaries on other artists, see Oguibe 1992a,
1993b, 1993c, 1995a, 1995b, 1995c, 1995e, 1995g, 1996,
n.d. For the more general essays, see Oguibe 1991b, 1993a,
1994a, 1994b, 1994c, 1995d, 1995f.

34. Oguibe 1993a.

35. Oguibe 1990c.

36. See Chapter 1.

37. Cole 1982.

38. Aniako̩r 1984; Boston 1977; Cole and Aniako̩r 1984,
24–34; Jeffreys 1951.

39. Adler and Barnard 1992, 47.

40. Oguibe 1991a.

41. Oguibe 1990b [1991]; "Blank Response" 1991: "Graffiti
Artist" 1991; "Late Items" 1991.

42. The drawings are found only in the Bayreuth edition (1992b)
and not in the Lagos one (Oguibe 1992c). Both include his
earlier poetry from *A Song from Exile* (Oguibe 1990a).

43. Oguibe 1990a.

44. Darwīsh 1980, xviii–xix, 54–55.

45. Adler and Barnard 1992; Cole and Ross 1977, 191–99.
46. See Ilona 1993–94, 87, for comments on Oguibe's "prodi-
    gious ability to cross artistic media and geopolitical space."
47. Oguibe 1994d.
48. See Hassan and Enwezor 1995, 25, for a 1992 installation of
    Oguibe's.
49. Ilona 1993–94, 89.
50. Oguibe 1991b, 1993a, 1994a, 1994b, 1994c, 1995d, 1995f,
    among others; also Olu Oguibe, video interview, March 24,
    1996.
51. See also Enwezor 1994; Hassan 1995.
52. Oguibe 1993a, in the Fernie reprint, 322.
53. Fisher 1994; Oguibe 1994a, 1994b.
54. For a good example of the kind of contemporary African art
    that Oguibe regrets is dominant in Euro/America, see Eck-
    hardt 1979, taking a position so extreme as to be almost a
    parody of itself. See also Odita's (1970) critique of some of
    this art.
55. Emmanuel Okechukwu Odita (1980), one of the Nsukka
    artists, now teaching in the United States, has also evolved a
    general theory of contemporary African art.
56. Oguibe 1995d, 30.

## CONCLUSION

1. Aig-Imoukhuede 1991, 83.
2. Shaw 1970.
3. Ottenberg 1959; Uchendu 1965.
4. The term *hybridity* has replaced the older term, *syncretism*,
   which has had a more limited range of meanings and interpretations. See Lavrijsen 1993; Miner 1956; Papastergiadis
   1994; Nicholas Thomas 1996.
5. On the art of the Aborigines, see, for example, Boulter 1994;
   Isaacs 1989; West 1988. For Native Americans, see Canadian Museum of Civilization 1993; Coe 1986; Wade 1986.
6. Ottenberg 1989a.
7. Kubik 1986.
8. Aas 1994b, 1.
9. A useful account of contemporary Nigerian women artists is
   found in C. Okeke 1992.
10. See various issues of *NKA: Journal of Contemporary African
    Art* and also Fisher 1994.
11. For Okeke, see the conversation of Uche Okeke and another
    senior Nigerian artist holding similar views, Bruce Ono-
    brakpeya, in "Conversation of Two Masters" 1995.

# BIBLIOGRAPHY

Notes: *Nigeria* changed its name to *Nigeria Magazine* with issue no. 64, 1960. Igbo is spelled Ibo in the older literature. Arochuku is sometimes spelled Arochukwu, Oṣogbo spelled Oshogbo, and Aṣante is also spelled Ashanti.


Aas, Norbert. 1992. *Uche Okeke: Auf dem Weg nach Kpaza.* Bayreuth: Iwalẹwa-Haus.

———. 1993. Uche Okeke, the German Experience: An Interim Report. Paper presented at the 2nd International Symposium on Contemporary Nigerian Art, Lagos, April 29–May 1. Unpublished.

———. 1994a. "Obiọra Udechukwu: Uli Art and Beyond." *NKA: Journal of Contemporary African Art* 1, 60–61.

———. 1994b. Conventions of Seeing and the So-Called Intellectual African Artists in Germany. Paper for the African Studies Association Annual Meeting, Toronto, Canada, November. Unpublished.

———. 1995. Obiọra Udechukwu's *Watermaid.* Paper presented at the Centre for West African Studies, University of Birmingham, England, October 10. Unpublished.

Aas, Norbert, and Ulf Vierke. 1993. *Obiọra Udechukwu.* Bayreuth: art/arc.

Achebe, Chinua. 1962a. *Things Fall Apart.* London: Heinemann.

———. 1962b. *The Sacrificial Egg and Other Short Stories.* Ọnitsha: Etudo Limited.

———. 1973. *Girls at War and Other Stories.* Garden City, N.Y.: Doubleday.

———. 1985. *The Trouble with Nigeria.* London: Heinemann.

Achebe, Chinua, Arthur Nwankwọ, Samuel Ifejike, Flora Nwapa et al. 1971. *The Insider: Stories of War and Peace from Nigeria.* Enugu: Nwankwọ-Ifejika and Co., Publishers.

Achebe, Chinua, and Dubem Okafọr (eds.). 1978. *Don't Let Him Die: An Anthology of Memorial Poems for Christopher Okigbo 1932–1967.* Enugu: Fourth Dimension Publishers.

Achebe, Chinua, and Obiọra Udechukwu (eds.). 1982. *Aka Weta: Egwu Aguluagu Egwu Edeluede.* Nsukka: Okike Magazine.

Achebe, Chinwe. 1986. *The World of Ọgbanje.* Enugu: Fourth Dimension Publishers.

Adenaike, A. O. [Tayọ]. 1979. The Oshogbo Experiment: Sixteen Years After. B.A. thesis, University of Nigeria, Nsukka, Department of Fine and Applied Arts.

———. 1980. *Childhood Fears: An Exhibition of Painting.* Lagos: Goethe Institut.

———. 1981. *Homage to Uli: 6–13 July, 1981.* London: Africa Centre.

———. 1982a. *Distorted Souls: An Exhibition of Drawings and Watercolours, 9–25 June, 1982.* Lagos: Goethe Institut.

———. 1982b. "The Influence of Uli Art on Contemporary Nsukka School Painting (Part I)." *Nigeria Magazine* 143, 28–52. [Part II never published.]

———. 1982c. The Influence of Uli Art on Contemporary Nsukka School Painting. M.F.A thesis, University of Nigeria, Nsukka, Department of Fine and Applied Arts.

———. 1983. *Faces of Time*. Lagos: National Council for Arts and Culture.

———. 1984. *The Subconscious: Watercolours and Drawings*. Lagos: Italian Cultural Institute.

———. 1986a. *We Live in the Deep*. Lagos: Goethe Institut.

———. 1986b. *Dialogue*. Lagos: Italian Cultural Institute.

———. 1990a. *Story-Telling*. Lagos: Italian Cultural Institute.

———. 1990b. *Fragments*. Washington, D.C.: Mbari Arts.

———. 1991. *Towards Essence*. Greensboro, South Carolina: Greensboro Cultural Center.

———. 1992. *Solemn Notes*. New Orleans.

———. 1993a. "Tributes: Salute to a Great Teacher." In Chika Okeke (ed.), *Uche Okeke: 60th Birthday Anniversary Retrospective Exhibition, Goethe Institut Lagos*. Enugu: Association of University of Nigeria Art Graduates, Art and Artists Conference Forum, Committee for Relevant Art and Society of Nigerian Artists, 5.

———. 1993b. *Impulses in 27 Watercolors*. Charleston, South Carolina: African American Gallery.

———. 1994a. *Statements*. Lagos: Italian Cultural Institute.

———. 1994b. *Recent Watercolors*. Denver, Colorado: Gallery 1619.

———. 1995a. "The Oshogbo Experiment." In Clementine Deliss (ed.), *Seven Stories about Modern Art in Africa*. London: Whitechapel, 202–7. Reprinted from his B.A. thesis, The Oshogbo Experiment: Sixteen Years After. 1979. University of Nigeria, Nsukka, Department of Fine and Appied Arts.

———. 1995b. *New Currents in Acrylics*. Seattle: Home of Simon Ottenberg.

Adler, Peter, and Nicholas Barnard. 1992. *Asafo African Flags of the Fante*. London: Thames and Hudson.

Afigbo, Adiele E. 1992. *Of Men and War, Women and History. Being a Valedictory Lecture Delivered by Professor Adiele Eberechukwu Afigbo . . . on 17th September 1992 at the University of Nigeria, Nsukka*. Nsukka: University of Nigeria, Institute of African Studies.

"African Art in City of London." 1961. *West African Review* 32:408, 51–53.

*Africus: Johannesburg Biennale*. 1995. Johannesburg: Transitional Metropolitan Council.

Afuba, Chris. n.d. Biography: Chris Afuba—Sculptor and Painter. Enugu(?): The author.

Agberia, John-Tokpabere. 1988. Ladi Kwali: A Study of Indigenous and Modern Techniques of Abuja Pottery. M.A. thesis, University of Ibadan.

Agoro, Ọladeinde Ọlasunkanmi. 1980. Aina Ọnabolu, Pioneer of Modern Art Tradition. B.A. thesis, University of Nigeria, Nsukka, Department of Fine and Applied Arts.

Ahamba, Samuel M. c. 1940. *Ọgugu Igbo Nke Mbu*. Port Harcourt(?): C.M.S. Nigeria Bookshops. [Illustrations by C. C. Ibeto.]

Aig-Imoukhuede, Frank. 1983. "Introduction." In Tayọ Adenaike, *Faces of Time*. Lagos: National Council for Arts and Culture 4.

———. 1991. *A Handbook of Nigerian Culture*. Lagos: Department of Culture.

Ajayi, Frank. 1985. *Handbook on Art Methodology: Book I*, rev. ed. Ikere-Ekiti: The author.

AKA Circle of Exhibiting Artists. 1986. *AKA 86: Inaugural Exhibition Catalogue*. Enugu: AKA Circle of Exhibiting Artists.

———. 1987. *AKA 2nd Annual Exhibition Catalogue*. Enugu: AKA Circle of Exhibiting Artists.

———. 1988. *AKA 88: 3rd Annual Exhibition Catalogue*. Enugu: AKA Circle of Exhibiting Artists.

———. 1989. *AKA 89: Fourth Annual Exhibition Catalogue*. Enugu: AKA Circle of Exhibiting Artists.

———. 1990. *AKA 90: Fifth Annual Exhibition Catalogue*. Enugu: AKA Circle of Exhibiting Artists.

———. 1991. *AKA '91: 6th Annual Exhibition Catalogue*. Enugu: AKA Circle of Exhibiting Artists.

———. 1992. *AKA '92: Annual Art Exhibition*. Enugu: AKA Circle of Exhibiting Artists.

———. 1993. *AKA '93: Annual Exhibition Catalogue*. Lagos: Lordgate Limited.

———. 1994. *AKA '94: Annual Exhibition Catalogue*. AKA Circle of Exhibiting Artists.

———. 1995. *AKA 10th Annual Exhibition Catalogue*. Enugu: AKA Circle of Exhibiting Artists.

Akantu, Fred, with Tunde Ọlanipekun. 1991. "The Thing about Salons." *Evening Times* (Lagos), Thursday, January 24, 7.

Akinosho, Toyin. 1984. "Forays into the Subconscious. Tayọ Adenaike recently mounted an exhibition of his works at the Italian Cultural Institute." *The Democrat* (Lagos), May 20, 5.

———. 1985. "The Arts: Society of Nigerian Artists in Doldrums." *The Guardian* (Lagos), August 21, 12–13.

———. 1993. The Zaria Rebels and the Evolution of Nigerian Art. Paper presented at the 2nd International Symposium on Contemporary Nigerian Art, Lagos, April 29–May 1. Unpublished.

Akolo, J. B. 1987. "Art Education and Cultural Imperatives." *Nigeria Magazine* 55:2, 20–29.

Akpaide, U. U. 1976. "So What's New." In El Anatsui, *Wooden Wall Plaques by El Anatsui: 2–9 February 1976*. Nsukka: Asele Art Gallery, Exhibition 1. Catalogue, 2.

Akpan, N. Y. 1972. *The Struggle for Succession 1966–1970: A Personal Account of Civil War Activities*. London: Cass, 1976.

Akpederi, Joni. 1986. "Journey into the Mind: Two Artists Reveal Different Strokes in Their Paintings." *African Guardian* (Lagos), March 20, 43.

Alaneme, Benjamin C. U. 1971. Designs of the Ibo People of the East Central State of Nigeria. B.A. thesis, University of Nigeria, Department of Fine and Applied Arts.

Albert, Isaac Ọlawale. 1993. *Inter-Ethnic Relations in a Nigerian City: A Historical Perspective of the Hausa-Igbo Conflicts in Kano 1953–1991.* Ibadan: Institute of African Studies, University of Ibadan, French Institute for Research in Africa, Occasional Publication 2.

Allagoa, Lawrence. 1967. "Exhibition Centre's New Home." *Nigeria Magazine* 93, 114–27.

Amaeshi, Basil. 1977. "Sources for West African Studies: Some Non-Alphabetic Writings of West Africa." *Libri International Library Review* 27:1, 1–9.

An Artist. 1964. "Exhibitions." *Nigeria Magazine* 80, 69–72.

*An Exhibition of Marada Design: Contemporary Fashion Using Traditional African Designs, Featuring Mary Ezewuzie and Ada Udechukwu.* 1984. Nsukka: The Gallery, Department of Fine and Applied Arts, University of Nigeria, Nsukka.

Anafulu, Joseph C. 1978. "Christopher Okigbo, 1932–1967: A Bio-bibliography. *Research in African Literatures* 9:1, 65–78.

Anatsui, El. 1976. *Wooden Wall Plaques by El Anatsui.* Nsukka: Asele Art Gallery, Exhibition 1. Catalogue.

———. 1979. *Broken Pots: Sculpture by El Anatsui.* British Council, Enugu, November 5–10; Institute of African Studies, University of Nigeria, Nsukka, November 21–30.

———. 1982. *El Anatsui: Sculptures, Photographs, Drawings, 20 Feb–5 Mar 1982.* Lagos: Goethe Institut.

———. 1987a. *Venovize. Ceramic Sculpture by El Anatsui, Ghana Internationl Artist. Monday 16–Friday 27 February.* Redruth, England: Faculty of Art and Design, Cornwall College of Further and Higher Education.

———. 1987b. *Pieces of Wood: An Exhibition of Mural Sculpture.* [Lagos: Franco-German Auditorium.]

———. 1991. *Old and New: An Exhibition of Sculptures in Assorted Wood by El Anatsui.* Lagos: National Museum.

———. 1992. The Modern African Artist as Rebel: A Personal Perspective. Paper Presented at the Ninth Triennial Symposium on African Art, Iowa City. Unpublished.

———. 1995. *El Anatsui.* London: October Gallery.

Anatsui, El, and Ọlu Ọguibe. 1993. "Sankofa: Go Back an' Pick: Three Studio Notes and a Conversation." *Third Text* 23, 39–52.

Anatsui, El, and Ndubisi Ọnah. 1988. *An Exhibition of Sculptures in Wood: "Thoughts and Processes," by El Anatsui and Ndubisi Ọnah.* Lagos: Italian Cultural Institute.

Anatsui, El, and Liz Willis. 1988. *Walls and Gates: An Exhibition of Sculptures and Paintings. El Anatsui—Liz Willis. Avant Garde Gallery, Kaduna, November 18–30, 1988.*

Aniakọr, Chike. 1972. *The Visions of My Ikenga. Exhibition of Drawings, Prints and Paintings at the National Museum Onikan, Lagos 29–25th December 1972.* N.p.: n.p.

———. 1973. "Structuralism in Ikenga: An Ethnoaesthetic Approach." *Ikenga* (Nsukka) 2:1, 8–18.

———. 1975. "Poems and Drawings." *African Arts* 8:4, 42–43.

———. 1978. Igbo Architecture: A Study of Forms, Functions, and Typology. Ph.D. dissertation, Indiana University, Department of Art History, Bloomington.

———. 1980. "Contemporary Nigerian Artists and Their Traditions." *Black Art: An International Quarterly* 4:2, 40–54.

———. 1982. "Igbo Aesthetics: An Introduction." *Nigeria Magazine* 141, 3–15.

———. 1984. "Ikenga Art and Igbo Cosmos." *Ikoro* (Nsukka) 5:1/2, 59–71.

———. 1985. "The Concept and Symbolism of the Centre in African Architecture." In Edith Ihekweazu (ed.), *Readings in African Humanities: Traditional and Modern Cultures.* Enugu: Fourth Dimension Publishers, 29–46.

———. 1986. "The State of Igbo Art Studies." *Nigeria Magazine* 54:1, 9–17.

———. 1990a. "Visual Arts: Critical Appraisal of Cultural Policy for Nigeria." In *Creative Dialogue: SNA at 25.* Lagos: Society of Nigerian Artists, 60–64.

———. 1990b. "El Anatsui: Visual Incantations." *Art Papers* (Atlanta) 14:4, 14–17.

———. 1991. "El Anatsui: Visual Incantations in Wood." *International Review of African American Arts* 9:3, 51–56.

———. 1992. *Ọjadili: The Clever Wrestler.* Enugu: Fourth Dimension Publishers.

———. 1995a. "What Is Uli?: The Emergence of a Modern Art Idiom." *Uli Art: Master Works, Recent Works. April 17–June 5, 1995.* New York: Skoto Gallery, 2–5.

———. 1995b. "The Adaptive Potential of Nigerian Indigenous Architecture and Building Technology." *USO: Nigerian Journal of Art* 1:1, 25–40.

———. n.d. (1992 or later). Songs of Tears and Laughter (A Collection of Poems). Unpublished manuscript.

Aniakọr, Chike, et al. 1989. *Legacy of Images: The Sculptures of Okpu Eze: Bronze, Wood and Pigments.* Enugu: New Africa Centre.

Anyakọra, Charles L. N. 1975. The Pioneers: The Lives and Works of Two Nigerian Transitional Contemporary Artists. B.A. thesis, University of Nigeria, Nsukka, Department of Fine and Applied Arts.

Anyakọra, Ngọzi. 1991. "Reminiscences of a Pioneer Student of Fine Arts, University of Nigeria, Nsukka." In *Homage—Artgrads—UNN Exhibition. Catalogue, 1991.* Nsukka: ARTGRADS—UNN, 6–7.

Appiah, Kwame Anthony. 1992. *In My Father's House.* New York: Oxford University Press.

Aradeon, Susan B. 1987. "Contemporary Nigerian Art, Tradition and National Identity." *Nigeria Magazine* 55:1, 1–10.

Aragbabalu, Omidiji. 1960. "Introducing Two Young Artists with

Much Promise." *Daily Service* [Lagos], February 20, 18.

Ardener, E. W. 1954. "Some Ibo Attitudes to Skin Pigmentation." *Man* 54, article 101, 71–73.

Arinze, Emmanuel Nnakenyi. 1991. "The Gift of Wood." In El Anatsui, *Old and New: An Exhibition of Sculptures in Assorted Wood by El Anatsui.* Lagos: National Museum.

Armstrong, Robert Plant. 1971a. *The Affecting Presence: An Essay in Humanistic Anthropology.* Urbana: University of Illinois Press.

———. 1971b. "Aesthetic Continuity in Two Yoruba Works." *African Arts* 4:3, 40–43, 68–70.

Arnot, A. S. 1937. "Art and an Industry in Arochuku." *Nigeria* 12, 10–14.

———. 1950. "Uli Body Painting and Aro Embroidery." *Nigerian Field* 15:3, 133–37.

Aronson, Lisa. 1980. "Patronage and Akwete Weaving." *African Arts* 13:3, 62–66, 91.

———. 1989a. "Akwete Weaving: Transition and Change." In Beate Engelbrecht and Bernhard Gardi (eds.), *Man Does Not Go Naked: Textilien und Handwerk aus africanischen und anderen Ländern.* Basel: Ethnologische Museum für Völkerkunde, *Basler Beiträge zur Ethnologie* 30, 35–64.

———. 1989b. "To Weave or Not to Weave: Apprenticeship Rules among the Akwete Igbo of Nigeria and the Baule of the Ivory Coast." In Michael W. Coy (ed.), *Apprenticeship from Theory to Method and Back Again.* Albany: State University of New York Press, 149–62.

*Art from the Frontline: Contemporary Art from Southern Africa.* 1990. London: Frontline States/ Keric Press.

"Art Gallery: Exhibition Centre, Marina, Lagos." 1962. *Nigeria Magazine* 74, 91–95.

*Arte—Sociedad—Reflexión: Quinta bienal de la Habana, Mayo 1994.* 1994. Havana: Secretaría de Estado de Cultura.

*Artifacts.* 1992–. Lagos: Artifacts Company Ltd.

Ashiwaju, Garba (ed. in chief), Edith Uche Enem (ed.), S. O. Oputa and B. J. Abegunde (asst. eds.). 1977. *The National Theatre and Makers of Modern Nigerian Art.* Lagos: Nigeria Magazine.

Asuquo, Edef M., and Odumegu M. Onuoha. 1985. Central Analysis of Cartoons in Nigerian Newspapers. B.A. thesis, University of Nigeria, Nsukka, Department of Mass Communication.

Azuonye, Chukwuma (ed.). 1972. *Nsukka Harvest: Poetry from Nsukka 1966–1972.* Nsukka: Odunke Publications.

———. 1984. "The Romantic Epic of the Anambra Igbo: An Introductory Survey." *Uwa Ndi Igbo: Journal of Igbo Life and Culture* 1, 4–16.

———. 1985a. "The Epic as Work Poetry: A Case Study of the Tradition of Ita among the Anambra Igbo Fisherfolk." *Black Orpheus* 5:2, 8–13.

———.1985b. "The Epic of Ozoemene Ndive. An Encounter from the Second Night of a Performance by Onwuraa Ikem of Abo Ivite Aguleri, edited and translated by Chukwuma Azuonye." *Black Orpheus,* new series 5:2, 14–45.

———. 1990. "Kaalu Igirigi: An Ohafia Singer of Tales." In Isidore Okpewho (ed.), *The Oral Performance in Africa.* Ibadan: Spectrum Books.

———. 1991. "Reminiscences of the Odunke Commmunity of Artists: 1966–1990." *ALA Bulletin: A Publication of the African Literature Association* 17:1, 20–26.

Azuonye, Chukwuma, and Obiora Udechukwu. 1984. "Enu-Ny-ili-Mba: An Encounter from the Ameke Okoye Epic as Performed by Jeveizu Okaavo of Aguleri." *Uwa Ndi Igbo: Journal of Igbo Life and Culture* 1, 20–41. [In Igbo and English.]

Azuru, A. 1980. Cartoons: A Medium of Communication in Modern Nigeria. B.A. thesis, University of Nigeria, Nsukka, Department of Fine and Applied Arts.

Bankier, Joanna, and Deirdre Lashgari (eds.). 1983. *Women Poets of the World.* London: Collier and Macmillan.

Bascom, William. 1969. "Creativity and Style in African Art." In Daniel P. Biebuyck (ed.), *Tradition and Creativity in Tribal Art.* Berkeley: University of California Press, 98–119.

Bastian, Misty L. 1993. Useful Women and the Good of the Land: The Igbo Women's War of 1929. Department of Anthropology, University of Chicago. Unpublished.

Battestini, Simon P. X. 1991. "Reading Signs of Identity and Alterity: History, Semiotics and a Nigerian Case." *African Studies Review* 34:1, 100–16.

Beier, Ulli. 1960a. *Art in Nigeria 1960.* Cambridge: Cambridge University Press.

———. 1960b. "Three Zaria Artists: Ulli Beier Comments on an Ibadan Exhibition." *West African Review* 31, 37–41.

———. 1961a. "Contemporary Nigerian Art." *Nigeria Magazine* 68, 27–51.

———. 1961b. "Ibrahim Salahi." *Black Orpheus* 10, 48–50.

———. 1961c. "Uche Okeke." In Uche Okeke, *Drawings: Uche Okeke.* Ibadan, Mbari Publications, no pagination.

———. 1962a. "Nigerian Folk Art." *Nigeria Magazine* 75, 26–32.

———. 1962b. "Demas Nwoko and Uche Okeke." Typescript translation from the French from the catalogue of their exhibition at Galerie Lambert, Paris, May 9–31, 1962. Manuscript Division, Library of Congress, Harmon Foundation Collection.

———. 1962c. *Ibrahim el Salahi.* Ibadan: Mbari Publications, African Artists Series 2.

———. 1965. "Experimental Art School." *Nigeria Magazine* 86, 199–204.

———. 1968. *Contemporary Art in Africa.* New York: Praeger.

———. 1980. *Neue Kunst in Afrika: Das Buch zur Ausstellung.* Berlin: Dietrich Reimer Verlag.

———.1981. "An Interview with Obiora Udechukwu." *Okike* 20, 53–68.

———. 1983. *Ibrahim El Salahi. Gesprach mit Ulli Beier, Bayreuth, Sept. 1983. Conversation with Ulli Beier, Bayreuth, Sept. 1983.* Bayreuth: Iwalewa-Haus.

———. 1990. *Ibrahim el Salahi: Identity and Exile.* Bayreuth: Iwalẹwa-Haus.

———. 1991. *Thirty Years of Oshogbo Art.* Bayreuth: Iwalẹwa-Haus.

———. 1993. *In a Colonial University.* Bayreuth: Iwalẹwa-Haus.

Bello, Sule (ed.). 1991a. *Culture and Decision Making in Nigeria.* Lagos: National Council for Arts and Culture.

———. 1991b. *Documentation and Cultural Development.* Lagos: National Council for Arts and Culture.

Bello, Sule, and Y. Nasidi (eds.). 1991. *Culture, Economy and National Development. Proceedings of the National Seminar Events of NAFEST '89.* Lagos: National Council for Arts and Culture.

Ben Amos, Paula. 1967. "A Modern Nigerian Sculptor." *Nigeria Magazine* 94, 248–52.

Benson, Peter. 1986. *Black Orpheus, Transition, and Modern Cultural Awakening in Africa.* Berkeley: University of California Press.

Berns, Marla. 1986. *The Essential Gourd: Art and History in Northeastern Nigeria.* Los Angeles: University of California, Museum of Cultural History.

"Blank Response." 1991. *Daily Telegraph* (London), March 22.

Boston, John. 1977. *Ikenga Figures among the North-West Igbos and the Igala.* London/Lagos: Ethnographica/Federal Department of Antiquities, Nigeria.

Boulter, Michael. 1994. *The Art of Utopia: New Directions in Contemporary Aboriginal Art.* Sydney: Craftsman House.

Brokensha, David. 1969. "Ori Olokun: A New Cultural Center." *African Arts* 2:3, 32–35.

Brook, Donald. 1958. "Anglicising African Art." *West Africa* 42:2144, 465.

Brown, Evelyn S. 1966. *Africa's Contemporary Art and Artists.* New York: Harmon Foundation.

Butler, Vincent F. 1963. "Cement Funeral Sculpture in Eastern Nigeria." *Nigeria Magazine* 77, 117–24.

———. 1964. "Reader's Letters: Cement Funeral Sculptures." *Nigeria Magazine* 80, 3, 80.

Campbell, Bọlaji. 1993. The Sacred on the Secular: Patterns of Similarities in Uli and Yoruba Paintings. Paper presented at the 2nd International Symposium on Contemporary Nigerian Art, Lagos, Nigeria, April 29–May 1. Unpublished.

Campbell, Bọlaji, with R. I. Ibigbami, P. S. O. Arẹmu, and Agbo Fọlarin (eds.). 1993. *Diversity of Creativity in Nigeria. A Critical Selection from the Proceedings of the First International Conference on the Diversity of Creativity in Nigeria.* Ifẹ: Department of Fine Arts, Ọbafemi Awolowo University.

Campbell, Kenneth F. 1983. "Nsibidi Update: Nsibidi Actualize." *Arts d'Afrique Noire* 47, 33–44.

Campschreur, Willem, and Joost Divendal (eds.). 1989. *Culture in Another South Africa: Festival and Conference.* New York: Olive Branch Press.

Canadian Museum of Civilization (ed.). 1993. *In the Shadow of the Sun: Perspectives on Contemporary Native Art.* Hull: Canadian Museum of Civilization, Canadian Ethnology Service, Mercury Series Paper 124.

Cardew, Michael. 1971. *Pioneer Pottery.* New York: St. Martin's Press. Reprint of 1969 edition.

———. 1988. *A Pioneer Potter: An Autobiography.* London: Collins.

———. 1993. *Pottery in Nigeria: Incorporating a Preliminary Survey of Pottery in West Africa 1950.* Washington, D.C.: Smithsonian Institution Library, National Museum of African Art Branch. Reprint of 1986 edition.

Carroll, Kevin. 1966. *Yoruba Religious Carving: Pagan and Christian Sculpture in Nigeria and Dahomey.* New York: Praeger.

*Celebrating Africa. Modern and Traditional African Textiles: Ada Udechukwu—Babajide Olujimi Gureje (Kente Creations). Silver Ware from the Niger: Achmet Dizi.* 1993. Lagos: Goethe Institut.

Centre Georges Pompidou. 1989. *Magiciens de la Terre.* Paris: Editions du Centre Pompidou.

Centro Atlantico de Arte Moderno. 1991. *Africa Now.* Las Palmas de Gran Canaria: Centro Atlantico de Arte Moderno.

Chappel, T. J. H. 1977. *Decorated Gourds in North-Eastern Nigeria.* London/Lagos: Ethnographica/Nigeria Museum.

Chidume, Charles Ejike. 1973. "Uche Okeke—A Profile." *Nimo: Cultural Magazine of the Omega Fraternity Nimo* 1:1, 15–17.

Chikamnele, Ehieze Ngọzi. 1994. Interpretation of Designs on Ukara Cloth of the Ekpe Secret Cult. B.A. thesis, University of Nigeria, Nsukka, Department of Fine and Applied Arts.

*Christian Arts in Nigeria. Holy Trinity Cathedral, Parish Hall, Ọnitsha, June 1979.* 1979. Ọnitsha: Cathedral Doors Committee, Holy Trinity Ọnitsha.

Chukuegga, Aggu [S. A. O. Chukueggu]. 1952. "History of the Kemalu Juju." *Nigeria* 39, 252–53.

Clark, Garth. 1976. *Michael Cardew: A Portrait.* New York: Kodansha International.

Coe, Ralph T. 1986. *Lost and Found Traditions: Native American Art: 1965–1985.* Seattle: University of Washington Press.

Cole, Herbert M. 1982. *Mbari: Art and Life among the Owerri Igbo.* Bloomington: Indiana University Press.

———. 1988. "The Survival and Impact of Mbari Sculpture." *African Arts* 21:2, 54–65, 96.

Cole, Herbert M., and Chike Aniakọr. 1984. *Igbo Arts: Community and Cosmos.* Los Angeles: Museum of Cultural History, University of California.

Cole, Herbert M., and Doran H. Ross. 1977. *The Arts of Ghana.* Los Angeles: Museum of Cultural History, University of California.

Coleman, James S. 1958. *Nigeria: Background to Nationalism.* Berkeley: University of California Press.

*Commonwealth Nigerian Art: An Exhibition Assembled by the Society of Nigerian Artists.* 1968. London: Commonwealth Institute Art Gallery.

*Configura 2: A Conversation between Obiọra Udechukwu and Ulli Beier.* 1995. Bayreuth: Iwalẹwa-Haus, University of Bayreuth.

"Conversation of Two Masters." 1995. *Glendora Review: African Quarterly of the Arts* 1:2, 25–31.

Courtney-Clarke, Margaret. 1990. *African Canvas.* New York: Rizzoli.

Critic [pseud.]. 1963. "Art Gallery: Mbari Mbayọ." *Nigeria Magazine* 78, 223–28.

Crowder, Michael. 1961. "The Chase Manhattan Sculpture." *Nigeria Magazine* 70, 285–89.

———. 1962a. "Nigeria's Artists Emerge." *West African Review* 33:417, 30–36.

———. 1962b. "Art Gallery: Akolo." *Nigeria Magazine* 74, 91.

———. 1978. "The Contemporary Nigerian Artist: His Patrons, His Audience, and His Critics." *Présence Africaine* 105/106, 130–45.

———. 1981. "Patronage and Audience in Nigeria." *Black Orpheus,* new series 4:1, 68–74.

Danford, J. A. 1949. "Art in Nigeria." *African Affairs: Journal of the Royal African Society* 48:190, 37–47.

———. 1950. "Nigerian Art." *Nigeria* 33, 153–74.

Darrah, G. G. and Safy Quel (eds.). 1992. *Bruce Onobrakpẹya: The Spirit in Ascent.* Lagos: Ovumaroro Gallery Production.

Darwīsh, Mahmud. 1980. *The Music of Human Flesh.* London: Heinemann.

Dayrell, Elphinstone. 1910. "Some 'Nsibidi' Signs." *Man* 67, 112–14.

———. 1911. "Further Notes on Nsibidi Signs and Their Meanings from the Ikom District, Southern Nigeria." *Journal of the Royal Anthropological Institute* 41, 521–40.

Deliss, Clementine (ed.) 1995. *Seven Stories about Modern Art in Africa.* London: Whitechapel Gallery.

*Demas Nwoko—Uche Okeke.* 1961. [Exhibition catalogue, at Mbari Ibadan, July 20, 1961–August 9, 1961.]

"Didi Museum: A Leader in Private Museums." 1990. *Lagos Life,* November 8, 7.

*Diversity: An Exhibition of Paintings by Tayọ Adenaike and Nsikak Essien.* 1979. Enugu: British Council.

Dmochowski, Zbigniew. 1990. *An Introduction to Nigerian Traditional Architecture. Volume 3. South-Eastern Nigeria.* London/Lagos: Ethnographica/National Commission for Museums and Monuments.

Dolly Fiterman Gallery, n.d. Works by Uche Okeke [One-page list.].

Duerden, Dennis. 1953. "Is There a Nigerian Style of Painting?" *Nigeria* 41, 51–59.

———. 1959. "African Art and Its Critics." *Ibadan* 6, 14–17.

———. 1961. "Mbari Ibadan's Arts Club." *West African Review* 32:408, 41–44.

Dwyer, G. 1985. "A Burly North Sea Symposium." *International Sculpture* 4:4, 8–9.

East Central State. 1971. *East Central State Arts Festival 1971.* Enugu: Government Printer.

East Central State Arts Council. 1972. *Arts Festivals Syllabus 1972.* Enugu: Government Printer.

Ebọng, Ima. 1991. "Négritude: Between Mask and Flag—Senegalese Cultural Ideology and the 'Ecole de Dakar.'" In Susan Vogel, assisted by Ima Ebọng, *Africa Explores: 20th Century African Art.* New York/Munich: Center for African Art/Prestel, 198–229.

Echezọnem, Osodi. *Nigerian Constitution and Nigerian Cultures.* New York: Carlton Press.

*Echo. U.N.N. Silver Jubilee Exhibition: Nsukka Students' Art 1970–1984.* 1985. Nsukka: University of Nigeria, Nsukka, Department of Fine and Applied Arts.

Eckhardt, Ulrich. 1979. *Kunst aus Afrika.* Berlin: Heinemann.

Edigbe, Jos. 1990. *Artwork Collectors and Art-Scenes in America, Italy, Syria, Nigeria, and West-Germany.* Lagos/Los Angeles: Artifacts International for Genent Co.

Egbo, J. A. 1994. "Ọkwa Ọji (Kola Nut Vessel): Its Cultural Value in Igboland." *Nigerian Heritage: Journal of the National Commission for Museums and Monuments* 3, 90–103.

Egonwa, Osa. 1986. "Improving Art Literary Practice in Nigeria: Notes to Non-Artist Art Writers." *Nigeria Magazine* 54:4, 37–43.

Egudu, R. N. 1972. "Social Values and Thought in Traditional Literature: The Case of Igbo Proverbs and Poetry." *Nigerian Libraries* 8:2, 63–84.

———. 1977. *Four Modern West African Poets.* New York: Nok Publishers.

Ekekwe, Ngọzi Chidinma. 1994. Six Nsukka Printmakers. Special project for the B.A. degree, University of Nigeria, Nsukka, Department of Fine and Applied Arts.

Ekom, Ernest. 1966. "The Two Mbaris." *Nigeria Magazine* 89, 160–62.

Ekwensi, Cyprian. 1956. "New Movement in Nigerian Art." *West Africa* 40:2045, 422.

———. 1966. "High Price of Nigerian Art." *Nigeria Magazine* 88, 36–41.

———, [C. O. D.]. n.d. *Ikolo the Wrestler and Other Ibo Tales.* London: Thomas Nelson and Sons.

Ekwueme, Laz E. N. 1993. *Teasers, Poems, Proverbs, and Puns.* Yaba, Lagos: Lenaus Printing and Publishing.

Emeka, Laurence. 1989. "Eri: The Founder of the Igbo Nation." *Ụwa Ndi Igbo* 2, 41–43.

Enekwe, Ọnuọra O. 1987. *Igbo Masks: The Oneness of Ritual and Theatre.* Lagos: Nigeria Magazine.

Enwezor, Okwui. 1994. "Redrawing the Boundaries: Towards a

New African Art Discourse. *NKA: Journal of Contemporary African Art* 1, 3–7.

Enwọnwu, Ben. 1956. "Letters to the Editor: New Movement in Nigerian Art." *West Africa* 40:2049, 516.

———. 1963. "Into the Abstract Jungle: A Criticism of the New Trend in Nigerian Art." *Drum* (Nigeria edition) 146, 25–29.

———. 1969. "The Battle for Cultural Freedom." *Journal of the New African Literature and the Arts* 7/8, 90–92.

*Exhibition of Nigerian Traditional and Contemporary Art.* 1978. Lagos: no publisher.

*Exhibition of Sculptures at the Hotel Presidential Enugu 30 September–4 October 1972.* 1972. [Organized by Mbari Traditional Art Centre, Eke-Nguru, Mbaisẹ, East Central State.] Enugu: Government Printer.

*Exhibition of Wood Carvings from Mbaisẹ. C.E.C. 11th–21 March 1971.* Nsukka: Association of Fine Arts Students, University of Nigeria, Nsukka.

"Exhibitions." 1964. *Nigeria Magazine* 80, 69–72.

Eze, A. Okpu. 1989. *Legacy of Images: The Sculpture of Okpu Eze: Bronze, Wood, and Pigments.* Enugu: New Africa Centre.

———. 1995. "Impact of Folklore on Nigerian Visual Art." *USO: Nigerian Journal of Art* 1:1, 11–24.

Eze, Nebechianya J. C. 1978. The Zaria Art Society. B.A. thesis, University of Nigeria, Nsukka, Department of Fine and Applied Arts.

*Fabric Dimensions: The Art of Ada Udechukwu and Elizabeth Ọhene.* 1990. Enugu: Dawn Functions.

Federal Department of Culture, Nigeria. 1981. *The Nucleus: A Catalogue of Works in the National Collection on the Inception of the National Gallery of Modern Art.* Lagos: Federal Department of Culture.

*FESTAC '77.* 1977. London/Lagos: Africa Journal Limited.

Fisher, Jean (ed.). 1994. *Global Visions: Towards a New Internationalism in the Visual Arts.* London: Kala Press in association with The Institute of International Visual Arts.

Fọlarin, Agbo. 1987. "Notes on Creative Experimentation—Nigerian Contemporary Arts Example." *Nigeria Magazine* 55:3, 66–68.

Forsyth, Frederick. 1977. *The Making of an African Legend: The Biafran Story.* London: Penguin Books.

Fosu, Kojo. 1993. *20th Century Art of Africa,* rev. ed. Accra: Artists Alliance.

Frankel, Peter. 1958. "Enwọnwu's African Queen." *Ibadan* 2, 21–22.

Franklin, Daniel P., and Michael J. Baun (eds.). 1995. *Political Culture and Constitutionalism: A Comparative Approach.* Armonk, N.Y.: M.E. Sharpe.

Gailey, Harry A. 1970. *The Road to Aba: A Study of British Administration Policy in Eastern Nigeria.* New York: New York University Press.

"Gallery Labac." 1967. *Nigeria Magazine* 93, 128–33.

Gaudibert, Pierre. 1991. *L'Art africain contemporain.* Paris: Diagonales.

Gervasoni, Marie-George (ed.). *XLIV Exposizione Internationale d'Arte: La Biennale di Venezia.* 1990. Milan: Gruppo Editoriali Fabbri Milan.

*Glendora Review: African Quarterly on the Arts.* Lagos: 1995–.

Goepper, Roger. 1963. *The Essence of Chinese Painting.* Boston: Boston Book and Art Shop.

Goethe Institut, Lagos. 1979. *Twenty Years Goethe Institut Lagos: German Cultural Centre in Nigeria.* Lagos: Goethe Institut.

"Graffiti Artist." 1991. *The Voice* (London), April 2.

*Guide to the Nigerian Museum: Lagos.* n.d. Lagos: Nigerian National Museum.

Hackett, Rosalind I. J. 1987. *New Religious Movements in Nigeria.* Lewiston: Edwin Mellen Press, African Studies 5.

———. 1989. *Religion in Calabar: The Religious Life and History of a Nigerian Town.* Berlin/New York: Mouton/de Gruyter.

Harney, Elizabeth. 1996. "Les chers enfants 'sans papa.'" *Oxford Art Journal* 19:1, 42–52.

Harris, Michael D. 1992. "Beyond Aesthetics: Visual Activism in Ile-Ifẹ." In Rowland Abiọdun, Henry J. Drewal, and John Pemberton III (eds.), *The Yoruba Artist: New Theoretical Perspectives on African Arts.* Washington, D.C.: Smithsonian Institution Press, 201–15.

Hassan, Salah M. 1995. "The Modernist Experience in African Art. Visual Expressions of the Self and Cross-Cultural Aesthetics." *NKA: Journal of Contemporary African Art* 2, 30–33, 72.

Hassan, Salah M., and Okwui Enwezor (curators). 1995. *New Visions: Recent Works by Six African Artists.* Eatonville, Fla.: Zora Neale Hurston National Museum/Ithaca, N.Y.: African Studies and Research Center.

Hemmerich, Anne. c. 1944. Untitled, typed manuscript for an exhibition of contemporary art, Lagos. 11 pages.

Highet, Juliet. 1969. "Five Nigerian Artists." *African Arts* 2:2, 34–41.

Hobsbawm, Eric, and Terence Ranger (eds.). 1984. *The Invention of Tradition.* Cambridge: Cambridge University Press.

Ibeto, C. C. c. 1962. *Nigeria:* The Account of My Life. Manuscript, Library of Congress, Manuscript Division, Harmon Foundation Collection. 3 pages.

"Ibo Body Designs from Arochuku." 1946. *Nigeria* 25, 321.

*Ifẹ Art School 1974–1984.* 1984. Lagos: National Council for Arts and Culture, Evolution in Nigeria Art Series, 2.

Igboanugo, P. S. C. 1976. Review: "Homage to Christopher Okigbo." *Nigeria Magazine* 120, 22–28.

Igbokwe, Joe. 1995. *Igbos: Twenty Five Years after Biafra.* Lagos: Advent Communications.

Ike, Chukwuemeka. 1976. *Sunset at Dawn: A Novel of the Biafran War.* London: William Collins Sons. Reprinted 1993, Ibadan: University Press.

Ikwuemesi, C. Krydz. 1991. "Chike Aniakọr: Painter, Art Historian." *The Outlook*, February 14, 12–13.

———. 1992a. "Historical and Aesthetic Notes on Uli." *The Eye* 1:1, 8–10.

———. 1992b. Uli as Creative Idiom: Study of Udechukwu, Aniakọr, and Obeta. B.A. Project Paper, University of Nigeria, Nsukka, Department of Fine and Applied Arts.

Ilona, Anthony. 1993–94. "Ọlu Ọguibe: Recent Works." *Third Text* 25, 87–89.

Iloaputaife, Ijeọma. 1976. Cartoon in Society (with Special Reference to Nigeria). B.A. thesis, University of Nigeria, Nsukka, Department of Fine and Applied Arts.

Imoagene, Oshomha. 1990. *The Ibo of E. Central Nigeria.* Ibadan: New-Era Publishers, Know Your Country Series 3.

*Incroci del Sud. Affinities. Arte Contemporanea del Sudafrica. . . . Affinities: Contemporary South African Art.* 1993. Rome: Palazzo Giustinian Lolin, Fundazione Levi, Sala 1.

Iroh, Eddie. 1979. *Toads of War.* London: Heinemann.

Isaacs, Jennifer. 1989. *Aboriginality: Contemporary Paintings and Prints.* St. Lucia: University of Queensland Press.

Ishaka, Peter. 1990. "Great Works, Good Bucks." *Newswatch* (Lagos) 12:7, August 13, 45.

Jahn, Janheinz. 1966. *A History of Neo-African Literature: Writing in Two Continents.* Translated from the German by Oliver Coburn and Ursula Lehrburger. London: Faber and Faber.

James, Vicky. 1995. "Kenneth Murray: Father of Museum Movement in Nigeria." *Nigerian Heritage: Journal of the National Commission for Museums and Monuments* 3, 69–74.

Jari, Jacob. 1995a. "The Eye Manifesto." In Clementine Deliss (ed.), *Seven Stories about Modern Art in Africa.* London: Whitechapel Gallery, 212.

———. 1995b. "The Eye Society." In Clementine Deliss (ed.), *Seven Stories about Modern Art in Africa.* London: Whitechapel Gallery, 213–14.

Jarmon, Charles. 1980. *Nigeria: Reorganization and Development since the Mid-Twentieth Century.* Leiden: E.J. Brill.

Jeffreys, M. D. W. 1951. "The Winged Solar Disk in Ibo Itshi Facial Scarification." *Africa* 21:2, 93–111.

Jẹgẹdẹ, Dele. 1981. "'Made-In-Nigeria' Artists: Problems and Anticipations." *Black Orpheus,* new series 4:1, 31–45. Also published in *Nigeria Magazine* 144, 1983, 22–37.

———. 1983. Trends in Contemporary Nigerian Art: A Historical Analysis. Ph.D. dissertation, Indiana University, Department of Fine Arts. Ann Arbor, Mich.: University Microfilms International, no. 8317173.

———. 1984. "Patronage and Change in Nigerian Art." *Nigeria Magazine* 150, 29–36.

———. 1988. "Contemporary African Art." *Art Papers* 12:4, 22–26.

——— (ed.). 1990. *Creative Dialogue: SNA at 25.* Lagos: Society of Nigerian Artists.

———. 1994. Art in a State of Anomie: The Nigerian Case. Unpublished.

———. 1995. "The Essential Ẹmọkpae." In Clementine Deliss (ed.), *Seven Stories about Modern Art in Africa.* London: Whitechapel Gallery, 198–201.

———. n.d. (c. 1994). Art as a Weapon in the War against Oppression in Nigeria. Unpublished paper.

Jemkur, J. F. 1992. *Aspects of the Nok Culture.* Zaria: Ahmadu Bello University Press.

Johnson, Vivien. 1994. *Aboriginal Artists of the Western Desert: A Biographical Dictionary.* Sydney: Craftsman House.

Jones, G. I. 1984. *The Art of Eastern Nigeria.* Cambridge: Cambridge University Press.

Kalu, Ogbu U. 1978a. "Writing in Pre-Colonial Africa: A Case Study of *Nsibidi*." In Ogbu U. Kalu (ed.), *African Cultural Development: Readings in African Humanities.* Enugu: Fourth Dimension Publishers, 76–85.

———. 1978b. "Nsibidi: Pictographic Communication in Pre-Colonial Cross-River Basin Societies." *Cahiers d'Etudes des Religions Africaines* 12, 97–106.

———. 1991. The Balm of Gilead: Christianity and Inner Healing of War Wounds in Igboland. Unpublished paper for a seminar on "Healing the Social Wounds of War," Windhoek, Namibia, August 29–September 2, to be published in *Healing the Social Wounds of War,* ed. Murray Last, Edinburgh University Press.

Kelly, Bernice M. (comp.), and Janet L. Stanley (ed.). 1993. *Nigerian Artists: A Who's Who and Bibliography.* London: Hans Zell.

Kennedy, Jean. 1968. "I Saw and I Was Happy: Festival at Oshogbo." *African Arts* 1:2, 8–16, 85.

———. 1992. *New Currents, Ancient Rivers: Contemporary African Artists in a Generation of Change.* Washington, D.C.: Smithsonian Institution Press.

Kirk-Greene, A. H. M. (ed.). 1971. *Crisis and Conflict in Nigeria: A Documentary Sourcebook 1966–1969,* 2 vols. London: Oxford University Press.

———. 1975. *The Genesis of the Nigerian Civil War and the Theory of Fear.* Uppsala: Scandinavian Institute of African Studies, Research Report 27.

Kubik, Gerhard. 1986. "African Graphic Systems with Particular Reference to the Benue-Congo or 'Bantu' Language Zone." *Muntu* (Libreville) 4/5, 71–135.

Kure, Marcia Wok. 1994. Ndidi Dike and Ọmọlara Ige. Two Contemporary Female Nigerian Artists. B.A. thesis, University of Nigeria, Nsukka, Department of Fine and Applied Arts.

"Lagos Art Galleries." 1967. *Nigeria Magazine* 92, 2–28.

Lamb, Venice. 1975. *West African Weaving.* London: Duckworth.

Lamb, Venice, and Judy Holmes. 1980. *Nigerian Weaving.* Lagos: Shell Petroleum Development Company of Nigeria.

Lancaster, Michael. 1962. "Art Gallery: Murals at U.C.I." *Nigeria Magazine* 74, 94.

Laṣekan, Akinọla. 1942. *Drawing Made Easy*. Lagos: African Art and Craft Studio.

———. 1949. *The Nigerian Joker*. Lagos: Ribway Printing Press, 2d impression.

———. 1962. "Wanted: Sublime Art." *West African Pilot* (Lagos), August 22.

———. 1989. "Problems of Contemporary African Artists." *Kurio Africana: Journal of Art and Criticism* 1:1, 24–33, 2d ed. [Reprinted from an unstated earlier source.]

"Late Items." 1991. *African News*. London: School of African and Asian Studies, University of London, April.

Lavrijsen, Ria (ed.) 1993. *Cultural Diversity in the Arts*. Amsterdam: Royal Tropical Institute.

Law, Sabu. 1969. "Contemporary Works of Art Need a Home in Nigeria." *Nigeria Magazine* 100, 348–56.

Lawal, Babatunde. 1977. "The Search for Identity in Contemporary Nigerian Art." *Studio International* 985:192, 145–50.

Lehmann, Arno. 1966. *Christian Art in Africa*. St. Louis: Concordia Publishing House.

Lévi-Strauss, Claude. 1971. "The Science of the Concrete." In Carol P. Jopling (ed.), *Art and Aesthetics in Primitive Societies: A Critical Anthology*. New York: Dutton, 225–49.

Lindfors, Bernth. 1973. *Folklore in Nigerian Literature*. New York: Africana Publishing Company.

———. 1982. *Early Nigerian Literature*. New York: Africana Publishing Company.

Macgregor, J. K. 1909. "Some Notes on *Nsibidi*." *Journal of the Royal Anthropological Institute* 39, 209–19.

Madiebo, Alexander A. 1980. *The Nigerian Revolution and the Biafran War*. Enugu: Fourth Dimension Publishers.

Madumere, Ifeọma Perpetua. 1993. Discovering Rowland E. Ndefo. Project paper for Nigerian Certificate of Education (N.C.E.), Anambra State College of Education, Nsugbe, Department of Fine and Applied Arts.

Madumere, Irene Chinedum N. 1988. The Adoptive Potential of Using Nsibidi Writing for Textile Design and Production. B.A. thesis, University of Nigeria, Nsukka, Department of Fine and Applied Arts.

Malan, Nancy E. 1973. "Photographs in the Harmon Foundation Collection." *African Arts* 6:3, 32–33.

"Matriarchal Folklorist Zulu Sofọla Steps into Ancestry." 1995. *Guardian* (Lagos), October 4, 25.

Mbadugha, Chike. 1958. *Zik of Africa by "Lash."* Ọnitsha: Zik'sway Bookshop.

McClusky, Pamela. 1987. *African Art: From Crocodiles to Convertibles in the Collection of the Seattle Art Museum*. Seattle: Seattle Art Museum.

McFarlan, Donald. 1957. *Calabar: The Church of Scotland Mission: Founded 1946*. London: Thomas Nelson and Sons.

Meek, Charles K. 1937. *Law and Authority in a Nigerian Tribe*. Oxford: Oxford University Press.

Meyerowitz, H. V. 1937. "Meditations about an Art Exhibition." *Nigeria* 11, 70–73.

Miller, Judith von D. 1975. *Art in East Africa: A Guide to Contemporary Art*. London/Nairobi: Frederick Muller/ Africa Book Services Ltd.

Miner, Horace. 1956. "Body Rituals among the Nacirema." *American Anthropologist* 58:3, 503–7.

Moore, Gerald. 1968. "Poetry and the Nigerian Crisis." *Black Orpheus* 2:3, 10–13.

Moughtin, J. C. 1984. *Hausa Architecture*. London: Ethnographica.

Mount, Marshall W. 1989. *African Art: The Years since 1920*, 2d ed. New York: Da Capo.

Munonye, John. 1966. *The Only Son*. London: Heinemann.

Murray, K. C. 1938a. "Painting in Nigeria." *Nigeria* 14, 112.

———. 1938b. "The Exhibition of Wood-Carvings, Terracottas, and Water-Colours: The Work of Five Nigerians Trained under the Nigerian Government, Held at the Zwemmer Gallery, London, 6th July to 7 August 1937." *Nigerian Field* 7:1, 12–15.

Museum of Modern Art, Oxford. 1990. *Art from South Africa*. Oxford: Museum of Modern Art.

Na'Allah, Saidu. 1980. *Gwari Pottery and the Potter Training Centre Abuja*. Ph.D. dissertation, Columbia University. Ann Arbor, Mich.: University Microfilms International.

National Archives and Records Administration, Still Picture Branch. n.d. *Contemporary African Art from the Harmon Foundation*. Capital Heights, Md.: National AudioVisual Center.

National Council of Women's Societies. 1987. *Nigerian Women in Arts 2nd–7th March, 1987*. Lagos: National Gallery of Crafts and Design.

Ndubisi, Ngọzi M. 1991. Uche Okeke: Formative Years (1956 to 1963). B.A. thesis, University of Nigeria, Nsukka, Department of Fine and Applied Arts.

Nduka, Toyin. 1994. "Woman, me: Ada Udechukwu's Lyrical Journey." *Festac News* (Lagos), April 24, 6.

*New Culture*. Ibadan: New Culture Studies: 1978–79, 1:1–11 (all published).

"News from Denmark." 1996. *ACASA Newsletter* [Arts Council of the African Studies Association] 46, 6.

Ngerem, Nathaniel N. 1986. Trends in Contemporary Nigerian Cartoons. B.A. thesis, University of Nigeria, Nsukka, Department of Fine and Applied Arts.

Nicolls, Andrea. 1987. Igbo Pottery Traditions in the Light of Historical Antecedents and Present-Day Realities. Ph.D. dissertation, Indiana University, Bloomington, Department of Art History.

Nigeria. 1953. *Report on the Kano Disturbances 16th, 17th, 18th and 19th May, 1953*. Lagos: Government Printer.

———. 1988. *Cultural Policy for Nigeria*. Lagos: Federal Government Printer.

*Nigerian Art—Kindred Spirits*. 1990. A CoProduction of WETA, Washington, D.C. and the Smithsonian Institution. Television program aired Wednesday, May 2, 1990, with accompanying texts of sections aired and of outtakes.

*Nigerian Art Exhibition: March 18–April 1, 1982*. 1982. Bonn: Nigerian Information and Cultural Centre. German edition: *Nigerianische Kunst-Ausstellung: 18 Marz bis 1. April 1982*. 1982. Bonn: Nigerianisches Informations- und Kulturzentrum.

Nigerian Council for the Advancement of Art and Culture, Lagos Branch. 1960. *Exhibition of Nigerian Arts and Crafts: 1st–22nd October 1960*. Lagos: Nigerian Council for the Advancement of Art and Culture, Lagos Branch.

*Nigerian-German Prints Exhibition. An Exhibition of Prints from the Workshop Held at the University of Nigeria, Nsukka, October 20–31, 1986 and Prints by the Workshop Director Winfried Schmidt*. 1986. Lagos and Nsukka: Goethe Institut and French Culture Centre, Department of Fine and Applied Arts, University of Nigeria, Nsukka.

"Nigerian Master Artists Adorn the New Murtala Mohammed [sic] Airport." 1979. *New Culture* 1:4, 34–38.

*Nigerian National Exhibition January/February 1977: Contemporary Visual Arts. Lagos State Cultural Centre, Eleke Crescent, Victoria Island*. 1977. Lagos: Visual Arts Committee.

*Nigerian Wood-Carvings, Terracottas, and Watercolours. 6th July 1937 to 7th August 1937*. 1937. London: Zwemmer Gallery.

Njọku, John E. Eberegbulam. 1990. *The Igbos of Nigeria: Ancient Rites, Changes, and Survival*. Lewiston: Edwin Mellen Press, African Studies 14.

*NKA: Journal of Contemporary African Art*. New York: 1994–.

Nkurumeh, Barthosa. 1992. Printmaking in Nsukka School: The Influence of Traditional Igbo Art and Life. Paper presented at the 9th Triennial Symposium on African Art, Arts Council of the African Studies Association, University of Iowa, Iowa City, April 22–26. Unpublished.

Nnachy, D. L. K. 1940. "Ite Odo—Ohafia War Dance." *Nigeria* 20, 281.

Nsukka Analyst. 1994. *Marginalisation in Nigerian Polity: A Diagnosis of "The Igbo Problem" and the National Question*. Nsukka: The Nsukka Analysis.

Nwankwọ, Arthur A. 1972. *Nigeria: The Challenge of Biafra*. London: Collings.

Nwankwọ, Nkem. 1964. *Danda*. London: Andre Deutsch.

Nwapa, Flora. 1966. *Efuru*. London: Heinemann.

Nwọga, D. I. 1971. "The Concept of Satire among the Igbo." *The Conch* 3:2, 30–45.

———— (ed.). 1982. *Rhythms of Creation: A Decade of Okike Poetry*. Enugu: Fourth Dimension Publishers.

———— (comp. and ed.). 1984. *Critical Perspectives on Christopher Okigbo*. Washington, D.C.: Three Continents Press.

Nwoko, Demas. 1979. "The Aesthetics of African Art and Culture: Art and Artist: The Performing Arts." *New Culture* 1:11, 3–5.

Nwoko, Piu Eke. 1973. Aspects of Uli Body Painting from Ufuma. B.A. thesis, University of Nigeria, Nsukka, Department of Fine and Applied Arts.

Nzewi, Meki. 1994. "Das Kollektiv der Upa-Malerinnen." In *Agua Mmiri Wasser: Kunst als Mittlerin—Brasilien—Nigeria—Deutschland*. Osnabruck: Deutsche Bundesstiftung Umwelt, 48–59.

Ọbafemi, Olu. 1993. *Forty Years in African Art and Life: Reflections on Ulli Beier*. Bayreuth: Iwalẹwa-Haus.

Obiechina, Emmanuel. 1980. *Christopher Okigbo: The Poet of Destiny*. Enugu: Fourth Dimension Publishers.

Ọdita, Emmanuel. 1966. "Some Observations on Contemporary African Art." *Journal of the New African Literature and the Arts* 2, 60–63.

————. 1970. Review of Ulli Beier, *Contemporary Art in Africa*, New York: Praeger, 1968. *Africa Report*, January, 39–40.

————. 1980. "Contemporary African Art: Theory of Bintu, Kuntu, Skokian and Awo." *Search, Research and Discovery in the Arts* (Ohio State University) 3:2, 4–9.

Odutokun, Gani. 1993a. "Bruce Onobrakpẹya: 60th Birthday Retrospective Exhibition." *The Eye* 2:1, 4–6.

————. 1993b. "II. Obiọra Udechukwu: The Exploration of a Poetic Eye." In *So Far: Drawings, Paintings, Prints 1963–1993 by Obiọra Udechukwu*. Bayreuth: Boomerang Press, 9–11.

Ọfọmata, G. E. K. (ed.). 1978. *The Nsukka Environment*. Enugu: Fourth Dimension Publishers.

Ogbalu, F. C. (ed.). 1965. *Dimkpa Taa Aku, A Hu Ichere Ya*, 3d ed. Ọnitsha: University Publishing Co.

Ogbechiẹ, Sylvester O. 1988. Ben Enwọnwu in the Art Historical Account of Modern Nigerian Art. B.A. thesis, University of Nigeria, Nsukka, Department of Fine and Applied Arts.

————. 1990. "Sublime Presence: Ada Udechukwu's Fabrics and Designs." In Ada Udechukwu, *Fabrics and Designs*. Nsukka: Continuing Education Centre, University of Nigeria, Nsukka, no pagination.

————. 1992. Corporate Interaction in Contemporary Nigerian Art: A Study of the AKA Circle of Exhibiting Artists. M.A. thesis, University of Nigeria, Nsukka, Department of Fine and Applied Arts.

————. 1993. Revolution and Evolution in Modern Nigerian Art: Myths and Realities. 2nd International Symposium on Contemporary Nigerian Art, Lagos, April 29–May 1. Unpublished.

————. 1994. Revolution and Evolution in Modern Nigerian Art: Myths and Realities. Northwestern University. Unpublished.

————. 1995. Songs of the City: Ben Enwọnwu's Portrait of Queen Elizabeth II. Paper read at the 1995 Triennial Symposium of the Arts Council of the African Studies Association, New York. Unpublished.

Ogbechiẹ, Sylvester, and Nkiru Nzegwu. 1991. *Exhibition: Ben Enwọnwu at 70*. N.p.: n.p.

Ogedengbe. 1963. "Reader's Letters: Cement Funeral Sculptures." *Nigeria Magazine* 78, 153.

Ọguibe, Ọlu. 1987. "Anatsui's Pieces of Wood." *West Africa* 3630, 663–64.

———. 1988. "*. . . unbind me.*" Lagos: Didi Museum.

———. 1989a. "Women as a Metaphor in Obiọra Udechukwu's Art." *Kurio Africana: Journal of Art and Criticism* 1:2, 52–60.

———. 1989b. *Statements: Recent Art and Poetry.* Lagos: Syrian Club.

———. 1989c. The Image of Woman in Contemporary Nigerian Art: 1970 to the Present. M.A. thesis. University of Nigeria, Nsukka, Department of Fine and Applied Arts.

———. 1990a. *A Song from Exile.* Bayreuth: Boomerang Press.

———. 1990b. [actually 1991]. *Statement from the Artist. On the Censorship of My Work by the Commonwealth Institute.* London: The author.

———. 1990c. *The Emperor and the Poet.* Bayreuth: Iwalẹwa-Haus.

———. 1991a. *Ọlu Ọguibe: Works and Words.* London: Bhownagree Gallery, Commonwealth Institute.

———. 1991b. "Introduction." In *Paradox of the New: Art from Africa.* Bradford, England: South Square Gallery, sponsored by Savannah Gallery, London, no pagination.

———. 1992a. "El Salahi." In *Ibrahim El Salahi.* London: Savannah Gallery, no pagination.

———. 1992b. *A Gathering Fear: Poems with Drawings by the Author.* Bayreuth: Boomerang Press.

———. 1992c. *A Gathering Fear (Poems),* 2d ed. Lagos: Kraft Books.

———. 1993a. "In the 'Heart of Darkness.' 1993." *Third Text* 23, 3–8, reprinted in Eric Fernie (ed.), *Art History and Its Methods: A Critical Anthology.* London: Phaidon, 1995, 314–22.

———. 1993b. "Ethiopian Footprints: The Work of Falaka Yimer. In *Falaka Yimer.* London: Savannah Gallery, no pagination.

———. 1993c. "Introduction." In *8 African Women Artists.* London: Savannah Gallery, no pagination.

———. 1994a. "New Internationalism." *NKA: Journal of Contemporary African Art* 1, 24–28.

———. 1994b. "A Brief Note on Internationalism." In Jean Fisher (ed.), *Global Visions: Towards a New Internationalism in the Visual Arts.* London: Kala Press, 50–59.

———. 1994c. "Seen/Unseen." *NKA: Journal of Contemporary African Art* 1, 52–55.

———. 1994d. *Songs for Catalina.* London: Savannah Publications.

——— (ed.). 1994e. *Sojourners: New Writing by Africans in Britain.* London: Africa Refugee Publishing Collective.

———. 1995a. "Uzọ Egọnu: A Discourse of Reversals." *NKA: Journal of Contemporary African Art* 2, 12–17.

———. 1995b. *Uzọ Egọnu: An African Artist in the West.* London: Kala Press.

———. 1995c. "Emmanuel Jẹgẹdẹ: Joy of the Living Race." *NKA: Journal of Contemporary African Art* 2, 62–63.

———. 1995d. "Art, Identity, Boundaries: The Rome Lecture." *NKA: Journal of Contemporary African Art* 3, 26–33.

———. 1995e. "Jacob Lawrence: The Migration Series." *NKA: Journal of Contemporary African Art* 3, 70–75.

———. 1995f. Theory and Practice in Modern African Art. Unpublished.

———. 1995g. "A Painter's Progress." *West Africa* 4079, 1974–76.

———. 1996. "El Anatsui: In the Public Space." *Third Text* 35, 69–77.

———. n.d. El Anatsui. Unpublished manuscript.

Ọguibe, Ọlu, and Ulli Beier. 1994. *The Relocated Artist: Ọlu Ọguibe Talks to Ulli Beier.* Bayreuth: Iwalẹwa-Haus.

Ọguibe, Ọlu, and Jonathan Lessor. 1987. *Homage to Olumọ: An Exhibition of Paintings and Drawings.* Abeokuta.

Ọguibe, Ọlu, and Greg Odo. 1988. *Art on the Street: An Exhibition of Drawings and Paintings.* Nsukka: University of Nigeria.

Ogunwa, Denrele. 1995. "A Man of the Earth. Denrele Ogunwa Talks to a Foremost African Sculptor." *West Africa,* October 9–15, 1575–77.

*Ọjaadili [Igbo Play] Ọdunke Artists.* 1979. Ibadan: University Press Limited. [In Igbo]

Ọji, Ugonma Mercy. 1994. A Comparative Analysis of Omu-Aro and Nsibidi Symbols in Arochukwu Cultural Context. B.A. thesis, University of Nigeria, Nsukka, Department of Fine and Applied Arts.

Ojukwu, Dili. 1989. "Up, Up They Go. Nigerian Art Works Attract Higher Prices." *African Guardian* (Lagos) 4, December 4, 33–35.

Okafọr, Chizube A. O. 1980. Rowland Ndefo: The Man and His Works. B.A. thesis, University of Nigeria, Nsukka, Department of Fine and Applied Arts.

Okediji, Moyọ. 1989. "Ọnaism in *The Nucleus.*" *Kurio Africana: Journal of Art and Criticism* 1:1, 89–99.

——— (ed.). 1992. *Principles of 'Traditional' African Culture.* Ibadan: Bard Books.

Okeke, Chika. 1990. "Lyrics of a Lost Totem: Another View of Udechukwu's Verse." *The Guardian* (Lagos), August 13, 37.

———. 1991. "Towards Better Art Criticism." *Daily Times,* July 27, 15.

———. 1992. "Nigerian Women Artists—Amazons of a New Order." *Classique* (Lagos), October 5, 27.

——— (ed). 1993a. *Uche Okeke: 60th Birthday Anniversary Retrospective Exhibition, Goethe Institut, Lagos.* Enugu: Association of University of Nigeria Art Graduates, Art and Artists Conference Forum, Committee for Relevant Art and Society of Nigerian Artists.

————.1993b. "Moving On, Looking Backwards—Udechukwu's Retrospective." *The Eye* 2:2, 4–6.

————. 1994. "Slashing Wood, Eroding Culture: Conversation with El Anatsui." *NKA: Journal of Contemporary African Art* 1, 34–40.

————. 1995. "The Quest: From Zaria to Nsukka. A Story about Nigeria." In Clementine Deliss (ed.), *Seven Stories about Modern Art in Africa*. London: Whitechapel Gallery, 40–75.

Okeke, Josiah. 1993. A Survey of the Murray School with a Retrospective Study on C. C. Ibeto. Manuscript, University of Nigeria, Nsukka, Department of Fine and Applied Arts.

Okeke, Uche. 1961. *Drawings: Uche Okeke*. Ibadan: Mbari Publications.

————. 1963. Art in Nigeria. Speech delivered at the Queen's College, Enugu, December 16, under the auspices of the British Council. Unpublished. Copy in the United States Library of Congress, Manuscript Division, Harmon Foundation Collection.

————. 1969a. *Kunst und Kunsthandwerk aus Biafra*. Bergweg: Zentrale der Aktionskomitees Biafra/Sudan.

————. 1969b. *Biafra Weihnachten 69*. Bonn: Zentral der Aktions-Komitees Biafra-Sudan.

————. 1970. *Geschichte der Ibo-Kunst*. Dortmund: Dortmund Kulturamt, *Dortmunder Vorträge*, Reihe A, Heft 97.

————. 1971a. *Tales of Land of Death: Igbo Folk Tales*. Garden City, N.Y.: Doubleday and Co., Zenith Books.

————. 1971b. *Vierzig Gedichte. Aus dem Englischen ubertragen von Herbert Kummer*. Dortmund: Verlag Wull and Co., Kleine Reihe Lyrik und Prosa.

————. 1971c. "The Story of Contemporary Art of Nigeria's Eastern States." *Ikorok* 1:2, 35–46.

————. 1972a. "Painters from Nsukka." In *New Painters from Nsukka 1972. Bons Nwabiani and Obiọra Udechukwu at the British Council Centre 15 Ogui Road Enugu. Monday 24 to Monday 31 July 1972*. N.p., n.p., 2.

————. 1972b. "Ekeama." *African Arts* 5:2, 50–51. [Movement IV only.]

————. 1973. "Ekeama (Ọgbanje Drama)." *Nimo: Cultural Magazine of the Omega Fraternity Nimo* 1:1, 19–29. [Movements I and II only.]

————. 1975. "Panorama of Nigerian Art." *Nigeria Magazine* 115/116, 34–55.

————. 1976a. "Igbo Drawing and Painting. Two Little Known Art Forms." *Ufahamu* 6:2, 106–15.

————. 1976b. "Introduction." Introductory paper for the Symposium of Nigerian Contemporary Art, March 21–26. Nsukka: University of Nigeria. Unpublished.

————. 1977a. "The Search for a Theoretical Basis for Contemporary Nigerian Art." *Nigerian Journal of the Humanities* (Benin City) 1:1, 60–66. Reprinted in Okeke 1982a, 20–25.

————. 1977b. *Igbo Art*. Nimo: Asele Institute.

————. 1978a. Towards a Rational Policy of Art Patronage in Nigeria. Paper presented at the Seminar: Interrelationship of the Fine Arts and Performing Arts in Nigeria, University of Lagos, Center for Cultural Studies, February 12, 18. Unpublished. Subsequently published in U. Okeke 1982a, 29–35.

————. 1978b. "The Art Culture of the Nsukka Igbo." In G. E. K. Ọfọmata (ed.), *The Nsukka Environment*. Enugu: Fourth Dimension Publishers, 271–85.

————. 1978–79. "An Introduction to Contemporary Nigerian Art." *New Culture* (Ibadan) 1:1, 14–23; 1:2, 12–18.

————. 1979a. "History of Modern Nigerian Art." *Nigeria Magazine* 128/129, 100–118.

————. 1979b. "Towards a Rational Policy of Art Patronage in Nigeria." *New Culture* 1:4, 14–20.

————. 1982a. *Art in Development—A Nigerian Perspective*. Edited by LeClair Grier Lambert. Nimo/Minneapolis: Documentation Centre, Asele Institute, Nimo/African American Cultural Center, Minneapolis.

————. 1982b. *Design Inspiration through Uli*. Minneapolis: The author.

————. 1982c. *Uche Okeke: Selection of 35 Works Created from 1958 to 1981*. Minneapolis: no publisher. [Reprographs of 35 of his works, with a 3-page text.]

————. 1985. *Art Culture of Anambra State: The Eri. Heritage*. Nimo: Asele Institute.

————. 1988. *Treasures of Asele Institute*. Lagos/Nimo: Italian Cultural Institute/Asele Institute.

————. 1993a. *Creative Conscience*. Nimo: Asele Institute.

————. 1993b. *Uche Okeke: Biodata. Sixtieth Anniversary Edition*. Nimo: Documentation Centre, Asele Institute.

————. 1995a. "Natural Synthesis." In Clementine Deliss (ed.), *Seven Stories about Modern Art in Africa*. London: Whitechapel Gallery, 208–9.

————. 1995b. "Growth of an Idea." In Clementine Deliss (ed.), *Seven Stories about Modern Africa*. London: Whitechapel Gallery, 210–11.

————. 1995c. Modern African Art: Its Role as a Catalyst of Development in the 20th Century. Paper presented at the Royal African Society Symposium on the African Arts, London, September 29–October 1. Unpublished.

————. n.d. *Natural Synthesis: Collected Notes 1959–1970*. No place: The author.

Okeke, Uche, and C. U. V. Okechukwu. 1978. "Igbodo Art and Culture." In G. E. K. Ọfọmata, *The Nsukka Environment*. Enugu, Fourth Dimension Publishers, 307–14.

Okeke, Uche, and Ego Uche-Okeke. 1978. *A Retrospective Exhibition of Uche Okeke: Drawing, 1957–1978. Lagos: Goethe Institute 8–22 November 1978*. N.p.: n.p.

Okereke, Emma[nuel] Chukwudi. 1979. Art and Conflict: The Visual Art in Biafran Propaganda. B.A. thesis, University of Nigeria, Nsukka, Department of Fine and Applied Arts.

Okigbo, Christopher. 1962. *Heavensgate*. Ibadan: Mbari Publications.

———. 1971. *Labyrinths: With Path of Thunder*. London, Ibadan: Heinemann, Mbari Pubications.

*Okike*. Nsukka: Okike Magazine. 1971–.

Okonta, Ike. 1988. "Testament of a Lost Generation." *African Concord*, March 1, 44–45.

Ọkpara, Chukwuemeka Vincent. 1993. C. C. Ibeto: His Life and Contributions to the Contemporary Nigerian Art. B.A. Project, University of Nigeria, Nsukka, Department of Fine and Applied Arts.

Ọkparọcha, John. 1976. *Mbari: Art as Sacrifice*. Ibadan: Daystar Press.

*Okpu Eze: New Dimensions: Present of the Past. Wood Sculptures, Installations and Paintings. National Museum, Onikan, Lagos, August 15–22, 1992*. 1992. Enugu: New Africa Centre.

Ọlọidi, Ọla. 1977. *The New Direction. Experiment on the Training of University Art Students. Produced for the Lagos International Trade Fair, November 27–December 11*. Nsukka: University of Nigeria, Nsukka, Department of Fine and Applied Arts, Art History Section.

———. 1978a. FESTAC National Art Exhibition and Nigerian National Aspiration. Paper presented at the Seminar: The Interrelationship of the Arts in Nigeria, University of Lagos, Centre for Cultural Studies, February 12, 18. Unpublished.

——— (ed.). 1978b. *Introducing Ana Gallery*. Nsukka: University of Nigeria, Nsukka, Department of Fine and Applied Arts.

———. 1979. "Abstraction in Modern African Art." *New Culture* (Ibadan) 1:9, 9–13.

———. 1980. "De-Africanization and Europeanization: The Non-Acknowledgement of African Influence on Modern Art." *Kiabara: Journal of the Humanities, University of Port Harcourt* 3:1, 93–112.

———. 1981. "Elitism and Modern African Artists." *Nigeria Magazine* 134/135, 71–84.

———. 1984. Modern Nigerian Art: Implementation, Growth and Development from 1900 to 1960. Ph.D. dissertation, University of Nigeria, Nsukka, Department of Fine and Applied Arts.

———. 1985. "Introduction." In *Echo. U.N.N. Silver Jubilee Exhibition: Nsukka Students' Art 1970–1984. Ana Gallery, Dept. of Fine and Applied Arts U.N.N. 13–23 Feb. 1985*. Nsukka: University of Nigeria, Department of Fine and Applied Arts, 1–5.

———. 1986. "Growth and Development of Formal Art Education in Nigeria, 1900–1960." *Transafrican Journal of History* 15, 103–26.

———. 1989. "Constraints on the Growth and Development of Modern Nigerian Art in the Colonial Period." *Nigerian Journal of the Humanities* 5/6, 29–51.

———. 1991a. "Defender of African Creativity: Aina Ọnabolu, Pioneer of Western Art in West Africa." *Africana Research Bulletin* (Freetown) 17:2, 21–49.

———. 1991b. "The Progression of Sculptural Aesthetics." In El Anatsui, *Old and New: An Exhibition of Sculptures in Assorted Wood by El Anatsui*. Lagos: National Museum.

———. 1993a. "Tribute to the Late Professor Chuka Amaefunah." *The Eye* 2:2, 34–35.

———. 1993b. "Obiọra Udechukwu: Fulfilled but Still after Clarity of Vision." In Obiọra Udechukwu, *So Far, Drawings, Paintings and Prints 1963–1993*. Bayreuth: Boomerang Press, 11–13.

———. 1995a. "Three Decades of Modern Nigerian Art (1960–1990): General Observations and Critique." *USO: Nigerian Journal of Art* 1:1, 66–73.

———. 1995b. "Art and Nationalism in Colonial Nigeria." In Clementine Deliss (ed.), *Seven Stories about Modern Art in Africa*. London: Whitechapel Gallery, 192–94. Reprinted from *Nsukka Journal of History* 1989, 92–110.

———. 1995c. "Imageries of Contemporary Nigerian Art." In *Contemporary Nigerian Art: Catalogue of an Exhibition at the Headquarters of the World Intellectual Property Organisation (WPO). Geneva, September 25–29, 1995*, 6–9.

Ọlọrukọọba, B. K. 1991. *Art for Senior Secondary Schools*. Zaria: Ahmadu Bello University Press.

Oludare, J. A. 1981. The Career of a Nigerian Independent Artist: Akinọla Laṣekan. B.A. thesis, University of Nigeria, Nsukka, Department of Fine and Applied Art.

Ọnabolu, Aina. 1920. *A Short Discussion on Art*. Lagos.

———. 1925. *Catalogue of Pictures by Aina Ọnabolu and Drawings by His Pupils. Glover Memorial Hall, Lagos, Nov–Dec 1925*. Lagos.

Ọnabolu, Dapo. 1963. "Art Gallery: Aina Ọnabolu." *Nigeria Magazine* 79, 295–98.

Onobrakpẹya, Bruce. 1995. "The Zaria Art Society." In Clementine Deliss (ed.), *Seven Stories about Modern Art in Africa*. London: Whitechapel Gallery, 195–97.

Ọnwudinjọ, Chukwunyem F. 1987. Cartoon in Contemporary Nigerian Society: A Reappraisal. B.A. thesis, University of Nigeria, Nsukka, Department of Fine and Applied Arts.

Ọnwuejeọgwu, M. Angulu. 1981. *An Igbo Civilization: Nri Kingdom and Hegemony*. London/Benin City: Ethnographica/Ethiope Publishing Corporation.

Ọnwuzurọha, Martin Osita. 1980. Society of Nigerian Artists. B.A. thesis, University of Nigeria, Nsukka, Department of Fine and Applied Arts.

Onyeneke, A. O. 1987. *The Dead among the Living: Masquerades in Igbo Society*. Nimo: Holy Ghost Congregation and Asele Institute.

*Original Prints from the Third Nsukka Workshop 1987*. 1987. Nsukka: Department of Fine and Applied Arts, University of Nigeria, Nsukka.

Ọrjih, Chinze Scholastica. 1985. Cartoon in Nigeria: With Emphasis on the Effects of Change of Government on the Cartoonists. B.A. thesis, University of Nigeria, Nsukka, Department of Fine and Applied Arts.

Ottenberg, Simon. 1959. "Ibo Receptivity to Change." In W. J. Bascom and M. J. Herskovits, *Continuity and Change in African Cultures*. Chicago: University of Chicago Press, 130–43.

———. 1968. *Double Descent in an African Society: The Afikpo Village-Group*. Seattle: University of Washington Press, American Ethnological Society, Monograph Series 47.

———. 1971. *Leadership and Authority in an African Society: The Afikpo Village-Group*. Seattle: University of Washington Press, American Ethnological Society, Monograph Series 52.

———. 1972. "Humorous Masks and Serious Politics among Afikpo Ibo." In Douglas Fraser and Herbert M. Cole (eds.), *African Art and Leadership*. Madison: University of Wisconsin Press, 99–121.

———. 1973. "Afikpo Masquerades: Audience and Performers." *African Arts* 6:4, 32–35, 94–95.

———. 1975. *The Masked Rituals of Afikpo: The Context of an African Art*. Seattle: University of Washington Press.

———. 1979. "Analysis of an African Masked Parade." In Justine Cordwell and Ronald A. Schwarz (eds.), *The Fabrics of Culture: The Anthropology of Clothing and Adornment*. The Hague: Mouton, 177–97.

———. 1989a. *Boyhood Rituals in an African Society: An Interpretation*. Seattle: University of Washington Press.

———. 1989b. "We Are Becoming Art Minded: Afikpo Arts 1988." *African Arts* 22:4, 58–67, 88.

———. 1994. "Introduction." In *AKA '94 Annual Art Exhibition*. Enugu: AKA Circle of Exhibiting Artists, 7.

———. n.d. Christian and Indigenous Religious Issues in the Work of Four Contemporary Eastern Nigerian Artists. Paper presented at the Tenth Triennial Symposium on African Art, April 19–23, 1995, New York University, New York. Unpublished.

"Our Authors and Performing Artists—II." 1966. *Nigeria Magazine* 89, 133–40.

Owomoyela, Oyekan. 1979. *African Literatures: An Introduction*. Waltham, Mass.: Crossroads Press.

Oyebọla [Oyelọla], Pat. 1981. "The Visual Artist and His Audience: Past, Present and Future." *Black Orpheus*, new series 4:1, 75–79.

Oyelọla, Pat. 1976. *Everyman's Guide to Nigerian Art*. Lagos: Nigeria Magazine Cultural Division, Nigeria Magazine Special Publication 5.

*Pageants of the African World*. 1980. Lagos: Nigeria Magazine.

Papastergiadis, Nikos. 1994. *The Complicities of Culture: Hybridity and 'New Internationalism.'* Manchester: Cornerhouse, Cornerhouse Communiqué 4.

*Paradox of the New: Art from Africa*. 1991. Bradford, England: South Square Gallery.

Perham, Margery. 1937. *Native Administration in Nigeria*. Oxford: Oxford University Press.

Pieterse, Cosmo, and Dennis Duerden (eds.). 1972. *African Writers Talking: A Collection of Radio Interviews*. New York: Africana Publishing Corporation.

Poynor, Robin. 1987. "Naturalism and Abstraction in Owo Masks." *African Arts* 20:4, 56–61, 91.

*Prints from Nsukka: 4th Printmaking Workshop 1990*. 1990. Nsukka: Department of Fine and Applied Arts, University of Nigeria, Nsukka.

*Programme for the Funeral Ceremonies of a Mother in a Million. Madam Monica Mgboye Okeke (Akọbuije) 1910–1994*. 1994. Nimo: no publisher.

Rattray, R. S. 1923. *Ashanti*. London: Oxford University Press.

———. 1927. *Religion and Art in Ashanti*. London: Oxford University Press.

Reed, Dorothy B. 1996. Engendered Spirits: Politics and Performance in an Urban Masquerade Festival in Nigeria. Ph.D. dissertation, University of California, Santa Barbara, Department of Art History.

*Research in African Literatures*. Austin: University of Texas. 1970–.

*Revue Noire*. Paris: 1991–.

Ruprecht, Ronald. 1988. "Kunst in Nigeria seit 1950." In *Kunstreise nach Afrika: Tradition und Moderne*. Bayreuth: Iwalẹwa-Haus.

St. Jorre, John de. 1972. *The Brothers' War: Biafra and Nigeria*. Boston: Houghton Mifflin.

Schmidt, Nancy. 1965. An Anthropological Analysis of Nigerian Fiction. Ph.D. dissertation, Department of Anthropology, Northwestern University.

Schmidt, Winfried. 1988. "Moderne nigerianische Kunst: Die Nsukkaschule und ihre Herkunft aus der traditionellen Wand- und Korpermalerei." In *Kunstreise nach Afrika: Tradition und Moderne*. Bayreuth: Iwalẹwa-Haus, 93–110.

Schmidt, Winfried, and Obiọra Udechukwu. 1985. *Invitation: Dialogue with Prints. Winfried Schmidt—Obiọra Udechukwu*. October 22–November 22. Lagos: German Cultural Centre.

Schwab, Peter. 1971. *Biafra*. New York: Facts on File.

"Sculptor Wins Japanese Prize." 1995. *The Guardian* (Lagos), October 21, 22.

Senghor, Léopold. 1956. "The Spirit of Civilisation or the Laws of African Negro Culture." *Présence Africaine*, new series 8–10, 51–64.

———. 1966. "The Function and Meaning of the First World Festival of Negro Arts." *African Forum* 1:4, 5–10.

———. 1967. "Standards critiques de l'art africain." *African Arts* 1:1, 6–9, 52.

Shaw, Thurstan. 1970. *Igbo-Ukwu: An Account of Archaeological Discoveries in Eastern Nigeria*, 2 vols. Evanston, Ill.: Northwestern University Press.

Sibigam, Emmanuel C. 1987. Sixteen Years of Printmaking: A Survey of the Nsukka School. B.A thesis, University of Nigeria, Nsukka, Department of Fine and Applied Arts.

*Silver Jubilee National Art Exhibition 25th Anniversary. Sept. 26–Oct. 1, 1985.* 1985. Lagos: National Council for Arts and Culture.

*Simon Obiekeziẹ Okeke: Painter, Sculptor, Curator.* 1976. Enugu: Ministry of Social Development, Youth, Sports and Culture.

*Sixteen Paintings and Prints.* 1994. London: Savannah Gallery.

Smith, Fred. 1986. "Compound Entryway Decoration: Male Space and Female Creativity." *African Arts* 19:3, 52–57.

Society of Nigerian Artists. 1964. *Inaugural Exhibition January 16–22, 1964. Exhibition Centre, Marina, Lagos.* Lagos: Society of Nigerian Artists.

Ṣoyinka, Tunde. 1995. *Beauty Will Save the Republic: An Exhibition of Paintings, Drawings and Cartoons by Tunde Ṣoyinka. Lagos, Didi Museum 23–31st August, 1995.* Lagos: Didi Museum.

Stanley, Janet. 1992. "In Memoriam: Jean Kennedy: September 22, 1919–November 30, 1991. *African Arts* 25:2, 38, 96.

Studio Museum in Harlem. 1990. *Contemporary African Artists: Changing Traditions.* New York: Studio Museum in Harlem.

*Susanne Wenger: New Sacred Art Exhibition, Muson Centre.* 1994. Lagos: Muson Centre.

Sze, Mai-mai. 1963. *The Tao of Painting,* 2d ed. (2 vols. in one). New York: Pantheon, Bollingen Series 49.

Talbot, P. Amaury. 1912. *In the Shadow of the Bush.* London: Heinemann.

Tamuno, Tekena N., and Samson C. Ukpabi (eds.). 1989. *Nigeria since Independence: The First 25 Years. Volume VI: The Civil War Years.* Ibadan: Heinemann Educational Books.

Taylor, Eric. 1962. "Commercial Art at Zaria." *Nigeria Magazine* 73, 64–65.

*Textile and Clothing.* 1984. Lagos: National Gallery of Crafts and Design.

*The Eye: A Journal of Contemporary Art.* Zaria: The Eye Society. 1992–.

"*The Muse* Interviews Obiọra Uudechukwu: An Association of Nigeria Authors Award Winner, a Poet and Painter." 1993. *The Muse* 23.

*Third Text.* London: 1987–.

Thomas, Nicholas. 1996. "Cold Fusion." *American Anthropologist* 98:1, 9–16.

Thomas, Northcote W. 1913. *Anthropological Report on the Ibo-Speaking Peoples of Nigeria. Part I. Law and Custom of the Ibo of the Awka Neighbourhood, S. Nigeria.* London: Harrison and Sons.

Thomas, Peter. 1968. "'Ride Me Memories': A Memorial Tribute to Christopher Okigbo (1932–1967)." *African Arts* 1:4, 68–70.

Thompson, Robert Farris. 1971. *Black Gods and Kings.* Los Angeles: Occasional Papers of the Museums and Laboratories of Ethnic Arts and Technology, University of California, 2.

———. 1978. "Black Ideographic Writing: Calabar to Cuba." *Yale Alumni Magazine,* November, 29–33.

———. 1982. *Flash of the Spirit: African and African-American Art and Philosophy.* New York: Random House.

"Thorn Figure Carving." 1938. *Nigeria* 14, 134–36.

Tutuọla, Amos. 1958. *The Brave African Huntress.* London: Faber and Faber.

Ubagu, Susan. 1984. The Adaptation of Uli Motifs to Contemporary Igbo Women's Dress Patterns. B.A. thesis, University of Nigeria, Nsukka, Department of Fine and Applied Arts.

Uche-Okeke, Nwakaego Eunice. 1975. Uche Okeke: His Works and Thoughts on Art. B.A. thesis, University of Nigeria, Nsukka, Department of Fine and Applied Arts.

Uchendu, Victor. 1964. "Kola Hospitality and Igbo Lineage Structure." *Man* 64:53, 47–50.

———. 1965. *The Igbo of Southeast Nigeria.* New York: Holt, Rinehart and Winston.

Udechukwu, Ada. 1990. *Fabrics and Designs.* Nsu ka: Continuing Education Centre, University of Nigeria, Nsukka.

———. 1992. *Uli: Different Hands, Different Times. Paintings, Drawings, Textiles and Ceramics, Sculpture. By Ndidi Dike, Bridget Egbeji, Elizabeth George, Mgbadunnwa Ọkanumee, Ego Uche-Okeke, Ada Udechukwu, Chinwe Uwatse. Catalogue of an Exhibition Held at the Continuing Education Centre, University of Nigeria, Nsukka 14–17 July 1992.* Nsukka: The author.

———. 1993. *Woman, me.* Bayreuth: Boomerang Press.

———. 1994. "Introduction." In *Marcia Kure: Paintings * Drawings.* Nsukka: Institute of African Studies Museum, University of Nigeria, Nsukka.

Udechukwu, Obiọra. 1972. Lyrical Symbolism: Notes on Traditional Wall Painting from Agulu. B.A. thesis, University of Nigeria, Nsukka, Department of Fine and Applied Arts.

———. 1975. *Homage to Christopher Okigbo.* Nsukka: Ọdunke Publications.

———. 1977. Folklore and Fantasy in Contemporary Nigerian Art. M.F.A. thesis, University of Nigeria, Nsukka, Department of Fine and Applied Arts.

———. 1978. "Observations on Art Criticism in Nigeria." *Nigeria Magazine* 126/127, 35–43.

———. 1979a. "Nigerian Political Cartoonists in the 1970s." *New Culture* 1:10, 13–20.

———. 1979b. "Igbo Traditional Design and Con mporary Dress Wears." *Anụ* 3, 1–14.

———. 1980a. "Obiọra Udechukwu: Towards Essence and Clarity." *Nigeria Magazine* 132–133, 43–46.

———. 1980b. *Obiọra Udechukwu: Five Themes Fifty-Five works. An Exhibition of Drawings, Watercolours, and Prints.* Lagos: Goethe Institut.

———. 1981a. *No Water: An Exhibition of Drawings, Water-*

*colours and Prints by Obiọra Udechukwu. Catalogue.* Nsukka: Ọdunke Publications.

———. 1981b. "'Uli' and 'Li': Aspects of Igbo and Chinese Drawing and Painting." *Nigeria Magazine* 134/135, 40–50.

———. 1981c. "Line, Space, Simplicity and Spontaneity: Aspects of Igbo and Chinese Drawing and Painting." *Ugo* 1:4, 26–33.

———. 1982a. *Obiọra Udechukwu.* Bayreuth: Iwalẹwa-Haus.

———. 1982b. "The Unusual and Beautiful." In El Anatsui, *El Anatsui: Sculptures, Photographs, Drawings 20 Feb–5 Mar 1982.* Lagos: Goethe Institut.

———. 1984a. "Aesthetics and the Mythic Imagination: Notes on Christopher Okigbo's *Heavensgate* and Uche Okeke's *Drawings.*" In D. I. Nwọga (ed.), *Critical Perspectives on Christopher Okigbo.* Washington, D.C.: Three Continents Press, 78–85.

———. 1984b. "Ọgwugwa Aja Iyiazi Nri." *Ụwa Ndi Igbo* (Nsukka) 1, 55–60. [In Igbo with a short English summary.]

———. 1984c. *Obiọra Udechukwu: Selected Sketches 1965–1983.* Lagos: National Council for Arts and Culture.

———. 1984d. "Further Notes on the Epics of Ameke Okoye and Ọzọemene Ndive." *Ụwa Ndi Igbo: Journal of Igbo Life and Culture* 1, 17–19.

———. 1984e. "Igbo Traditional Design and Contemporary Dress Wear." *Anu* 3:1, 14.

———. 1985a. *Rhythms of Hunger: An Exhibition of Recent Work by Obiọra Udechukwu.* London: Commonwealth Institute, Bhownagree Gallery.

———. 1985b. *Onye Ndidi . . . a Series of Drawings and Watercolours on the Theme of Patience.* Lagos: Instituto Italiano di Cultura.

———. 1988. *"Uli" Drawings and Prints by Obiọra Udechukwu.* Harare: P.G. Gallery, National Gallery of Zimbabwe.

———. 1989a. *Nsukka Landscape: Paintings and Prints by Obiọra Udechukwu.* Lagos: Italian Cultural Institute.

———. 1989b. "Traditional Wall Paintings: Modern Art from Nigeria." In *The Art and Living: Artwork Collectors and Art Scenes in America, Italy, Syria, Nigeria and West Germany.* Lagos: Communication Arts Company, vol. 2.

———. 1990a. *What the Madman Said: Poems by Obiọra Udechukwu. Drawings by the Author.* Bayreuth: Boomerang Press.

———. 1990b. *Obiọra Udechukwu: Drawings, Watercolours, Prints.* Washington, D.C.: Mbari Art.

———. 1991a. "Agha a dirọ mma" or "War is not good": The Biafran War through the Eyes of Artists. Unpublished revised paper from a seminar, "Healing the Social Wounds of War," Windhoek, Namibia, August 29–September 2, to be published in *Healing the Social Wounds of War,* ed. Murray Last, Edinburgh University Press.

———. 1991b. *Uli: Traditional Wall Painting and Modern Art from Nigeria. An Exhibition at Iwalẹwa-Haus, Bayreuth, Germany (June–July 1989), and at the Goethe Institut—German Cultural Centre (January–February 1990),* rev. ed. Lagos/Bayreuth: Goethe Institut/Iwalẹwa-Haus.

———. 1993. *So Far: Drawings, Paintings, Prints 1963–1993.* Bayreuth: Boomerang Press.

———. 1994. "Art: A Bridge of Understanding: Working with Renate." In *Footprints: A Bridge of Culture and Friendship.* Lagos: Goethe Institut.

———. 1995. Of Appraisals and Appraisers: The Criticism of Nigerian Art 1983–1993. Paper presented at the Tenth Triennial Symposium on African Art, April 19–23, 1995, New York University. New York: Arts Council of the African Studies Association. Unpublished.

Udechukwu, Obiọra, and Chika Okeke (eds.). n.d. *Ezumeezu: Essays on Nigerian Art and Architecture, a Festschrift for Demas Nwoko.* Lagos: Vista Books, forthcoming.

*Ufahamu.* Los Angeles: African Activist Association, African Studies Center, University of California. 1970–.

Ugonna, Nnabuenyi. 1982. "Igbo Satiric Art: A Comment." In F. C. Ọgbalu and E. N. Emenanjo (eds.), *Igbo Language and Culture: Volume Two.* Ibadan: University Press Limited, 65–79.

Ukheugbe, Osasuyi. 1986. Ori Olokun School: Its Contribution to Modern Nigerian Art. B.A. thesis, University of Nigeria, Nsukka, Department of Fine and Applied Arts.

Ukpabi, S. C. 1971. "Nsukka before the Establishment of British Administration." *Odu: A Journal of West African Studies,* new series 6, 101–10.

*Uli Art: Master Works, Recent Works. April 17–June 5, 1995.* 1995. New York: Skoto Gallery.

Umegakwe, Emmanuel. 1967. "Artist Uche Okeke." *Catholic Life* (Calabar), September, 8–10.

United States National Archives and Records Administration, Still Picture Branch, College Park, Md. Collection of Harmon Foundation photographs.

*Upa Paint-Drawing: Ama Dialog Exhibition January 21–27, 1995.* Lagos: National Museum.

*USO: Nigerian Journal of Art.* Lagos: National Gallery of Art. 1995–.

*Ụwa Ndi Igbo: Journal of Igbo Life and Culture.* Nsukka: Okike Arts Centre. 1984–.

Van Allen, Judith. 1976. "'Aba Riots' or 'Women's War'? Ideology, Stratification and the Invisibility of Women." In Nancy J. Hafkin and Edna G. Bay (eds.), *Women in Africa: Studies in Social and Economic Change.* Stanford, Calif.: Stanford University Press, 59–86.

Vogel, Susan, assisted by Ima Ebọng. 1991. *Africa Explores: 20th Century African Art.* New York/Munich: Center for African Art/Prestel.

Wade, Edwin L. (ed.). 1986. *The Arts of the North American Indian: Native Traditions in Evolution.* New York: Hudson Hills Press.

Wangboje, S. Irein. 1977. "Western Impact on Nigerian Arts." *Nigeria Magazine* 122/123, 100–124.

———. 1991. *A Textbook of Art for Junior Secondary Schools.* Ibadan: Evans Publishers.

Weller, Doris. 1992. *Doris Weller: Earthview.* Lagos: Mercedes-Benz ANAMMCO.

———. 1994. "Die Kunst der Roten Erde. The Art of the Red Earth." In *Agua Mmiri Wasser: Kunst als Mittlerin—Brasilien—Nigeria—Deutschland.* Osnabruck: Deutsche Bundesstiftung Umwelt, 12–15.

*Werbung für Biafra: Kunst und Politik im nigerianischen Burgerkrieg 1967 bis 1970.* 1985. Bayreuth: Iwalẹwa-Haus.

West, Margie K. C. (ed.). 1988. *The Inspired Dream: Life as Art in Aboriginal Australia.* Queensland: Queenland Art Gallery.

Wẹwẹ, Adetọla F. 1989. "Thematic Growth in Nigerian Contemporary Paintings: 1920–1964. *Kurio Africana: Journal of Art and Criticism* 1:2, 80–88.

Whipper, Audrey. 1982. "Riot and Rebellion among African Women: Three Examples of Women's Clout." In Jean F. O'Barr (ed.), *Perspectives on Power: Women in Africa, Asia and Latin America.* Durham, N.C.: Duke University, Center for International Studies, 50–72.

Whiteman, Kaye. 1994. "Ben Enwọnwu (1921–94)." *West Africa* 227: February, 309.

Wilks, Ivor. 1975. *Aṣante in the Nineteenth Century: The Structure and Evolution of a Political Order.* London: Cambridge University Press.

———. 1993. *Forests of Gold: Essays on the Akan and the Kingdom of Aṣante.* Athens: Ohio University Press.

Willett, Frank. 1986. "Nigerian Thorn Carvings: A Living Monument to Justus Akeredolu." *African Arts* 20:1, 48–53, 98.

———. 1989. "Nigerian Life in Miniature: In Memory of Justus Akeredolu." *African Arts* 22:4, 80–81.

Williams, Denis. 1962. "The Mbari Publications." *Nigeria Magazine* 75, 69–74.

Willis, Elizabeth W. 1986. Form and Content in Traditional Uli Painting. M.F.A. thesis, University of Nigeria, Nsukka, Department of Fine and Applied Arts.

———. 1987. "A Lexikon of Igbo *Uli* Motifs." *Nsukka Journal of the Humanities* 1, 91–120.

———. 1989. "Uli Painting and the Igbo World View." *African Arts* 23:1, 62–67, 104.

———. 1997. Uli Painting and Identity: Twentieth Century Developments in Art in the Igbo-speaking Region of Nigeria. Ph.D. dissertation, University of London, School of Oriental and African Studies, Department of Art and Archaeology.

Wonodi, Okogbule. 1971. *Dusts of Exile.* Ifẹ: P.P.P., Pan African Pocket Poets, vol. 3.

Younge, Gavin. 1988. *Art of the South African Townships.* New York: Rizzoli.

*Zaria Art School: Ahmadu Bello University, Zaria, Nigeria.*

1990. Lagos: National Council for Arts and Culture, Evolution in Nigerian Art 5.

Zerby, Lewis, and Margaret Zerby. 1971. *If I Should Die before I Wake: The Nsukka Dream.* East Lansing: Michigan State University Press.

*Zweites Symposion Nordseeküste: Kunstler vor dem Deich. Theme: "Wetter." 20 Oktober bis 17 November 1984. Cuxhaven.* 1984.

## VIDEO INTERVIEWS

Stored at the Elisofon Photographic Archives, National Museum of African Art, Smithsonian Institution, Washington, D.C.

Tayọ Adenaike, June 13, 1994, at the National Museum of African Art, Smithsonian Institution, Washington, D.C. Taping by Amy Staples, interview by Simon Ottenberg.

Tayọ Adenaike, June 30, 1994, at the National Museum of African Art, Smithsonian Institution, Washington, D.C. Taping by Amy Staples, interview by Simon Ottenberg.

Tayọ Adenaike, April 24, 1996, creating a watercolor at the National Museum of African Art, Smithsonian Institution, Washington, D.C. Taping by Amy Staples, no voice.

El Anatsui, May 29, 1994, at his studio at Nsukka. Taping and interview by Simon Ottenberg.

Chike Aniakọr, June 7, 1994, at his home on the campus, University of Nigeria, Nsukka. Taping and interview by Simon Ottenberg.

Chike Aniakọr, April 3, 1996, creating an ink, wash, brush and pen work, at the National Museum of African Art. Taping by Amy Staples, interview by Simon Ottenberg, Amy Staples, and Andrea Nicolls.

Sylvester Ogbechiẹ. June 19, 1994, at the National Museum of African Art, Smithsonian Institution, Washington, D.C. Taping by Amy Staples, interview by Simon Ottenberg.

Ọlu Ọguibe, March 24, 1996, at his home in Chicago. Taping and interview by Simon Ottenberg.

Chika Okeke, May 14, 1994, at his home at Nsukka. Taping and interview by Simon Ottenberg.

Uche Okeke, May 26, 1994, at his home, Asele Institute, Nimo. Taping and interview by Simon Ottenberg.

Kaego Uche-Okeke, May 26, 1994, at her home, Asele Institute, Nimo. Taping and interview by Simon Ottenberg.

Ada Udechukwu, May 22, 1994, at her home on the campus, University of Nigeria, Nsukka. Taping and interview by Simon Ottenberg.

Ada Udechukwu, November 5, 1995, at her home on the campus, University of Nigeria, Nsukka. Taping and interview by Simon Ottenberg.

Obiọra Udechukwu, June 4, 1994, at his studio at Nsukka. Taping and interview by Simon Ottenberg.

# INDEX

Anidi, Obiọra, 153, 192
Anku, Seth, 225
Antal, Sandro, 130
*Anu, a Magazine of Igbo Culture,* 72
Anyakọra, N., 51
*anyanwu* (sun), 58, 93
Appiah, Kwame Anthony, 103
architecture, decoration of, 4. *See also mbari* designs; *uli* wall murals
Argent, Charles, 86
Arochuku, missionary center at, 23
Aroko (Yoruba) symbols, 165
Art and Arts Conference Forum (AACF), 105
art centers, contemporary, 106–7. *See also* cultural centers
art criticism, contemporary, 106
art education: establishment of, 18, 21, 43; expansion of, 103–4, 106
*Art Facts* (journal), 109
art galleries, Nigerian, 23–24, 104–5
*Art in Development* (U. Okeke), 78
*Art in Nigeria in 1960* (Beier), 24
art markets, contemporary, 104–6, 109, 260–61
art materials. *See* media (art materials)
art movements, definition of, 6
*Art on the Street* (exhibition, 1988), 227
art patronage, contemporary, 72, 104–6, 260
art salons, 106
Art Society, Zaria NCAST ("Zaria Rebels"), 32–35, 86, 253
art/arc, 130
Arte Amazonas (Manuas, Brazil, 1992), 175, 177
Arts and Crafts Pavilion, Lagos, 42
arts festivals, 105
Asele (female spirit of creativity), 49, 62, 267n.16
Asele Art Studio/Gallery, Nsukka, 71, 78, 82, 159
Asele Institute, Nimo, 66, 71, 72, 76, 82–83
assemblages, 226. *See also* installation art
Association of Fine Arts Students, Zaria NCAST, 35
Aṣante symbolism, 158
Auchi Polytechnic, 103, 107
Awka carved doors, 159
Azikiwe, Nnamdi, 19, 51, 269n.14
Azuonye, Chukwuma, 72, 116, 125

Badunka (male spirit of manipulative skills), 62
Baldwin, James, 227
Bamun scripts, 165
basketry, 230, 256
Beier, Georgina Betts, 23
Beier, Suzanne Wenger, 23
Beier, Ulli, 17, 23, 24, 34, 35, 43, 86, 120, 122, 129, 130, 143, 147, 223, 224, 260
Ben Enwọnwu College of Fine Art. *See* University of Nigeria, Nsukka, art school at
Benin art, 266n.18
Bhownagree Gallery, London, 239
Biafran art exhibition (Germany, 1969), 67, 116
*Biafran Cultural Workshop Exhibition,* 115
Biafran Directorate of Propaganda, 66, 115
bilingualism, 6
Bisiri, Yẹmi, 22
Black Art movement, 226
*Black Orpheus* (journal), 24
Bolange script, 165
Boomerang Press, 275n.9
Bowert, Ruth, 67
British Academy style, 17, 32, 34
British colonialism, 2, 3–4, 17, 139, 231, 256–57

British Council, 24, 50, 72, 75, 105, 129, 260; "Art in Education" workshop (1965), 50
British Council, Ibadan, 42
British Council, Port Harcourt, 50
*Broken Pots* (exhibition, 1979), 159
Brown, James, 181
Buhari, Jerry, 104
Buraimoh, Jimoh, 107
burnt designs, on wood, 157

Cadbury Poetry Prize, Association of Nigerian Authors, 140
Camp, Sokari Douglas, 104, 109
Campbell, Bọlaji, 104, 109, 256
Cardew, Michael, 23
cartoons, 104
ceramics. *See* pottery
"cerebral art," 121
Champman, Paul, 278n.2
Chi (destiny spirit), 5
*Childhood Fears* (exhibition, 1980), 183, 184–85, 191
Christian Art Fairs, Archdiocese of Ọnitsha, 83
Christopher Okigbo All-Africa Prize for Literature, 232
Chukueggu, S. A. O., 20, 236
Chukwu (heavenly god), 5, 61–62
Clark, P. J., 50
clay. *See* pottery
Clem (basketmaker), 225
Coalition of Nigerian Artists (CONA), 105
Cole, Herbert M., 87, 99, 236
colonialism, 2, 3–4, 17, 139, 164, 231, 256–57
colors, of *uli* designs, 2, 52, 59–60, 89, 256
Committee on Relevant Art (CORA), 105
Commonwealth Arts Festival (1965), 50
Commonwealth Institute, London, 238
communication, visual, 259
Community of Arts, Cummington, Mass., 163
*Conch, The* (journal), 73
*Configura 2* (art project), 147, 177
*Contemporary African Painting and Drawings by Uche Okeke* (exhibition), 272n.27
contemporary art: development of, 2, 17–25, 72–73, 103–9; Euro/American attitudes toward, 12–13; in Lagos, 3, 17, 72; political issues in, 107; style and content of, 108; variations in, 98, 104, 107
*Contemporary Art in Africa* (Beier), 24
*Contemporary Nigerian Prints, Drawings and Paintings* (exhibition), 272n.27
*Contemporary Visual Arts* (exhibition, 1977), 78
Cornwall College of Further and Higher Education, Redruth, England, 162, 163
corporate sponsorship, 106
Cross River Akwanshi carved stone monuments, 159
Crowder, Michael, 34, 43, 107
cultural centers, 23, 43–44, 72
cultural revival, Igbo, 257
curative spirits, 5
curvilinear designs, 7–8, 121, 182, 205

Dale, David, 104
dance, African, 4, 21
Darwîsh, Maḥmûd, 241
Dawn Functions Nigeria Limited, 190
*Design Inspiration through Uli* (U. Okeke), 78
*Dialog mit Grafik* (exhibition, 1985), 275n.4
*Dialogue* (exhibition, 1986), 190

Dickinson, Emily, 220
Didi Museum, Lagos, 105
Dike, Ndidi (Didi), 104, 219, 261, 262
Dike, Paul Chike, 109, 272n.26
Diop, David, 158
*Distorted Souls* (exhibition, 1982), 183, 185
divination, 5
dramatic traditions. *See* dance; literature; masquerade tradition; music
Duckworth, E. H., 21
Duerden, Dennis, 31
Dunlap, Margaret, 51

Eastern Nigeria Library, Enugu, 50
Eastern Nigerian Festival of the Arts, 50, 114
Eastern Nigerian Theatre Group, 50
Echeruo, Kevin, 11
*Economist* (London), 247
education, European-style, 6, 21
Egọnu, Uzọ, 22, 109, 232, 248
Eicher, Joanne, 78
Ejagham cultural group, 1
Ejiogu, Ngozi, 115
*eke* (python), 52, 58, 185, 236, 238
Ekeadam, F. N., 35, 268n.18
Ekekwe, Ngọzi, 78
Ekọng, Afi, 23
Ekpe secret society (cult), 125, 192
Ekwensi, C. O. D. (Cyprian), 43, 267n.6
Ekwueme, Alex, 78
"Elegy for Alto" (Okigbo), 228
Enugu, cultural center at, 45, 49–50, 51, 86
Enugu Musical Society, 269n.7
Enwezor, Okwui, 233, 263
Enwọnwu, Ben, 18, 20–21, 31, 32, 34, 248, 253, 275n.42
Eri (mythic founder of Anambra Igbo area), 61–62, 79
Esie (Yoruba) terra-cottas, 161
Essien, Nsikak, 104
Esso Independence Calendar painting competition (1959), 43
Euba, Akin, 107
Euro/American modern art: attitudes toward African art in, 12–13; familiarity with, 8–10
Ewe cultural group, 155, 156, 160
Exhibition Centre, Lagos, 42
*Exhibition of Marada Design, An* (1984), 206
*Exhibition of Mosaics and Stained Glass Windows* (1963), 45
exhibition spaces, Nigerian, 23–24, 104–5
expatriates, British and German, 21, 24
experimental art, 252
*Eye, The* (journal), 109
Eye Society, The, 105, 109
Eze, Joseph, 113
Eze, Nebechianya, 32
Eze, Okpu, 22
Ezeani, Gertrude, 52
Ẹmọkpae, Erhabọr, 22
Ezewuzie, Mary, 206

*Faces of Time* (exhibition, 1983), 187
Fagg, Bernard, 31
Fakẹyẹ, Bisi, 104
Fakẹyẹ, Lamidi, 21, 23
Fante cultural group, 157
Federal Department of Culture, Nigerian, 104
fertility spirits, 5